W9-AGN-174

Earth Science

Authors

Samuel N. Namowitz

Former Principal and
Earth Science Teacher
Charles Evans Hughes High School
New York, NY

Nancy E. Spaulding

Earth Science Teacher
Elmira Free Academy
Elmira, NY

Contributing Writer

Margaret A. LeMone, Ph.D.

Scientist
National Center for Atmospheric Research
Boulder, CO

Content Consultants

Frederick H. Carr, Ph.D.
Associate Professor of Meteorology
School of Meteorology
University of Oklahoma
Norman, OK

Jack K. Fletcher, Ed.D.
Director, Hummel Planetarium
Assistant Professor of Astronomy
Eastern Kentucky University
Richmond, KY

Jack L. Mason, Ed.D.
Director of Secondary Education
Geology Teacher
Emory and Henry College
Emory, VA

Robert W. Ridky, Ph.D.
Associate Professor of Geology
Department of Geology
University of Maryland
College Park, MD

Stephen A. Swift, Ph.D.
Research Associate
Woods Hole Oceanographic Institution
Woods Hole, MA

HEATH
D.C. HEATH AND COMPANY
Lexington, Massachusetts / Toronto, Ontario

The Earth Science Program

Earth Science, Pupil's Edition
Earth Science, Teacher's Annotated Edition
Earth Science Laboratory Investigations, Pupil's Edition
Earth Science Laboratory Investigations, Teacher's Annotated Edition
Earth Science Teacher's Resource Binder
Earth Science Overhead Transparencies
Earth Science Computer Test Bank
Earth Science Computer Test Bank, Teacher's Guide
Computer Software: Mountains and Crustal Movement ▪ Dating and Geologic Time

Editorial Development: Linda Zust Reddy, Marianne Pratt Knowles, Elizabeth A. Jordan
Book Designer: George McLean
Production Coordinator: Maureen LaRiccia
Readability Testing: J & F Readability Service, Charlottesville, VA
Cover Photograph: Mt. Everest by Galen Rowell (Peter Arnold, Inc.)

Teacher Reviewers

Donald B. Adams
Santa Rita High School
Tucson Unified School District
Tucson, AZ

Jeanne A. Endrikat
Lake Braddock Secondary School
Burke, VA

Shirley Harrison
Kalispell Junior High School
Kalispell, MT

Venton H. Haskins, Ph.D.
Central High School
Springfield, MO

Wayne A. Lueck
Niles Township High School—North Division
Skokie, IL

Kathy L. Salomon
The Bishop's School
La Jolla, CA

Charles F. Spain
Lincoln High School
Des Moines, IA

Richard C. Walter, Jr.
Manheim Central School District
Manheim, PA

F. Earl Wenzel
Teacher and Chairman
Science Department
Penfield Central Schools
Penfield, NY

Field Test Teachers

Grateful acknowledgment is given to the teachers and students who participated in the field testing of this program.

Harlan A. Meints
Charter Oak-Ute High School
Charter Oak, IA

Thomas Schroeder
Colfax High School
Colfax, CA

David Ramos
Sir Francis Drake High School
San Anselmo, CA

Anthony L. Occhiuzzi
Tempe High School
Tempe, AZ

Everett A. Sorenson
Roosevelt Junior High School
Blaine, MN

Howard R. Dirksen
Greenhills High School
Cincinnati, OH

Michael G. Walters
Riverview Gardens Senior High School
St. Louis, MO

Curt Wing
Minnechaug Regional High School
Wilbraham, MA

Sister Carol Ann Grandlich
Kenneth J. Kessenich
Larry Velk
Pius XI High School
Milwaukee, WI

C. Wayne Davis
Swatara Junior High School
Oberlin, PA

Gary Rose
Churchville Chili Senior High School
Churchville, NY

James Romansky
Bay Shore High School
Bay Shore, NY

John D. Klara
Staley Junior High School
Rome, NY

Published simultaneously in Canada
Printed in the United States of America
International Standard Book Number: 0-669-16291-4
5 6 7 8 9 0

To the Student

Why take earth science? At this point in your school career, you may not have much choice about the courses you take. You have a class in each of several subject areas (English, social studies, mathematics, etc.), and the science course offered at your school for your grade level happens to be earth science. But have you ever thought about why an earth science course is offered in the first place?

You live on Earth. This may seem obvious, but think about what it means. Everything you have or use, whether it is this book, your breakfast, your favorite clothes, the bus you rode to school in, or anything else, comes from materials found on Earth. Any place that you are likely to visit or live is on Earth. Everything you see or hear takes place on Earth, in its atmosphere, or in the universe of which Earth is a part.

Since you will be involved in so many aspects of Earth and the universe in your lifetime, it makes sense that you should know something about them. Also, with an understanding of earth science, you will be able to make more informed choices about how you conserve and use Earth's resources. These are the reasons for why you are taking a course in earth science.

Like any worthwhile experience, your earth science course will require some time and effort on your part. Even good students often need help to know how to best use their time and apply their effort. For this reason, some suggestions follow to assist you toward a successful, pleasant, and worthwhile experience.

Listen in class. Your teacher will help you to understand the basic concepts and master the important facts. Listen carefully in class and take good notes. Take some time to review your notes after class, even if no homework is assigned for that day. If there is something you do not understand, ask about it the next time your class meets. Students who listen in class and review the material often find that they spend less time in the long run doing homework or preparing for tests.

Do the assignments faithfully. Whether the assignment is reading the book, answering questions, or writing up a laboratory report, it is important to keep up with the work. Students who keep up with their work find their earth science experience far more enjoyable.

Read your textbook carefully. A textbook cannot be read as quickly as a magazine or novel. As you read a textbook, be sure you understand every sentence. Some students find it helpful to read assignments out loud at home so they can both see and hear the words.

Look at the illustrations. Read the captions that go with them. The illustrations show examples or diagrams of the topics covered in the written part of the text. They will help you to better understand the material in the reading.

Do the Topic Questions at the end of each lesson. These questions help you review the important points in each topic. See whether you can answer them without looking back at the topic, but be sure to look up anything that you do not know.

At the end of every chapter, you will find materials designed to help you review and strengthen your knowledge of the chapter material.

Read the Summary. The summary highlights important points in the chapter. As you read the summary, try to recall the concept described in each item. Think of examples of each concept.

Review the Vocabulary. You should be able to define or give an example of each term in the list. If you find that you are uncertain about a term, look back in the chapter and review the topics in which that term appears.

Do the Review. The Review helps you find out which chapter concepts you know, and which concepts you may need to study more than others.

Try the Interpret and Apply. The Interpret and Apply questions require a different kind of thinking than the Topic Questions or Review. To answer Interpret and Apply questions, you may need to use ideas and information from more than one topic in the chapter. These questions assess how well you can identify relationships among ideas. Or you may be asked to apply an idea from the chapter to a new situation. Here's where you have an opportunity to see the relevance of earth science in today's world.

Try the Critical Thinking. Critical Thinking exercises require you to use or analyze new information in light of the concepts you learned in the chapter. Typically, you will be asked to interpret data in graphs and charts.

One last suggestion—**Read the biographies** that appear in each chapter. Each one is about a real person who chose some aspect of earth science as a career. Think about how each person spends his or her day, and whether his or her career is something that you would enjoy doing.

Once you know what to look for, you will find examples and applications of earth science all around you. Whether you live in a city or in the country, you can observe changes in the weather, stars, and planets in the sky, the effects of rain and snow on rocks and buildings, and many other phenomena that are part of earth science.

The rewards of a successful study of earth science are many. For one, there is the satisfaction of mastering a subject that can sometimes be difficult. More important, the knowledge you gain here can give you a lifetime of pleasure in observing and appreciating the world in which you live.

CONTENTS

CHAPTER 28 Atmospheric Pressure and Winds 468

CHAPTER 29 Air Masses and Fronts 486

CHAPTER 30 Storms and Weather Forecasts 498

CHAPTER 31 Climate and Climate Change 514

UNIT ONE
Structure of a Dynamic Earth

▲
Minerals are part of Earth's structure, yet minerals have structures of their own. What does this mineral's shape tell about its structure?

▲
What do volcanoes reveal about the structure inside Earth?

Oil is found underground within certain kinds of structures. How do geologists on the surface know where to drill for oil? ▶

What is Earth's Structure?

Earth's *structure* refers to the way Earth is put together. Parts of Earth's structure are easily seen. Other parts are hidden from view because they are too small, too large, or are buried underground. Earth scientists strive to understand Earth's structure at many levels, large and small. Look at the photographs. What does each reveal about the structure of a dynamic Earth?

Since early times, people have noticed that ships appear to sink as they sail away. How is this a clue to Earth's overall structure? ▶

How is a steep structure on Earth's surface shown on a flat map? ▼

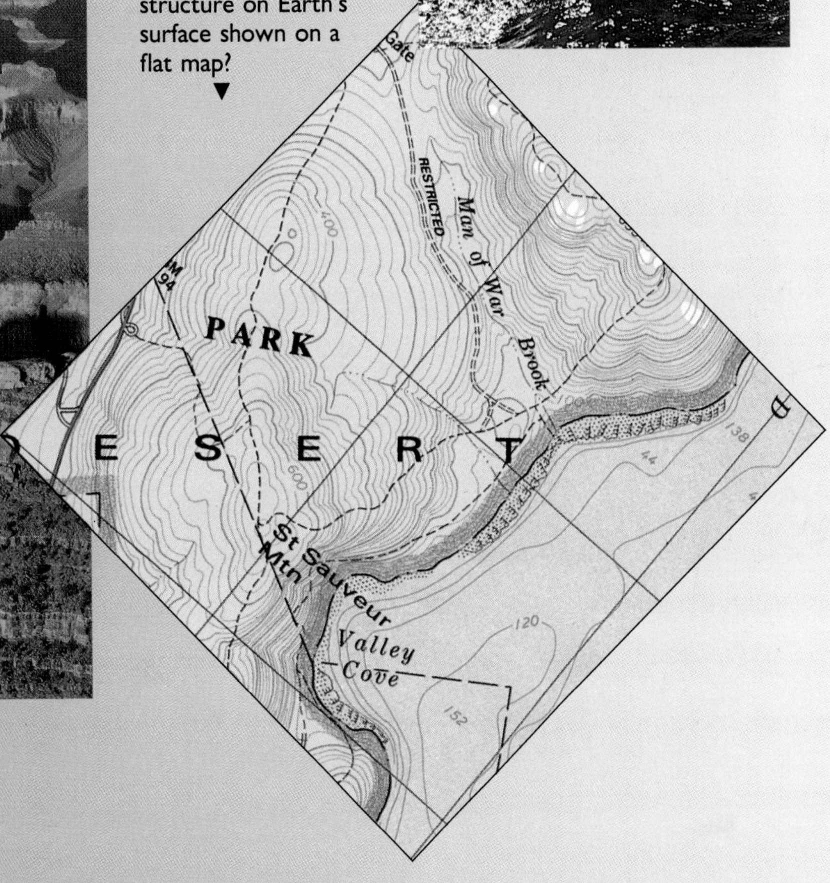

▲
Rock layers make up the structure of these cliffs. What do layers reveal about the way the rocks formed?

CHAPTER

1

Introduction to Earth Science

▲
Rock mounds from a lava flow cover trees, houses, and a highway in Hawaii.

How Do You Know That . . .

Earth is changing? The mounds in the photograph were formed when hot lava flowed over houses, trees, and the highway, then cooled. The lava flow has closed almost 2 kilometers of highway. The people living nearby must detour almost 100 kilometers just to buy groceries and pick up their mail. The lava came from Kilauea, a volcano in Hawaii that has erupted frequently in recent years. People living there are used to volcanic eruptions. Eruptions like this one, however, cause far more damage than most. Lava flows are just one way Earth's activities affect our lives.

I What Is Earth Science?

Topic 1 Branches of Earth Science

A volcano erupts in Hawaii, destroying several homes and covering a major highway. An earthquake destroys a city in Central America. A 3-kilogram meteorite travels millions of kilometers through outer space and crashes through the roof of a home in Connecticut. Tornadoes weave erratic paths through the Great Plains, causing loss of life and property. Storms and high waves lash the coast of California, resulting in floods, landslides, and extensive erosion.

All of these occurrences are earth science *events*—that is, each causes a change. However, *Earth* includes more than the solid earth. It also includes Earth's oceans and atmosphere, and the universe of which Earth is a part. To which branch of earth science does each event belong? The volcano and earthquake are part of **geology**, the study of Earth's surface and interior. The meteorite belongs to the branch of earth science called **astronomy**, the study of the universe. Tornadoes belong to **meteorology**, the study of Earth's atmosphere. The Pacific Coast events—like many others—involve more than one branch of earth science. These events involve meteorology, geology, and **oceanography**, the study of the oceans.

OBJECTIVES

A Identify the major branches of earth science and describe events that occur in each branch.

B Define *geology* and list several activities of geologists.

C Explain how astronomers obtain information and list some topics and materials they study.

D Describe the work and activities of meteorologists and oceanographers.

1.1 Shoreline phenomena are studied by a variety of earth scientists including meteorologists, oceanographers, and geologists.

1.2 This geologist has donned protective clothing in order to gather data from an active volcano. What are some of the dangers involved?

Topic 2 Activities of Today's Geologists

Geologists are scientists who study the origin, history, and structure of Earth and the processes that shape its surface. Like other scientists, geologists are important in today's world. They explore Earth's crust to discover new sources of oil, uranium, and geothermal power. They search for new deposits of important metallic and nonmetallic minerals. They help plan water supply systems for towns and cities. They devise measures for flood control. They do research in forecasting earthquakes and volcanic eruptions. They make topographic maps showing details of Earth's surface and geologic maps to show Earth's rock structure. Using the observations made by spacecraft, geologists can make maps of the moon and nearer planets.

Topic 3 What Astronomers Do

Unlike geologists and most other scientists, astronomers deal mainly with objects and happenings beyond their physical reach. To study the universe beyond the planet Earth, astronomers must use telescopes and other instruments. They study radiations sent out by objects in space and learn about the stars and planets from these radiations. Satellites, lunar explorers, and space probes have been most useful to astronomers.

Many astronomers specialize in studies of the planets and their moons. Some devote their time mainly to comets. Others may be interested in the origin of the universe or the life cycles of stars. Still others work on ways of discovering whether or not life exists anywhere else in the universe.

Do astronomers have any outer-space materials to study? The answer is yes. Meteorites have fallen to Earth from other parts of the solar system. Between 1969 and 1972, *Apollo* astronauts landed on the moon and brought moon rocks back to Earth. In addition, astronauts and space probes—*Mariner, Pioneer, Viking, Voyager,* and others—have provided many photographs and observations of members of the solar system.

1.3 A scientific milestone was reached in 1969 when the first astronauts landed on the moon.

Topic 4 What Meteorologists Do

Earth's atmosphere covers Earth's entire surface and reaches a height of hundreds of kilometers. The weather is created in its bottom layer. Today jet planes fly above the weather, and artificial satellites go much higher. Therefore, scientists are very interested in the upper atmosphere too.

The meteorologists known best are the weather forecasters. Standing behind the forecasters are many others. Some study the effects of solar energy in changing the weather. Still others are concerned with the important problems of air pollution. A number of meteorologists are investigating changes in the *climate,* or long-term weather. Then there are those doing research on such problems as hurricane control, thunderstorms, tornadoes, and long-range forecasting.

1.4 Meteorologists are able to track the dynamic forces within the atmosphere and to make weather predictions based on atmospheric conditions.

Topic 5 What Oceanographers Do

Since the oceans cover nearly three fourths of Earth's surface, oceanographers have many problems to solve. Oceanographers work from special research ships to measure the ocean depths and map the ocean floor. They drill into the ocean floor to study its rocks and its history. They locate deposits of valuable minerals.

Oceanographers also track and map ocean currents. They chart the movements of icebergs that break off from the glaciers of Greenland and Antarctica. They study the plant and animal life of the deep sea and of the surface waters. They do research to discover the effects of the ocean on weather and climate. From studying great ocean waves and undersea earthquakes, oceanographers are able to develop warning systems for coastal regions threatened by these phenomena.

1.5 This special diving suit allows oceanographers to dive deep below the surface and to remain below for long periods of time.

TOPIC QUESTIONS

Each topic question refers to the topic of the same number.

1. **(a)** What branches of science are included in earth science? **(b)** Name one event that can occur in each of these branches of science.
2. List at least four activities performed by geologists.
3. **(a)** How can astronomers study space beyond Earth? **(b)** Name three specialized topics studied by astronomers. **(c)** What are some outer-space materials available to astronomers?
4. Name at least three activities carried on by meteorologists.
5. Briefly describe at least four activities of oceanographers.

Margaret LeMone
Meteorologist

Margaret LeMone is a scientist at the National Center for Atmospheric Research in Boulder, Colorado. She is interested in the structure and evolution of thunderstorms into lines (such as squall lines and hurricane bands) and in how they affect the winds in the atmosphere.

Dr. LeMone's study of thunderstorm lines involves some exciting methods of data collection. She has flown through or directed other research aircraft through numerous thunderstorms, mostly over the central Atlantic Ocean. She has also used data collected from aircraft and tall towers to study air currents heating the lowest few kilometers of the atmosphere. The data help her understanding of how these air currents relate to the organization of cumulus clouds into lines ("cloud streets"). Computer modeling is also a part of her study of clouds and thunderstorms.

Dr. LeMone has been active in the American Meteorological Society, serving as councillor, head of its Board of Women and Minorities, and president of its Denver-Boulder Chapter.

II The Origin of Earth

Topic 6 Where Earth Science Begins: The Solar System

Where should the study of earth science begin—land, oceans, atmosphere, or sky? A good choice seems to be the origin of the planet Earth. Earth, however, is only one member of a whole family of planets circling the sun. So we begin with the origin of the whole family, which is called the solar system.

A **hypothesis** is an informed guess that tries to explain how or why an event occurs. A good hypothesis explains known facts. Every hypothesis about the origin of the solar system has to consider the following six facts:

1. All planets move around the sun (revolve) in the same direction.
2. The paths, or orbits, of the planets around the sun are all nearly circular.
3. Most of the orbits are in nearly the same flat surface (plane).

OBJECTIVES

A Define *hypothesis* and list some facts that a hypothesis of the origin of the solar system must explain.

B Describe the origin of the solar system according to the protoplanet hypothesis.

C Discuss the origin and characteristics of Earth's oceans, atmosphere, internal structure, and continents, and describe Earth's internal structure.

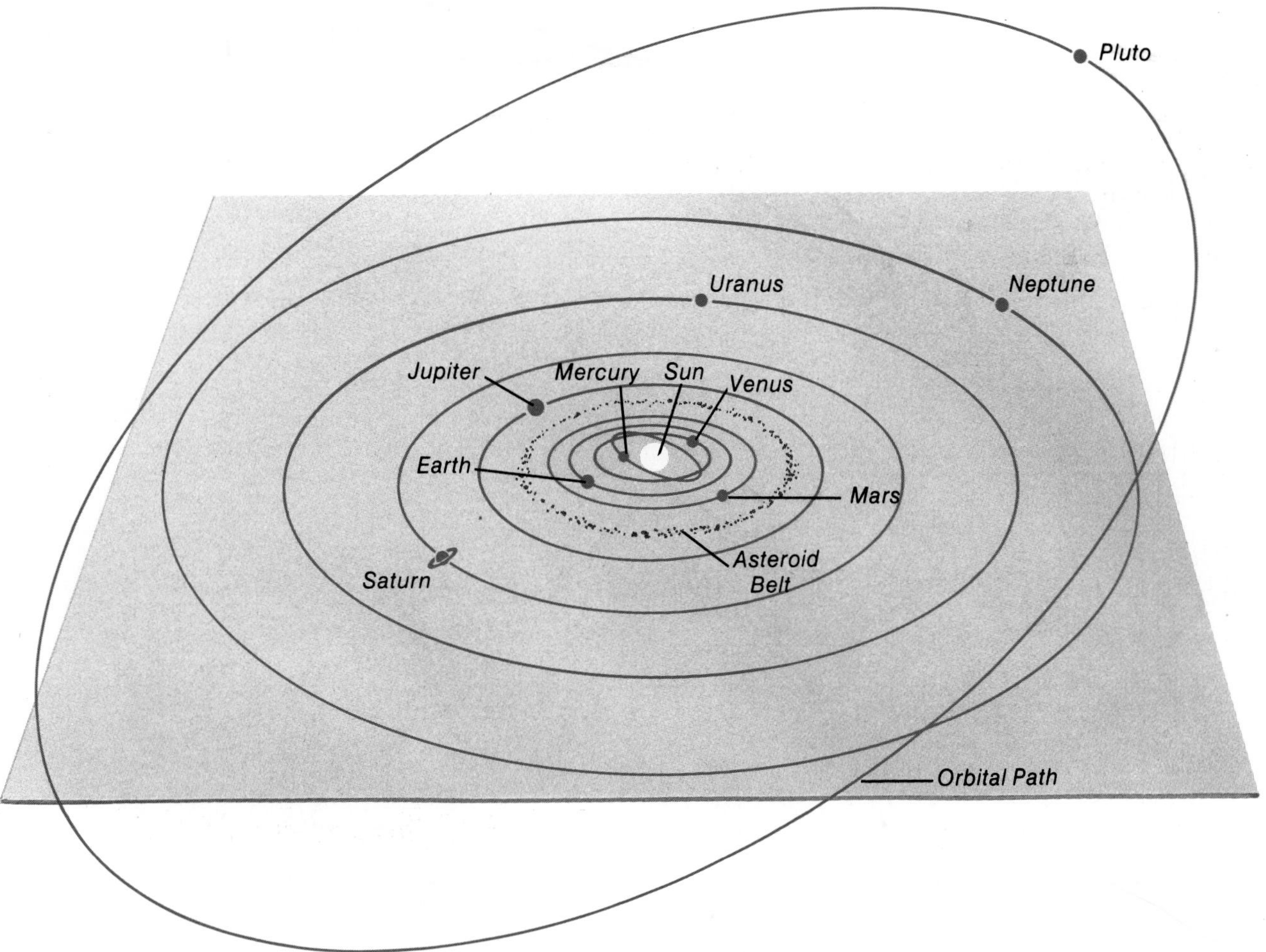

1.6 This artist's conception of the solar system illustrates the orbits of the nine planets revolving around the sun.

4. The sun turns on its axis (rotates) in almost the same plane as the planets and in the same direction that the planets revolve.
5. Most of the planets rotate in the same direction as the sun.
6. Seven of the nine planets have moons. Most of the moons revolve around the planets in the same direction that the planets revolve around the sun.

The hypothesis that many astronomers favor—because it best explains the facts listed above—is the **protoplanet hypothesis**. It was first proposed about 1944 by a German astronomer, von Weizsacker, and modified by an American astronomer, Kuiper, in 1950.

Topic 7 The Protoplanet Hypothesis

The protoplanet hypothesis suggests that about 5 billion years ago a great cloud of gas and dust rotated slowly in space. The cloud was at least 10 billion kilometers in diameter. As time passed, the cloud shrank under the pull of its own gravitation or was made to collapse by the explosion of a passing star. Most of the cloud's material gathered around its own center. Its shrinking made it rotate faster, like a spinning whirlpool. The compression of its material made its interior so hot that a powerful reaction, hydrogen fusion, began and the core of the cloud blazed into a newborn sun.

About 10 percent of the material in the cloud formed a great platelike disk surrounding the sun far into space. Friction within the disk caused most of its mass to collect in a number of huge whirlpools or eddies. These eddies shrank into more compact masses called **protoplanets** and later formed planets and moons. Some uncollected material remains even today as comets, meteoroids, and asteroids.

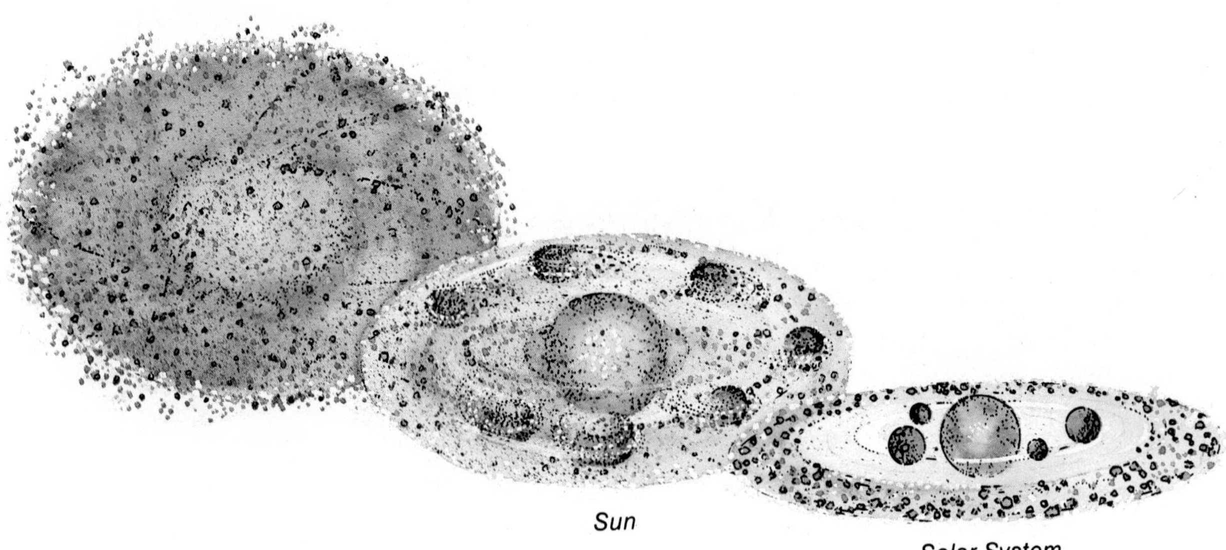

1.7 According to the protoplanet hypothesis, a great cloud of gas and dust was gradually transformed into the planets and natural satellites that make up the solar system.

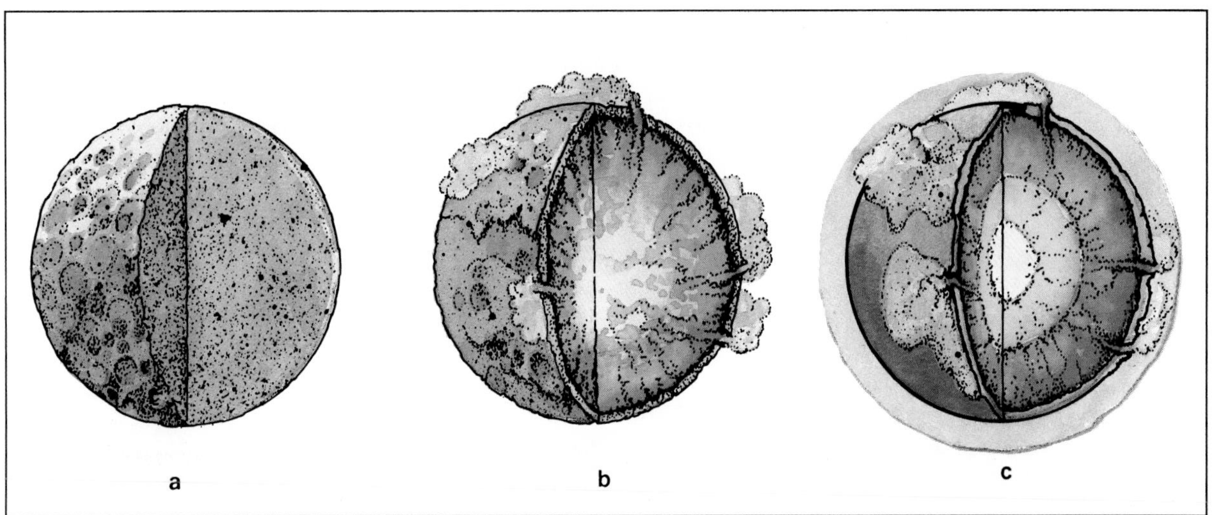

1.8 According to the model, the protoplanet Earth (a) had no oceans or atmosphere. As the intense heat of Earth's interior built up, volcanic eruptions began to occur (b). Repeated huge eruptions produced volumes of volcanic gases. The steam in these gases condensed upon reaching the surface (c) to form Earth's oceans.

Topic 8 **Origin of the Oceans**

Scientists now agree that when Earth first formed, it had neither oceans nor atmosphere. As the protoplanet changed to the planet Earth, it grew hotter. There were three sources of heat: compression, radioactive minerals, and bombardment by showers of meteorites. Radioactive minerals are natural sources of energy, much of which becomes heat energy. Meteorites produce heat both by friction and by impact.

When Earth became hot enough, the common element iron melted. The molten iron sank toward the center of Earth, forming a dense core. As the molten iron sank, it partially melted other earth materials that it touched (Topic 10). Water and gases that had been trapped in those materials were released. The molten earth materials separated into layers. As the materials separated, the steam and gases that they had held escaped to the surface in volcanic eruptions. The steam that escaped condensed into water that slowly accumulated as oceans.

Topic 9 **Origin of the Atmosphere**

The atmosphere that surrounds Earth today includes about 78 percent free nitrogen and 21 percent free oxygen. *Free* means these gases are not combined with other elements. The remaining 1 percent is mostly other gases, such as argon, carbon dioxide, and helium. (Water vapor is in the atmosphere too, but the amount varies with weather and climate.)

This present mixture of gases is very different from what scientists think Earth's original atmosphere must have been. The original atmosphere is thought to have come from volcanoes. It would have been like the mixture of gases that now erupts from volcanoes.

This mixture usually is over 50 percent water vapor with large amounts of carbon dioxide and sulfur gases. However, the mixture contains no free oxygen!

Almost all forms of life on Earth need free oxygen. Where, then, did it come from? Scientists think the atmosphere's first free oxygen came from the breakup of water molecules by sunlight in the upper atmosphere. When simple green plants came into existence, they added more free oxygen to the atmosphere by **photosynthesis**. In this process, green plants manufacture sugars and starches from carbon dioxide and water in the presence of sunlight. In photosynthesis, more than half of the oxygen present in the carbon dioxide and water is not used. This excess oxygen is released into the atmosphere as free oxygen.

Topic 10 **Structure of the Solid Earth**

A *model* is a picture that shows a concept, event, or object that cannot be seen in its natural state. For example, no one can directly see the inside of Earth. Yet geologists today have a fairly clear model of Earth's structure from its surface to its very center. Since the center is nearly 6400 kilometers from the surface, most of this model is based on indirect evidence. This indirect evidence will be discussed in the chapter on earthquakes.

For now, consider the Earth model that geologists describe. At its center is a spherical **inner core** 1200 kilometers in diameter. The inner core is made of solid iron and nickel. Surrounding the inner core is an **outer core** about 2250 kilometers thick made of liquid iron and nickel. Then comes a 2900-kilometer-thick layer of heavy rocks rich in compounds of iron, magnesium, and silicon. This layer, called the **mantle**, reaches almost to Earth's surface. The

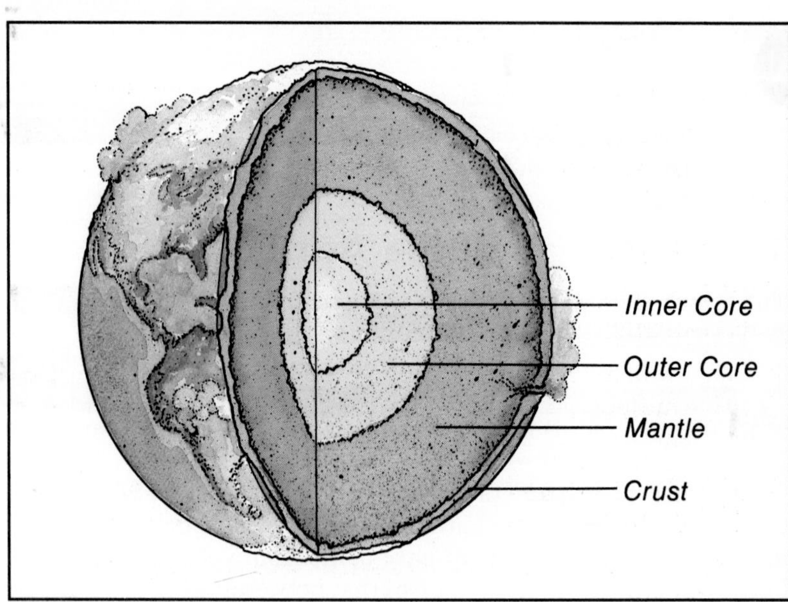

1.9 A simple model of Earth's interior reveals distinct layers between the core and the surface.

mantle is covered by a layer of lighter rocks called the **crust**. The crust ranges in thickness from about 10 kilometers below the ocean basins to about 65 kilometers below the continents. Mines and wells go deep into the crust, but none have reached the mantle.

Was Earth layered like this when it formed more than 4 billion years ago? Probably not. If the protoplanet hypothesis is correct, the original surface of Earth looked much like the moon does today. Below its surface, Earth was probably composed of the same kind of material all the way to its center.

How then did Earth develop its layers of core, mantle, and crust? Many geologists think that as the temperature of the newly formed Earth increased, large quantities of iron and nickel in its rocks melted. Great streams of these hot, heavy liquids flowed toward Earth's center. On their way down they melted lighter rock materials and forced them up to the surface. At the surface the light rock became solid and formed Earth's crust. The mantle formed between the crust and the core.

Topic 11 How the Continents Formed

One hypothesis suggests that when the melted iron and nickel sank into Earth's core, it forced out enough light rock to form an immense single continent. Another suggestion is that the continents were formed by great lava flows from erupting volcanoes over hundreds of millions of years. In either case, today's continents are quite different from those that first formed on Earth's surface. In the billions of years following their origin, the continents have undergone many changes. Later chapters will explain the evidence for these changes, how they occurred, and what caused them.

TOPIC QUESTIONS

Each topic question refers to the topic of the same number.

6. **(a)** What is a hypothesis? **(b)** What is the solar system? **(c)** List at least three facts that should be considered by a hypothesis that explains the origin of the solar system.

7. Briefly describe the protoplanet hypothesis.

8. **(a)** Describe three ways Earth got hotter in its early history. **(b)** Describe how the oceans formed.

9. **(a)** How does the present atmosphere differ from Earth's original atmosphere? **(b)** How did Earth's atmosphere get its free oxygen?

10. **(a)** Make a simple labeled diagram showing the model of Earth. **(b)** Explain how Earth's interior got its layered structure.

11. Briefly describe one hypothesis that explains the forming of continents.

CHAPTER 1 REVIEW

Summary

Geology, astronomy, meteorology, and oceanography are the branches of earth science. Some earth science events are included in more than one branch.

Geologists study and explore Earth's surface and internal structure. Astronomers study the universe beyond Earth.

Meteorologists study Earth's atmosphere to understand the processes that control weather and climate.

Oceanographers study ocean currents and waves, the ocean floor, and other aspects of Earth's oceans.

A hypothesis is an informed guess that tries to explain how or why an event occurs. The protoplanet hypothesis is an explanation of the origin of the solar system.

According to the protoplanet hypothesis, the solar system originated as a great rotating cloud of dust and gas that shrank into compact masses called protoplanets.

Compression, radioactive decay, and bombardment by showers of meteorites heated the protoplanet Earth. Steam that was released by the heat condensed into water to form oceans. Other gases formed the atmosphere.

The original atmosphere contained large amounts of carbon dioxide and sulfur gases but no free oxygen. Free oxygen was formed later from the breakup of water molecules and in the process of photosynthesis.

Earth's interior contains an inner core, outer core, and mantle surrounded by a thin rock crust at the surface.

The continents are thought to have formed either from light rock that was forced to Earth's surface or by great lava flows from erupting volcanoes.

Vocabulary

astronomy
crust
geology
hypothesis
inner core
mantle
meteorology
oceanography
outer core
photosynthesis
protoplanet
protoplanet hypothesis

Review

Match terms in List **A** with phrases in List **B.**

List A

1. astronomers
2. radioactive minerals
3. crust
4. earth science
5. event
6. geologists
7. volcanic eruptions
8. hypothesis
9. inner core
10. mantle
11. space probes
12. oceanographers
13. meteorologists
14. outer core
15. photosynthesis
16. protoplanet

List B

a. scientists who study Earth's oceans
b. process that adds free oxygen to the atmosphere
c. an informed guess that explains an event
d. Earth layer rich in iron, magnesium, and silicon
e. compact masses that became planets and moons
f. an occurrence that causes a change
g. Earth layer made of solid iron and nickel
h. scientists who study solid Earth
i. layer of lighter rock found at surface
j. a possible heat source for a young Earth
k. scientists who study the universe
l. Earth sphere made of liquid iron and nickel
m. *Mariner, Pioneer, Viking,* and *Voyager*
n. the study of Earth, its oceans, atmosphere, and the universe
o. scientists who study Earth's weather and climate
p. original source of oceans and atmosphere

Interpret and Apply

On your paper, answer each question in complete sentences.

1. Describe an earth science event that is related to more than one branch of earth science and explain how it is related to those branches.
2. Information about an object or event that can be obtained by direct observation is called *direct evidence.* For information about objects and events that cannot be observed first-hand, scientists rely on *indirect evidence.* Which branches of earth science are able to use a lot of direct evidence? Which branches use mostly indirect evidence? Explain your answers.
3. Review the protoplanet hypothesis described in Topic 7. Which of the six facts listed in Topic 6 can be explained by the protoplanet hypothesis?
4. Which facts listed in Topic 6 are *not* explained by the protoplanet hypothesis? Explain your answer.
5. A good hypothesis not only explains known facts; it also correctly predicts new facts. Based on the hypotheses about the formation of Earth (Topics 8–11), predict some features that should be true of other planets.

Critical Thinking

A skill needed by all earth scientists is graph reading. The graph below shows world population from the population in the year 1750 to the expected population in the year 2000. The straight lines that meet at the lower left corner of the graph are the two *axes* (singular: axis) of the graph. The x-axis is the horizontal line at the bottom of the graph. The y-axis is the vertical line on the left side of the graph.

1. Which axis (x or y) shows population?
2. What was the world population in 1950?
3. What is the population expected to be in the year you graduate from high school?
4. In which year was the world population 1 billion?
5. What was the world population in 1960?
6. In which year was the world population 2 billion?
7. How long did it take world population to increase from 1 billion to 2 billion?
8. In which year was the world population 4 billion?
9. How long did it take world population to increase from 2 billion to 4 billion?
10. What is different about the time it took the world population to double from 1 billion to 2 billion and the time it took to double from 2 billion to 4 billion?
11. According to the graph, will the doubling time from 4 billion to 8 billion be greater or less than the time for the previous doubling?

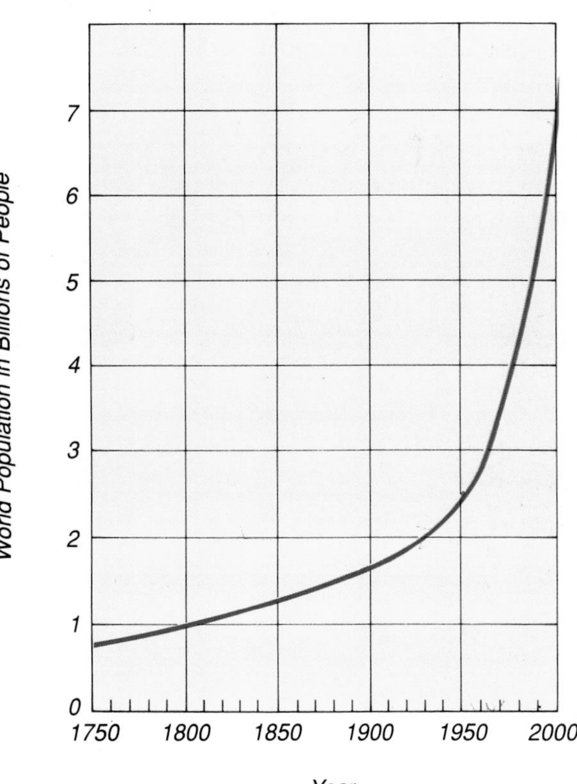

CHAPTER

2

Earth's Shape, Dimensions, and Internal Heat

▲ Even though this vast area appears to be flat, it is not. How can you tell that it is not flat?

How Do You Know That . . .

Earth is not flat? This expanse of land has an area of hundreds of square kilometers. Nearly three hours are required just to drive across it. This area certainly looks flat, but it is not. Laid out on this area is a 16-kilometer racetrack used to set land speed records. If Earth were flat, an observer standing at one end of the track would be able to see to the other end, but this is impossible. Does this show that Earth is a sphere? No, it merely shows that Earth is not flat. We need other evidence to prove that Earth is a sphere.

I Earth's Shape and Size

Topic 1 Earth Is Spherical

Is Earth flat or round? Until 1522 most people believed Earth was flat. In that year one of Magellan's ships completed the first trip all the way around Earth. Long before the explorer Magellan, however, early scientists thought that Earth was shaped like a ball. In geometry the ball shape is called a *sphere,* so the early scientists said that Earth is spherical.

The spherical model of Earth is based on such evidence as the following:

1. The mast of a ship was the first part to appear over the horizon. It was the last part to disappear. The traditional cry of the lookout in a sailing vessel is, "I see a mast."
2. When ships sailed north or south, sailors observed that the nighttime sky changed in appearance. The North Star rose higher in the sky as they sailed northward. It sank in the sky as they sailed southward. The position of the North Star changed so gradually and so evenly that it could only be explained in one way. The ship was sailing on a spherical surface. When ships sailed far enough south, constellations such as the Big Dipper could no longer be seen, but new ones such as the Southern Cross appeared in the sky. Would this be true on a flat Earth? Compare Figures 2.1(a) and 2.1(b).
3. An eclipse of the moon occurs when Earth's shadow falls on the moon. During an eclipse of the moon, the edge of Earth's shadow as it moves across the moon is always the arc of a circle. Only a sphere casts a circular shadow, no matter what position it is in.

OBJECTIVES

A List several evidences that Earth is nearly spherical.

B Define *oblate spheroid* and explain the effect of Earth's shape on the weight of an object.

C Describe and use Eratosthenes' method of measuring Earth's circumference.

D Compare Earth's polar and equatorial dimensions and discuss the amount of land and water area on Earth's surface.

2.1 (a) The angle of the North Star above the horizon changes as the latitude of the observer changes. This is evidence that Earth is spherical. (b) If Earth were flat, the North Star would be overhead at all latitudes.

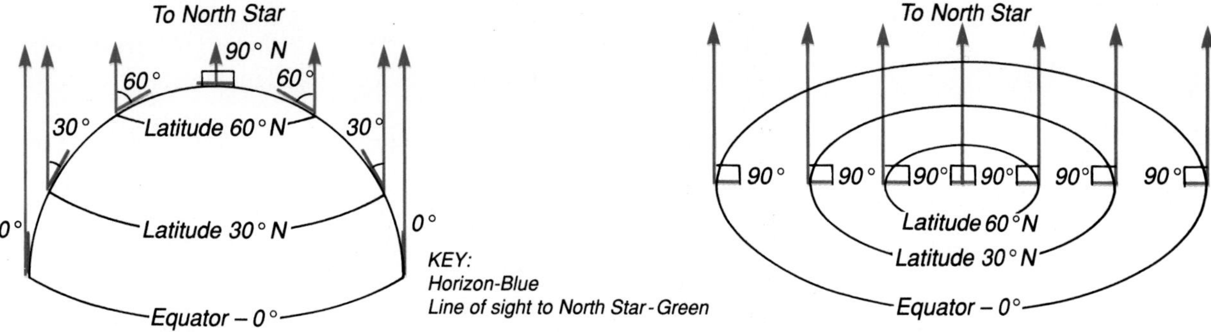

Angular distance of North Star above is the angle between the horizon and the line of sight. (Because of distance to North Star, all lines of sight are parallel.)

The evidence listed above is, of course, still visible today, although a lookout is much more likely to see a smokestack than a mast. But now everyone can see the evidence. Many photographs of Earth have been taken by orbiting spacecraft. Other photographs of Earth have been taken from the moon by the *Apollo* astronauts.

2.2 A photograph of Earth taken from outer space provides concrete evidence of Earth's spherical shape.

Topic 2 The Sphere Is Not Perfect

Gravity provides further evidence that Earth is a sphere. The weight of an object is simply a measure of the force with which gravity pulls it toward Earth's center. The weight changes if the object's distance from the center of Earth changes. The further an object is from Earth's center, the less it weighs. Measurements show that a given object weighs almost the same everywhere on Earth's surface. What does this statement mean? It means that all of Earth's surface is almost equidistant from Earth's center. This means that Earth is almost spherical.

Why almost? Careful measurements show that the weight of an object is not exactly the same all over Earth. An object that gives a reading of 195 newtons on a spring scale at sea level at Earth's North Pole or South Pole loses weight as it approaches the equator, where it gives a reading of only 194 newtons. What does this result mean? For one, the object must be nearer Earth's center at the poles than at the equator. In other words, Earth is not a perfect sphere. It is slightly flattened at the poles, and it bulges at the equator. This shape is called an **oblate spheroid**. The flattening is caused by Earth's rotation.

Topic 3 Measuring Earth's Circumference

How do you measure the distance around Earth?

In principle, the method is simple. Take two points a substantial distance apart on Earth, with one directly north of the other. The line joining these points will be part of a circle that goes around Earth through the North Pole and South Pole. Measure the distance between the two points. Find out what part of the whole circle that part is (you shall see how in a moment). Then multiply the measured distance by the number of parts needed to make the whole circle. This calculation gives the north-south distance around Earth. This distance is called the *circumference* of Earth.

The first scientific measurement of Earth's circumference was probably made by the Greek astronomer Eratosthenes (er uh TOS thuh neez) more than 2000 years ago. Eratosthenes, who lived in Alexandria, heard of a famous well in the city of Syene (sie EE nee) in southern Egypt. Once a year, at noon on the longest day of the year, the sun shone straight down to the bottom of this deep vertical well. This occurrence meant that the sun was directly overhead in Syene at that moment. At noon on the same day in Alexandria, the sun was 7.2° below the overhead point. Since Alexandria was supposed to be directly north of Syene, the two cities must be separated by 7.2° on a circumference of Earth. The whole distance around Earth is 360°, the total number of degrees in a circle, and 7.2° is one-fiftieth of a circle. Eratosthenes multiplied the distance between Syene and Alexandria by 50 and obtained his answer for Earth's circumference.

2.3 Eratosthenes used the difference in the angle of the sun's rays at two locations in his calculation of Earth's circumference.

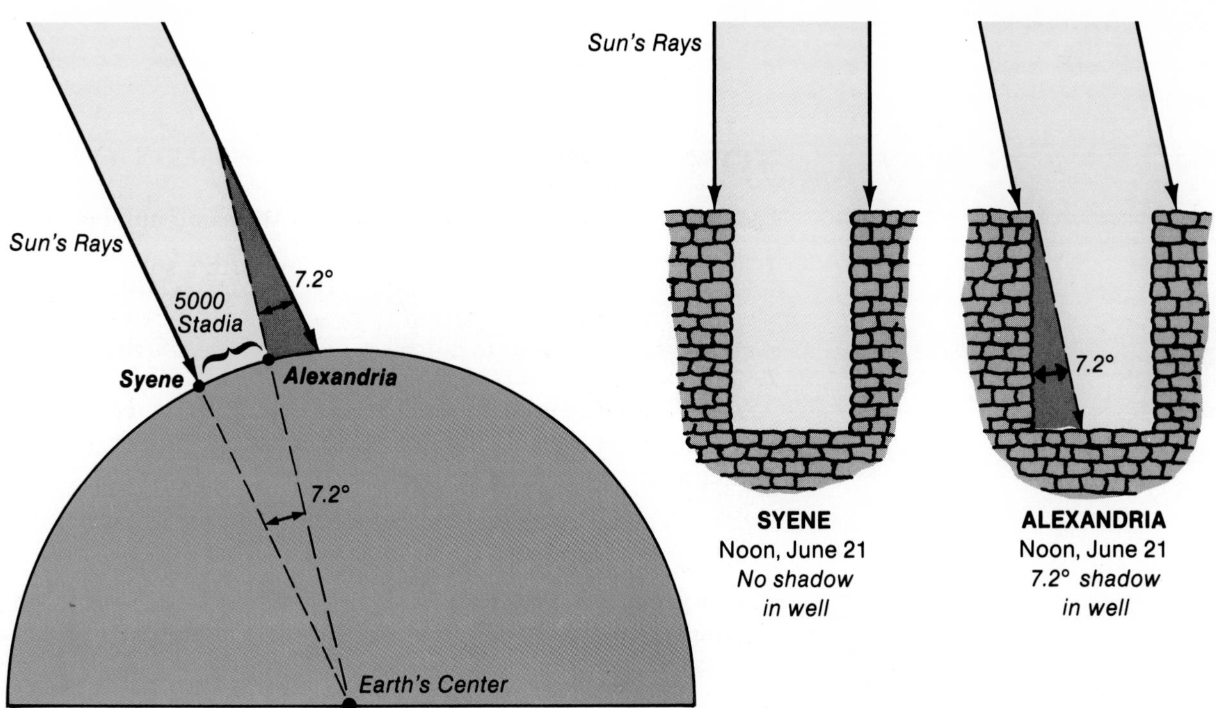

What was Eratosthenes' answer? The distance between the two cities was 5000 stadia (a stadium was about 185 meters). Multiplied by 50, this gave a circumference of 250 000 stadia, or 46 250 kilometers. Despite a number of inaccuracies in his assumptions, Eratosthenes had come remarkably close to the real size of Earth's circumference (about 40 000 kilometers). If you look at a map of Egypt, you may discover one—perhaps two—of Eratosthenes' errors. (Syene is now called Aswan.)

Topic 4 Earth's Dimensions

The method used by Eratosthenes is still used today to measure Earth's circumference. Today, however, the data used are gathered by more precise instruments and methods. Modern instruments used to measure Earth include lasers, satellites, and ground-based satellite tracking stations. Here are a few of the important dimensions of Earth. (Remember Earth bulges at the equator and is flattened at the poles.)

Circumference at Equator	40 074 kilometers
Circumference at Poles	40 007 kilometers
Diameter at Equator	12 756 kilometers
Diameter at Poles	12 714 kilometers

The total surface area of Earth is about 510 million square kilometers. Of this, about 149 million square kilometers stand above sea level as continents and islands. The remaining 361 million square kilometers are covered by oceans. Thus, the percentage of land is only about 29 percent, while that of water is about 71 percent.

TOPIC QUESTIONS

Each topic question refers to the topic of the same number.

1. **(a)** Describe two pieces of evidence for Earth's spherical shape that have been known for thousands of years. **(b)** What modern evidence enables us to see that Earth is spherical?

2. **(a)** How do the effects of gravity show that Earth is almost spherical? **(b)** What is an oblate spheroid? **(c)** How do the effects of gravity show that Earth is an oblate spheroid?

3. **(a)** What two measurements did Eratosthenes need to determine Earth's circumference? **(b)** Explain how he used these measurements to find Earth's circumference.

4. **(a)** Compare Earth's equatorial and polar diameters. **(b)** Compare the amount and percent of land and water areas on Earth's surface.

II Earth's Density and Temperature

Topic 5 Earth's Density

Properties of small objects are fairly easy to determine. Properties of the whole Earth must often be measured indirectly. Earth's density is an example. **Density** is a measure of the amount of material (mass) in a given space (volume). The density of an object or substance is determined using the following equation.

$$\text{density} = \frac{\text{mass}}{\text{volume}} \quad \text{or} \quad D = \frac{m}{V}$$

For example, suppose you have a small block of the metal lead. By taking measurements, you find that the block has a mass of 90.4 grams (90.4 g) and a volume of 8 cubic centimeters (8 cm^3). The density of lead is found as follows.

$$D = \frac{m}{V} = \frac{90.4 \text{ g}}{8 \text{ cm}^3} = 11.3 \text{ g/cm}^3$$

The formula D = m/V can also be used to determine Earth's density. The mass of Earth is calculated from its gravitational force, that is, the force with which it attracts objects of known mass to its surface. The volume of Earth can be calculated from its dimensions. Dividing Earth's volume into its mass gives an average density of 5.5 grams per cubic centimeter.

A similar calculation for the rocks of Earth's crust gives an average density of only 2.8 grams per cubic centimeter. How can the density of Earth's rocks (2.8 grams per cubic centimeter) be so much less than its average density (5.5 grams per cubic centimeter)? In order to have an average density value this high, the materials inside Earth must have densities much greater than 5.5 grams per cubic centimeter. The model of Earth's interior is based partly on the difference between Earth's average density and crustal density. Earth's core is thought to be mostly iron and nickel. Iron and nickel are dense enough to account for the difference. The density of iron is just under 8.0 grams per cubic centimeter. The density of nickel is a little more than 8.0 grams per cubic centimeter.

Topic 6 Temperatures Below the Surface

Have you ever visited an underground cave? In summer, caves are pleasantly cool. Deep caves stay at about the same temperature all year. Neither the sun's heat nor winter cold penetrates Earth below about 20 meters. At this depth, the temperature usually remains equal to the average yearly temperature of the particular place—except in areas of hot springs and volcanoes.

OBJECTIVES

A Define *density* and calculate the density of an object given its mass and volume.

B Give the values for Earth's average density and the density of its crust; relate these values to the model of Earth's layers.

C Discuss sources of heat inside Earth; describe the temperatures of Earth's interior and the evidence for these values.

2.4 Density is the mass in a unit volume of a substance. The two objects on the balance have the same volume. Which object is more dense?

Below a depth of 20 meters, however, is a different situation. Beginning at this depth, the temperature of the ground rises. This temperature rise has been measured thousands of times in deep mines, tunnels, water wells, and oil wells. The increase in temperature differs from place to place, but for the outer crust it averages about 1 degree Celsius (1°C) for every 40 meters in depth.

Direct temperature measurements are only available for a few thousand meters down. Temperature is estimated for depths below that. A temperature rise of 1°C in 40 meters is a very high rate. If that rate continued all the way to Earth's center, the inner core would have a temperature of about 150 000°C. Evidence from earthquakes (Chapter 15) indicates that the inner core is solid, which would be very unlikely at such a high temperature. The inner core is probably no hotter than 7000°C. If the model is correct, the rise in temperature must become more gradual somewhere below the first few thousand meters of Earth's crust.

Topic 7 **What Makes the Crust Hot?**

If Earth's crust gets hotter with increasing depth, there must be some source of heat in the rocks. Most of the heat appears to come from radioactive elements. Radioactive elements give off energy that can be absorbed as heat. Some radioactive elements include uranium, thorium, and a form of potassium. Another possible source of heat is friction between rock masses during movements of Earth's crust. There may also be some heat left over from the original heat of Earth's interior.

Like other planets, Earth loses heat to outer space. The rocks of Earth's crust, however, do not transfer heat very well. Therefore, Earth loses its interior heat slowly. The heat loss is uneven, for several reasons. Some rocks lose heat more quickly than others. The thickness of the rock crust varies. The percentage of radioactive elements is not the same in all rocks. Thus, different amounts of heat loss are measured at different places on Earth's surface.

2.5 Hot springs and geysers at Earth's surface provide evidence that a major heat source exists below the crust.

TOPIC QUESTIONS

Each topic question refers to the topic of the same number.

5. **(a)** A 100-gram rock has a volume of 35 cubic centimeters. Find the density of the rock. **(b)** What is Earth's average density? **(c)** What is the average density of Earth's crust? **(d)** What do these two values indicate about the density of Earth's core?

6. **(a)** Why does an underground cave stay at about the same temperature all year? **(b)** What is the average rate that temperature rises with depth in the outer crust? **(c)** What evidence suggests that this rate does not continue all the way to Earth's core?

7. **(a)** What is thought to be the major source of heat for Earth's crust? **(b)** List some reasons why the heat given off by the crust is different in different places.

Map Skills

Questions 1 and 2 refer to the map of Earth on pages 588–589.

1. Which hemisphere (north or south) has most of Earth's land area? Which hemisphere has most of Earth's water area?

2. What Earth property is impossible to show on this map? How does the shape of the map attempt to show this property?

Dr. James W. Head III
Geologist

Dr. James W. Head III is Professor of Geological Sciences at Brown University. Dr. Head does research on the processes that form and change the surfaces and crusts of planets. He also does research on how these processes form historical records that are preserved on the planets. By studying the history of a planet's crust, scientists are able to learn a great deal about the geologic events that shaped the planet over millions of years.

Dr. Head has helped to plan unmanned lunar and planetary exploration and has helped to train astronauts for space shuttle missions. He received his B.S. degree in 1964 from Washington and Lee University and his Ph.D. from Brown University in 1969. The recent space probes and advances in space technology since that time have made Dr. Head's field of study very busy indeed.

CHAPTER 2 REVIEW

Summary

Evidence that Earth is spherical includes observations of sailing ships, the changing appearance of the nighttime sky over Earth's surface, eclipses of the moon, and photographs of Earth from space.

Earth's rotation causes it to be flattened at the poles and to bulge slightly at the equator. Such a shape is called an oblate spheroid.

The weight of an object depends on its distance from Earth's center; an object's weight is less the further it is from Earth's center. Because Earth is not a perfect sphere, an object weighs slightly less at the equator than it does at the poles.

Earth's circumference can be calculated if the angle and surface distance between any two points on its surface are known. Eratosthenes is thought to be the first person to calculate Earth's circumference.

Earth's diameter is slightly less at the poles, slightly more at the equator. Most of Earth's surface is covered by oceans.

The density of an object is found by dividing its mass by its volume ($D = m/V$).

Earth's average density is 5.5 grams per cubic centimeter. The density of its crust averages 2.8 grams per cubic centimeter. Earth's iron-nickel core is its densest part.

Temperatures increase with depth in Earth's outer crust. Evidence indicates that the temperature does not increase at the same rate all the way to Earth's interior.

Earth's internal heat is mainly from radioactive elements such as uranium and thorium. Earth's original heat and friction between moving rock masses may be other sources of heat. The rate at which Earth loses heat to outer space varies over Earth's crust.

Vocabulary

density
oblate spheroid

Review

Number your paper from *1* to *18*. On your paper write the word that best completes each sentence.

1. The way a sailing ship gradually appears over the horizon is one evidence that Earth is ______.
2. The North Star rises higher in the sky as an observer travels toward the ______
3. During an eclipse of the moon, Earth's shadow on the moon is always an arc of a ______.
4. Only a ______ casts a circular shadow from every position.
5. Because Earth is almost spherical, an object's ______ is nearly the same anywhere on Earth's surface.
6. An object weighs ______ the further it is from the center of Earth.
7. An object weighs slightly ______ at Earth's poles than at Earth's equator.
8. Eratosthenes used the difference between the angle of the sun at Syene and Alexandria and the distance between those two cities to calculate Earth's ______.
9. An object like Earth that is flattened at the poles and bulges at the equator is said to have the shape of a ______.
10. Earth's diameter at the equator is ______ than its diameter at the poles.
11. Most of Earth's surface is covered by ______.
12. ______ is the measure of the amount of mass in a given volume.
13. The density of Earth's ______ is much less than the average density of Earth.
14. The densest part of Earth is its nickel-iron ______.
15. The temperature of Earth's outer crust ______ 1°C for every 40 meters in depth.
16. If the temperature change were constant all the way to Earth's core, then the core would have to be ______. Earthquake evidence suggests that this is not the case.

17. The major source of heat inside Earth is ____ elements such as uranium and thorium.
18. Earth's original heat and ______ between moving rock masses may be sources of heat inside Earth.

Interpret and Apply

On your paper, answer each question.

1. During a total eclipse of the sun, the moon's shadow falls on Earth. The moon's shadow is always a circle. What does this suggest about the shape of the moon?
2. What should happen to the weight of an object as it is moved from a valley to a nearby mountaintop?
3. Planet X has a spherical shape. Two points on Planet X are 10° of arc apart. The distance between these same two points is 1500 kilometers. **(a)** What is the circumference of Planet X? **(b)** Is Planet X larger or smaller than Earth? (Refer to Topic 3.)
4. Rotating objects are affected by centripetal force, a force that pushes away from the center of rotation. For a rotating sphere, centripetal force is strongest at the equator. Explain how Earth's rotation causes it to have the shape of an oblate spheroid.
5. If Earth did not rotate, would an object at the equator weigh more or less than it does now? Why? (Refer to Interpret and Apply item 4.)
6. What is the density of an object with a mass of 10 grams and a volume of 5 cubic centimeters?
7. An object will float in a liquid if it is less dense than that liquid. The density of water is 1 gram per cubic centimeter. A particular block of wood has a mass of 3.21 grams and a volume of 3 cubic centimeters. Will the wood float in water? Why or why not?
8. **(a)** An object has a mass of 6 grams and a volume of 2 cubic centimeters. Find its density. **(b)** The object described in Part **(a)** is cut in half. What is the density of each half?

Critical Thinking

Scientists try to reduce sources of error in their measurements. Eratosthenes did well at measuring Earth's circumference with the information available to him. However, there were several sources of error in the information he used. How many sources of error can you find? Refer to Topic 3, to the map of Egypt, and to the other information listed below. List the errors you find on your paper.

In Eratosthenes' time, travelers had to stay near sources of water.

The sun is overhead at noon on the longest day of the year for locations on the Tropic of Cancer.

Eratosthenes estimated the distance from Alexandria to Syene based on the distance a camel could walk in a day and the number of days it took a camel to walk to Syene from Alexandria.

When size estimates are made by multiplying part of a whole item, using a larger part of the whole leads to more accurate results.

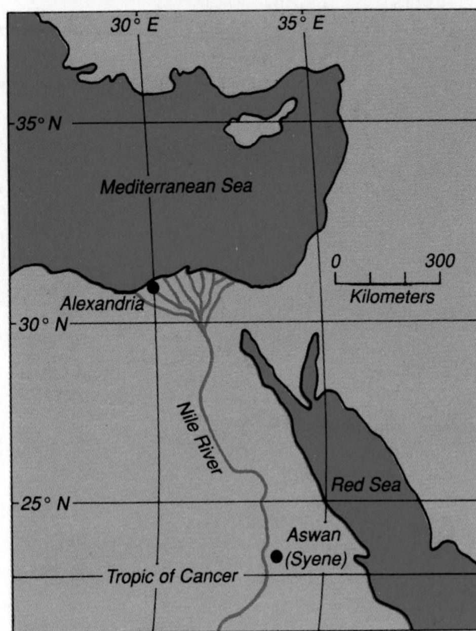

CHAPTER

3 Atoms to Minerals

▲ An amethyst can be cut into many shapes, but amethyst crystals in nature have the same shape.

How Do You Know That . . .

Gemstone shapes are different from natural crystal shapes? The lovely violet mineral shown is amethyst, a kind of quartz. The gemstones surrounding the mineral are also amethyst. The amethyst gems have been artificially cut to have shapes different from the shape of the crystal. Gemstones can be cut to almost any shape. However, the natural crystal shape of a gemstone mineral is always the same. How does the arrangement of mineral particles determine crystal shape?

I Atomic Structure of Matter

OBJECTIVES

A Explain the properties of matter in terms of the particle model.

B Define *element* and *atom*, and describe the particles, structure, and size of the atom.

C Determine the number of protons and neutrons in an atom from its atomic number and atomic mass; define *isotope*.

D Define *compound* and *molecule* and compare the properties of compounds with those of elements and mixtures.

Topic 1 Earth's Matter

You already know that Earth has layers. Earth's outermost layer, its crust, is made of rock. Rocks are made of minerals. What makes up minerals? To understand the materials that make up Earth's crust, you must first learn what makes up all earth materials—matter.

What is matter? **Matter** is anything that has mass and volume. *Mass* is the material in an object or substance. Mass is often discussed in terms of weight, but mass and weight are not the same. Weight is the force of gravity on an object or substance. If the force of gravity is very weak, as in outer space, an object has no weight, but it still has mass. *Volume* is the amount of space that is taken up by an object or substance. A sample of earth material—for example, a bucket of sand—has mass and volume and therefore is matter.

Scientists have developed a model to explain observations about matter. According to the model, all matter is made of particles. These particles are so small that they cannot be seen, not even with a microscope. Even though there are only about one hundred kinds of basic particles, there are about 3000 different kinds of minerals and many thousands of other substances.

Topic 2 Elements and Atoms

All matter is composed of elements. An **element** is a substance that cannot be broken into simpler substances by ordinary chemical means. The names of many elements are already familiar. Oxygen and nitrogen are elements in the atmosphere; gold, silver, and iron are examples of metallic elements. Each element has a symbol as well as a name. Usually the symbol is the first letter or two of the element's name; for example, the symbol for hydrogen is H, and the symbol for helium is He. Some elements take their symbols from their Latin or Greek name. For example, the symbol for gold is Au, from the Latin name for gold, *aurum*.

What makes up elements? More than 150 years ago the English chemist John Dalton stated his concept of the particle model—that each element is made up of tiny particles called atoms. Dalton defined the **atom** as the smallest part of an element that has all the properties of that element. Today scientists know that the atom itself is made from still smaller particles. Furthermore, all atoms—from every kind of element—contain the same kinds of particles! Let us look closer at the structure of an atom.

3.1 The position of a single propeller blade is difficult to determine while the blades are in motion. The motion of electrons is similar because electrons fill the space in which they move, but the position of one electron is difficult to determine.

Topic 3 Model of an Atom

How does one imagine an atom? The atom is extremely small and complex. The model of the atom's structure has changed many times since the days of John Dalton. A large part of the atom model of today is based on complex mathematics. The pictures of atoms that you see in this book are used to help you visualize the structure and properties of atoms. However, these pictures do not show how atoms actually look.

Imagine charged particles moving at high speed about a central nucleus (plural, nuclei). The moving charged particles are **electrons**. Their motion creates a cloud of charge surrounding the nucleus. The exact path an electron takes in moving about the nucleus has never been determined. The motion of electrons in the cloud is like the area occupied by the blades of a moving fan. The position of a fan blade cannot be determined while the blades are in motion. The same idea holds for the motion of an electron.

The nucleus of an atom contains **protons** and **neutrons**. Each proton also has an electric charge, but it is unlike that of the electron. The electron's charge is negative and the proton's charge is positive. The amount of the proton's positive charge is exactly equal to the amount of the negative charge of an electron. The neutron carries no charge. An atom has as many electrons in the cloud around the nucleus as it has protons in the nucleus. The atom is electrically neutral, since protons and electrons have equal but opposite charges.

The atom is tiny. An atom of iron, for example, is about 25 ten-millionths of a meter in diameter. Yet most of its volume is empty space! The diameter of the nucleus is, on the average, about one hundred-thousandth of the diameter of the space in which its electrons move. This tiny space contains the more massive atomic particles. The proton is 1836 times heavier than the electron, and the neutron is slightly heavier than the proton. More than 99.9 percent of the mass of an atom is in its nucleus.

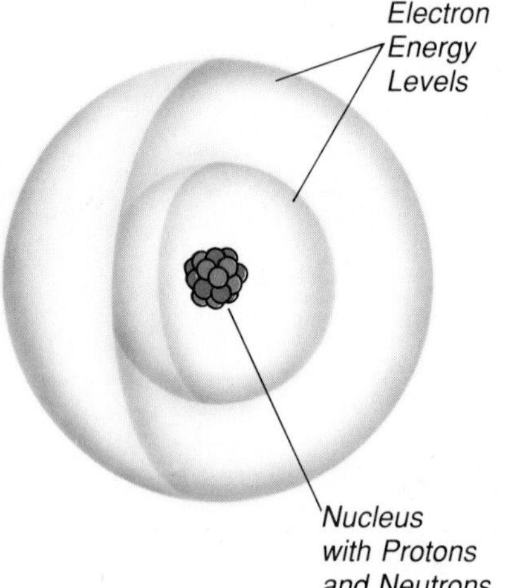

3.2 This model of the atom shows a central nucleus surrounded by electrons.

Topic 4 Examples of Atomic Structure

The simplest and lightest of all atoms is ordinary hydrogen, the symbol for which is H. Ordinary hydrogen has a nucleus with one proton. It is the only atom without neutrons. A single electron occupies the electron cloud surrounding the nucleus.

The second lightest of the elements is helium, He. The nucleus of a helium atom has two protons. Two electrons in its cloud electrically balance the two positively charged protons in the nucleus. The helium nucleus also contains two neutrons, as shown in Figure 3.3. These neutrons make up about half the mass of a helium atom.

The third lightest element is lithium, Li. The lithium atom has three protons in its nucleus and three electrons in the electron cloud outside the nucleus. The nucleus also includes four neutrons. For atoms that have more than two electrons the electron cloud is divided into energy levels, as the model in Figure 3.2 illustrates. Two of lithium's three electrons move about the nucleus in an energy level like that of the helium atom, but the third electron lies beyond the first two in an energy level of its own.

This scheme of electron structure continues. As the number of electrons increases new energy levels exist, but in every atom the number of electrons equals the number of protons. The largest number of energy levels in any atom is seven. The number of electrons differs from level to level, but the innermost level never holds more than two electrons. Other levels may hold up to 32 electrons.

With each change in the number of protons and electrons, there is a change in the properties of the atoms. The heaviest of the natural elements, uranium, U, has 92 protons in its nucleus. Its 92 electrons are distributed in its seven energy levels as follows: 2, 8, 18, 32, 21, 9, 2. Do they add up to 92?

3.3 Atoms are three-dimensional. These models of hydrogen, helium, and lithium show the numbers of electrons, protons, and neutrons.

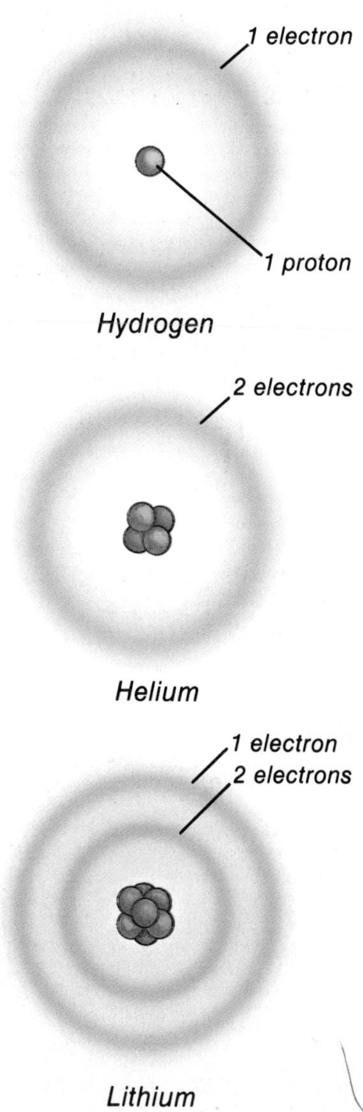

Topic 5 Atomic Number and Mass Number

The **atomic number** is the number of protons in an atom. This value is 1 for hydrogen; 2 for helium; 3 for lithium; and 92 for uranium. The atomic number of oxygen is 8. The oxygen atom, therefore, has 8 protons in its nucleus and 8 electrons in its electron cloud—2 in the first energy level and 6 in the second.

How many neutrons are there in a nucleus? There is no simple rule relating the number of neutrons to the number of protons. However, the **mass number** of the element gives the average number of protons and neutrons in an atom. To find the number of neutrons in an atom, simply subtract the atomic number (number of protons) from the mass number.

number of neutrons = mass number − atomic number

For example, the atomic number of potassium is 19; its mass number is 39. The potassium nucleus, therefore, contains 19 protons and (subtracting 19 from 39) 20 neutrons. How many electrons move about the nucleus? Since the number of electrons must equal the number of protons, the answer is 19 electrons. Try another example: If uranium, whose atomic number is 92, has a mass number of 238, its atom must include 92 electrons, 92 protons, and 146 neutrons. Check to see if these values are correct.

A periodic table of the elements appears in the Appendix on pages 578–579. Notice that there are more than 100 different elements. No more than 90 of these occur naturally on Earth, although scientists have created synthetic elements in the laboratory. In the periodic table, elements are listed horizontally in order of atomic number and vertically by similar chemical properties. Each element, indicated by its symbol, is in its own box in the periodic table. The box for potassium is shown in Figure 3.4. Each element's box includes information about atoms of the element. Refer to the periodic table when you need information for an element.

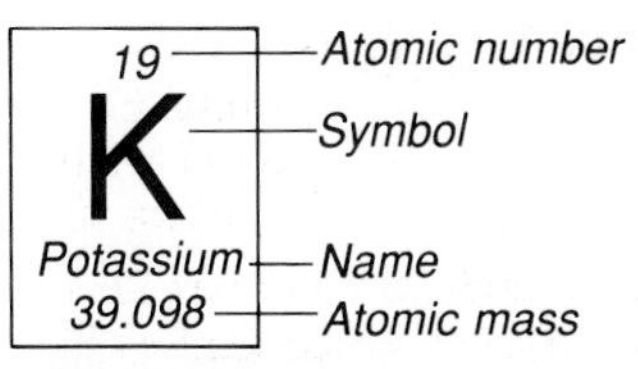

3.4 The box for potassium

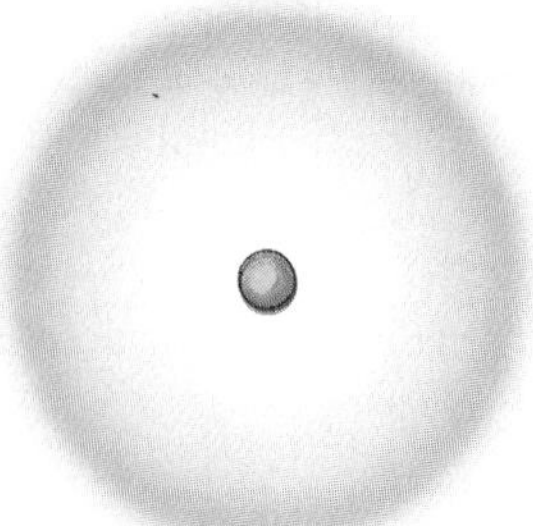

Common Hydrogen
Mass Number = 1
Atomic Number = 1

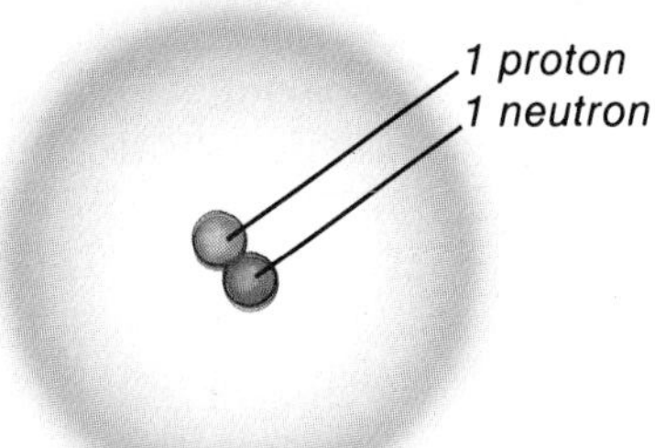

Deuterium
Mass Number = 2
Atomic Number = 1

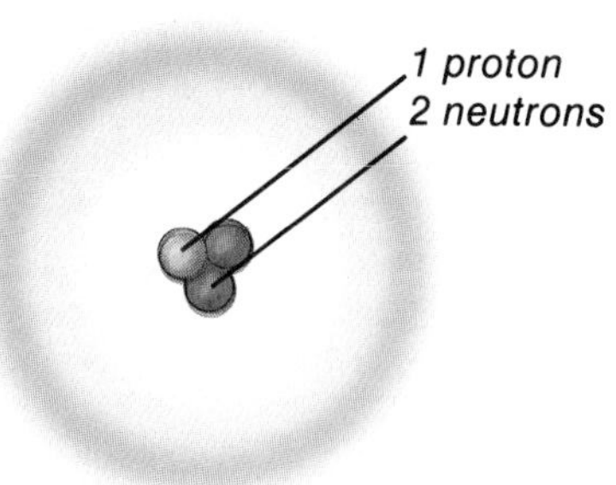

Tritium
Mass Number = 3
Atomic Number = 1

3.5 Each hydrogen isotope has the same number of protons and electrons but different numbers of neutrons.

Topic 6 Isotopes

The identity of an atom depends only on the number of protons and not on the number of neutrons. Many elements have atoms with the same number of protons but different numbers of neutrons. **Isotopes** are atoms of the same chemical element with different mass numbers.

Hydrogen has three isotopes. Ordinary hydrogen has one proton and no neutrons in its nucleus. Its atomic number is 1; its mass number is also 1. However, hydrogen has a second isotope with 1 proton and 1 neutron in its nucleus. Its atomic number is 1, but its mass number is 2. This isotope is known as "heavy hydrogen" or *deuterium* (doo TEER ee um). It is much less common than ordinary hydrogen. The third isotope of hydrogen is rare. Known as *tritium* (TRIT ee um), it has a mass number of 3 with a nucleus of 1 proton and 2 neutrons.

You may have heard of carbon-14, the heavy isotope of carbon. Each ordinary atom of carbon-12 has a nucleus of 6 protons and 6 neutrons. Carbon-14 atoms (mass number, 14) have nuclei with 6 protons and 8 neutrons.

Uranium has a number of isotopes. Ordinary uranium, described in Topic 5, has a mass number of 238, with 146 neutrons in its nucleus. Uranium-235 (mass number, 235), however, has only 143 neutrons in its nucleus. All isotopes have 92 protons in the nucleus.

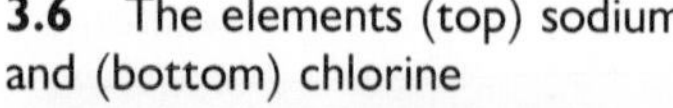

3.6 The elements (top) sodium and (bottom) chlorine

Topic 7 Compounds

So far only elements have been discussed. However, most minerals—in fact, most substances—are compounds. A **compound** is a substance that contains two or more elements chemically combined. Dalton said that an atom is the smallest part of an element. The smallest part of a compound that still has all the properties of that compound is a **molecule**. A molecule consists of at least two atoms. In a molecule, each element is present in a definite proportion to the other elements. For example, a molecule of water always contains two atoms of the element hydrogen and one atom of the element oxygen.

A compound can have properties entirely unlike the elements of which it is made. For example, water is certainly different from hydrogen and oxygen. Hydrogen and oxygen are gases, but water is a liquid. Another example is salt, which is a compound of the elements sodium and chlorine. Sodium and chlorine are shown in Figure 3.6; salt is shown in Figure 3.7. Both sodium and chlorine are poisonous by themselves. Yet when these two elements are chemically combined they form salt, a compound most people can eat safely with their food.

Compounds should not be confused with mixtures. In a *mixture* the individual elements or compounds keep their own properties and can be present in any proportions. Most mixtures can be separated easily by physical means—for example, picking them apart, dissolving those that are soluble, or sifting out the different substances by grain size. Salt water is an example of a mixture. It can be separated by evaporating the water. The elements in a compound, however, can only be separated by chemical means. For example, water can be decomposed into hydrogen and oxygen by passing a strong electric current through it.

3.7 The compound sodium chloride, as it occurs in nature

TOPIC QUESTIONS

Each topic question refers to the topic of the same number.

1. (a) What is matter? (b) Describe the particle model of matter.
2. (a) What is an element? (b) What is an atom? (c) Who was John Dalton?
3. (a) Name and describe the three kinds of particles that make up atoms. (b) Identify where in the atom each kind of particle is located.
4. (a) Describe the structure of an atom of each of these elements: hydrogen, helium, and lithium. (b) In what ways are atoms of different elements alike? (c) In what ways are atoms of different elements different?
5. (a) Define atomic number. (b) Define mass number. (c) How many protons, neutrons, and electrons are in an ordinary atom of sodium? (Show your work.)
6. (a) What is an isotope? (b) List the numbers of protons, neutrons, and electrons for carbon-12, carbon-14, uranium-238, and uranium-235.
7. (a) Define compound. (b) What is a molecule? (c) Describe how a compound is different from a mixture and give an example of each.

OBJECTIVES

A Identify a substance as a mineral or nonmineral based on its structure and origin.

B Identify the most common elements in Earth's minerals; define *native mineral*.

C Define and describe the formation of ionic and covalent bonds and identify the general element combinations that form each kind of bond.

D Describe some ways minerals form.

II Chemical Composition of Minerals

Topic 8 What Is a Mineral?

All matter is made of elements, including the rocks and minerals of Earth's crust. What makes a mineral different from other forms of matter? Several things must be true for a material to be called a mineral. A mineral

1. occurs naturally,
2. is a solid,
3. has a definite chemical composition (that is, its elements are combined in definite proportions),
4. has its atoms arranged in an orderly pattern, and
5. is *inorganic* (it was not formed by any process involving plants, animals, or other organisms).

A substance that fits this description is a **mineral**.

Which earth materials are minerals? Examples of familiar minerals include quartz, halite (rock salt), mica, gold, and diamond. Each of these minerals occur naturally in Earth's crust. Each is a solid at normal surface temperatures. Each has a definite chemical composition. The atoms in each mineral are arranged in orderly patterns. None is made by any process involving plants or animals.

What kinds of earth materials are not minerals? Water is not a mineral because it is not a solid. The glass in a window is not a mineral because window glass does not occur naturally. A pearl is not a mineral because it is formed by an oyster. Coal is not a mineral because it is made from plant remains, it lacks a definite composition, and its atoms are not arranged in an orderly way.

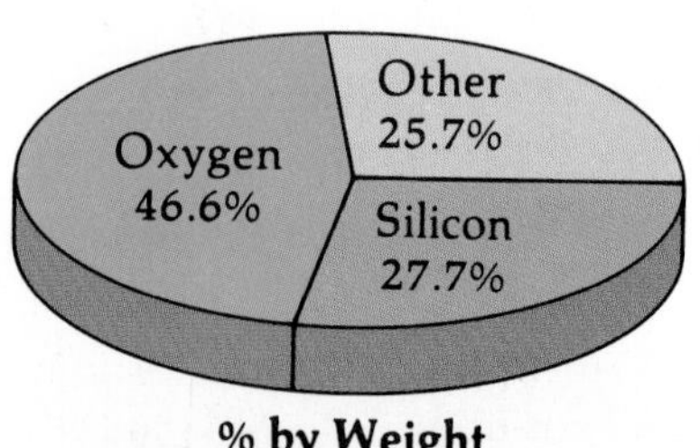

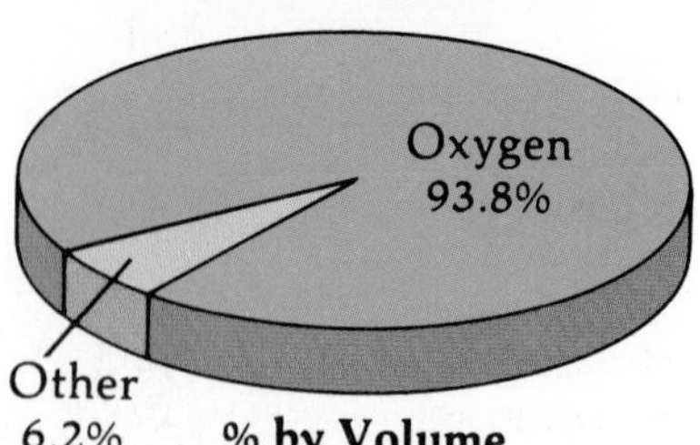

3.8 The percentage of oxygen in Earth's crust is significant in terms of weight and volume.

Topic 9 Minerals May Be Elements or Compounds

Of all the elements in Earth's crust, a mere eight make up 98.5 percent of the crust's total mass. These eight elements, which are listed in the table below, are almost always found combined with other elements as chemical compounds. The two most abundant elements, oxygen and silicon, are found in more than 90 percent of the minerals in the crust.

Oxygen is a significantly larger portion of the crust than silicon. By mass, oxygen is nearly 50 percent of Earth's crust while silicon is about 28 percent. By volume, the difference is much more marked. Oxygen, by volume, makes up nearly 94 percent of the crust, while silicon is less than 1 percent. The reason for this difference is that the space taken up by an oxygen atom in a compound is more than the space taken up by a silicon atom.

The Eight Most Common Elements in Earth's Crust

Name	Chemical Symbol	Percent by Mass	Percent by Volume
Oxygen	O	46.6	93.8
Silicon	Si	27.7	0.9
Aluminum	Al	8.1	0.8
Iron	Fe	5.0	0.5
Calcium	Ca	3.6	1.0
Sodium	Na	2.8	1.2
Potassium	K	2.6	1.5
Magnesium	Mg	2.1	0.3

3.9 Native minerals, such as the copper sample shown, are elements that occur uncombined in nature.

Most minerals are compounds. Quartz is a compound of silicon and oxygen. Most sand is composed of quartz. Halite (rock salt) is a compound of sodium and chlorine. The mineral galena, an ore of lead, is a compound of lead and sulfur. A few minerals, however, are made of only one element. Minerals composed of single elements are called **native minerals**, or native elements. Examples of native minerals are gold (Au), silver (Ag), copper (Cu), sulfur (S), and diamond (C).

Topic 10 Ionic Bonds in Minerals

How do atoms of different elements stay together in a mineral that is a compound? For one type of compound, the answer lies in electric attraction. In its normal state each atom has an equal number of protons and electrons. It is electrically neutral. If an atom gains one or more electrons, it becomes negatively charged. If an atom loses one or more electrons, it becomes positively charged. An atom in a charged condition, either negative or positive, is called an **ion**. Groups of atoms may also form ions.

Since opposite charges attract each other, ions of opposite charges may bond together to form compounds. For example, positively charged sodium ions are bonded with negatively charged chlorine ions in the compound sodium chloride, or table salt. Sodium chloride is found in nature as the mineral halite. Many other minerals contain ions.

How do atoms lose or gain electrons to form ions? Consider the element sodium. You can see from the sodium model in Figure 3.6 that its outer energy level contains only one electron. Sodium reacts with many elements in order to lose this outer electron. Chlorine is reactive for the opposite reason. Its outer energy level is short one electron, so it reacts with other elements to gain an electron. When sodium and chlorine react, sodium loses its outer electron, which chlorine gains. Both sodium and chlorine have become charged particles, or ions, and both are now chemically stable. The force of attraction, or **ionic bond**, between the oppositely charged ions holds them together.

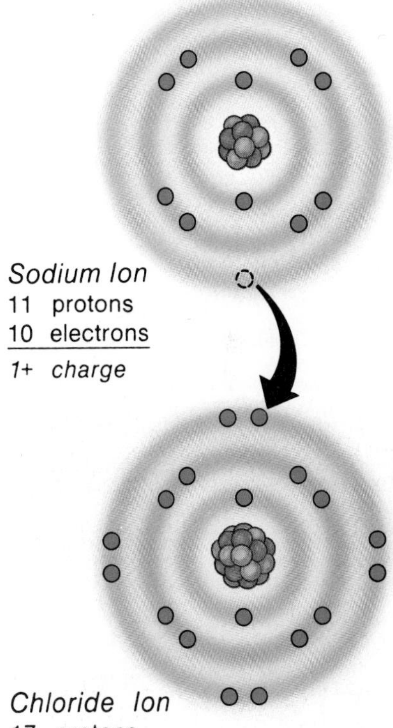

3.10 Ions are formed when electrons are transferred between atoms. Sodium chloride consists of a positive sodium ion that has transferred one electron to chlorine to form a negative chloride ion.

Nonmetal	Metal (Metalloid)
O Atom 0.132 nm	Si Atom 0.234 nm
O^{2-} Ion 0.28 nm	Si^{4+} Ion 0.082 nm

Diameters are measured in nanometers (nm). There are 1 billion nanometers in 1 meter.

3.11 Negative ions tend to be larger than the nonmetal atoms from which they formed. Positive ions tend to be smaller than the metal atoms from which they formed.

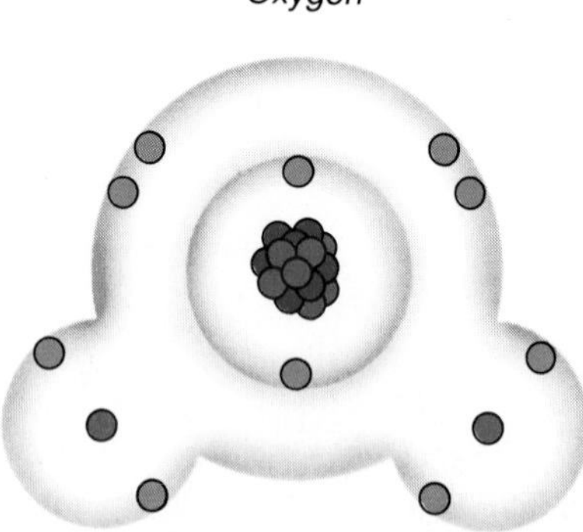

3.12 In a water molecule, two hydrogen atoms and one oxygen atom share eight electrons in a covalent bond.

Elements that lose electrons easily and form positive ions are classed as **metals**. They include gold, silver, iron, copper, lead, aluminum, sodium, potassium, calcium, zinc, and many others. Metals appear on the left side of the periodic table. Notice that most pure elements are metals.

Elements that gain electrons easily and form negative ions are classed as **nonmetals**. They include nitrogen, oxygen, fluorine, chlorine, phosphorus, and sulfur. Nonmetals appear on the right side of the periodic table. The ions of nonmetals are generally much larger than the ions of metals.

Topic 11 Covalent Bonds in Minerals

Ionic bonds form easily between metals and nonmetals. How can a compound form from two nonmetals? Compounds also form when elements combine and share electrons. For example, two atoms of hydrogen and one atom of oxygen share electrons in a molecule of water. In a molecule of carbon dioxide, one carbon atom and two oxygen atoms share electrons. The kind of attachment where electrons are shared by atoms is called a **covalent bond**. Covalent bonds are common between nonmetal elements, and many minerals contain covalent bonds. The common mineral quartz contains the elements silicon and oxygen combined by covalent bonds.

Some elements—such as helium, neon, and argon—do not readily gain, lose, or share electrons, and form a limited number of compounds. They are described as *noble gas* elements. Because noble gases do not form compounds easily, they are not found combined in any minerals.

Topic 12 How Minerals Form

Minerals can form in several ways. Many minerals form out of molten earth material, or magma. Atoms in magma are free to move around each other. As magma cools, its atoms move closer together. As the atoms move closer together, they are able to combine to form mineral compounds. Many different minerals can form out of one magma mass. The kinds of minerals that form depend in part on which elements are present and in what amount. The rate at which the magma cools determines the size of the mineral grains that form (Topic 13).

Some kinds of minerals form when water containing dissolved ions evaporates. Halite forms when salt water evaporates. As the water molecules evaporate into water vapor, the sodium and chlorine ions arrange themselves into the mineral halite. Other minerals also form by evaporation. Minerals can also be changed into different minerals by heat, pressure, or the chemical action of water.

TOPIC QUESTIONS

Each topic question refers to the topic of the same number.

8. **(a)** List and describe the five factors that determine whether a substance is a mineral. **(b)** Give several examples of minerals. **(c)** Explain why window glass, pearl, water, and coal are not minerals.

9. **(a)** What are the most common elements in Earth's crust? **(b)** How do the common elements usually occur? **(c)** Explain why oxygen and silicon are important elements in Earth's crust. **(d)** What name is given to those few minerals that are composed of only one element? Give examples.

10. **(a)** What is an ion? **(b)** Describe how ions form. **(c)** What is an ionic bond? **(d)** Define metal and nonmetal and give an example of each.

11. **(a)** Describe a covalent bond. **(b)** What is a noble gas element?

12. Describe two ways minerals can form.

Dr. Keith G. Cox
Mineralogist

Keith G. Cox is a specialist in the field of mineralogy. He received his bachelor's degree from Oxford University in England. In 1956, he became a research student in the Research Institute of African Geology at the University of Leeds and did fieldwork in the Karroo volcanic region of South Africa. In describing his fieldwork in South Africa, he tells how "quite by accident" he was "directed by a local diamond prospector to the Matsoku Kimberlite pipe, a mine which at that time was not known to scientists." Kimberlite is the kind of ancient volcanic rock in which diamonds are found and mined, and its further study became a specialty of Dr. Cox.

Dr. Cox was a lecturer at the University of Edinburgh for seven years and is now university lecturer in the Department of Earth Sciences at Oxford University, his alma mater. He is the coauthor of textbooks on rocks and a former editor of the *Journal of Petrology* (petrology is the study of rocks) and of *Earth and Planetary Science Letters.*

OBJECTIVES

A Discuss the origin of mineral crystals and give examples.

B Explain the importance of silicate minerals; describe the silica tetrahedron and the arrangement of silica tetrahedra in several minerals.

C Relate a mineral's atomic arrangement to its crystal shape, hardness, cleavage, and density.

III Structure of Minerals

Topic 13 Minerals Have Crystalline Structure

Minerals are often found in the form of beautiful crystals. **Crystals** have regular geometric forms featured by smooth surfaces or crystal faces. Each mineral always has its own crystal form, with angles between particular faces always measuring the same number of degrees. A repeating arrangement of smaller units determines the shape of the crystal. Quartz crystals have a long, regular, six-sided shape. The building blocks that cause this shape in quartz will be discussed in Topic 14. The crystals of halite (sodium chloride), pyrite (iron sulfide), and galena (lead sulfide) are cubes. Diamond crystals have an octahedral (eight-sided) shape.

Mineralogists reasoned that the crystal form of a particular mineral was probably the result of a regular geometric arrangement of its ions or atoms. In 1912, X rays were first used for studying the internal structure of crystals. These X-ray photographs showed the arrangement of particles in crystals of the various minerals.

Consider the arrangement of sodium and chlorine ions in a halite crystal. Opposite charges attract, so each positively charged sodium ion becomes attached to a negatively charged chloride ion. As the ions line themselves up alternately, the result is the orderly arrangement that is seen as crystals. Thus in examining Figure 3.13 you see that every sodium ion is actually surrounded by six chloride ions. Every chloride ion is surrounded by six sodium ions. This cubic arrangement is repeated throughout the crystal.

When large numbers of ions are free to arrange themselves during the growth of the mineral, large perfect crystals may form. More often, however, conditions in Earth's crust limit crystal growth. Crystals are hemmed in by other crystals while they are all still tiny and imperfect. A magnifying glass or microscope can reveal crystal faces not apparent to the unaided eye.

In some crystals, atoms share electrons in covalent bonds. In diamond, for example, carbon atoms are arranged in a network pat-

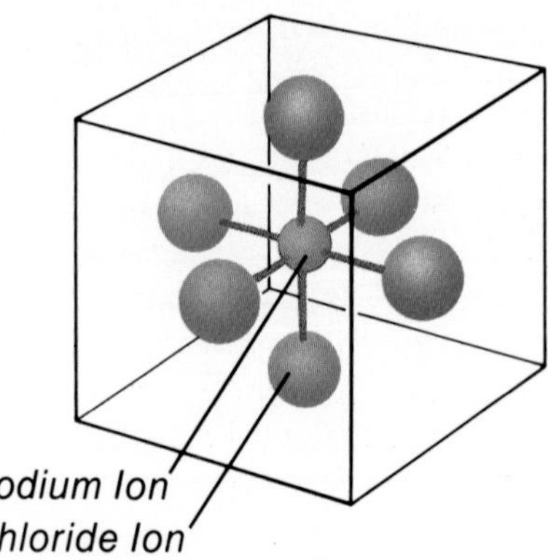

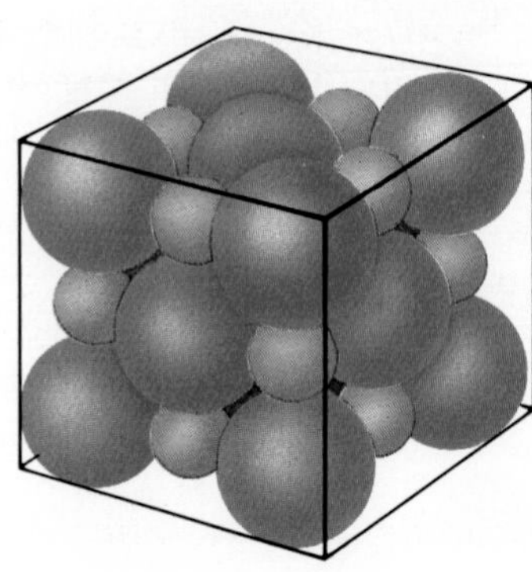

3.13 The crystalline arrangement of sodium chloride shows that each unit consists of one ion surrounded by six ions of opposite charge. Each individual unit has a cubic shape.

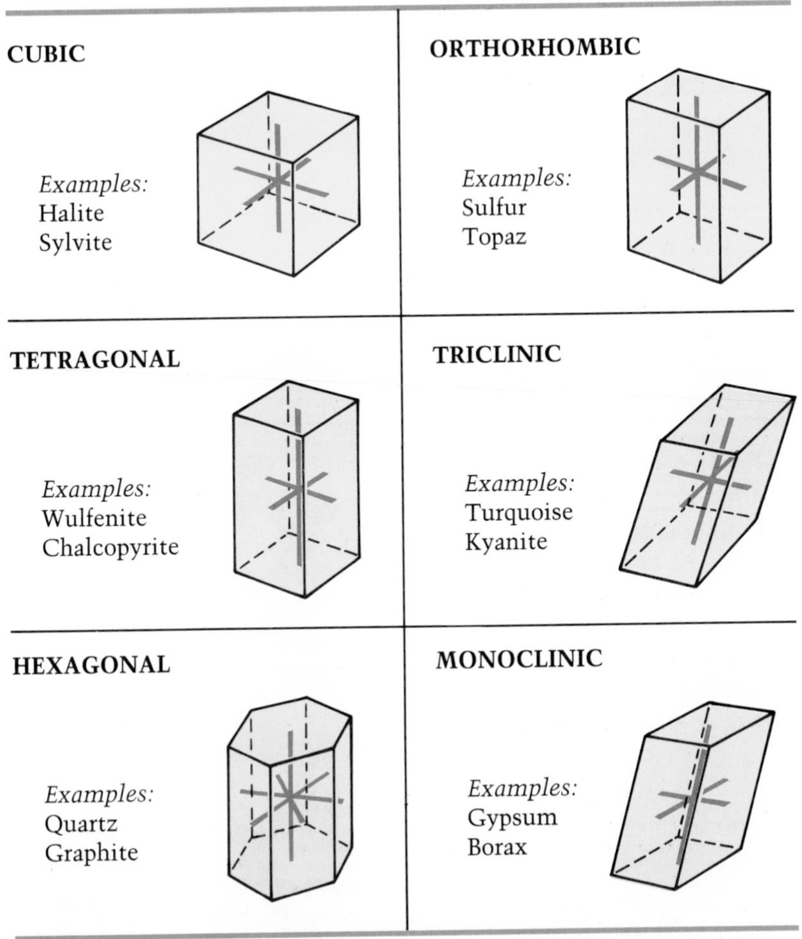

3.14 Mineral crystal shapes belong to one of six crystal *systems*, or families of related shapes.

tern. Each carbon atom shares one electron with each of four other atoms. Covalent bonds can also occur between atoms of different elements. Many minerals are covalently bonded.

Topic 14 The Silica Tetrahedron

More than 90 percent of the minerals in Earth's crust are members of a mineral family called **silicates**. These are compounds of the elements silicon and oxygen, plus one or more metallic element, such as aluminum or iron. In all silicates, the basic building block is four oxygen atoms packed closely around a silicon atom. This unit is held together by covalent bonds between the silicon atom and oxygen atoms. If imaginary lines are drawn to connect the centers of the four oxygen atoms, they make a geometric figure called a tetrahedron. So the basic unit, with the silicon atom in the center, is known as the **silica tetrahedron**. Its geometric representation (Figure 3.15) is less realistic but easier to use in illustrations. Incidentally, the word *silica* merely means "silicon plus oxygen."

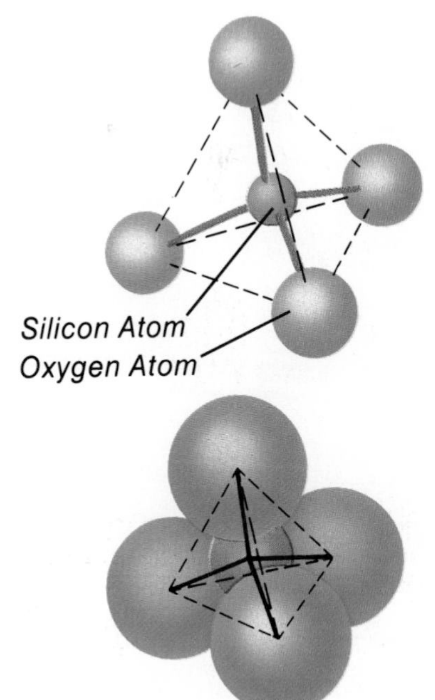

3.15 A silica tetrahedron consists of a silicon atom bonded covalently to four oxygen atoms. The bonds shown represent shared electrons.

3.16 Many properties of silicate minerals depend on the arrangement of their silica tetrahedrons.

Some Bonding Arrangements for Silica Tetrahedrons

IONIC

Silica tetrahedrons with positive iron or magnesium ions attached to negative SiO_4 ions as in the mineral olivine.

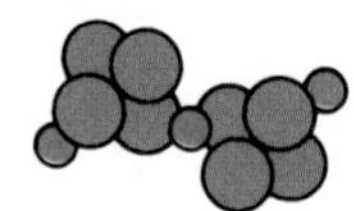

SINGLE CHAINS

Silica tetrahedrons sharing electrons to form single chains of tetrahedrons as in pyroxene.

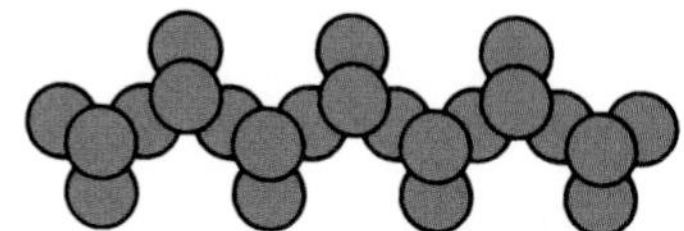

DOUBLE CHAINS

Silica tetrahedrons sharing electrons to form double chains as in amphibole.

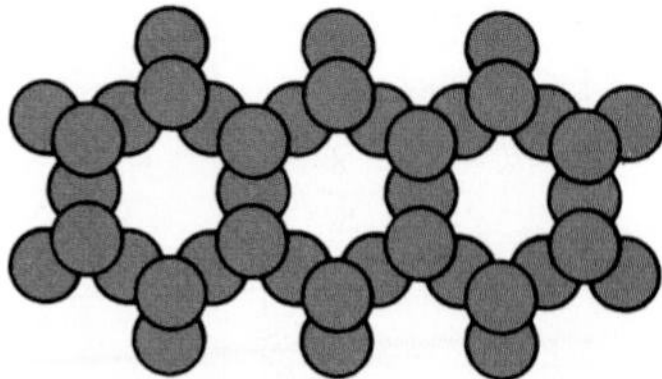

SHEETS

Silica tetrahedrons sharing electrons to form sheets of tetrahedrons as in mica.

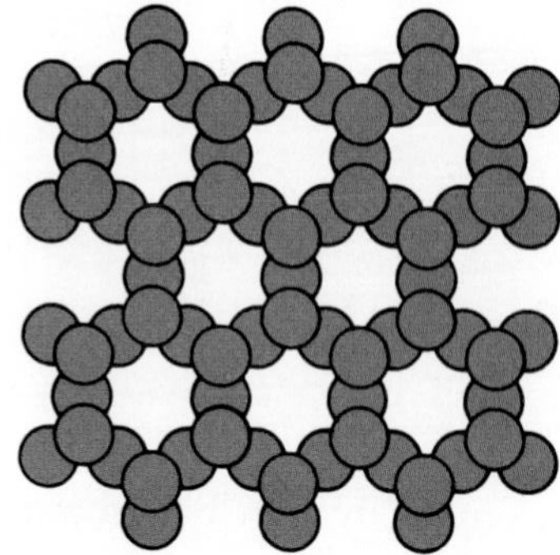

Topic 15 Crystals and Physical Properties

The orderly arrangement of the atoms or ions in a mineral helps to explain other properties of the mineral besides its crystal shape.

A mineral is *solid* because of the close packing of its ions or atoms and the strong forces of attraction among them. An increase in temperature weakens the bonds between particles. Therefore, solids melt into the loose groups of particles in a liquid, or they vaporize into a gas in which individual particles are far apart.

The *hardness* of a mineral depends on the arrangement of its ions or atoms and the strength of the electric forces among them. A good example of this property is seen in the element carbon. In one arrangement carbon forms diamond, the hardest natural mineral.

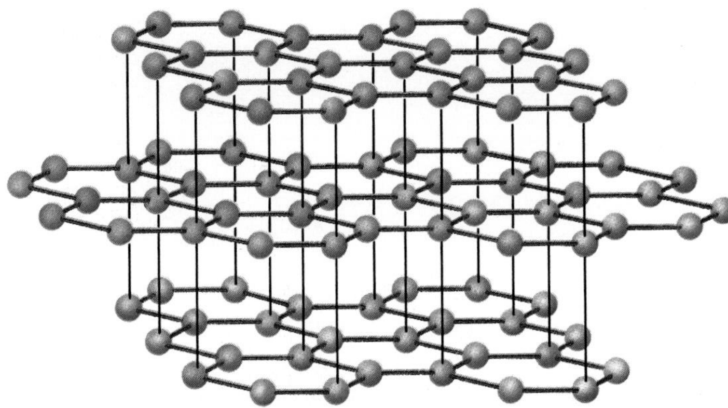

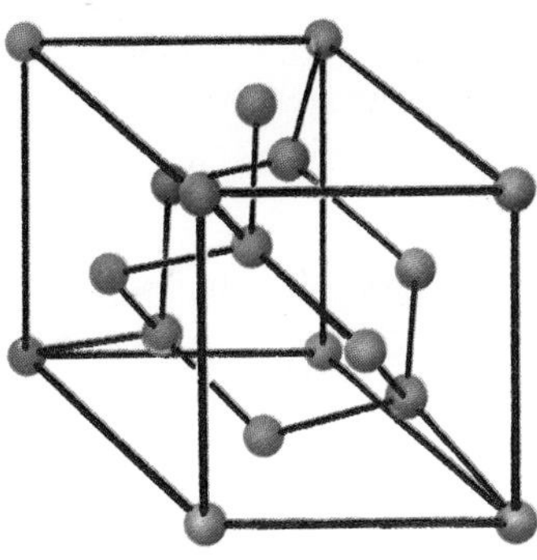

3.17 Graphite (left) consists of layers of carbon atoms bonded in interlocking hexagonal rings. Diamond (right) is a network of carbon atoms. The bonds between the layers of carbon atoms in graphite are weak. The bonds between carbon atoms in diamond are strong. Thus the properties of graphite differ greatly from those of diamond.

Diamond consists of a tetrahedral network of carbon atoms. In another arrangement, carbon forms graphite, a very soft mineral that flakes easily. Carbon atoms are arranged in layers or sheets in the graphite structure.

The *cleavage* of a mineral is its tendency to split or separate along flat surfaces. The planes along which the mineral splits are directions of weak bonds among the ions or atoms of the mineral. Halite splits into cubes between layers of ions. Quartz, with its strong network of atoms, does not split along any plane.

Remember that the density of a mineral is the ratio of its mass to its volume. This property depends on the mass of the ions or atoms of the mineral, but it also depends on how closely they are packed together. The density of the loosely packed mineral graphite is about 2.3 g/cm^3, but that of closely packed diamond is 3.5 g/cm^3. Both minerals are pure carbon.

Let us now summarize the characteristics of a mineral as described in this chapter.

1. A mineral is an element or compound found in nature.
2. Its ions or atoms usually are arranged in regular patterns that give it a crystalline structure.
3. It has a characteristic chemical composition.
4. It has definite physical properties.
5. It is inorganic.

TOPIC QUESTIONS

Each topic question refers to the topic of the same number.

13. **(a)** What is a crystal? **(b)** Describe why crystals form, in terms of the atoms or ions in a mineral. **(c)** Why are some crystals large and perfect, while others are small and irregular?

14. **(a)** What are the silicate minerals? **(b)** How are the atoms arranged in the silica tetrahedron unit?

15. How does the crystalline structure of a mineral explain its **(a)** solid nature, **(b)** hardness, **(c)** cleavage, and **(d)** density? **(e)** Summarize the characteristics of a mineral.

CHAPTER 3 REVIEW

Summary

Matter is anything that has mass and volume.

An element is a substance that cannot be broken down by ordinary chemical means. An atom is the smallest part of an element that still has all the properties of that element.

Protons and neutrons are particles in the atomic nucleus; electrons occur in a cloud surrounding the nucleus. Protons have a positive charge, electrons have a negative charge, and neutrons have a neutral charge.

Atomic number is the number of protons in an atom. Mass number is the total mass of particles in the nucleus of an atom (protons plus neutrons).

Isotopes are atoms of the same chemical element with different numbers of neutrons in their nuclei and therefore different mass numbers.

In a compound, two or more elements are combined chemically. A compound can have properties different from those of the elements of which it is made.

A mineral is a naturally occurring inorganic solid with a definite chemical composition and orderly atomic arrangement.

Eight elements make up 98.5 percent of the total mass of Earth's crust. Most elements occur combined with other elements.

Ionic bonds form between metals that lose electrons to form positive ions and nonmetals that gain electrons to form negative ions.

Covalent bonds tend to form between nonmetal atoms that share electrons.

Some minerals form characteristic crystal shapes.

Silicate minerals make up over 90 percent of Earth's crust. The silicate minerals are built around the silica tetrahedron.

The crystal shape, hardness, cleavage, and density of a mineral are determined by the internal arrangement of its atoms or ions.

Vocabulary

atom	ion	molecule
atomic number	ionic bond	native mineral
compound	isotope	neutron
covalent bond	mass number	nonmetal
crystal	matter	proton
electron	metal	silica tetrahedron
element	mineral	silicate

Review

Write the letter of your answer on your paper.

1. Matter is defined as anything that has (a) mass and weight, (b) weight and size, (c) mass and volume, (d) molecules.
2. A substance that cannot be broken down by chemical means is a (a) mixture, (b) metal, (c) ion, (d) element.
3. The smallest part of an element that has all the properties of the element is the (a) ion, (b) atom, (c) proton, (d) molecule.
4. Which is NOT part of an atom? (a) electron (b) energy level (c) nucleus (d) mixture
5. The mass number of an element is the sum of its (a) ions and protons, (b) protons and neutrons, (c) protons and electrons, (d) electrons and ions.
6. Isotopes are atoms of the same element that differ in the number of (a) ions, (b) electrons, (c) protons, (d) neutrons.
7. A substance made of two or more elements chemically combined is a (a) mineral, (b) atom, (c) mixture, (d) compound.
8. Which is NOT true of a mineral? (a) solid (b) organic (c) orderly atomic structure (d) definite chemical composition
9. A substance NOT considered a mineral is (a) calcite, (b) diamond, (c) glass, (d) quartz.
10. Which is NOT a native mineral? (a) copper (b) gold (c) halite (d) sulfur
11. Atoms that have lost electrons are (a) metal ions, (b) nonmetal ions, (c) noble gases, (d) isotopes.

12. The two most abundant elements in Earth's crust are (a) aluminum and iron, (b) iron and oxygen, (c) oxygen and silicon, (d) silicon and aluminum.
13. Nonmetal elements share electrons in (a) covalent bonds, (b) mixtures, (c) ionic bonds, (d) atoms.
14. Minerals can form from magma when (a) the magma cools, (b) atoms come closer together, (c) atoms form mineral compounds, (d) all of the above.
15. Which is NOT true of crystals? (a) They are regular shapes. (b) They are always formed from ions. (c) Each mineral has a crystal shape. (d) They are studied with X rays.
16. How many oxygen atoms are in a single silica tetrahedron? (a) 1 (b) 2 (c) 3 (d) 4
17. Two minerals composed of carbon but with different atomic structures are (a) quartz and calcite, (b) calcite and graphite, (c) graphite and diamond, (d) diamond and quartz.

Interpret and Apply

Answer each question in complete sentences.

1. Would a single atom be considered matter? Would a single electron be considered matter? Explain your answers.
2. Using the periodic table in the Appendix, identify elements a–c. (When using the table, round off atomic masses to the nearest whole number to find the mass number.) **(a)** atomic number = 7, mass number = 14; **(b)** atomic number = 26, number of neutrons = 20; **(c)** number of neutrons = 20, number of electrons = 19.
3. A container holds a mixture of sand, salt, and iron filings. **(a)** Describe a method for separating the substances in the mixture. **(b)** The sand is a compound of silicon and oxygen. Could the silicon and oxygen be separated by any of the methods described in part **(a)**?
4. Is ice in a glacier a mineral? Is the mercury in a thermometer a mineral? Explain.
5. Most minerals that contain metal atoms do not look like metals. Why is this true?

Critical Thinking

Different silicate minerals have different ratios of silicon atoms to oxygen atoms. For example, in quartz there is 1 silicon atom for every 2 oxygen atoms, a silicon to oxygen ratio of 1 to 2 (1:2). The drawings below show the structural models of some silicate minerals. The silicon atoms are shown by dashes because they are hidden by an oxygen atom. Questions 1–3 refer to Model A.

1. How many oxygen atoms are shown?
2. How many silicon atoms are shown?
3. What is the ratio of silicon to oxygen in Model A?

Questions 4–6 refer to Model B.

4. How many oxygen atoms surround the silicon atom indicated by the X?
5. How many of these oxygen atoms are shared with other silicon atoms?
6. Two shared oxygens count as one whole oxygen. What is the ratio of silicon to oxygen in Model B?
7. Compare Models A and B with the models in Figure 3.16. What are the names of the bonding arrangements represented by Models A and B?

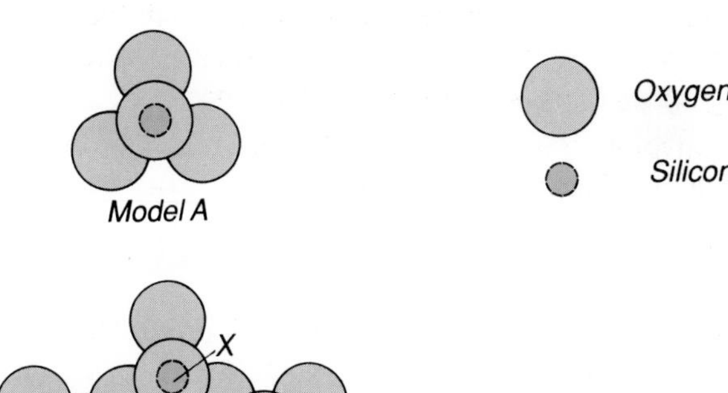

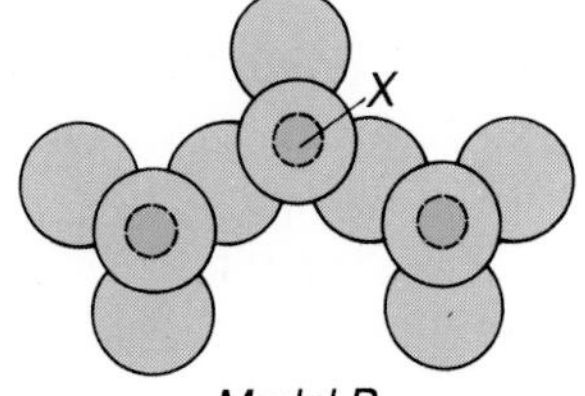

CHAPTER

4 How to Know the Minerals

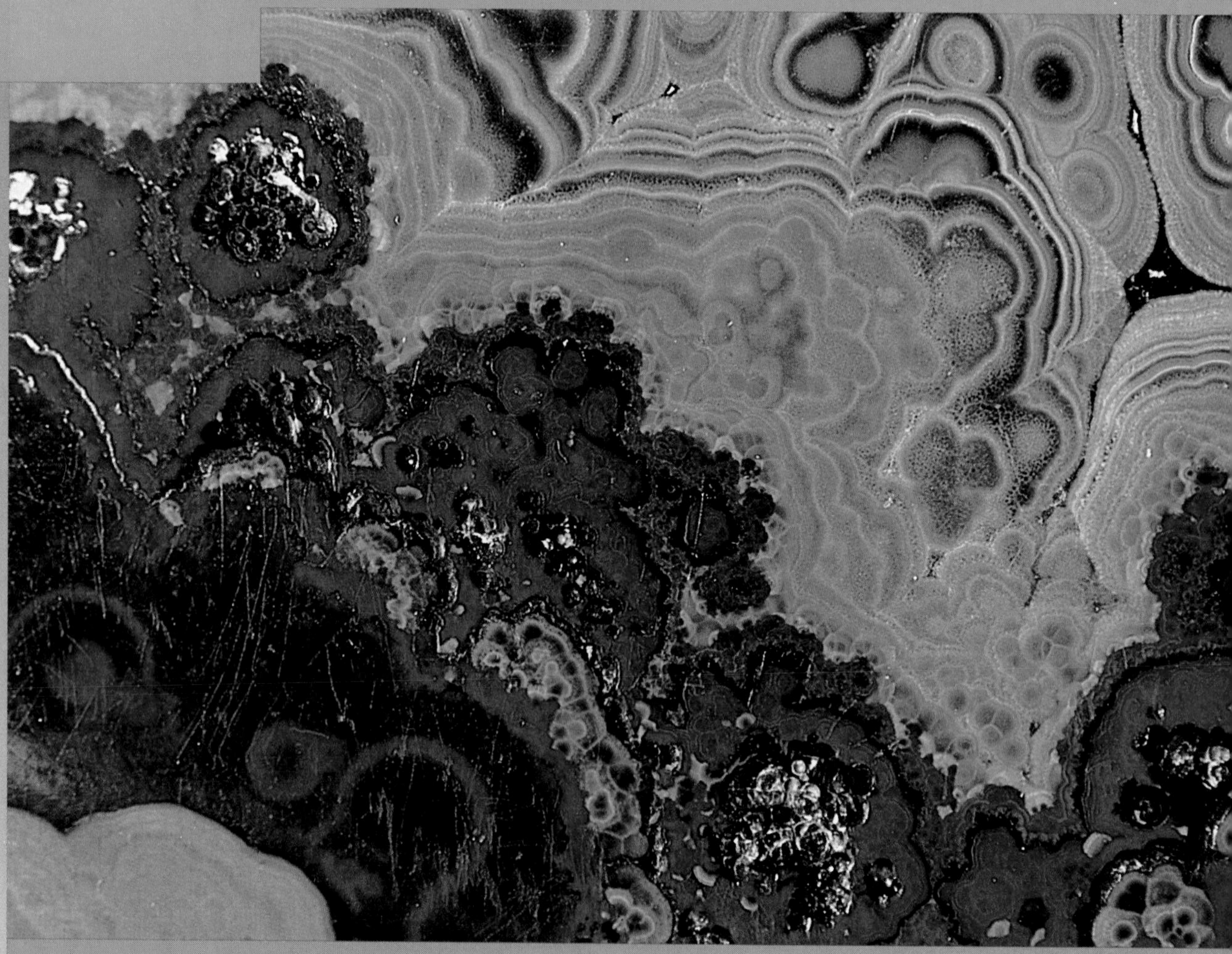

▲
Malachite is easily recognized by its characteristic green color. The blue mineral is azurite, which commonly occurs with malachite.

How Do You Know That . . .

The minerals shown above are azurite and malachite? Some minerals have distinct properties, such as color or crystal shape. Azurite is easily recognized by its blue color; malachite is recognized by its green color. The two minerals often occur together, as they do in this sample. Other minerals are not as easy to recognize. Often, a number of different properties must be observed and tested before a mineral is correctly identified.

I Identifying Minerals

Topic 1 Rock-Forming Minerals

Over 2000 minerals are known. Many of them, such as gold and diamond, are rare. Other minerals, such as quartz, feldspar, mica, and calcite, are common. Common minerals that make up most of the rocks in Earth's crust are called **rock-forming minerals.** Most rock-forming minerals are silicate minerals.

Minerals that occur in rocks are not always large crystals. However, even small mineral grains can be identified, in most cases.

The minerals in rocks are usually identified by their physical properties. Some of these properties can be determined by looking at the mineral with the unaided eye (inspection) and by simple physical tests. Simple chemical tests may also be used. The study of minerals and their properties is called **mineralogy.**

Topic 2 Identification by Inspection

The color, luster, and crystal shape of a mineral may be observed by inspection.

Color is the first and most easily observed mineral property. Some minerals have very characteristic colors that help identify them. For example, cinnabar, an ore of mercury, is red. Malachite (MAL uh kite), an ore of copper, is green.

Color, however, is the least useful property for mineral identification. One reason is that many different minerals have similar colors. For example, orthoclase feldspar, calcite, and other minerals all can have a milky-white color. Also, traces of impurities can turn colorless minerals into colored minerals. For example, pure quartz is colorless or white. A small amount of iron gives quartz a purple color. A small amount of titanium results in pink quartz. A third reason not to rely on color is that some minerals change color when exposed to air. In air, the brass-yellow color of chalcopyrite (kal koe PIE rite) tarnishes to bronze. The brownish-bronze of bornite turns purple. (Both chalcopyrite and bornite are copper ores.)

The **luster** of a mineral is the way the mineral shines in reflected light. Lusters are either metallic or nonmetallic. A mineral with metallic luster shines like polished metal. Examples of minerals with metallic luster are galena and pyrite. A mineral that does not shine like a metal has a nonmetallic luster. Several terms are used to further describe nonmetallic lusters. A vitreous luster, like shining glass, is seen in quartz. Mica has a pearly luster, like a pearl. The

OBJECTIVES

A Name some rock-forming minerals and identify the group to which most belong.

B Discuss the usefulness of color and crystal shape in mineral identification.

C Describe and give examples of mineral luster, streak, cleavage, fracture, and hardness.

D Define *specific gravity*, explain how it is determined, and calculate specific gravity given the necessary data.

E Describe other tests for specific mineral identification.

4.1 The colors of (top) cinnabar and (bottom) malachite can be used to identify these minerals.

a

b

4.2 (a) Galena has metallic luster. (b) Sphalerite is nonmetallic.

mineral sphalerite (SFAL er ite), an ore of zinc, can have a resinous luster, like wax, or a glassy luster. The hard, brilliant luster of diamond is called adamantine (add uh MAN teen). Other terms that are used to describe luster are greasy, oily, dull, and earthy.

Crystal shape is sometimes helpful in identifying a mineral. When minerals have enough time and room to form, their ions or atoms arrange themselves into patterns. These patterns lead to flat-faced, regularly shaped crystals (Chapter 3, Topic 15). Such crystal faces, however, are rare. More often the mineral grains in rocks lacked room to grow. The mineral grains in most rocks are so small or so imperfect that crystal faces are hard to find.

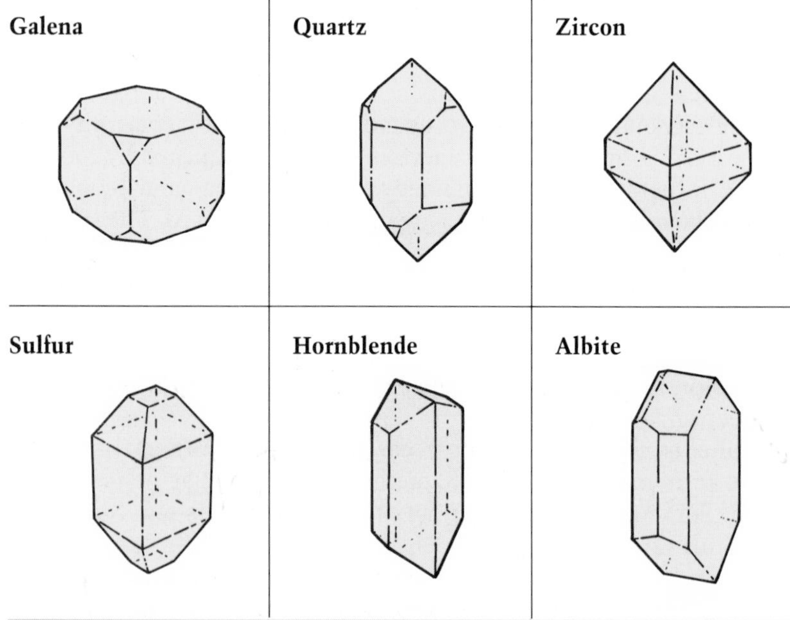

4.3 Crystal shape can be used for mineral identification.

Topic 3 Identification by Simple Tests

Some mineral properties can be determined by simple tests. The streak, cleavage, and hardness of a mineral, for example, can be tested easily. The **streak** of a mineral is the color of its powder. The streak is obtained by rubbing the mineral on an unglazed white tile, called a streak plate. For many minerals, the streak is not the same color as the mineral. Iron pyrite is brass-yellow. The streak of iron pyrite is always greenish-black. Hematite, another iron-bearing mineral, can be brown, red, or silver. Its streak, however, is always reddish-brown. Although the color of a mineral may vary, its streak rarely does. As a rule, the streak of a metallic mineral is at least as dark as the hand specimen. The streak of a nonmetallic mineral is usually colorless or white.

The **cleavage** of a mineral is its tendency to split easily or to separate along flat surfaces. Cleavage surfaces can be observed even on tiny mineral grains. Therefore, cleavage is a useful property for mineral identification. Mica splits very easily, and always in the same direction (Figure 4.4(a)). Mica is said to have one perfect cleavage. Feldspar splits readily in two different directions, at or near right angles (Figure 4.4(b)). It is said to have two good cleavages. Calcite and galena cleave in three directions. They are said to have three good cleavages.

a

4.4 Mineral cleavage varies. (a) Mica only cleaves well in one direction. (b) Feldspar cleaves in two directions.

b

Not all minerals have cleavage. Some minerals, however, tend to break along non-cleavage surfaces. When minerals break along other than cleavage surfaces, they are said to have **fracture**. *Conchoidal* (kon KOY dul), or shell-like, fracture can be seen in the mineral flint or the rock obsidian (Figure 4.5). The fracture surface is smoothly curved like the inside of a clam shell. Fibrous or splintery fracture leaves a jagged surface with sharp edges, as in native copper. Uneven or irregular fracture leaves a generally rough surface, as in the cinnabar sample in Figure 4.1.

The **hardness** of a mineral is its resistance to being scratched. Diamond is the hardest of all minerals. It will scratch any other mineral against which it is rubbed. On the other hand, talc is the softest of all minerals. All other minerals scratch talc.

In order to give a specific measure to hardness, the mineralogist Friedrich Mohs devised a hardness scale. In this scale, ten well-known minerals are given numbers from one to ten. They are arranged from softest (talc) to hardest (diamond). The differences in hardness between one step in the scale and the next are about the same for all except the last. Diamond, number ten, is several times harder than corundum, number nine.

From *Mohs' scale* you can find the approximate hardness of any common mineral. All you need is a copper penny, a knife blade or metal nail file, and a small glass plate. If a mineral is harder than number 5 but softer than number 6 in the hardness scale, it has a hardness of about 5½.

4.5 This rock, obsidian, shows conchoidal fracture. Many minerals—for example, quartz—also have conchoidal fracture.

Mohs' Scale of Hardness

Hardness	Mineral	Simple Test
1	Talc	Fingernail scratches it easily.
2	Gypsum	Fingernail scratches it.
3	Calcite	Copper penny just scratches it.
4	Fluorite	Steel knife scratches it easily.
5	Apatite	Steel knife scratches it.
6	Feldspar	Steel knife does not scratch it easily; it scratches window glass.
7	Quartz	Hardest common mineral; it scratches steel and hard glass easily.
8	Topaz	Harder than any common mineral
9	Corundum	It scratches topaz.
10	Diamond	Hardest of all minerals

Hardness should not be confused with brittleness. Glass is a brittle substance that breaks easily when dropped. Glass, however, is harder (resistant to scratching) than copper and other metals.

In doing a scratch test for hardness, the powder rubbed off the softer mineral may look like a scratch on the harder mineral. For example, when calcite is rubbed against glass, the calcite may appear to have scratched the glass. Rub this "scratch" with your finger. It may prove to be powder that comes off and leaves the glass unscratched. The calcite is obviously softer than the glass. A real scratch can be felt with the fingernail.

Topic 4 Specific Gravity

Specific gravity is another property that is helpful in identifying a mineral. Specific gravity is the ratio of the weight of a mineral to the weight of an equal volume of water. In other words, the specific gravity of a mineral tells you how many times as dense as water the mineral is.

Nearly all minerals are denser than water. Their specific gravities are greater than 1. Typical nonmetallic minerals—such as quartz, feldspar, calcite, and talc—have specific gravities of slightly less than 3. Typical metallic minerals—such as the iron ores hematite and magnetite—have specific gravities of about 5. Other metallic minerals are much denser. Gold has a specific gravity as high as 19.3 when pure.

The specific gravity of a mineral is found as suggested by the definition. The weight of the mineral sample is found by weighing it in air. Then the mineral sample is weighed again while it is underwater. This second weighing indirectly gives the weight of a volume of water that is equal to the volume of the mineral sample. The sample weighs less submerged because of the buoyant effect of the water. *Archimedes' principle* states that this loss in weight is equal to the weight of the displaced water. The displaced water is equal in volume to the mineral sample that displaced it. Thus it can be stated that

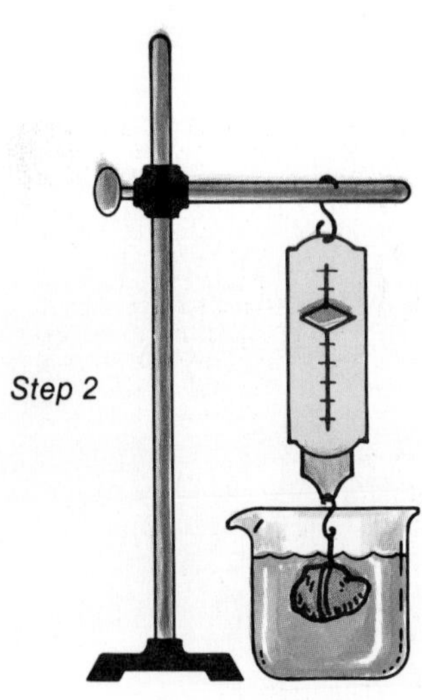

4.6 A mineral's weight in water and in air is used to find specific gravity.

$$\text{Specific gravity} = \frac{\text{weight of sample in air}}{\text{weight of equal volume of water}}$$

$$= \frac{\text{weight of sample in air}}{\text{loss of weight in water}}$$

For example, suppose a specimen weighs 50 newtons in air and 30 newtons in water. (A newton is a unit of weight equal to about 0.25 pounds.) The weight loss is 50 newtons − 30 newtons, or 20 newtons. The specific gravity of the specimen is calculated as follows.

$$\frac{50 \text{ N}}{20 \text{ N}} = 2.5$$

In other words, the specimen is 2.5 times as heavy as an equal volume of water.

Topic 5 The Acid Test

Calcite is the principal mineral in limestone and marble. Calcite is easily identified by a simple chemical test. Calcite is calcium carbonate, $CaCO_3$. If a drop of cold, weak hydrochloric acid is placed on calcite, the drop of acid fizzes. The bubbles are carbon dioxide gas. Other minerals also react to acid, but they are not as reactive. They may require using stronger acid, heating the acid, or powdering the mineral.

Topic 6 Special Properties of Minerals

There are many other properties that are used to help identify mineral samples. A few particularly interesting ones follow.

Some minerals are magnetic and can be picked up by a magnet. The best example is magnetite, an iron ore. Lodestone, a kind of magnetite, itself acts as a magnet.

Halite (rock salt) can be identified by its taste.

Fluorescence is the state of glowing while under ultraviolet light. It is seen in some samples of fluorite, calcite, and other minerals. Some samples of the minerals willemite (zinc silicate), sphalerite (zinc iron sulfide), and others continue to glow after the ultraviolet light is turned off. They are said to be *phosphorescent.*

Some minerals, such as the uranium minerals carnotite and uraninite, are *radioactive.* They give off subatomic particles that will activate a Geiger counter.

The mineral calcite splits light rays into two parts. One ray travels straight through the mineral. The other ray is bent. This causes two images to be seen when an object is viewed through a transparent specimen of calcite. This property, shown in Figure 4.7, is called *double refraction.*

The topics in Lesson II describe some important rock-forming minerals. The table "Properties of Some Common Minerals" on pages 576–577 lists other minerals.

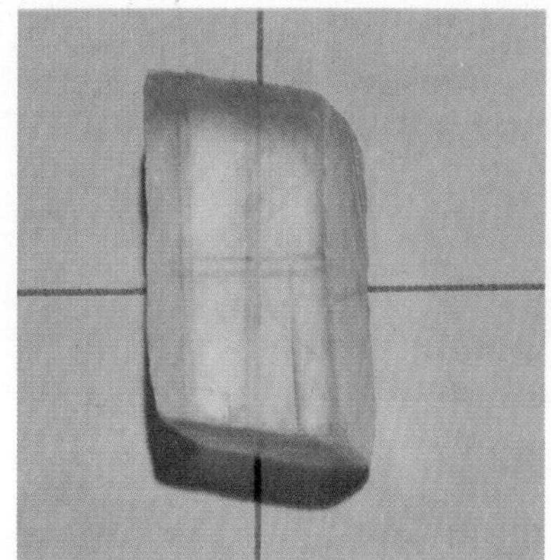

4.7 This mineral is a transparent variety of calcite called Iceland spar. It splits light rays and forms a double image of the red lines. This sample also shows the rhombic shape of calcite.

TOPIC QUESTIONS

Each topic question refers to the topic of the same number.

1. **(a)** What are rock-forming minerals? List some examples. **(b)** How are minerals usually identified? **(c)** What is mineralogy?

2. **(a)** Give three reasons why it is difficult to identify a mineral by its color alone. **(b)** What is luster? Name different types of luster and give examples of minerals with those lusters. **(c)** Why is crystal shape not usually helpful in mineral identification?

3. **(a)** Explain what a mineral streak is, how it is obtained, and how the streak of metallic and nonmetallic minerals differ. **(b)** Define cleavage. Give examples of minerals that can be identified by cleavage. **(c)** Define mineral fracture and give some examples. **(d)** What is mineral hardness? How is it determined?

4. **(a)** What is specific gravity? **(b)** Compare the specific gravity of the average metallic and nonmetallic minerals. **(c)** A mineral sample weighs 76 newtons in air and 51 newtons in water. Find its specific gravity.

5. Describe the acid test for a mineral.

6. Give examples of minerals that can be identified by **(a)** magnetism, **(b)** taste, **(c)** fluorescence, **(d)** phosphorescence, **(e)** radio activity, and **(f)** double refraction.

Laurence R. Kittleman
Geologist

Laurence R. Kittleman is a geologist who is interested in volcanic rocks. He began his study at Colorado College, where he earned his B.S. degree in geology. He continued with an M.S. at the University of Colorado and a Ph.D. from the University of Oregon. His professional career has included work with the U.S. Department of Energy and at the University of Oregon's Museum of Natural History. Here he served as curator of geology and as museum director. He has done research on the volcanic rocks of Oregon. Another of his interests is the geology of prehistoric dwelling places. Dr. Kittleman wrote *Canyons Beyond the Sky*, an earth-science adventure novel for middle-school readers.

II Descriptions of Rock-Forming Minerals

OBJECTIVES

A Identify and describe the two most common types of silicate minerals.

B Define and give examples of ferromagnesian silicates.

C Contrast silicate minerals and carbonate minerals, and distinguish between the two principal carbonate minerals.

D Identify and describe some iron-bearing minerals.

Topic 7 Silicates: From Silica Tetrahedrons

In Topic 14 of Chapter 3, the silica tetrahedron was discussed as nature's most important building block for minerals. All of the following minerals are made of silica tetrahedrons, either alone or combined with other elements.

(a) *Quartz* is made entirely of silica tetrahedrons bound tightly together. Quartz has the chemical formula SiO_2. Its chemical name is silicon dioxide. The chemical formula and name indicate that there are two oxygen atoms for every silicon atom in quartz.

Several properties help identify quartz. Quartz has a glassy or greasy luster. Its fracture is shell-like or irregular. Quartz is number 7 in Mohs' scale of hardness. It is the hardest of the common minerals. The color of quartz varies. Pure quartz is colorless or white, but many colored varieties exist. Among these are pink rose quartz, purple amethyst, and brown or gray smoky quartz.

Quartz is the second most abundant mineral in Earth's crust. It is an important part of all granites. Sandstone and quartzite are formed almost entirely of quartz. Most sands consist mainly of grains of quartz.

(b) The **feldspar** family includes the most common and most abundant of all minerals. In feldspars, the silica tetrahedrons have been joined together by ions of aluminum and other metals. Feldspars are usually divided into two groups.

Feldspars in which the other metal is potassium are called *potash* feldspars. Like quartz, they are a part of all granites. Potash feldspars have a hardness of 6. They also have two good cleavages that meet at a right angle. They are easily identified in granite by their light colors—white, yellow, gray, or pink. Their smooth cleavage surfaces also aid identification. The most common potash feldspar is *orthoclase,* which means "right-angled breaking."

4.8 (a) Orthoclase feldspar, (b) pure quartz, (c) rose quartz

a

b

c

a

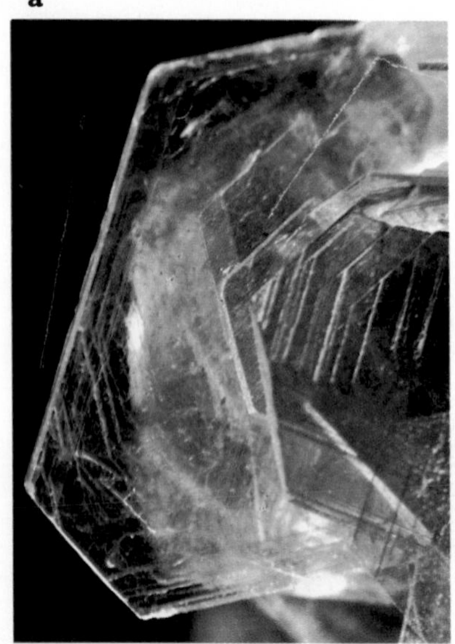
b

4.9 (a) Plagioclase feldspar, (b) muscovite mica, (c) hornblende, (d) augite

Feldspars in which the other metal is sodium, calcium, or both are called *soda-lime* feldspars. They also have two good cleavages. However, the angle formed by the two cleavages of soda-lime feldspars is not quite a right angle. Because of this, they are also called *plagioclase* (slant-breaking) feldspars. Most varieties are white or gray, but some are dark green or bluish. Plagioclase feldspars are less abundant in granites than are the potash feldspars. However, they are very prominent in darker rocks, such as diorite and granodiorite (to be described in Chapter 5). Two common varieties of plagioclase feldspar are *albite* and *oligoclase.* They can be distinguished from orthoclase by the fact that one cleavage surface is marked by fine parallel lines called striations.

(c) Mica minerals are soft silicates found in many rocks. Flat, shiny mica flakes are easily picked out of rocks, such as granite and gneiss. *Muscovite* mica, also known as white mica, is silvery white. *Biotite* mica is dark brown or black. Both are soft—each has a hardness of about 2.5. Each has one perfect cleavage.

(d) *Talc* is the softest mineral—number 1 on Mohs' scale. It is white, gray, or greenish in color. It has one good cleavage and has a soapy feel. Pure talcum powder is ground talc.

(e) Amphiboles are a family of complex silicate minerals. They tend to form long, needlelike crystals. The most common amphibole is *hornblende*. Hornblende is a shiny dark green, brown, or black mineral. It has two good cleavages that meet at oblique angles. (See Figure 4.9(c)). Hornblende has a hardness of 5 to 6.

Hornblende is also an example of a **ferromagnesian silicate.** These silicates can belong to almost any of the silicate families, but they all contain atoms of iron and magnesium. Ferromagnesian silicates are always dark in color.

(f) Pyroxenes have cleavage surfaces that meet nearly at right angles (90°). *Augite* (AW jyte) is the most common member of the pyroxene family. It is also a ferromagnesian silicate. Augite is dark green, brown, or black. It has two good cleavages and has a hardness between 5 and 6. It can be distinguished from hornblende by its poorer luster; its short, stout crystals; its cleavage surfaces that

c

d

a

b

meet nearly at right angles.

Both hornblende and augite are common minerals in many dark crystalline rocks.

(g) *Olivine* is an olive-green ferromagnesian silicate. It is found in dark crystalline rocks. It belongs to a silicate family in which single silica tetrahedrons are bonded by metal ions. It is glassy, shell-like in fracture, and very hard—about 6.5. It is found in some meteorites.

(h) *Garnets* may be dark red, brown, yellow, green, or black. They are very hard (from 6.5 to 7.5) and are used as abrasives. Clear crystals are used as gems. Garnets are found in many crystalline rocks.

(i) *Kaolinite* or *kaolin* is an aluminum silicate. It is formed by the weathering of feldspar and other silicate minerals. It is the principal mineral in clay and in shale. Pure kaolin is white, but impurities usually make it yellow. Less often it is red, brown, green, or blue. It has an earthy (crumbly) fracture. Its hardness is between 1 and 2.5. It feels greasy and, when breathed on, it gives off a typical earthy odor.

Summary: There are several main groups of silicate minerals. Only common examples from some of the groups have been described here. The properties and structures of silicate minerals differ. However, all varieties have the silica tetrahedron as their basic building block.

c

4.10 (a) Garnet, (b) kaolinite, (c) olivine

Topic 8 Carbonate Minerals: Calcite and Dolomite

While some minerals are built of silica tetrahedrons, others are built of other groups of atoms. The **carbonate** group is made of one carbon atom combined with three oxygen atoms and has a negative charge of two ($-CO_3^{2-}$). A carbonate mineral is made of carbonate groups joined with various metal ions. The rocks limestone and marble are made almost entirely of carbonate minerals.

4.11 Calcite is the most common carbonate mineral.

a

b

4.12 (a) Azurite, (b) dolomite in marble

The most common carbonate mineral is *calcite*. Calcite is calcium carbonate, chemical formula $CaCO_3$. Pure calcite is colorless or white. Impurities may make it almost any color. It has a hardness of 3. Calcite has three perfect cleavages that meet at oblique angles. Its cleavages give it a very strong tendency to break into little flat-sided rhombs when dropped or struck. Calcite rhombs are shown in Figures 4.7 and 4.11. Calcite is easily identified by the acid test described in Topic 5.

Colorless transparent calcite is called *Iceland spar.* Iceland spar has the unusual property of double refraction (see Topic 6).

Dolomite is calcium magnesium carbonate. It has a hardness of 3.5 to 4. Like calcite, it cleaves into rhombs. Dolomite is not as reactive to acid as calcite is, and does not easily bubble in the acid test. It must be scratched or powdered, or the acid must be heated or concentrated. Dolomite usually occurs as coarse or fine grains in dolomitic limestones and marbles.

The copper carbonates *malachite* and *azurite* and the iron carbonate *siderite* react to the acid test. They do not react as easily as calcite. These carbonates are best identified by their color. Malachite is always green. Azurite is always blue. Siderite is usually brown or yellow-brown.

Topic 9 Iron Oxides and Sulfides

Some minerals contain large amounts of the metal element iron. These minerals are not as common as the silicate or carbonate minerals. However, they are economically important (Chapter 6, Topic 9). In these minerals, iron tends to be combined with either oxygen or sulfur to form an *oxide* or *sulfide.* An oxide is a mineral consisting of a metal element combined with oxygen. A sulfide is a metal element combined with sulfur. Each iron-bearing mineral has its own identifying properties.

a

b

4.13 (a) Magnetite, sometimes called lodestone; (b) pyrite, or fool's gold

Hematite is the most common iron oxide mineral. It has a hardness of 5 to 6 on Mohs' scale. Most hematite is red and has an earthy luster and crumbly fracture. Some hematite samples are silvery and have a metallic luster. All hematite samples leave a red-brown streak on a streak plate.

Magnetite is a black magnetic iron oxide. It has a hardness of 5.5 to 6.5. It occurs in many rocks in the form of small grains or crystals. Its name refers to the fact that it is attracted to a magnet. *Lodestone* is a highly magnetic variety of magnetite. It is a natural magnet. The first magnetic compass needles were made from lodestone.

Pyrite is iron sulfide. It is the most common sulfide mineral. Its color ranges from pale brass to golden-yellow. Its hardness is about 6. Pyrite frequently occurs in 6- or 12-sided crystals. Because of its golden color and high metallic luster, it is sometimes mistaken for gold. A common name for pyrite is fool's gold.

TOPIC QUESTIONS

Each topic question refers to the topic of the same number.

7. **(a)** Which of the silicate mineral groups is most abundant? **(b)** Name the two main feldspar groups and describe the general properties of each group. **(c)** Name and describe the two forms of mica. **(d)** What are ferromagnesian silicates? Give three examples. **(e)** Compare and contrast hornblende and augite. To which group does each belong? **(f)** Discuss the properties and importance of quartz, garnet, kaolinite, and talc.

8. **(a)** How are carbonate minerals different from silicate minerals? **(b)** Compare and contrast calcite and dolomite.

9. **(a)** Describe the forms of hematite. What identifying property do all forms of hematite exhibit? **(b)** Describe magnetite. Distinguish between magnetite and lodestone. **(c)** Describe pyrite. How is the composition of pyrite different from that of hematite and magnetite?

CHAPTER 4 REVIEW

Summary

Rock-forming minerals make up most of the rocks in Earth's crust. Most rock-forming minerals are silicates.

Minerals are identified by their properties.

Color, luster, and crystal shape can be determined by simple inspection of a mineral.

Color is the most obvious property of a mineral, but it is often the least useful for identification. Crystal shape is sometimes useful.

Minerals have either metallic or nonmetallic luster. Vitreous, pearly, resinous, adamantine, greasy, dull, and earthy are all kinds of nonmetallic luster.

Streak, cleavage, fracture, and hardness of a mineral can be determined with simple tests.

Specific gravity is the ratio of the weight of a mineral to the weight of an equal volume of water.

Other properties used to identify minerals are reaction to acid, magnetism, taste, fluoresence, radioactivity, and double refraction.

Silicate minerals are made of silica tetrahedrons combined in various structures. Feldspar minerals, quartz, and mica are the most common silicate minerals.

Amphiboles are silicate minerals that form long, needlelike crystals. Pyroxenes are silicates that form shorter, stouter crystals. Hornblende is a common amphibole; augite is a common pyroxene.

Ferromagnesian silicates include any dark silicate mineral containing iron and magnesium. Hornblende, augite, and olivine are examples.

Calcite and dolomite are the two most important carbonate minerals.

Several minerals contain large amounts of iron combined with oxygen (oxides) or sulfur (sulfides). Hematite and magnetite are iron oxides; pyrite is iron sulfide.

Vocabulary

amphibole	ferromagnesian silicate	mineralogy
carbonate	fracture	pyroxene
cleavage	hardness	rock-forming minerals
color	luster	specific gravity
crystal shape	mica	streak
feldspar		

Review

Match definitions, List **A**, with terms, List **B**.

List A

1. study of minerals and their properties
2. minerals that make up Earth's crust
3. unreliable for mineral identification
4. vitreous, resinous, pearly, and adamantine
5. tendency of a mineral to split
6. measured by Mohs' scale
7. color of mineral powder
8. ratio of the weight of a mineral to the weight of an equal volume of water
9. bubbles easily in acid
10. state of glowing under ultraviolet light
11. hardest common mineral
12. orthoclase and plagioclase
13. muscovite and biotite
14. hornblende, augite, olivine
15. silicate family that includes hornblende but not augite
16. mineral made mostly of $(-CO_3^{2-})$ groups
17. all samples exhibit red streak

List B

a. amphibole
b. calcite
c. carbonate
d. cleavage
e. color
f. feldspars
g. ferromagnesian silicates
h. fluorescence
i. hardness
j. hematite
k. luster
l. mica
m. mineralogy
n. pyroxene
o. quartz
p. rock-forming minerals
q. streak
r. specific gravity

Interpret and Apply

On your paper, answer each question.

1. Why is color a useful property for identifying malachite, but not quartz?
2. The hardness of a streak plate is about 6. Why would the streak of corundum be difficult to determine?
3. Both calcite and galena have three directions of cleavage. How does the shape of a cleavage fragment of calcite compare with that of a cleavage fragment of galena? (Refer to the table of mineral properties on pages 576–577 in the Appendix.)
4. A specimen of quartz weighs 13.25 newtons in air and 8.25 newtons in water. What is the specific gravity of the quartz specimen?
5. Name one property that would readily distinguish each pair of minerals. **(a)** feldspar and quartz **(b)** magnetite and hornblende **(c)** talc and mica **(d)** calcite and fluorite **(e)** cinnabar and malachite **(f)** pyrite and sphalerite **(g)** halite and calcite **(h)** hematite and pyrite

Critical Thinking

Eight rock-forming minerals are shown in the chart. Listed across the top are rocks made up of those minerals. Copy the 0–100% scale from the chart onto the edge of your paper. Use the scale to read the volume percentages of a mineral in a rock. For example, to find the percent volume of quartz in tonalite, slide your scale to the vertical line marked tonalite. Place the zero of your scale at the line between quartz and plagioclase. Read the percentage volume of quartz at the line between quartz and orthoclase. You should read close to 35% quartz.

1. Find the percent of plagioclase feldspar in tonalite.
2. What percentage of the volume of peridotite is pyroxene?
3. Which rock contains 40% orthoclase feldspar, 35% quartz, 12% plagioclase feldspar, 8% biotite, and 5% amphibole?
4. What name would be given to a rock that contained 60% plagioclase feldspar, 20% amphibole, 15% pyroxene, and 5% biotite?
5. Describe the composition of a quartz diorite.

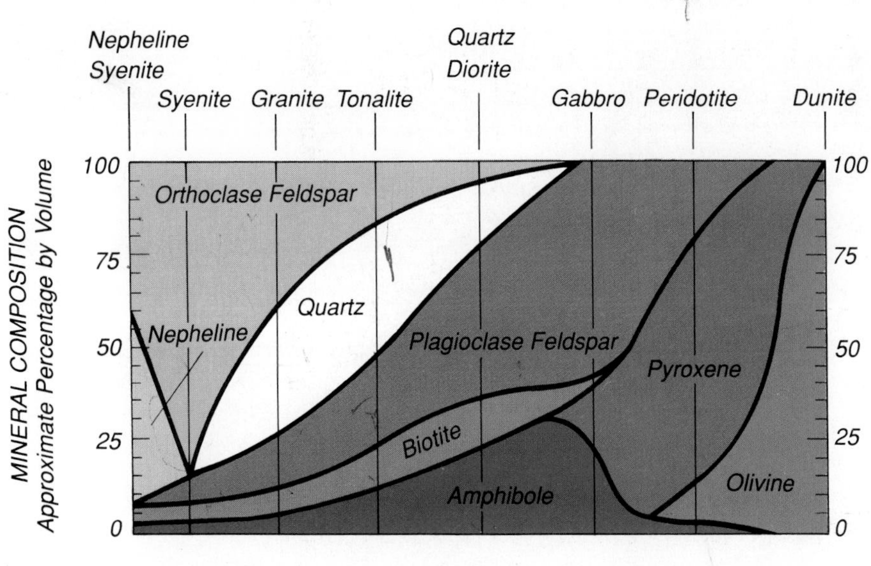

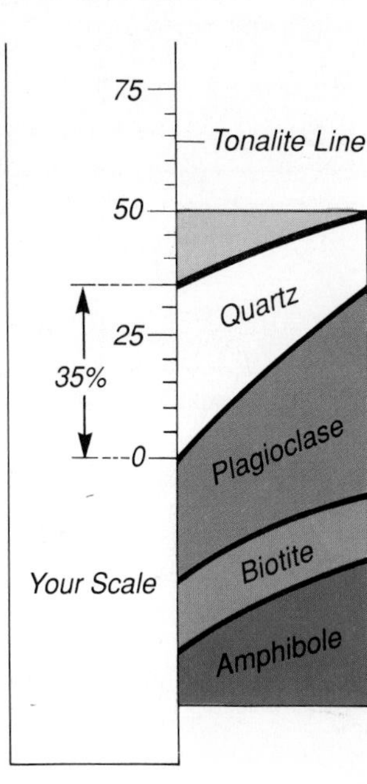

CHAPTER

5

How Earth's Rocks Were Formed

▲
This formation is made of granite, an igneous rock.

How Do You Know That . . .

Rocks are made from minerals? Obtain several different rocks. Examine each with a magnifying glass. Are mineral grains visible in every rock? Can you recognize clear quartz grains, shiny mica flakes, or black bits of hornblende or augite? How hard is each rock? Can you scratch any with a paper clip? Check to see whether layers are visible in any of the rocks. Does the rock appear to have broken along those layers? What else do you notice about the rocks?

I Igneous Rocks

Topic 1 Uniformity of Process

Modern geology is said to have begun in 1795. In that year the Scottish geologist James Hutton described a new concept, called **uniformitarianism.** Before Hutton, most geologists thought that the physical features of Earth had been formed by sudden spectacular events, or catastrophes. In their view, these catastrophes caused the formation of mountains, canyons, waterfalls, and almost all landforms.

James Hutton's ideas were quite different. After years of studying landforms and rocks, he came to the conclusion that "the present is the key to the past." This statement included two concepts. (1) The geologic processes now at work were also active in the past. (2) The present physical features of Earth were formed by these same processes, at work over long periods of time.

According to Hutton, a canyon or a river valley need not be formed by a sudden splitting of Earth's crust. Instead, it can be formed by the slow and steady wearing away of the land. This was done, said Hutton, by the very same river now running in the canyon, doing for thousands and thousands of years what it is still doing today.

OBJECTIVES

A Explain the principle of uniformitarianism and relate it to the formation of igneous, sedimentary, and metamorphic rocks.

B Discuss differences between plutonic and volcanic igneous rocks.

C Define *rock texture* and list some factors that control the texture of an igneous rock.

D Name and describe members of the granite, diorite, and gabbro igneous rock families.

Topic 2 Three Groups of Rocks

The study of rocks is an important part of understanding Earth processes. A **rock** can be generally defined as a group of minerals bound together in some way.

Hutton's principles of uniform processes have been used by geologists to explain the origin of rocks. Geologists have noted, for example, that erupting lava hardens into rocks. These rocks are similar to others that have been found in many places on Earth. Geologists have seen that sands and clays sometimes harden into rocklike materials. Such materials resemble present-day sandstone and shale. They have observed that when hot lava flows over other rocks, it changes those rocks. From many studies like these, geologists have concluded that all rocks of the crust form in one of three general ways:

Igneous rocks are formed by the cooling and hardening of hot molten rock from inside Earth. This hot molten rock is called **magma.**

5.1 James Hutton

Sedimentary rocks are formed by the hardening and cementing of layers of sediments. The sediments may consist of rock fragments, plant and animal remains, or chemicals that form on lake and ocean bottoms.

Metamorphic rocks are formed when rocks that already exist are changed by heat and pressure into new kinds of rocks.

Topic 3 Recognizing Igneous Rocks

Granite, a common igneous rock, does not form on Earth's surface. Instead, granite forms from magma that cools deep underground. As magma cools, elements in it form distinct, interlocking mineral grains. Rocks that form underground from cooled magma are called **plutonic,** or *intrusive,* igneous rocks. Such rocks are seen at the surface only after the rock that covers them is worn away.

Magma that pours onto Earth's surface during a volcanic eruption is called *lava.* The rock that forms when the lava cools is called **volcanic,** or *extrusive,* igneous rock. Volcanic rocks also form out of volcanic dust and ash. Volcanic rocks are similar to plutonic rocks in mineral composition. However, they lack distinct mineral grains.

5.2 After lava flows onto the surface, it begins to cool and harden. It eventually becomes volcanic, or extrusive, igneous rock.

Topic 4 Kinds of Magma

From the study of plutonic and volcanic rocks, geologists have learned that there are many kinds of magma. There are two general kinds that are the most common. Both kinds are hot solutions of silicates. Both have temperatures ranging from about 600°C to 1200°C. However, these magmas differ in chemical composition. One kind has a high percentage of silica (SiO_2). It does not have much calcium, iron, or magnesium, which are common in dark-colored minerals. This high-silica magma is thick and slow flowing. When it hardens, it forms rocks that have mainly light-colored minerals. These light-colored, high-silica rocks are called **felsic** (feldspar + silica) rocks. Granite is a common felsic rock. It contains light-colored minerals such as quartz and orthoclase feldspar. Most plutonic rocks are felsic.

The second kind of magma has a much lower percentage of silica. It has a higher percentage of calcium, iron, and magnesium. This low-silica magma is hotter, thinner, and more fluid than the felsic type. When it solidifies, it forms rocks that contain mostly dark ferromagnesian minerals. These dark-colored, low-silica rocks are called **mafic.** They have a high percentage of magnesium and iron (ferric) bearing minerals. Basalt is a mafic rock. It contains a number of dark minerals such as hornblende, augite, and biotite. Most volcanic rocks are mafic.

5.3 In a coarse-grained igneous rock like the granite shown in (a) and (b), the individual mineral grains can easily be seen.

a

b

Topic 5 Textures of an Igneous Rock

Rocks are grouped not only by their minerals but also by their textures. A rock's **texture** depends on the size, shape, and arrangement of its mineral crystals. Igneous rock textures range from glassy-smooth, such as obsidian, to coarse-grained, such as granite.

Crystal size is the most important factor affecting texture. The crystal size in an igneous rock depends mostly upon how fast the magma hardens. When rock is in the liquid state, its atoms are free to move around and arrange into crystals. The longer the magma stays liquid, the longer the atoms are free to move, and the larger the crystals become. A second factor that affects crystal size, and thus rock texture, is the amount of gas dissolved in the magma. Dissolved gases help ions move around in the magma. A high percentage of dissolved gases helps crystals to grow faster. Thus the crystals grow large in a relatively short time.

Magmas trapped deep within the crust hardens very slowly. The rocks that form from these magmas have large mineral grains of fairly uniform size. Such plutonic rocks have a granular, or coarse-grained, texture. The most familiar example is granite.

Magmas that reach Earth's surface as lava harden rapidly. The volcanic rock that forms has tiny crystals. The crystals are usually too small to see without a microscope. These rocks have fine-grained textures. A good example is basalt.

5.4 A porphyry

In some cases magma flowing onto the surface hardens so rapidly that there is no time at all for crystals to develop. The rocks that form under these conditions—for example, obsidian—are as smooth as glass. They are said to have a glassy texture.

Topic 6 Porphyritic Texture

Some igneous rocks have two distinctly different textures. In these rocks, large crystals are surrounded by a fine-grained mass of rock. Such a rock is called a **porphyry** (POR fur ee).

One explanation of how a porphyry forms involves two stages of cooling. In the first stage the magma is at a great depth. Here it cools slowly enough so that large crystals of one mineral can form. The rest of the magma remains liquid. Then the magma moves upward, possibly melting through overlying rock, until it comes close to the surface. Here the rest of the magma cools into a fine-grained rock around the larger first-stage crystals.

Topic 7 Families of Igneous Rocks

5.5 (top) Rhyolite, (bottom) gabbro

Remember that rocks can be described in terms of texture and mineral composition. Igneous rocks are grouped into families according to mineral composition. Each family has coarse-grained, fine-grained, and glassy members.

The *granite family* forms from felsic magmas. All the rocks in this family consist mainly of orthoclase feldspar and quartz. Other minerals likely to be present are plagioclase feldspar, mica, and some hornblende. Orthoclase and quartz are light in color. Thus, the rocks in this family are usually light-colored. In this family granite is coarse-grained, rhyolite is fine-grained, and obsidian and pumice are glassy. These rocks have different textures, but all have similar chemical compositions.

The *gabbro family* forms from mafic magmas. The rocks in this family are made mainly of dark plagioclase feldspar and augite. Other likely minerals are olivine, hornblende, and biotite. These rocks are generally dark in color and more dense than rocks in the granite family. In this family, gabbro is coarse-grained, basalt is fine-grained, and basalt glass is glassy.

The *diorite family* has a composition and color between those of the granite and gabbro families. Diorite, the coarse-grained member, has less quartz than granite. It has less dark plagioclase than gabbro. Andesite is the fine-grained member of the diorite family.

Some igneous rocks do not fit into any of these families. Granodiorite is a coarse-grained rock. It has a composition between those of granite and diorite. Also of interest are three coarse, dark heavy rocks that may be like the rock of Earth's mantle. Pyroxenite is nearly all pyroxene. Dunite is almost all olivine. Peridotite is a mixture of pyroxene and olivine.

Topic 8 Descriptions of Common Igneous Rocks

Specific igneous rocks can be recognized by their minerals and textures. *Granite* is made of quartz, orthoclase feldspar, and at least one other mineral, such as mica or hornblende. Quartz grains look like little chips of cloudy or grayish glass. Feldspar often has smooth cleavage surfaces. It is usually white, gray, pink, or orange. Mica, usually black biotite, occurs in shiny little flakes. Hornblende occurs as tiny, dull black chunks or sticks. Granites range in color from light to medium grays and pinks. Feldspar makes up the largest part of granite. Because of this, the color of the feldspar has the greatest effect on the overall color of the rock. Granites have coarse-grained textures.

Granite is the most common continental igneous rock. It occurs in the Rockies, the Adirondacks of New York State, the Black Hills in South Dakota, the White Mountains of New Hampshire, and in many other mountainous areas. Granite is plutonic. Because granite forms far beneath the surface, its presence at the surface shows that erosion removed thousands of meters of overlying rocks since the rock first cooled from magma.

Felsite is the general name for any light-colored, fine-grained rock in the granite family. *Rhyolite* is an example. It is a fine-grained, light gray to pink rock.

Obsidian is volcanic glass of the granite family. Obsidian contains many of the same minerals as granite and other light-colored rocks, so it is grouped with those rocks. However, obsidian is usually dark brown or black. The dark color is due to tiny amounts of dark-colored minerals scattered throughout the rock. Obsidian is hard and brittle. An important property of obsidian is conchoidal, or shell-like, fracture.

Pumice is formed from felsic lava that hardened while steam and other gases were still bubbling out of it. It looks like a sponge with many small holes in it. Because of its many air holes, pumice is sometimes light enough to float on water.

The most common rock of the gabbro family is *basalt.* It is a fine-grained rock that ranges in color from dark green to black. Basalt is the igneous rock of the ocean floor. On land, it is the most common rock formed from flows of lava. Large areas of basalt occur in the lava flows of Iceland, the Hawaiian Islands, and in the Columbia and Snake River Plateaus in the western United States.

Gabbro has about the same composition as basalt. However, because it cooled slowly deep underground, gabbro is coarse-grained. Gabbros are very dark in color. *Diabase* has a composition similar to gabbro. Its texture is finer than gabbro but coarser than basalt.

Basalt glass is like obsidian but has a mafic composition. *Scoria,* like pumice, is full of holes. Scoria, however, is made of denser minerals, so not all scoria floats.

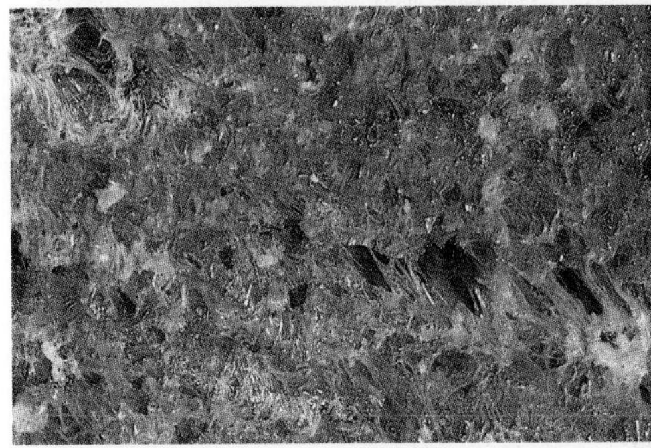

5.6 (top) Pumice, (bottom) close-up of pumice

5.7 (top) Diorite, (bottom) pyroxenite

Summary Table: Common Igneous Rocks

Texture and Origin	Felsic or Light-Colored Rocks		Medium-Colored Rocks	Mafic or Dark-Colored Rocks	
	Colors: white, tan, gray, pink, red *Minerals:* feldspar (mostly orthoclase), quartz; also some mica and hornblende		*Colors:* gray, green *Minerals:* feldspar (mostly plagioclase), hornblende, augite, biotite	*Colors:* dark green, dark gray, black *Minerals:* plagioclase feldspar, augite; also olivine, hornblende, biotite	
	With Quartz	*Almost No Quartz*	*Without Quartz*		
Glassy: cooled quickly at surface of Earth	Obsidian Pumice		Obsidian	Basalt glass Scoria	
Fine-grained: cooled slowly at or near surface	Rhyolite (Felsite)	Trachyte (Felsite)	Andesite	Basalt Diabase	
					No Feldspar
Coarse-grained: cooled very slowly, usually at great depths	Granite Pegmatite	Syenite Granodiorite	Diorite Granodiorite	Gabbro	Peridotite Pyroxenite Dunite

TOPIC QUESTIONS

Each topic question refers to the topic of the same number.

1. **(a)** Before James Hutton, how had geologists explained the origin of landforms? **(b)** What two principles make up Hutton's uniformitarianism?

2. **(a)** Give two examples of the ways in which geologists have applied Hutton's principles to describe the origins of rocks. **(b)** Identify and describe the three main groups of rocks.

3. **(a)** What is the difference between magma and lava? **(b)** Where do plutonic rocks form? **(c)** Where do volcanic rocks form?

4. **(a)** How do felsic magmas differ from mafic magmas in color, temperature, mineral composition, and the kind of rock each forms? **(b)** Which kind of magma is more likely to form a plutonic rock? Which will likely form a volcanic rock?

5. **(a)** List two factors that affect the texture of an igneous rock. **(b)** How are textures of plutonic rocks different from textures of volcanic rocks? **(c)** How does a rock with a glassy texture form?

6. **(a)** What is a porphyry? **(b)** How is a porphyry thought to form?

7. **(a)** Describe the granite family and list its coarse-grained, fine-grained, and glassy members. **(b)** Describe the gabbro family and list its members. **(c)** What is the diorite family?

8. List and briefly describe the common igneous rocks.

II Sedimentary Rocks

Topic 9 Kinds of Sediments

Although most of Earth's crust is made of igneous rock, most of its surface is covered by sedimentary rocks. Sedimentary rocks form when sediments harden into rocks. There are three main kinds of sedimentary rock.

Clastic sedimentary rocks are formed from fragments of other rocks. Examples of clastic sedimentary rocks are shale, sandstone, and conglomerate.

Chemical sedimentary rocks are formed from mineral grains that fall out of a solution (precipitate) by evaporation or by chemical action. Rock salt and some limestones are examples of chemical sedimentary rocks.

Organic sedimentary rocks are formed from the remains of plants and animals. Coal is an example. Limestones made of shell fragments are also examples.

OBJECTIVES

A Describe the three major processes by which sedimentary rocks are formed and give examples of rocks formed by each process.

B Discuss sediment sorting and relate it to rock stratification.

C Explain the origin of fossils, ripple marks, mud cracks, nodules, concretions, and geodes.

Topic 10 How Clastic Rocks Form

Rock fragments that form clastic sedimentary rocks come from the weathering of rocks that already exist. Fragments range in size from large pebbles and gravels down to sand, silt, and microscopic flakes of clay. Winds, waves, and glaciers all can pick up and move these particles. However, running water collects and moves the greatest amount. As particles are moved by running water, they are smoothed and rounded by rubbing against each other and against the stream bed. The farther the particles travel, the more rounded they become. Sediments are deposited when a stream slows down. This occurs when the stream flows into the quiet water of a lake or the ocean. Waves and currents may then spread the sediment over great distances.

How do loose sediments become rock? In coarse sediments such as gravels and sands, the particles do not stick together unless they are cemented. Ocean water, lake water, and groundwater all contain natural cements in the form of dissolved minerals. These include *silica* (from quartz), *lime* (from calcite), and *iron-oxide* cements (from iron-containing minerals). When these dissolved minerals settle into the spaces between sand grains or pebbles, they bind the fragments together. The cement transforms loose sediments into firm, cemented rock.

The pressure of overlying sediments is sometimes enough to make fine sediments such as clay or silt stick together, even without cement. More often, however, cement is needed to hold the rock together. Cements give their own colors to rocks. Cemented rocks may be gray or white from silica or lime, or red, brown, or rust-colored from iron cement.

5.8 Most sediments are deposited by running water. Running water also smooths and rounds sediments, such as the rocks in this stream bed.

Topic 11 Sorting of Sediments

When a river flows into a lake or ocean, it drops its sediment load as it slows down. The first sediments to be dropped are larger pebbles and gravels. These settle to the bottom in the shallow areas near shore. Next to settle are the smaller sands and finally, in calm water, the silts and clays.

The process of sorting does not always produce perfect separation. Sand is sometimes found mixed with pebbles and gravels in shallow water or with silts and clays in deeper water.

In time, the sediments become cemented together into sedimentary rocks. Pebbles and gravels become conglomerate. Sands form sandstones. Silts and clays form shale.

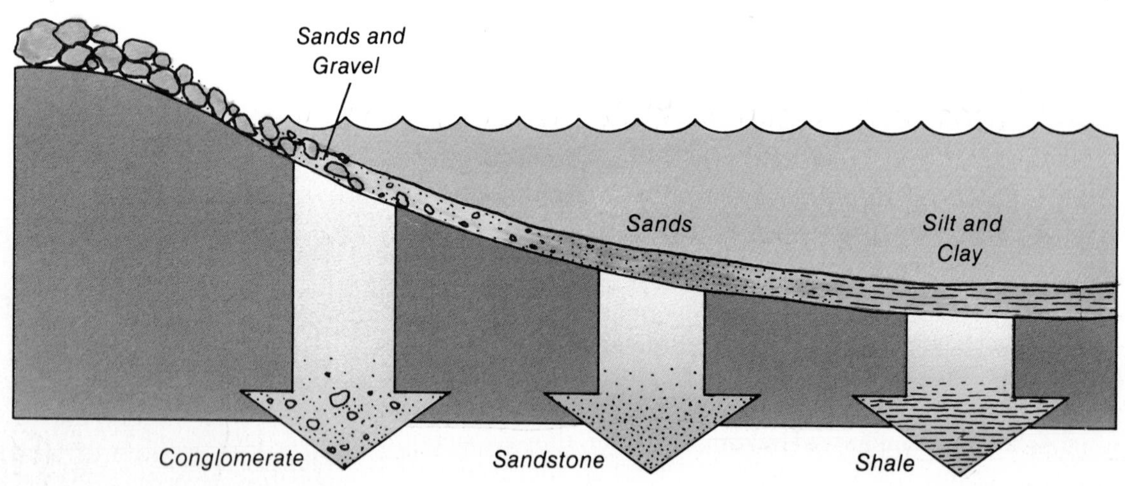

5.9 The kinds of sediment deposited on the ocean floor vary with the distance from shore.

Topic 12 Conglomerate, Sandstone, and Shale

Conglomerate is the coarsest of the clastic rocks. It is a cemented mixture of rounded pebbles and sand grains that were deposited in rough water. The pebbles in conglomerate may be any rock material. Quartz is most common because it is so durable.

Most *sandstones* are made largely of grains of quartz. The cement in a rock seldom fills all the spaces between the grains. Sandstones may have up to 30 percent air space in them. The air spaces mean that sandstone is both *porous* (filled with small holes) and *permeable* (water is able to pass through it). Sandstones are rough, gritty, and durable if well cemented.

The clays found in *shale* are usually tiny flakes of the mineral kaolin. The spaces between the clay particles in shale are so tiny that water cannot pass through the rock. This makes shale *impermeable.* Shales are smooth, soft, and easily broken.

5.10 Conglomerate is a cemented rock of pebbles and sand grains.

5.11 (left) Sandstone, (right) shale

Topic 13 Sedimentary Rocks of Chemical Origin

Sea, lake, swamp, or underground waters often contain dissolved minerals. Chemical sediments are formed when these minerals fall out of solution. This can occur through evaporation or through chemical action, the combining of dissolved ions to form new minerals. The most common chemical sediments are limestone, rock salt, and rock gypsum.

Limestones of chemical origin are formed from tiny grains of calcite deposited from sea or lake waters. The most common ones are called compact limestone. They are usually gray or tan, dense, and smooth to the touch.

Rock salt is the natural form of common table salt (sodium chloride). It occurs as a sedimentary rock in thick layers in many parts of the world. Rock salt is almost pure halite.

Rock gypsum, like rock salt, occurs in layers. It also occurs as nearly pure veins of the mineral gypsum.

5.12 (top) Rock salt, (bottom) rock gypsum

Topic 14 Sedimentary Rocks of Organic Origin

Organic sediments come from the remains of animals and plants. The most important rocks that come from organic sediments are limestone and coal. Coal will be discussed in Chapter 6.

The lime in organic limestones is the mineral calcite. Calcite is dissolved out of rocks on land, carried to the ocean (or lake) by streams, and taken from the water by lime-forming organisms to make their shells.

Great numbers of lime-forming animals and plants live in the shallow ocean water near shore. These include clams, mussels, oysters, sea snails, corals, microscopic algae, and many others. When

5.13 What sort of rock might these sediments form?

5.14 (above) Cross-bedding occurs when sediment is deposited at an angle. (right) The layers of these rocks show stratification. The lines between the layers show bedding planes.

they die, their lime shells pile up on the shallow ocean floor. The shells may be whole but are more often broken into fragments by the grinding action of the waves. In time the shells become cemented into limestones. The limestones that form near the shore may contain a good deal of clay. Those that form farther from shore may be almost pure lime.

Since most limestones are composed of the mineral calcite, they can readily be identified by the acid test (Chapter 4, Topic 5).

Topic 15 Sedimentary Features: Stratification

Sedimentary rocks show special features that help to identify them. One of these is **stratification**—arrangement in visible layers. How does stratification develop?

When any change occurs in the kind of sediments being laid down in one place, new rock layers are formed. For example, if a coarse clay is deposited on a fine one, layers of different shale will form, one on top of the other. If sand is deposited on clay, a layer of sandstone will form on a layer of shale. In this way sedimentary rocks become layered. Their beds or layers are separated by bedding planes. Bedding planes are usually horizontal. *Cross-bedding* may develop when beds are deposited by the wind in leaning positions on sand dunes, or deposited by rivers on deltas and sandbars.

The sediment changes that lead to stratification happen for a number of reasons. For example, the river that brings the sediment to the ocean or lake may be wearing away new kinds of rock. It may carry larger amounts and more kinds of pebbles, sand, and clay during flood times. The river may carry its sediments farther out to sea than before. Or, it may drop the sediments closer to shore.

Topic 16 Fossils in Sedimentary Rocks

As sediments pile up, animals and plants that die in the area are buried. The soft parts of the animals and plants usually decay. The hard parts may remain as fossils when the sediments turn to rock. **Fossils** are the remains, impressions, or any other evidence of plants and animals preserved in rock. The shells of clams, mussels, and snails are often found in layers of sandstone, limestone, and shale. More often, the shells themselves have dissolved but were replaced by other minerals that took the shapes of the shells. Other fossils are formed when a shell or a skeleton, such as that of a fish, leaves an impression in the rock layer. These are seen when the rock layers are split apart. Plants can also form impressions in rocks. Plant remains or impressions are usually found in rocks formed from swamp sediments.

5.15 Organic limestone contains fossils of lime-bearing organisms. The fossils in this limestone are easily seen.

Topic 17 Ripple Marks and Mud Cracks

Animals and plants are not the only remains preserved in sedimentary rocks. Many sandstones show *ripple marks* on the surface of a bedding plane. Ripple marks are formed by the action of winds, streams, waves, or currents on sand. Many of them are preserved when the sand becomes sandstone. Fresh ripple marks can be seen today on any sandy beach or stream bed. *Mud cracks* develop when deposits of wet clay dry and contract. If the cracks are later filled with different materials, they are fossilized when the clay becomes shale rock. Fresh mud cracks can be seen wherever muddy roads or puddles of water dry out after a rain.

Topic 18 Nodules, Concretions, Geodes

Limestones often contain lumps of fine-grained silica called *chert.* Geologists call the lumps *nodules.* Round masses of calcium carbonate, called *concretions,* often occur in layers of shale. Both structures were probably deposited from a solution, bit by bit, around a piece of fossil material in the rock. Chert that is dark gray or black is called *flint.* Flint is typically hard and fine-grained.

Limestones sometimes contain small hollow spheres of silica rock. The hollows may be lined with crystals of quartz or calcite. These spheres are called *geodes* (JEE odes). Geodes seem to have been formed by groundwater. First, the water dissolved some of the limestone and formed cavities in it. Then the groundwater deposited quartz or calcite crystals in the cavities.

5.16 Sedimentary features: (top) geode, (bottom left) ripple marks, (bottom right) mud cracks

Summary Table: Common Sedimentary Rocks

	Color	Distinguishing Feature	Origin
breccia	variable	contains angular fragments surrounded by finer grains	clastic
coal	shiny to dull black	found in beds located between other sedimentary rocks	organic
conglomerate	variable	contains rounded pebbles held together by cement	clastic
rock salt	colorless to white	cubic crystals	chemical
gypsum	white, gray, brown, red or green	grains range in size from very fine to very large, can have a very crumbly texture	chemical
limestone	variable—white, gray, yellow, red, brown	found in thick layers on cliffs, may contain fossils	organic
sandstone	white, gray, yellow, red	fine or coarse grains held together by cement	clastic
shale	yellow, red, gray, green, black	dense but soft, breaks easily	clastic

TOPIC QUESTIONS

Each topic question refers to the topic of the same number.

9. **(a)** Compare the total amount of sedimentary rock on Earth's surface with the total amount of sedimentary rock in Earth's crust. **(b)** Name, describe the origin, and give examples of the three groups of sedimentary rocks.

10. **(a)** What substance collects and moves the greatest amount of sediment? **(b)** What kinds of materials can act as mineral cement in clastic sedimentary rocks? **(c)** How can fine particles be formed into rock without cement?

11. **(a)** Explain how sediments are sorted when they are deposited in water. **(b)** Name the rock that is formed from each kind of sediment.

12. **(a)** Describe conglomerate. **(b)** Explain why sandstone is permeable. **(c)** How does the composition of shale explain the fact that it is impermeable?
13. **(a)** Describe how chemical sediments are formed. **(b)** Name three examples of chemical sedimentary rocks.
14. Explain the origin of organic limestones.
15. What is stratification? How does it develop in sedimentary rocks?
16. What are fossils? How do they form in sedimentary rock?
17. How do ripple marks and mud cracks form in sedimentary rocks?
18. **(a)** What is a nodule and how is it thought to form? **(b)** What is a geode? How is it formed?

Suzanne Webel
Exploration Geologist

A childhood interest in rocks turned into a career for Suzanne Webel. She is now an independent consultant searching for petroleum in the Rocky Mountains.

Suzanne's job is to select the places where the chances of drilling a successful well are greatest. She first visits all of the road cuts and other places where the rocks of the exploration area can be observed and sampled. Then she examines the records of oil wells that have already been drilled in the area to find out more about the rocks below the surface. Finally, she fits all of this information together and decides not only which rock layers could have oil but where in the layer the oil is most likely to be trapped.

Once the site is selected, Suzanne is then involved in every aspect of the drilling. She inspects the rocks that the drill brings to the surface to see whether her interpretations and predictions about the rocks are correct. She finds her work exciting, challenging, and highly rewarding.

III Metamorphic Rocks

OBJECTIVES

A Explain the difference between dynamic metamorphism and thermal metamorphism.

B Describe the effects of metamorphism on rocks; name and describe some metamorphic rocks and identify the rock from which each formed.

C Describe the rock cycle and discuss different orders of rock-forming events within the cycle.

Topic 19 What Metamorphic Rocks Are

Marble, slate, gneiss (NICE), and quartzite are examples of rocks that do not fit into either of the first two classes. These rocks are not formed from either magma or sediment. Yet in many ways they are like members of the first two groups. Marble resembles some limestones. Slate looks similar to shale. Quartzite looks like crystallized sandstone. Gneiss contains minerals like those in granite.

These resemblances are not mere coincidence. The rocks in these pairs are related. One actually is formed from the other through changes produced by natural forces. These metamorphic (*meta*, change; *morph*, form) rocks are formed from existing rock by the action of heat, pressure, and chemicals.

5.17 The twisted patterns in this metamorphic rock were caused by extreme heat and pressure.

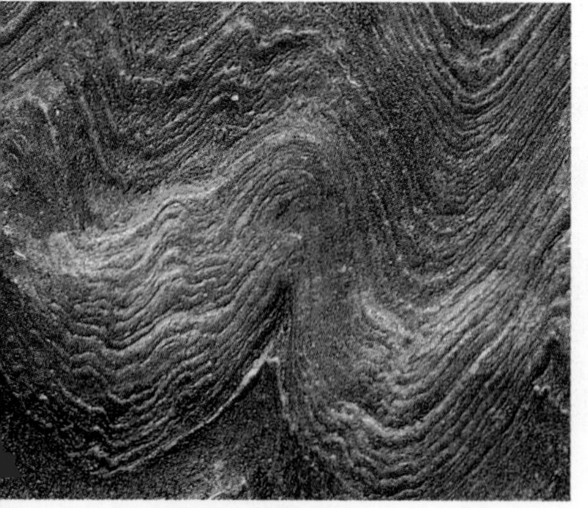

Topic 20 Dynamic Metamorphism

Most of the metamorphic rock of Earth's crust is formed by the process of **dynamic metamorphism.** Dynamic metamorphism occurs when large areas of rock are under intense heat and pressure. This process causes them to change form. This occurs during mountain-building movements. At such times, layers of rock deep in the crust are under high temperature and high pressure. Heat from the friction of the moving rock layers is added to the heat already in the deeply buried rocks. The pressure on the rocks comes from both the great weight of the overlying rocks and the squeezing pressure of the moving rock masses. Hot water, steam, and other liquids and gases in the deep rocks join with the heat and pressure. These forces work together and produce striking changes in the rocks. Dynamic metamorphism takes place over very large areas. For this reason, it is also called *regional metamorphism.*

5.18 (left) Sandstone, (right) quartzite

What happens to rocks that are metamorphosed? Pressure squeezes their grains closer together. The squeezing makes them more dense and less porous. However, pressure alone does not produce all of the changes. Heat and chemicals may rearrange the particles. Minerals may be reformed in the rock, or new minerals may be formed. Two examples of metamorphic rocks are quartzite and marble. Quartzite is metamorphosed sandstone and, like most sandstone, is made of quartz. Marble is metamorphosed limestone and, like limestone, is made of calcite. Both quartzite and marble are dense, crystalline rocks.

5.19 Through metamorphism, shale (top) becomes slate (bottom).

Topic 21 The Metamorphism of Shale

When shale undergoes dynamic metamorphism, many changes can occur. The rock becomes more dense and more crystalline. The elements recombine to form new minerals that are not found in shale, such as mica and hornblende. The pressures on the rocks squeeze the flakes of mica or the needles of hornblende into parallel layers. The new rocks split easily along these layers. This new feature in the rocks is called *foliation.*

The first rock formed from shale during dynamic metamorphism is *slate.* In slate, the foliation layers are microscopically thin. If metamorphism goes further, a shiny rock called *phyllite* (FILL yte) is formed. More intense metamorphism produces a flaky rock called *schist,* in which the foliation layers are easily seen.

Schists can be formed from many different rocks, such as shales, impure sandstones, and basalt. The result is that there are many varieties of schist. These are usually named for their principal mineral. Mica schist, talc schist, and hornblende schist are examples.

Gneiss is another metamorphic rock that is formed from a variety of rocks. It can be formed from shale, granite, conglomerate, and many others. Gneiss has the coarsest foliation of all the metamorphic rocks. Its minerals are arranged in cardboard-thick parallel bands. Bands of light-colored minerals such as quartz and feldspar alternate with dark minerals such as hornblende or biotite.

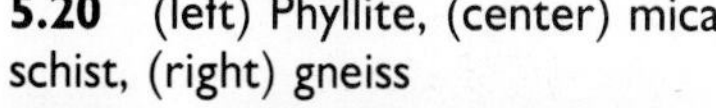

5.20 (left) Phyllite, (center) mica schist, (right) gneiss

Topic 22 Thermal Metamorphism

A second kind of metamorphism is **thermal metamorphism.** This process occurs when hot magma forces its way into overlying rock. The heat of the magma bakes the rocks that are in contact with it. Thus, the process is also called *contact metamorphism.* Hot liquids and gases from the magma also enter the intruded rock and react with its minerals. These effects rarely reach more than a hundred meters into the intruded rock. Much less rock is affected than in dynamic metamorphism. Changes in the rock are usually less drastic, and foliation is not produced.

Hornfels is a rock formed from shale by thermal metamorphism. It is very fine-grained, dense, and very hard.

Relation of Principal Sedimentary Materials, Sedimentary Rocks, and Metamorphic Rocks

Sedimentary Material	Sedimentary Rock	Metamorphic Rock
Pebbles, gravel, sand	Conglomerate	Quartzite conglomerate Gneiss (also from granite and rhyolite)
Sand grains (usually quartz)	Sandstone	Quartzite
Clay (usually kaolin), silt	Shale, mudstone	Slate, phyllite, hornfels, schist
Lime (shells, fragments, or grains)	Limestone	Marble

Topic 23 The Rock Cycle

Classifying the rocks of the crust according to their origin shows how closely related they are. The igneous rocks may be thought of as the primary, or parent, rocks of the crust. As these are attacked by weathering and erosion, sediments form. The sediments are turned into sedimentary rocks. If these rocks are buried beneath other sediments and are involved in movements of Earth's crust, they may become metamorphic rocks.

If crustal movements force rocks deep into Earth's crust, they may reach temperatures so high that they melt into magma. The magma may then harden into igneous rocks to complete the rock cycle.

The rock cycle has many shortcuts and detours. Igneous rocks may be metamorphosed directly. Sedimentary rocks may be weathered without being metamorphosed. Metamorphic rocks may be metamorphosed or weathered a second time. The story of the rock cycle is outlined in Figure 5.21. In brief form, it is a large part of the story of geology.

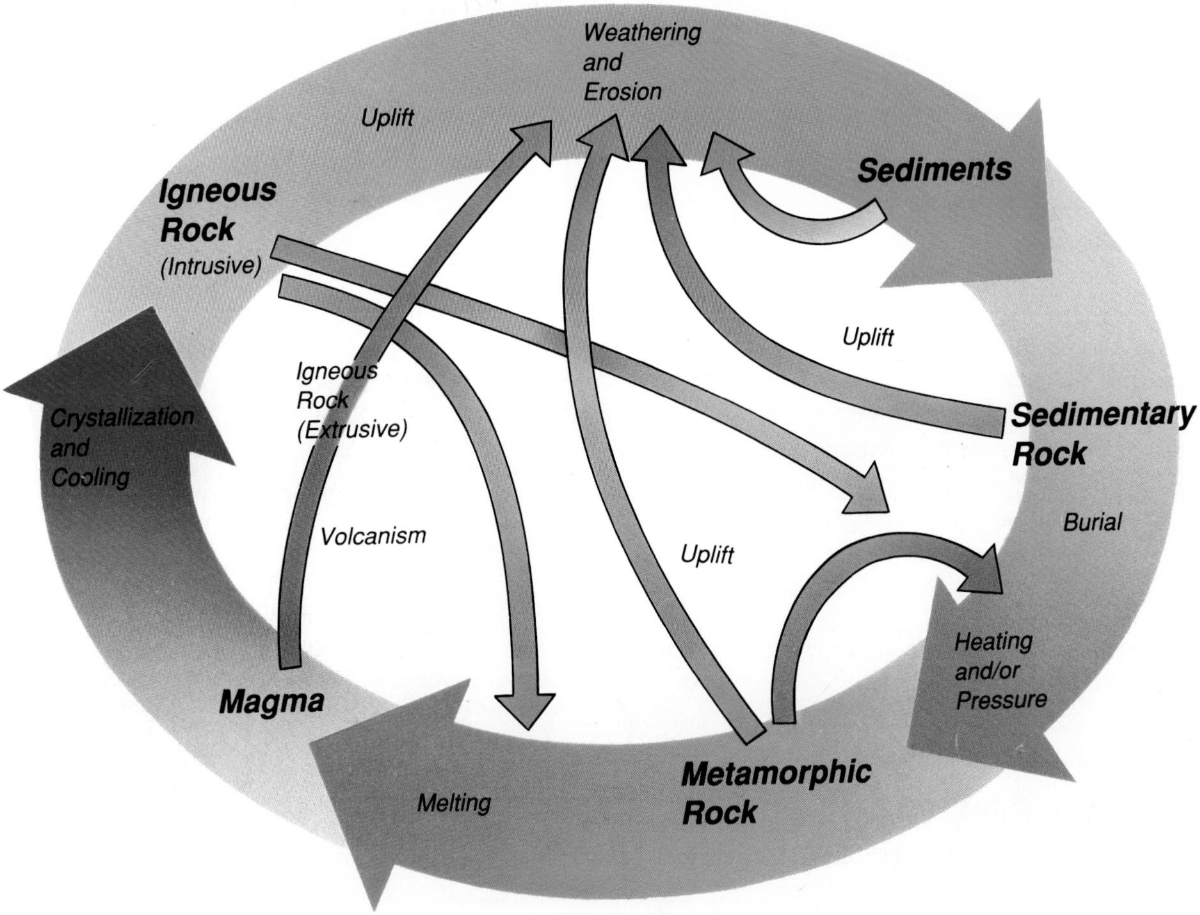

5.21 The rock cycle summarizes the formation and breakdown of igneous, sedimentary, and metamorphic rocks.

TOPIC QUESTIONS

Each topic question refers to the topic of the same number.

19. Define metamorphic rock and list four examples.

20. **(a)** Explain the process of dynamic metamorphism. **(b)** What general changes does metamorphism cause in rocks? **(c)** In what ways does metamorphism change sandstone? Limestone?

21. **(a)** What changes occur in shale during dynamic metamorphism? **(b)** What rocks are formed from shale as metamorphism progresses? **(c)** Describe schist and gneiss.

22. **(a)** What causes thermal metamorphism? **(b)** How do the effects of thermal metamorphism compare with those of dynamic metamorphism?

23. **(a)** List the general steps of the rock cycle. **(b)** Identify two shortcuts in the rock cycle.

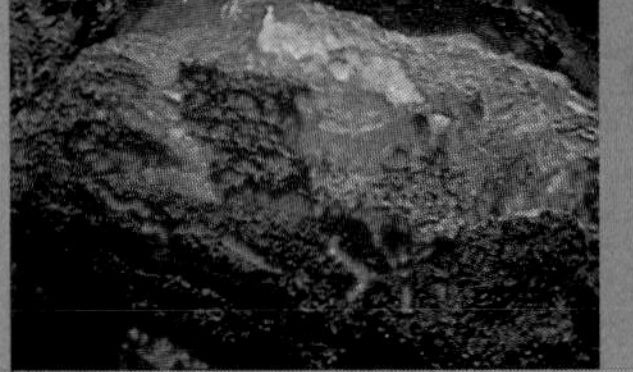

CHAPTER 5 REVIEW

Summary

The same processes that form and shape Earth's crust today also formed features in the past. This is the principle of uniformitarianism.

Plutonic igneous rocks form from magma deep in the crust and have distinct mineral grains. Volcanic igneous rocks form from lava at or near the surface and lack distinct grains.

Felsic magmas form light-colored, silica-rich rocks such as granite. Mafic magmas form dark-colored, ferromagnesian-rich rocks such as basalt.

Igneous rock texture depends mainly on the rate at which magma cools. The slower magma cools, the coarser the texture. A porphyry is a rock with two distinct textures.

Igneous rocks are grouped into families by mineral composition. Each family has members with different textures.

Sedimentary rocks are grouped by the kind of sediment from which they form: clastic, chemical, or organic.

Clastic sediments are often sorted by water action before pressure and mineral cements turn them into rock.

Sedimentary rocks often occur in visible layers. These form when different sediment types are deposited on top of each other.

Fossils, ripple marks, mud cracks, nodules, concretions, and geodes are all features of sedimentary rock layers.

Metamorphic rocks are formed when heat or pressure or both changes the density, minerals, and structure of existing rocks.

Dynamic metamorphism results from the heat and pressure of mountain-building and affects large areas. Thermal metamorphism results when hot magma is in contact with rock; it affects small areas.

The rock cycle shows how the formation of igneous, sedimentary, and metamorphic rocks are interrelated.

Vocabulary

chemical
clastic
dynamic metamorphism
felsic
fossils
igneous
mafic
magma
metamorphic
organic
plutonic
porphyry
rock
sedimentary
stratification
texture
thermal metamorphism
uniformitarianism
volcanic

Review

On your paper, write the word or words that best complete each sentence.

1. The principle of uniformitarianism states "The present is the _______ to the past."
2. Molten rock underground is called _______.
3. Depending on where they form, igneous rocks are _______ (intrusive) or volcanic (extrusive).
4. Depending on their mineral composition, igneous rocks are felsic (silica-rich) or _______ (ferromagnesian-rich).
5. Igneous rocks that cool slowly in the crust are likely to have a _______ texture.
6. A rock with two different textures is a _______.
7. Quartz and _______ are the two most important minerals in the granite family.
8. The most important member of the gabbro family is the fine-grained rock from lava flows, _______.
9. _______ rocks are classified as clastic, chemical, or organic.
10. Silica, lime, and iron are natural _______ that bind sediments into sedimentary rocks.
11. When streams drop sediments, heavy pebbles and gravels are left near shore, but _______, silt, and clay are left farther away.
12. A sedimentary rock made of rounded pebbles and sand grains is called _______.

13. A sedimentary rock made of tiny calcite grains or of fossil shell bits is ______.
14. When different kinds of sediments are laid down on top of each other, ______ results.
15. A ______ is some evidence of a plant or animal, preserved in rock.
16. The bedding planes of some sedimentary rocks show ripple marks and ______ cracks.
17. A lump of silica that forms in limestone is called a ______ .
18. If sedimentary or igneous rocks are subjected to heat and pressure, they become ______ rocks.
19. Dynamic (regional) metamorphism affects a large area, while ______ (contact) metamorphism affects only a small area.
20. ______ forms when limestone undergoes metamorphism.
21. Three metamorphic rocks that form from shale are ______, phyllite, and schist.
22. In the rock cycle, igneous rocks weather to form ______, which becomes sedimentary rocks.

Interpret and Apply

On your paper, answer each question in complete sentences.

1. Using the terms *felsic, mafic, plutonic,* and *volcanic,* compare each pair of igneous rocks. (a) granite and gabbro (b) granite and rhyolite (c) gabbro and basalt (d) rhyolite and basalt
2. Why are fossils more likely to be formed in shale and sandstone than in conglomerate?
3. Why are fossils less likely to be found in metamorphic rocks than in the sedimentary rocks from which those metamorphic rocks formed?
4. Explain several ways of distinguishing white marble from white quartz.
5. If the heat and pressure of dynamic metamorphism caused a rock to melt, would the rock that results still be considered a metamorphic rock?

Critical Thinking

The graph shows a classification system for sandstones that are made of varying amounts of three minerals: kaolin, feldspar, and quartz. Each corner shows a rock made up of 100% of the named mineral. The side opposite the same corner shows rocks with 0% of that mineral, but 100% of the other two. Determine the composition of a sandstone by finding the amount of each mineral in that sandstone. For example, to find the amount of feldspar at point X, start at the "0% Feldspar" side. Count the red lines from this side to point X. There are 5 lines. Each line is 10%; point X is on the 50% feldspar line. Likewise, it is on the 30% kaolin line, and the 20% quartz line. It also falls within the graywacke area. Thus, point X shows a graywacke with 50% feldspar, 30% kaolin, and 20% quartz.

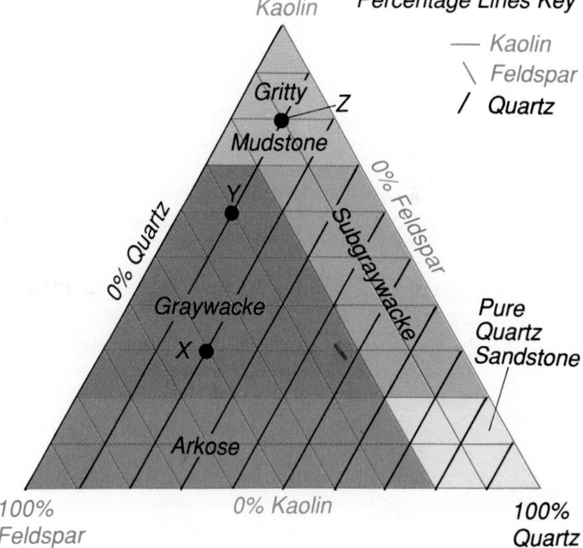

1. What is the composition and name of the sandstone at point Y?
2. What is the composition and name of the sandstone at point Z?
3. A sandstone has 40% quartz, 30% feldspar, and 30% kaolin. What kind is it?
4. Oriskany Sandstone is an oil and gas source in New York and Pennsylvania. It has 95% quartz, 5% other minerals. What kind is it?

CHAPTER

6

Resources and Our Environment

▲
If the soil in this field is managed wisely, it will produce healthy crops for many years.

How Do You Know That . . .

Earth's resources are limited? Some of Earth's resources, such as oil and coal, cannot be replaced once they are used. Other resources, such as the soil in the field shown above, are reusable. However, even resources such as soil and water are limited. Unless the soil in this field is managed carefully, it may lose its ability to support healthy crops. How does the use of Earth's resources affect the environment?

I Renewable Environmental Resources

OBJECTIVES

A Compare renewable and nonrenewable resources.

B Identify the sources of solid and gaseous air pollutants.

C Describe factors that affect the usability of land and soil.

D Identify sources of water pollution.

Topic 1 Renewable versus Nonrenewable Resources

A great deal of attention is being given to the protection of the environment. Earth's **environment** includes all of the resources, influences, and conditions at Earth's surface. Some of the most important resources are basic to life on Earth—air, water, land, and sunlight. Other resources have become vital to the world economy since the late nineteenth century. These include energy resources, such as coal and oil, as well as raw materials, such as metal ores.

Earth's resources can be grouped as renewable and nonrenewable. A **renewable resource** is one that can be replaced in nature at a rate close to its rate of use. Examples are oxygen in the air, trees in a forest, food grown in the soil, and solar energy from the sun.

A **nonrenewable resource** is one that is used up faster than it can be replaced in nature. Many of Earth's resources are nonrenewable. These include metals such as gold, silver, iron, copper, and aluminum; nonmetals such as sand, gravel, limestone, and sulfur; and energy sources such as coal, oil, natural gas, and uranium. Some geological resources can be recycled after use. Most of them, however, especially the energy resources, are destroyed by use. These same resources are being used at an alarming rate.

Topic 2 Air

Air is a renewable resource. Dry air is made up of about 78 percent nitrogen and 21 percent oxygen. Together these two gases make up about 99 percent of the air by volume. The other 1 percent is argon, carbon dioxide, and other gases.

For living things, the two most important gases in the air are oxygen and carbon dioxide. Oxygen is used by all plants and animals in respiration. **Respiration** is the process by which food is changed to energy. Carbon dioxide is a by-product of respiration. Carbon dioxide is used in photosynthesis. **Photosynthesis** is the process by which plants make sugars and starches. Oxygen is a by-product of photosynthesis. Thus nature restores oxygen and carbon dioxide to the air about as fast as they are used up.

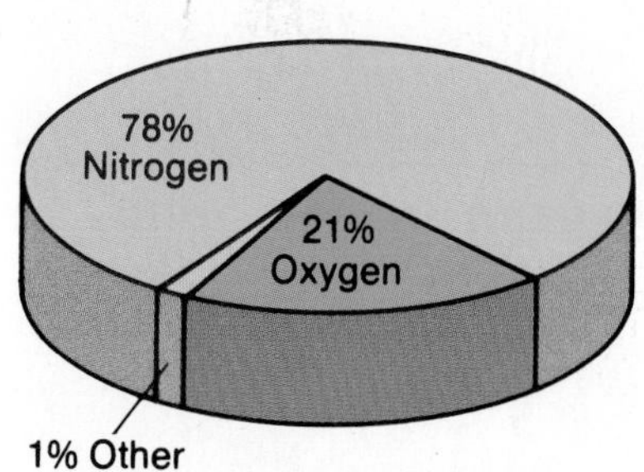

6.1 Nitrogen and oxygen occupy about 99 percent of air by volume. The remaining 1 percent is a mixture of other gases.

Topic 3 **Air Pollution**

Pollution occurs when some part of the environment is changed in a way that makes it unfit for human, plant, or animal use. One way pollution occurs is when harmful substances, called *pollutants*, enter the air. Most air pollutants exist as solids or gases. Common solid pollutants found in the air include soot, dust from soil, and plant pollen. Soot enters the air mainly from the smoke of coal-burning furnaces. Such furnaces are used to generate electricity in some power plants. Plant pollen is a natural pollutant. It is disturbing to people who are allergic to it.

The main air pollutants that exist as gases are sulfur dioxide, carbon monoxide, oxides of nitrogen, and hydrocarbons. Sulfur dioxide enters the air when coal and fuel oil are burned. It is a poisonous gas that is irritating to the nose and throat. When sulfur dioxide combines with droplets of water in the air, it forms a harmful acid (Topic 21). The other gas pollutants are mainly from the burning of fuels in car and truck engines. Many gases in the exhaust from such engines are poisonous. The nitrogen oxides and hydrocarbon gases form smog. These gases are the main cause of smog in many urban areas. Poisonous lead compounds enter the air when leaded gasoline is burned. For this reason, leaded gasoline is being phased out of use in the United States.

Topic 4 **Land and Soil**

About 29 percent of Earth's surface is land. The usefulness of land depends on a number of factors. Factors include the land's steepness, the local climate, and whether the soil is suitable for growing food. One use of land is as a foundation for buildings. Not all land is suitable for this purpose. If the land is too soft, too hilly, or in an area with a hostile climate, it will generally not be used to build on.

6.2 Cultivation and irrigation are used to increase the productivity of land resources.

Soil is a mixture of mineral matter and organic matter. Together these substances affect the fertility of the soil. **Fertility** is the ability of the soil to grow plants. The types of mineral matter and organic matter in a soil determine the kind of plant that will grow best there. For example, a soil that is fertile for potatoes may be less fertile for wheat. This is because the nutrients needed to grow potatoes are different from the nutrients needed to grow wheat. Soil is generally thought to be a renewable resource. The nutrients in soil can be replaced by natural and artificial fertilization.

Soil is used to grow the rooted plants needed by humans and other animals to live. Cultivated soils provide the grains, fruits, and vegetables needed for human nutrition. Trees, which provide timber for buildings and fuel, also grow on soil. Grasses grown on soil provide food for livestock. However, less than 25 percent of Earth's land can be used to grow crops. Rough terrains, such as mountain regions, often have no soil cover. Temperature and available water also affect the usability of land. Polar regions are too cold to grow crop plants, while desert regions are too hot and dry.

6.3 Severe environmental conditions such as droughts have a serious impact on the renewability of land resources.

Topic 5 Problems in Land and Soil Use

Although land and soil are generally thought to be renewable, several problems limit their renewability. One problem is that the areas with the most fertile soil are often the areas with the greatest population density. Few crops are grown in mountain areas, deserts, or polar regions . . . few people live in those same areas. Most crops are grown on level land in moderate climates. Most people live on fairly level land in moderate climates. In some areas of the world, the conflict between land for housing and land for crops is a critical problem. In Japan, about 85 percent of the land surface is mountainous. The amount of land suitable for farming is, therefore, quite limited. The bulk of the Japanese population, including farmers, lives in the same 15 percent of the country. As a result, the conflict between using land for housing or for farming is a critical one.

A second problem in land and soil use is **soil depletion.** Crop plants use certain nutrients in the soil, as do natural grasses. When natural grasses die, the nutrients are returned to the soil. When crops are harvested, however, the nutrients are removed from the soil. In time, the soil can become so lacking in nutrients that it will no longer grow a usable crop. The problem of soil depletion can be managed through good farming practices. Fields can be left to rest. A crop can be allowed to return to the soil. Or, the kind of crop grown on a field can be changed from year to year. These practices are not always followed, however, because they can be very expensive in the short term.

A third problem in soil use is **desertification.** This occurs in areas where plant cover has been removed by farming or by farm animals. When this happens, the bare soil can be easily removed by wind or rain, like the soil in a desert. The lost soil is difficult to replace. The land has become nonrenewable.

Salinization is a problem in desert areas. With water, some desert soils are very fertile. However, water brought in to irrigate a desert contains minerals. The dry air of the desert causes water to evaporate rapidly. When this happens, minerals in the water, such as salt, are left behind on the soil surface. In time, the soil surface has so much mineral matter that crops can no longer be grown. Such soil is difficult to reclaim.

Topic 6 Water

Seventy-one percent of Earth's surface is covered by ocean water. Oceans average nearly four kilometers in depth. However, ocean water is salt water. Most uses of water require fresh water found in lakes, rivers, and the ground. Water is necessary to all life-forms on Earth. Vast amounts of water are also used for sanitary purposes, in agriculture, and by industry.

Unlike air, water resources are not evenly spread around Earth. Large parts of Earth's surface cannot be lived in because they lack fresh water. Other regions have severe droughts from time to time. As a result, these regions are not well suited for people to live.

Water is a renewable resource because it evaporates back into the air after use and returns to Earth as rain. This cycle of water will be discussed in Chapter 9.

Topic 7 Water Pollution

Like air, water can become polluted. There are several sources of water pollutants. Untreated or poorly treated sewage is one source. Phosphates and nitrates from fertilizers and manure also pollute water. Poisonous wastes from factories, oil spills on the ocean, and even hot water can pollute water.

Harmful germs from sewage may affect shellfish beds. Germs in polluted water also cause such diseases as typhoid and hepatitis. Sewage has caused the closing of some beaches because of fears that swimmers might become ill.

Phosphates and nitrates that enter lake water lead to the growth of some algae and other microscopic organisms. When these organisms die, they are eaten by other organisms that use up oxygen. The oxygen-using organisms multiply rapidly. Then the oxygen of the lake is used up faster than it can be replaced. When this happens, fish and other animals in the lake die from lack of oxygen. The damaging of a lake by accidental fertilizing is called **eutrophication** (YOU truh fi KAY shun).

6.4 Poisonous waste flows into this polluted river. Notice the strange color of the water.

Poisonous wastes from factories may build up in the fish that live in rivers and lakes. The fish are then unfit to eat. The poisons may kill birds that feed on the fish. These poisons include insecticides, pesticides, lead, mercury, and many other by-products of industrial processes.

Oil spills can happen when oil tankers run aground or when offshore oil wells leak. The oil is poisonous to some living things. It may suffocate others. It gets into feathers, keeping birds from swimming or flying. Ocean currents can move oil spills some distance away from the point of the spill. Oil spills can then be washed ashore, fouling beaches and marshes.

Thermal pollution is caused by hot-water wastes. Warm water does not hold oxygen gas as well as cold water does. Some factories and most nuclear power reactors use water to cool equipment. The water is taken from nearby streams, lakes, or rivers, and flows around a hot object. The water absorbs some heat from the object. Then it is returned to its source, usually at a higher temperature. As water warms, it cannot hold as much oxygen. Low oxygen levels lead to the growth of harmful bacteria and foul-smelling green algae. This kills fish and amphibians in the lake or river and affects wildlife that feeds on these animals.

6.5 Volunteers work to clean up an oil spill on a California beach.

TOPIC QUESTIONS

Each topic question refers to the topic of the same number.

1. **(a)** What are renewable resources? List some examples. **(b)** What are nonrenewable resources? List some examples.
2. **(a)** How is oxygen used by living things? **(b)** How is oxygen returned to the air? **(c)** How is carbon dioxide used by living things? **(d)** How is carbon dioxide returned to the air?
3. **(a)** When is the environment considered to be polluted? **(b)** What solid pollutants are most often found in the air? **(c)** What gases most often pollute the air?
4. **(a)** What are some uses for land and soil? **(b)** List some factors that make land or soil difficult to use. **(c)** What determines the fertility of soil?
5. **(a)** Describe the conflict between farming and housing. **(b)** What is soil depletion? How can it be controlled? **(c)** How does desertification occur? **(d)** How does salinization occur?
6. **(a)** List some sources of fresh water. **(b)** Identify some uses of water. **(c)** How does the amount of water in different places on Earth affect where people live? **(d)** Why is water a renewable resource?
7. **(a)** Describe how eutrophication occurs. **(b)** Describe some ways other than eutrophication that water can become polluted.

OBJECTIVES

A Define the terms *ore mineral, mineral resource,* and *mineral reserve.*

B Identify the ores and uses of various metals.

C Identify various nonmetal resources and their uses.

II Nonrenewable Resources: Metals and Nonmetals

Topic 8 Minerals and Ores

All metallic elements and many important nonmetallic elements can be obtained from minerals. Some of the elements are attached to other elements. Since these elements are not chemically bound, they are easily separated. Gold and silver are good examples of such elements. More commonly, the metal or nonmetal is combined with another substance. It must then be chemically separated to be useful. In either case, the needed element is often only a small part of the rock in which it occurs.

If the rock has enough of the element to make the separation profitable, the rock is called an ore. Iron ore and copper ore are examples of rocks from which elements can be removed. The valuable mineral is called the **ore mineral.** The rest of the rock is the **gangue** (gang). Quartz, feldspar, calcite, and dolomite are common gangue minerals.

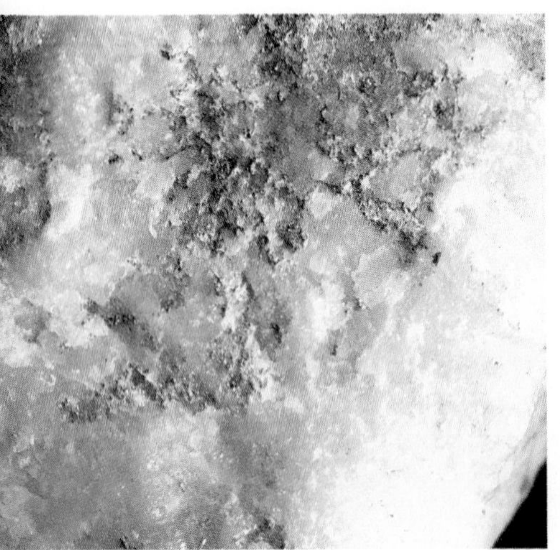

6.6 Gold often occurs in association with quartz.

Mineral resources are nonrenewable. Thus, it is important to know how much of each resource is available for the future. Surveys have been made for this purpose. In these surveys, the amount of a *resource* is an estimate of the total amount of the mineral thought to exist. Mineral **reserves** are the amount of known deposits of a mineral in ores that are worth mining at the present time. Knowing how fast a particular mineral is being used makes it possible to figure out about how long the supply will last.

Ores deep in the ground are usually removed through underground mines reached by tunnels. Ores close to the surface are removed through great holes called open-pit mines.

Topic 9 Some Important Metals and Their Ores

Iron is a metal essential to modern society. Steel is made from iron. Steel is used to make large structures such as skyscrapers, bridges, tunnels, ships, planes, trains, and cars. It is used for objects as small as pins and stainless-steel kitchen utensils. The common ore minerals of iron are its oxides, *hematite* and *magnetite.* The main iron ore deposits in the United States are in the Lake Superior region of Michigan, Wisconsin, and Minnesota. The high-grade ores from this area have been used up. However, great quantities of lower-grade ore, called *taconite,* remain. They are the source of millions of tons of iron each year.

Copper is used in electrical wiring and in making brass. Its main ore mineral is *chalcopyrite* (kal koe PIE rite). About 20 percent of the copper used in the United States is imported. World copper reserves are not large. They will be used up in about 60 years if present rates of use continue.

Aluminum is used for cans, cookware, and structural materials. Aluminum is the third most common element in Earth's crust (after oxygen and silicon). Nevertheless, *bauxite,* a compound of aluminum, oxygen, and water, is the only major source of aluminum. Bauxite is abundant in the world as a whole, but not in the United States, which imports 90 percent of the bauxite ore it uses.

Zinc is combined with copper to make brass. Galvanized iron is iron coated with a thin layer of zinc to prevent rusting. The main ore of zinc is *sphalerite* (SFAL er ite), a compound of zinc and sulfur. About half of the zinc used in the United States is imported. World reserves should last about 40 years at the present rate of use.

Lead is used in storage batteries, solder, and shielding around radioactive materials. Most lead ore is *galena,* a compound of lead and sulfur. World reserves of lead are enough for about 50 years. A small amount of the lead used in the United States is imported.

Some metals are scarce in the United States and must be entirely imported. Examples of such metals include platinum, magnesium, cobalt, chromium, tin, and nickel.

6.7 Open-pit copper mine in Bingham Canyon, Utah

6.8 Major mineral resources occur throughout the world.

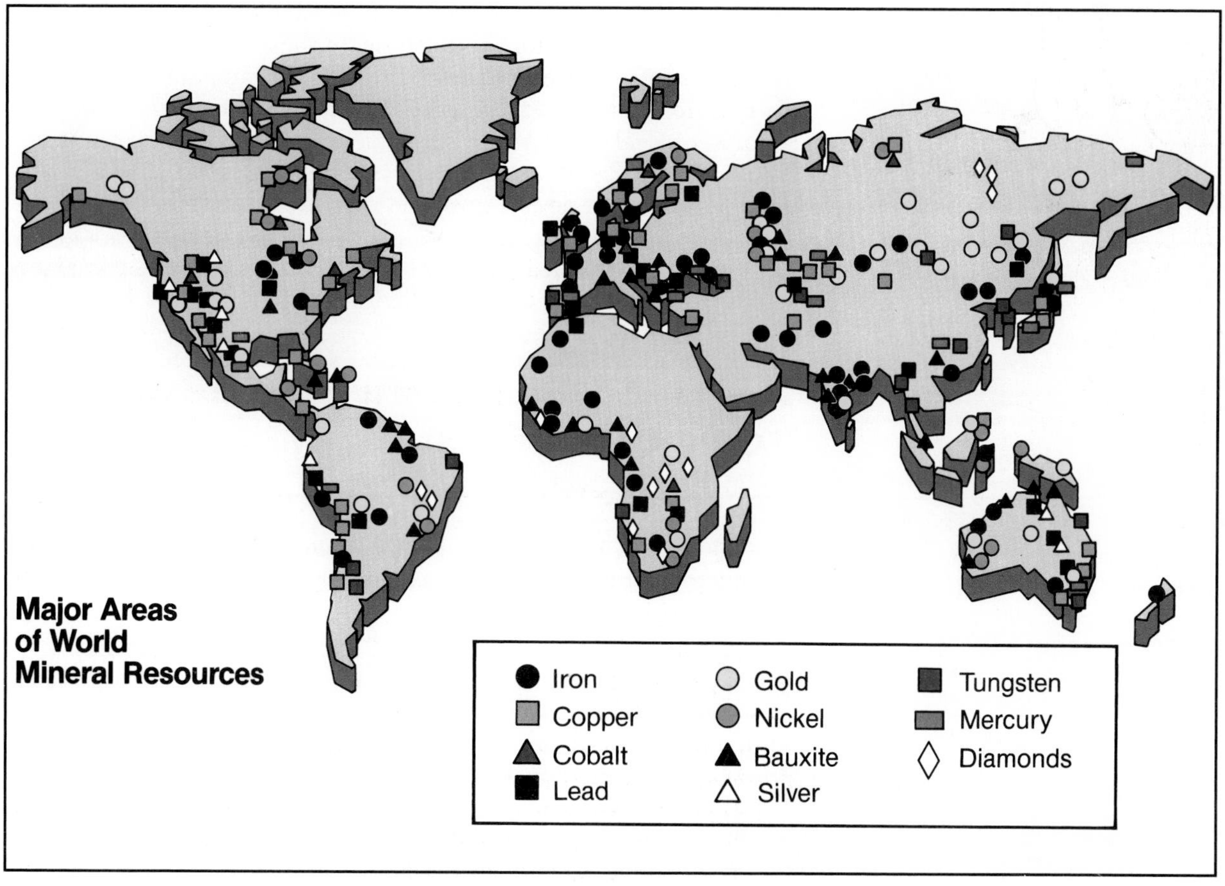

Major Areas of World Mineral Resources

Iron
Copper
Cobalt
Lead
Gold
Nickel
Bauxite
Silver
Tungsten
Mercury
Diamonds

Topic 10 **Important Nonmetals**

Unlike most metallic minerals, most nonmetallic mineral resources are used in the form in which they come out of the ground. No treatment is needed to extract them from other compounds. The main nonmetallic resources are such simple materials as sand, gravel, building stone, rock salt, talc, and graphite.

Sand, gravel, and crushed stone come from quarries. A quarry is a small open-pit mine where these materials occur naturally. The United States has enough of these construction materials.

Materials used as soil fertilizers are also nonmetals. These include phosphate rock, potash, and nitrates. All are mined or produced in the United States.

Salt is plentiful in the United States, with mines in New York, Michigan, Ohio, Texas, and Louisiana. It is an important raw material in the chemical industry. Salt is also used for melting ice from highways and for preserving foods. Gypsum is a common mineral used to make plasterboard and other plaster products.

Sulfur occurs as a native element in the salt mines of Louisiana and Texas. Sulfur is used as a soil conditioner, as a fungicide, and in the manufacture of sulfuric acid. Graphite, a form of carbon, is used in dry cells and as a lubricant. Talc is crushed to make talcum powder and is used as a filler in paints and rubber.

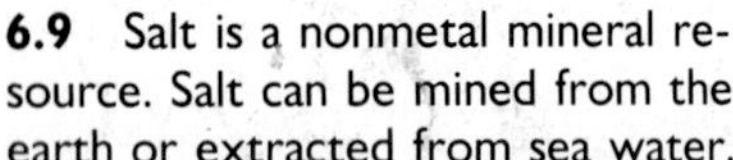

6.9 Salt is a nonmetal mineral resource. Salt can be mined from the earth or extracted from sea water.

TOPIC QUESTIONS

Each topic question refers to the topic of the same number.

8. **(a)** What is an ore mineral? **(b)** What is the gangue? **(c)** What is the difference between mineral reserves and mineral resources?

9. **(a)** What are the common ore minerals of iron and copper? **(b)** What are the important ores of aluminum, zinc, and lead? **(c)** Identify some metals that the United States must import.

10. **(a)** How do most nonmetallic mineral deposits differ from metallic mineral deposits? **(b)** List some nonmetal materials used in construction. **(c)** What are phosphate rock, potash, and nitrates used for?

III Nonrenewable Energy Resources

OBJECTIVES

A Describe the origin, occurrence, and uses of various fossil fuels.

B Describe how uranium is used to generate electricity.

Topic 11 Energy Use

Energy is defined as the ability to do work. Water, wind, animals, and even human muscles can supply energy for work. People's use of energy has increased dramatically in the last century. At one time wood, which can be burned for heat, light, and cooking, was the major source of energy in the world.

Today, the world's use of energy is greater than ever. Yet only 5 percent of that energy comes from renewable sources like water power and wind. The rest comes from nonrenewable sources of energy such as coal, petroleum, and natural gas.

Coal, petroleum, and natural gas are called **fossil fuels** because they formed from the remains of plants and animals that lived long ago. Burning these fuels releases the energy stored in them. Fossil fuels are nonrenewable because they are burned at rates millions of times faster than they are forming today.

Topic 12 Fossil Fuels: Coal

Coal is an organic sedimentary rock. It is formed from such plant materials as mosses, ferns, and parts of trees. All organic material contains the elements carbon, hydrogen, and oxygen. When plant or animal materials are buried in swamp waters—usually under sand or clay—they slowly decay. They gradually lose most of their hydrogen and oxygen and are left with most of their carbon. As the sediment ages and is compacted over time, it changes. A compressed mass of plant remains in which the mosses, leaves, and twigs can still be seen is called *peat*. Over the hundreds of years that are needed for peat to form, hydrogen and oxygen are lost. This concentrates the carbon that remains. *Lignite,* a soft brown coal that forms when peat is compressed and aged, is about 40 percent carbon. After thousands of years of compression, bituminous coal may form. *Bituminous,* or soft coal, may be up to 85 percent carbon. Soft coal burns readily, but it produces a lot of smoke. Regional metamorphism may change bituminous coal to *anthracite,* or hard coal. Anthracite is about 90 to 95 percent carbon. As the percentage of carbon increases, the amount of energy given off by burning the coal increases.

6.10 The carbon content of different kinds of coal depends on the age of the material and on the heat and pressure that affected it.

Deep coal deposits are worked in underground mines. Shallow deposits are worked in open-pit mines called strip mines. The main use of coal in the United States today is to run power plants that generate electricity. Coal is also used in making steel and as a raw material in many chemical factories. World reserves of coal could last hundreds of years at the present rate of use.

Topic 13 Fossil Fuels: Petroleum and Natural Gas

The word *petroleum* means "rock oil." Petroleum, like coal, is a sedimentary material of organic origin. It is a mixture made mainly of liquid hydrocarbons, which are compounds of hydrogen and carbon. Gasoline and kerosene are hydrocarbons.

Scientists think that petroleum was formed by slow chemical changes in plant and animal materials buried under sand and clay in shallow coastal waters. Some of the hydrocarbons formed were liquids, and some were gases. As the sediments became compacted, the hydrocarbons were squeezed into pores and cracks of nearby sandstones or limestones. These rocks also contained sea water. The lighter, mixed hydrocarbon liquids (petroleum) rose above the water, and the natural gas collected above the petroleum.

Why haven't the petroleum and gas kept rising and escaped from the rock in the millions of years since they formed? Probably a good deal did. The petroleum found today was sealed in by an impermeable rock layer, such as shale. Such rock structures are called *oil traps.* Figure 6.12 shows the most common kind of trap, the anticline, or upfold.

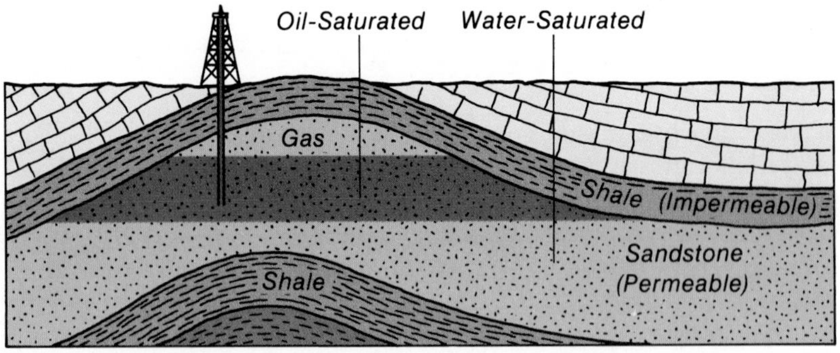

Oil-Saturated
Water-Saturated
Gas
Shale (Impermeable)
Sandstone (Permeable)
Shale

6.11 Oil and natural gas are often found trapped in sedimentary layers that are located beneath a layer of impermeable rock. By drilling through the impermeable layer, the oil and gas can be extracted from the permeable layer.

Wells are drilled into oil-bearing rock to release the oil. The pressure of the natural gas helps bring the oil to the surface. Unless the drilling is carefully controlled, the high pressure causes wasteful oil gushers. Even with modern technology, only about 40 percent of the oil is pumped out of a given well.

Natural gas often occurs with petroleum. Yet it may also exist in great deposits of gas alone. It is a mixture of hydrocarbon gases, mostly methane. Natural gas is an efficient fuel for use in heating.

When petroleum is refined, it is separated into many different hydrocarbons. Gasoline is used in automobiles. Kerosene and fuel oil are used for heating. Other oils are used as lubricants. Both petroleum and natural gas are used as the raw material in making such substances as plastics, fertilizers, dyes, and medicines.

At the present rate of use, United States reserves of petroleum are expected to last between 30 and 50 years. United States reserves of natural gas are expected to last between 40 and 60 years. Other reserves may be found, but usage is also likely to increase.

Topic 14 Uranium

Although uranium is not a fossil fuel, it is a fuel, that is, a source of energy. It is used in nuclear reactors to generate electricity. Uranium is a metal. Energy is obtained from certain kinds of uranium during a reaction that can be triggered within the nucleus of the uranium atom. Such a reaction is called atomic fission. The chain of events in atomic fission is illustrated in Figure 6.12. Atomic fission releases huge amounts of energy. The fission of one gram of uranium releases as much energy as the burning of nearly 3 tons of coal or 14 barrels of oil.

A nuclear power plant can be used to produce electricity. In a nuclear power plant, uranium is fissioned in a special vessel called a nuclear reactor. Water under high pressure is pumped through the reactor. The energy given off by the fission reaction heats the water. This hot water is used to heat other water, which becomes steam. The steam is pumped into turbines, which generate electricity. This system is quite similar to the one used when electricity is generated from coal. In both cases, the fuel (either uranium or coal) turns water to steam. The steam then runs a turbine.

The main ores of uranium are the black mineral *uraninite* and the yellow mineral *carnotite*. Both are oxides of uranium. Uranium is the fourth most important source of energy, behind oil, natural gas, and coal, in the world today. At present rates of use, United States uranium reserves will last about 30 years.

The major world producers of energy resources are not always the major consumers. Figures 6.14 and 6.15 show the locations of major energy producers and consumers of the world.

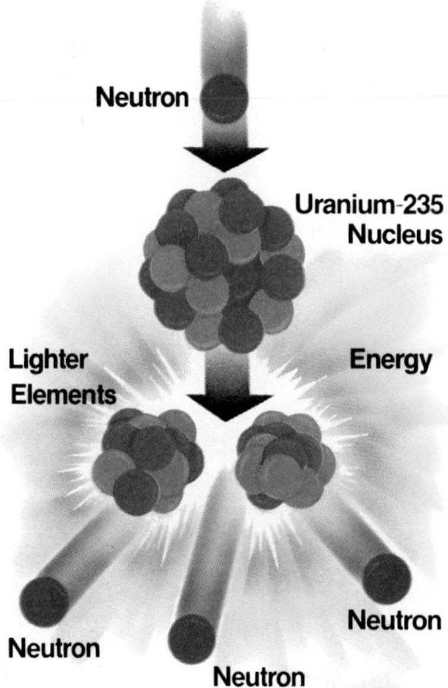

6.12 An atom of a certain isotope of uranium, U-235, can be made to split (fission) by hitting it with neutrons.

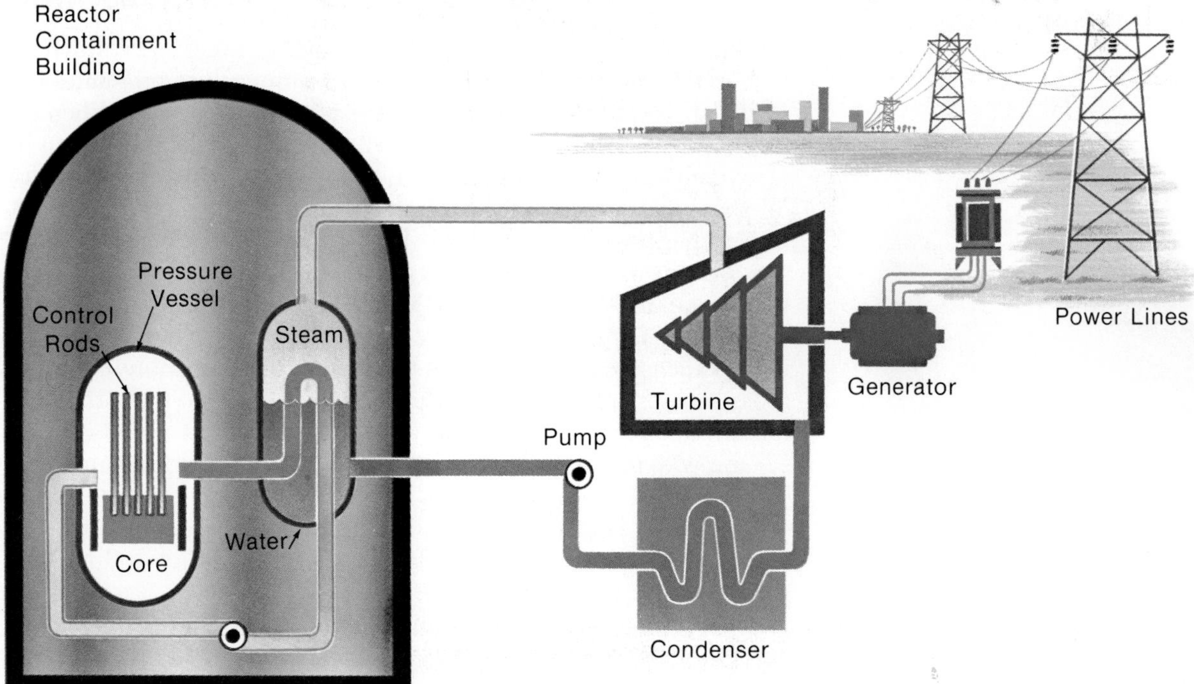

6.13 The energy released by fissioned uranium atoms can be used to generate electricity.

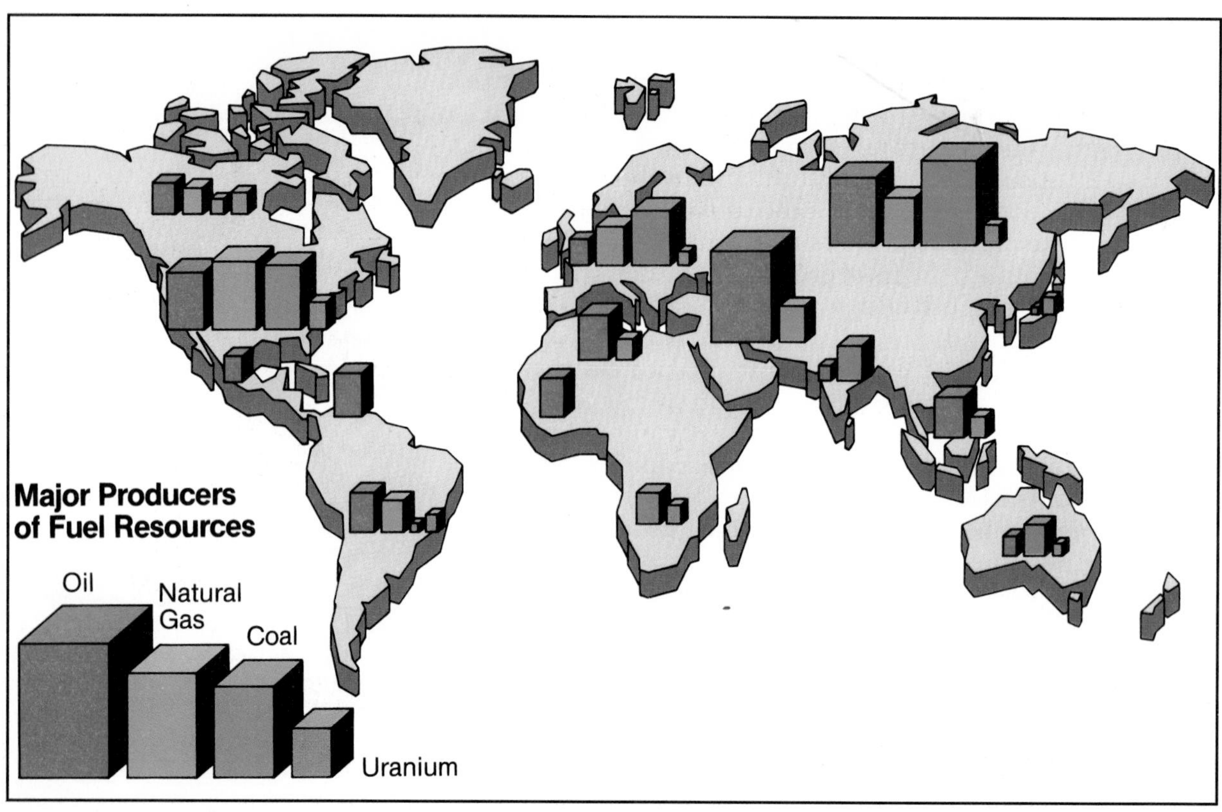

6.14 The locations of the major world fuel producers

Topic 15 Other Fossil Fuels and Gasohol

Coal and oil are presently the least expensive fossil fuels. In Utah, Colorado, and Wyoming there are vast amounts of oil shale. *Oil shale* contains a high percentage of carbon compounds. When oil shale is heated, oil in vapor form is driven off. The oil vapor can be recovered as liquid oil. At present, this process is too expensive for oil shale to compete with oil from wells.

Another possible source of oil is *tar sand.* Great deposits of tar sands occur in the Athabaska region of Canada. The pore spaces in these sands are filled with tar. This tar seems to be the dried residue of petroleum. Oil can be removed from these sands, but the process is too expensive at present. It is estimated that the amount of oil in the oil shales and tar sands of the world is 50 percent more than the remaining oil resources.

One way to conserve oil resources is to use fuel mixtures that contain smaller amounts of fossil fuel. *Gasohol* is a mixture of gasoline (usually 90 percent) and alcohol from corn or other grain crops (usually 10 percent). Gasohol can be used instead of 100 percent gasoline in auto engines. This reduces the use of gasoline. At present, gasohol costs more than gasoline. However, the mileage an automobile gets per gallon of gasohol is greater than that per gallon of gasoline.

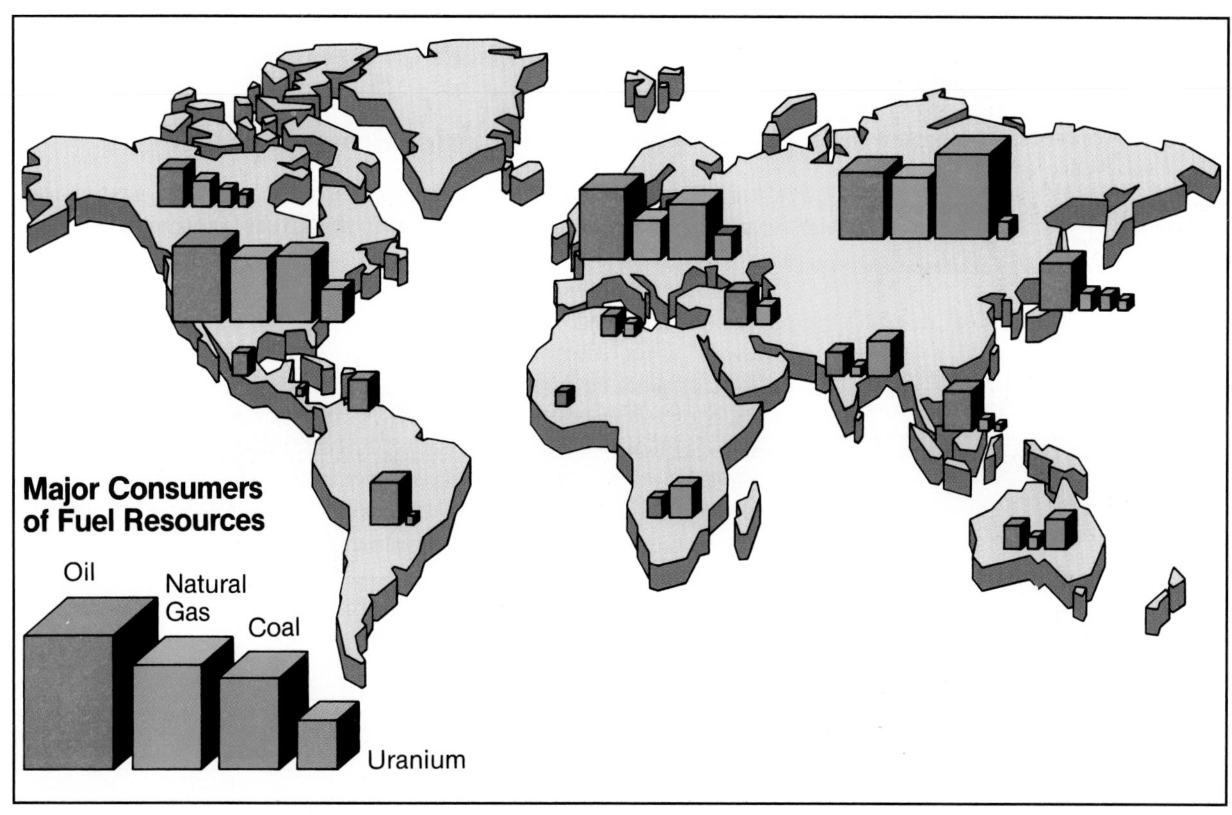

6.15 The locations of the major world fuel consumers

TOPIC QUESTIONS

Each topic question refers to the topic of the same number.

11. (**a**) Define *energy* and list some sources of energy. (**b**) Define *fossil fuel.* (**c**) Why are fossil fuels considered nonrenewable energy sources?

12. (**a**) Describe the formation of coal. (**b**) Compare the percentages of carbon found in lignite, soft coal, and hard coal. (**c**) What are the main uses of coal in the United States?

13. (**a**) What is petroleum and how does it form? (**b**) What is an oil trap? (**c**) What are some products of refined petroleum? (**d**) List some substances made from oil and gas.

14. (**a**) How is uranium used as an energy source? (**b**) Explain how a nuclear reactor generates electricity. (**c**) How does uranium rank as an energy source in the world today?

15. (**a**) How is oil removed from oil shale? (**b**) What is tar sand? (**c**) What is gasohol? (**d**) Explain why oil shale, tar sand, and gasohol are not commonly used at present.

OBJECTIVES

A Identify and describe properties of renewable energy sources.

B Describe the advantages and disadvantages of various alternative energy sources.

IV Alternative Energy Sources

Topic 16 Renewable Energy Sources

Some energy resources are replaced in nature almost as fast as they are used, and are said to be renewable resources. Water power, wind power, solar energy, and geothermal energy are examples of renewable energy sources. Water power is renewed by falling rain. Wind power is renewed every time the wind blows. Solar energy is renewed when the sun shines. Geothermal energy comes from rocks that will be hot for many years.

Each of these energy resources is limited in some way. Water power can be used only in areas where dams can be built for water storage. Wind power can be used only in areas with strong, steady winds. Solar energy varies with the time of day, the season, and the location. Geothermal energy is presently useful only in areas with hot bedrock near the surface. Thus, although these energy sources use no fuel and are nonpolluting, none are usable everywhere.

Topic 17 Water Power

The major use of *water power* today is to produce electricity. Water power is the most efficient way to generate electricity. When burning coal or atomic fission is used, the energy must first heat water to change it into steam. The steam then turns the blades of a turbine to generate electricity. With water power, the turbine blades are turned directly by the moving water. Electricity generated in this way is called *hydroelectric power*. Unfortunately, hydroelectric power can only be used in areas with rivers suitable for damming. Today, only 15 percent of the electricity used in the United States comes from hydroelectric power.

Efforts are underway to generate electricity from tides. The water of Earth's oceans rises and falls with the tides. Water levels can differ from 1 to 10 meters in height. When this water is held back and released slowly, its motion can be used to spin a turbine to produce electricity. Currently, a tidal-powered plant exists at the mouth of La Rance River in France.

6.16 Hydroelectric plants produce electricity without burning a fuel; therefore, such plants are nonpolluting.

Topic 18 Wind Power

Wind power depends on the force of moving air against a windmill. The amount of power produced depends on the speed of the wind, the diameter of the blades on the windmill, and the efficiency of the windmill. In some areas, vast arrays of windmills, called *windmill farms,* produce significant amounts of electrical energy for their local area. There are problems with using wind power, however. Windmills are noisy. They also interfere with television and radio reception. There is also the problem of energy storage. No good method has been found to store the energy produced during strong winds for use during calmer periods.

Topic 19 Solar Energy

Solar energy uses the limitless energy of the sun to provide both heat and electricity. When solar energy is used to heat buildings, the system may be passive or active. In *passive solar heating systems,* the building is designed to collect and store solar energy. For example, a special window might let sunshine into the house but not let heat escape. An outside wall might be made of a material that heats easily in the sunshine and then gives up its heat to the inside of the house. For passive heating systems, important factors include the materials used to build the house, the location of the house relative to the sun, and the landscaping around the house.

An *active solar heating system* has three parts. First, a solar collector facing the sun absorbs heat. This heat is transferred to a storage area. Second, the storage area stores the heat energy until it is needed. Third, a system moves the heat throughout the building. The same system can also be used to heat water and to cool the building in summer.

Solar cells have been used to generate electricity for spacecraft since the start of the space age. These cells convert sunlight into electricity. Recent advances in the design of solar cells may lead to power plants that can produce millions of watts of electrical power.

Another experiment using solar energy to make electricity uses a field of large mirrors. The mirrors focus sunlight on a receiver. The receiver then heats the water, which changes into steam. The steam then drives a turbine.

6.17 Rooftop solar panels are a common sight in some areas of the country.

6.18 At the Geysers power plant in California, naturally occurring, high-pressure steam is used to run electricity generators.

Topic 20 **Geothermal Energy**

Geothermal energy is heat from the interior of Earth. The heat may be brought to the surface by steam or hot water. If the steam or hot water can be piped into a power plant to run a generator, the geothermal energy is changed into electric energy. Hot water from geothermal areas can also be piped into homes for heating and cooking. Only a few countries generate electricity using geothermal energy. The largest geothermal power plant in the world is in an area called the Geysers, located in California. This power plant is driven by superheated, highly pressurized steam. The steam rises naturally out of deep hot rock. Most other geothermal sources, however, are drilled and controlled like oil wells.

Since hot rock can be found in all parts of Earth's crust at some depth, scientists are thinking of ways to use it at any location. One plan underway at Fenton Hill, New Mexico, involves pumping cold water into an underground reservoir hollowed out in the hot rocks. The water is left underground to warm. Then it is pumped back to the surface to generate electricity and heat homes.

Geothermal energy has many advantages. For example, it needs no fuel, and gives off little pollution. It also has disadvantages. Geothermal power plants are usually far from population centers. The energy must be moved a long way to be used. The superheated steam and superheated water is very corrosive. It requires expensive piping and other equipment. Hot water drawn from the ground must be returned to the ground to prevent cave-ins. For these reasons, geothermal energy presently provides much less than one percent of the world's total supply of energy.

TOPIC QUESTIONS

Each topic question refers to the topic of the same number.

16. **(a)** Identify some renewable energy sources. **(b)** Describe reasons each resource is limited.

17. **(a)** Why is water power a more efficient method of generating electricity than coal or nuclear energy? **(b)** Describe how energy can be gained from tides.

18. **(a)** List three factors that affect the amount of energy produced by a windmill. **(b)** What are windmill farms? **(c)** What are some disadvantages in using windmills?

19. **(a)** What is a passive solar heating system? **(b)** List the parts of an active solar heating system. **(c)** What do solar cells do?

20. **(a)** Describe the origin of geothermal energy. **(b)** Describe the Geysers geothermal power plant in California. **(c)** What is important about the geothermal energy plant being developed at Fenton Hill, New Mexico? **(d)** What are the advantages and disadvantages of geothermal energy?

V Environmental Problems and Solutions

OBJECTIVES

A Discuss the causes and effects of acid rain and toxic wastes.

B Identify environmental concerns associated with the use of nuclear reactors.

C Describe several measures that can be taken to conserve nonrenewable resources.

Topic 21 Acid Rain

A negative result of our modern society is the pollutants emitted into the air by industry. Nitrogen and sulfur oxides are released into the air from the burning of soft coal and from car exhaust. These gases react with water vapor in the air and form drops of nitric acid and sulfuric acid. These polluted drops of rain are quite acidic. This type of precipitation is called **acid rain.**

Acid rain has many harmful effects on the environment. Soils where acid rain falls become so acidic that forest growth is reduced and crops may be harmed. Lakes become too acidic to support fish. Stone buildings and monuments weather rapidly as the fall of acid rain increases.

Acid rain can be lessened by reducing air pollution. Pollution from sulfur dioxide can be cut down by burning low-sulfur fuels. Special equipment can be used to remove soot and poisonous gases from the exhaust from factories. Pollution-control devices on cars and trucks can be used to change exhaust gases to harmless substances. In some places where acid rain has already affected the soil and water, lakes and land can be treated with substances to partly neutralize the acid.

6.19 Lime is being added to this lake to help neutralize the acid from acid rain.

Topic 22 Toxic Wastes

Toxic wastes are the extremely poisonous by-product of some industrial processes. Unlike pollution, these poisons usually do not enter the environment directly but are left at various locations. Unless disposed of with care, these wastes can pollute the soil and water around them. For many years, toxic wastes were dumped with little care, and their locations were not written down. In some cases, houses were built on top of old toxic waste dumps. When the toxic waste was later discovered, hundreds of families had to be moved.

The Environmental Protection Agency (EPA) has identified almost 19 000 places across the United States where toxic wastes have been dumped. Over 500 of those sites are thought to be a serious threat to public health and the environment. These sites are scheduled to be cleaned up. Other sites will be added to the cleanup list as money becomes available. Strict rules now govern the disposal of any toxic wastes.

Topic 23 Nuclear Waste Disposal

The use of nuclear reactors leads to two important environmental problems. The first is that nuclear reactors produce by-products that are dangerously radioactive for many years. No satisfactory way has been found for the safe storage or disposal of these nuclear wastes. The second problem is the chance of an accident at a nuclear plant. Such accidents can have awful results. There may be immediate injuries, and the radioactivity may make the area around the plant unfit for people and animals for many years.

Topic 24 Conserving the Nonrenewables

6.20 Recycling of metals conserves both the metal resources and some of the energy resources that would be needed to process new metals.

At present rates of use, many metallic and nonmetallic minerals are likely to be used up in the next 100 years. The only way to deal with this situation is through conservation. Nonrenewable resources are conserved by cutting down on waste, reusing materials, and coming up with substitutes that use more common materials.

Scrap iron, aluminum cans, and the silver in photographic film are examples of metals that are being reused. Glass is made from sand and other minerals. In many states, bottles are returned for recycling or reuse. Glass fibers are replacing copper wire for lines that carry telephone conversations and computer information. Plastic and fiberglass are used instead of metals in cars, airplanes, and other construction. Research is going on to develop high-technology ceramics for use in automobile engines and industrial applications. These are just a few examples of possible conservation measures.

In the field of energy, conservation of nonrenewable resources depends mostly on more efficient use of fuels. Fuel conservation is done by using lighter, smaller cars with more efficient engines.

Are there any new sources of minerals and fuels that are not yet being used? Oil cannot ever be thought of as a renewable resource. However, new deposits may be found. Most of the present-day search for oil is in areas off the shores of continents. The oceans are also possible sources of many important elements such as manganese, cobalt, copper, nickel, and bromine. Methods still have to be developed to recover these resources in a profitable way.

TOPIC QUESTIONS

Each topic question refers to the topic of the same number.

21. **(a)** How does acid rain form? **(b)** What effect does acid rain have on the environment? **(c)** How can acid rain be controlled?
22. **(a)** What are toxic wastes? **(b)** What agency is responsible for finding and cleaning up toxic waste sites?
23. Identify two problems with the use of nuclear reactors.
24. **(a)** What three things can be done to conserve nonrenewable resources? **(b)** Give examples of how some resources are being conserved.

Dr. Betty Miller
Researcher

One of the critical needs of our nation is a complete and precise knowledge of all of our untapped energy and mineral resources. Dr. Betty Miller of the U.S. Geological Survey is working to obtain these data for one especially important resource—petroleum. She does this by collecting and compiling all of the information that is available about the rocks of a particular area. She then carefully studies all of the data and, with the help of a computer, decides where petroleum is most likely to be found. The final step in her work is to prepare a detailed report, complete with maps, that identifies these areas.

Dr. Miller's most recent areas of study have been the wilderness lands of 11 western states. These areas have been set aside by the government to remain in a natural state. In the event of an energy crisis, however, the resources there could be used. That is why it is so important to continue making an inventory of the nation's crucial energy and mineral resources.

CHAPTER 6 REVIEW

Summary

Renewable resources are replaced by nature. Nonrenewable resources are not replaced by nature.

Air is a renewable resource, but it can be polluted.

The usability of land depends on its terrain, climate, and soil. Problems with soil use are depletion, desertification, and salinization.

Fresh water is used for sanitation, farming, and industry. Rain renews the water supply, but water can become polluted.

Mineral resources are the total amount of a mineral. Mineral reserves are the amount of mineral that can be mined profitably.

Nonmetallic mineral resources are used in the form in which they come out of the ground.

Fossil fuels form from the remains of plants and animals. Fossil fuels are nonrenewable, yet they are the primary energy source used today.

The atoms of some forms of uranium can be made to fission, releasing energy that can be used to generate electricity.

Oil can be obtained from both oil shales and tar sands, but it is presently too expensive to do so.

Renewable energy sources, such as water power, wind power, solar energy, and geothermal energy, use no fuel and do not pollute.

Acid rain, toxic wastes, and the disposal of nuclear wastes are problems that must be addressed.

Nonrenewable resources need to be conserved and recycled. Alternative energy sources must be developed to slow the use of such resources.

Vocabulary

acid rain	nonrenewable resource	reserves
desertification	ore mineral	respiration
environment	photosynthesis	salinization
eutrophication	pollution	soil depletion
fertility	renewable resource	toxic wastes
fossil fuels		
gangue		

Review

Choose the best answer for each question.

1. An example of a renewable resource is (a) gold, (b) oxygen, (c) iron, (d) sulfur.
2. Which substance is returned to the air by photosynthesis? (a) pollen (b) sulfur dioxide (c) carbon dioxide (d) oxygen
3. An example of a solid air pollutant is (a) dust, (b) nitrogen oxide, (c) carbon monoxide, (d) sulfur dioxide.
4. Soil fertility is the ability of the soil to (a) absorb water, (b) release oxygen, (c) support buildings, (d) grow plants.
5. The removal of soil nutrients by crops is (a) salinization, (b) eutrophication, (c) soil depletion, (d) desertification.
6. Which is NOT a source of fresh water? (a) oceans (b) lakes (c) rivers (d) ground
7. Eutrophication results from (a) germs in sewage, (b) phosphate and nitrite enrichment, (c) poisonous wastes, (d) oil spills.
8. The amount of a mineral that can be profitably mined at present is the (a) ore, (b) gangue, (c) resource, (d) reserve.
9. The metal used to make steel is (a) aluminum, (b) copper, (c) iron, (d) lead.
10. A nonmetallic resource used to remove ice is (a) gypsum, (b) salt, (c) sulfur, (d) graphite.
11. Which is NOT a fossil fuel? (a) coal (b) oil (c) natural gas (d) uranium
12. Which kind of coal contains the highest percentage of carbon? (a) peat (b) lignite (c) soft coal (d) anthracite
13. Gasoline and kerosene are made from (a) petroleum, (b) natural gas, (c) coal, (d) peat.
14. The energy from fission first (a) turns turbines, (b) cools water, (c) produces electricity, (d) heats water to steam.
15. Which can be removed from tar sands? (a) peat (b) petroleum (c) lignite (d) gas
16. Which is true of renewable energy sources? (a) all use sunlight and water (b) none use up fuels (c) all are usable everywhere (d) all are inexpensive

17. The most efficient way to produce electricity is by (a) coal, (b) water power, (c) oil, (d) nuclear fission.
18. Wind power depends on (a) splitting atoms, (b) direct sunlight, (c) moving air, (d) heat from Earth.
19. A collector, a storage area, and a transport system are sometimes used in (a) water power, (b) wind power, (c) solar energy, (d) geothermal energy.
20. Geothermal power depends on (a) heat from Earth, (b) direct sunlight, (c) moving air, (d) splitting atoms.
21. Acid rain is NOT (a) a result of air pollution, (b) more acidic than regular rain, (c) good for lakes, (d) reduced by using low-sulfur fuels.
22. The group that watches and cleans up toxic waste sites is the (a) United States Geological Survey, (b) Environmental Protection Agency, (c) Federal Bureau of Investigation, (d) National Science Foundation.
23. Which is NOT a concern with nuclear energy? (a) radioactive wastes (b) chance of accidents (c) storage of wastes (d) poor energy yields
24. Eliminating waste, recycling, and using substitutes are ways of conserving (a) nonrenewable resources, (b) renewable resources, (c) nonrenewable energy sources, (d) renewable energy sources.

Interpret and Apply

On your paper, answer each question in complete sentences.

1. Explain why wood is a renewable resource.
2. What kinds of problems would result if everyone heated their homes with wood?
3. The noise level at a pep assembly probably would not be considered noise pollution, but the same noise level in the hallway outside your classroom would. Why?
4. Explain why it is possible to increase reserves of a mineral but not resources of a mineral.
5. Which produces more energy, burning peat or burning an equal volume of anthracite? Why?
6. Figure 6.14 shows major producers of oil, natural gas, coal, and uranium. Figure 6.15 shows major users. Find the United States on both maps. How does U.S. production of each fuel compare with U.S. consumption?

Critical Thinking

The graph shows the concentration of pollutants per cubic centimeter of air in a city over a two-day period. Use the graph to answer the questions.

1. How does the concentration of pollutants at 6 A.M. Tuesday compare with concentration of pollutants at 6 A.M. Wednesday?
2. At what times does the concentration of pollutants peak on both days?
3. What could be the cause of the pollution peaks on the two days?
4. Falling rain tends to clean pollutants from the air. What evidence is there in the graph that no rain occurred Tuesday?
5. If these trends continue into Thursday, July 12, at what time would the greatest amount of pollutants probably be observed on that day?

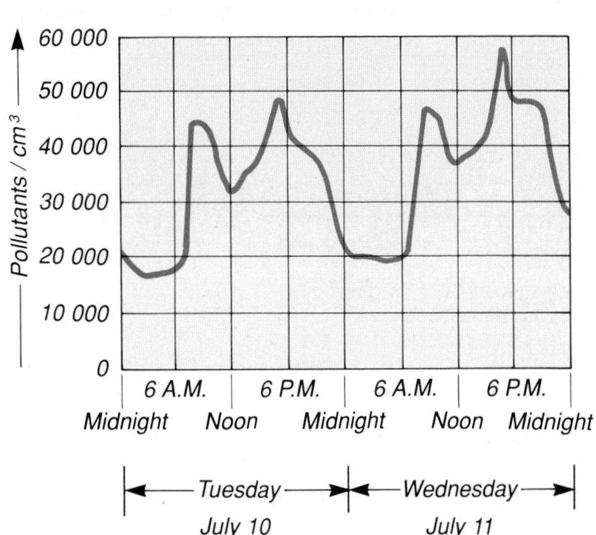

CHAPTER 7

Using Topographic Maps

▲ This orienteering group depends upon the accuracy of maps when traveling in an unknown area.

How Do You Know That . . .

Maps are accurate representations? When you use a map, you take for granted that someone made it carefully. However, there are problems that mapmakers encounter in producing accurate maps. See if you can make an accurate map. Try drawing a map to be used by friends or relatives from another county or state to find your home for the first time. If you have never done this before, you may begin to appreciate the work of a mapmaker.

I Map Projections, Location, Scales

Topic 1 Making Accurate Map Projections

A map shows all or part of Earth's surface on a *plane,* or flat surface. Since Earth is a sphere, its surface is like the skin of an orange. Making a map of half of Earth is like making the skin of half an orange fit the flat surface of a table. The orange skin will be distorted, that is, torn or stretched out of shape. Making a single map of the whole Earth is even more difficult and requires more distortion. On the other hand, if a small section of an orange skin is removed, it can be flattened with little distortion. The smaller the area mapped, the less distorted the map will be.

The ideal map would show shapes, distances, and directions correctly, but no map can do all of those things. Still, mapmakers have developed many ways, called **map projections,** for showing the curved Earth on a flat surface. Some map projections show true shapes while distorting distances and directions. Other map projections show true distances and directions but distort shapes. Maps of small areas, however, can be made with very little distortion of any kind.

There are many kinds of map projections. Mercator, gnomonic, and polyconic are three examples. The *Mercator* projection shows the whole world (except the extreme polar regions) on one continuous map. These maps show true directions as straight lines. The

OBJECTIVES

A Describe how three different map projections deal with distortion.

B Describe how longitude and latitude are used to locate points on Earth.

C Define *great circle* and identify a use for great-circle routes.

D Identify three ways map scales are indicated and discuss the differences between a small-scale map and a large-scale map.

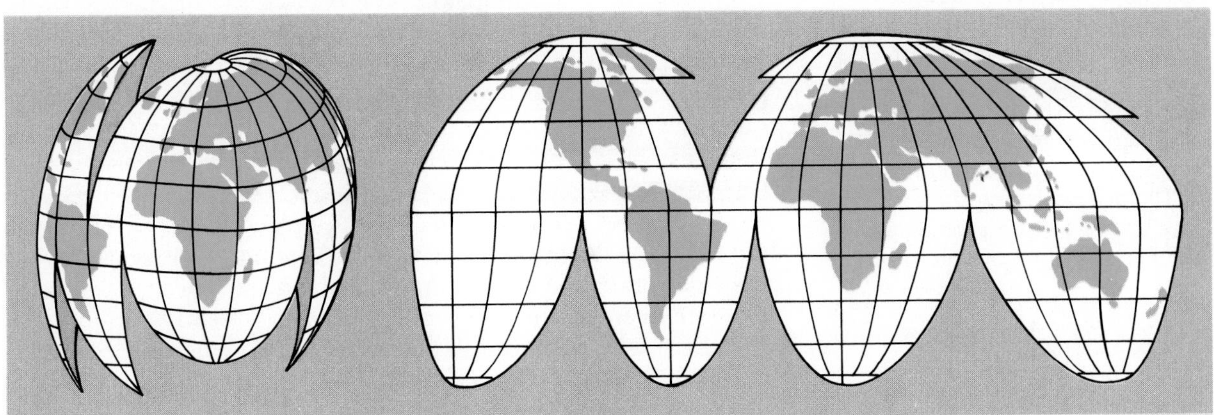

7.1 Mapping the entire Earth on a flat surface is difficult because of Earth's spherical shape.

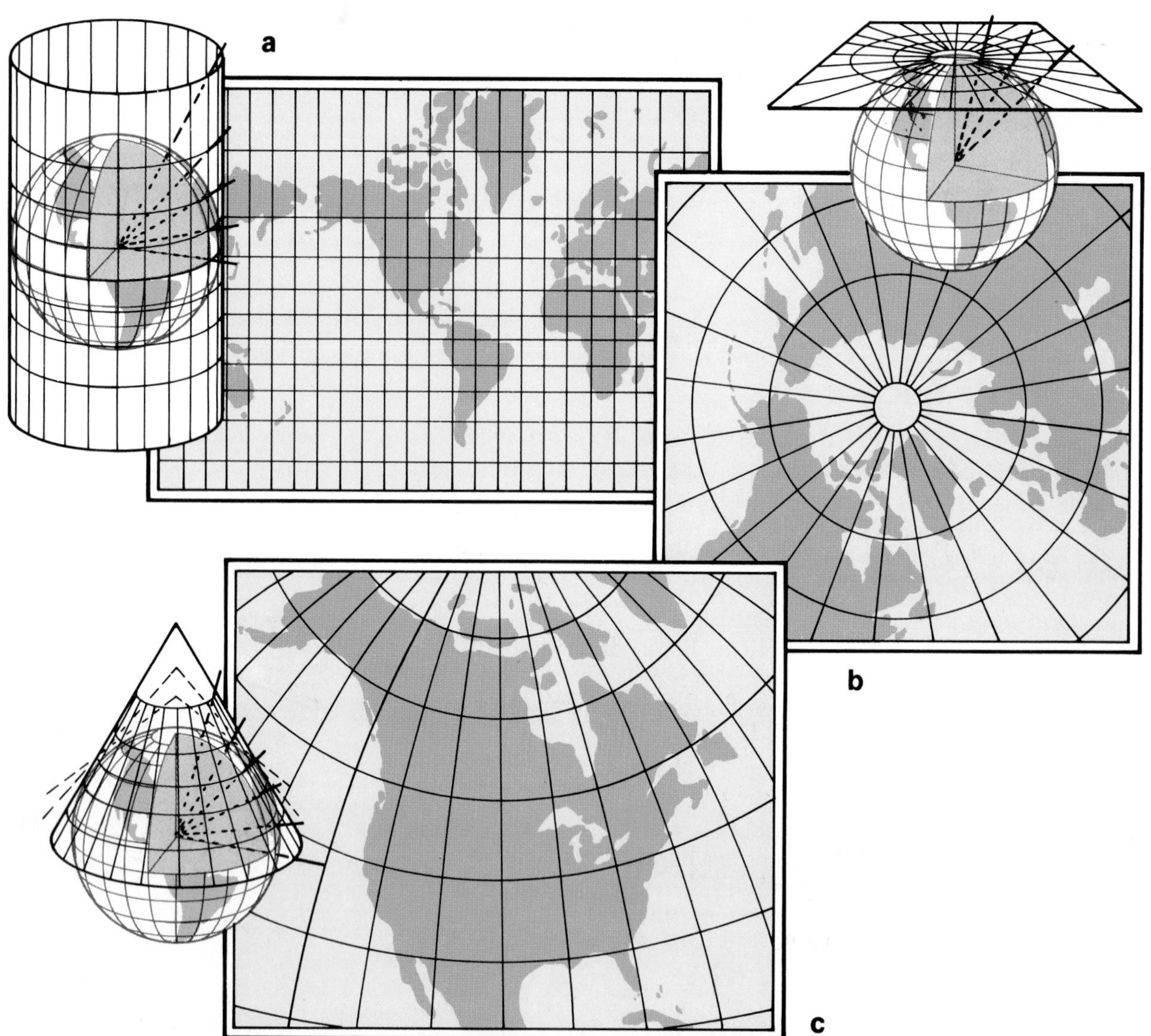

7.2 (a) A Mercator projection shows true direction in straight lines but distorts distance in high latitudes. (b) The gnomonic projection can be used to plot the shortest distance between two points, but direction and distance are distorted. (c) The polyconic projection is a more accurate representation and is useful in making topographic maps.

major problem with a Mercator projection is that high latitudes are enlarged tremendously. For example, a Mercator projection shows the island of Greenland in the North Atlantic Ocean to be nearly the same size as the continent of North America, even though North America is actually about 12 times larger than Greenland.

The *gnomonic* (noe MAHN ik) projection shows the shortest route between two points as a straight line. This projection is useful in planning for long airplane flights and ocean trips. However, directions and distances are not true on gnomonic projections, and other maps must be used along with them.

For small areas, the *polyconic* projection is nearly correct in all respects. It is therefore well suited to the making of topographic maps (Topics 6–13). The United States Geological Survey uses this projection to make topographic maps.

Usually maps are made with north at the top, south at the bottom, east to the right, and west to the left. In polar view maps, north is toward the center, while east and west are opposite directions around the concentric circles. On any map, however, the location of places on the surface of Earth is shown by means of latitude and longitude (Topics 2 and 3). No matter what projection is used or what distortions a map has, all maps must show the same latitude and longitude for any particular point on Earth's surface.

Topic 2 Latitude: Distance North and South

Latitude is distance in degrees north and south of the equator. Latitude is measured by parallels. **Parallels** are imaginary lines that circle the world from east to west parallel to the equator. The latitude of the equator is zero degrees (0°). The points farthest from the equator are the two poles of Earth, the North Pole and the South Pole. Since the poles are located one quarter of the circular distance around Earth from the equator, their latitudes are 90° N and 90° S, respectively. (One fourth of a circle is 1/4 of 360, or 90.) Latitudes between the equator and the poles have values between 0° and 90°. For example, 30° N and 30° S latitudes mark the locations of parallels that are one third of the way between the equator and each pole. In the same way, 60° N and 60° S latitudes mark the locations of parallels that are two thirds of the way between the equator and the poles.

One degree of latitude is 1/360 of Earth's circumference measured at the poles. The circumference at the poles is about 40 000 kilometers (25 000 miles). Thus, the distance on land of a degree latitude is about 112 kilometers (70 miles) (40 000 divided by 360 equals about 112 kilometers). Each degree latitude is divided into minutes, 1 degree latitude (1°) being equal to 60 minutes (60′). Since one minute of latitude is 1/60 of a degree, its length is about 1.85 kilometers (1.16 miles). Notice that the length of degrees and minutes of latitude does not change over Earth's surface.

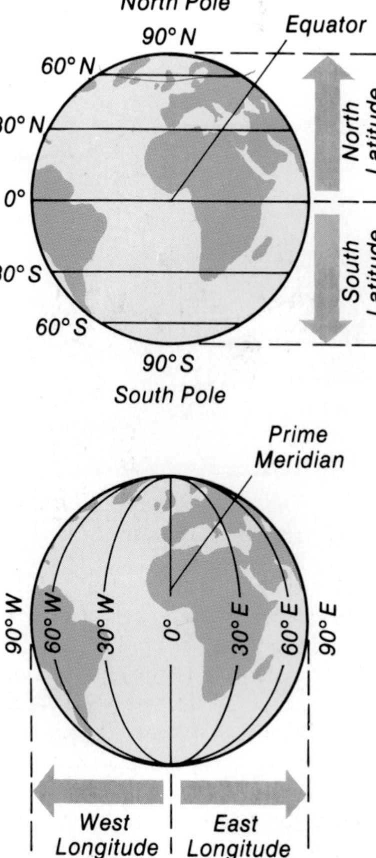

7.3 Latitude is measured in degrees north or south of the equator. Longitude is measured in degrees east or west of the prime meridian.

Topic 3 Longitude: Distance East and West

While the east-west parallels are used to mark off distance north and south on Earth's surface, distances east and west (longitude) are noted with meridians. A **meridian** is a half circle that runs in a north-south direction from the North Pole to the South Pole. The *prime meridian* was declared to be the starting line for the worldwide longitude system. The prime meridian passes through Greenwich (GREN ich), England, a town outside London and the location of a major observatory for Earth measurements. **Longitude** is the distance in degrees east or west of the prime meridian. The longitude of the prime meridian is 0°. If you move in either direction from the prime meridian, the furthest you can get is 180° away (one half of a full circle of 360°). The 180th meridian (180° east and west) is halfway around Earth from the prime meridian. The half of the world that is west of the prime meridian has west longitude. The half that is east of the prime meridian has east longitude.

Longitude degrees, like latitude degrees, are divided into minutes, and 1 degree of longitude equals 60 minutes of longitude. Unlike parallels, meridians are closer together the farther they are from the equator. There is no set number of kilometers or miles in a degree of longitude. At the equator, 1 degree of longitude is about as long as 1 degree of latitude. Moving toward the poles, the length in kilometers of a degree of longitude gets smaller and smaller, reaching zero at Earth's North and South Poles.

Topic 4 **Great Circles**

Circles drawn on the surface of any sphere may be either great circles or small circles. A **great circle** is a circle whose plane passes through the center of the sphere. Perhaps it is simpler to say that any circle that divides the sphere in half is a great circle. All other circles drawn on the sphere are called small circles.

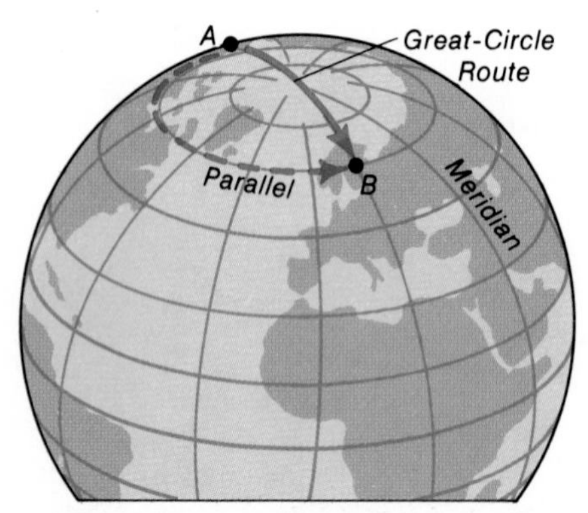

7.4 The great-circle route from *A* to *B* is much shorter than the route along the parallel.

On Earth, the equator is a great circle. All other parallels are small circles. Each meridian is half of a great circle. The meridian opposite it in the other hemisphere is the other half of the same great circle. Great circles may also be drawn in slanting positions between the equator and the poles. Think of an orange, which may be cut in half in any direction.

Figure 7.4 shows a *great-circle route* between two points, *A* and *B*, that are on the same small-circle parallel. Great-circle routes are the shortest routes between two points on a sphere. They are almost always the most desirable routes for airplane travel. Great-circle routes between cities at high latitudes pass over or near the poles. To find a great-circle route between any two points on a globe, simply stretch a string between the two points.

Topic 5 **Map Scales**

The scale of a map tells how the map compares in size with the piece of Earth's surface that it shows. With many world maps the distortion of distance varies so much over the map that no single scale can be given. Small-scale maps, such as topographic maps, do not have this problem.

A **map scale** is usually defined as the ratio of distance on the map to distance on Earth. This ratio may be shown on the map in three different ways:

1. Verbally as a simple statement, such as "1 centimeter represents 50 kilometers" or "1 inch to 100 miles."

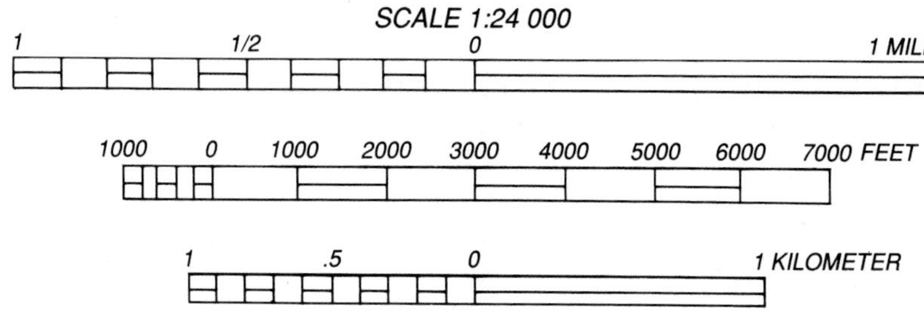

7.5 A topographic map has a numerical scale (1:24 000) and three graphic scales (milès, feet, and kilometers).

2. Graphically by a line divided into equal parts and marked in kilometers, miles, or other units of length.
3. Numerically, usually by writing a fraction to show what part of the true distances the map distances really are. The fraction is known as the representative fraction, or R.F. For example, the scale 1/1 000 000 (also written 1:1 000 000) means that any distance on the map is one millionth of its true length on Earth. This may also be expressed by saying that 1 unit of length on the map represents 1 000 000 of the same units on Earth.

Maps are always much smaller than the pieces of land they show. The more closely the map approaches the land in size, the larger its scale is. A map of the United States on a sheet of paper would have to use a very small scale, such as 1 inch (of paper) to 300 miles (of Earth). On the other hand, a large wall map of the same area would use a larger scale, such as 6 inches (of paper) to 300 miles (of Earth), usually expressed as 1 inch to 50 miles. A still larger scale such as 1 inch to 1 mile would use a sheet of paper 300 feet long (the length of a football field) and almost as wide to show all of the United States.

7.6 Map scales vary according to the size of the area shown on the map.

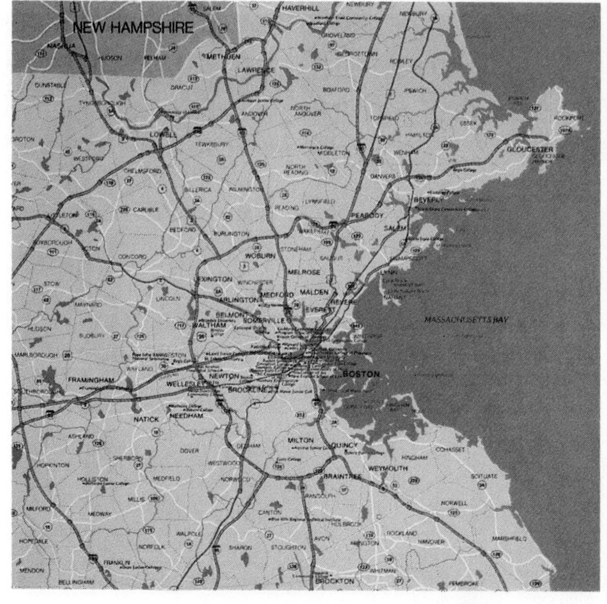

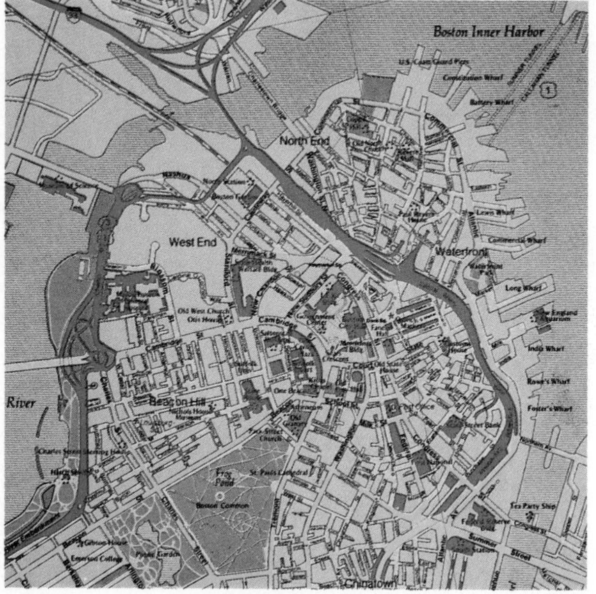

TOPIC QUESTIONS

Each topic question refers to the topic of the same number.

1. **(a)** What are some problems in making maps? **(b)** What three factors would an ideal map show correctly? **(c)** What is a map projection? **(d)** Name three map projections and identify the features that make each one useful.
2. **(a)** What is latitude and how is it measured? **(b)** State the latitudes of the equator, the North Pole, the South Pole, and the parallels halfway between the equator and the poles. **(c)** How long in kilometers is one degree of latitude?
3. **(a)** What is longitude and how is it measured? **(b)** Where is the starting meridian for the longitude system? **(c)** Where is the 180th meridian? **(d)** Why is there no set distance in kilometers for a degree of longitude?
4. **(a)** What are great circles? **(b)** Why are great circles important in air and ocean travel?
5. **(a)** Explain what a map scale is. **(b)** List three ways of expressing a map scale and give examples of each. **(c)** Distinguish between a large-scale map and small-scale map.

Peg Rawson
Cartographer

A cartographer is a mapmaker. Peg Rawson is a cartographer for the U.S. Geological Survey, the major maker of contour, or topographic, maps in this country. She says that mapmaking has three basic steps. The first step is to take photographs of the land surface being mapped from an airplane. This provides the cartographer with a bird's-eye view of the land features. The next step involves field work in the area.

Cartographers go to the area being mapped and note features not identifiable on the photographs, such as specific locations of benchmarks, schools, or hospitals. The next step involves placing the photographs in a stereoplotter. When viewed through the stereoplotter, the ground surface in the photographs appears in three dimensions. This makes elevation differences easy to see. The cartographer can then draw an accurate map of the ground surface which shows not only elevation but also rivers, highways, cities, and other features.

Peg Rawson has recently been working on ways to make greater use of computers in mapmaking. The major effort is to develop programs that change the information on a map into a form that is understandable to a computer.

II Parts of a Topographic Map

Topic 6 Showing Elevation—Contours

In order to show landforms, maps must show the *relief* (the highs and lows) of Earth's surface. Relief can be shown in many ways, such as shading, coloring, or miniature sketching of landforms. Topographic maps show relief with **contour lines,** that is, lines drawn to connect points at the same elevation (height above sea level). Contour lines show both exact elevations and the shape of the land. Contour lines are best explained by a drawing. Figure 7.7(a) is a sketch of an island in the sea. This island is 6 miles long, 3 miles wide, oval shaped, and 113 feet high at its highest point. In an ordinary map, the island would appear as shown in Figure 7.7(b). The shoreline shows the shape of the island at sea level, and the scale indicates the length and width of the island. However, the map gives no information about the height of the island, how steep it is, or about its shape above sea level.

A mapmaker would survey the island and turn this map into a contour map. The mapmaker would first locate and mark on the map all of the points that were 20 feet above sea level. All points 20 feet above sea level are then joined with a contour line. Every point on this contour line is 20 feet higher than the shoreline. The shoreline is also a contour line—at zero feet above sea level.

Using an interval of 20 feet, a mapmaker then draws contour lines showing where the island reaches the 40-foot, 60-foot, 80-foot, and 100-foot elevations above sea level. The **contour interval** is the difference in elevation between two consecutive contour lines, in this case, 20 feet. Contour intervals differ depending on the relief of the land. If the land is high and steep, a mapmaker uses a large contour interval such as 50 feet or 100 feet. If the land slopes gently or is nearly level, a mapmaker uses a small contour interval such as 10 feet, 5 feet, or even 1 foot. For moderately steep land such as the island, a 20-foot contour interval is used.

Do not confuse the contour interval, which is difference in height, with distance along the ground. The distance along the ground between any two points is found with the map scale. Using the scale in Figure 7.7(d), note that between *A* and *B* the island reached the 20-foot elevation in one mile. Between *C* and *D* the same height is reached in only one third of a mile. Obviously, then, the island is steeper between *C* and *D*. Instead of figuring each time, use the rule that where the contour lines are close, the slope is steep; where the contour lines are far apart, the slope is gentle.

To make the reading of contour lines easier, every fifth line is made heavier and its elevation is marked. The other contour lines are not numbered, but the contour interval is stated at the bottom of the map. Notice that the contour lines show three things—elevation of the land, steepness of its slopes, and the shape of the land at various heights.

OBJECTIVES

A Describe how contour lines show the elevations, shape, and slope of the land.

B Name and compare the two series of topographic maps published by the USGS.

C Identify the meanings of some symbols and colors used on topographic maps.

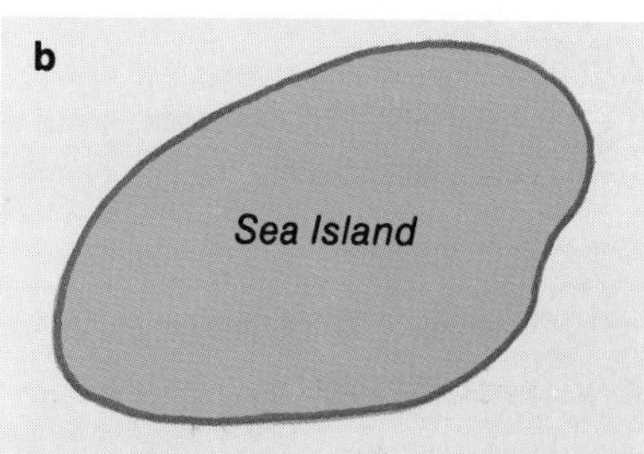

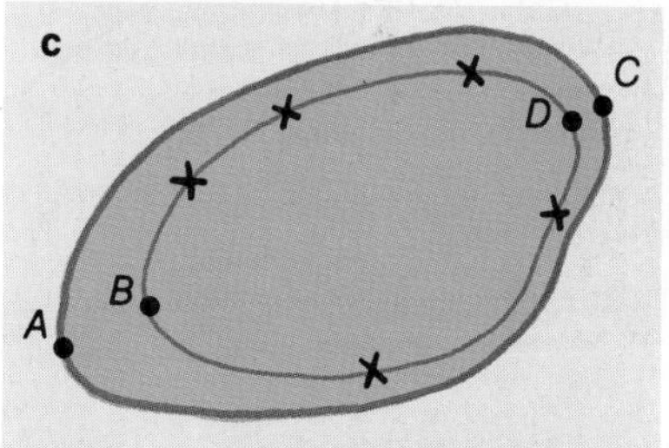

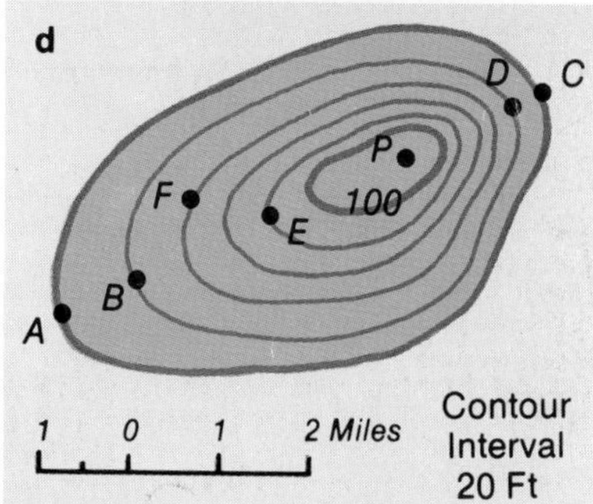

7.7 Mapping a sea island

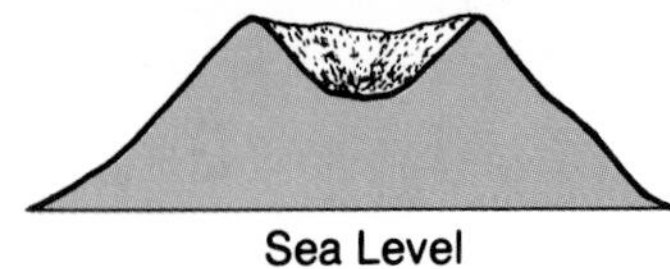

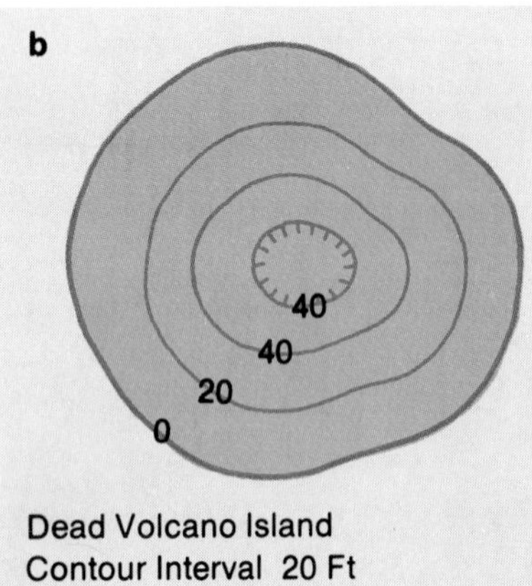

7.8 (a) Sketch of an island volcano, (b) contour map of the same island with contours showing its crater

7.9 A bench mark is an elevation reference point for surveyors.

Topic 7 Depression Contours

Moving inland from sea level does not always result in higher elevations. In climbing a volcano, for example, the highest point is reached at the rim of the crater. The crater is a lower area, or depression, inside the rim. This lower area is shown on a topographic map by the use of **depression contours.** These lines are drawn like contour lines but are marked on the inside (Figure 7.8).

In reading depression contours, the first one is read at the same elevation as the ordinary contour that comes before it. Thereafter, each depression contour is lower than the one that comes before it by an amount equal to the contour interval of the map. If the land rises in the middle of the depression, this is shown with a regular contour. In such a case, the first regular contour has the same altitude as the last depression contour that encloses it.

Topic 8 Bench Marks, Spot Elevations

In mapmaking, surveyors find the exact elevation of many points in the map area. These may be shown on the map in a number of ways. A **bench mark** point is a location whose exact elevation is known and is noted on a brass or aluminum plate. This plate is permanently set into the ground at the location surveyed. Bench marks are shown on the map by the letters *BM*. Numbers give the elevation to the nearest foot. A survey point for which there is no bench mark is shown on the map by a triangle and the elevation.

Spot elevations are the elevations of road forks, hilltops, lake surfaces, and other points of special interest. These points are usually shown on the map by a small cross. Numbers giving elevations checked by surveyors are printed in black. Unchecked elevations are printed in brown. Water elevations are shown in blue.

Topic 9 U.S. Geological Survey Maps

The United States Geological Survey (USGS) issues standard topographic maps, called quadrangles, in two main series.

1. The 15-minute quadrangle series. This represents quadrangles that cover one-fourth degree of latitude (15 minutes) and one-fourth degree of longitude. Each map, or sheet, is named for a part of the quadrangle, for example, the Brooklyn sheet. The area covered by each sheet in the 15-minute series is about 18 miles (north to south) by 13 miles (east to west). The scale used on most of these sheets is 1:62 500. This means that 1 inch on the map represents 62 500 inches (nearly a mile) on Earth's surface. (The exact number of inches in a mile is 63 360, but the number 62 500 is used to simplify calculations.) The contour interval found most often on these sheets is 20 feet.
2. The 7.5-minute quadrangle series. This uses a scale of 1:24 000 (1 inch on the map = 24 000 inches, or exactly 2000 feet, on land). This scale is more than twice as large as the scale on the

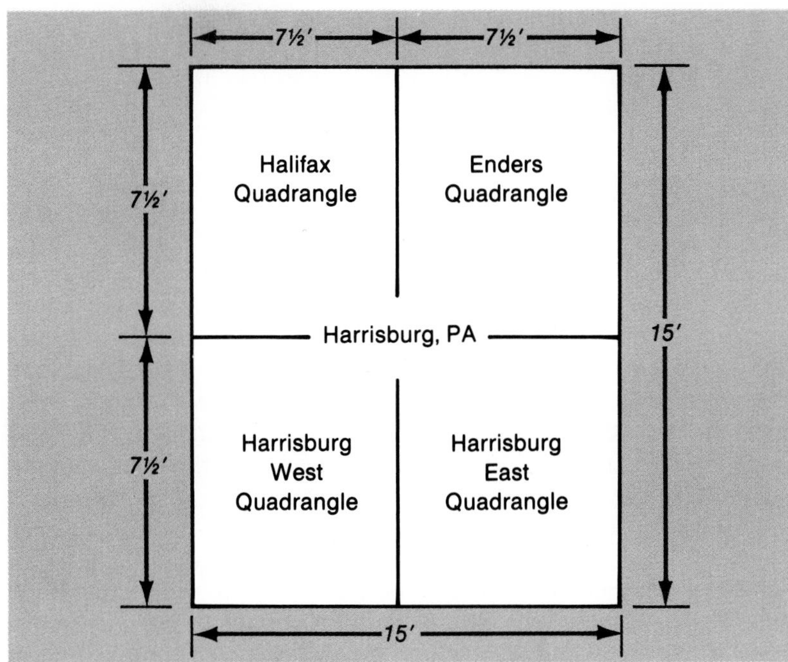

7.10 Four 7.5-minute quadrangles fit into one 15-minute quadrangle of the Harrisburg, Pennsylvania, area.

15-minute map. It gives much greater detail. Each map sheet shows an area 7.5 minutes from north to south and 7.5 minutes from east to west.

The features of a contour map are shown in three colors. Contour lines are always printed in brown. Roads, buildings, railroads, and other works built by people are printed in black. Water features—such as rivers, lakes, and swamps—are shown in blue. Many maps also show woodland areas in green, highways in red, and densely developed areas, such as cities, in pink.

TOPIC QUESTIONS

Each topic question refers to the topic of the same number.

6. **(a)** How are contour lines drawn on maps? **(b)** How does a contour map show whether a slope is gentle or steep? **(c)** Define *contour interval* and give examples of large and small contour intervals. **(d)** Distinguish between the use of the contour interval and the map scale.

7. Explain the meaning, use, and rules for drawing and reading depression contours.

8. **(a)** What is a bench mark? **(b)** How is a bench mark point shown on a map? **(c)** What are spot elevations? How are they shown?

9. **(a)** Describe the area, scale, and most common contour interval of a U.S. Geological Survey 15-minute topographic sheet. **(b)** What is the scale of a 7.5-minute quadrangle sheet? **(c)** Describe the use of color on topographic maps.

OBJECTIVES

A Use a topographic map to read distances and elevations and calculate the average slope of an area from such information.

B Identify landforms and estimate steepness from contour lines.

C Draw a profile from a contour map.

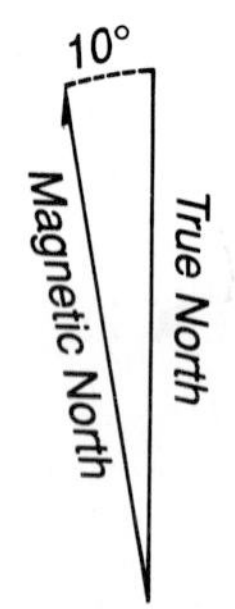

7.11 Topographic maps show the magnetic declination of the area they represent.

III Reading a Topographic Map

Topic 10 Reading the Contour Map

Almost all maps show directions in some way. Most maps show direction with parallels and meridians (Topics 2 and 3). If a map does not show parallels or meridians, the map should have an arrow pointing to the North Pole or true north. Except for a few areas on Earth, a compass points, not to true north, but to the Magnetic North Pole, or magnetic north. The **magnetic declination** is the difference in the angle between true north and magnetic north. This angle is different over Earth's surface. Each topographic map gives the angle of the magnetic declination for the area it shows.

If the scale of a map is given verbally, distances on the map may be measured with a ruler. When a graphic scale is printed on the map, the distance between two points can be marked off with a straightedge, such as the edge of a sheet of paper. A piece of string may also be used. The marked straightedge is held against the scale for reading. Zigzag distances along roads or rivers may be marked off one after the other on the edge of a sheet of paper before measuring against the graphic scale.

When a point is on a contour line, its exact elevation is known. Any point between two contour lines is higher than the last contour line but lower than the next contour line. For example, a point between the 100-foot line and the 120-foot line may be any elevation from 101 feet to 119 feet. The elevation of points between two contour lines can be estimated. For example, a point halfway between the 20-foot and 40-foot contour lines would have an estimated elevation of about 30 feet.

Each elevation given on a contour map represents height above sea level. Only those contour maps that include a seacoast will start from sea level. To figure the elevation of any point, start from the marked contour line that is nearest to that point.

Topic 11 Landforms on Contour Maps

The map distance between contour lines indicates the steepness or levelness of the land. When contour lines are far apart, the land is fairly level. Grassy Terrace in the northwest corner of Figure 7.12, for example, does not have contour lines, so it must be level.

Where contour lines run very close together, the land is very steep. If contour lines coincide, it means that the higher ground is directly above the lower ground. Such contour lines indicate a cliff. An example of this formation is Sheer Cliff in Figure 7.12.

Closed circles or ovals at the end of a rising series of contours show the tops of hills, as at *J, K, L, M,* and *N.* The exact elevation of

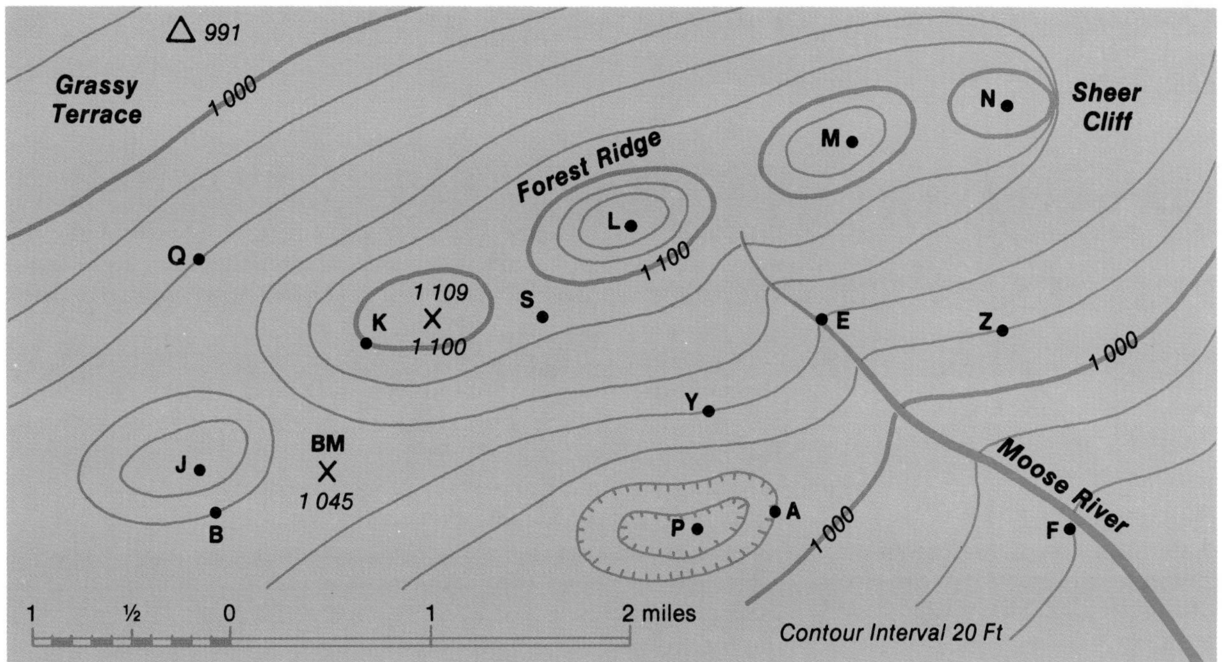

7.12 Simple landforms are easily identified on a contour map.

the top of a hill may be indicated, as at *K*. Hills or mountains that are long and narrow are called ridges. These may include a number of peaks. Ridges are shown by long oval contour lines, as at Forest Ridge in Figure 7.12.

Where a river has cut a valley, contour lines plainly show the valley. As each contour line comes near the valley, it can stay at the elevation it represents only by bending in the direction of the high land from which the river flows. This rule may be used to figure out the direction in which a river flows. The direction the river flows can also be figured out by noticing the elevations of marked contour lines. A river flows from higher to lower elevations.

The steepness of a river is shown by the closeness of the contour lines that cross it. The width of a valley is approximately shown by the width of the V made by a contour line where it crosses a river.

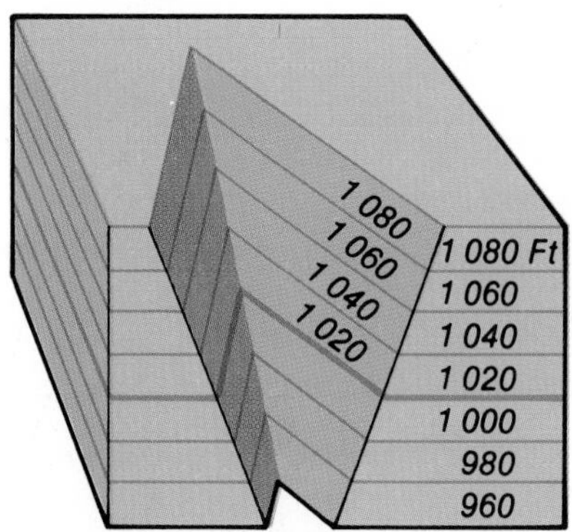

7.13 Contour lines bend upstream where they cross a river valley.

Topic 12 The Average Slope

The **average slope,** or *gradient*, between any two points of a hill, mountain, river, trail, or road can be determined from a contour map. If you know how many feet the hill drops in a given distance, you can find the average slope using the following equation.

$$\textbf{Average slope} = \frac{\textbf{change in elevation (ft)}}{\textbf{distance (mi)}}$$

Both the drop in elevation and the distance between two points can easily be read from a contour map. For example, a trail is four miles long, as measured by the scale on the map. The beginning of the trail is at the 1060-foot contour, and the end of the trail is at the 960-foot contour. Calculate the average slope of the trail in this way.

$$\textbf{Average slope} = \frac{\textbf{1060 ft} - \textbf{960 ft}}{\textbf{4 mi}} = \frac{\textbf{100 ft}}{\textbf{4 mi}} = \textbf{25 ft/mi}$$

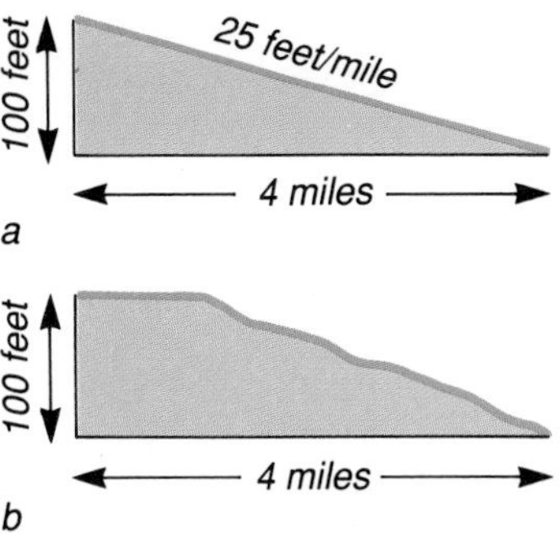

7.14 (a) Average slope of a trail; (b) the actual slope may vary.

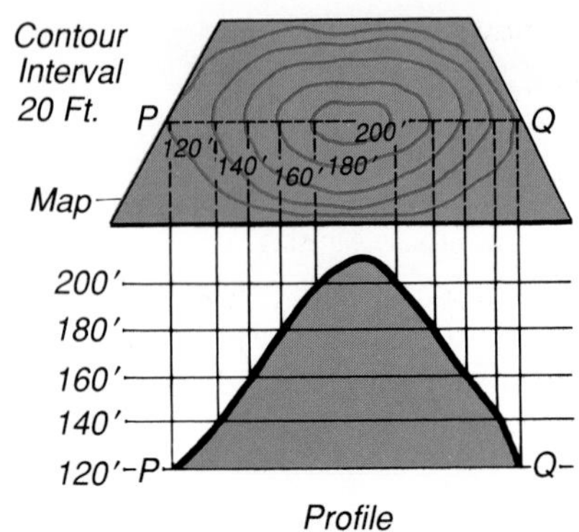

7.15 A profile—a line showing the changes in elevation across a section of a topographic map—can be made as shown in this sketch.

Topic 13 Profiles from Contour Maps

It is easy to make a **profile** that shows the ups and downs of a line across any part of a contour map. Wherever the line meets a contour, the exact height above sea level is known. Plotting these points on a vertical scale results in a profile.

A profile is done most easily by placing the bottom edge of a sheet of paper on top of the line to be followed. At each point where the line crosses a contour, make a mark on the edge of the paper. Record the height of the contour next to its mark on the paper. When all points are marked, use the vertical scale to raise each point to its proper height. (Plotting is easier if graph paper is used.) Vertical scales are usually stretched out compared to the horizontal scale. This is to make the differences in elevation more visible. An example of a vertical scale is ⅛ inch = 20 feet. Of course, it is important to keep the points the same horizontal distance apart as they were on the map. Once the elevated points have been plotted, they are joined to make the profile.

TOPIC QUESTIONS

Each topic question refers to the topic of the same number.

10. **(a)** How is direction found on a contour map? **(b)** How is distance measured on a contour map? **(c)** How is the elevation of a point determined on a contour map?

11. How does a contour map show each of the following: **(a)** level areas, **(b)** cliffs, **(c)** hilltops, **(d)** ridges, **(e)** river valleys, **(f)** the steepness of a slope?

12. **(a)** Explain the meaning of the average slope between two points. **(b)** How is average slope determined?

13. **(a)** What does a profile show? **(b)** How is a profile made from a contour map?

Map Skills

The following questions refer to the topographic map of Monadnock, NH, on page 582 in the Appendix.

1. What is the name of the tallest feature on the map?
2. Locate Gap Mountain in the southwest part of the map. Which side of Gap Mountain would be the more gentle climb? How can you tell?
3. Why would a fire lookout be located on top of Monadnock Mountain, rather than on top of Gap Mountain?

IV Modern Methods of Mapmaking

OBJECTIVES

A List and describe some methods of remote sensing.

B Explain the function of a false-color image and identify some uses of computer-drawn images.

Topic 14 Remote Sensing

Making an accurate topographic map requires finding the exact location of many points on land. The first topographic maps were made using only *ground survey*. In ground survey, a surveying team collects the necessary data while standing on the ground surface. Each map drawn by ground survey takes a long time to complete. Today, most maps are made by **remote sensing,** that is, by gathering data about the land from above the surface. Remote-sensing data is commonly collected using equipment placed onboard airplanes or satellites. The methods used in remote sensing are quicker and easier than those used in ground surveys. Also, maps made from remote-sensing data are far more detailed and accurate.

The oldest method of remote sensing is **photogrammetry.** This is a method for determining the position and elevation of surface features from aerial photographs. Photogrammetry was used to produce the accurate maps of the moon that made possible the choice of safe landing sites for the *Apollo* missions.

Radar has proven to be a very valuable tool in remote sensing. Unlike aerial photography, radar can be used even when the surface is dark or hidden by clouds. The radar system used to study Earth is called **imaging radar.** Like all radar systems, imaging radar sends out a signal and then "listens" for the signal to echo off Earth's surface. The signal used in imaging radar is aimed, not at the surface beneath the airplane or spacecraft, but off to one side. This scatters the signal and returns many different echoes, instead of just one, to the radar receiver. Called **side-looking radar,** this method provides far more information about the surface than an ordinary radar echo. Computers are used to turn the radar data into images of Earth's surface.

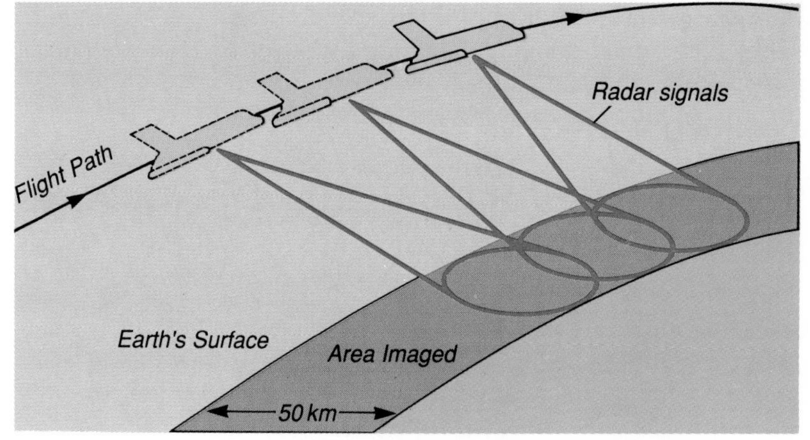

7.16 Side-looking radar involves scattering radar signals from an aircraft. The radar signals bounce back to the craft. Computers process the information into an image.

A newer method of remote sensing uses ***Landsat*** satellites. These satellites do not take actual photographs of the ground. Instead, they use sensors to detect wavelengths of solar energy reflected from the ground surface. The data collected by the sensors in the satellites are sent to ground stations, where computers turn them into images of Earth's surface. *Landsat* scanners do not provide the kind of information about surface elevations that is needed to make a topographic map. Instead, the scanners gather data about other features of Earth's surface (Topics 15 and 16). *Landsat* satellites orbit Earth about 700 kilometers above the surface. Their sensors scan the ground directly below the satellite in 185-kilometer wide strips. The location of each strip changes with each orbit of the satellite. In this way, a single *Landsat* can scan all of Earth every 16 days.

7.17 In this false-color image of Niagara Falls, calm water is black, rough water is blue, trees and grass are red, and buildings are blue-gray.

Topic 15 Computer Imaging

Computer imaging is used to make maps from the data collected by *Landsats* and imaging radar. *Landsat* sensors are designed to detect wavelengths of green light, red light, and infrared (heat) energy. These wavelengths were chosen so that certain surface features, such as rock structures and kinds of plants, would show more clearly. *Landsat* sensors are more sensitive to differences in wavelength than the human eye. For example, two wavelengths of light may appear to the eye as the same shade of red. The *Landsat* sensor, however, clearly records the difference. When the image is processed by computer, two very different colors can be assigned to each wavelength. The different colors make each wavelength easier to see on the map. The resulting picture is called a **false-color image.** In a standard *Landsat* false-color image, healthy vegetation appears bright red, cities appear blue or blue-gray, and clear water appears black.

False-color images can also be made from radar data. Radar images are made from a signal sent from an airplane or spacecraft. By processing the radar echo data through a computer, it is possible to draw topographic maps of the surface. Colors are added to the map by the computer to make specific surface features more visible. The radar-imaging data can also be used to make three-dimensional images of features, as if features were viewed from the ground. Such an image is shown in Figure 7.18.

7.18 This side view of California's Mount Shasta was generated by a computer from imaging radar data.

Topic 16 Uses of Computer-Drawn Maps and Images

Computer-drawn maps and images have many uses, and new uses are being found all the time. One of the most important is mapmaking. Remote sensing has made it possible to draw highly accurate and detailed maps of even the most remote and inaccessible areas of Earth.

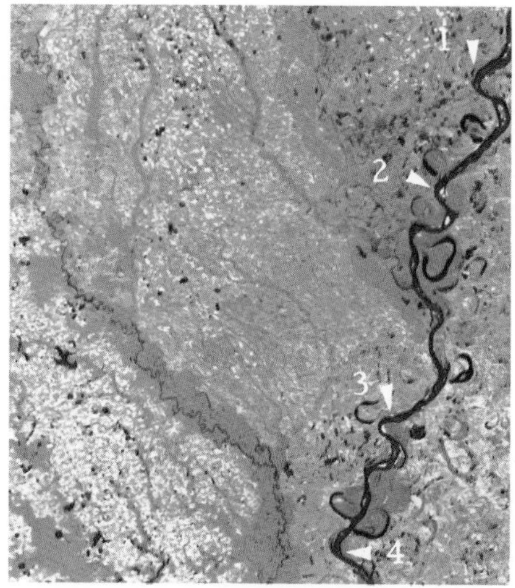

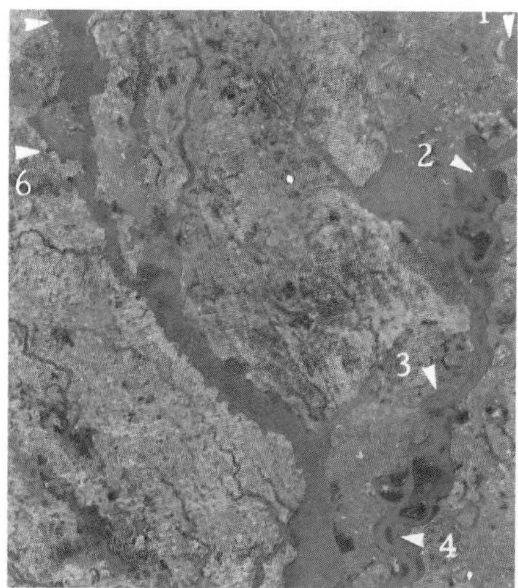

7.19 Computer images made from satellite data help locate areas of environmental and safety concerns, such as this floodplain area along the Mississippi river. (left) During the dry autumn season, (right) during spring flooding

The uses of computer-generated images of Earth go far beyond mapping. In farming and forestry, computer-generated images make it possible to find out the health of a particular crop or stand of trees, and to estimate the yield of each crop. Remote-sensing methods can detect hazardous waste sites, oil slicks, and other water and air pollutants. Prospecting for oil and mineral resources is often done using false-color imaging. False-color radar imaging has even detected features below the surface, like ancient riverbeds, that were previously unknown.

Satellite imaging has revolutionized meteorology. The day-to-day weather maps that appear in newspapers and on television are made from data gathered by weather satellites. In addition to helping weather prediction, such maps also provide a detailed permanent weather record.

These are just a few of the applications for computer-generated satellite imaging. Remote-sensing data are also used in oceanography, commercial fishing, wildlife biology, archaeology, military applications, and in monitoring the effects of acid rain. The current uses have only begun to tap the potential information that is available through modern methods of mapmaking.

TOPIC QUESTIONS

Each topic question refers to the topic of the same number.

14. **(a)** How were the first topographic maps made? **(b)** What is remote sensing? **(c)** List three methods of remote sensing used today and identify the method by which each collects data.

15. **(a)** What are false-color images and why are they used? **(b)** Why can radar images be used to map surface elevations?

16. List some areas of study in which maps and other images generated from remote-sensing data are used.

CHAPTER 7 REVIEW

Summary

A flat map of a curved surface is distorted. Different map projections are used to minimize distortion of shape, distance, or direction.

Latitude indicates distances north and south of the equator. Longitude indicates distances east and west of the prime meridian.

Map scales compare the size of the map with Earth's surface. Map scales can be verbal, graphic, or numerical, and vary with the size of the area shown by the map.

Contour lines show the elevations, shape, and slope of the land. Hollows in the land are shown by depression contours.

Topographic maps are drawn in the 15-minute and 7.5-minute series. Colors are used to indicate different kinds of features on topographic maps.

Direction, distance, elevation, and average slope can be determined from a topographic map.

A map profile shows changes in elevation across a section of a topographic map.

The use of remote-sensing methods allows mapmakers to produce accurate maps of many places on Earth.

Computers are used to turn remote-sensing data into detailed maps and false-color images. Satellite images are used in many areas of science and research.

Vocabulary

average slope
bench mark
contour interval
contour line
depression contour
false-color image
great circle
imaging radar
Landsat
latitude
longitude
magnetic declination
map projection
map scale
meridians
parallels
photogrammetry
profile
remote sensing
side-looking radar

Review

Match the phrases in List **A** with the terms in List **B.**

List A

1. major problem when a flat map is made of spherical Earth
2. map projection used to draw topographic maps
3. distance in degrees north and south of the equator
4. east-west lines used to measure latitude
5. north-south lines used to measure longitude
6. used to locate shortest distance between two points on Earth
7. example of numerical scale
8. line drawn through points with the same elevation
9. used to show craters and hollows on a map
10. places where exact elevations are shown on permanent plates
11. USGS map series showing greater detail
12. angular difference between true north and magnetic north
13. shown by contour lines far apart
14. shown by contour lines close together
15. numerical value for gradient of land surface
16. shows elevation changes across a map section
17. methods include *Landsat* and imaging radar
18. method that enhances different wavelengths

List B

a. average slope
b. bench-mark points
c. contour
d. depression contour
e. distortion
f. false-color imaging
g. gnomonic
h. great-circle route
i. ground survey
j. latitude
k. level land
l. longitude
m. magnetic declination
n. meridians
o. parallels
p. polyconic
q. profile
r. remote sensing
s. steep land
t. 1:1 000 000
u. 7.5-minute quadrangle
v. 15-minute quadrangle

Interpret and Apply

On your paper, answer each question in complete sentences.

1. Globes are true representations of Earth's surface. Why aren't they used instead of maps?
2. Where are north, south, east, and west on a gnomonic projection of the Southern Hemisphere? (Figure 7.2 shows map projections.)
3. Why are high-latitude polar regions enlarged on a Mercator projection? (Figure 7.2 shows map projections.)
4. A map is drawn so that 1 centimeter on the map represents 100 meters along the ground. What is the numerical scale of this map? Is this a large-scale or a small-scale map? (Note: There are 100 cm in 1 m.)
5. For places in the Northern Hemisphere, the southern edge of a topographic map is slightly wider than the northern edge. Explain why this is so.
6. What is the average slope between two points that are 5 kilometers apart and differ in elevation by 200 meters?
7. Answer questions a through i about Figure 7.12. (a) What is the maximum elevation of hilltops *J*, *L*, *M*, and *N*? (b) How high are points *S*, *Y*, *Z*, *A*, and *B*? (c) What is the height, from base to top, of Sheer Cliff? (d) From *L*, in what directions are *J*, *N*, *Q*, and *Y*? (e) In what direction does Moose River flow? (f) At what elevation does Moose River start? (g) How many feet on the average does Moose River drop per mile? (h) How far is it from *Q* to *Y*? (i) What is the feature at *P* called? What is the lowest possible elevation for *P*?

Critical Thinking

The profile below was drawn from a topographic map. Use the profile to answer questions 1–6.

1. What is the difference in elevation between point *B* and point *A*?
2. What is the map distance between point *B* and point *A*?
3. Determine the average slope in feet per mile between point *A* and point *B*.
4. Determine the average slope in feet per mile between point *C* and point *D*.
5. The relief of an area is the difference between the highest and lowest point. What is the total relief of the profile?
6. The vertical exaggeration of a profile is the amount by which the vertical scale is expanded compared to the true scale. The horizontal scale in feet is the true scale. Compare the vertical scale with the true scale. What is the vertical exaggeration of this profile?

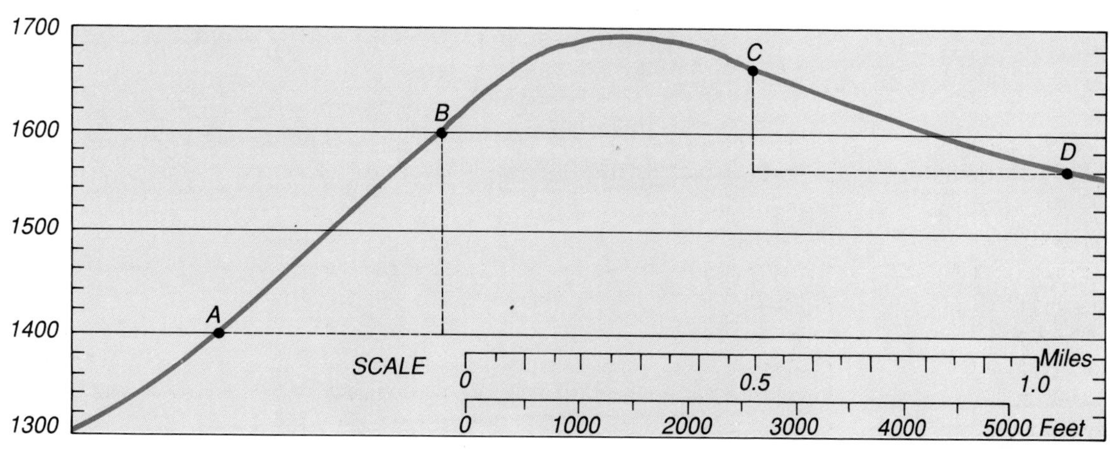

UNIT TWO
Forces That Attack the Surface

Water cascades over a cliff. How does running water shape the land?

This hole suddenly appeared in Florida. It grew larger for weeks, swallowing cars, swimming pools, and homes. How did it begin?

These houses were built on the ground, well away from the water's edge. What happened to the land beneath them?

What wears away Earth's surface?

Earth's surface is under attack. Hard rains pound the land. Swift streams tear chunks out of mountains. Glaciers grind out valleys. Ocean waves rip up shorelines. Gravity pulls rocks and soil down hillsides, burying roads and damming rivers. What evidence does each photograph show of the constant attack on Earth?

Much of North America was once covered by huge masses of ice. How did the ice affect the landscape? ▼

In moments, this highway was buried under a mass of soil and rock that took days to clear away. What forces cause such a change? Can such changes be predicted? ▶

CHAPTER

8

Weathering, Soils, and Mass Movement

▲ The older photograph shows how Cleopatra's Needle appeared in 1880, when it first arrived in New York. The newer photograph shows the monument as it appears today.

How Do You Know That . . .

Air and moisture affect rocks? The photographs show a monument called Cleopatra's Needle. It was carved in Egypt around 1450 B.C. The sides of the monument are carved with hieroglyphs, the writing of ancient Egypt. Cleopatra's Needle stood in the dry, hot Egyptian desert for over 3000 years. During all that time, the hieroglyphs remained distinct. In 1880, the monument was moved to New York City. Almost immediately, the hieroglyphs began to fade. In only a few years in the wet and variable climate of New York, the Egyptian writing became indistinct.

I Weathering

Topic 1 Weathering and Erosion

Cleopatra's Needle was carved from granite, a hard, tough, crystalline rock. Although it is tough, granite, like other rocks, is changed by the atmosphere. Some of the minerals that make up granite change to clay. Other minerals dissolve. Chips and flakes of still other minerals break away from the rock surface. Eventually, the surface of the rock crumbles, or weathers. **Weathering** is the breakup of rock due to exposure to the atmosphere.

Why do rocks weather? Rocks like granite form deep underground where pressure is great and temperatures are high. When these rocks are raised to Earth's surface, the pressures and temperatures are much less. Water and oxygen, which are lacking deep in the crust, are present at the surface. Weathering of rocks is due in part to the difference between conditions at depth and conditions at the surface.

What happens to materials that form by weathering? Rain and melting snow wash them from the rock face. Gravity pulls them to lower levels. Finally, these materials are washed into a stream. There they become part of the stream's sediment. This sediment helps the stream wear down, or erode, the land. The stream is an agent of erosion. **Erosion** is the removal and transport of earth materials by natural agents. Agents of erosion include streams, rivers, glaciers (ice in motion), wind (air in motion), waves and currents (water in motion), and gravity.

Topic 2 Types of Weathering

Weathering includes many processes. These processes are grouped under two headings—mechanical weathering and chemical weathering. **Mechanical weathering,** or disintegration, takes place when rock is split or broken into smaller pieces of the same material without changing its composition. The breaking of a rock cliff into boulders and pebbles is an example of mechanical weathering.

Chemical weathering, or decomposition, takes place when the rock's minerals are changed into different substances. Water and water vapor are important agents of chemical weathering. The formation of clay minerals from feldspar is an example of chemical weathering.

OBJECTIVES

A Explain why weathering occurs, distinguish between weathering and erosion, and name several agents of erosion.

B Distinguish between mechanical and chemical weathering and identify processes by which each occurs.

C Discuss the effect of weathering on several common minerals and rocks.

D Identify some factors that control the rate at which a rock weathers.

Mechanical weathering processes and chemical weathering processes are often studied separately. However, the two processes seldom occur alone. The fact that water vapor is present in the air almost everywhere means that chemical weathering occurs almost everywhere. In different parts of the world, one process may be more important than the other. However, mechanical and chemical weathering almost always act together.

Topic 3 Types of Mechanical Weathering

Mechanical weathering happens in many ways. Common mechanical weathering processes are frost action, wetting and drying, action of plants and animals, and the loss of overlying rock and soil.

Water takes up about 10 percent more space when it freezes. This expansion puts great pressure on the walls of a container. For example, think about a pail of water left outdoors in freezing weather. The force of freezing water may split the pail. In the same way, water held in the cracks of rocks wedges the rocks apart when it freezes. This process is called **ice wedging,** or frost action. Ice wedging often occurs in places where the temperature varies from below the freezing point of water (0°C) to above the freezing point. In the northern United States and in other places in which there are frequent freezes and thaws, ice wedging is the most damaging of all weathering processes.

Ice wedging occurs mostly in porous rocks and in rocks with cracks in them. Bare mountaintops, especially, are subject to ice wedging. Vast fields of large, sharp-cornered boulders are often found on such mountaintops. Ice wedging also causes potholes on paved streets and highways. Here it is helped by *ice heaving.* Ice heaving happens when water in the ground freezes and lifts the pavement above it. When the ice thaws, the pavement collapses, leaving the pothole.

Repeated *wetting and drying* is especially effective at breaking up rocks that contain clay. Clays swell up when wet and shrink when dry. Constant swelling and shrinking causes rocks that contain clay, such as shale, to fall apart.

Small plants, such as lichens (LIE kens) and mosses, grow on rocks. They wedge their tiny roots into pores and crevices. When

8.1 The process of ice wedging was partly responsible for the damaging cracks that formed in the porous rocks shown on the right.

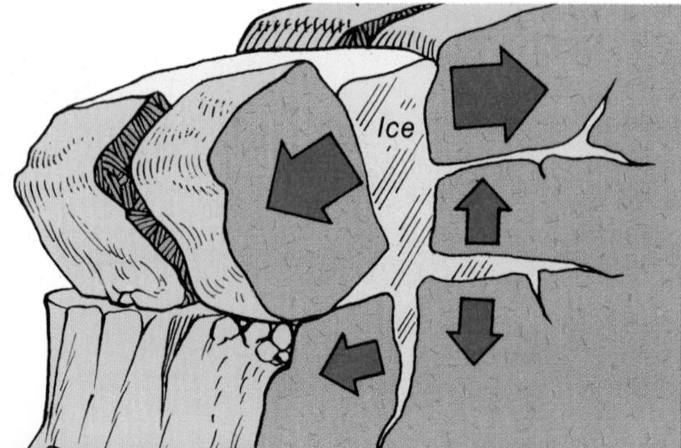

8.2 When lichens grow on rocks, their tiny roots act like wedges to split the rock.

the roots grow, the rock splits. Larger shrubs and trees may grow through cracks in boulders. Ants, earthworms, rabbits, woodchucks, and other animals dig holes in the soil. These holes allow air and water to reach the bedrock and weather it.

Granite is a rock formed far below Earth's surface. It is exposed when the rocks on top of it are worn away. The removal of the rocks reduces the pressure on the granite. When this happens, the relief from pressure lets the granite expand. Upward expansion leads to long curved breaks, or *joints.* The joints are parallel to the surface and occur in exposed peaks or outcrops. This process is *sheet jointing.* From time to time, large sheets of loosened rock break away from the outcrop. This process is called **exfoliation** – the peeling of surface layers. Rounded mountain peaks called exfoliated domes are formed in this way. In the United States spectacular exfoliated domes occur in Yosemite National Park, California. Other famous granite domes are Stone Mountain in Georgia and Sugarloaf Mountain near Rio de Janeiro, Brazil.

a

8.3 **(a)** Sheet jointing on a granite outcrop produces cracks in the rock, thereby exposing more of the rock surface to weathering. **(b)** Half Dome in Yosemite National Park, California, is an exfoliation dome. Its surface shows plainly where large sheets of rock have peeled away.

b

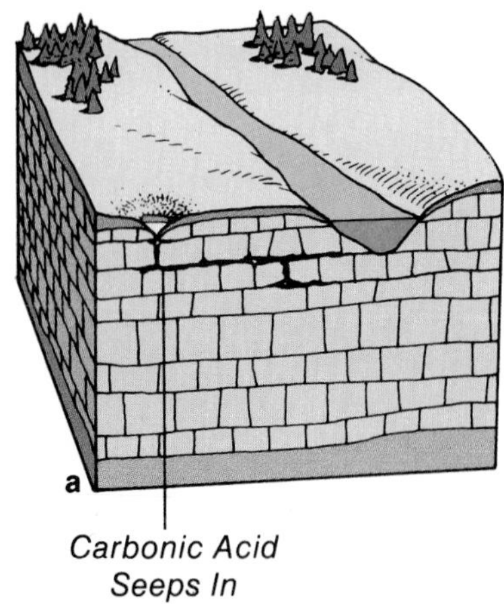

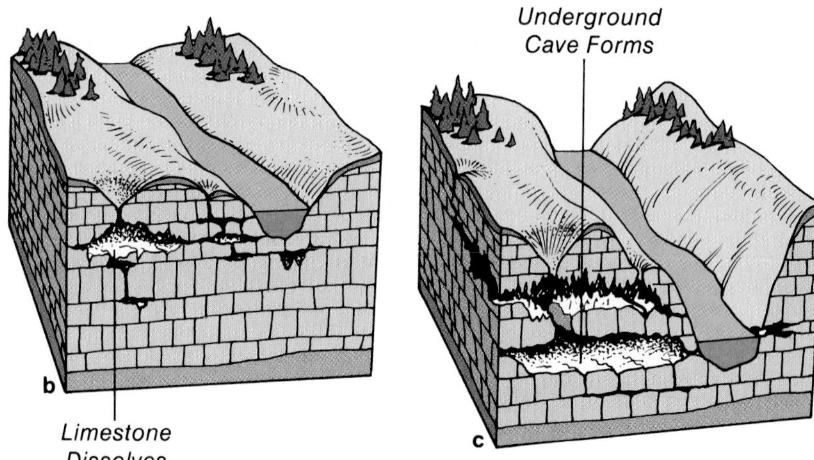

8.4 When carbonic acid seeps into bedrock made of minerals that dissolve easily, such as calcite, the bedrock dissolves and is carried away. The result is an underground cavern.

Topic 4 Chemical Weathering

Chemical weathering of rock results mainly from the action of rainwater, oxygen, carbon dioxide, and acids of plant decay. There are several ways in which these chemical agents work.

The chemical reaction of water with other substances is called **hydrolysis.** Common minerals that undergo hydrolysis include feldspar, hornblende, and augite. When these minerals are exposed to water, they slowly unite with it and form clay.

The chemical reaction of oxygen with other substances is called **oxidation.** Iron-bearing minerals are the ones most easily attacked by oxygen. These include magnetite, pyrite, and the dark-colored ferromagnesian silicates—hornblende, augite, and biotite. Oxidation of these minerals results in kinds of rust, or iron oxides. If the iron in these minerals combines with oxygen alone, the rust is the red iron oxide hematite. When water is also present, rusting occurs more quickly, and the brown rust limonite is formed. The hematite and limonite formed by weathering are often the reason for the reddish and brownish colors of soils and rocks at exposed surfaces.

Carbon dioxide dissolves easily in water. When it does, it forms a weak acid called **carbonic acid.** This compound is the acid in carbonated soft drinks. Carbonic acid attacks many common minerals, such as feldspar, hornblende, augite, and biotite mica. The acid dissolves out elements such as potassium, sodium, magnesium, and calcium. When this occurs, the original mineral is changed into a clay mineral.

Carbonic acid has a greater effect on calcite than on the minerals listed above. Carbonic acid dissolves calcite completely. Unless the calcite is impure, no clay is left over. The dissolving action of carbonic acid has hollowed out great underground caverns in limestone bedrock. Gypsum and halite also dissolve, slowly but surely, in carbonic acid.

Acids that are formed by the decay of plants and animals are dissolved by rainwater and carried through the ground to the bedrock. Like carbonic acid, these acids attack minerals.

8.5 Carbonic acid created this cave by dissolving limestone bedrock. (Luray Caverns, Virginia)

Carbon dioxide and sulfur compounds released by industries unite with water in the atmosphere to form acid rain (Chapter 6, Topic 21). Increasing amounts of acid rain in the environment increases the rate of chemical weathering.

Chemical weathering occurs most quickly at the corners and edges of rock outcrops and boulders. These areas are more exposed to chemicals. This process rounds the rock and is called *spheroidal* (sfir OY dl) *weathering.* Boulders rounded this way are spheroidal boulders.

8.6 Acids from decaying plant and animal matter dissolve in rainwater and chemically attack minerals.

Topic 5 Which Minerals and Rocks Resist Most?

There are several overall effects of weathering on the major rock-forming minerals and their rocks.

Quartz does not react very much to water, oxygen, or acids. It is almost unchanged by chemical weathering. Because it is hard and does not have cleavage, it also resists mechanical weathering. In time, however, quartz is broken into pebbles and sand grains.

Feldspar, hornblende, biotite mica, augite, calcite, and gypsum are all affected by chemical and mechanical weathering. Mechanical weathering breaks these minerals into small fragments. Chemical weathering turns these fragments into clay minerals. Some minerals, such as calcite, gypsum, and halite, are also dissolved and carried off in solution.

Most igneous rocks and many metamorphic rocks weather more rapidly in wet climates than in dry ones. These rocks often have cracks that are widened by mechanical weathering. They contain minerals that are easily attacked by chemical weathering. The first weathering products from igneous and metamorphic rocks are

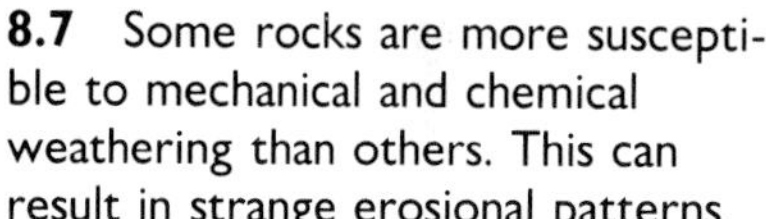

8.7 Some rocks are more susceptible to mechanical and chemical weathering than others. This can result in strange erosional patterns.

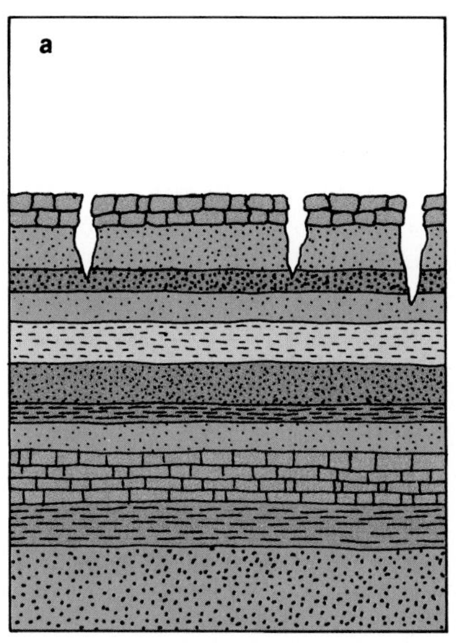

boulders, pebbles, sands, and some clay minerals. In time, even boulders are turned into clay. Pebbles and sands may also be left if the rocks contain quartz or other chemically resistant minerals.

Sandstones, quartzites, and quartz-pebble conglomerates are only as durable as the cements that hold them together. When the cement gives out, the rocks fall apart into the grains that make them up. Rocks cemented with calcite are subject to faster weathering. Rocks that are cemented with silica (quartz that dissolved and reformed as cement) are more durable. Quartzites and silica-cemented sandstones and conglomerates are among the most lasting of all rocks.

Shales, weakest of the sedimentary rocks, split easily between layers. In time they crumble into the clays from which they were formed.

Marbles and limestones are fairly resistant to mechanical weathering. However, the calcite that makes up marble and limestone undergoes slow attack by acids in water. In moist climates there is much dissolved acid, and rocks made of calcite are less durable than quartzites or sandstones. In dry climates there is very little dissolved acid, and limestones may be among the most durable of rocks.

Topic 6 The Rate of Weathering

8.8 Weathering and erosion by rainwater has occurred along weak vertical joints, resulting in this spectacular formation in Bryce Canyon, Utah.

There are several factors that affect the rate of weathering. One is that rocks themselves weather at different rates. Less-resistant rocks, such as shale, are weathered away relatively quickly. More-resistant rocks, such as granite and gneiss, take much longer to weather away. When rocks of different resistance are in the same place, spectacular landscapes are sometimes formed. An example is seen at Bryce Canyon in Utah (Figure 8.8). Each rock layer in Bryce Canyon has its own rate of weathering. In some places, remnants of more-resistant rock have protected the layers of less-resistant rock beneath. The taller formation in Figure 8.8 has a cap of more-resistant rock.

An important factor that affects the rate at which rock weathers is the amount of rock surface that is exposed. When a rock is broken into smaller pieces by mechanical weathering, the rock has more surface area. This means that more surface is exposed to chemical weathering. Thus, breaking a rock into smaller pieces causes the rock to weather away faster.

Climate is also an important factor in rock weathering. In general, warm, wet climates favor chemical weathering processes. Cold or dry climates favor mechanical weathering processes.

Keep in mind the fact that, under average conditions, weathering is a very slow process. For example, it is estimated that limestone dissolves as little as one twentieth of a centimeter in a hundred years. At this rate, it would take 60 million years to dissolve away a 300-meter layer of limestone. During the same time, however, other weathering processes would remove far more rock.

TOPIC QUESTIONS

Each topic question refers to the topic of the same number.

1. **(a)** Why do rocks weather? **(b)** Distinguish between weathering and erosion. **(c)** Identify some agents of erosion.
2. **(a)** Define mechanical weathering and give an example. **(b)** Define chemical weathering and give an example.
3. Explain how rocks are weathered by **(a)** frost action, **(b)** plants and animals, **(c)** wetting and drying, and **(d)** unloading of overlying rock.
4. **(a)** What substances cause chemical weathering? **(b)** Explain how rocks are weathered by hydrolysis, oxidation, and natural acids. **(c)** How do spheroidal boulders form?
5. **(a)** Which rocks and minerals are affected mostly by mechanical weathering? **(b)** Which rocks and minerals are affected mostly by chemical weathering? **(c)** Why do igneous and metamorphic rocks weather rapidly in wet climates? **(d)** What factor determines the resistance of sedimentary rocks?
6. Identify three factors that control the rate at which a rock weathers.

Dr. Juergen Reinhardt
Field Geologist

Weathered outcrops of bedrock can be a problem to a field geologist who needs fresh, unweathered samples for study. Dr. Juergen Reinhardt of the U.S. Geological Survey has been studying the rocks of several areas in the southeastern United States. The hot, humid climate there results in badly weathered outcrops. Getting fresh material presents a continual problem. The rocks of recently made roadcuts, for example, tend to be relatively fresh. But not all of the rocks that Dr. Reinhardt needs can be found in roadcuts. Some can be obtained only after hiking away from highways or canoeing along creeks. Still others are available only by going down steep cliffs using special equipment. In all of these cases, the outcrop is likely to be somewhat weathered. The exposure must then be dug into or chipped away until fresh rock is found. In some areas Dr. Reinhardt must even drill hundreds of meters beneath the surface to obtain fresh samples.

Dr. Reinhardt makes frequent and careful records of the material he observes for later use in making maps and in writing reports of his fieldwork.

OBJECTIVES

A Define *soil*, explain the difference between residual soil and transported soil, and describe a mature soil profile.

B Relate climate to soil formation; identify and describe the major types of soils.

C Identify and describe several types of mass movement.

D List and describe some methods of soil conservation.

II Soils, Mass Movements, and Soil Conservation

Topic 7 Soils: Result of Weathering

Weathering has attacked the rocks of Earth's surface since the beginning of geologic time. It has helped to wear down mountains and to shape countless landforms in this and past ages. Weathering has led to valuable mineral deposits and materials for sedimentary rocks. Most important, it has helped form a priceless resource—Earth's life-supporting soil. Without soil there could be no life on land. **Soil** is made of loose, weathered rock and organic material in which plants with roots can grow. The rock material in soil contains three noticeable parts: sand, clay, and silt.

The material from which a soil is formed is called its **parent material.** Often this material is the bedrock beneath the soil. Soil that has bedrock as its parent material is **residual soil.** The soil of the famous Blue Grass region of Kentucky is an example of a residual soil. The parent material in the Blue Grass region is the limestone bedrock. In other places, deposits left by winds, rivers, and glaciers have covered over the bedrock. Soils formed from such materials are called **transported soils.** The soils of New England and much of the midwestern United States are examples of transported soils. Their parent material is loose soil, boulders, sands, and gravels left by glaciers after the Ice Age.

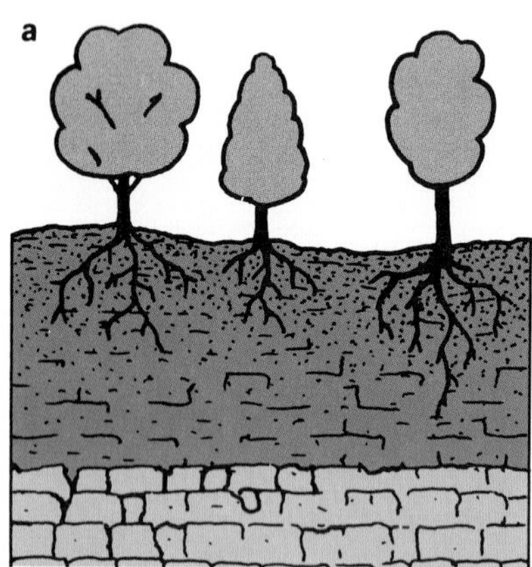

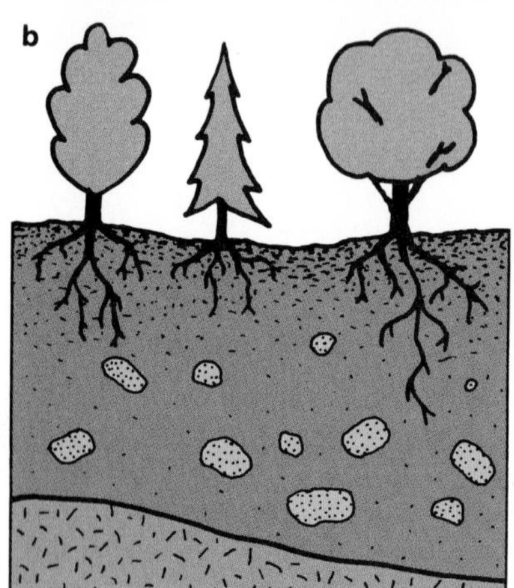

8.9 (a) The parent material for residual soil is the underlying bedrock. **(b)** Transported soil is formed from deposits left by wind, water, or a glacier. Notice that it does not resemble underlying bedrock.

Topic 8 A Mature Soil Profile

Scientists who study soil dig through layers of soil until they reach the parent material. The cross section of earth exposed by the digging is called the **soil profile.** In most mature soils, three distinct zones, or horizons, can be seen in the soil profile. These are named the A-, B-, and C-horizons. Beneath them is the parent material.

The A-horizon is **topsoil.** Its color is generally gray to black. Topsoil tends to be darker than soil in other horizons because it has organic material, or humus. Humus forms from decayed plant and animal materials. Although both sand and clay are in topsoil, most of the clay is washed to the B-horizon. The sand that is left tends to make topsoil sandy.

The B-horizon begins with the **subsoil.** Much of the clay in the topsoil is washed to the subsoil. Thus, the B-horizon contains more clay. The color, usually red or brown, is from iron oxides that formed in the A-horizon and then washed down. The B-horizon may contain soluble minerals that were washed into it, such as calcium and magnesium carbonates.

The C-horizon has slightly weathered parent material, such as rock fragments. Near the bottom of the C-horizon, these fragments sit on top of the unweathered bedrock.

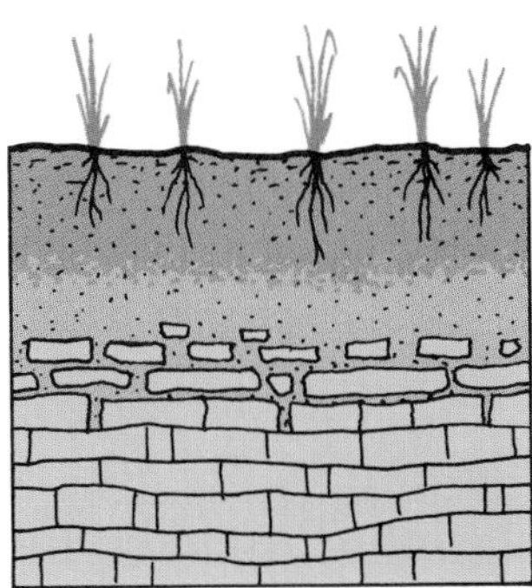
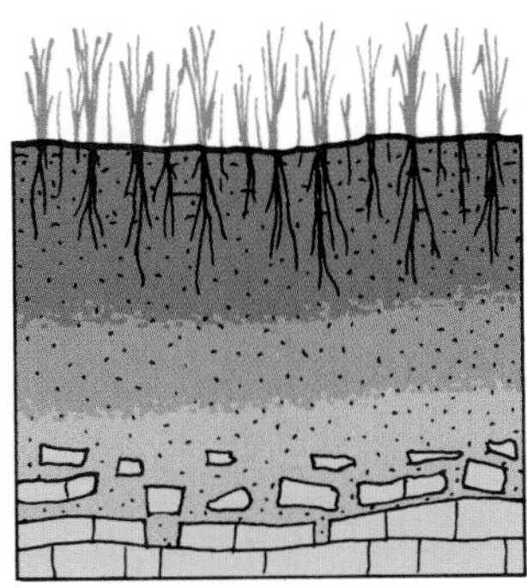

8.10 Mature soil develops from the gradual weathering of parent material.

Topic 9 Soil Types and Climates

Soil scientists have learned that the most important factor affecting soil is the climate. Once a soil has matured, the parent material no longer has much effect on soil type. The soil formed from granite in a wet tropical climate is very different from the soil formed from granite in a desert. At the same time, mature soils in a wet tropical climate strongly resemble each other no matter what their parent material is.

A *tropical soil* forms in the areas that have constant high temperature and heavy rainfall. Warm, wet conditions speed up chemical weathering, and soil forms quickly. The soil profile that results may be more than three meters thick. Frequent heavy rains wash nutrients out of the soil. Thus, tropical soils are relatively infertile. They must be fertilized heavily if they are used to grow crops.

Grassland soils form in areas that receive enough rainfall for heavy grass, but not enough for trees. The soil profile is usually less

8.11 Note the three distinct horizons in this soil profile.

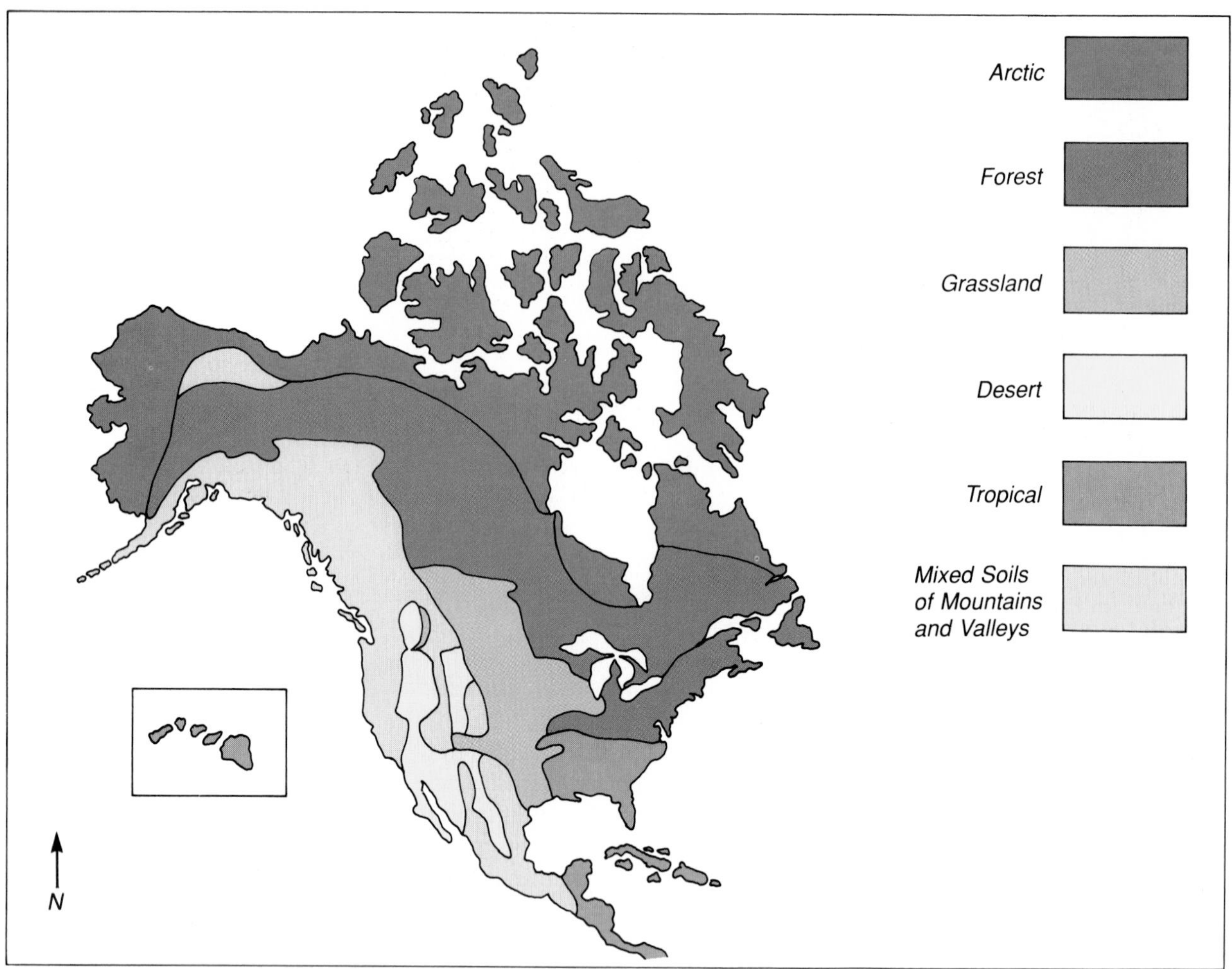

8.12 Map of soil types in North America

than a meter thick. The A-horizons are black or deep-brown. Grassland soils are very rich in organic matter and, as a result, are very fertile soils. Grassland soils are good for growing wheat and similar grains.

Forest soils form in humid regions that have cool seasons and forests of hardwood and evergreen trees. These soils have very well developed A-, B-, and C-horizons. However, the soil profile in forests is usually less than a meter in total thickness. Forest soils are not very fertile.

Desert soils form in very dry climates. Their profiles are seldom more than a few centimeters from top to bottom. Nutrients that would be washed from the soil in a wet climate stay in a desert soil. Such soils often have a great deal of calcium. These soils can be very fertile when they are watered.

Arctic soils form at high elevations and high latitudes. The surfaces of these soils are poorly drained and boggy. The bottom layers are constantly frozen (permafrost). The soil profile is very shallow, often only a few centimeters thick.

8.13 Talus forms on a slope at the base of a weathered cliff.

Topic 10 Mass Movements

Soil partially protects bedrock beneath it from weathering. On steep slopes, however, loose soil is easily removed by erosion and gravity. This removal continually exposes a fresh bedrock surface to weathering. Gravity, then, is an aid to weathering and erosion. Gravity is largely responsible for the fact that steep slopes weather more rapidly than gentle slopes.

Wherever the ground slopes, gravity causes soil and rock fragments to fall, slide, or move at very slow speeds to lower levels. Such movements of loose earth material down a slope is called **mass movement.** There are several important types of mass movement, some of which have a profound effect on people and the landscape.

Creep is a slow, imperceptible downslope movement of the soil. Creep can be noticed by its effects. Creep causes fence posts, poles, and other objects fixed in the soil to lean downhill. Water in the soil probably adds to creep.

Talus is the result of mass movement near steep slopes. *Talus* is a pile of rock fragments at the base of a cliff. The fragments are weathered from the cliff and pulled down by gravity. Talus hides the lower part of the cliff. Talus piles rest against the cliff at angles as steep as 40 degrees. Talus is common wherever there are cliffs.

A **landslide** is the sudden movement of a mass of bedrock or loose rock down the slope of a hill, mountain, or cliff. An *avalanche* is a landslide made from masses of snow, ice, soil, or rock, or mixtures of these materials. Landslides are likely to occur on steep slopes, especially those caused by erosion or by mining. Small landslides, or *slumps,* are common on cliffs, steep hills, and roadcuts next to highways.

8.14 This mudflow formed when loose sand and rock mixed with water during a heavy rainfall.

A **mudflow** is the rapid movement of a water-saturated mass of clay and silt. A *mud avalanche* is an especially fast and large mudflow. A mud avalanche in Columbia, South America, in 1985 was triggered by a volcanic eruption. The heat from the eruption melted part of the volcano's ice cap. The mixture of water and volcanic ash buried towns below the volcano and killed 25 000 people.

It is possible to avoid such catastrophic loss of life and property by understanding what leads to landslides and mudflows. Steep slopes, which are common in mountain regions, often experience mass wasting. A road or house that is built on or into the side of a steep slope is at risk of being damaged by a landslide. The risk is even greater in areas near volcanoes and earthquakes, since eruptions and tremors can trigger landslides.

It is best not to build roads or houses on steep slopes. However, people who live in such places can still avoid injury by knowing when the danger of landslide is greatest, and leaving the area at that time. Landslides often happen after very heavy rains or during spring melting of snow. Rain and snowmelt contribute to landslides in two main ways. The first is by adding weight. Water is very heavy. Soil that is soaked with water is more likely to be pulled downslope by gravity than dry soil. The second way water contributes to mass wasting is by reducing friction. Water is a good lubricant. When enough rain has fallen to saturate the soil, a layer of water builds up between the soil and the bedrock beneath it. When this happens, the whole mass of soil may be pulled down the slope, riding on top of a layer of water. People living in areas that are in danger of landslides can avoid injury by leaving the area during heavy rains and spring melts.

Topic 11 Soil Conservation

Soil erosion is the removal of topsoil by the action of running water or wind. Each year, the streams and rivers of the United States carry away 4 billion metric tons of sediment. The sediment was removed from the land by soil erosion. Winds blow away another 1 billion metric tons. This loss of topsoil reduces soil fertility and crop production. Soil erosion has become a serious environmental and economic problem.

Soil erosion can be reduced by a number of soil conservation methods. One method is the planting of *windbreaks,* belts of trees along the edges of fields. These trees slow the wind and reduce wind erosion. Windbreaks are important on level plains where strong winds may blow nearly all the time.

A second method of reducing soil erosion is *contour farming.* Instead of plowing up and down a hillslope, the crops are planted in rows parallel to the land contours. This prevents water from flowing rapidly downhill and carrying the soil with it. Flattening hillslopes into *terraces* also slows stream flow and, in turn, reduces soil erosion.

8.15 The crop on this hillside has been planted in contours, which reduce the effects of soil erosion.

Another method of reducing soil erosion is *strip cropping*. In this method, a crop that leaves bare ground between rows is alternated with a crop that completely covers the ground. For example, the ground between rows of corn plants is bare, while alfalfa is a crop that covers the ground. By planting alternating strips of a field with corn and alfalfa, soil erosion can be reduced.

Still another method of reducing soil erosion is a technique called *no-till*. In this method, plowing, planting, fertilizing, and weed control are all done at the same time. Once the field is planted, the ground does not need to be disturbed again until harvest. When the soil is left alone, there is less of a chance that it will be carried away by the wind.

TOPIC QUESTIONS

Each topic question refers to the topic of the same number.

7. **(a)** What is soil and why is it important? **(b)** What is parent material? **(c)** How is the parent material of a residual soil different from that of a transported soil?
8. List and briefly describe the three horizons of a mature soil.
9. **(a)** What is the most important factor affecting soil type? **(b)** List and briefly describe five types of soil.
10. **(a)** What is mass movement and what is its cause? **(b)** Identify and describe several kinds of mass movements.
11. **(a)** Why is soil erosion a problem? **(b)** Identify and briefly describe some methods of reducing soil erosion.

CHAPTER 8 REVIEW

Summary

Weathering occurs when rocks are exposed at Earth's surface. Agents of erosion transport weathered earth materials.

Mechanical weathering breaks rocks without changing their composition. Chemical weathering changes the composition of the rocks.

The way a rock weathers depends on its mineral content and cement.

Some factors that determine the rate at which rock weathers are mineral composition, particle size, and climate.

Soil is loose, weathered material capable of supporting rooted plants. Soils may be residual or transported, depending on the parent material.

A soil profile shows the soil layers: A-horizon (topsoil), B-horizon (subsoil), and C-horizon. Each layer has its own characteristics.

The major factor in soil formation is climate. Examples of soil types are tropical, forest, grassland, desert, and arctic soils.

Gravity pulls loose soil and rock downhill in mass movements. Examples of mass movements include creep, landslides, and mudflows.

Soil erosion reduces soil fertility and crop production. Windbreaks, contour plowing, terracing, strip cropping, and no-till planting can be used to conserve soil.

Vocabulary

carbonic acid	oxidation
chemical weathering	parent material
creep	residual soil
erosion	soil
exfoliation	soil erosion
hydrolysis	soil profile
ice wedging	subsoil
landslide	topsoil
mass movement	transported soil
mechanical weathering	weathering
mudflow	

Review

On your paper, write the term that best completes each sentence.

1. Weathering is due in part to differences between conditions at depth and those at Earth's ______.
2. Streams and rivers, glaciers, wind, and other natural agents that break up and move rocks are called ______.
3. ______ weathering breaks rocks in smaller pieces without changing their composition.
4. ______ weathering changes the minerals in the rock into different minerals.
5. ______ occurs when water enters a crack in a rock and expands as it freezes.
6. In hydrolysis, minerals such as feldspar, hornblende, and augite unite with water and form ______.
7. Rocks like sandstone are only as durable as the ______ that holds them together.
8. Breaking a rock into smaller pieces increases its ______ and, as a result, the rate at which the rock weathers.
9. Warm, wet climates favor ______ weathering, while cold and dry climates favor ______ weathering.
10. The ______ material of a residual soil is the bedrock beneath the soil.
11. ______ soils are formed from deposits left by winds, rivers, or glaciers.
12. The dark, humus-rich A-horizon of a soil profile is also called the ______.
13. Fine materials from the A-horizon are washed to the B-horizon, or ______.
14. ______ soils form in areas that have constant high temperatures and heavy rainfall.
15. ______ soils are especially fertile soils on which wheat and other grains grow well.
16. A ______ is the sudden movement of a mass of loose material down the slope of a hill, mountain, or cliff.
17. Windbreaks, contour plowing, strip cropping, and the no-till method are all ways of reducing ______.

Interpret and Apply

On your paper, answer each question in complete sentences.

1. How is the weathering of a bare mountain peak different from the weathering of bedrock under a forest soil?
2. Why are streets and highways damaged so much more in the winter months than in the summer months in most of the United States? Compare the processes of weathering in the two seasons.
3. Sandstones cemented by lime usually weather much more rapidly than those cemented by silica. Why?
4. What should be the content of a residual soil that formed in a humid climate from granite composed of quartz, feldspar, and black mica?
5. Which horizon of a soil profile is most weathered? Explain.
6. Using the soil map of the United States in Figure 8.12, determine the soil type for your area.
7. What effect would a long, dry period have on the frequency of landslides and mudslides?
8. Soil erosion is usually the result of human use of the land surface. Are there any ways in which human use has been beneficial to the soil?

Critical Thinking

The type of weathering that dominates in an area depends upon the climate in that area. The major factors that control climate are precipitation (rain and snow) and temperature. The graph shows the relationship between precipitation, temperature, and weathering. For example, a climate with an average yearly temperature (AYT) of 5°C and average yearly precipitation (AYP) of 75 centimeters would have moderate chemical weathering with frost action. Use the graph to answer the questions.

1. Determine the major type of weathering that occurs in Washington, D.C., AYT, 23°C; AYP, 104 cm.
2. If the AYT in Washington, D.C., dropped 26°C but the AYP stayed the same, what kind of weathering would dominate?
3. Phoenix, Arizona, has an AYT of 20°C and an AYP of 20 cm. How would the climate in Phoenix have to change for moderate chemical weathering to become dominant?
4. According to the graph, no frost action occurs at a mean annual temperature above 13°C. What is a possible reason?
5. In general, how does a climate with strong chemical weathering differ from a climate with strong mechanical weathering?

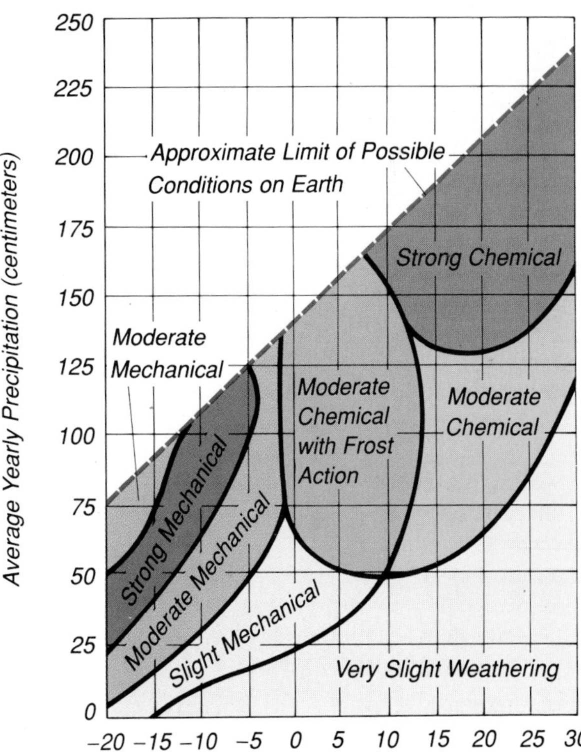

CHAPTER 9

Water Moving Underground

▲ Old Faithful Geyser in Yellowstone National Park, Wyoming

How Do You Know That . . .

Water exists beneath Earth's surface? The following investigation will give you a clue. Fill a plastic container to the top with coarse gravel or marble chips. Is the container really full? Estimate the amount of air space in the container. Check your estimate by filling another container of equal volume with water. Pour the water into the container with the gravel until it can hold no more water. Compare your estimate with your observation. Carefully pour the water off the gravel and back into the water container. Was all the water removed from the gravel?

I Fresh Water and Water Budgets

Topic 1 All the World's Water

How much water is there on and in the whole Earth? Scientists estimate the answer to be about one and one third billion cubic kilometers. The number is so large that it is difficult to picture. How much of Earth's water is salt water? How much is fresh water? This question is important because most uses of water require fresh water. With the growth of industry and the increase in population, the need for fresh water becomes more and more critical.

More than 97 percent of all Earth's water is in the ocean as salt water. Less than 3 percent is fresh water. Of this 3 percent, more than two thirds is frozen in the ice caps and glaciers of Greenland, Antarctica, and high mountain regions. Therefore, only about one half of one percent of all Earth's water is usable fresh water.

Where is this fresh water located? A tiny part of it flows on the surface in rivers and streams. About 100 times that amount is stored in lakes and swamps. However, most of the fresh water is in the ground. By one estimate, the amount of groundwater is 50 times as much as all the water in rivers and lakes! It is thousands of times as much as in all Earth's rivers at any given moment.

Topic 2 The Water Cycle

The **hydrosphere** is the water of Earth's surface. The hydrosphere includes groundwater, running water, lakes, and oceans. The movement of water from one part of the hydrosphere to another is described by the hydrologic cycle, or **water cycle.** The path of water in the water cycle is shown in Figure 9.2.

Sunlight provides the energy that evaporates water from the surface of Earth. Most of the water vapor comes from the ocean, but some comes from the continents. Winds carry the water vapor over the continents. Part of the water vapor condenses into clouds, then falls as rain or snow.

Some of the rain returns to the ocean from rivers and streams as runoff. Some seeps into the ground to become groundwater. Some returns to the air by *evaporation* from the ground or by *transpiration* from plant leaves. Hydrologists (scientists who study the hydrosphere) usually combine evaporation and transpiration in the term **evapotranspiration.**

OBJECTIVES

A Describe the distribution and quantity of fresh water on Earth.

B List the parts of the hydrosphere and describe the movement of water in the water cycle.

C Identify the conditions under which groundwater surplus, usage, deficit, and recharge occur.

D Compare the climates of different areas by comparing their water budgets.

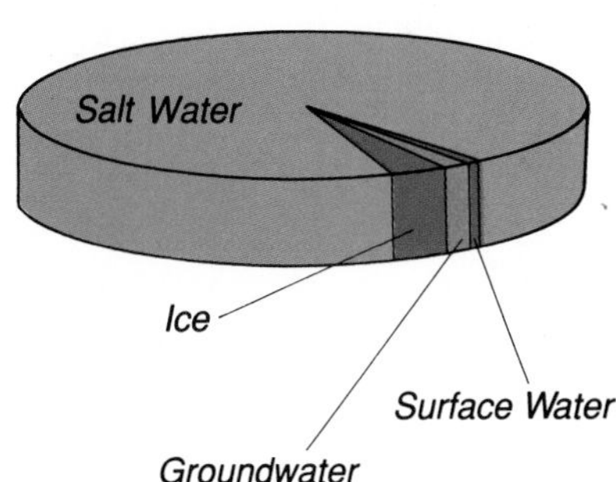

9.1 Less than three percent of Earth's water is fresh water, and less than one third of the fresh water is available as surface or groundwater. The rest is frozen.

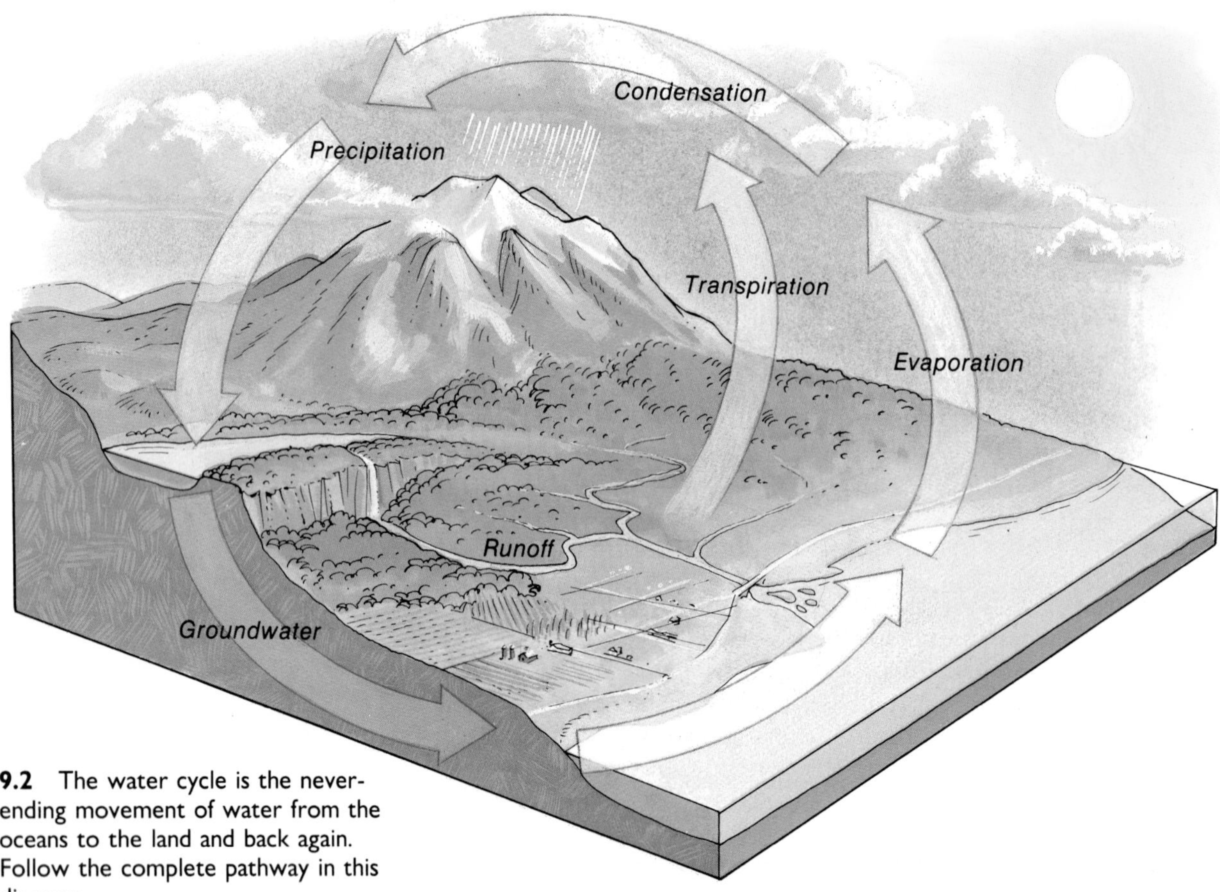

9.2 The water cycle is the never-ending movement of water from the oceans to the land and back again. Follow the complete pathway in this diagram.

When runoff from the continents returns to the ocean, one turn of the water cycle is completed. Other routes are possible. For example, water that evaporated from the ocean could return to the ocean as rain.

The water cycle is a never-ending process. The salt water of the ocean supplies fresh water to the continents over and over again.

Topic 3 The Water Budget

A budget is a statement of expected income and expected outgo. In a balanced budget of any kind, income and outgo are equal. A **water budget** describes the income and outgo of water for a region. In a water budget, the income is rain or snow. The outgo includes water lost by use, by runoff, and by evapotranspiration.

The evapotranspiration of an area is controlled by air temperature. When air temperature is high, plants growing in the ground need and use more moisture. At such times, evapotranspiration is high. When air temperature is low, plants do not need or use as much moisture; thus, evapotranspiration is low.

If it rains during a time when the plants need little moisture, the extra moisture soaks into the soil, where it is stored between the

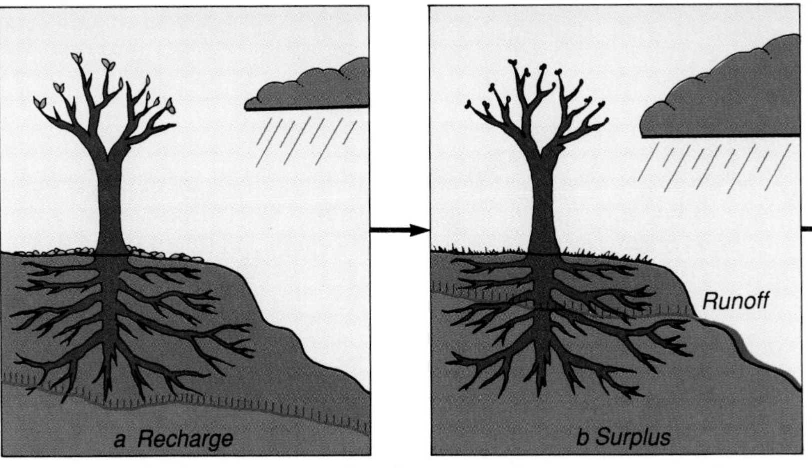

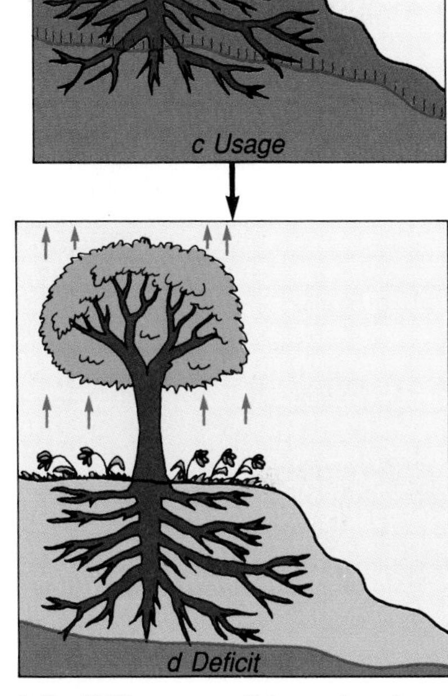

grains of soil. This is a time of soil water **recharge.** During recharge, the soil water storage is filling. Figure 9.3(a) illustrates conditions during recharge. If the rain continues so that the soil becomes saturated, the surplus water raises the water table (Topic 7) or becomes part of the stream runoff. Thus, a moisture **surplus** occurs when two conditions are true: the rainfall is greater than the need for moisture and the soil water storage is filled, as in Figure 9.3(b).

If the need for moisture is greater than the rainfall, the plants can draw water from the soil water supply. This is a time of soil water **usage,** Figure 9.3(c). If the need for moisture continues to be greater than the rainfall, all of the water available in the soil may be used up. A water **deficit** occurs when the need for moisture is greater than the rainfall and the soil water storage is gone (Figure 9.3(d)).

9.3 Different conditions of moisture input and need lead to phases in the yearly water budget cycle of an area.

Topic 4 **Water Budget Graphs**

Each location on Earth has its own unique water budget. Water budgets can be summarized by *water budget graphs.* Each water budget graph shows two kinds of information: moisture need and moisture supply. Periods of water usage, deficit, recharge, and surplus can be determined from data on the water budget graph. Three examples of water budget graphs are shown in Figures 9.4 and 9.5, and are discussed in the following paragraphs.

Phoenix, Arizona (Figure 9.4), is located in a dry desert climate in the southwestern United States. The rainfall in Phoenix is very low all year. The need for moisture is great almost all year. Because of these conditions, Phoenix has a moisture deficit nearly all year. The only recharge of water occurs in December and January, but that moisture is used up before April.

Hartford, Connecticut (Figure 9.5(a)), is located in the humid eastern part of the United States. Temperatures in Hartford, even in summer, are not as high as those in Phoenix. Thus, the moisture need in Hartford is never as great as in Phoenix. Rainfall in Hartford is abundant all year long. Plants generally do not use up all of the moisture stored in the ground. As a result, Hartford does not have a moisture deficit. The water usage of summer is quickly recharged in the fall. Thus, Hartford has a moisture surplus more than half the year.

9.4 Water budget graph for Phoenix, Arizona

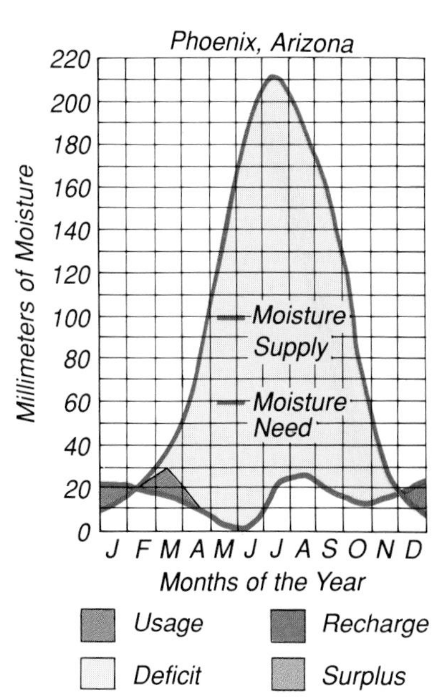

Little Rock, Arkansas (Figure 9.5(b)), has a climate in between those of Phoenix and Hartford. In summer, Little Rock is not as hot as Phoenix nor as cool as Hartford. Summer rainfall at Little Rock is greater than at Phoenix but not as great as at Hartford. The water storage at Little Rock is used up before summer is over, and a period of water deficit occurs. However, the water storage in Little Rock is recharged in the fall. A water surplus starts in December and continues until the next summer.

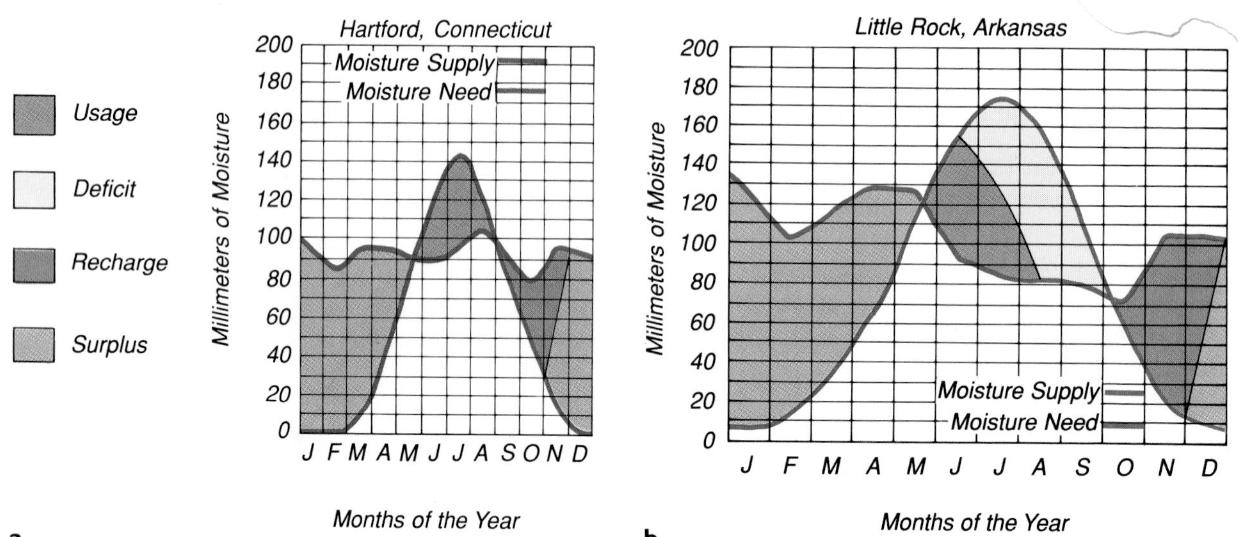

9.5 Water budget graphs for **(a)** Hartford, Connecticut, and **(b)** Little Rock, Arkansas

TOPIC QUESTIONS

Each topic question refers to the topic of the same number.

1. **(a)** Compare the percentage of salt water and fresh water on Earth. **(b)** What portion of Earth's fresh water is frozen into ice caps and glaciers? **(c)** Where is most of Earth's usable fresh water located?

2. **(a)** List the parts of the hydrosphere. **(b)** Identify the energy source for the water cycle. **(c)** What kinds of things can happen to rain that falls on Earth's surface? **(d)** What is evapotranspiration?

3. **(a)** What is a water budget? **(b)** How are temperature and evapotranspiration related in a water budget? **(c)** What occurs during a time of moisture recharge? **(d)** Under what two conditions does a moisture surplus occur? **(e)** What occurs during a time of moisture usage? **(f)** Under what two conditions does a moisture deficit occur?

4. **(a)** Identify the kinds of information shown by a water budget graph. **(b)** Describe the water budgets of Phoenix, Arizona, Hartford, Connecticut, and Little Rock, Arkansas.

II Water in the Ground

Topic 5 Can Rocks Hold Water?

The amount of water that soil or rock can hold depends upon the amount of space, called pore space, that lies between the grains of the material. **Porosity** is the percentage of a material that is pore space.

The porosity of a material depends upon a number of factors. One factor is particle shape. Rounded particles have a lot of space between them—picture the space between glass marbles in a jar. Flat or angular particles fit together more closely than rounded particles, and thus have less total pore space—picture the small amount of space between pennies in a jar. Another factor affecting porosity is sorting. The percentage of pore space is greatest in well-sorted materials—that is, materials in which the particles are all the same size. Where the material is poorly sorted—as in a mixture of gravel, sand, and silt—small particles fill the spaces between the large particles, which greatly reduces the total porosity. Deposits of well-rounded particles of gravel, sand, or silt that have little or no cement between grains may be more than 40 percent pore space.

OBJECTIVES

A Define *porosity* and *permeability* and list some factors that control each.

B Identify and describe underground regions above and below the water table, list factors that determine water table depth, and explain the importance of the water table.

C Describe an artesian formation.

D Identify some methods of obtaining groundwater and describe ways of dealing with two problems in groundwater usage.

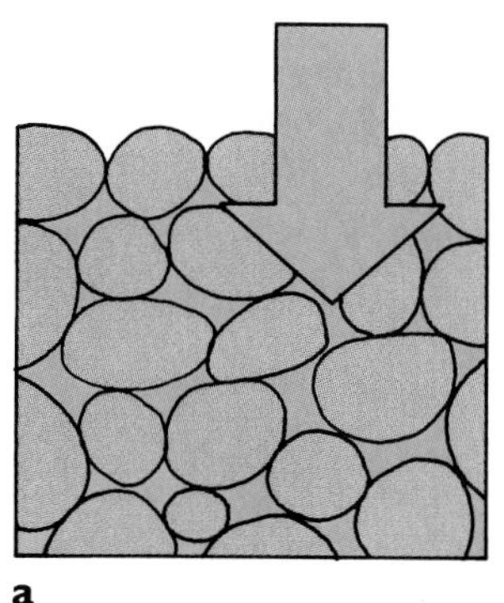
a

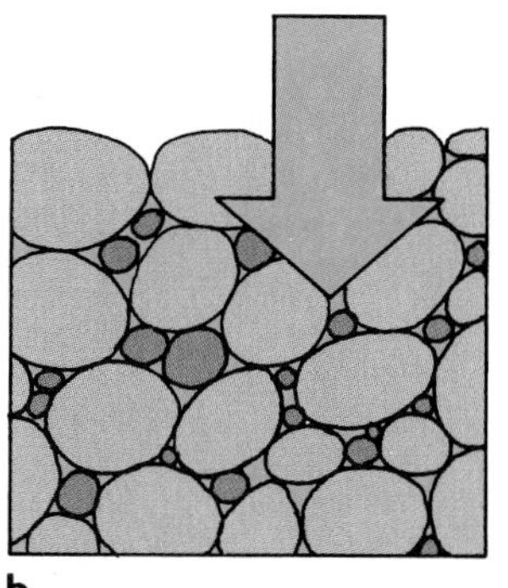
b

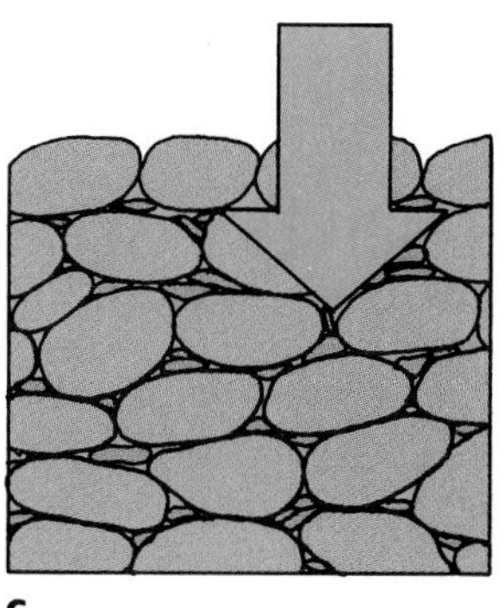
c

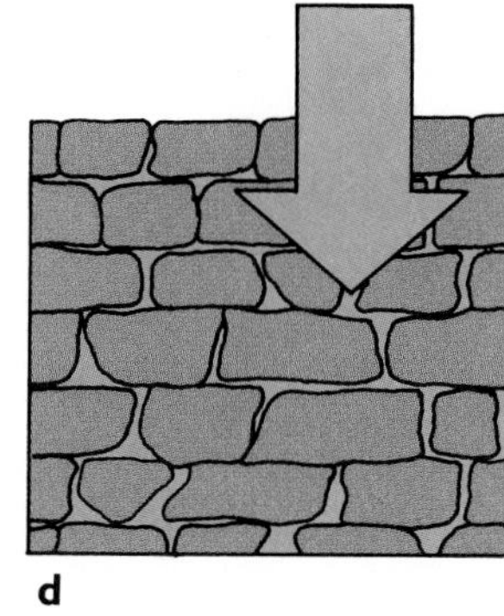
d

9.6 Different earth materials have different amounts of pore space. **(a)** All sand, lots of pore space; **(b)** sand mixed with silt, less pore space; **(c)** sandstone, cement reduces pore space; **(d)** limestone, porous because of cracks and fissures

Topic 6 Can Rocks Transmit Water?

Porosity describes the pore space in a material, but it does not describe whether water can pass through the material. **Permeability** is the rate at which water or other liquids pass through the pore spaces of a rock. In general, permeability increases with grain size because large-grained materials have large pore spaces. Water passes easily through materials with large pore spaces, such as sand and gravel. It passes slowly through finer materials, such as silt. A material that water cannot pass through is **impermeable.** Clays and shales, which are very fine-grained, are usually impermeable.

It is possible for a material to be highly porous but not at all permeable. An example is pumice. Pumice has many holes, or pores, but the holes are not connected. Thus, water cannot pass through pumice. On the other hand, a nonporous rock such as limestone may become permeable if cracks develop in the rock. The cracks transmit the water.

Some of the water that passes through a sediment or rock will stick to the particles. This film of water is *capillary water.* It can be removed only by evapotranspiration. For materials made of small particles, such as shale, capillary water may fill the pore space. When the pore space is filled, the material is impermeable.

Topic 7 Forming the Water Table

When rain falls to the ground, it enters the pores in the soil and sticks to the particles. If enough rain falls, the upper layers of soil will not be able to absorb all the water. When this happens, the water continues downward until it reaches an impermeable material. The water then begins to fill the pore spaces above the impermeable material. As rain continues, the water level in the ground rises higher as more pore spaces are filled. The *zone of saturation* is that part of the ground where all pore spaces are filled. The surface of the zone of saturation is the **water table.**

From the water table to the surface, the ground can still hold more water. This section is called the *zone of aeration* because air can enter this region. It includes three parts. Just above the water table is the *capillary fringe.* In the capillary fringe, water rises from the water table by capillary action. (A familiar example of capillary action occurs when a paper towel is dipped in water. Just as water rises into the towel, water rises into the soil just above the water table.) Above the capillary fringe is a section that is dry except during rains. Just below the soil surface is the soil water, a film of capillary water that sticks to the grains of topsoil.

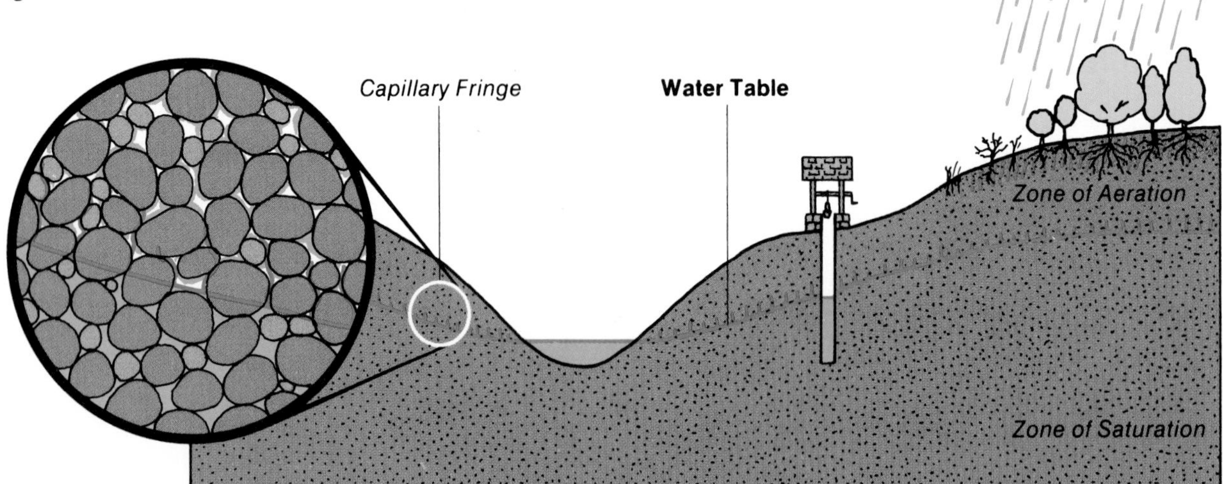

9.7 The depth of the water table varies, mainly due to the amount of rainfall and the structure of underground formations.

Topic 8 Water Table Depth and Use

How far under the surface is the water table? The depth depends upon many things. Some factors include the amount of rainfall, the season, the slope of the ground surface, the thickness of the soil, the climate, and the time between rains.

In places such as swamps, lakes, and rivers, the water table is at the surface. In desert regions, the water table may be hundreds of meters below the surface. In woods, fields, and farmlands, it is likely to be within a few meters of the surface. In hilly country, it is generally nearer the surface in valleys than in hills, but it has its own hills and valleys much like the overlying surface.

The water table is important in several ways. Seepage of water from the water table keeps streams flowing between rains and maintains the water levels of swamps and lakes. The water table also supplies drinking water to springs and wells.

Topic 9 Ordinary Wells and Springs

In places where the water table does not reach the surface, the groundwater is reached by digging or driving wells into the ground. A well of this type, known as an *ordinary well,* contains water from its bottom up to the level of the water table. Recall that the depth of the water table depends in part on the season. A well must reach below the lowest level to which the water table is likely to fall in dry weather. If it does not, it will not provide water all year. As the water table rises and falls with weather changes, so does the level of the water in the well.

On a hillside where the water table meets the surface, groundwater may flow out as a *hillside spring.* Hillside springs are more common in mountainous areas.

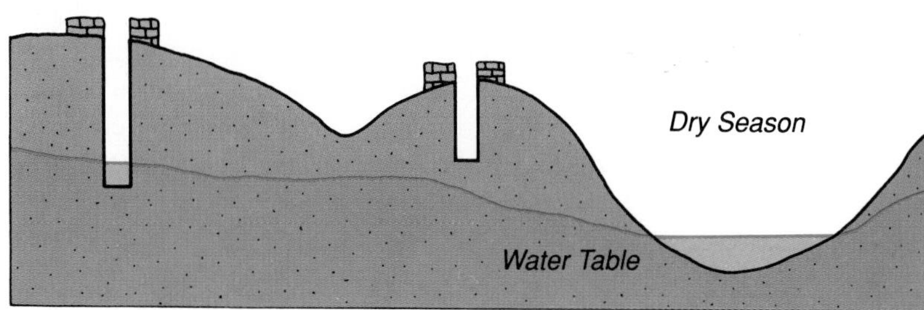

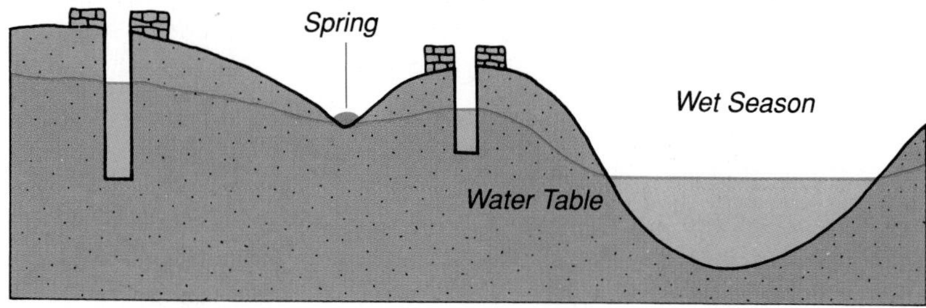

9.8 Wells and springs are fed by the water table. Changes in the water table affect the availability of surface and well water.

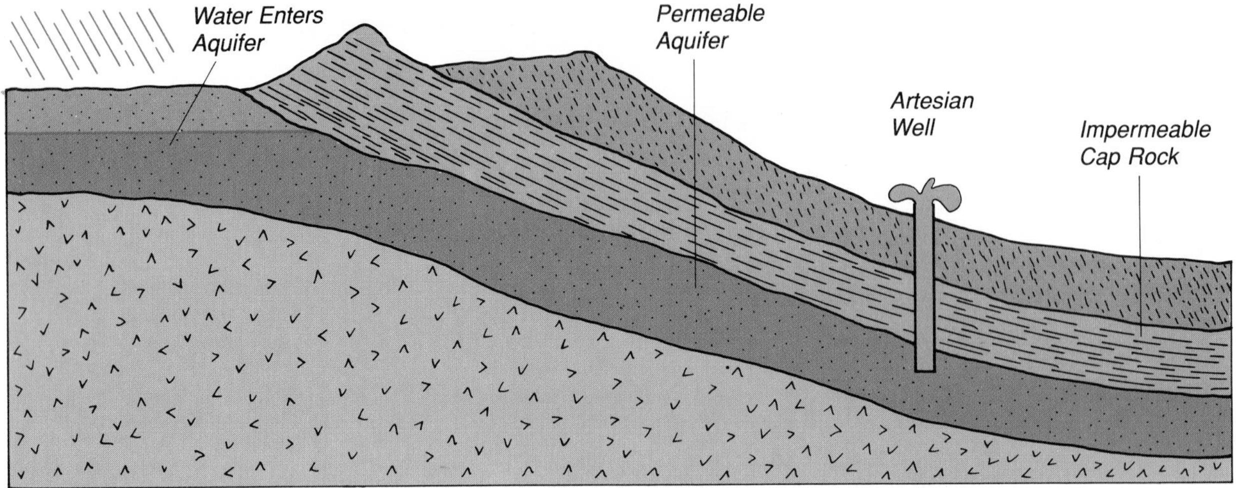

9.9 The rainwater that enters the aquifer of an artesian formation is trapped under an impermeable rock layer. From there it may travel a great distance underground before returning to the surface through an artesian well or spring.

Topic 10 Artesian Formations

In many parts of the world, beds of permeable materials occur near the surface on hillsides and mountainsides. When the permeable bed dips underground between impermeable beds, a "sandwich" of permeable and impermeable rocks is formed. This arrangement is an **artesian formation** (Figure 9.9). Rain that enters the permeable bed is trapped by the impermeable beds above and below.

The upper impermeable layer of an artesian formation, usually shale or clay, is the *cap rock*. The permeable layer, usually sandstone or gravel, is the **aquifer** (water bearer). The water trapped in the aquifer follows a sloping course underground. Gravity pulls the water along this course.

One of the best-known artesian formations in the United States carries water hundreds of kilometers underground from the Rocky Mountains to the Great Plains. Its aquifer is a porous sandstone more than 30 meters thick called the Dakota sandstone. Its cap rock is shale.

Topic 11 Artesian Wells

Great quantities of water may enter the aquifers of artesian formations where the aquifers are at the surface. Like the water in a great sloping pipe, the water in the aquifer is under pressure. When wells are drilled into the aquifers at lower elevations, water rises in the wells. It may even spout into the air if water pressure is great enough. These are *artesian wells,* that is, wells in which water comes from an aquifer that lies beneath an impermeable layer.

Artesian wells differ greatly in depth. Generally, as the distance from the source of the water increases, the depth of the aquifer increases. On the Great Plains, wells that are hundreds of kilometers from the mountains may go down more than a thousand meters to reach the aquifer.

Artesian formations may be broken naturally by cracks in the cap rock called fissures. Artesian springs, or *fissure springs,* rise through these cracks. Such a spring may form an oasis in a desert (Figure 9.10).

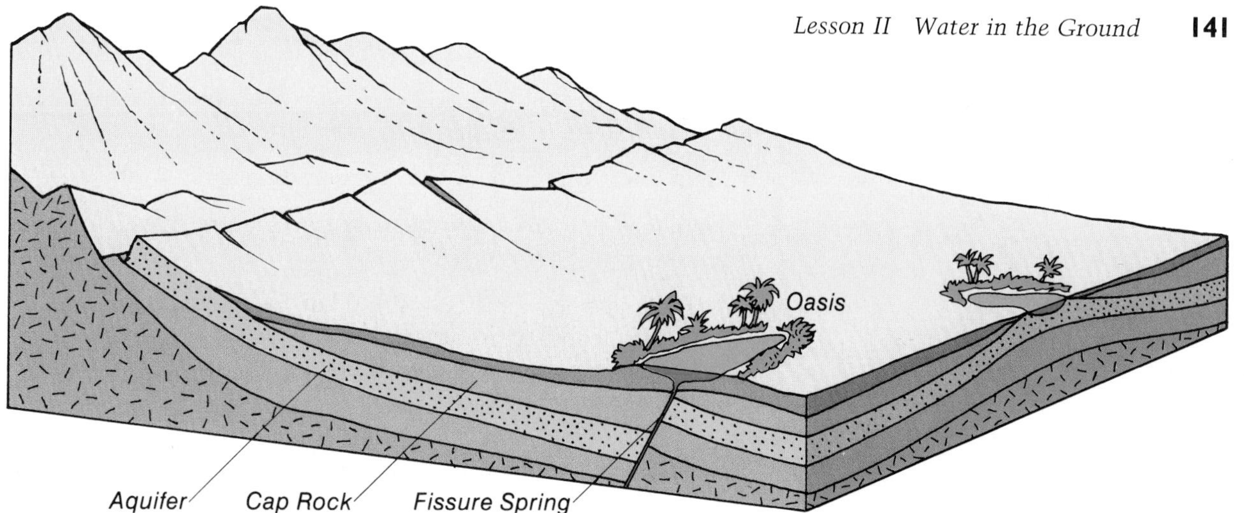

9.10 This oasis is located over a spot where a fissure spring has risen through a crack in the impermeable layer.

Topic 12 Conserving Groundwater

Groundwater supplies are not limitless. The amount of water returned to the ground in a given area must be at least equal to the amount removed by wells and springs. If more groundwater is removed than can be returned, the water table will drop. A drop in the water table lowers the water level of wells and springs. This may cause the wells or springs to go dry. In coastal areas, wells are affected in a different way. Fresh groundwater in these areas rests on top of salt water. As fresh water is used, salt water from the ocean seeps in, replacing the fresh water that has been removed from the ground. When this occurs, wells and springs become unusable.

Pollutants can enter the groundwater. Groundwater is recharged by rain seeping down through the soil. Any polluting agent in the soil becomes part of the groundwater. In agricultural areas, this includes nitrates from fertilizers that are applied to the soil, as well as pesticides applied to plants. Toxic chemicals from accidental spills, careless disposal, or rotting underground storage containers all can become part of the groundwater. Even salt, used to melt ice on highways in the winter, seeps down into the groundwater with the melting snow and spring rains.

What can be done? In areas where heavy groundwater use has lowered the water table, artificial methods of groundwater recharge are used. A former practice was to pour used water into sewers, where it became part of the runoff. Instead, water is pumped back underground through wells, or it is pumped into ponds and allowed to seep back into the groundwater naturally. Many states now require large commercial users of groundwater to purify and return the water they use.

Groundwater pollution is a more difficult problem. As yet, no simple or inexpensive way to purify polluted groundwater is known. However, further pollution can be reduced or prevented. One way is by restricting the use of pesticides and fertilizers. Another is by disposing of toxic wastes in such a way that they cannot enter the environment.

TOPIC QUESTIONS

Each topic question refers to the topic of the same number.

5. **(a)** What is porosity? **(b)** Identify two factors that determine the porosity of a material.
6. **(a)** What is permeability? **(b)** What is the relationship between permeability and grain size? **(c)** Define impermeable. **(d)** What is capillary water and how is it removed?
7. Locate and describe the **(a)** zone of saturation, **(b)** zone of aeration, **(c)** capillary fringe, and **(d)** water table.
8. **(a)** List some natural factors that cause the depth of the water table to vary. **(b)** How deep is the water table in swamps, lakes, deserts, and farmland?
9. **(a)** Explain what an ordinary well is. **(b)** Where do hillside springs occur?
10. **(a)** Describe the arrangement of rock layers in an artesian formation. **(b)** What is an aquifer?
11. **(a)** What is an artesian well? **(b)** What is a fissure spring?
12. **(a)** Why is the water table dropping steadily in some areas? **(b)** How do pollutants enter groundwater? **(c)** How can groundwater be recharged artificially? **(d)** How can groundwater pollution be reduced or prevented?

Dr. Ruth Patrick
Limnologist

The drinking water of nearly half of the population of the United States comes from groundwater. Because of this, concern over groundwater contamination has been growing. Dr. Ruth Patrick is one of the scientists at the Academy of Natural Sciences in Philadelphia who have been studying the problem. Dr. Patrick learned that there are many sources of groundwater contamination—human wastes are just part of the problem. Manufacturing and agricultural activities can also make groundwater unfit to drink. In some areas radioactivity from rocks containing uranium causes contamination. In others it is arsenic from hot springs. In coastal areas salt water creeps into and contaminates wells that have been overused.

Dr. Patrick points out that "one of the major difficulties in dealing with groundwater contamination is that it occurs underground, out of sight." Cleaning it up is therefore difficult, expensive, and sometimes, impossible. She says that the best solution to groundwater contamination is prevention.

III Groundwater Characteristics

OBJECTIVES

A Explain why groundwater is nearly the same cool temperature all year.

B Discuss the origin of hot springs, including paint pots, geysers, and fumaroles.

C Discuss the origin of minerals in groundwater and list some factors that control the mineral content of groundwater.

Topic 13 Groundwater Is Usually Cool

At a depth of about 20 meters under the surface, soil and rock are protected from weather changes. The temperature at that depth remains at the average yearly temperature of the location all year. In most parts of the United States, the average temperature is between 5°C and 15°C. The water of an ordinary well or spring is close to the same temperature as the ground around it. Therefore, the water is relatively cool in summer and does not freeze in winter. In polar regions, where the average temperature is below freezing, there can be no wells or springs, for the water in the ground is always frozen. This permanently frozen ground, which may be hundreds of meters deep, is called *permafrost.*

Topic 14 Hot Springs, Geysers, and Fumaroles

Below the 20-meter depth, heat from Earth's interior raises underground temperatures at the rate of about 1°C for every 40 meters of depth. Water from deep artesian wells or springs may therefore be much warmer than water from ordinary wells or springs. Fissure springs that originate a thousand meters below the surface may be warm springs or even hot springs, such as those at Warm Springs, Georgia, or Hot Springs, Arkansas.

Groundwater may be hot without coming from great depth. In many regions of recent volcanic activity, igneous rock near the surface is still hot enough to boil water. In such places the groundwater may come to the surface as boiling hot springs. If the hot water comes up through thick, sticky clays, the result is a sputtering spring called a *paint pot,* or mud volcano.

Geysers are boiling hot springs that periodically erupt as gushers of hot water and steam. There are only a few places in the world where geysers occur. The most familiar may be Yellowstone National Park in Wyoming. Old Faithful in Yellowstone is famous for both its height and its frequency. The average time between its eruptions is about 66 minutes, although the time may be as short as 35 minutes or as long as 80 minutes. An eruption lasts several minutes and reaches a height of 45 meters or more.

Why does a geyser erupt violently, instead of simply overflowing as an ordinary hot spring does? The difference seems to be that the ordinary hot spring rises from its source through a wide tube. The geyser's tube, in contrast, has one or more constrictions, such as a partly blocked water pipe, that interfere with the upward flow of heated water. Because of the constriction, the water at the bottom

9.11 This paint pot is a hot spring that reaches the surface through sticky clays formed by weathering.

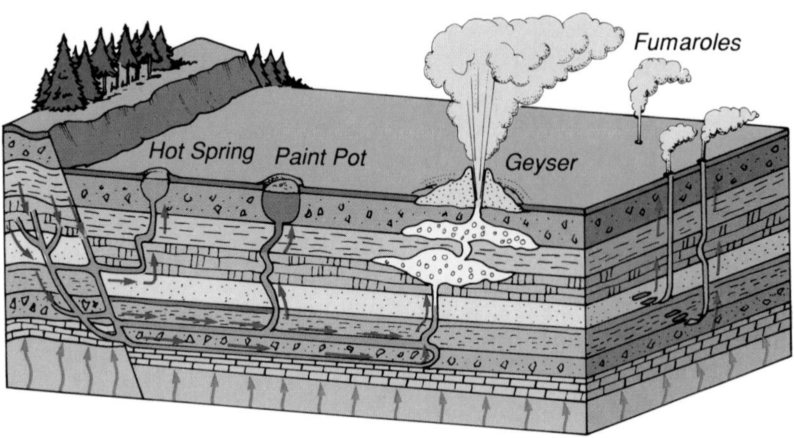

9.12 Heating and pressurization of groundwater causes geothermal phenomena, such as geysers, hot springs, and fumaroles. Red arrows represent heating. Blue arrows represent pathways for groundwater and steam.

of a geyser's tube is under pressure. It becomes superheated to a temperature far above its surface boiling point but does not yet turn into steam because of the pressure. When steam eventually does form, it forces its way up the tube and pushes some of the superheated water up to the surface. The pressure at the bottom of the tube is relieved, and the superheated water explodes into steam. The steam blows out the water above it, and the geyser erupts.

Fumaroles (FEW muh roles) are fissures in the ground from which steam and hot gases escape. They are found in volcanic regions where fairly recent eruptions have occurred. A fumarole field is the source of the geothermal energy at the Geysers in California (Chapter 6, Topic 20). Other commercial fumarole fields are located in Italy, Japan, Iceland, New Zealand, Mexico, and the Soviet Union.

Topic 15 The Minerals in Groundwater

The water in clouds and in rain comes from water that evaporated from Earth's oceans and land. When water evaporates, it leaves impurities behind. Therefore, rainwater contains almost no dissolved mineral matter, although it may contain dissolved gases and liquids. When rainwater seeps into the ground, however, the situation changes. As groundwater passes through the lower soil layers or bedrock, it dissolves minerals. Much of the dissolved mineral matter remains in the groundwater. The kind of rock through which water passes, the distance the water travels underground, and the water temperature all affect the kind and amount of mineral matter dissolved in groundwater.

Hard water contains a substantial amount of ions that were dissolved from mineral matter. The ions are usually calcium, magnesium, or iron. Of these ions, calcium (from calcite) is the most common cause of water hardness. The dissolved minerals in hard water interfere greatly with its use. In laundering, these minerals react with soap to form scum instead of suds. In boiler tubes and hot-water pipes, dissolved minerals form deposits called boiler scale.

Artesian water is usually harder than ordinary groundwater. Artesian water travels farther and may be warmer, so it can dissolve more mineral matter than ordinary groundwater. By contrast, ordinary groundwater is almost always harder than river water. Because limestone is largely calcite, almost all the water is hard in regions that have limestone bedrock.

Topic 16 Mineral Springs

A spring containing so much dissolved mineral matter that it cannot be used for ordinary drinking or washing purposes is called a *mineral spring.* The high mineral content of the water may be due to any of the following factors:

1. The water passes through very soluble rock (such as the salt beds in Michigan).
2. The water contains large quantities of gases that form acids when mixed with water, such as carbon dioxide (Saratoga Springs, New York) or hydrogen sulfide (White Sulphur Springs, West Virginia).
3. The water is very hot (Hot Springs, Arkansas). Minerals dissolve better in hot water than in cold water. Therefore, water from hot springs usually has a high mineral content. When the hot water cools at the surface, some of the mineral matter is deposited around the spring. Such deposits are discussed in Topic 19.

Many mineral spring areas have become health resorts. In desert regions, however, alkali (bitter) mineral springs may be poisonous. In southwestern United States, for example, alkali springs may carry borax, sodium carbonate, and sodium sulfate in solution.

TOPIC QUESTIONS

Each topic question refers to the topic of the same number.

13. **(a)** Why do spring water and well water stay cool in summer? **(b)** Why doesn't well water freeze in winter months? **(c)** What is permafrost?

14. **(a)** Why is the water of very deep artesian wells warmer than ordinary well water? **(b)** Explain the heat source of boiling hot springs and geysers. **(c)** What is a paint pot? **(d)** What causes a geyser? **(e)** What is a fumarole?

15. **(a)** What factors determine the amount and kind of mineral matter dissolved in groundwater? **(b)** What is hard water? **(c)** Compare the hardness of water in ordinary wells, artesian wells, and rivers. **(d)** Why is all the water hard in a limestone region?

16. What three factors cause a high mineral content in a mineral spring?

OBJECTIVES

A Describe the formation of several features that result from erosion by groundwater.

B Identify karst topography by its characteristic features.

C List materials that are deposited by groundwater; discuss the role of groundwater in cementing rocks.

IV Caverns and Mineral Deposits

Topic 17 How Caverns Form

Limestone is not a porous rock. However, limestone formations are frequently split, both by fissures that run down from the surface and by cracks that run horizontally between the beds. Groundwater always contains some carbonic acid. Carbonic acid forms when carbon dioxide gas in the air dissolves in falling rainwater. As groundwater flows through cracks and fissures in limestone, carbonic acid slowly dissolves the limestone and carries the ions away in solution.

After thousands of years, the vertical fissures may be enlarged into circular surface openings. During the same time, the cracks between the beds become networks of underground tunnels, sometimes many kilometers long and hundreds of meters high. The surface openings are called *sinkholes,* or sinks. The tunnels are *caverns,* or caves. Sinkholes also form when parts of the cave roof falls in. Water in sinkholes below the water table forms sinkhole ponds or lakes.

A natural bridge may be formed when a surface river disappears into a fissure in the bedrock, runs underground a short distance, and then gushes out a crack on the face of a cliff. As the fissure and the crack are enlarged, part of the cliff is left as a natural bridge.

Limestone is a common surface or near-surface bedrock, and it dissolves more easily than other types of rock. As a result, limestone caverns are found in many parts of the world. Some of the best-known caverns in the United States are Carlsbad Caverns in New Mexico, Mammoth Cave in Kentucky, Luray Caverns in Virginia, Howe Caverns in New York, Oregon Caves in Oregon, and Wind Cave in South Dakota.

9.13 This pond occupies a sinkhole in a limestone region.

Topic 18 Karst Topography

In regions of caverns, most rainwater enters the ground through sinkholes and fissures. Thus there are very few surface rivers. Lost rivers are formed when surface streams disappear underground and flow out of caves many kilometers away. Regions characterized by sinks, sinkhole ponds, lost rivers, and underground drainage are said to have *karst topography.* This name comes from the Kars Plateau region of Yugoslavia. Karst topography forms in areas with bedrock made of calcite, dolomite, or other minerals that dissolve easily. The Mammoth Cave region of Kentucky has karst topography. Other karst regions in the United States are found in Florida, Tennessee, and Indiana.

Topic 19 Mineral Deposits by Groundwater

The minerals dissolved in groundwater are deposited in a variety of ways. Where groundwater drips from the roof of a limestone cave, it slowly deposits some of the calcite. Deposits shaped like icicles hang from the roof along the routes of the dripping water. These slender calcite formations are *stalactites.* On the floor beneath the stalactites, blunt, rounded masses called *stalagmites* are formed. When stalactites and stalagmites meet, columns, or pillars, are made. Stalactites, stalagmites, and pillars are all examples of *dripstone.* Dripstone is a calcite deposit formed from dripping water in caverns. Dripstone can form only when a cave is above the water table, where water can evaporate.

Calcite deposits around mineral springs are called *travertine* (TRAV er teen). Among the most famous travertine deposits are the delicately colored terraces around Mammoth Hot Springs in Yellowstone National Park. Here the hot water pours out of long hillside fissures in limestone bedrock, depositing some of its dissolved calcite as it cools. Algae grow on the moist terraces, producing a variety of beautiful colors.

9.14 The travertine covering these terraces was deposited when mineral-rich hot spring water evaporated.

Around the openings of geysers, a white porous substance called *geyserite* is deposited. Geyserite is silica dissolved from the hot igneous rock through which the geyser waters pass on their way to the surface. Hot groundwater often leaves deposits of minerals in bedrock cracks and fissures. Such mineral veins may contain quartz, calcite, gold, and silver.

Petrified wood is formed when minerals dissolved in groundwater replace the decaying wood of buried trees. As each microscopic particle of wood is replaced by a grain of mineral matter, many details of the wood structure are reproduced. The petrified trees of Arizona, which formed in this way, consist of silica.

Perhaps the most important groundwater deposit is the cement that binds together the sand grains and pebbles of sedimentary deposits to form rocks. While calcite is the most common cementing mineral, silica and iron oxides also serve as natural cements.

TOPIC QUESTIONS

Each topic question refers to the topic of the same number.

17. **(a)** Explain how groundwater forms sinkholes, caverns, natural bridges, and sinkhole ponds. **(b)** Why are limestone caves common?

18. Describe karst topography and give examples.

19. **(a)** Explain how stalactites and stalagmites are formed. **(b)** What is dripstone? **(c)** Explain the origin of travertine, geyserite, and petrified wood.

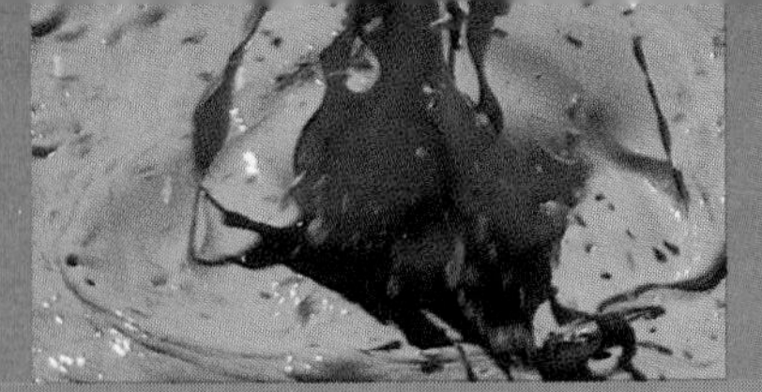

CHAPTER 9 REVIEW

Summary

Less than three percent of Earth's water is fresh, and over half of that is frozen. Most usable fresh water is underground.

The hydrosphere includes all of Earth's waters. The movement of water within the hydrosphere is described by the water cycle.

A water budget relates the recharge, surplus, usage, and deficit of soil water to the moisture needs and moisture supply of an area.

Porosity is the percent of a material that is pore space. Permeability is the rate at which a liquid passes through a porous material.

The water table is the top of the water-saturated region of the ground. The depth of the water table depends on climate, season, and location.

Groundwater can be obtained from natural springs or by making a well that reaches below the water table.

Several methods are used to recharge groundwater. Groundwater pollution can be prevented but it is difficult to clean up.

Groundwater has nearly the same cool temperature all year. However, in areas of volcanism, groundwater may be very hot and hot springs may result.

Bedrock type, dissolved gases, and water temperature affect the kind and amount of mineral matter in groundwater.

Carbonic acid in groundwater dissolves limestone, forming features of karst topography.

Stalactites, stalagmites, travertine, geyserite, petrified wood, and the cement that binds sedimentary rocks are all groundwater deposits.

Vocabulary

aquifer	porosity	surplus
artesian formation	recharge	usage
deficit	hydrosphere	water budget
evapotranspiration	impermeable	water cycle
geysers	permeability	water table

Review

Number your paper from *1* to *15*. Write the letter of your answer on your paper.

1. Where is most usable fresh water located? (a) oceans (b) glaciers (c) lakes and rivers (d) underground
2. What is the source of energy for the water cycle? (a) solar energy (b) gravity (c) running water (d) ocean tides
3. Rainfall is greater than moisture need, and the soil is saturated. Which will occur? (a) deficit (b) recharge (c) surplus (d) usage
4. Which is the most likely description for a material with high porosity? (a) well-sorted, round grains (b) well-sorted, angular grains (c) unsorted, round grains (d) unsorted, angular grains
5. The rate at which liquids pass through a material is called (a) porosity, (b) permeability, (c) capillarity, (d) rate of recharge.
6. The water table is between (a) zone of aeration and capillary fringe, (b) soil water and capillary fringe, (c) capillary fringe and zone of saturation, (d) capillary fringe and bedrock.
7. A hillside spring occurs in places where the ground surface meets with the (a) zone of aeration, (b) capillary fringe, (c) water table, (d) bedrock.
8. Water often rises on its own in an artesian well because it is (a) under an impermeable layer, (b) under a permeable layer, (c) in a pipe, (d) under pressure.
9. Which is most likely to cause the water table to drop? (a) salt water seeping into wells (b) rainwater seeping into the ground (c) pumping water from the ground (d) pumping used water into the ground
10. The temperature of ordinary well or spring water is usually (a) warm all year, (b) warm in summer and cool in winter, (c) cool in summer and warm in winter, (d) cool all year.

11. Hot water bubbling up through thick, sticky clay may cause a (a) paint pot, (b) artesian spring, (c) fumarole, (d) sinkhole.
12. Which would probably contain the most dissolved minerals? (a) artesian spring water (b) hillside spring water (c) ordinary well water (d) river water
13. Which does NOT usually affect the mineral content of a spring? (a) acid-forming gases (b) bedrock solubility (c) water temperature (d) local surface temperature
14. Caverns, sinkholes, and other features of karst topography form best in areas where the bedrock is (a) granite, (b) shale, (c) limestone, (d) sandstone.
15. Stalactites, stalagmites, and pillars are most likely to form in (a) artesian formations, (b) limestone caves, (c) hillside springs, (d) area of impermeable bedrock.

Interpret and Apply

On your paper, answer each question in complete sentences.

1. In cold climates less water enters the ground during winter than in any other season. Why?
2. Compare the porosity and permeability of well-sorted sand with a mixture of sand and silt.
3. What is likely to happen to the distance between the ground surface and the water table if rainfall increases but evapotranspiration is unchanged?
4. How is a hillside spring different from a fissure spring?
5. In what ways is the water from a well 10 meters deep likely to be different from the water from a well 1000 meters deep?
6. Why does dripstone form only when a cave is above the water table?
7. In some regions, petrified wood is composed of silica. In other regions, it is composed of calcite. Why?

Critical Thinking

The graph shows a water budget for Springfield, Illinois, an area that has four seasons. Use the graph to answer questions 1–4.

1. If moisture need increases with air temperature, what is the warmest month?
2. What is the value for moisture need in January? Why?
3. Which months have the most rainfall?
4. In which month does the water storage finish refilling?

Compare the graph for Springfield with the three graphs in Figures 9.4 and 9.5 and answer questions 5–6.

5. Identify one way in which all four locations are alike.
6. Based on moisture need, how do summer and winter temperatures in Springfield compare with those in Little Rock?

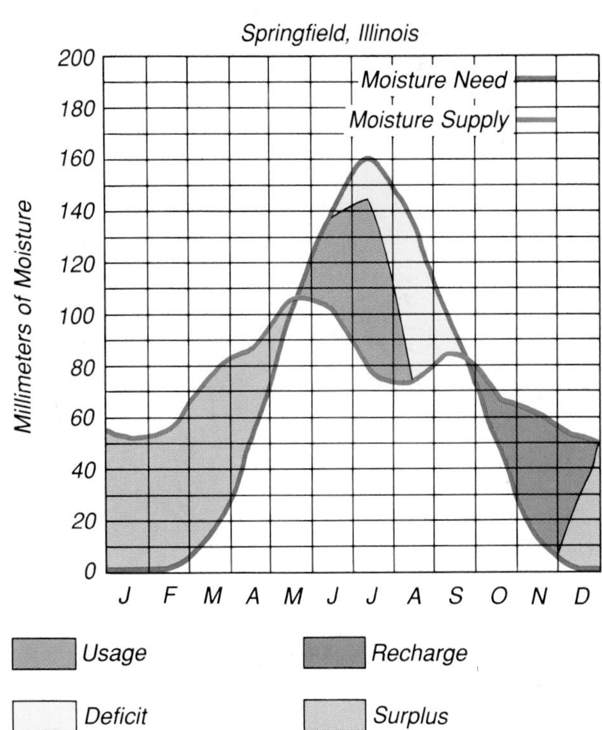

CHAPTER

10 Running Water

▲ Running water is a powerful agent of erosion.

How Do You Know That . . .

Solid sediment can be moved by running water? Pour enough clay into a tall, clear container to form a layer two or three centimeters deep. Cover this layer with the same depth of sand and then with two or three centimeters of coarse gravel or marble chips. Cover all the layers with about 15 centimeters of water. With a spoon, mix the sediment together until the layers have completely disappeared. Stop stirring and observe the order and arrangement of the sediments as they settle. Which materials settle first? Which settle last? Why?

I Stream Erosion and Transportation

OBJECTIVES

A Explain how running water gets its energy from the sun.

B Describe three ways in which running water breaks up bedrock.

C Describe the three ways running water transports rock material.

D Discuss the relationship between stream speed, discharge, and carrying power.

Topic 1 Running Water and Its Energy

Of all the agents of erosion, running water is the most effective in wearing down the surface of Earth. Running water includes all the water that falls on Earth as rain, snow, or other precipitation and then moves downhill under the pull of gravity. It begins with drops of water moving down hillsides. Running water comes together until it forms great rivers such as the Mississippi and the Amazon.

Like the other agents of erosion, running water gets its energy from the sun. The sun lifts water from the oceans by evaporation. Winds created by the sun's heating of the atmosphere carry the water vapor over the continents. When the water falls as rain or snow and runs back to the sea, it is using the sun's energy to erode the lands.

Topic 2 Running Water Attacks Bedrock

Like all agents of erosion, running water wears down the land in two ways. It breaks up bedrock and removes weathered and eroded rock and soil materials.

Running water breaks up the bedrock over which it flows primarily by mechanical means. Using sand, pebbles, and even boulders as its cutting tools, running water grinds and hammers away at its bed. The grinding action is called **abrasion.** Abrasion also causes the cutting tools themselves to be worn down, especially at their edges. In time, abrasion produces the rounded boulders, pebbles, and sand grains that are commonly found in the beds of streams and rivers.

Cutting tools are very important for stream erosion. However, even clear water can break up the rock of a streambed if it runs fast enough. Rapidly flowing water has a lifting effect that splits off and moves rock fragments.

Running water's chemical attack on bedrock consists of dissolving soluble minerals. Limestone, marble, and sandstone that is held together with lime cements are affected in this way. Rivers flowing over such rocks form pits and holes in the riverbed, and widen existing cracks and holes.

Topic 3 Water Removes Weathered Rock

When rain runs down even the gentlest of slopes, it carries some weathered rock material with it. Eventually this material reaches a larger and more permanent body of running water such as a tiny brook. The brook is probably part of some river system. The sediment carried by the brook finds its way through larger and larger streams until it reaches the main stream. Once in the main stream, the water may be carried to a lake. Eventually the water is carried to the ocean.

Rivers carry rock material in three ways. Some mineral matter is carried in **solution.** This is material that has dissolved from bedrock. Most of the solution load comes to the river from the groundwater that constantly seeps into streams. The most common minerals carried in solution are compounds of calcium and magnesium, especially in limestone regions.

When river water looks muddy, it is carrying rock material in **suspension.** Suspended material includes clay, silt, and fine sand. Although these materials are heavier than water, they are stirred up and kept from sinking by the turbulence of stream flow. Turbulence includes swirls and eddies that form in water from friction between the stream and its bed and banks. The faster the stream flows, the more turbulent and muddy it becomes. A rough bed also increases turbulence. (See Figure 10.1.)

Sand, pebbles, and boulders that are too heavy to be carried in suspension may be carried as **bed load,** especially during floods. Boulders and pebbles roll or slide on the riverbed. Large sand grains are pushed along in jumps and bounces.

Geologists estimate that the rivers of the United States carry about 25 percent of their load in solution, about 50 percent in suspension, and about 25 percent as bed load. In general, the suspended load increases with human use of the land. On the other hand, streams flowing from undisturbed areas may have only 25 percent of the load in suspension but 75 percent in solution.

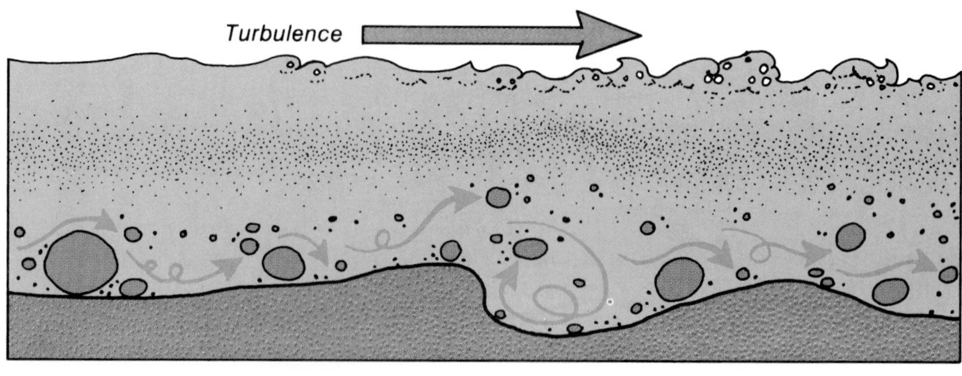

10.1 This diagram shows the rock materials carried by a stream, the name of the carrying process, and the level at which each material is normally found.

Topic 4 Carrying Power and Load

The **carrying power** of a stream is indicated by both the total amount of sediment in the stream and by the size of the particles being moved by the stream. The carrying power depends upon the speed of the stream and its discharge. Stream **discharge** is the volume of water flowing past a given point in the stream at a given time. Discharge is usually expressed in cubic meters per second or cubic feet per second. Streams moving at high speed with high discharge can carry both a large amount of sediment and larger sizes of sediment particles than slow-moving streams with small discharge. Thus, the carrying power of a stream increases as the speed and discharge of the stream increases.

The speed of a stream depends mainly upon the steepness, or gradient, of its bed. Speed also increases with increased discharge. During floods the discharge of a river increases tremendously, and its carrying power may be hundreds of times as great. For this reason much of the erosion caused by moving water occurs during floods. If all the sediment is removed from the bed during a flood, the river can erode deeper into its bedrock.

When the speed of a river doubles, the ability of the stream to carry larger particles in suspension more than doubles. At normal times the lower Mississippi River may carry nothing larger than silt in suspension. During a flood, the river may tear out bridges.

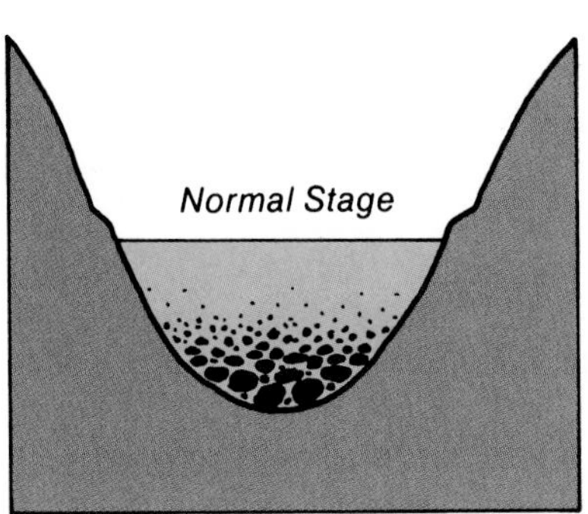

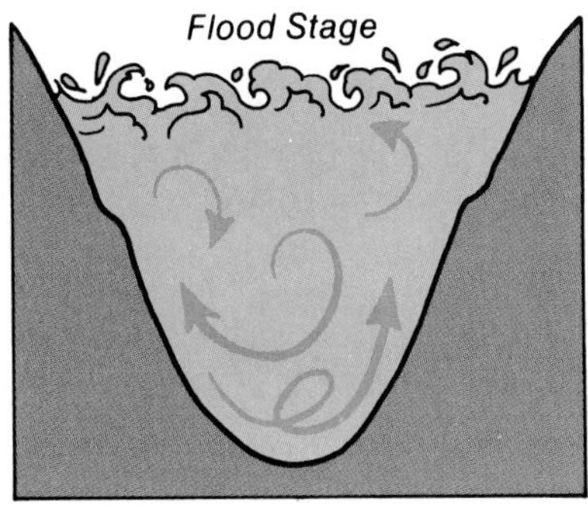

10.2 When a river is at flood stage, it flows much faster than normal. It picks up the sediments from the bottom and scours the rock of the riverbed.

TOPIC QUESTIONS

Each topic question refers to the topic of the same number.

1. **(a)** Define *running water.* **(b)** How does running water get its energy from the sun?
2. How does running water break up bedrock?
3. List the three ways rivers carry materials and the most common materials carried by each.
4. **(a)** What two factors indicate the carrying power of a stream? **(b)** What affects the carrying power of a stream? **(c)** What is a stream's discharge? **(d)** Why does erosion of a riverbed increase so much during flood times?

OBJECTIVES

A Explain how rivers form V-shaped valleys and canyons.

B Describe what occurs as a river approaches its base level.

C Define *headward erosion* and identify some features that result from headward erosion.

D Define *stream divide* and *drainage basin* and locate these features for a river system.

II The River Valley

Topic 5 V-Shaped Valleys and Canyons

The streams of mountain regions and high plateaus are likely to have formed relatively recently. Such young, or youthful, streams typically have V-shaped valleys. This shape occurs because youthful streams tend to flow at high speeds, which easily scour the streambed. At the same time, the upper valley walls are widened by weathering and erosion.

Valleys with very steep, almost vertical sides are features of scenic interest. Steep valleys are called canyons, gorges, or chasms. The Grand Canyon of the Colorado River, Royal Gorge of the Arkansas River in Colorado, and Ausable Chasm in New York State are examples.

How long does it take a river to make a canyon? The time depends upon the kind of rock the river must erode, the amount of water and sediment in the river, the climate of the area, as well as several other factors. The Colorado River is thought to have taken millions of years to cut the mile-deep canyon into the rocks of the Colorado Plateau. Other rivers in wetter climates may take less time to cut canyons in softer rock.

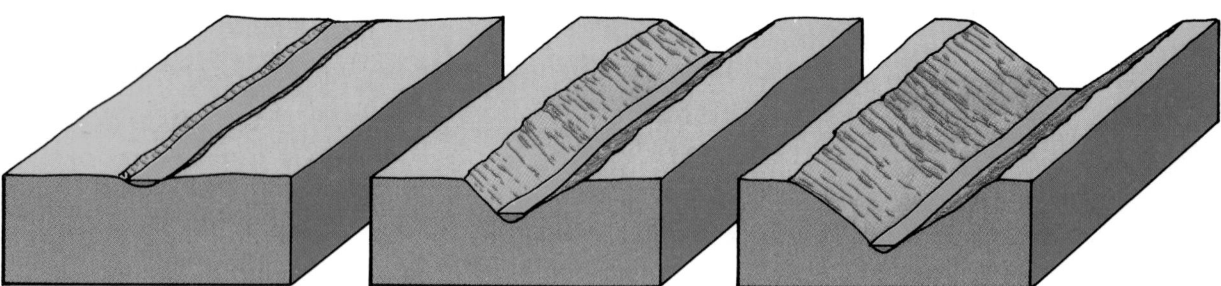

10.3 Young river valleys are V-shaped because while the river is cutting into the valley floor, the valley walls are being worn back by weathering and tributary streams.

Topic 6 Base Level: Widening the Valley

A stream cannot cut its bed any lower than the level of the stream, river, or body of water into which it flows. The level is called the **base level** of the stream. For streams that flow into an ocean, the base level is sea level. For streams that flow into lakes or rivers, the base level is the level of the lake or river.

As a stream approaches its base level, the slope of the streambed and the speed of the stream decrease. As a result, the stream cuts into its bed much more slowly. Meanwhile, the valley walls continue to be attacked by weathering, erosion, tributary streams, and the river itself. (See Topic 13.) The result is a wider valley with a broad floor and gentle sloping walls.

10.4 (a) This young river flows fast. Its valley floor is wearing down much faster than its sides. **(b)** This is also a fast-flowing river, but in this valley the walls are also eroding. This V-shaped valley is noticeably different from the nearly vertical walls in (a).

Topic 7 **Lengthening the Valley**

When a hillside is stripped of its trees and shrubs, it loses its protective covering. A single heavy rain may form a miniature stream valley. This valley is likely to be V-shaped and to have tributaries running into it. When the rain ends, the stream may disappear, but the small valley remains. Such a feature is called a **gully.**

Gullies grow in length, width, and depth every time it rains. The term **headward erosion** means the wearing away of land at the head of the gully or stream valley. Headward erosion makes the gully longer.

As a gully grows in length and depth, the stream may cut below the water table. When this occurs, the stream becomes a permanent stream. When the tributary gullies also cut below the water table, a river system is born. Most of the world's river systems probably began in this way.

Even in deserts, water is the main agent of erosion. Desert cloudbursts cause many small streams to flow temporarily. In dry regions of soft clay beds, these temporary streams form many small gullies with steep slopes. Early explorers found some of these badly-eroded regions so difficult to travel through that they called them badlands. Among the best-known badlands in the United States are those in South Dakota, North Dakota, and Nebraska.

a

b

10.5 (a) Headward erosion will cause this gully to become deeper and larger. **(b)** The Badlands National Monument contains a giant maze of gullies.

Topic 8 Divides and Drainage Basins

The high land that separates one gully from the next, or one river valley from the next, is called a **divide.** The major divide of the United States, called the Great Continental Divide, is located in the Rocky Mountains. Rain falling east of the Great Continental Divide eventually flows into the Atlantic Ocean. Rain falling west of the Great Continental Divide flows into the Pacific Ocean.

A river and all of its tributaries is called a river system. The **drainage basin,** or **watershed,** of a river includes all of the land that drains into the river, either directly or through its tributaries.

The largest single drainage basin in the United States is the Mississippi River system. Its western divide is the Great Continental Divide in the Rocky Mountains. Its eastern divide is a lesser continental divide in the Appalachian Mountains. To the north in Wisconsin and Minnesota, a low divide separates the Mississippi system from land sloping toward the Great Lakes and the Arctic Ocean. Within these three divides lies two fifths of the area of the United States (excluding Alaska and Hawaii).

10.6 Each river has its own drainage basin that is separated from the next basin by a high ridge called a divide. A river system often has tributaries from different sources.

Topic 9 **Stream Piracy**

Stream piracy, or *stream capture,* is an interesting result of the lengthening of a river by headward erosion. In Figure 10.7, two rivers are separated by a divide. As headward erosion continues, the headwaters of river *A* wear through the divide and capture the headwaters of river *B*. River *A* has grown larger and extended its drainage basin at the expense of its neighbor, river *B*.

Does stream piracy occur often? Geologists think that stream piracy has been an important factor in the early growth of many great river systems.

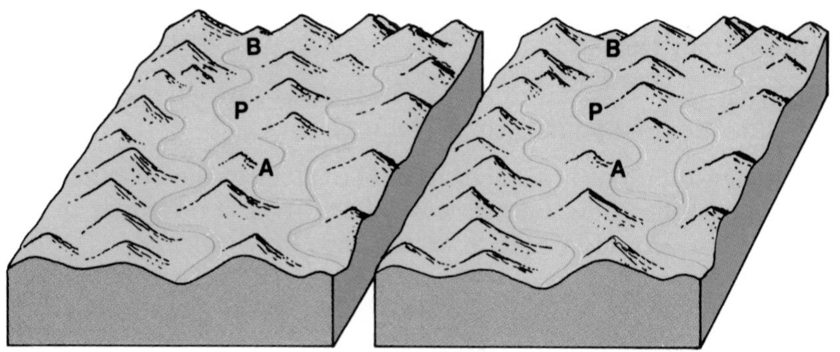

10.7 Stream piracy is illustrated as stream A extends its source by headward erosion until it captures stream B at point P.

10.8 The Delaware Water Gap

Topic 10 Water Gaps and Wind Gaps

As a river cuts into its valley, it may meet an unusually resistant rock formation. As time passes, this rock formation will wear away more slowly than the surrounding rock. A narrow cut called a **water gap** forms in the ridge through which the river runs. An example is the gap in the Delaware River through the Kittatinny Mountain ridge in New Jersey and Pennsylvania.

Occasionally a gap occurs without any river in it. This abandoned water gap is a *wind gap.* These features may have formed when the water of the gap was captured by a neighboring river.

TOPIC QUESTIONS

Each topic question refers to the topic of the same number.

5. **(a)** Why does a youthful river have a V-shaped valley? **(b)** What is a canyon? Give some examples. **(c)** What factors determine the time needed for a river to form a canyon?
6. **(a)** What is a river's base level? **(b)** Describe the changes in a stream as it approaches its base level.
7. **(a)** What is a gully? **(b)** How are gullies related to rivers?
8. **(a)** What is a divide? **(b)** What is a drainage basin?
9. What is stream piracy and how does it occur?
10. **(a)** What is a water gap? How does it form? **(b)** What is a wind gap? How is it thought to form?

Map Skills

Questions 1–3 refer to Topographic Map: Harrisburg, PA, which appears on page 584.

1. What is the general direction, or trend, in which the ridges of Blue Mountain and Second Mountain lie?
2. Blue Mountain ridges appear on both sides of the Susquehanna River. What ridge on the west of the river corresponds to the ridge of Second Mountain east of the river?
3. How does the direction of flow of the Susquehanna River compare to the trend of these ridges?

III Waterfalls and River Deposits

OBJECTIVES

A Explain the formation of potholes and plunge pools.

B Describe some ways in which a waterfall may occur.

C List some factors that cause streams to deposit their loads.

D Explain the origin of flood plains, meanders, cutoffs, oxbow lakes, entrenched meanders, deltas, and alluvial fans.

Topic 11 Potholes and Plunge Pools

A stream running over an irregular bed develops small whirlpools in many places. As sand, pebbles, and small boulders swirl around in the whirlpools, they grind deep oval or circular holes. These basins are called **potholes.** The particles responsible for forming a pothole are often found at its bottom.

Potholes occur in any kind of rock. For example, potholes in the James River at Richmond, Virginia, have been ground out of hard granite. Potholes also come in all sizes. Most of the James River potholes are less than 1 meter deep. Some potholes in the Mohawk River valley near Little Falls, New York, are over 3 meters deep. Very large potholes are called *plunge pools.* Such potholes are commonly found at the bases of waterfalls. An example occurs at the base of Niagara Falls.

10.9 Potholes are small oval or circular basins ground out of a rocky streambed by whirlpool action.

Topic 12 Waterfalls and Their Recession

Streams running through steep mountain regions flow over ever-changing slopes. The riverbed may be steep enough to form white water rapids. It may level out into a lake or pond, or the stream may plunge over a cliff to form a waterfall.

The steep slopes and cliffs of rapids and waterfalls occur for many reasons. The Great Falls of the Potomac occur where the Potomac River flows over hard igneous rocks onto soft sedimentary rocks. The falls in Yosemite Valley in California were formed when

10.10 Niagara Falls carries all the water flowing out of the Great Lakes from Lake Erie to Lake Ontario.

10.11 Whirlpool action at Niagara Falls rapidly erodes the weak shales at the base of the falls. This erosion undermines the tough limestone layer at the top. From time to time the limestone breaks off, and the waterfall recedes.

glaciers eroded one valley more deeply than others. The two great falls on the Yellowstone River in Yellowstone National Park are the result of intrusions of igneous rock. Other rapids and waterfalls occur for many other reasons.

Rapids and waterfalls are temporary features of streams because these are locations where stream erosion is greatest. One way in which streams erode at waterfalls is by *undermining.* The water falling into the plunge pool at the base of the waterfall erodes the rock there, leaving the rocks at the top of the falls to overhang (Figure 10.11). From time to time, pieces break off the top. Each time this breakage occurs, the waterfall recedes farther upstream. The rate of undermining and recession is fastest when the rocks contain fractures or are poorly cemented.

A famous example of a waterfall that recedes by undermining is Niagara Falls. Here the falls are the result of a nearly flat-lying, 20-meter-thick layer of tough dolostone. The rocks underneath the dolostone are almost all thin beds of shale. The rapidly eroding shale undermines the dolostone. The base of the waterfall is littered with huge blocks of fallen dolostone.

The Niagara Gorge marks the path of recession of Niagara Falls. The gorge extends from the base of the falls to Lake Ontario, a distance of about 11 kilometers. At the end of the Ice Age 11 000 years ago, Niagara Falls was located on or near Lake Ontario. The recession of the falls since that time carved the gorge.

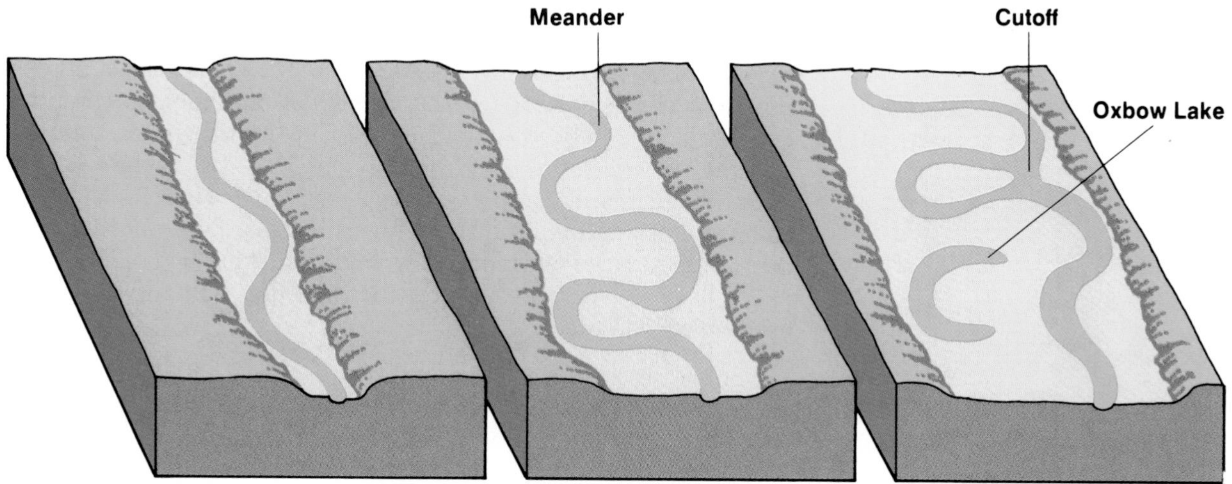

10.12 Meanders are formed as a riverbed gradually shifts toward the outside of a bend in the river.

Topic 13 Meanders and Oxbow Lakes

In times of heavy rains, a river may overflow its banks and cover part of the valley floor. This part of the valley floor is the **flood plain.** At first the flood plain is narrow, but as time passes it becomes wider. Why? As a river cuts its bed lower and lower, its slope and speed decreases. The river is more easily deflected sideward, and its course becomes more winding. The banks and valley walls are eroded, and the valley floor is widened.

When a river swings around a bend, the fastest-moving water is on the outside of the bend. Erosion is most rapid there. The water is shallowest on the inside of the bend. Sediment is often deposited there. In time, the riverbed is shifted toward the outside of its bend. If one bend shifts to the right, the next bend shifts to the left. As this pattern continues, the river eventually forms a series of broad curves across a wide flood plain. The broad curves are called **meanders** (mee AN ders).

10.13 This aerial view of the Yukon River shows a meandering river with an oxbow in the upper right corner.

There is a limit to how large a meander can become. As it swings wider and wider, the curve becomes a loop that the river breaks through. The breakthrough is called a *cutoff.* Then the river drops mud and silt at the ends of the abandoned meander. In time the deposits completely separate the meander from the river, forming an **oxbow lake.**

Entrenched meanders are deep canyons with meandering courses that are found on some high plateaus. Entrenched meanders are thought to have formed when the surrounding plateau was raised high above sea level after the meanders had already developed on a flood plain.

Topic 14 **Why Rivers Deposit Sediment**

A river may deposit a part of its load of sediment with each decrease in either speed or discharge.

A river's speed decreases when its slope decreases, its bed widens, or it meets an obstruction in the form of a curving bank or a rock outcrop. However, the greatest loss of speed occurs when the river empties into a sea or a lake. At this point all its remaining sediment is deposited.

A river's discharge may decrease if it passes through an arid region where it loses water by evaporation into the air and seepage into the ground. (In humid regions, rivers usually grow larger as they approach a sea and acquire new tributaries.) Discharge may also decrease when people divert water for farmland irrigation or city water supplies.

10.14 **(a)** Three stages in the growth of a river delta **(b)** *Landsat* image of the Mississippi River delta

a

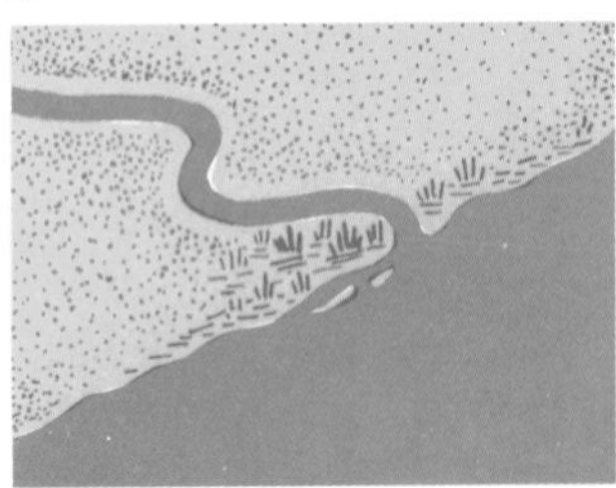

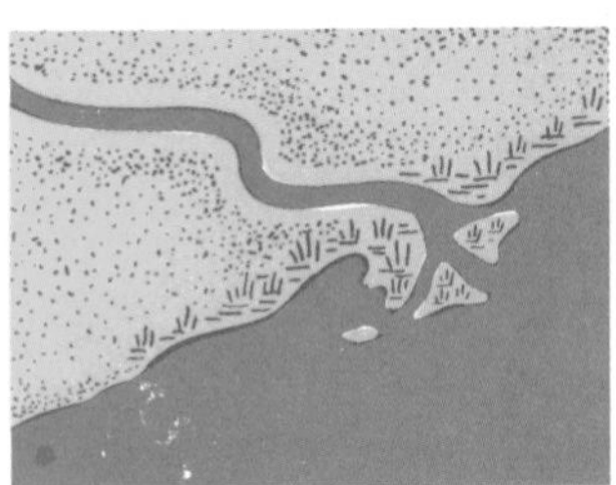

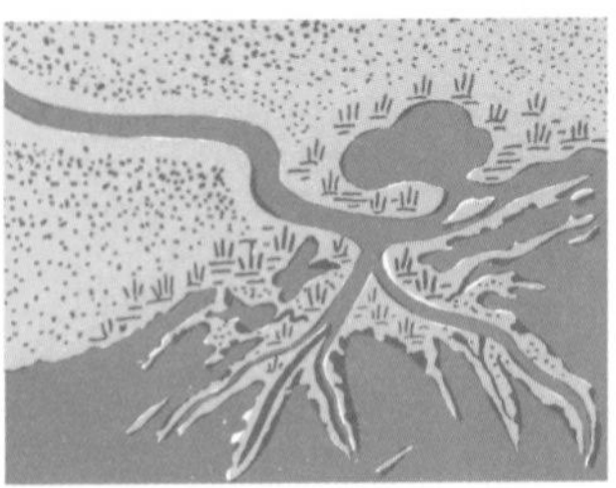

b

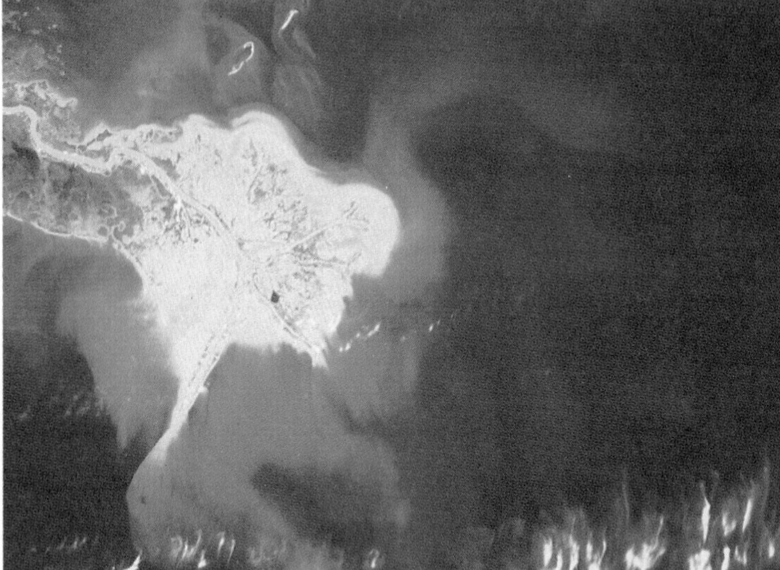

Why does a river leave so much sediment on its valley floor after a flood? As the flooding waters subside, the river's ability to hold its sediment is greatly diminished by losses in both discharge and speed.

Topic 15 Deltas and Alluvial Fans

The Mississippi, the Nile, and other great rivers have level, fan-shaped deposits at their mouths. These deposits are called **deltas.** Deltas form when the river flows into a quiet body of water, such as a lake, a gulf, or an inland sea. The river water comes almost to a standstill. Most of its sediment drops at the river's mouth. The river is split into channels by its own deposits and drops more sediment. As the deposit grows in size, it may resemble the shape of the Greek letter Δ (delta). A river flowing over its delta splits into branches called distributaries. Rivers that flow into an open ocean rarely form deltas because strong waves and currents usually carry the sediment away as fast as the river delivers it.

In dry regions, a steep mountain stream may meet dry, level land at the base of the mountain, rather than a lake. When it reaches the land, it slows down greatly. As a result, the stream drops a large part of its sediment load, and a fan-shaped deposit forms. This deposit differs from a delta in several ways. For one, the deposit is formed on land, not in water. Second, the sediments of these deposits are coarse sands and gravels, rather than the fine silts and clays of deltas. Also, their surface is sloping, not flat like a delta. These sloping deposits are called **alluvial fans.** Alluvial fans are most common in desert or semidesert regions. In the United States many of these formations occur at the foot of the Rocky Mountains and the Sierra Nevadas.

10.15 This alluvial fan formed as sediments were washed down from the slopes above.

TOPIC QUESTIONS

Each topic question refers to the topic of the same number.

11. **(a)** How do potholes form? **(b)** What is a plunge pool?
12. **(a)** What are the conditions that led to the formation of the Great Falls of the Potomac, the falls of Yosemite Valley, and the falls of the Yellowstone River? **(b)** How does the action in plunge pools make Niagara Falls recede?
13. **(a)** What is a flood plain? **(b)** How does a meander develop? **(c)** How does an oxbow lake form? **(d)** How do geologists think entrenched meanders form?
14. Name some factors that can cause a river's speed and discharge to decrease, leading to deposition.
15. **(a)** Explain how a delta forms. **(b)** Which rivers do not form deltas? Why? **(c)** How is an alluvial fan formed? **(d)** How does an alluvial fan differ from a delta?

Saundra Duncan
Water Quality Chemist

The water quality of streams and rivers is a growing concern in many areas of the United States. In an effort to determine the present quality of the nation's running water, the U.S. Geological Survey regularly samples and tests streams throughout the country. Saundra Duncan is a chemist at the Denver Central Laboratory, where water samples collected west of the Mississippi River are sent for testing. She says that the samples are tested for many different substances. These include metals such as sodium, potassium, calcium, and aluminum, and ions such as chloride, bicarbonate, sulfate, and bromide. Tests are also made for dangerous pollutants such as PCB's, dioxane, DDT, and benzene.

Ms. Duncan points out that the function of her lab is not to oversee the cleanup of problem streams but to try to define the conditions as they now exist. Once that is done, her lab may then try to predict what effect additional industries or people will have on the water quality of the watershed tested.

IV The Flood Plain and Floods

OBJECTIVES

A Describe the origin of levees and back swamps.

B Describe the conditions that lead to normal flooding and conditions that lead to flash flooding.

C Discuss the formation of natural dams.

D Describe methods used to prevent floods.

Topic 16 Sediment on the Flood Plain

During floods, great rivers like the Mississippi River carry large amounts of sediment. When such a river overflows onto its flood plain, the speed of the river slows and its sediment load is immediately deposited. Thick deposits build up alongside the stream banks. These deposits form elevated ridges called natural **levees.**

Beyond the levees the flood plain is lower, and the sediments are a finer texture. The flood plain slopes away from the river, and swamps, called *back swamps,* may form in the lowest areas. New tributaries may also form and flow through the back swamps. Some may flow for many kilometers parallel to the main stream before breaking through the levee to join the main stream.

Flood plains are among the most fertile agricultural areas in the world. The fertility of a flood plain is due partly to the minerals and soil nutrients that each flood deposits on the valley floor. Flood plains in arid regions, such as that of the Nile River in Egypt, were of great importance in the development of early civilization.

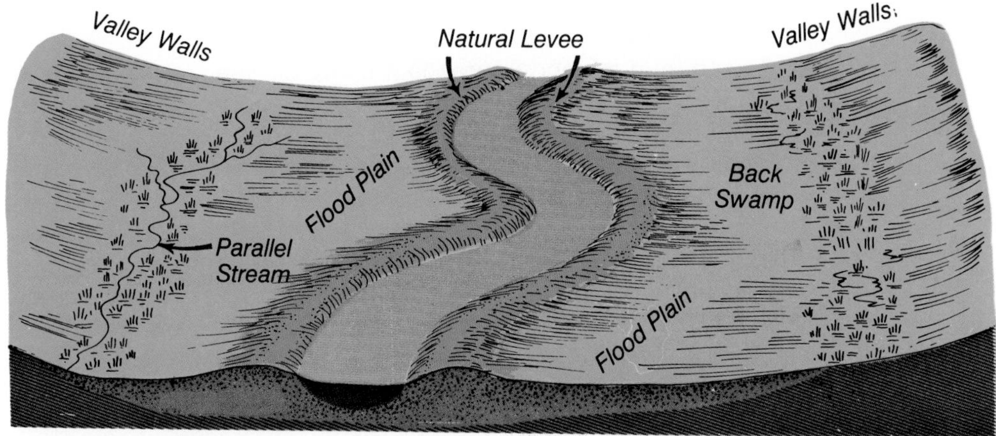

10.16 (top) The flood plain slopes away from the natural levee toward an area where back swamps form. (bottom) A natural levee along the Mississippi River

Topic 17 **Main Causes of River Floods**

River floods can be destructive as well as constructive. As a result, the causes and control of floods are of great importance.

Most river floods result from heavy or long-lasting rains, the rapid melting of winter snows, or both. A single cloudburst may cause a **flash flood,** especially if the cloudburst occurs over the narrow valley of a young mountain stream. Towns at the bases of such valleys suffer severe damage when hit by flash floods. Such floods are common in many parts of the United States.

Large rivers such as the Ohio, Missouri, and Mississippi do not have flash floods. Their floods result from many days of steady rainfall over large parts of their vast drainage basins. In winter and early spring, thaws (warm spells that melt snow) increase the runoff, especially when the ground is still frozen. Frozen ground is not porous. During a thaw, melted snow cannot soak into the ground.

Topic 18 **Other Causes of River Floods**

When a dam forms across a river, it floods the valley above the river up to the height of the dam. Dams are built to create reservoirs. Dams also form naturally.

A common type of natural dam is the ice jam. An ice jam may form when a frozen river breaks up in winter or spring thaws. Other natural dams may result when a volcano erupts and deposits ash, cinders, or lava across streams. Dams caused by landslides are even more common.

Many bad floods have been caused by the failure of reservoir dams. The famous Johnstown, Pennsylvania flood of 1889 happened when a dam made of earth collapsed after days of heavy rain. The dam had been built to make a reservoir three kilometers above Johnstown. When the dam broke, the water in the reservoir burst down on the sleeping city, drowning more than 2200 people.

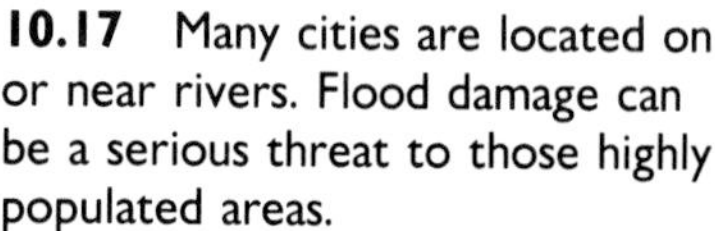

10.17 Many cities are located on or near rivers. Flood damage can be a serious threat to those highly populated areas.

In 1963, a massive landslide poured into a reservoir in the Italian Alps. The dam held, but a surge of water swept over the dam and destroyed the town of Longarone, drowning 3000 people.

Topic 19 Preventing Floods

Can floods be prevented? The causes of floods are largely natural. The removal of natural vegetation, such as trees, shrubs, and grass, usually increases runoff. In areas where vegetation has been removed, reforestation (the replanting of trees and other vegetation) helps to prevent floods. Replanting is most important in the headwater parts of a river's drainage basin.

If floodwaters are already swelling the river's tributaries, can they be contained before they overflow the main stream? If dams are built across headwaters and tributaries, excess runoff can be stored in reservoirs. An example of this method of flood control is seen in the Tennessee River system, where 26 dams have been built to control the river.

10.18 In emergency situations people build artificial levees to control flooding.

Great rivers such as the Ohio, Missouri, and Mississippi must rise above their natural levees to overflow. Here the usual method of flood control is to build up the levees. Artificial levees are made by placing sandbags or other materials on top of natural levees.

What can be done to control flooding near a river's mouth? On the lower Mississippi, spillways are used. Spillways are channels that run through the 10 to 17 back swamps parallel to the main stream and then flow into the Gulf of Mexico. At certain points on the flood plain, water is guided into these spillways to relieve the flooding in the Mississippi itself. In general, flood problems are becoming more severe because more land is being cleared of vegetation as it is being developed. Land that is covered with buildings and pavement does not absorb water, so development increases problems with runoff. It is essential that lakes, ponds, swamps, and other natural storage areas for rainwater not be filled in or used for building purposes.

TOPIC QUESTIONS

Each topic question refers to the topic of the same number.

16. **(a)** How do natural levees form? **(b)** Where do back swamps form? **(c)** Why are flood plains fertile?

17. **(a)** What is a flash flood? **(b)** What causes floods in large rivers?

18. Name three kinds of natural dams and explain how they form.

19. Explain how each of the following helps to prevent floods: **(a)** reforestation, **(b)** building of dams, **(c)** artificial levees, **(d)** spillways.

CHAPTER 10 REVIEW

Summary

Running water includes all the water that falls on Earth and is moved downhill by gravity. It gets its energy from the sun.

Running water breaks up bedrock by abrasion, by lifting particles, and by dissolving soluble minerals. The particles that result are carried by solution, in suspension, and as bed load.

The carrying power of a stream refers to the amount of sediment it carries and the size of particles it can carry. Carrying power increases as stream speed and discharge increase.

Youthful streams form V-shaped valleys and steep-sided gorges and canyons.

Base level is the lowest level to which a stream can erode its bed.

Headward erosion is the process by which a stream lengthens its valley. Stream piracy is a result of headward erosion. Gullies can grow into stream systems through headward erosion.

A drainage basin, or watershed, includes the area drained by a river and all of its tributaries. A divide is the high land between drainage basins.

Features that result from stream erosion include water gaps, wind gaps, waterfalls, potholes, and plunge pools. Some plunge pools are involved in waterfall recession.

Features that occur on flood plains include meanders, cutoffs, oxbow lakes, levees, and back swamps.

A decrease in either speed or discharge causes a river to deposit its load. Deltas and alluvial fans are sediment deposits left by a river when it loses speed at its mouth.

Steady rains over large areas of a watershed cause large rivers to flood. Natural damming, or the failure of a dam, also lead to floods. Flash floods result from cloudbursts over small stream valleys.

Flooding can be prevented by reforestation, damming tributary streams, building artificial levees, and using spillways.

Vocabulary

abrasion
alluvial fan
base level
bed load
carrying power
delta
discharge
divide
drainage basin or watershed
flash flood
flood plain
gully
headward erosion
levees
meanders
oxbow lake
pothole
solution
stream piracy
suspension
water gap

Review

Match the terms in List **A** with the definitions in List **B.**

List A

1. evaporation
2. abrasion
3. bed load
4. solution
5. carrying power
6. canyon
7. base level
8. gully
9. stream divide
10. drainage basin
11. stream piracy
12. water gap
13. pothole
14. undermining
15. flood plain
16. sediment
17. delta
18. levee
19. flash flood
20. ice jam
21. artificial levee

List B

a. grinding action of particles in a streambed
b. high land between two river systems
c. ridge-shaped deposits formed on riverbanks by flooding streams
d. streambed holes scoured out by particles trapped in whirlpools
e. natural dam resulting from breakup of frozen river
f. small V-shaped valley
g. a rounded river stone
h. method by which streams carry dissolved material

i. a river, its tributaries, and all land drained by the river
j. whirlpools eroding base of cliff, causing it to overhang
k. deposits at river mouths
l. abandoned water gap
m. measure of total amount of sediment and of particle sizes carried by a stream
n. process by which water is lifted from ocean by sun
o. steep-sided valley
p. capture of one stream by another through headward erosion
q. part of river valley that is underwater during floods
r. broad curves in river on valley floors
s. narrow cut in resistant rock through which a river flows
t. stream deposits at base of steep mountain
u. moves by rolling, sliding, or bouncing
v. materials carried by a river
w. occurs when cloudburst hits narrow valley
x. lowest level to which a stream can erode its bed
y. placing sandbags on top of natural levees

Interpret and Apply

On your paper, answer each question in complete sentences.

1. Compare the carrying power of a small, fast-flowing stream in the Rocky Mountains with that of the lower part of the Mississippi River.
2. **(a)** Using the data in Topic 12, determine the average rate of recession of Niagara Falls, in meters per year. **(b)** The rock layers of Niagara are not perfectly horizontal but dip into the ground toward Niagara's source. Explain how continued recession will change the height of Niagara Falls.
3. Why is a meandering river like the Rio Grande an unsatisfactory boundary between the United States and Mexico?
4. Can a tributary form a delta where it enters the main stream of the river system? Explain.
5. Over a 4-day period in spring of 1972, Hurricane Agnes dropped 35 centimeters of rain on the Susquehanna River watershed. Record flooding occurred 36 to 48 hours after the heaviest rain. Why didn't the flooding occur during the rain?

Critical Thinking

The graph shows the relationship between particle diameter, in centimeters, and speed of stream flow, in centimeters per second, needed to keep the particle in suspension. The graph also shows the size range for clay, silt, sand, pebbles, cobbles, and boulders. Use the graph to answer questions 1–4.

1. If a particle has a diameter of 0.05 centimeters, what is the particle called?
2. What is the name of the particle that stays in suspension at the slowest stream speed?
3. What is the minimum stream speed needed to carry a boulder in suspension?
4. Name the particles that would be in suspension in a stream moving at 100 cm/s.

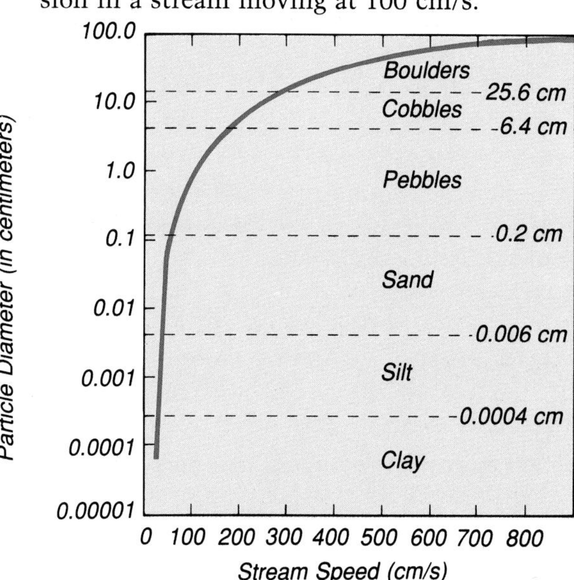

CHAPTER

11

Glaciers

▲ Margerie Glacier, Glacier Bay, Alaska

How Do You Know That . . .

Glaciers form from snow? To see how solid ice can form from snow, take a handful of snow or crushed ice and squeeze it between your hands. Keep applying pressure until you notice a change in the snow or ice particles. What does squeezing seem to do to the particles of snow or ice? What happens when you stop applying pressure? What would cause the packing of snow to form glaciers?

I Types of Glaciers

Topic 1 The Problem of the Strange Boulders

In the early 1800's, European geologists noted that many rock outcrops in northern regions had polished and scratched surfaces. These were unlike the rock outcrop surfaces of more southern regions. Giant boulders had compositions that differed from the bedrock on which they rested. The boulders could sometimes be traced to outcrops many kilometers north. Pebbles and other sediments were strange to the locality in many places.

Geologists agreed that these materials could not be explained by stream action. Before the late 1800's many geologists hypothesized that all this had happened in one great flood. They thought floodwater had carried the boulders, scoured the bedrock, and deposited sediments over a wide area. Because they thought water had moved the foreign materials, geologists called all such material *drift,* a name still in use.

Meanwhile, another explanation was being offered. A study of existing glaciers in the Alps Mountains of Europe showed how bedrock is attacked by glacial erosion and how boulders and soils are carried downslope. Sometimes deposits were found kilometers down the valley from the glacier front or high above the glacier on the valley walls. In those cases geologists reasoned that the glacier had been longer and thicker. A number of geologists then used this reasoning to explain the drift that covered so much of northern Europe. They concluded that great ice sheets had covered the drift area during a long ice age.

The person who is known for this idea is the famous Swiss naturalist Louis Agassiz (AG ah see). Agassiz did much research to prove his theory, and he worked hard to publicize it.

Topic 2 What Is A Glacier?

Imagine a steep valley high in the Alps Mountains of Switzerland. No river runs in this valley. Instead, the entire valley floor is covered by a mass of snow-covered ice, hundreds of meters thick. This ice mass can be followed up the valley for many kilometers. It begins in huge fields of ice and snow just below the very highest peaks.

Careful study would show that the ice in this valley moves downhill at the rate of several meters a day. At the lower part of the

OBJECTIVES

A Summarize the observations that led Louis Agassiz to propose that glaciers had once covered large parts of Europe.

B Describe how firn becomes a glacier.

C Describe the occurrence and appearance of a valley glacier.

D Identify two kinds of ice sheets.

11.1 This view of the edge of a glacier shows where a huge chunk of ice broke off. Notice the sizes and kinds of materials left by the ice.

valley, the ice thins out and suddenly ends. Milky-colored water runs out from beneath the ice and flows down the valley. This long, slow-moving, wedge-shaped stream of ice is a **valley glacier.**

Imagine a great landmass in the polar latitudes of the far north or south. The climate is so cold that only snow falls. For thousands of years snow has been falling, building up, and changing to ice. Almost the whole landmass is covered by the thick mass of ice. Only the highest mountain peaks reach above the ice.

The ice is thousands of meters thick, and it moves outward from its center in all directions toward the seacoasts. In some places it reaches the sea by traveling through low valleys. Here great chunks of ice break off to float away as icebergs. This moving mass of ice, far larger than a valley glacier, is called an **ice sheet.**

Topic 3 **The Snow Line**

Glaciers are born in areas always covered by snow. These are areas where more snow falls than melts each year. Some snow is always left to add to the buildup of previous years. Climates cold enough to cause such conditions may be found in any part of the world. Air temperatures drop with greater height above sea level and with greater distance from the equator.

Even in equatorial areas, then, permanent snows may be found on high mountains. Farther from the equator the mountains need not be so high for snow to exist. In the polar areas permanent snows may be found even at sea level. The lowest level that permanent snows reach in summer is called the **snow line.** A mountain that is completely covered with snow in winter, but from which the snow is all melted by summer, has no snow line.

The snow line is highest near the equator and lowest near the poles. As climates become colder with greater latitude (distance from the equator), less height is needed to reach a snow line. The position of the snow line also changes with the total yearly snowfall and the amount of exposure to the sun. Thus the height of a snow line is not the same for all places in the same latitude.

11.2 The nearly horizontal snow line on these Colorado peaks represents the lowest level that permanent snows reach in the summer.

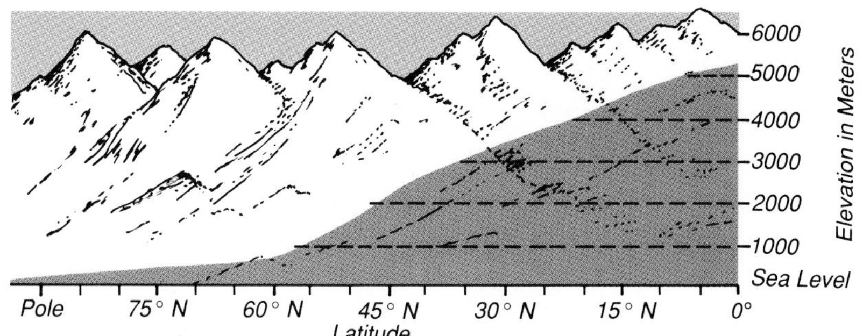

11.3 This diagram shows approximately how the elevation of the snow line varies with latitude.

Topic 4 **Birth of a Glacier**

Except for bare rock cliffs, the mountain above the snow line is buried in snow. Great basins below the highest peaks are filled with snow hundreds of meters thick. In the huge snow fields freshly fallen snow becomes compressed and recrystallizes into a rough, granular ice material called **firn,** or *névé* (NAY vay).

Figure 11.4 illustrates the development of a valley glacier. The granules of firn start off no larger than fine buckshot. The firn is like the ice of a packed snowball. As the firn becomes thicker, its crystals may grow as large as kernels of corn. The lower layers of firn change to solid ice because they are compressed by the weight of the top layers. This ice begins to flow downward or outward because of the weight of the overlying firn and snow. This moving mass of ice and snow has become a valley glacier.

a

b

c

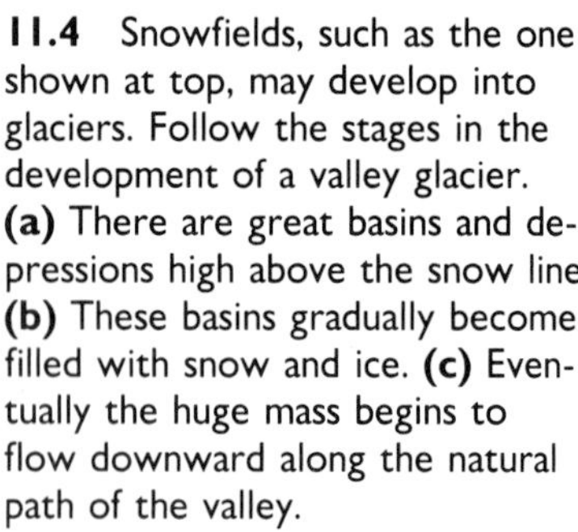
11.4 Snowfields, such as the one shown at top, may develop into glaciers. Follow the stages in the development of a valley glacier. **(a)** There are great basins and depressions high above the snow line. **(b)** These basins gradually become filled with snow and ice. **(c)** Eventually the huge mass begins to flow downward along the natural path of the valley.

Topic 5 **Where Valley Glaciers Occur**

Valley glaciers are also known as *alpine* glaciers. They occur in all parts of the world where mountains stretch above the snow line. This includes all continents except Australia.

The smallest valley glaciers may be as little as two thousand meters long, a few hundred meters wide, and less than a hundred meters deep. The largest may be over a hundred thousand meters long, several thousand meters wide, and hundreds of meters thick. The world's largest valley glaciers are in southern Alaska. Here mountains with a snow line at about 1500 meters reach to heights above 6000 meters. The world's largest mountains, the Himalayas, also have very large glaciers.

11.5 A valley glacier in the Swiss Alps

Topic 6 Where Ice Sheets Occur

Ice sheets form in polar areas where the snow line is close to sea level and wide areas are above the snow line. Ice sheets are roughly circular or oval in shape. Small ice sheets called **ice caps** are found in Iceland, Baffin Island, Spitsbergen, and other large islands of the Arctic Ocean. An ice cap may have an area of several thousand square kilometers.

The larger ice sheets of Greenland and Antarctica are called **continental glaciers.** The Greenland glacier is about 1 700 000 square kilometers in area and up to 3 kilometers thick. It covers all of Greenland except a narrow part of the coast.

The Antarctic glacier covers a larger landmass with an area of about 12.5 million square kilometers. Here the ice reaches a thickness of nearly 5 kilometers. Along the coast the ice may descend more than 1.5 kilometers below sea level. Farther inland great mountain peaks called **nunataks** project through the ice.

TOPIC QUESTIONS

Each topic question refers to the topic of the same number.

1. **(a)** What is drift? **(b)** How did Louis Agassiz explain the drift that covered parts of northern Europe?
2. **(a)** Define valley glacier. **(b)** Define ice sheet.
3. **(a)** Define snow line. **(b)** How does the snow line change with latitude?
4. **(a)** What is firn? **(b)** How does firn become a glacier?
5. Where are valley glaciers generally found?
6. What is the difference between ice caps and continental glaciers? Give examples of each.

II Glacier Movement

OBJECTIVES

A Describe the motion of ice within a glacier and the factors that affect its motion.

B Describe factors that determine the location of the ice front.

C Describe the origin and location of several kinds of moraine.

D Explain several ways in which glaciers erode the land and compare erosion by a continental glacier with erosion by a valley glacier.

Topic 7 How Glaciers Move

A glacier's own weight is an important factor in its movement. The weight of overlying layers of ice and snow push down on lower layers of the glacier. The weight also causes grains of ice to partially melt and refreeze. As this happens, the ice grains slip over each other, and the glacier moves downhill.

Geologists have studied the movement of glaciers by driving rows of stakes into the ice across a valley. They observe the positions of the stakes regularly. They have found that some glaciers move only a few centimeters a day, while others move as much as 3000 centimeters a day. They have learned that glaciers move more rapidly at the surface than at the base and faster in the center than at the sides, where friction with valley walls slows their flow. Geologists have seen that glaciers move more rapidly after winters of heavy snowfall, on steep slopes, and in summer.

Like river valleys, glacial valleys have steep and gentle slopes. When a valley glacier comes to a steep slope, great fissures, or cracks, called **crevasses** form across the width of the glacier. These openings rarely go deeper than about 40 meters. Studies have shown that the glacier ice is brittle to about that depth. Below 40 meters, the ice is more flexible from the pressure of overlying ice.

11.6 Aerial view of huge crevasses in a glacier

Topic 8 How Far Glaciers Move

As a valley glacier moves into lower, warmer levels, it thins steadily because of melting and evaporation. Most glaciers extend below the snow line. A glacier is thinnest at the elevation where the ice melts as fast as it moves. Under normal conditions the glacier ends here, at its **ice front.**

A glacier always moves forward. However, as long as the rates of movement and melting are equal, the ice front is stationary. After a winter of heavy snows, which add pressure to the bottom ice, a glacier may move faster than normal and advance beyond its usual limit. On the other hand, in very warm summers, it may melt faster than normal, causing the ice front to move back, or recede.

In regions such as Alaska and Greenland, the snow line is close to sea level. Many glaciers reach the sea. Even here they do not melt as fast as they move. As they extend into the sea, great blocks break off to become icebergs. This process is called **calving.**

In Antarctica, where the snow line is at sea level, the ice sheet reaches the coastline almost everywhere. In a number of places the ice sheet extends beyond the coast far into the sea in huge ice shelves. The largest of these, the Ross Ice Shelf, is hundreds of kilometers wide and about a third of a kilometer thick at its sides. The icebergs that break off from an ice sheet are huge. One such iceberg was about 65 kilometers long.

Topic 9 Glaciers Transport Loose Rock

Like rivers, glaciers remove loose rock from the valleys through which they move. There seems to be almost no limit to the size and amount of material carried by a glacier. Particles, ranging in size from fine powder to giant boulders, are picked up by a glacier from its valley floor. Often rocks fall into a glacier from the valley walls. Other material may be brought to it by tributary glaciers.

Large amounts of rock material build up in several areas of a moving glacier. When these materials are deposited, they form **moraines.** Material carried in the bottom of the glacier before it is deposited is called *ground moraine.* The two long lines of rock pieces that pile up along the valley sides of a glacier are called *lateral* (side) *moraines*. Sometimes two glaciers come together to form a single larger glacier. Then their inside lateral moraines are joined to form a single *medial* (middle) *moraine.* At the ice front, rock pieces brought forward by the glacier's motion build up as the ice melts. These pile up as an *end moraine.* An end moraine may grow very large if the ice front does not move for a long time, since glacier movement and melting will constantly add material to it.

Rock flour is a mixture of fine sand and silt formed by the crushing of rock under a glacier. The meltwater pouring out of a glacier is likely to be filled with suspended rock flour. This gives the water a milky white color, so it is called *glacial milk*.

11.7 These icebergs broke off from Portage Glacier near Anchorage, Alaska. Notice the glacier in the background.

11.8 The material that will form moraines is clearly visible in this glacier as dark parallel bands. (Lamplugh Glacier, Alaska)

11.9 The large parallel scratches on this rock are striations, which were carved by a glacier.

Topic 10 Glaciers Leave Their Mark

Glaciers erode the bedrock largely by using pieces of rocks as cutting tools. These pieces are dragged over the bedrock by the forward movement of the glacier. Particles of fine sand, acting like sandpaper, smooth and polish the bedrock. Coarse sand, pebbles, and sharp boulders leave long parallel scratches called **striations.** Striations show the general direction of ice movement. If the bedrock is soft, pebbles and small boulders may dig in so deeply as to leave long parallel grooves. The pebbles and boulders carried by the glacier also show signs of wear, becoming flattened and scratched.

Glacial erosion shapes bedrock into many forms. Outcrops of bedrock may become smooth and polished on the side facing a glacier. The opposite side may be left steep and rough where the glacier freezes and plucks away loose blocks of rock. Such outcrops look like resting sheep and are called **roches moutonnées** (rosh moo toe NAY), meaning "sheep rocks." Potholes are ground out beneath glaciers in whirlpools formed by meltwater falling into crevasses.

Frost action and glacial erosion at the head of a glacier wear away the walls of mountain peaks. A semicircular basin called a **cirque** (SERK) is formed at the head of the glacial valley.

When two cirques are formed next to each other on a peak, the divide between them may become narrow and sharp. Such a divide is called an **arête** (ah RET), or knife-edge ridge. When three or more cirques cut into the same peak, they may cut away so much that a spectacular pyramid-shaped peak is left. Such peaks are called **horns,** or *matterhorns,* after the Matterhorn in Switzerland.

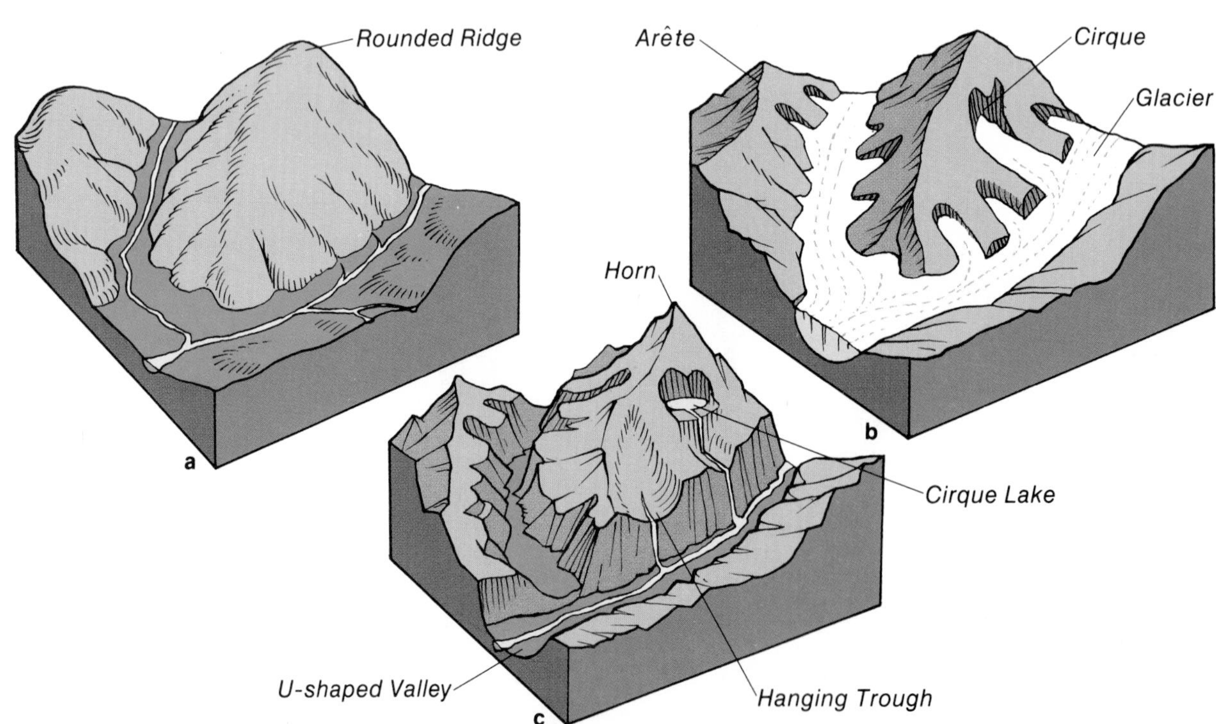

11.10 Glacial erosion of mountain peaks often leaves steep, jagged formations.

Topic 11 Recognizing Glacial Valleys

A river touches only a small part of its valley floor. A valley glacier, on the other hand, touches the entire valley floor and a large part of the valley walls as well. As it moves, a valley glacier scours away the rock until it flattens the entire valley floor and makes the valley walls nearly vertical. The resulting formation is called a **glacial trough**—a glacial valley that is roughly U-shaped.

Main valley glaciers are usually much thicker than their tributary glaciers. Thus, they erode their valleys more powerfully. The effects of this erosion can be seen in regions where a change of climates has caused glaciers to disappear. The main valleys are much deeper than the tributary valleys. The tributary U-shaped valleys are called *hanging troughs.* The rivers that have formed in the hanging troughs plunge over the cliffs, forming *hanging trough waterfalls.* Glacial troughs, hanging troughs, and hanging trough waterfalls are common in all glaciated mountains. A famous hanging trough waterfall is Yosemite Falls in California.

11.11 A U-shaped glacial valley, or trough

Topic 12 What Continental Glaciers Do

Like valley glaciers, continental glaciers remove loose rock and soil. They smooth, striate, and groove bedrock. They form roches moutonnées and other features. However, erosion of mountain areas by continental glaciers differs in several ways from erosion by valley glaciers. A continental glacier deepens and widens valleys that are parallel to its direction of movement. Since a continental glacier covers most mountaintops, it grinds down the peaks and leaves them polished and rounded. Valley glaciers, by contrast, sharpen mountain peaks by grinding away at their sides.

TOPIC QUESTIONS

Each topic question refers to the topic of the same number.

7. **(a)** What causes glaciers to move? **(b)** At what times do glaciers tend to move fastest? **(c)** What are crevasses?
8. **(a)** What determines the location of the ice front of a glacier? **(b)** What causes an ice front to recede? **(c)** How are icebergs formed? What is this process called?
9. **(a)** What are the sources of material that are carried by a glacier? **(b)** Where are ground, lateral, medial, and end moraines located in respect to a glacier? **(c)** Define rock flour.
10. **(a)** Describe the formation of roches moutonnées. **(b)** What is a cirque? **(c)** How are arêtes and horns related to cirques?
11. Describe the shape and origin of glacial troughs, hanging troughs, and hanging trough waterfalls.
12. How does erosion by continental glaciers differ from that by valley glaciers?

III Deposits by Glaciers

OBJECTIVES

A Discuss the origin and properties of till and outwash.

B List some features of glacial deposition and explain how each occurs.

C Name and describe three types of lakes resulting from glaciation.

Topic 13 Deposition Occurs

Most of the rock material carried by glaciers is deposited by melting. The name *drift* is used for all deposits of glacial origin.

There are two kinds of drift. Unsorted and unstratified rock materials deposited directly by the ice is called **till**. Till deposits may be left under a moving glacier or along its sides. The second kind of drift, called **outwash**, includes deposits made by streams of glacial meltwater. Like all stream deposits these are sorted and stratified.

11.12 A lateral moraine is visible on the left side of the photograph. (Alberta, Canada)

Topic 14 Glaciers Leave Moraines

When a glacier melts, its rock load remains in nearly the same places as in the glacier. The ground moraine forms a thin, fairly even deposit over the whole area. Lateral and medial moraines form ridges running in almost the same direction as the glacier.

The end moraine forms a ridge along the ice front. The longer the ice front stays in one place, the larger the end moraine becomes. When a receding ice front stops in new places for any length of time, new end moraines are formed behind the main one. These are called *recessional moraines*.

Even a stationary ice front moves back and forth slightly with the seasons. End moraine deposits are spread over a broad belt in front of a glacier. Furthermore, no two parts of the ice front deposit exactly the same amount of material. For these reasons, end and recessional moraines are likely to have irregular hills and hollows, rather than being a single straight ridge. End moraines of continental glaciers may be hundreds of kilometers long, several kilometers wide, and a tenth of a kilometer high. The end moraine marking a glacier's farthest advance is called its *terminal moraine*.

The materials of the moraines range from boulders to clays. They are mixed in widely varying amounts and are unstratified. Large glacial boulders that have been transported into an area are called **erratics.** Erratics differ in composition from the local bedrock.

11.13 Aerial view of a swarm of drumlins

Topic 15 Drumlins

Drumlins are long, smooth, canoe-shaped hills made of till. They usually are found in swarms. They all point in the direction of glacier movement. A typical drumlin may be 400 meters long, 100 meters wide, and 25 meters high.

Drumlins were probably formed when an advancing glacier ran over an earlier glacial moraine, sweeping it into long strips. Swarms of drumlins are found in southeastern Wisconsin, south of Lake Ontario in New York State, and near Boston, Massachusetts.

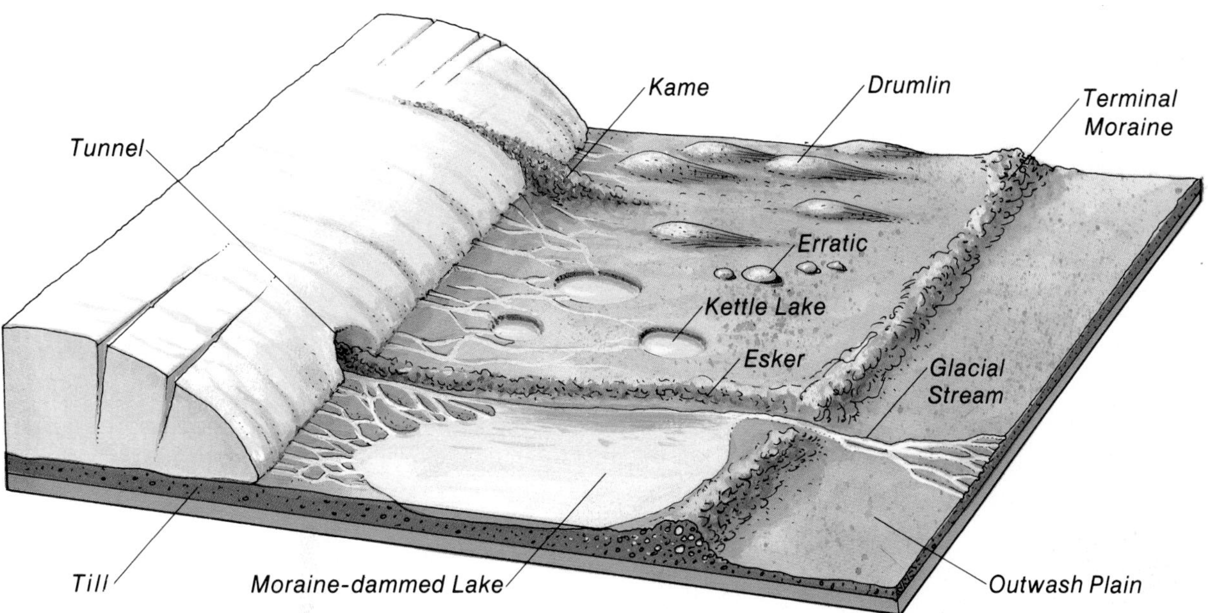

11.14 Notice the different kinds of deposits and formations left by a glacier.

Topic 16 Outwash Plains and Eskers

Glacial meltwater pours out at the ice front in streams filled with rock flour, sand, and gravel. These streams form gently sloping stratified deposits that may reach for kilometers beyond the terminal moraine. The deposits look like alluvial fans. In front of large glaciers, they overlap and form broad flat areas called **outwash plains.**

Much of the water of a melting glacier falls to the bottom of the ice through crevasses. Subglacial streams are formed that run in tunnels beneath the ice and come out at the ice front. The winding tunnels of these streams become partly filled with roughly stratified sands and gravel. When the glacier melts, the deposits slump down at the sides and form long, widening ridges called **eskers**.

Eskers are found in the glaciated states of the Mississippi Valley, the north central states, central New York, and Maine. Eskers usually run in about the same general direction as the direction of ice movement.

Topic 17 Kames, Kettles, and Deltas

Kames (KAYMS) are small, cone-shaped hills of stratified sand and gravel. They are formed when streams from the top of the glacier deposit their sediments at the ice margin or into lakes on the top of the ice. These pile up in heaps as the ice thins and are finally lowered to the ground surface.

Kettles are circular hollows found on terminal moraines and outwash plains. Kettles are formed in two steps. First, moraine or outwash deposits bury large blocks of ice left as the glacier recedes. Then the ice melts, leaving the kettles.

11.15 St. Mary's Lake, Glacier National Park, Montana

When glacial streams empty into lakes or beyond the ice front, *deltas* are formed. These are made up largely of layers of gravel and coarse sand. Fine sands and clays may spread evenly over the whole lake floor.

Topic 18 **Lakes Made by Glaciers**

Glaciation of an area leaves many new basins or depressions in the land surface. If these basins are permanently filled with water, they form lakes, ponds, or swamps, depending on how large and deep they are. Three important types of lakes that come from glaciation are cirque lakes, kettle lakes, and moraine-dammed lakes.

Cirque lakes are formed when water fills the rock-floored cirque basins left by alpine glaciers. Cirque lakes and rock-basin lakes are also called *tarns*. Examples of cirque lakes are Lake Louise in the Canadian Rockies and St. Mary's Lake in Montana.

Kettle lakes form in large numbers in the kettle holes of moraines and outwash plains. They are common in Minnesota, Wisconsin, New York, and New England.

Moraine-dammed lakes are formed where river valleys are blocked by glacial moraines. The river rises to the height of the moraine dam and floods its valley to form a long, usually narrow lake. Many of the larger lakes of the northern United States came about in this way. Examples are Lake George in New York and Long Lake in Maine.

In many cases, lakes were formed by both glacial erosion that scoured out river valleys and deposition that dammed the rivers. The Finger Lakes of central New York State were formed in this way. Many of their former tributary valleys were left as hanging troughs high above the main troughs. The Great Lakes have a more complicated history. However, they also lie in basins that were deepened and then dammed by glacial moraines.

TOPIC QUESTIONS

Each topic question refers to the topic of the same number.

13. How do till deposits differ from outwash deposits?
14. **(a)** What are recessional moraines? **(b)** Why are end moraines usually broad and irregularly hilly? **(c)** What is a terminal moraine? **(d)** What are erratics?
15. Describe the appearance and possible origin of drumlins.
16. **(a)** Describe an outwash plain. **(b)** How are eskers formed?
17. **(a)** How are kames formed? **(b)** How are kettles formed? **(c)** How do melting glaciers form deltas?
18. Describe three types of lakes resulting from glaciation.

IV The Ice Age

Topic 19 How It Happened

About a million years ago it was as cold in much of northern North America and northern Europe as it is today in Greenland. Great ice sheets developed over central and eastern Canada and northern Scandinavia. In North America the ice sheets developed over an area that extends as far south as where the Ohio and Mississippi rivers meet and eastward to central Long Island. Much of the north central and northeastern parts of the United States were covered by ice. In Europe the ice sheets covered most of Scandinavia, the British Isles, Denmark, Belgium, northern France, and the Baltic countries and reached far into Germany and Russia.

In North America there were three centers in which the snow and ice were thickest. These centers of accumulation were the Labrador center east of Hudson Bay, the Keewatin center west of Hudson Bay, and the Cordilleran center in the Canadian Rockies.

From the Labrador center came the ice that covered eastern Canada and the northeastern United States. From Keewatin came the ice that covered central Canada and the north central United States. The Cordilleran ice sheet covered the Canadian Rockies down to their foothills but did not move south. At that time there were valley glaciers in the mountains of the western United States, but they were far larger than they are today.

The ice sheets advanced and receded four major times during the million-year period as the climate changed from cold to warm and back again. The last time the ice sheets receded was about 11 000 years ago. Many geologists think we are now in a warm, or *interglacial,* period that will be followed by a return of the ice sheets in perhaps 20 000 years. Others think that this warm period will last millions of years.

OBJECTIVES

A List some evidences for glaciation found in North America.

B List the facts supporting a theory of glacial climate.

C Describe several hypotheses for the occurrence of an ice age.

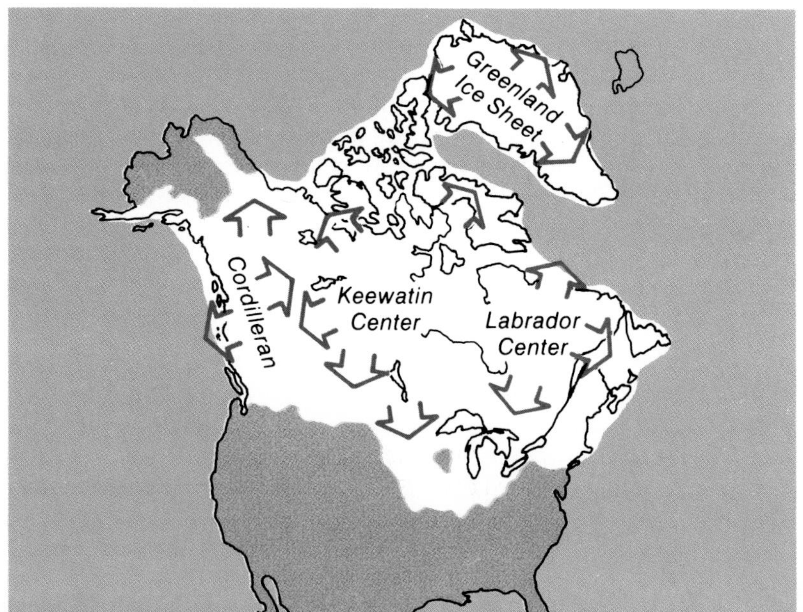

11.16 The entire area in white was covered by ice sheets during the Ice Age. Notice the uncovered area south of Lake Superior.

11.17 These smoothly polished rocks provide evidence of glacial erosion.

Topic 20 Ice Age Evidence

Proof that there were ice ages is given in the many glacial features that have been described. The southern limit reached by some advances of ice sheets is marked by terminal moraines. One of these is the Long Island, New York, moraine that extends almost 225 kilometers from Brooklyn to Montauk Point. Other terminal moraines stretch from New Jersey through Pennsylvania, Ohio, Indiana, and westward to Puget Sound in the State of Washington. The edge of the ice sheet illustrated on the map in Figure 11.16 was determined by the location of these terminal moraines. South of the terminal moraines, outwash plains are found in many places.

Much of the northern United States and Canada is covered by drift. There are many glacial boulders in the glacial-till soils. Exposed bedrock is striated and polished, even on mountaintops. North-south valleys are shaped into glacial troughs. East-west valleys are partly filled with drift. Kames, eskers, drumlins, and moraines are found in many places. Lakes and swamps are far more common in glaciated areas than in the unglaciated areas to the south. In the Rockies and the Sierra Nevadas, glacial markings occur high upon the valley walls. This shows that much larger glaciers filled these valleys during the most recent Ice Age.

Topic 21 Causes of Glacial Climates

To explain why Earth was cold enough to have the recent Ice Age, certain facts must be considered:

1. This Ice Age began about 1 million years ago and included four major advances of the ice sheets.
2. Warm interglacial periods came after each advance. Earth may now be in an interglacial period.
3. Other ice ages have occurred from time to time in the past 600 million years.
4. During the last Ice Age, glaciers advanced and receded at the same time in both the Northern and Southern Hemispheres.

Geologists have proposed many hypotheses to account for ice ages. One idea is that the amount of heat energy given off by the sun changes. Ice ages may occur during periods when energy from the sun is less. Or the amount of energy reaching Earth might change due to volcanic dust in the atmosphere. Another possibility is that during periods of mountain building, more of Earth's land area lay above the snow line. More land under snow might change the climate enough for an ice age to begin. A fourth idea concerns the former position of continents on Earth's surface. If continents used to be in the way of currents between oceans, they may have prevented the mixing of cold and warm water. Without mixing between oceans, areas of Earth might become cold enough to start an ice age. Each of these hypotheses has its strong and weak points. Recent research has added to knowledge about the times and durations of the previous Ice Age. Geologists have also discovered evidence of many more ice ages in the distant past.

A hypothesis that explains much of the new evidence being found concerns changes in the motions of Earth itself. Changes in the tilt of Earth's axis and in the shape of its orbit might cause colder climates on some parts of Earth. Changes of this kind do take place over and over again at regular intervals in Earth's history, which might explain why ice ages happen periodically. Also, such changes in Earth's position could cause glacial climates in both hemispheres at the same time. Did the Ice Age occur because of changes in Earth's position and motion? Scientists must study all new evidence to see whether it supports the hypothesis, or to determine whether the hypothesis must be modified.

TOPIC QUESTIONS

Each topic question refers to the topic of the same number.

19. **(a)** What is a center of accumulation? **(b)** Describe the extent of the ice sheets in North America during the last Ice Age.

20. Identify the kind of evidence for the Ice Age found at the following locations: **(a)** Long Island, New York, to Puget Sound, Washington, **(b)** northern United States and Canada, and **(c)** Rockies and Sierra Nevadas.

21. **(a)** List four pieces of evidence that must be considered to explain why Earth was cold enough to have an ice age. **(b)** Describe some hypotheses about the cause of ice ages.

Luanne Whitbeck

Glacial Geologist

You know about outwash plains, but what are outwash trains? Luanne Whitbeck, while at the New York State Geological Survey, found an excellent example of an outwash train during her study of the glacial deposits near Lake George in New York. She says that trains are long, narrow bodies of outwash in the floor of a valley. Like an outwash plain, they formed from the sand, gravel, and other particles deposited by streams flowing from the melting ice.

Ms. Whitbeck notes that the outwash train is especially interesting because of the changes that occur within it. At the end of the train, where the glacier once stood, the outwash contains cobbles and other large particles. Farther away the particles become smaller. At the other end of the train, the outwash is a delta. The delta shows clearly the layering that is characteristic of such features. The delta rests on till that in turn rests on bedrock. With the kames, eskers, moraines, and other features that occur here, the area is an excellent place to study glacial deposits.

CHAPTER 11 REVIEW

Summary

Observations of rocks and drift deposits led Agassiz to propose that glaciers had once covered large parts of Europe.

The snow line is the lowest elevation of permanent snow. The snow line is highest near the equator and lowest near the poles.

Glaciers form from compressed snow called firn. A valley glacier is a slow-moving, wedge-shaped stream of ice. Ice caps and continental glaciers are examples of ice sheets.

Glaciers move most rapidly at the surface of their centers. The location of the ice front of a glacier depends on the rates of glacial movement and melting.

Icebergs form when pieces of glaciers that reach sea level break off in a process called calving.

Glaciers pick up and carry material of all sizes. The material may be carried as ground, lateral, or medial moraines and deposited as end moraines.

Valley glaciers and continental glaciers each leave characteristic landforms and erosional features.

Till is unsorted, unstratified material deposited directly by the ice. Outwash is sorted, stratified material deposited by meltwater from the ice.

Ice accumulated in three areas of North America and extended south to the present Ohio and Missouri Rivers.

The features of glacial erosion and deposition are evidence that glaciers once covered large parts of Canada and the northern United States.

There are several hypotheses about the cause of ice ages; a likely one concerns changes in the motion and position of Earth.

Vocabulary

arête
calving
cirque
continental glacier
crevasses
drumlins
erratics
eskers
firn
glacial trough
horn
ice caps
ice front
ice sheet
kames
kettles
moraine
nunataks
outwash
outwash plains
roches moutonnées
rock flour
snow line
striations
till
valley glacier

Review

On your paper, write the word or words that best complete each sentence.

1. Before Agassiz, geologists thought that scratched boulders and drift deposits in Europe had been left by a ______.
2. As distance from the equator increases, the elevation of the snow line ______.
3. The rough, granular ice that becomes a glacier is called ______.
4. Slow-moving, wedge-shaped streams of ice found in mountain areas are called alpine, or ______, glaciers.
5. The large ice sheets of Greenland and Antarctica are called ______ glaciers.
6. Glaciers move more rapidly at the ______ than at the base and in the ______ than at the sides.
7. The location of an ice ______ is a balance between the rate of ice movement and the rate of melting.
8. Calving occurs when large blocks of ice break off in the ocean to become ______.
9. Ground, lateral, medial, and end are kinds of ______.
10. Striations are long, parallel ______ in the bedrock that show the general direction of ice movement.
11. An arête is a sharp, narrow ridge between two semicircular basins, called ______.
12. A U-shaped valley carved by a glacier is called a ______.
13. Continental glaciers tend to leave ______, polished mountaintops.
14. Unsorted, unstratified material left by ice is ______, while sorted, stratified material left by meltwater is ______.

15. The ______ moraine marks the farthest advance of the ice, while the ______ moraine shows where the ice paused as it receded.
16. Long, smooth, canoe-shaped hills that commonly occur in swarms are called ______.
17. The gently sloping, stratified area beyond the farthest glacial front is an outwash ______.
18. ______ are small, cone-shaped hills of stratified sand and gravel that formed at the ice margin.
19. Kettle holes that fill with water become ______.
20. Ice built up at Labrador, Keewatin, and Cordilleran centers on the continent of ______.
21. Striated and polished mountaintops, glacial troughs, kames, eskers, and drumlins are all evidence of ______.
22. One hypothesis is that glacial climates result from changes in the tilt of Earth's ______ and in the shape of Earth's ______ around the sun.

Interpret and Apply

On your paper, answer each question in complete sentences.

1. How should the total yearly snowfall and the direction a mountainside faces affect the position of the snow line?
2. Why should glaciers move faster in warm weather than in cold weather?
3. One danger of walking on a glacier is the chance of falling into a hidden crevasse. What should you look for in the surrounding area to tell you when the danger of a crevasse is greater?
4. After the ice sheet retreated from New England, valley glaciers existed for some time in the White Mountains of New Hampshire. What evidence would show this?
5. Compare the amount of sediment carried by the Mississippi River system today with the amount that was probably carried 11 000 years ago.
6. Many eskers go up and down hills. How is that possible?
7. Moraine-dammed lakes often have many irregular inlets and bays. Why?
8. In Wisconsin, fossil evidence of a forest has been preserved between two till layers. What does this indicate about the length of the interglacial period between the formation of the two till layers?

Critical Thinking

The graph shows changes in worldwide temperatures over the past 200 000 years. Ice ages occurred when worldwide temperatures were coolest. Interglacial periods occurred when worldwide temperatures were warmer.

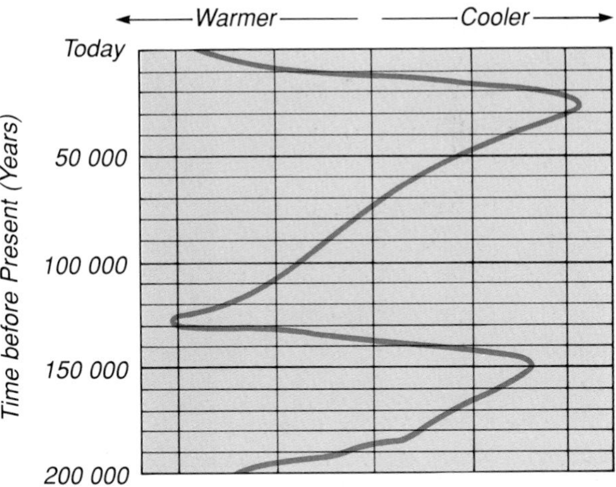

1. How do today's worldwide temperatures compare with those of 150 000 years ago?
2. Compare the temperatures of 20 000 years ago with those of 120 000 years ago.
3. According to the graph, how many ice ages occurred during the past 200 000 years? When did they occur?
4. How does the length of time for an ice age to develop compare with the length of time for an ice age to end?
5. When would the next ice age be expected?

CHAPTER

12 Effects of Winds, Waves, and Currents

▲
This toadstool rock was formed by wind action.

How Do You Know That. . .

Wind causes erosion? Wind erosion is thought to have been a factor in shaping this unusual formation. The formation is called a toadstool rock. It is a flat slab of rock supported by a thin "stem." Although the rock of the slab looks like the rock of the stem, the two must have at least one difference. The slab rock must be slightly harder. It was able to resist wind erosion slightly better than the rock of the stem. The result is that the stem has been worn away faster than the slab above it, leaving the toadstool shape.

I Wind as an Agent of Change

Topic 1 Rock Materials Carried by Winds

Like rivers and glaciers, winds are agents of erosion. Winds act in two basic ways. Winds pick up and move sediment, and they drive sediment against rocks and other materials, causing weathering (Topic 2). Wind erosion and weathering are most effective where sands, silts, and clays lie loose and dry. Conditions for wind erosion are found in great deserts, such as the Sahara in Africa and the Mohave in the southwestern United States. On a smaller scale, these conditions occur on beaches and in semiarid regions.

When strong, steady winds lift great amounts of silt and clay from the topsoil, a **dust storm** occurs. Very destructive dust storms took place on the Great Plains in the 1930's. Long dry spells killed the soil's protective vegetation, leaving the soil exposed to wind erosion. Dust produced during some of the storms was carried high into the atmosphere.

Sand grains are much larger and heavier than clay and silt particles. Experiments with sand grains show that winds of at least 18 kilometers per hour are needed to move them. Sand grains do not move in a steady stream above the ground. Like sand grains in a riverbed, they move in short hops and bounces. Even during strong winds, most sand is carried within one meter of the ground.

Topic 2 Abrasion by Windblown Sediments

Windblown silt and clay particles are too small, and often too soft, to wear away most rocks. Sand grains, however, are larger and tend to be made of more abrasive materials. Sand grains driven by winds grind and scour anything they hit. Quartz sand grains, especially, can wear away many materials. In some desert areas, rocks and telephone poles may be undercut at the base by wind-blown sand. Some poles are even worn through.

Desert sand blasts grind boulders and small rocks into shapes called **ventifacts.** The side of a ventifact that faces the steady wind direction wears into a smooth flat surface, or facet. Figure 12.2 (a) shows how a facet can form. A second facet may form if the wind blows from different directions at different times of the year, or if the boulder is turned so that a new side faces the wind.

OBJECTIVES

A Identify conditions that lead to erosion by wind action and locate areas where such conditions are common.

B Discuss the actions of wind erosion and weathering and identify features resulting from wind action.

C Describe loess and discuss its origin.

D Describe conditions that result in four different sand dune shapes and describe how dune migration occurs.

12.1 Dust storms occur when winds are strong enough to lift and carry dry sand, silt, and clay particles.

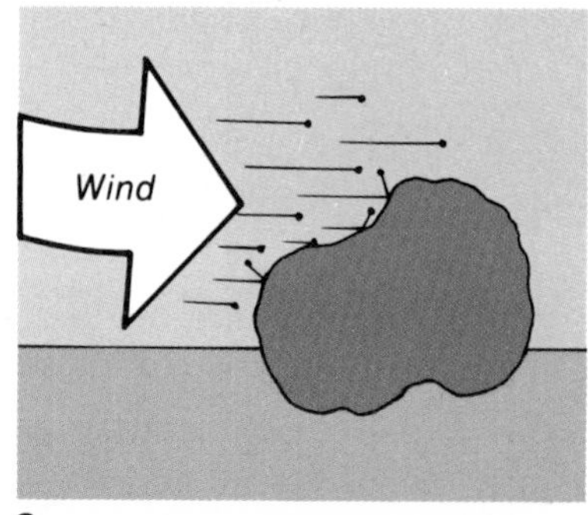

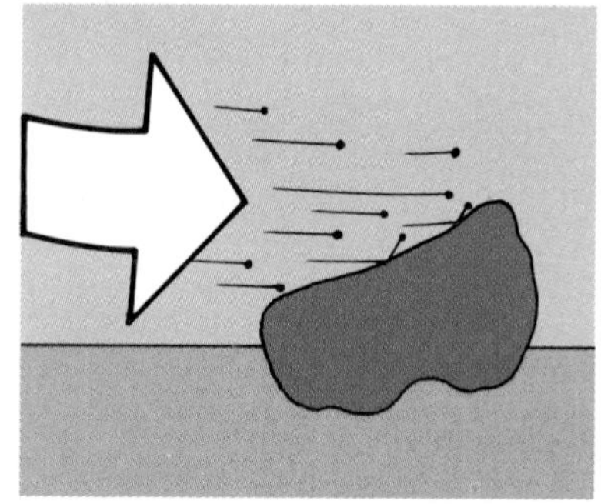
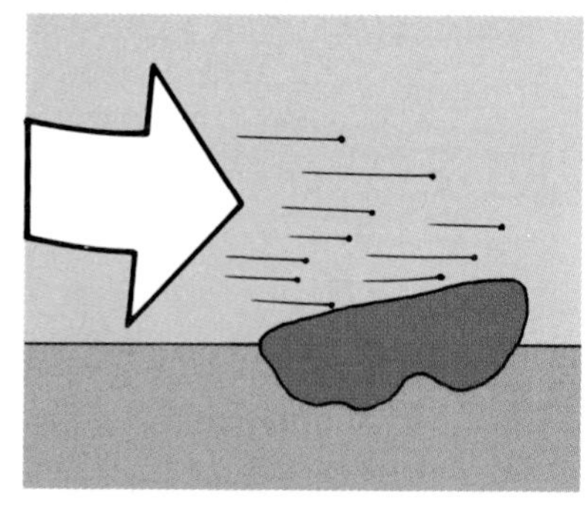

a

b

12.2 **(a)** This series of sketches shows how the abrasive action of windblown sand grinds the face of a boulder into a ventifact. **(b)** The shape of this ventifact gives a clue to the direction of the wind that formed it. The ventifact is surrounded by desert pavement.

Topic 3 **Deflation: An Erosional Effect**

Deflation is a geological term that describes the removal of loose rock particles by the wind. In many desert areas the sands and clays formed by weathering are blown away by the wind, leaving pebbles and boulders. Such a surface is called **desert pavement.** The surface surrounding the ventifact in Figure 12.2(b) is desert pavement. Desert pavement protects the materials beneath from further deflation. Stony surfaces of this type are common in the deserts of the southwestern United States and in the Sahara in Africa.

In semiarid regions, such as the Great Plains, deflation has formed thousands of hollows called **blowouts.** Most of these are shallow and small. Some are many thousand meters long and perhaps a hundred meters deep. If the bottom of the blowout reaches the water table, the wet ground stops further deflation. The growth of vegetation also stops further deflation. Some desert oases occur in deep blowouts that were probably formed by deflation.

Topic 4 **Loess**

Wind can deposit sediment as well as remove it. Large areas in China, northern Europe, and the north central United States are covered by deposits of material called **loess** (LES or LOW ess). Loess ranges in thickness from about 1 meter to about 100 meters. It is made of unlayered, yellowish particles that are the size of silt. Unlike ordinary silt, loess particles are angular in shape. Loess is made of particles from many different minerals and rocks. Loess holds together so well that when it erodes, it splits off vertically to form clifflike slopes.

Loess appears to be a wind-carried sediment. The particles are light and small enough to be carried by winds in dust storms. The main deposits of loess in the United States are in the upper Mississippi and Missouri river valleys.

The particles that make up loess deposits in the United States and Europe were probably picked up from the outwash left by glaciers. The loess of northern China, however, was probably blown into China from the great deserts of Mongolia.

Topic 5 Composition and Types of Sand Dunes

Sand dunes are hills of sand deposited by winds. They form when the sand piles up against shrubs, boulders, or other obstructions.

Sand dunes are found wherever there are strong winds and enough loose sand, such as in the Sahara. Sand dunes also form on sandy river flood plains in semiarid climates and on sandy beaches.

Most sand dunes are made of quartz sands, but there are exceptions. The dunes of White Sands National Monument in New Mexico are made of gypsum sands. Where limestone or coral is common, dunes are calcite sands. Dune sands may contain grains of other minerals, such as feldspar, mica, and magnetite.

If the winds blow steadily from one direction, dunes will have a long, gentle slope on the *windward* side and a shorter, steep slope on the sheltered *leeward* side. For example, winds blowing steadily from the west will form dunes with gentle slopes on their west sides and steep slopes on their east sides. Tiny sand ripples are likely to form on the windward slopes of sand dunes.

Dunes occur in many different shapes. The shape of a dune seems to depend on the supply of sand, the strength and steadiness of the winds, and the amount of vegetation present. Strong, steady winds blowing over a limited supply of sand usually form crescent-shaped dunes called *barchans* (BAR kans). The ends of a barchan point downwind. Where sand is more abundant, long continuous sand ridges called *transverse* dunes form at right angles to the wind. *Parabolic* (U-shaped) dunes often form around blowouts. Unlike barchans, the open ends of parabolic dunes face upwind. Transverse and parabolic dunes are commonly seen on beaches. *Longitudinal*

12.3 Crescent-shaped barchans in Death Valley, California

12.4 Here are four types of sand dunes: **(a)** barchans, **(b)** parabolic, **(c)** transverse, and **(d)** longitudinal. The arrows represent wind direction.

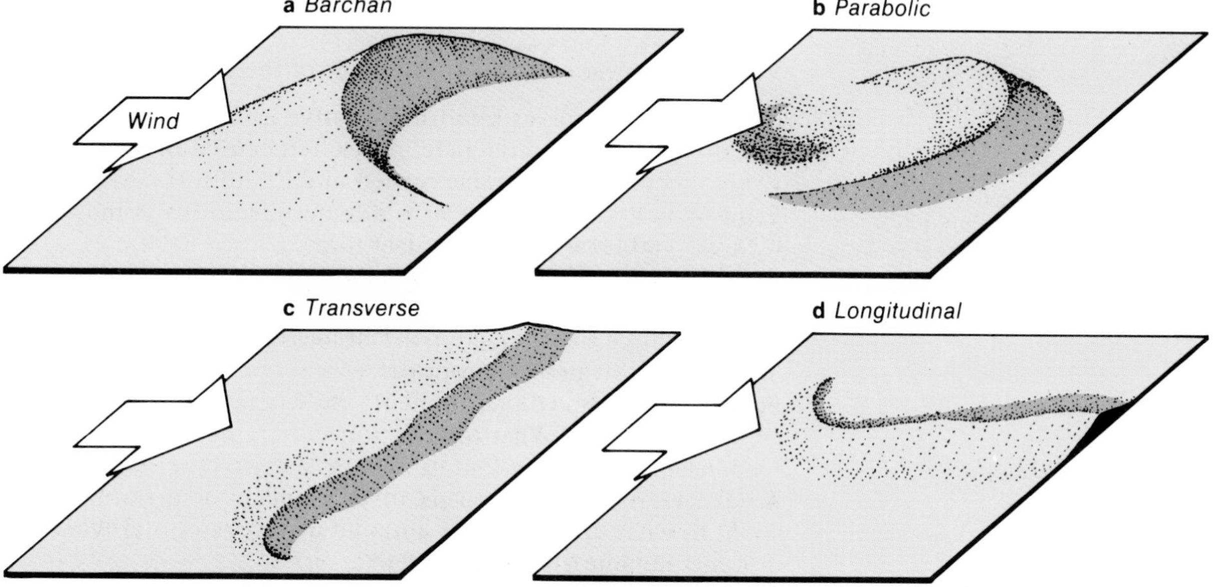

dunes form in desert regions with a moderate supply of sand. The winds that form these dunes often shift direction, but only slightly. Longitudinal dunes are long, straight ridges that are parallel to the general wind direction. Dunes in areas of widely changing wind directions may have shapes that are combinations of those just described.

Dunes range in size from a few meters high to more than a hundred meters high and many thousand meters long. Dunes often occur in groups that may cover a large area. About 800 000 square kilometers of the Sahara is covered by dunes.

Topic 6 **Migration of Dunes**

Each time the wind blows against the windward side of a sand dune, some of the surface sand is carried over the top. Then it falls down on the leeward side, also known as the slip face. As this process continues, the whole dune is moved in the leeward direction. The movement of a dune in this manner is called dune migration. The rate of migration may be as much as 30 meters per year.

Migrating dunes can bury towns, farms, and forests. However, not all dunes migrate. In humid beach areas, grasses and shrubs that grow on the dunes keep them from moving.

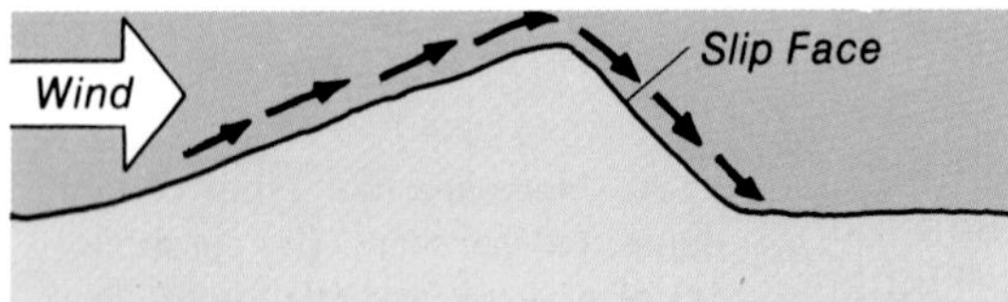

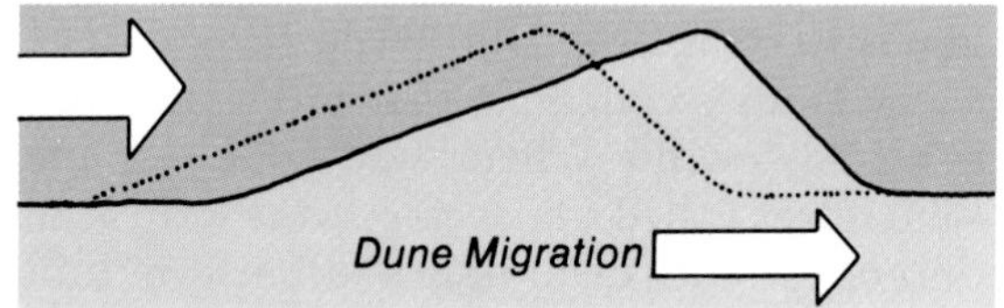

12.5 This dune migrates from left to right as sand is blown over the top and accumulates on the slip face.

TOPIC QUESTIONS

Each topic question refers to the topic of the same number.

1. **(a)** In what areas is wind most active as an agent of erosion? **(b)** What two materials are most often carried in dust storms? **(c)** Where are sand grains carried in dust storms?
2. **(a)** Which kind and size of windblown sediment is most abrasive? **(b)** How does a ventifact form?
3. **(a)** Describe deflation of sediment. **(b)** How is a desert pavement formed? **(c)** How is a blowout formed?
4. **(a)** Describe the characteristics of loess particles. **(b)** How is a loess deposit probably formed?
5. **(a)** How are sand dunes formed? **(b)** Where are sand dunes usually found? **(c)** What three factors determine the shape of sand dunes? **(d)** Identify four sand dune shapes.
6. **(a)** Describe what happens to the sand in a migrating dune. **(b)** In what direction does a sand dune migrate? **(c)** What prevents dune migration in humid areas?

II Waves in the Sea

Topic 7 Winds and Waves

An ocean wave is a rhythmic rise and fall of the water's surface. Waves seen at the seashore are generally produced one of three ways. The most common way is by wind. Waves are also formed by undersea earthquakes, and by the effects of the moon in producing tides.

When gusty storm wind blows over open water in an ocean or a lake, ripples form. If the wind continues to blow, or if it blows over a long distance, the ripples grow larger until they become waves. The height of a wind-formed wave depends on two factors: the length of time that the wind blows and the fetch. **Fetch** is the length of open water over which the wind blows. The fetch of a lake is shorter than that of an ocean. Thus, lake waves are not as high as ocean waves. Normal winds rarely produce ocean waves higher than 15 meters. However, hurricane winds can create waves 30 meters high after blowing for hours over a fetch of 1500 kilometers.

Gusts of strong winds that change speed and direction cause choppy seas. In choppy seas, each wave has a different height and length and may come from a different direction. As the waves clash and the winds tear the wave crests, foamy *whitecaps* are formed.

Even on calm days the sea is likely to have a steady movement of smooth waves. They come at regular intervals of up to ten seconds. These waves, called *swells,* are caused by winds and storms far out at sea.

OBJECTIVES

A Explain how wind produces water waves and list two factors affecting the height of a wind-formed wave.

B Identify the features of a water wave, find wave speed, and compare the speed, length, and origin of tsunamis with those of wind-formed waves.

C Describe the motion of water in a wave as the wave approaches shore.

D Describe the motion of the wave itself as the wave approaches shore.

E Name and explain the origin of some shoreline currents.

Topic 8 Features of Water Waves

When a wave passes through water, the water's surface rises and falls. **Wave height** is the difference between its high point, or *crest,* and its low point, or *trough.* **Wavelength** is the distance from one crest to the next. Strong winds make waves with long wavelengths. Waves produced during a storm often have wavelengths of more than 150 meters. On the average, the wavelength of an ocean wave is 20 to 30 times its height. A wave 2 meters high would have a wavelength of between 40 and 60 meters.

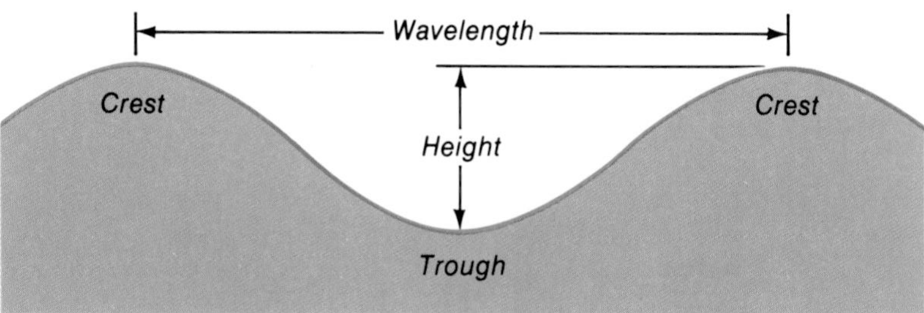

12.6 (below left) Wavelength is the distance from crest to crest. Height is the distance from crest to trough. (below right) Ocean waves are a powerful and constant erosional agent.

12.7 The size and speed of a tsunami make it an enormously destructive phenomenon.

The **period** of a wave is the time it takes one wavelength to pass a given point. Most ocean waves have a period that ranges from two seconds to ten seconds. To find the speed of a wave, divide its wavelength by its period.

$$\textbf{Speed} = \frac{\textbf{wavelength}}{\textbf{period}}$$

For example, what is the speed of a wave 24 meters long with a period of 4 seconds? The answer is 6 meters per second.

Waves with periods ranging from 5 to 60 minutes are called long waves. The best-known long wave is the **tsunami,** which is caused by an underwater earthquake. A typical Pacific Ocean tsunami may have a wavelength of 150 kilometers and a period of 12 minutes. Dividing 150 kilometers by 12 minutes gives a speed of 12.5 kilometers per minute (or 208 meters per second). When a wave of this speed reaches shore, it can cause great damage.

Water is not carried along with the motion of a wave. Instead, each water particle moves in place in a circular motion (Figure 12.8). (Objects floating in the water have the same kind of motion, which can be seen as objects bob up and down in the water.) As each water particle moves, it bumps into the next one and passes its energy along. In this way, the energy of the wave is passed through the water. The wave travels as far as its energy can carry it.

Wave motion also takes place below the surface. The water molecules move in smaller and smaller circles as depth increases. Motion ceases at a depth equal to about half the wavelength.

Most waves approach a shoreline at an angle. Yet when they reach shallow water, they tend to swing around until they approach the shoreline more or less head on. This bending of the wave is called **refraction.** How does refraction occur? As a wave comes in, the end closest to shore scrapes bottom first and slows down. The end that is still in deep water continues at its normal speed and tends to catch up. The result is that the wave approaches at a gentler angle, one that is more nearly parallel to the shore.

Refraction of ocean waves helps to explain why an uneven shoreline with shallow water is worn away quickly. Headlands are parts of a shore that stick out into the ocean. Coves are areas that are indented. Waves reach shallow water sooner at the headlands.

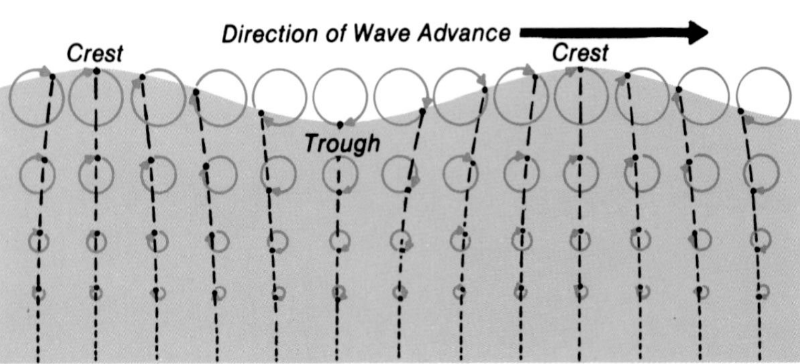

12.8 Water particles do not move forward with a wave. Instead, they move in place in a circular path.

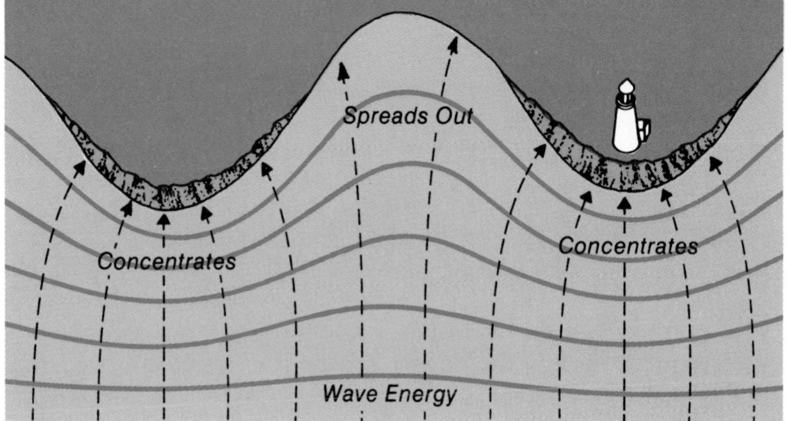

12.9 Refraction causes ocean waves to bend and approach the shoreline at a gentler angle. Because of refraction, wave energy tends to concentrate on headlands and spread out in coves.

Therefore, they slow down sooner in front of the headlands. The wave is bent until it is nearly parallel to, and is striking all three sides of, the headland (Figure 12.9). Wave action, and thus erosion, is reduced in shallow bays and coves.

Topic 9 **Origin of Breakers**

Waves usually approach the shoreline smoothly until they reach water so shallow that they touch the bottom. Recall from Topic 8 that this happens where water depth is about half the wavelength. For example, a wave with a wavelength of 20 meters will scrape bottom at 10 meters of depth.

As the wave scrapes the bottom, the circular motion of the wave is distorted, and the lower part of the wave slows down (Figure 12.10). At the same time the upper part of the wave moves ahead. Finally there is no longer enough water to support the wave. The crest falls over and breaks into surf that washes onto the beach. The next crest will fall over in about the same place. The line along which the crests break is called the *line of breakers.* The depth of water at the line of breakers is one to two times the height of the waves.

The surf formed by breaking waves is a powerful agent of erosion. On rocky shorelines it pounds the rocks and cliffs and wears them down. On beaches it scours the bottom and moves sediments along the shoreline.

12.10 Breakers form when waves reach shallow water—usually where the water depth is one or two times the height of the original wave.

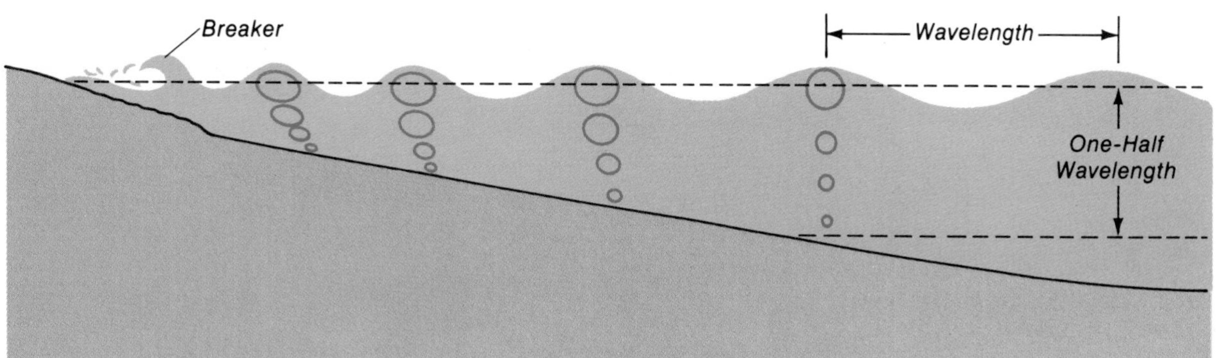

Topic 10 Shoreline Currents

Waves, like the winds that form them, may come from any direction. Thus, most waves strike shorelines at angles. When waves break, large amounts of water and sand are pushed up the beach at an angle. The motion of water up the beach is called **swash.** Most of the water runs back down the beach under the next wave in a gentle current called **backwash.** A very strong backwash is sometimes called *undertow.* Backwash drags sand almost straight back toward the sea. Each breaking wave repeats the process of pushing sand up at an angle (during swash) and pulling it straight back (during backwash). The sand drifts down the beach in a zigzag path (Figure 12.11 (a)). The water beyond the line of breakers is also pushed toward shore by waves and pulled back by backwash. This movement forms a **longshore current** that runs almost parallel to shore. Swimmers in the surf often discover that they have been moved along the beach by a longshore current. Longshore currents are important in the movement of sand and in the formation of sandbars.

Rip currents are much more dangerous than backwash. Rip currents are strong surface currents that flow away from the beach. They may form where too much water builds up in the surf zone. This can occur where two longshore currents meet head-on, where breakers bring in more water than backwash can return, or where water is held back by a headland, breakwater, or an underwater sandbar. The piled-up water flows rapidly back to the sea through a gap in the barrier.

Since rip currents can reach speeds of up to five kilometers per hour, they are a serious hazard for swimmers. Swimmers often can avoid rip currents by knowing what to look for. The water in a rip current may carry a lot of sand, which makes the current visible. Waves around a rip current may be steeper than the surrounding waves, or the line of breakers may be further out to sea. For a swimmer who is caught in a rip current, the best thing to do is to swim parallel to shore. Do not try to swim against the rip current.

12.11 **(a)** Swash and backwash carry sand down the beach in a zigzag path. Water beyond the line of breakers is carried in a longshore current. **(b)** An aerial view of waves along the beach

a

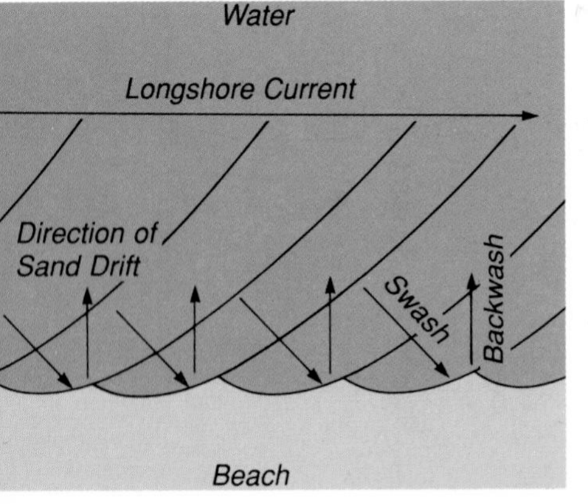
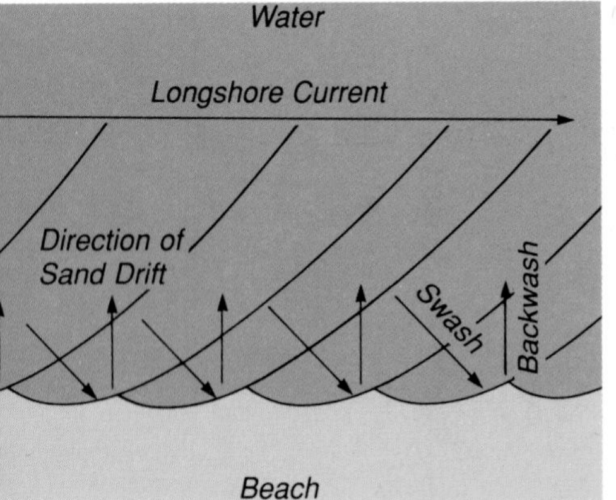

b

TOPIC QUESTIONS

Each topic question refers to the topic of the same number.

7. **(a)** How are most waves produced? **(b)** What two factors affect the height of wind-formed waves? **(c)** What are swells and what is their cause?
8. **(a)** Explain the meaning of wavelength, crest, trough, period. **(b)** Find the speed of a wave that has a length of 12 meters and a period of 3 seconds. **(c)** Describe the motion of water molecules in a wave. **(d)** What is wave refraction and how is it caused? **(e)** What effect does wave refraction have on uneven shorelines and why?
9. **(a)** What causes breakers and surf to form? **(b)** How deep is the water at the line of breakers? **(c)** Why is surf important geologically?
10. **(a)** What are swash and backwash? **(b)** Describe the motion of water and sand in a longshore current. **(c)** What is a rip current? **(d)** How can a rip current be recognized?

Dr. Orrin Pilkey, Jr.
Marine Geologist

Beach erosion by waves and currents has become a serious problem along the Atlantic coast of the United States. As much as a meter of shoreline is being removed from some areas each year.

Dr. Orrin Pilkey, Jr., of Duke University is one of several marine geologists who are studying the problem. He has found that the erosion involves more than the shoreline we see; the ocean floor offshore is also being removed. This means that the edge of the continental shelf is creeping closer to shore. Dr. Pilkey explains that this gives deep water ocean waves less distance to lose their energy and, as a result, they strike the beach with greater force and do more damage.

Dr. Pilkey has also found that sea walls or other obstacles do not help to save beaches but, in fact, speed up erosion. The waves crashing against the sea wall carry away far more sand than they would if they could roll gently onto a beach.

To date, no method of slowing beach erosion has proved to be very effective for very long. Most marine geologists, including Dr. Pilkey, expect the problem to get worse.

OBJECTIVES

A Name and describe some features of shoreline erosion and shoreline deposition.

B Define *beach* and discuss factors that affect the kind of materials that make up a beach.

C Describe the formation of coral reef structures.

III Shoreline Features

Topic 11 How Waves Erode Rock Materials

Waves erode the shoreline in a number of ways. Breaking storm waves may strike rock cliffs with a force of thousands of kilograms per square meter. Such breakers easily remove large masses of loose sand and clay. Bedrock is split by water driven into cracks and fissures. The bedrock is also scoured away by the grinding of sands and pebbles. Boulders that fall from rock cliffs are pounded into pebbles and sand. Sea water dissolves minerals from rocks such as limestone.

When waves strike the headlands of a deep-water shoreline, they may cut away the rock up to the high-tide level. If the rock is soft, it is worn away quickly, creating a notch. The materials overhanging the notch collapse. When this happens, a **sea cliff** is formed. These cliffs wear back rapidly, in some cases as fast as a meter a year.

In harder rock materials a notch may deepen until it becomes a *sea cave*. Waves may cut through the walls of sea caves to form *sea arches.* Arches may also form when waves cut through vertical cracks in narrow headlands. If the roof of a sea arch falls in, a tall, narrow rock island called a *stack* remains.

All of these features can be seen on the coasts of California, Oregon, Washington, and Maine, on the Gaspé peninsula of Canada, and in many parts of the Mediterranean Sea.

12.12 Sea stacks on the coast of New Brunswick, Canada

12.13 A lagoon is an area protected from strong winds and waves, often by a baymouth bar or other sandbar.

Topic 12 Attached and Unattached Sandbars

On irregular shorelines, longshore currents carry away most of the sand and pebbles eroded from the headlands. Where a longshore current passes across the mouth of a bay or cove, some of the sediment is carried inland by waves. There it may form a sand or pebble beach.

Many times, however, the current carries enough sand to form a **sandbar** across the mouth of the bay. The sandbar seems to grow right out of the end of the headland. Such a bar, attached at one end, is called a *spit.* In time it may grow completely across the bay to become a *baymouth bar.* In some places bars form between islands and the mainland.

Waves and crosscurrents may drive the end of a spit toward the shore. A spit with a curved end is called a *hook.* Sandy Hook in New Jersey is a well-known hook. Other famous hooks are Rockaway Beach on Long Island, New York, and the tip of Cape Cod in Massachusetts.

Sandbars usually protect the water behind them from strong winds and waves. The protected areas are called **lagoons.** As time passes, lagoons may fill with sediment and become salt marshes. Jamaica Bay is the lagoon behind the Rockaway Beach hook. It is an important shelter for shorebirds, as are many other lagoons.

Sandbars may also form on coasts with straight shorelines. These bars are not attached to the shoreline. Instead, they run parallel to it at some distance from the shore. They are called **barrier islands.** They are found along the eastern coast of the United States from New York southward to Texas. Some well-known examples of barrier islands include Fire Island in New York, Atlantic City beach in New Jersey, and Hatteras in North Carolina. Galveston, Texas, and Palm Beach and Miami Beach, Florida, are also located on barrier islands. Padre Island, a barrier island in Texas, is about 160 kilometers long.

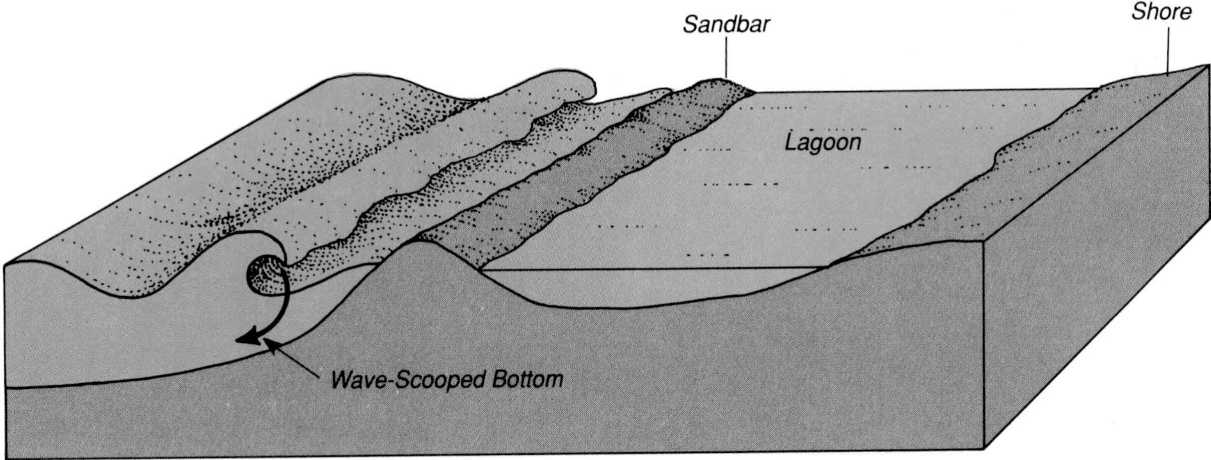

12.14 This diagram shows the relative positions of a sandbar, lagoon, and shore.

Barrier islands, sandbars, and beaches are not permanent features. The sand that makes these features is constantly being removed by waves, storms, and longshore drift. If enough new sand arrives at the beach or island (from rivers or from other beaches), then it remains. However, if the amount of sand removed is greater than the amount that arrives, then the beach or island erodes. In many parts of the country, rock walls have been built to protect houses and other property from beach erosion. Unfortunately, such structures often make the situation worse because they prevent waves from breaking normally. The energy of the waves hits the beach all at once, and the wave removes more sand than it otherwise would have. The best way to avoid property loss due to beach erosion is to avoid building on the beach.

Topic 13 **Beach Materials**

Geologists define a **beach** as the area between the high-tide level and the low-tide level. The gentler the seafloor, the wider the beach. Beaches may be sandy, pebbly, or even rocky. The makeup of a beach depends on both the material that is available and on the slope of the shoreline. Materials that make up a beach may come from the local area, or they may arrive from other beaches and rivers. Not all materials that arrive are left on the beach. If the seafloor is steep, sands and clays are washed out to sea by backwash, and pebble beaches are left. If the seafloor slopes gently, only clay is washed out, and sand beaches are formed.

Most beach sands are grains of durable minerals, such as quartz and some feldspar. Other materials commonly found in beach sands are grains of magnetite and flakes of muscovite mica. The makeup of beach sand, however, depends not only on the durability of minerals but also on the minerals that are common in the source area. Beach sand that was weathered from granite is mainly quartz and feldspar. Beach sands on coral islands, such as Bermuda, are mainly coral (calcite) fragments.

Topic 14 Types of Shorelines

The shoreline of the Maine coast zigzags from headland to bay, covering a total of nearly 4000 kilometers. The straight-line distance along the coast, however, is about 300 kilometers. The coast of Maine is an example of an irregular shoreline. Other examples of this type of shoreline are the coast of Scotland and the northwest coast of Spain.

Most irregular shorelines appear to have formed when coastal areas were flooded by the sea. This flooding occurred either because the land sank or the sea rose, which the sea did at the end of the Ice Age. After the flooding, the drowned main valleys became short, deep, narrow bays. The divides between the valleys became headlands. The drowned tributary valleys became branches of the bays. Many hills were partly drowned and became islands. Some were completely drowned and became shallow areas called *shoals.* The shallowness of a shoal makes navigation by boat difficult.

The land along the Atlantic coast from New York to Florida is called a coastal plain. Much of this area also has an irregular shoreline formed by drowning of the land. However, the river valleys of the coastal plain were wide and gently sloped. Thus, the bays of the coastal plain are wider and longer than those in Maine. The water close to shore is not as deep as in Maine, and there are fewer islands. Chesapeake Bay is the drowned valley of the lower Susquehanna River and its tributaries. New York Bay is the drowned valley of the lower Hudson River. Similarly, San Francisco Bay is the drowned valley of the lower Sacramento River.

12.15 **(a)** The irregular shoreline of the Maine coast formed in a hilly area cut by river valleys. **(b)** The valleys were drowned by a rise in sea level. Valleys became bays, ridges became headlands, and hills became islands. **(c)** Erosion by waves and currents formed sea cliffs and attached sandbars.

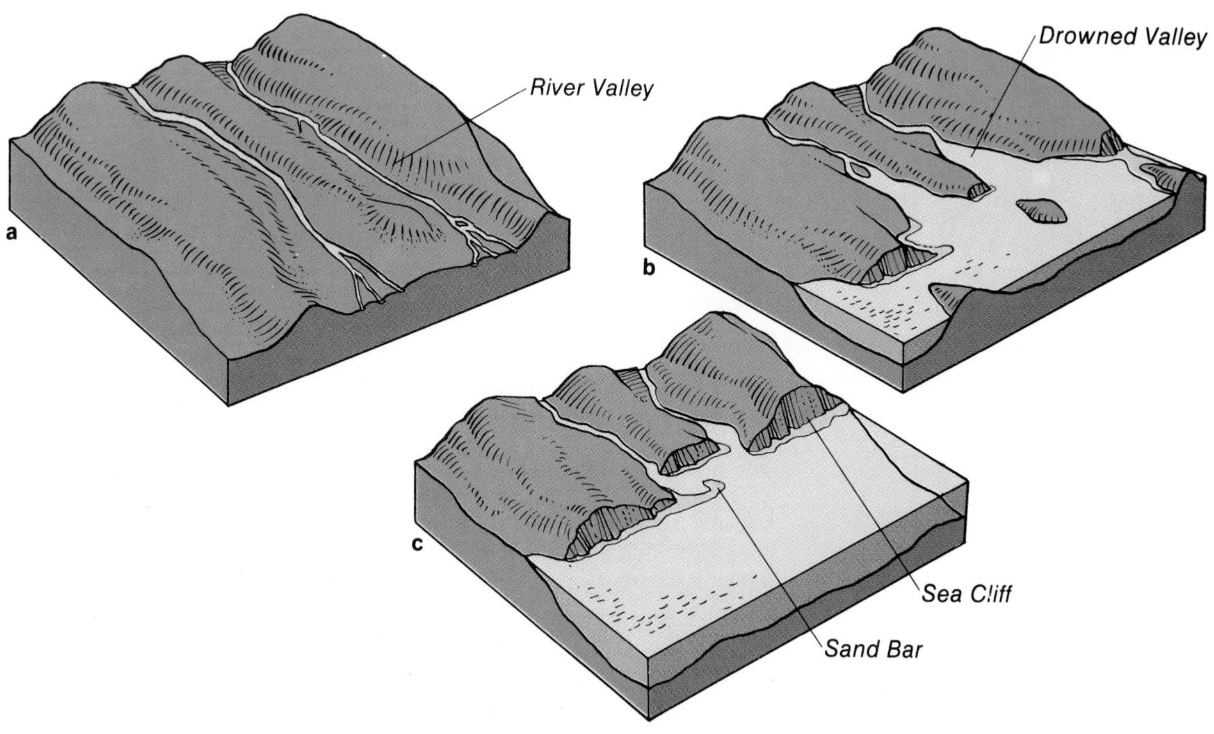

12.16 A deep fiord in Norway

During the Ice Age, glaciers in Norway, Alaska, and other near-polar regions reached the oceans. Glacial troughs (Chapter 11, Topic 11) were formed below the present-day sea level. When the Ice Age ended, the sea flooded the parts of the troughs below sea level. This formed long, deep, steep-sided bays called **fiords.** The tributary valleys of glacial troughs are hanging troughs. Where hanging troughs meet the main glacial trough, spectacular waterfalls drop down the walls of the fiord. Fiord shorelines are found in Greenland, Labrador, Chile, New Zealand, Norway, and Alaska.

Almost all of the west coasts of North America and South America—from Oregon to central Chile—have fairly straight or regular shorelines. A regular shoreline does not have many deeply indented inlets or drowned valleys, although it may have a number of shallow, wave-carved coves. The plate tectonic theory (Chapter 13) explains how these regular shorelines were formed. These shorelines are, for the most part, on the boundary line between two sets of plates. As the heavier Pacific Ocean plates meet the continental plates and plunge under them, mountains rise and deep undersea troughs form. Long lines of mountains run parallel to the coasts. The ocean floor slopes steeply to great depths near each shore. Each coast is bordered in many places by sea cliffs and stacks.

Topic 15 Corals, Coral Reefs, and Coral Atolls

Corals are tiny sea animals that live in colonies. They remain fastened to rocky seafloors in warm, clear, fairly shallow water. For corals to survive, the water temperature must be between 18°C and 21°C. The water depth must be no more than about 45 meters.

Since corals do not move, they depend on waves and currents to carry their food supply. They make their shells from the lime in sea water. When corals die, their shells remain, and new corals grow on

12.17 (left) Corals are tiny marine animals that live in groups. New corals tend to build their shells on top of old coral shells. (right) Over time, the shells of generations of corals build up a coral reef.

them. Large buildups of coral shells are called *coral reefs.* Corals do not grow above the surface of the water. However, as with sandbars, waves may pile coral shells above sea level. When these coral shell fragments are cemented together, they form coral limestone.

Coral colonies growing close to shore form **fringing reefs.** Fringing reefs can be seen in Florida and along many other semitropical and tropical coasts. A coral reef grows mainly on its ocean side, where ocean waves bring food that feeds new corals. When old corals die on the shore side of the reef, their shells are broken and scattered. Thus, a fringing reef slowly moves away from shore.

As a fringing reef grows oceanward, it becomes a **barrier reef.** The Great Barrier Reef of Australia is about 2000 kilometers long and up to 150 kilometers wide. The wide lagoon between the reef and the mainland is called the Inland Waterway.

An **atoll** is a narrow, ring-shaped island or chain of islands. Atolls are found mostly in open waters in the middle of the Pacific Ocean, far away from shores of continents. Most atolls are made of coral limestone, yet coral cannot grow in the deep water far away from shore. Therefore, there must have been a surface on which the coral atoll started to grow. Holes bored through the coral show that each atoll has grown on the slopes of a volcano. The formation of atolls is discussed further in Chapter 18.

TOPIC QUESTIONS

Each topic question refers to the topic of the same number.

11. What features are caused by wave erosion on irregular shorelines?

12. (a) How do the following originate: a spit, a baymouth bar, a hook? (b) What is a lagoon? (c) Explain why shoreline features made of sand cannot be considered permanent structures.

13. (a) What is a beach? (b) How does a pebble beach form?

14. (a) How were most irregular shorelines formed? (b) How do the bays between New York and Florida differ from those of the Maine coast? (c) What are fiord shorelines? Where do they occur? (d) Explain the origin of the regular shorelines of western North America and South America.

15. (a) What are corals? (b) How does a coral reef form? (c) What is a fringing reef? (d) Why does a coral reef grow mainly seaward? (e) What is a barrier reef? (f) What is an atoll?

CHAPTER 12 REVIEW

Summary

Wind erodes and weathers land by moving loose sediment. Desert pavement and blowouts result from wind erosion.

Loess is a silt-sized, wind-deposited sediment.

Sand supply, wind strength, and vegetation affect sand dune shape. Dunes migrate in the direction toward which the wind blows.

Most waves result from winds. Fetch and wind duration affect the height of a wind-formed wave.

A wave is described by its height, wavelength, period, and speed. A tsunami is a long, rapidly moving wave caused by an undersea earthquake.

Water moves in place as a wave passes. Water motion exists to a depth of about one half wavelength, the depth at which a wave begins to slow down.

Waves approaching a shoreline at an angle refract and approach the shore at less of an angle.

Swash, backwash, longshore currents, and rip currents move water and sediments on beaches.

Sea cliffs, sea caves, sea arches, and stacks result from shoreline erosion. Sandbars, spits, baymouth bars, hooks, lagoons, and barrier islands result from shoreline deposition.

Pebble beaches form on steep shorelines, sand beaches on gently sloping shorelines.

Irregular shorelines form when hilly, uneven coastal areas are flooded by the sea. The regular shorelines of western North and South America are the result of crustal plate collisions.

Corals are tiny, shell-building sea animals that build coral reef structures.

Vocabulary

atoll
backwash
barrier island
barrier reef
beach
blowouts
corals
deflation
desert pavement
dust storm
fetch
fiord
fringing reef
lagoon
loess
longshore current
period
refraction
rip current
sandbar
sea cliff
swash
tsunami
ventifact
wave height
wavelength

Review

Choose the best answer for each item. Write the letter of the answer on your paper.

1. An area that is LEAST likely to experience wind erosion is a (a) beach, (b) desert, (c) forest, (d) semiarid region.
2. Which material is likely to be the most abrasive in a wind storm? (a) quartz sand (b) calcite sand (c) silt (d) clay
3. A shallow depression formed by deflation is a (a) dune, (b) stack, (c) blowout, (d) spit.
4. Which particle size is closest to that of loess? (a) clay (b) silt (c) sand (d) pebbles
5. Barchan, transverse, parabolic, and longitudinal are kinds of (a) sea arches, (b) offshore sandbars, (c) sand dunes, (d) coral reefs.
6. When sand is blown from the windward side of a dune to the leeward side, the dune will (a) migrate to leeward, (b) weather into clay, (c) stand in vertical cliffs, (d) migrate to windward.
7. The fetch of a wave is the (a) height of the wave, (b) speed of the wave, (c) speed of the wave-forming wind, (d) distance over which the wave-forming wind blows.
8. The distance from the crest of one wave to the crest of the next is (a) wavelength, (b) period, (c) fetch, (d) trough.
9. Wave motion begins to touch bottom at a depth of about (a) ½ wavelength, (b) 1 wavelength, (c) 1½ wavelengths, (d) 2 wavelengths.
10. The process by which waves are turned to be more parallel to the shoreline is called (a) ventifaction, (b) deflation, (c) refraction, (d) erosion.

11. Longshore currents are (a) strong seaward-flowing currents, (b) gentle seaward-flowing currents, (c) important movers of sand, (d) a kind of tsunami.
12. Which feature results from shoreline erosion? (a) spit (b) stack (c) hook (d) lagoon
13. A beach near a steeply sloping sea floor is likely to be covered with (a) mud, (b) silt, (c) sand, (d) pebbles.
14. Which mineral is most common in beach sands made from coral fragments? (a) quartz (b) calcite (c) gypsum (d) magnetite
15. A glacial trough that was drowned by the sea is a (a) atoll, (b) stack, (c) spit, (d) fiord.
16. A ring-shaped coral island is a (a) atoll, (b) barrier reef, (c) ventifact, (d) tsunami.

Interpret and Apply

On your paper, answer each question in complete sentences.

1. How would visibility in a sand storm compare with visibility in a dust storm?
2. Why is quartz sand a better tool of wind erosion than gypsum sand or calcite sand? (The table *Properties of Some Common Minerals* on pages 576–577 may be helpful.)
3. Make sketches showing the windward and leeward sides of sand dunes for winds blowing steadily from (a) north, (b) south, (c) east, and (d) west.
4. How might the sand grains in a sand dune be different from the sand grains in a river delta?
5. Find the speed of a wave that has a wavelength of 300 meters and a period of 25 seconds.
6. At what depth would a 300-meter-long wave first be slowed by the seafloor? At what depth would a 10-meter wave be slowed?
7. Would there be a longshore current in a lagoon behind a long sandbar? Explain your answer.

Critical Thinking

Particle sizes in sand dunes and loess vary, as do the amounts of each particle size present. The graph below shows the percent of each particle in a sand dune sample and in a loess sample. Refer to the graph to answer questions 1–5.

1. What is the size range for medium sand?
2. Give the name, size range, and percentage of the most abundant particle in the sand dune sample and in the loess sample.
3. How does the percentage of coarse silt in the sand dune compare with the percentage of coarse silt in the loess?
4. How does the range of sizes for the sand dune compare with those of the loess?
5. Which sample shows better sorting? (Review the term *sorting* from Chapter 5.)

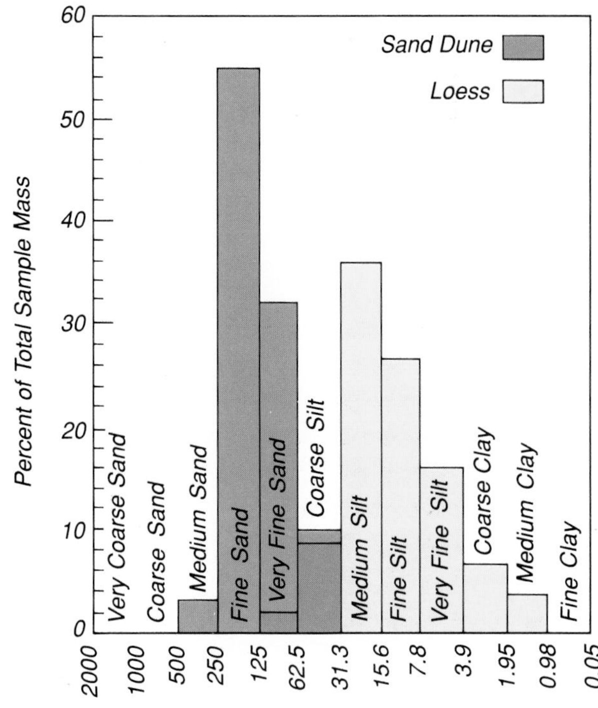

*1 micrometer (μm) = 1000 millimeters (mm)

UNIT THREE
Forces That Raise the Surface

▲
A movement in Earth's crust made these sediment layers break and shift. Why did Earth's crust move in this particular place?

▲
Rocks and dust explode out of Earth's interior during a volcanic eruption. Can volcanic eruptions be predicted?

Thousands of years ago, these folded rocks lay flat. What Earth forces bend solid rock? ▶

What raises Earth's surface?

Even as Earth's surface is worn away, it is pushed up from within. Unseen forces shift and mold Earth's face, making mountains, adding new material to the crust, raising land out of the sea. Look at the photographs. What evidence does each show of the powerful forces that shape Earth's crust?

Alaska's Mount McKinley, the highest peak in North America, is often shaken by earthquakes. Is there a reason high mountains and earthquakes occur together? ▼

Earthquakes can shatter buildings in a matter of seconds. Here, people in Mexico City look at the damage to their homes following a quake. Why are earthquakes common in some parts of the world, but not in others? ▼

CHAPTER

13 Plate Tectonics

▲
A *Paradoxides* fossil

How Do You Know That . . .

Earth's surface has changed? This fossil, found in an outcrop near Boston, Massachusetts, is called *Paradoxides. Paradoxides* is found in similar rocks along the east coast of North America, but nowhere else in North America. However, rocks containing *Paradoxides* are found in the British Isles. *Paradoxides* provides evidence that North America and the British Isles were once part of the same continent. The continent separated as an ocean basin formed between North America and Europe. Some parts of this continent remained on the North American side of the ocean, while other pieces went with the Euopean side.

I What Is Plate Tectonics?

Topic 1 Moving Plates Cover the Globe

OBJECTIVES

A Define *plate tectonics* and describe the relative motions of several plates.

B Locate and describe the lithosphere and the asthenosphere and relate both to plate tectonics.

The discovery that continents could be separated into parts that can then move about has led to a new understanding of Earth's outer layer. Scientists now know that Earth's surface consists of a number of rigid, but moving, pieces called *plates*. In some areas, the plates are moving away from each other. In other areas, the plates are moving together. The study of the formation and movement of these plates is called **plate tectonics.**

Earth's surface is divided into approximately a dozen plates (see Figure 13.1). Some of the plates, such as the North American Plate and the Eurasian Plate, are moving apart. The South American Plate and the African Plate are also moving apart. Other plates are moving together. The Indian Plate is colliding with the Eurasian Plate and the Nazca Plate is sliding under the South American Plate. In California, the Pacific Plate and the North American Plate are sliding past each other.

13.1 The major plates and some of the smaller plates are labeled on the map below. Notice that the large plates include both oceans and landmasses.

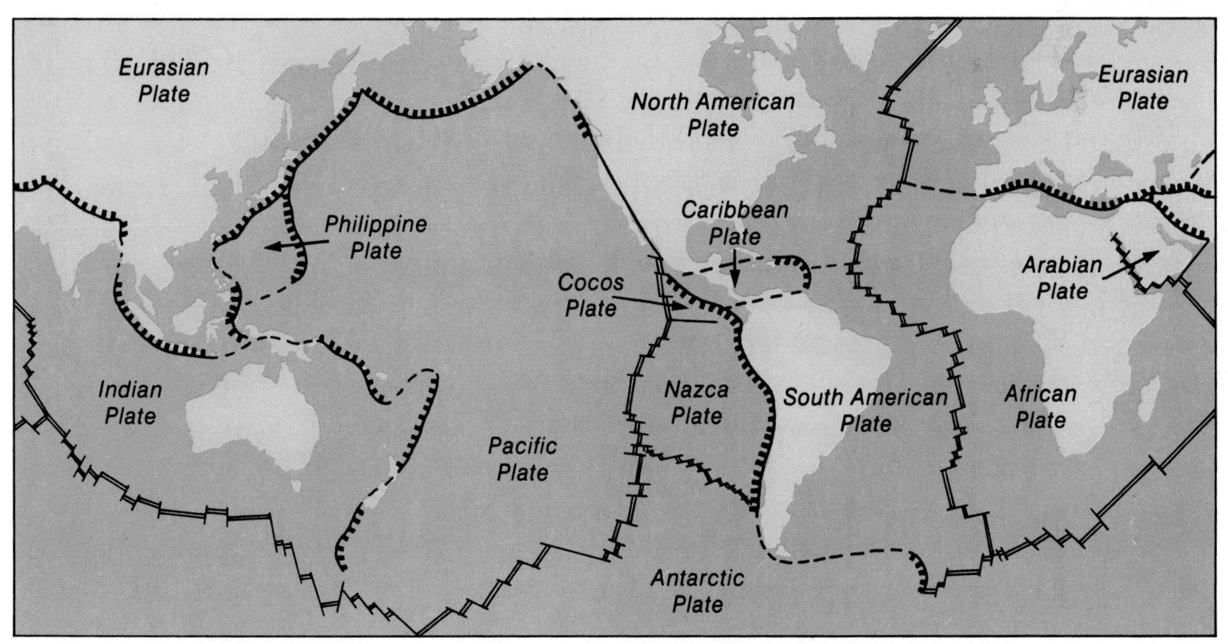

Topic 2 **How Thick Are the Plates?**

Plate tectonics has expanded the model of Earth's interior as described in Chapter 1. The crust and mantle were originally thought to represent two distinctly different materials. Now it is known that the crust and the uppermost portion of the mantle are very similar in both rock composition and physical properties. Together they make up a single solid layer called the **lithosphere.** The lithosphere is rigid but broken into plates that are able to move. It is about 100 kilometers thick.

The composition of the lithosphere is basically that of the igneous rock basalt. The continents, however, are a major exception. Continental crust has a composition more like that of the igneous rock granite. Because granite is less dense (lighter) than basalt, continents occur only as pieces embedded in the surface of the more dense (heavier) lithosphere.

Topic 3 **Why Do the Plates Move?**

The lithospheric plates rest upon a layer within the mantle called the **asthenosphere.** This layer is thought to cause plate movement.

The asthenosphere has a composition similar to the lithosphere above, but it has very different properties. The rock of the asthenosphere is partially melted. As a result, this layer is able to flow. Scientists think that this flow takes the form of very large and slow-

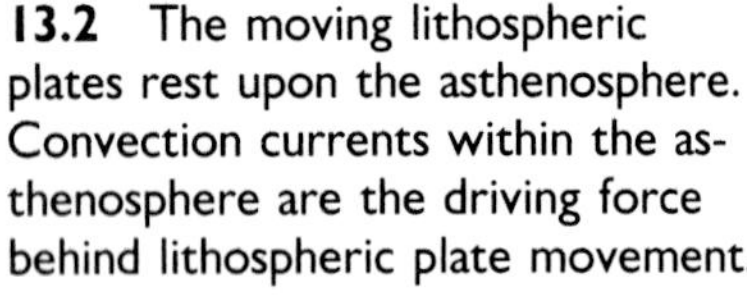

13.2 The moving lithospheric plates rest upon the asthenosphere. Convection currents within the asthenosphere are the driving force behind lithospheric plate movement.

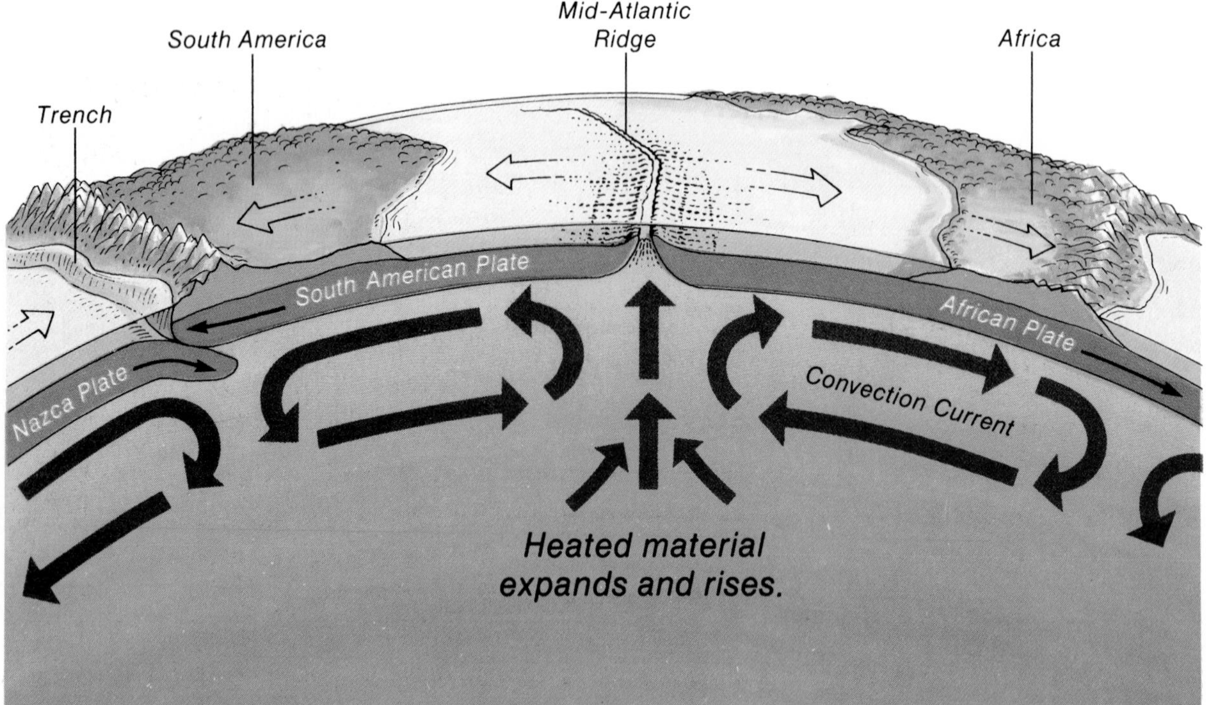

moving convection currents. Within such currents, material expands and rises upon heating but contracts and sinks upon cooling.

Where the convection currents within the asthenosphere are rising, new material continually arrives at Earth's surface and pushes older material aside. This push drives the lithospheric plates apart. The South American Plate and the African Plate are an example.

Where cooler, denser currents within the asthenosphere seem to be sinking, the plates of the lithosphere are pulled together. This motion is thought to be the reason for the Nazca Plate sliding beneath the South American Plate.

TOPIC QUESTIONS

Each topic question refers to the topic of the same number.

1. **(a)** What is plate tectonics? **(b)** Identify plates that are moving apart; moving together or colliding; and sliding past each other.
2. **(a)** Describe the structure and properties of the lithosphere. **(b)** How are the composition and density of continental crust different from that of the rest of the lithosphere?
3. **(a)** Where is the asthenosphere? **(b)** What is the major property of the asthenosphere? **(c)** How do the lithospheric plates move where convection currents are rising? **(d)** How do the plates move where convection currents are sinking?

Dr. Anita G. Harris
Geologist

A devil's advocate is someone who presents facts and arguments against an accepted concept. Dr. Anita G. Harris considers herself a devil's advocate with respect to plate tectonics. Although she does not argue against the movement of the plates, she does feel that those motions are used to explain too many aspects of Earth's history. She says that plate tectonics has been "oversimplified and overapplied."

After earning degrees from Brooklyn College, Indiana University, and Ohio State University, Dr. Harris became a specialist in conodonts at the U.S. Geological Survey. Conodonts are very tiny fossil pieces of an unknown marine animal found in sedimentary rocks. Dr. Harris collected many of her conodonts from the sedimentary rocks of the Appalachians. In the process, she developed a thorough understanding of the geologic history of that area. That understanding has caused her to question some of the conclusions of other geologists about the origin of certain areas of the Appalachians.

II Evidence for Plate Tectonics

OBJECTIVES

A Describe the theory of continental drift and list some evidences that Alfred Wegener used to support the theory.

B Discuss the relationship between earthquakes, volcanoes, and plate boundaries.

C Explain what is meant by normal and reversed polarity, discuss the pattern of magnetic polarity at spreading centers, and relate this pattern to plate tectonics.

D Discuss heat flow and elevation of the seafloor as evidence of seafloor spreading.

Topic 4 Africa and South America

The idea that Earth's solid surface might be moving and changing is not new. When the first reliable world maps were made in the seventeenth century, people noted the remarkable similarities in the shape of the west coast of Africa and the east coast of South America. The suggestion was eventually made that the two continents had once been part of a larger continent that had broken and moved apart. This idea was the start of a theory called *continental drift.*

The most famous version of the theory was proposed in 1912 by Alfred Wegener, a German scientist. In addition to the similarities in continental shape, Wegener found other evidence to show that Africa and South America must have been joined once. He noted that the fossil remains of *Mesosaurus,* a small reptile that lived 270 million years ago, are found in Brazil and in South Africa but are not found anywhere else on Earth. This peculiar distribution is easily explained if the two continents were joined at that time. Wegener also noted that some particularly distinctive rocks are found on both continents. The rocks at these locations would match nicely if the two continents were joined.

Wegener's theory of continental drift was debated for several years after its proposal. It was subjected to scorn and ridicule until the 1960's. At that time, new discoveries about such seemingly unrelated phenomena as earthquakes, volcanoes, magnetism, and crustal heat flow added support to Wegener's ideas. The theory of continental drift was expanded and became plate tectonics.

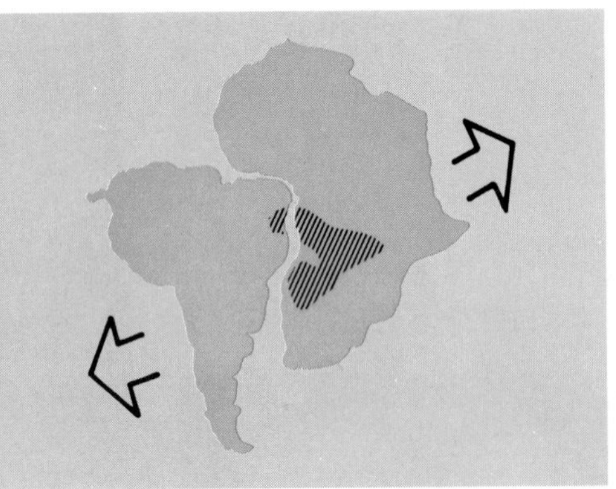

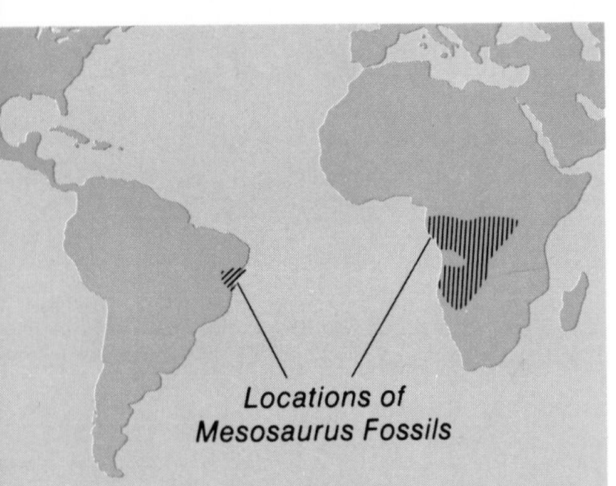

13.3 The theory of continental drift implies that Africa and South America were once joined. Fossil evidence on both continents seems to back the theory.

Topic 5 Earthquakes and Volcanoes

Scientists have long observed that earthquakes do not occur randomly throughout the world, but occur in rather limited belts. They have also noted that these same belts contain most of Earth's volcanoes. The locations of the belts became clear with the understanding of plate tectonics. The belts where earthquakes and volcanoes are located mark the location of *plate boundaries.*

It is not hard to understand why plate boundaries are active areas. These boundaries are places where one plate is moving relative to another plate. Stresses build up along the boundary, and when the stress becomes too great, fractures form and earthquakes occur. The boundaries are also areas of high heat flow, where molten rock moves upward to Earth's surface and forms volcanoes.

The largest active belt is the one that nearly surrounds the Pacific Ocean. In an average year, 90 percent of all the world's earthquakes occur there. Many famous volcanoes are found there also. Among them are Mount St. Helens in Washington State, Mount Katmai in Alaska, Mount Fujiyami in Japan, and Mount Mayon in the Philippine Islands.

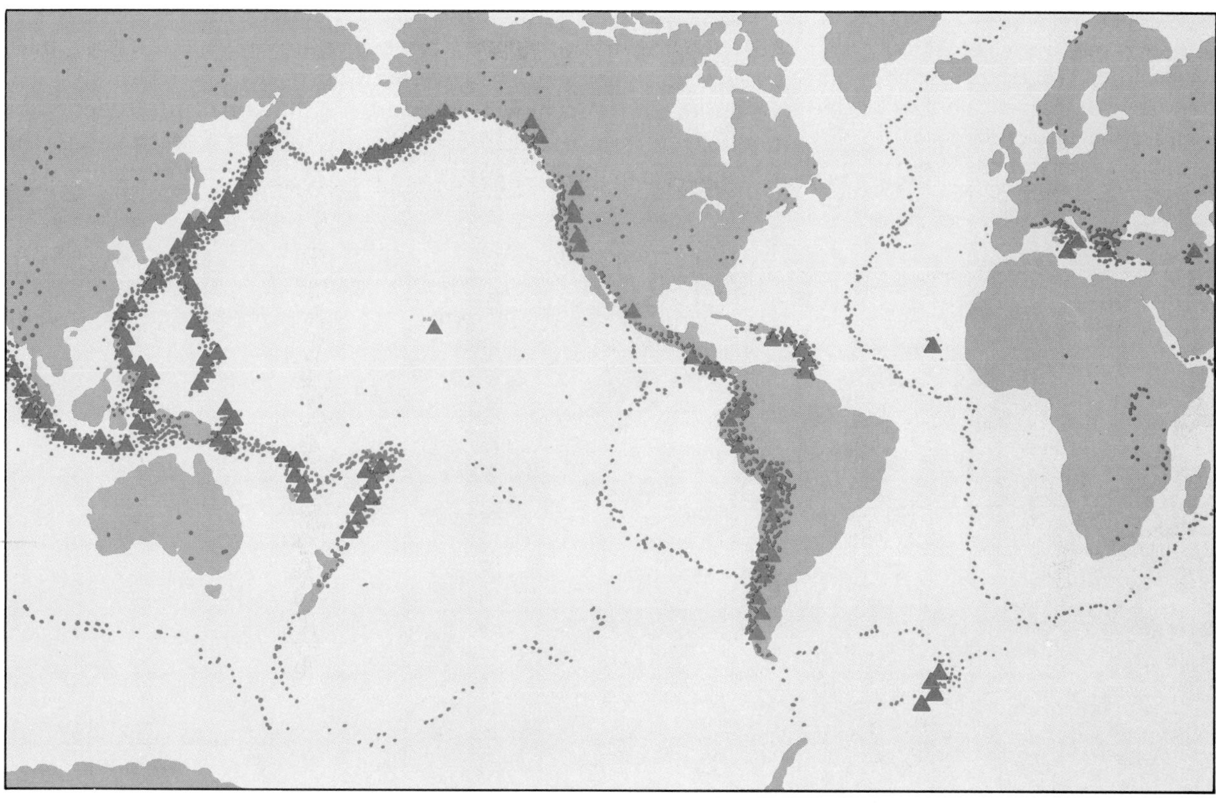

Volcanoes   Earthquakes

13.4 This map shows the locations of the world's earthquake and volcano belts. The belts are also the location of plate boundaries.

Topic 6 Magnetism

Some igneous rocks contain minerals that are magnetic. These minerals provide a record of the direction of Earth's magnetic poles at the time the rock formed. When this record was studied in igneous rocks on the continents, it was discovered that Earth's crust has apparently shifted or drifted since the rocks were formed. There is also evidence that Earth's magnetic poles had often been reversed. The present north magnetic pole became the south magnetic pole and the present south magnetic pole became the north magnetic pole. Scientists found that there have been four major periods of normal and reversed polarity within the past four million years (see Figure 13.5).

Magnetic polarity reversals also show in bands in the igneous rocks on the ocean floor. Where the lithospheric plates are moving apart, the polarity reversals occur in bands parallel to and on opposite sides of the plate boundaries. Scientists compared the magnetic bands found in the rock on both sides of the boundary with the actual age of the rock. They determined that the youngest rocks of the ocean floor are at the spreading plate boundaries, and that the ocean floor becomes increasingly older away from the boundaries.

13.5 There have been four major polarity reversals in the past four million years. Geologists use the knowledge of magnetic polarity to compare the ages of rocks near spreading centers on the ocean floor.

Using this observation, scientists theorize what happens in the areas where the lithospheric plates are moving apart. These areas are **spreading centers.** Lava wells up from deep within Earth and continuously forms new rocks there. At the same time, older rocks move away from the boundary equally in both directions. As the lithospheric plates move apart, they carry their continents with them.

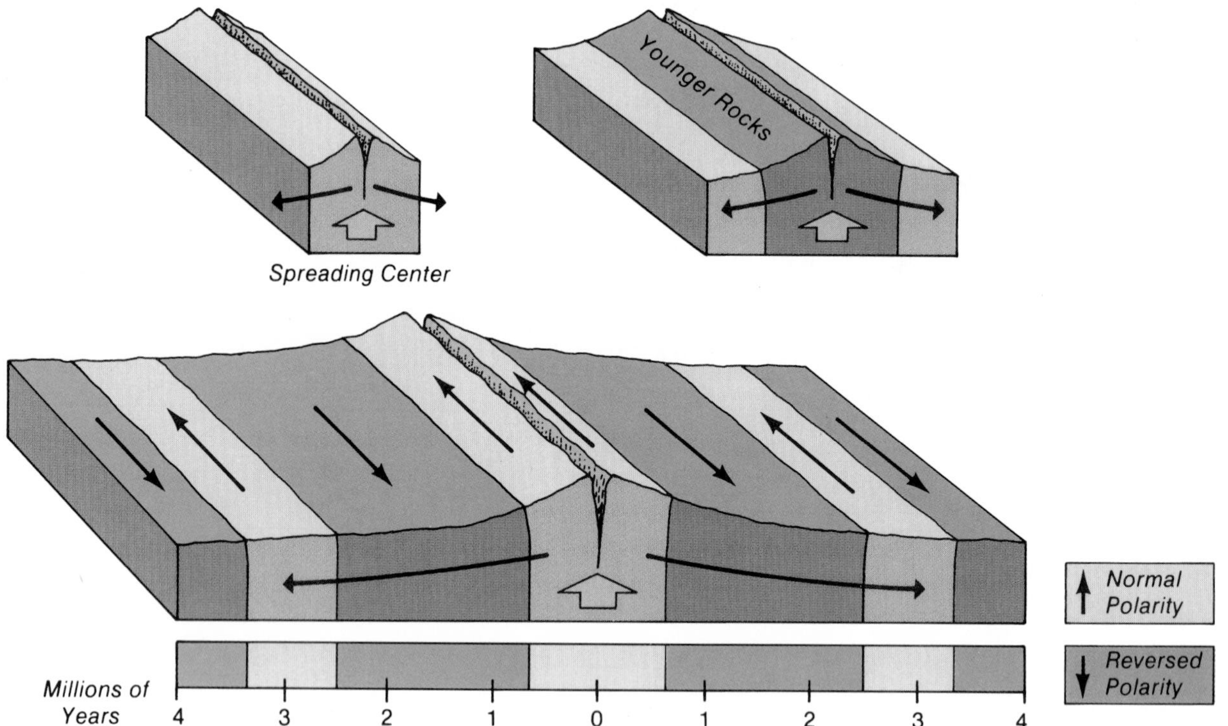

Topic 7 Heat Flow and Seafloor Elevation

If convection currents within the asthenosphere are the driving force behind the movement of the lithospheric plates, some evidence for their existence should be found at spreading centers. Heat flow provides that evidence.

Heat flow is a measure of the amount of heat leaving the rocks of the lithosphere. The values for heat flow are unusually high in the areas of spreading centers and decrease away from the centers. This is exactly what should happen if spreading centers are places where hot convection currents are rising and erupting new material onto the seafloor.

The elevation of the seafloor provides additional evidence of heat flow. Because heated materials expand, spreading centers have higher elevations than the rest of the seafloor. Elevations decrease away from spreading centers as the rocks cool and shrink.

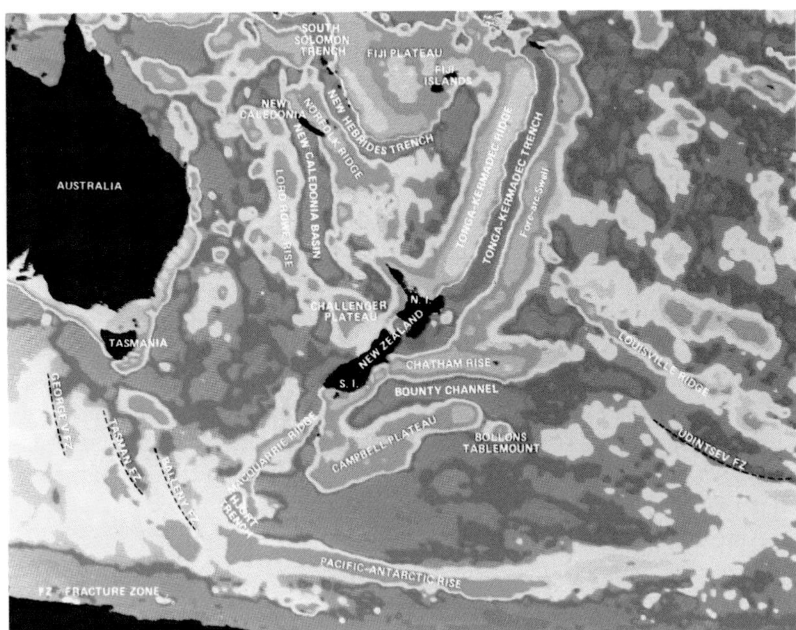

13.6 This *Landsat* photograph of the southeastern portion of the Pacific Ocean emphasizes heat flow on the ocean floor. Warmest areas are red; coolest areas are blue. Notice that the warmer areas are the higher elevations.

TOPIC QUESTIONS

Each topic question refers to the topic of the same number.

4. **(a)** What is the theory of continental drift? **(b)** List three pieces of evidence that Wegener used to support the theory of continental drift.

5. **(a)** Why do earthquakes and volcanoes occur at plate boundaries? **(b)** Where is the largest belt of active earthquakes and volcanoes? **(c)** Name four volcanoes that occur in this belt.

6. **(a)** Describe Earth's magnetic polarity when the magnetic poles are reversed. **(b)** What is the pattern of polarity reversals at spreading plate boundaries? **(c)** Describe the age of the rocks of the ocean floor relative to spreading plate boundaries. **(d)** What are spreading centers? What occurs there?

7. **(a)** What is heat flow? **(b)** What is the relationship between heat flow and distance from a spreading center? **(c)** How does heat flow provide evidence for rising convection currents at spreading centers? **(d)** What is the relationship between heat flow and seafloor elevation? Why?

OBJECTIVES

A Describe diverging boundaries, identify some features that occur there, and give examples.

B Discuss sliding plate boundaries and give an example.

C Describe collision boundaries and give several examples.

D Define *subduction*, identify and give examples of subduction boundaries, and list features that occur at each.

III Kinds of Plate Boundaries

Topic 8 Diverging Boundaries

Diverging boundaries are places where two lithospheric plates are diverging, or moving apart. In addition to the pattern of magnetic polarity that occurs there (Topic 6), diverging boundaries have *mid-ocean ridges.* Unlike mountain crests on land, mid-ocean ridges have deep valleys along their entire length. These valleys, called *rift valleys,* are both the boundary between the lithospheric plates and the place where new rocks form and push older rocks aside.

The rift valleys do not run smoothly along the ridge but are broken into segments. Movements along the *fracture zones* that separate the segments have been found to be a source of the earthquakes that occur along the ridge.

An example of a mid-ocean ridge is the *mid-Atlantic Ridge.* This ridge is the spreading center that separates the North American Plate from the Eurasian Plate and the South American Plate from the African Plate.

A second example of a mid-ocean ridge is the *East Pacific Rise.* This ridge separates the Nazca Plate from the Pacific Plate. Scientists who first studied the East Pacific Rise found hot springs bubbling up from the seafloor along the ridge. Some previously unknown organisms (Figure 13.9) were discovered living in the area around these hot springs. Recently, other hot springs with similar colonies of organisms have been found along other ridge systems including the mid-Atlantic Ridge.

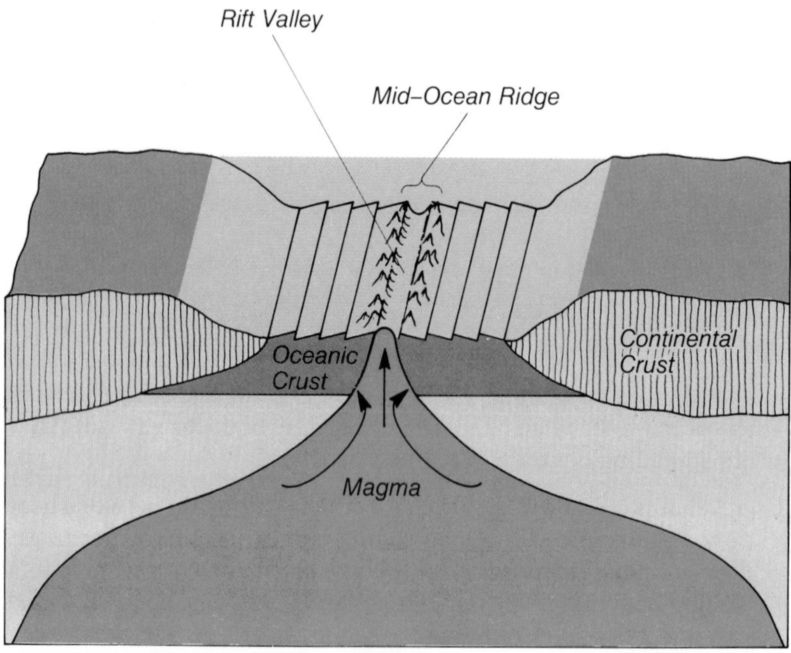

13.7 A mid-ocean ridge forms at a diverging boundary.

13.8 This rift in Iceland may be an extension of the mid-Atlantic Ridge. It is part of a spreading center.

13.9 (top) Basalt lava forms new ocean lithosphere at spreading boundaries. (bottom) Tubeworms are one kind of organism discovered in the hot-spring areas of the East Pacific Rise.

Topic 9 **Sliding Boundaries**

At the boundaries of some areas, the lithospheric plates are sliding past each other. In California, the North American Plate and the Pacific Plate are sliding past each other along the San Andreas Fault. A **fault** is a break or crack in Earth's crust along which movement has occurred. Southwestern California and the Pacific Plate are moving northwest with respect to the rest of the United States and the North American Plate.

The average rate of movement along the San Andreas Fault is five centimeters per year. However, some areas have not moved for over a century. These are thought to be the most likely places for future earthquakes.

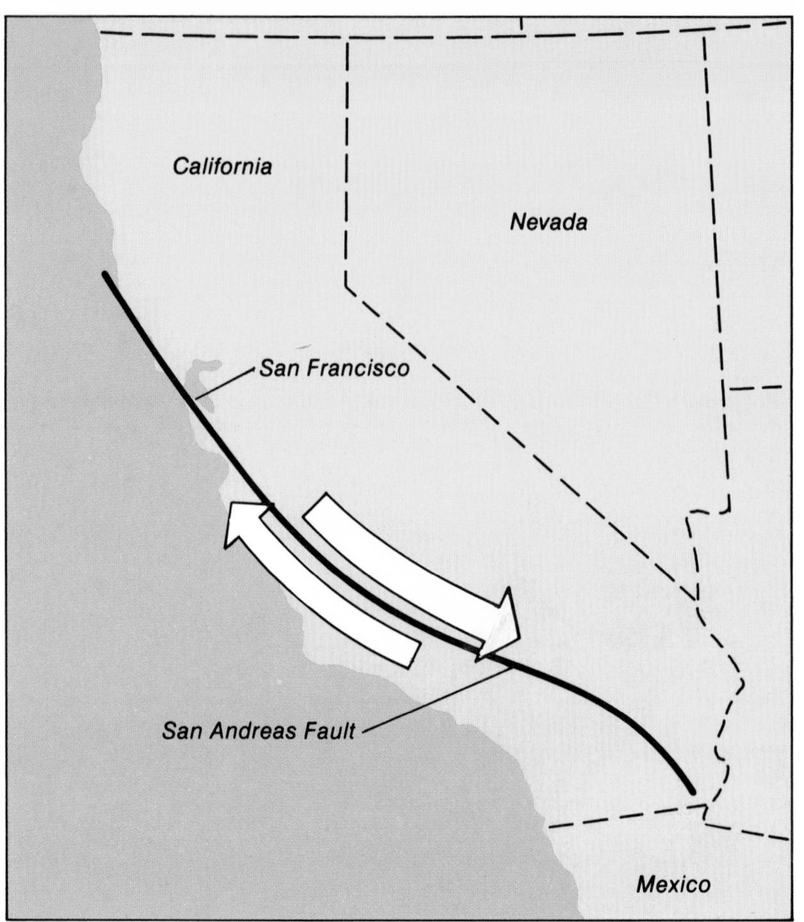

13.10 The San Andreas Fault is the boundary between two lithospheric plates that are sliding past each other. The arrow represents the direction of plate motion.

13.11 This orchard in California was offset during an earthquake that occurred in 1940.

Topic 10 Converging Boundaries: Collision

In addition to moving apart or sliding past each other, lithospheric plates can also move toward each other. A **converging boundary** forms when two plates come together, or converge.

If the converging plates are both carrying continents, they may be welded together into a single larger continent. This form of converging boundary is known as a **collision boundary.** The collision may cause the lithosphere at the boundary to be pushed upward into a mountain range.

The Himalayan Mountains are an example of a collision boundary that is still forming today. Here India is pushing northward into China at a rate of about 5 centimeters each year. The Indian subcontinent is now welded to the Eurasian continent. The result is not only the highest mountain range in the world but large numbers of major earthquakes as well.

Mountain ranges have also formed at other collision boundaries in the past. The Ural Mountains probably formed about 300 million years ago when Europe collided with Siberia and formed the Eurasian continent. The southern part of the Appalachian Mountains may have formed at about the same time, when North America and Africa collided. The Atlantic Ocean formed much later, when the two continents separated.

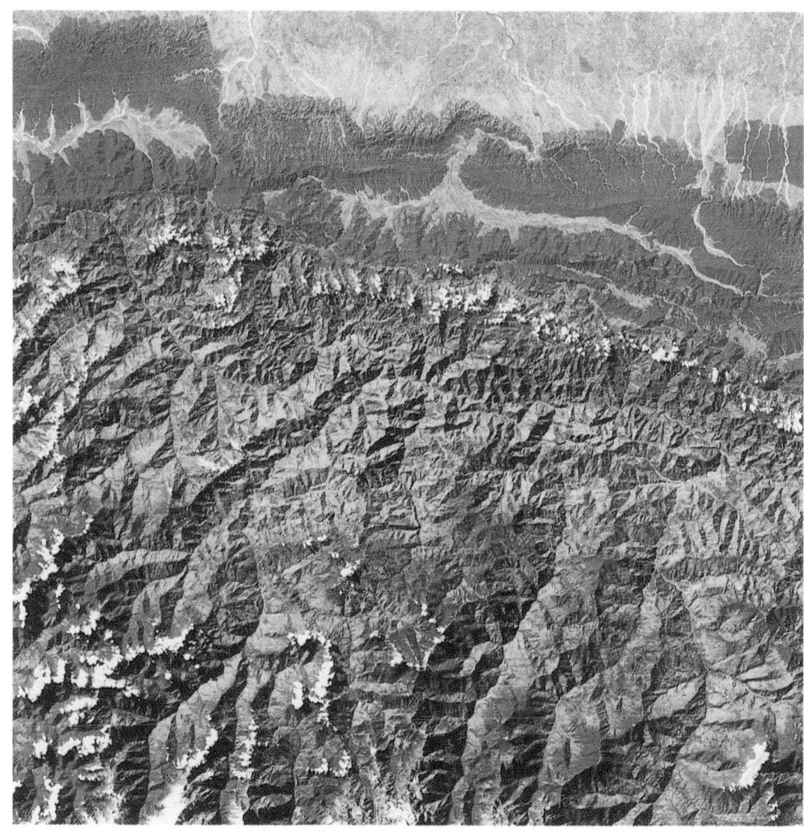

13.12 The converging of two continents at a collision boundary may result in the formation of a mountain range. This photograph is a *Landsat* image of the Great Smoky Mountains. These mountains may have formed when North America and Africa collided.

Topic 11 Converging Boundaries: Subduction

A **subduction boundary** is a form of converging boundary that occurs when one plate plunges down under another overriding plate. The plunging plate is said to be *subducting* beneath the overriding plate. A characteristic feature of a subduction boundary is a *deep-sea trench.* The deepest places in the ocean floor are in such trenches. Subduction boundaries occur in two ways—the convergence of two ocean plates or the convergence of an ocean plate with a continental plate.

When two ocean plates come together, the deep-sea trench that forms in the subducting plate is accompanied by the formation of a chain of volcanic islands on the overriding plate. For example, the Pacific Plate is subducting under the Philippine Plate. The Pacific Plate is pulled down to form the Mariana Trench, the deepest trench in the ocean. The leading edge of the Philippine Plate is marked by a chain of volcanic islands, the Mariana Islands. The rate of subduction here is about one centimeter per year.

When an ocean plate converges with a continental plate, the ocean plate, which is denser than the continental plate, subducts or slides under the continental plate. The deep-sea trench in the ocean

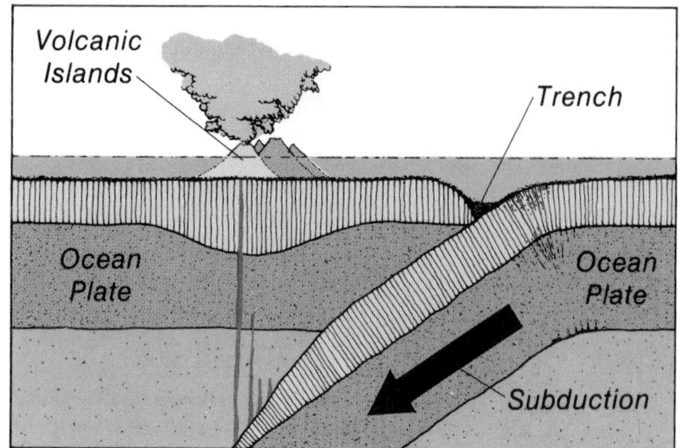

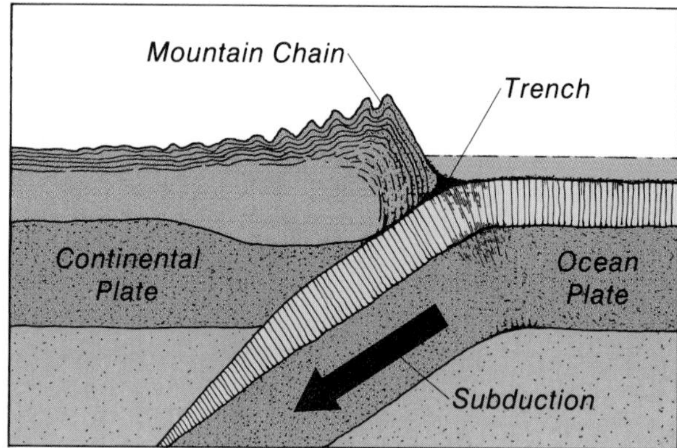

13.13 Two types of subduction: (left) two oceanic plates, and (right) an oceanic and a continental plate

plate is paralleled by a mountain chain on the continental plate. For example, on the west coast of South America, the Nazca Plate is subducting under the South American Plate. The Peru–Chile Trench occurs in the subducting Nazca Plate, and the Andes Mountains mark the edge of the South American Plate.

Two other facts are important about subduction boundaries. First, the earthquakes that occur with these boundaries originate deeper in the interior of Earth than at any other type of plate boundary. This is because the subducting plate is being pulled down into the asthenosphere. All other plate boundaries involve only the lithosphere and, as a result, have only shallow earthquakes.

The second important fact about subduction boundaries involves the deep-sea trenches that occur there. These trenches are the other half of the story that started at the mid-ocean ridges. The lithosphere that forms at the mid-ocean ridges eventually disappears into the interior by subducting at the deep-sea trenches.

TOPIC QUESTIONS

Each topic question refers to the topic of the same number.

8. **(a)** How are the plates moving at a mid-ocean ridge? **(b)** What two features occur at mid-ocean ridges? **(c)** Name and locate two mid-ocean ridges.

9. **(a)** How are the plates moving at a sliding boundary? **(b)** Give an example of a sliding boundary.

10. **(a)** What is a converging boundary? **(b)** What surface feature occurs at collision boundaries? Give some examples.

11. **(a)** What is happening to the plates at a subduction boundary? **(b)** What features are characteristic of the collision of two oceanic plates? **(c)** Give an example of this kind of plate boundary. **(d)** What features are characteristic of the collision of an oceanic plate and a continental plate? **(e)** Give an example of this kind of plate boundary. **(f)** Why do subduction boundaries have deeper earthquakes than any other type of plate boundary? **(g)** How are subduction boundaries related to mid-ocean ridges?

IV Continental Growth and Plate Tectonics

Topic 12 The Craton

The shapes of the continents have not always been as they exist today. The ancestors of the modern continents were smaller. Through tectonic processes, rock has been added to the margins of the ancient continent cores and the shapes that are currently familiar have gradually formed.

The ancient continent cores are called **cratons.** They are usually the oldest and most altered rock of the continent.

The North American craton is exposed at the surface in most of eastern Canada. Geologists call that part of the craton the *Canadian Shield.* The remainder of the craton lies below the surface from the Rocky Mountain system to the Appalachian Mountain system.

The North American craton shows the approximate shape of the continent 2.5 billion years ago. The remainder of North America has been added to the craton as the continent developed into its present dimensions.

OBJECTIVES

A Describe the North American craton.

B List some sources of material for continental growth.

C Define *thin-skinned thrusting* and identify a mountain range where thin-skinned thrusting is thought to have occurred.

D Define *terrane* and identify the properties used to identify terranes.

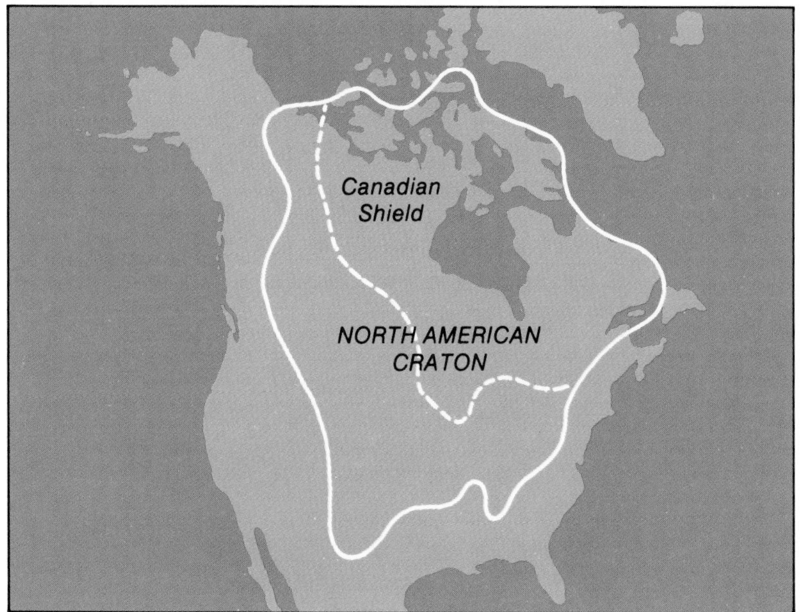

13.14 The craton of North America is made up of the oldest rocks on the continent. The exposed portion of the craton is called the Canadian Shield.

Topic 13 Sources of Growth Material

Earth material that is added to continents and causes their further development can come from several sources. One source is *deep-sea sediments.* When an oceanic plate plunges under a continental

13.15 Volcanic rock is one source of growth material that is added to continents.

13.16 The Appalachian Mountains may have formed during the time North America, Africa, and parts of Europe were converging.

plate in a subduction zone, some of the ocean-floor sediments may be scraped off and left behind. These sediments then become part of the continent on the other side of the subduction zone.

A second source of growth material is *volcanic rock.* Chains of volcanic islands are characteristic of many subduction zones. These volcanic chains may also contribute sediment, adding to the further expansion of a continent. There are places where volcanic rocks from former mid-ocean ridges are exposed on land.

A third source of growth material is the *sediments* deposited by rivers that flow across the continent. These sediments build up on continental margins. Unlike ocean-floor sediments and volcanic material, these sediments are not part of an active plate boundary.

Topic 14 Growth by Thin-Skinned Thrusting—The Southern Appalachians

Thin-skinned thrusting is the pushing of thin, horizontal sheets of rock from continental margins over great distances along nearly level fault surfaces. The stacking and shuffling of these thin sheets on the continental margins result in continental growth. Thin-skinned thrusting is thought to occur in many of the world's mountain ranges. It has been especially well studied in the Southern Appalachians.

The Appalachian Mountains are considered by many scientists to represent a typical mountain system. The Southern Appalachians are the part of the system south of Pennsylvania. The history of the Southern Appalachians is complex because it involves periods of both divergence and convergence. Only a general outline of what is thought to have happened is given here.

The ancestors of the continents of North America and Africa were originally part of the same larger continent. About 650 million years ago it split apart, forming an earlier version of the Atlantic Ocean. The closing of this ocean 150 million years later brought North America and Africa together again along with parts of Europe. It also pushed thin pieces of ocean floor, volcanic island, and other features typical of converging boundaries onto the continental margin. The Appalachian Mountains formed at this time as well. At a later date, the continents separated again to form the present Atlantic Ocean.

Topic 15 Growth by Terranes—Western North America

A **terrane** is a large block of lithospheric plate that has been moved, often a distance of thousands of kilometers, and attached to the edge of a continent. The attachment of terranes may have been the primary method of continent growth in western North America.

A terrane can be identified by three characteristics. First, each terrane block is bounded on all sides by major faults. Second, the rocks and the fossils found in them do not match those of neighboring terranes. And third, the magnetic polarity found in the terrane does not match that of neighboring terranes. All of the characteristics are strong evidence that the terranes formed in other places and were transported to their present locations.

An example of a terrane is the Cache Creek terrane of British Columbia in Canada. The rocks of this terrane are shallow-water limestones. They were deposited on oceanic crust. More important, the limestones contain fossil shells of tiny ocean animals called *fusulinids*. These shells are totally unlike fusulinid fossils found in rocks of the same age in other parts of North America. Instead, the Cache Creek fusulinids are very similar to shells found in Japan and large parts of Asia. From this evidence, scientists have hypothesized that the Cache Creek terrane had traveled thousands of kilometers across the Pacific Ocean before subduction processes welded it to the North American continent. Many other west coast terranes show evidence of similar histories.

13.17 The Cache Creek terrane contains fossils that resemble fossils found in Japan and other parts of Asia.

TOPIC QUESTIONS

Each topic question refers to the topic of the same number.

12. **(a)** What is a craton? **(b)** What is the Canadian Shield?

13. List three kinds of material that can become part of a continent.

14. **(a)** What is meant by thin-skinned thrusting? **(b)** Summarize the history of the Southern Appalachians.

15. **(a)** What are terranes? **(b)** List three characteristics that identify terranes. **(c)** What characteristic of the Cache Creek terrane was used to identify the original location of its rocks?

Map Skills

Refer to the map on pages 588–589 to answer these questions.

1. Locate the South American continent on the map. What is the relationship between the Peru–Chile Trench, the Andes Mountains, and the west coast of South America?

2. Compare this map with the map of volcanoes and earthquakes in Figure 13.4. Locate the Atlantic Ocean on both maps. What feature on this map occurs in the same location as the earthquakes in the Atlantic Ocean on the map in Figure 13.4?

3. Locate the Pacific Ocean on both maps. What occurs on the map in Figure 13.4 in the same place as the Aleutian Trench, Kuril Trench, Tonga Trench, and Mariana Trench of the map on pages 588–589?

CHAPTER 13 REVIEW

Summary

Plate tectonics is the study of the formation and movements of the rigid lithospheric plates that cover Earth's surface. Convection currents within the layer below the lithosphere are thought to move the plates.

Alfred Wegener proposed that the continents of Africa and South America are drifting apart. He used the shapes of the coastlines of the two continents, a reptile fossil, and some distinctive rocks as evidence.

Earthquakes and volcanoes occur at plate boundaries. A belt of earthquakes and volcanoes nearly surrounds the Pacific Ocean.

Minerals preserved in rocks show that Earth's magnetic poles have reversed several times in the past.

The pattern of polarity reversals at spreading centers indicates that new crustal material forms there. Heat-flow values and seafloor elevations provide supporting evidence.

Lithospheric plates move apart at diverging boundaries. Mid-ocean ridges occur at spreading centers. Rift valleys and fracture zones are features of mid-ocean ridges.

The North American Plate and the Pacific Plate form a sliding plate boundary at the San Andreas Fault in California.

The collision and welding of two continental plates result in a collision boundary.

Subduction boundaries occur when one lithospheric plate plunges beneath an overriding plate. Subduction boundaries have deep earthquakes.

The North American craton contains the oldest and most altered rocks of the continent. The Canadian Shield is the exposed part of the craton.

Deep-sea sediments, volcanic rocks, and river-deposited sediments all provide material for continental growth.

The formation of the Southern Appalachians involved thin-skinned thrusting.

Terranes are large blocks of lithosphere that have been moved and attached to continents. Terranes are identified by their faults, fossils, and magnetic polarity.

Vocabulary

asthenosphere
collision boundary
converging boundary
craton
diverging boundary
fault
lithosphere
plate tectonics
spreading centers
subduction boundary
terrane
thin-skinned thrusting

Review

On your paper, write the word or words that best complete each statement.

1. According to plate ______, Earth's surface consists of a number of rigid, but movable, pieces of lithosphere.
2. The lithosphere is made of the ______ and the upper part of the mantle.
3. Rising convection currents within the asthenosphere drive the lithospheric plate apart, while ______ convection currents pull the plate together.
4. Wegener used continent shape, fossils, and rocks to support his theory of ______.
5. Earthquakes and ______ occur at plate boundaries because of stresses that build up there.
6. The pattern of magnetic reversals indicates that the youngest rocks of the ocean floor are found at ______ centers.
7. Values for heat flow are ______ at spreading centers and decrease away from the centers.
8. The mid-Atlantic Ridge and the East Pacific Rise are locations where two lithospheric plates are moving ______.
9. The San Andreas Fault is the result of the Pacific Plate sliding past the North ______ Plate.
10. A collision boundary results when two ______ plates collide and weld together.

11. The subduction of the Pacific Plate under the Philippine Plate is an example of the convergence of two ______ plates.
12. The deepest earthquakes occur at ______ boundaries as old lithosphere is pulled down into the asthenosphere.
13. The Canadian ______ is the exposed part of the North American ______.
14. Deep-sea sediments, volcanic rocks, and river sediments are all sources of material that increase the size of ______.
15. Thin-skinned thrusting is thought to have been involved in the formation of the Southern ______ Mountains.
16. Terranes can be identified by their faults, fossils, and ______.

Interpret and Apply

On your paper, answer each sentence in complete sentences.

1. Coal deposits have been found in Antarctica. How do these deposits provide evidence for plate tectonics?
2. The Great Pyramid of Giza in Egypt was built more than 40 centuries ago. The structure faces slightly east of true north. Did the Egyptian surveyors make a mistake in laying out the foundation for the pyramid or is there some other explanation for this "error"?
3. How do the age of the seafloor, heat flow, and seafloor elevation relate to distance from a spreading center? Why?
4. The oldest rocks of the continents are almost four billion years old, while the oldest rocks of the ocean basin are not even one billion years old. Explain why this difference in age occurs and how it supports plate tectonics.

Critical Thinking

The graph shows a computer model of a slab of lithospheric plate plunging downward into the asthenosphere. The plunging plate is shown in red, and the plate colliding with the plunging plate is shown in blue. The dots represent earthquakes. The vertical axis of the graph shows depths, in kilometers, inside Earth. The horizontal axis of the graph shows distance, in kilometers, from the location where the plate starts to plunge. Temperatures inside Earth, in degrees Celsius, are indicated also.

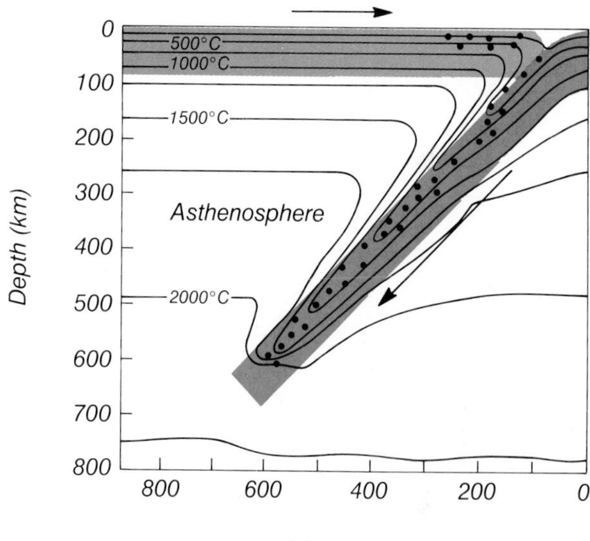

1. Determine the temperature of the asthenosphere at a distance of 600 kilometers and a depth of 100 kilometers.
2. What is the approximate depth of the earthquakes that occur at a distance of 200 kilometers from the point where the plate starts its plunge?
3. State the relationship between distance from the point of plunge and depth of an earthquake.
4. How does the temperature of the asthenosphere compare with the temperature of the plunging plate at a depth of 200 kilometers? At 400 km?
5. What is the approximate depth at which earthquake activity in the plunging plate stops?

CHAPTER

14 Volcanism and Plate Tectonics

▲ This nighttime view of an erupting volcano in Iceland shows the intense heat and powerful force of an eruption.

How Do You Know That . . .

Iceland is a volcanically active area? The erupting volcano is just one evidence of activity in Iceland. Craters and lava fields are common sights there. In fact, over one third of the island is volcanically active. Sometimes the volcanic activity causes harm to the people of Iceland. Poisonous gases that erupted from a volcano in 1783 killed two thirds of the island's livestock. During the famine that resulted, a fifth of the population starved to death. On the other hand, Icelanders make use of the volcanic activity. The groundwater is hot enough to heat homes, greenhouses, and even year-round swimming pools. Crops can be planted in hot areas while other areas are still under winter snows.

I Volcanism Releases Magma

Topic 1 Magma

The eruption of molten rock must surely be the most spectacular activity that accompanies the movement of lithospheric plates. Where does this molten rock come from and how does it move inside Earth? The answers are not simple because the processes occur deep underground where direct observation is not possible. Even so, several facts are known.

Molten rock underground is called **magma.** It forms wherever temperatures and pressures are high enough to melt rock. One region that meets this requirement is the asthenosphere (Chapter 13, Topic 3). At the asthenosphere, some minerals melt and become magma. Plate boundaries are also areas where rocks can be melted. The movements and stresses there produce enough heat to form magma.

Once the rock is melted, it has greater volume and thus is slightly less dense than the unmelted rock around it. The magma then moves upward, moving through fractures or melting crustal rock as it rises. If the magma reaches the surface, it erupts through an opening called a **volcano.**

The rate at which magma moves is determined primarily by its silica content. Silica is the major ingredient in all magma. Magmas with relatively high silica content are thick, light-colored, and slow moving. These are **felsic** magmas. In contrast, **mafic** magmas have relatively low silica content. They tend to be thinner and darker in color, and they flow more easily.

OBJECTIVES

A Identify some areas where rock underground can be melted.

B Explain the difference between magma and lava and describe the composition, properties, and behavior of mafic and felsic magmas and lavas.

C Name some gases that can occur in magma and discuss the relationship between the amount of gas and the nature of the eruption.

D Define *tephra* and give several examples.

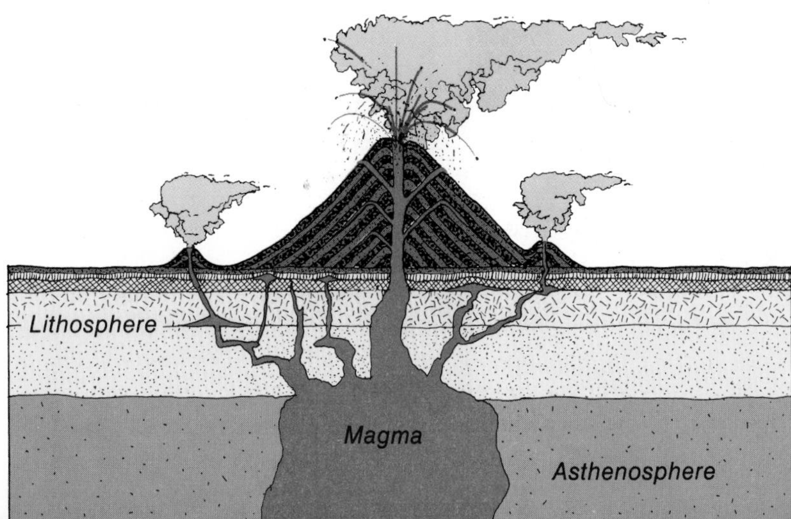

14.1 Magma rises from the asthenosphere through cracks in the lithosphere.

Topic 2 Gases in Magma

Many magmas contain dissolved gases that are given off as the magma erupts. The most important of these gases are water vapor, carbon dioxide, and sulfur. Other gases include hydrogen, which combines with atmospheric oxygen to form additional steam (hot water vapor). Carbon monoxide combines with oxygen to become carbon dioxide. Sulfur combines with both hydrogen and oxygen and forms the gases hydrogen sulfide and sulfur dioxide. Several other gases, such as chlorine and fluorine, are also given off.

The amount of gas dissolved in a magma is a major factor in the kind of eruption that results. As the magma reaches the surface, the pressure on it is greatly reduced. The gases dissolved in the magma come out of solution as bubbles. These bubbles can expand rapidly and even explode. As a result, magmas containing large amounts of dissolved gases tend to produce more explosive eruptions than magmas containing small amounts of gases.

Topic 3 Lava

Magma that reaches the surface is called **lava.** Its composition is somewhat different from that of the original magma because some gases have escaped and some new materials have been added from other rocks the magma has melted. Like magma, lava is classified by its silica content as either felsic or mafic. Like magma, felsic lavas are thick and stiff, while mafic lavas are thin and fluid.

The silica content of the original magma is also important to the type of eruption that occurs. Mafic magmas are more fluid. Thus, gases dissolved within them escape easily. As a result, their lavas pour out smoothly onto the surface. On the other hand, gases cannot move easily in less fluid, felsic magmas. The result is an explosive eruption.

14.2 Since there are different types of lava, lava flows have different appearances. **(a)** Aa lava flows are characterized by rough, jagged surfaces. **(b)** Pahoehoe lava flows are smooth with a ropelike surface.

a

b

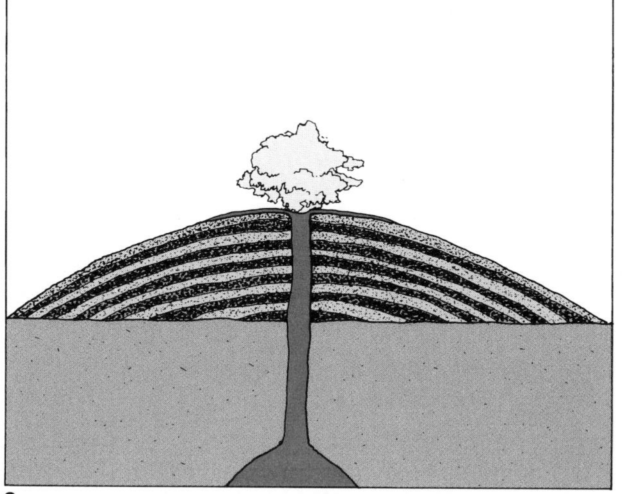

14.3 **(a)** Mafic magma is thin and fluid. It flows out of a volcano smoothly and covers a large area. **(b)** Felsic magma is very thick and contains much trapped gas. It erupts much more explosively than mafic magma.

Topic 4 **Lava Fragments**

Explosive eruptions produce solid fragments of lava called **tephra.** The smallest pieces of tephra (less than 2 millimeters in diameter) are called *ash.* Larger pieces (up to 64 millimeters) are called *lapilli.* The largest fragments (more than 64 millimeters) are called *blocks* and *bombs.* Blocks are erupted as solid pieces, while bombs are ejected as liquid and harden as they fall.

In some explosive eruptions, tephra combines with gases to form a dense, superheated cloud that travels along or close to the ground. The cloud may follow existing stream valleys and move at more than 100 kilometers per hour. One example of this type of eruption occurred in 1902 when Mount Pelee, a Caribbean volcano, destroyed the city of St. Pierre. The fiery blast shattered stone buildings and burned wooden ones. Within minutes, 30 000 people were smothered or burned to death.

14.4 Volcanic ash and cinders

TOPIC QUESTIONS

Each topic question refers to the topic of the same number.

1. **(a)** What is magma? **(b)** What condition is necessary in order for magma to form? **(c)** List two places where this condition can be met. **(d)** What causes magma to rise? **(e)** What is the major ingredient in magma? **(f)** List the properties of felsic and mafic magmas.

2. **(a)** List several gases that come from magma. **(b)** What effect does the amount of gases in a magma have on the kind of eruption that occurs?

3. **(a)** What is lava? **(b)** Why is the composition of lava different from that of its magma? **(c)** How are felsic lavas different from mafic lavas? **(d)** How are their eruptions different?

4. **(a)** What is tephra? **(b)** How are ash and lapilli different? **(c)** How do blocks form differently than bombs? **(d)** What kind of eruption destroyed St. Pierre?

OBJECTIVES

A Describe rift eruptions and features associated with them, and tell where they occur.

B Discuss and give examples of subduction zone eruptions, and discuss the features that occur there.

C Discuss the occurrence of hot spots and the features associated with them.

II Kinds of Eruptions

Topic 5 Rift Eruptions

Rift eruptions occur at long, narrow fractures in the crust. These fractures may be on the ocean floor or on land. Rift eruptions typically flow out smoothly and fluidly because the lava is basaltic and contains few gases.

Rift eruptions in the oceans occur at spreading centers, such as the mid-Atlantic Ridge and the East Pacific Rise. Here the lava oozes out and cools rapidly into rounded shapes that may look like pillows.

Rift eruptions on land may spread lava evenly over thousands of square kilometers. Lavas from the East African Rift system have covered large areas with basalt, forming a *basalt plateau.* The Columbia Plateau of Washington, Oregon, and Idaho is another example of a basalt plateau. During the past 50 million years, lava from rift eruptions has covered an area of over 200 000 square kilometers with up to 1500 meters of basalt. Other examples of basalt plateaus are the Karroo Plateau of South Africa, the Parana Plateau of South America, and the Deccan Plateau of India.

When the basalt of plateaus and other thick lava flows on land cool, they may display a unique pattern of closely packed, six-sided columns called *columnar jointing.* These columns are thought to form as shrinking lava cools and cracks. The columns are as high as the thickness of the basalt flows.

14.5 Columnar jointing is clearly visible in this basaltic sill.

Topic 6 Subduction Boundary Eruptions

Subduction boundary eruptions are the result of magma that forms at subduction boundaries (Chapter 13, Topic 11). Unlike the magma that forms at rifts, this magma tends to be thick and to contain large amounts of gases. As a result, subduction boundary eruptions usually are explosive, and the erupted material is mostly lava fragments (tephra). The volcanic cone that forms usually has very steep sides.

Most of the world's active volcanoes occur at subduction boundary eruptions. Many form the island chains that are typical of the west side of the Pacific Ocean. The most active volcanic chain is the islands of Indonesia. Other examples of volcanic chains resulting from subduction boundary eruptions are the Philippine Islands, the islands of Japan, and the Aleutian Islands off Alaska.

Subduction boundary volcanoes are also associated with young mountain ranges. The Cascades of Washington and Oregon, the mountains of Central America, and the Andes of South America all have active or recently active volcanoes.

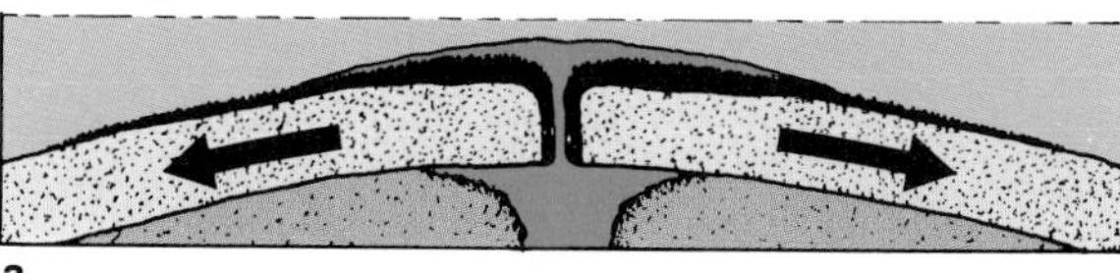

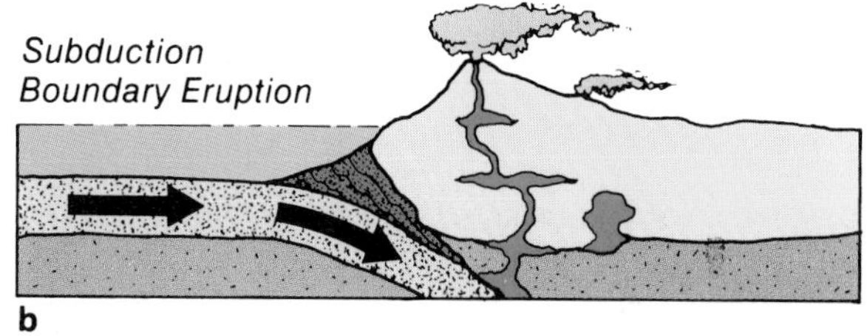

14.6 **(a)** Huge amounts of lava flow smoothly from a rift eruption, covering large areas with basalt. **(b)** Subduction boundary eruptions are usually more explosive.

Topic 7 Hot Spots

Not all volcanism occurs at plate boundaries. **Hot spots** are areas of volcanic activity in the middle of lithospheric plates.

The lava erupted at hot spots is similar to that of rift eruptions—it usually flows smoothly over the surface. However, unlike the lava that wells up at rifts, hot spot lavas form cones. The cones are usually broad and have gently sloping sides.

The cause of hot spots is not clear, although some kind of concentration of heat from radioactive sources in the asthenosphere is suspected. The location of the hot spot seems to remain the same even though the lithospheric plate above it moves. The result is a chain of extinct volcanoes marking former locations of the plate over the hot spot.

The most famous example of hot spot volcanism is the Hawaiian Islands. The island of Hawaii has active volcanoes and is now directly over the hot spot. To the northwest is a chain of extinct volcanic islands (see Figure 14.7). The rocks that form each island are increasingly older away from Hawaii. This indicates a steady movement of the Pacific Plate over the hot spot.

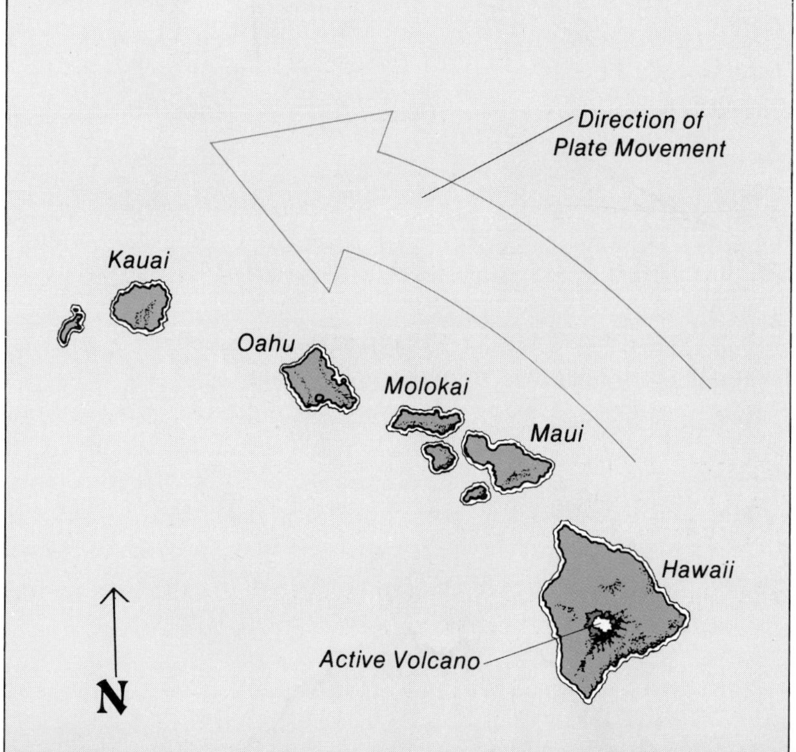

14.7 A chain of extinct volcanoes marks the movement of a lithospheric plate over a hot spot.

TOPIC QUESTIONS

Each topic question refers to the topic of the same number.

5. **(a)** Where do rift eruptions occur? **(b)** How does lava behave at rift eruptions? **(c)** Name two locations where rift eruptions occur in the ocean. **(d)** Give one example of a rift eruption on land. **(e)** What is a basalt plateau? Give some examples. **(f)** What is columnar jointing?

6. **(a)** How are subduction boundary eruptions different from rift eruptions? What causes the difference? **(b)** What is the shape of the volcanic cone that forms at subduction boundaries? **(c)** Name two landform features that form at subduction boundaries and give one example of each.

7. **(a)** What are hot spots? **(b)** How does lava behave at hot spots? **(c)** What is the shape of the volcanic cone that results? **(d)** What is thought to be the cause of hot spots? **(e)** How does the lithosphere behave relative to a hot spot? **(f)** How do the Hawaiian Islands support your answer to **(e)**?

Dr. Robert W. Decker
Volcanologist

Dr. Robert W. Decker has had a lifelong interest in volcanoes and volcanism. Following work in geology and geophysics at the Massachusetts Institute of Technology, he obtained a doctoral degree from the Colorado School of Mines. After joining the faculty of Dartmouth College to teach geophysics, Dr. Decker did volcanic research in Indonesia. While he was at Dartmouth, he did additional field work on volcanoes in Hawaii, Iceland, and Central America. He has also done work for the U.S. Geological Survey. In fact, he was studying Mount St. Helens for the USGS when it erupted in 1980.

Dr. Decker was scientist-in-charge of the Hawaiian Volcano Observatory from 1979 to 1984. Established in 1912, this famous laboratory is located on the edge of Kilauea's crater. From this site, Dr. Decker helped to oversee the monitoring of the volcano and the efforts to predict its activities. His current major interest is training geologists from developing countries about volcano-monitoring techniques.

III Examples of Volcanic Eruptions

Topic 8 Eldfell

Eldfell is a volcanic mountain on Heimaey, a small island off the south coast of Iceland located near the mid-Atlantic Ridge. Eldfell formed during a five-month period in 1973 from lava and tephra that flowed or was ejected from a newly opened fissure on the island. The tephra covered nearly half the island and burned or buried 50 homes in its only village, Vestmannaeyjar. The roofs of the other homes in the village had to be continually swept clear of tephra to prevent their collapse. The flowing lava added almost three square kilometers to the east side of the island. It also threatened to block the entrance of the village harbor. This was a serious problem because Vestmannaeyjar is Iceland's chief fishing port. The villagers attacked the lava flow by pumping seawater on it in the hope that the water would cool the lava enough to stop its advance. The pumping continued until the volcano fell silent four months later. The lava had stopped 165 meters short of the cliffs on the opposite side of the harbor, and the entrance to the harbor remained open.

Eldfell was an example of a rift eruption. Heimaey, along with the other areas of Iceland, is one of the few places in the world where a mid-ocean ridge is above sea level. Iceland is a part of the mid-Atlantic Ridge.

OBJECTIVES

A Discuss the cause and nature of the 1973 eruption of Eldfell, the 1980 eruption of Mount St. Helens, and the regular eruptions of Kilauea.

B Give the cause and some of the results of some famous volcanic eruptions of the past.

C Discuss the volcanism that occurs on the moon, Mars, and Io.

14.8 The village of Vestmannaeyjar was nearly buried by tephra from the eruption of Eldfell in 1973.

14.9 Mudflows and ash covered the area near Mount St. Helens after the eruption.

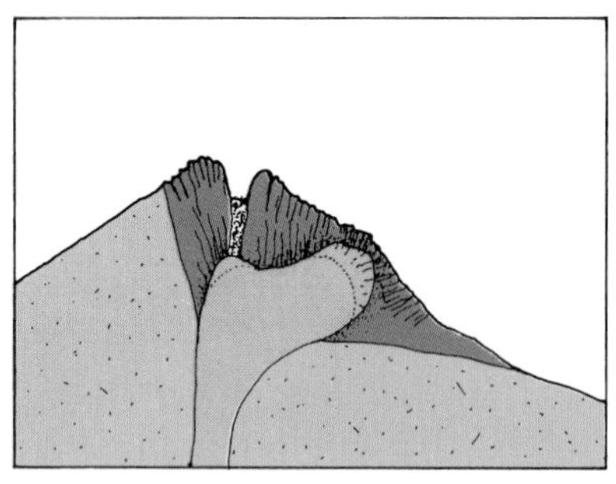

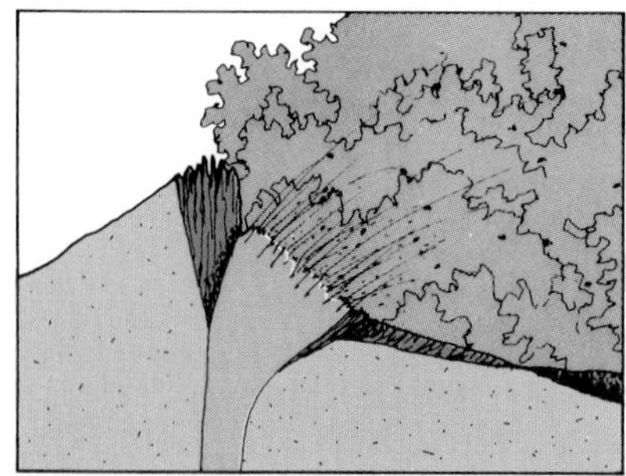

14.10 This was the series of events during the major eruption of Mount St. Helens in 1980.

Topic 9 **Mount St. Helens**

Mount St. Helens, located in Washington, is one of 15 major volcanoes in the Cascade Range. Its eruption in 1980 was the first volcanic activity in that range since 1921.

Signs of renewed activity in Mount St. Helens began in March 1980, two months before the major eruption. During that period, earthquake activity increased, a bulge in the north side of the cone grew larger, and small eruptions of steam and ash occurred. The major eruption involved four separate but related events:

1. An earthquake broke the bulge on the north side of the cone.
2. The bulge became a landslide.
3. An explosion of steam and superheated ash came from the magma, water, and gases that had been trapped under the bulge.
4. Mudflows formed when ash mixed with the melted snow and ice on the mountain.

The explosion blew down trees 25 kilometers away and rattled windows 160 kilometers away. The cloud of steam and ash was shot 20 kilometers into the air and its dust traveled around the world. Ash fall was heavy—2 to 5 centimeters—over hundreds of square kilometers. Mudflows and landslides accumulated to depths of over 180 meters in some areas.

Mount St. Helens and the other Cascade volcanoes are the result of subduction boundary volcanism. The two converging plates are the Juan de Fuca Plate and the North American Plate. The Juan de Fuca Plate is plunging eastward under the overriding North American Plate. The eruption that resulted at Mount St. Helens was typical of subduction boundary eruptions. It contained very little lava but large amounts of tephra and gases.

14.11 Spectacular lava flows have been a common feature during eruptions of Kilauea.

Topic 10 Kilauea

Kilauea is a volcano on the island of Hawaii. It has erupted at least once a year since 1952. Some of the eruptions have been spectacular.

Kilauea and the other active Hawaiian volcanoes result from a hot spot under the island (Topic 7). In the case of Kilauea, the magma is thought to come from a depth of at least 50 kilometers below the surface. After rising, it is stored in an irregular reservoir about four kilometers below the top of the volcano.

A unique feature of Kilauea is the lakes of lava that form in depressions in the gently sloping volcanic cone. The lava from the reservoir erupts onto the surface and flows through natural channels to these depressions. When the lava flow stops, the lake starts to harden into rock. Sometimes this takes 25 years. During that time, the lava lake provides volcanologists with great amounts of information on magma and the changes that occur as it hardens.

The lava flows from Kilauea often threaten homes and communities on the island. In 1986, a flow covered a stretch of Kalapana Highway. People who lived beyond the blocked area had to drive as much as 100 extra kilometers to get their mail and groceries.

Topic 11 Some Famous Eruptions

Most volcanoes that become famous occur at subduction boundaries. This is because most subduction boundary eruptions are violent.

Vesuvius and the other volcanoes of the Mediterranean are caused by the subduction of the African Plate beneath the Eurasian Plate. Because their lava is extremely thick and gas-rich, their eruptions are very explosive. Superheated steam and dense clouds of ash are common. The eruption of Vesuvius in A.D. 79 is probably the most famous volcanic eruption in history because it buried and preserved three Roman cities. Pompeii, the largest of the preserved cities, was buried in ash. Vesuvius has been active repeatedly since A.D. 79.

14.12 An aerial view of Crater Lake shows Wizard Island in the middle of the lake. The island is the top of a volcanic cone that formed inside the original huge caldera.

Krakatoa is a volcanic island in the Indonesian chain. Volcanic activity there is caused by the subduction of the Indian Plate under the Eurasian Plate. On August 27, 1883, an explosive eruption took place that has been described as "the most violent eruption of historic times." More than half of the island was destroyed and blown away in the explosion. The cloud over the volcano reached nearly 30 kilometers into the air.

The compression wave caused by the eruption broke windows 150 kilometers away, and the sound was heard 3000 kilometers away in Australia. Great sea waves flooded nearby coasts, and 36 000 people were drowned. The waves even reached the shore of South Africa, over 8000 kilometers away. The fine volcanic dust from the eruption was carried completely around the world by upper-air winds. It caused strangely beautiful sunrise and sunset skies for two years after the eruption.

Crater Lake in Oregon is all that remains of a volcano that erupted violently about 7000 years ago. The eruption deposited a blanket of ash as thick as 15 meters over distances of 50 kilometers. The top of the cone collapsed after the lava that had supported it flowed out through cracks in the sides and base. The huge crater, or caldera, that resulted has since filled with rain and melted snow to form a lake. It is the deepest lake in the United States.

Crater Lake, like the volcanoes in the Cascade Range, resulted from the subduction of the Juan de Fuca Plate under the North American Plate.

Topic 12 **Extraterrestrial Volcanism**

Lava flows on the moon erupted through cracks in the surface of the lunar lithosphere. Both the cracks and the heat needed to form the lava may have been the result of bombardment by huge rocks from space. The bombardment formed the basins that the lava later filled. The eruptions must have continued for some time because the lava flows overlap each other.

Could the lavas have resulted from lunar plate tectonics? There is no evidence that they did or that such activity exists on the moon today. The moon's lithosphere is too thick to either break or move.

The largest known volcanic cone in the solar system is on Mars. It is called *Olympus Mons.* The cone is 26 kilometers high and 500 to 600 kilometers across. There is a distinct caldera, or crater, at its top. Many other cones of different ages can be seen scattered around Mars' surface, especially in its northern hemisphere.

The huge size of the Martian volcanoes is evidence that Mars does not have moving plates near its surface. Mars also lacks other features that result from plate movements. There is no evidence on Mars of spreading centers, subduction boundaries, or folded mountains.

Io is a moon of Jupiter that has more than 100 active and inactive volcanoes. Although features on Io appear volcanic, the material that erupted from the volcanoes is not basalt. Scientists have proposed that the ejected materials are sulfur and sulfur dioxide.

Io is caught in a gravitational tug-of-war between Jupiter and two other moons. As a result, some parts of its surface regularly move up and down by as much as 100 meters. The heat produced by the friction of this up-and-down motion is thought to be great enough to cause volcanism.

14.13 Olympus Mons is the largest known volcanic cone in the solar system.

TOPIC QUESTIONS

Each topic question refers to the topic of the same number.

8. **(a)** Where is Eldfell? **(b)** What kinds of materials were ejected there? **(c)** What did the residents of Vestmannaeyjar do to save their harbor? **(d)** What kind of eruption was Eldfell?

9. **(a)** Where is Mount St. Helens? **(b)** What activities preceded the 1980 eruption there? **(c)** List the four major events that occurred with the eruption. **(d)** Identify some results of the eruption. **(e)** What causes the activity at Mount St. Helens and its neighboring volcanoes?

10. **(a)** Where is Kilauea? **(b)** What is the cause of volcanic activity there? **(c)** Why are the lava lakes of Kilauea important?

11. **(a)** What is the cause of the eruptions of Vesuvius and the other Mediterranean volcanoes? **(b)** Why are the eruptions of Vesuvius so explosive? **(c)** What is the cause of the volcanic activity at Krakatoa and the other Indonesian islands? **(d)** List some events that resulted from the eruption of Krakatoa. **(e)** What happened at Crater Lake after the volcano erupted? **(f)** What was the cause of the volcanic activity at Crater Lake?

12. **(a)** What is thought to have caused the lava flows on the moon? **(b)** Why is plate tectonics not likely on the moon? **(c)** What evidence is there that Mars lacks moving lithospheric plates like Earth's? **(d)** What is thought to be the cause of the volcanic activity on Io?

OBJECTIVES

A Identify and give examples of the various types of igneous intrusions.

IV Plutonic Activity

Topic 13 Plutons and Volcanism

Volcanoes and lava flows are the surface activities of volcanism. However, much more magma is active below Earth's surface. Magma forces its way into fractures in the bedrock. It squeezes in between rock layers. It pushes up overlying rocks to form domes. Great masses of magma solidify far below the surface to form the cores of mountains.

The rock masses that form when magma cools inside other rocks are called *igneous intrusions,* or **plutons.**

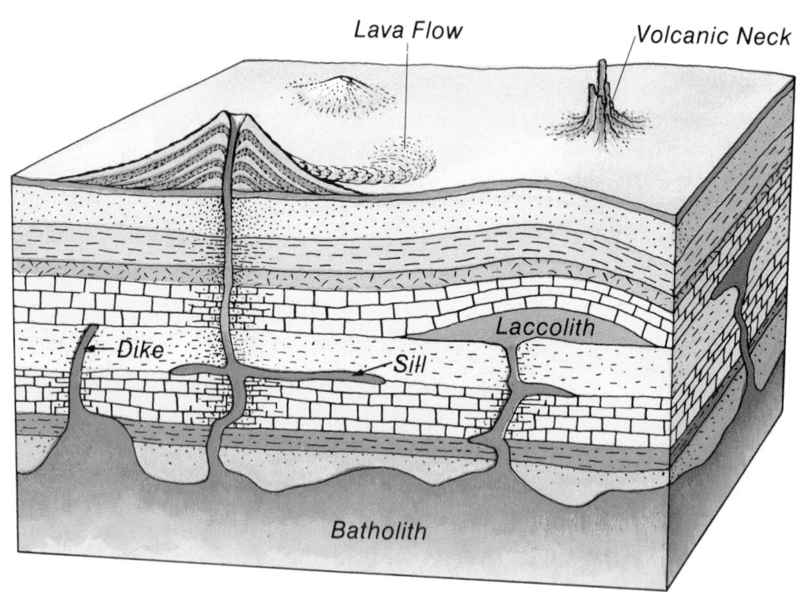

14.14 There are many volcanic formations below the surface where magma forced its way between existing rock layers. These formations are visible where erosion has removed the surface layer.

Topic 14 Dikes, Sills, Laccoliths, Necks

Dikes are flat sheets of igneous rock that cut across the rock layers they intrude. They form when magma is forced into vertical cracks. Dikes come in all lengths and thicknesses. They are common in old volcanic regions. Their rock is usually basalt or diabase.

In contrast to dikes, which cut across layers, are sills. **Sills** are sheets of igneous rock that are parallel to the layers they intrude. They form when magma is forced along bedding planes between rock layers. They too are usually basalt or diabase. They can be hundreds of meters thick and many kilometers long. The Palisades of the Hudson River in New York are the face of a great diabase sill that has been exposed by erosion. It is about 50 kilometers long.

14.15 Two basalt dikes

In some places, the magmas that intrude between rock layers are very stiff and unable to flow easily. Instead of spreading to form

14.16 (left) An igneous sill intruded between sedimentary layers at Big Bend National Park, Texas (right) A volcanic neck in Monument Valley, Arizona

sills, these magmas bulge upward to form domelike masses called **laccoliths.** The rock layers above the laccoliths are also pushed up into mountains. Laccoliths can be found in the Henry Mountains of Utah and the Black Hills of South Dakota.

When an extinct volcano is almost completely eroded, a **volcanic neck** may be left. A neck is the plug of hardened magma left in the vent from which lava flowed. One example of a neck is the famous Ship Rock in New Mexico. It is 400 meters high. Volcanic necks form the diamond-bearing rock of the great Kimberley mines of South Africa.

Topic 15 Batholiths and Stocks

Batholiths are the largest of all igneous intrusions. They form the cores of many of Earth's great mountain ranges. When erosion removes the overlying rock layers, the batholith rocks are exposed. They are usually either granite or granodiorite. The largest batholith in North America forms the core of the Coast Range of British Columbia. It is more than 1600 kilometers long and up to 250 kilometers wide.

A small batholith in which less than 100 square kilometers is exposed at the surface is called a **stock.**

TOPIC QUESTIONS

Each topic question refers to the topic of the same number.

13. What are plutons?

14. Describe the origin of a **(a)** dike, **(b)** sill, **(c)** laccolith, and **(d)** volcanic neck. Include examples for **(b)**, **(c)**, and **(d)**.

15. **(a)** What is a batholith? Give an example. **(b)** What kind of rock is usually found in batholiths? **(c)** What is a stock?

CHAPTER 14 REVIEW

Summary

Rock is melted in the asthenosphere and at plate boundaries. Molten rock underground is called magma; molten rock that reaches the surface is called lava.

Felsic magmas are rich in silica, thick, light-colored, and slow moving. Gases within the magma cannot easily escape, so felsic lavas tend to be associated with explosive eruptions.

Mafic magmas are poor in silica, thin, dark-colored, and fast moving. Gases within the magma escape easily, so mafic lavas pour out onto the surface smoothly.

Ash, lapilli, blocks, and bombs are examples of solid fragments of lava called tephra.

Lava flows out smoothly at rift eruptions on the seafloor or on land. On land, the eruptions may form huge lava plateaus. Columnar jointing is a feature of some of these thick lava flows.

The magma at subduction boundaries tends to result in explosive eruptions of tephra that form steep-sided cones. Island chains and young mountains are features of subduction boundary eruptions.

Hot spots form a string of volcanoes in the middle of moving lithospheric plates. The Hawaiian Islands are an example.

Eldfell is an example of a rift eruption; Mount St. Helens is a subduction boundary eruption; Kilauea is an example of a hot spot eruption.

Most famous eruptions of the past, including Vesuvius, Krakatoa, and Crater Lake, occurred at subduction boundaries.

The moon, Mars, and Jupiter's moon Io all show evidence of volcanic activity. The moon has extensive lava flows, Mars has a number of volcanic cones, and Io has over 100 volcanoes. None shows evidence of plate tectonics.

Magma that cools underground forms plutons. Examples of plutons, defined by their size and structure, are dikes, sills, laccoliths, volcanic necks, batholiths, and stocks.

Vocabulary

batholith	pluton
dike	rift eruption
felsic	sill
hot spot	stock
laccolith	subduction boundary eruption
lava	tephra
mafic	volcanic neck
magma	volcano

Review

Number your paper from *1* to *20.* Match the phrases in List **A** with the terms in List **B.**

List A

1. molten rock underground
2. molten rock that reaches Earth's surface
3. molten rock that is silica-rich, thick, light-colored, slow moving, and likely to cause explosive eruptions
4. water vapor, carbon dioxide, sulfur dioxide, and hydrogen sulfide
5. ash, lapilli, blocks, and bombs
6. mid-Atlantic Ridge and East Pacific Rise
7. Columbia, Karroo, Parana, and Deccan
8. closely packed, six-sided columns of some thick lava flows
9. location of island chains, young mountain ranges, and most of the world's volcanoes
10. areas of volcanic activity in the middle of lithospheric plates
11. volcanic mountain on an island near Iceland that erupted lava and tephra in 1973
12. 1980 eruption in the Cascade Range
13. famous explosive eruption of A.D. 79 that buried the city of Pompeii
14. source of "the most violent eruption of historic time"
15. enormous volcano of Mars
16. volcanic moon of Jupiter
17. igneous intrusion between rock layers; Palisades of the Hudson River
18. Henry Mountains and Black Hills

19. Ship Rock, New Mexico
20. largest igneous intrusion; core of the Coast Ranges of British Columbia

List B

- **a.** basalt plateaus
- **b.** batholith
- **c.** columnar jointing
- **d.** dike
- **e.** Eldfell
- **f.** felsic
- **g.** gases in melted rock
- **h.** hot spot
- **i.** Io
- **j.** Krakatoa
- **k.** laccolith
- **l.** lava
- **m.** mafic
- **n.** magma
- **o.** Mount St. Helens
- **p.** Olympus Mons
- **q.** rift eruptions
- **r.** silica
- **s.** sill
- **t.** stock
- **u.** subduction boundaries
- **v.** tephra
- **w.** Vesuvius
- **x.** volcanic neck

Interpret and Apply

On your paper, answer each question in complete sentences.

1. Earthquake activity often occurs before a volcano erupts but dies out as soon as the eruption starts. Propose a reason.
2. What relationship would be expected between the particle sizes within a tephra deposit and the distance from the volcanic source of the tephra?
3. The rate of movement of subducting plates differs from one subduction zone to another. How would this fact explain why Indonesia usually has one major volcanic eruption each year while the Cascades have only occasional eruptions?
4. At hot spot volcanoes in Africa, lavas of several ages are piled on top of each other. What would this indicate about the movement of the African Plate?
5. A layer of volcanic ash is found paralleling the sedimentary layers of a thick sequence of limestone. Would the ash layer be considered a sill? Explain.

Critical Thinking

The graph shows some of the islands of the Hawaiian Island chain (compare with Figure 14.7). The vertical axis of the graph shows the approximate age of the volcanic rocks found on each island, and the horizontal axis shows the distance of each island from Hawaii.

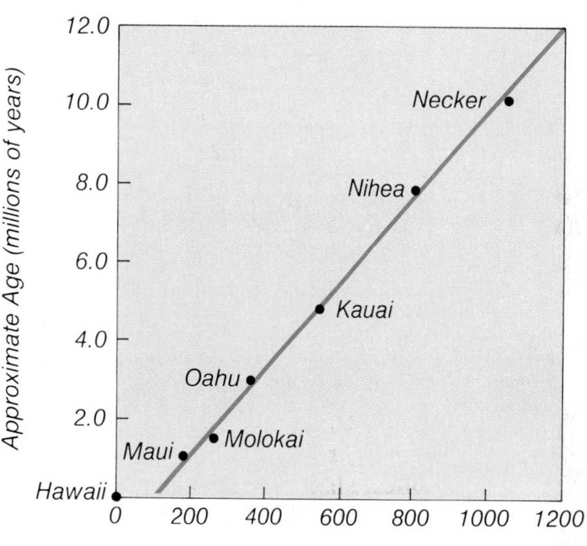

1. If an island were located 700 kilometers from Hawaii, what would be the expected age of the rocks of the island?
2. How far away from Hawaii would an island be on which the rocks were dated at 4.0 million years?
3. What evidence is there on the graph that Hawaii is currently over the hot spot?
4. Which island was over the hot spot about 5.0 million years ago?
5. According to the graph, which island is the oldest?
6. What is the age difference between the rocks of Oahu and the rocks of Molokai?
7. Assuming an age of 8.0 million years for the rocks of Nihea, determine the rate of motion, in centimeters per year, of the Pacific Plate in this area.

CHAPTER

15

Earthquakes and Plate Tectonics

▲ Walls and buildings in Whittier, California, collapsed during the 1987 earthquake.

How Do You Know That . . .

An earthquake is a sudden release of stress in Earth's crust? You can demonstrate this. Take a long, thin stick. (A piece of wood about the size of a meterstick or yardstick will work.) Hold one end down firmly at the side of your desk. Allow most of the stick to project beyond the desk. Using your free hand, push down gently on the overhanging end of the stick. Why does the stick bend rather than break? What happens to the stick if you suddenly let go of the overhanging end? A similar release of stress in Earth's crust can cause tremendous damage.

I Earthquakes Result from Stress

Topic 1 What Is an Earthquake?

Earthquakes are very common. More than a million occur each year. That is about one every 30 seconds. Most of these are too small to be noticeable on all but the most sensitive earthquake recording instruments. However, more than 3000 earthquakes strong enough to move sections of Earth's crust are recorded each year. Several hundred earthquakes move Earth's surface significant distances, and about 20 cause severe changes.

An **earthquake** is a shaking of Earth's crust caused by a release of energy. Like volcanoes, earthquakes are a result of the motions of the lithospheric plates. However, the area affected by an earthquake is much larger.

A severe earthquake in a populated area can be especially hazardous. Often the collapse of buildings caused by the ground shaking is only the beginning of the devastation. Explosions and fires start from broken electric wires or broken gas mains. Diseases spread when sewage lines are broken and water supplies become contaminated. Food shortages may occur as normal supply routes—roads, railroads, airport runways—become unusable. Coastal locations long distances from the earthquake may flood under the huge waves called tsunamis (Chapter 12, Topic 8). Earthquakes are the most destructive of natural disasters.

Topic 2 Causes of Earthquakes

Earthquakes can occur for many reasons. The ground can shake from the eruption of a volcano, the collapse of a cavern, or even from the impact of a meteor. However, the major cause of earthquakes is the stress that builds up between two lithospheric plates.

Most of the time, friction between plates prevents movement along the plate boundary. Instead, the stresses cause the plates to deform, or change shape. Eventually, the stresses become great enough to overcome the frictional forces, and the plates suddenly move. This movement causes an earthquake. The plates then snap back to the shapes they had before they were deformed but at new locations relative to each other. This explanation for the cause of an earthquake is called the **elastic-rebound theory** and is fundamental to an understanding of earthquakes.

OBJECTIVES

A Define *earthquake*, list problems caused by earthquakes, and discuss several causes of earthquakes.

B Define *focus* and *epicenter* and identify the significance of the depth of the focus.

C Name and describe the kinds of waves produced by earthquakes.

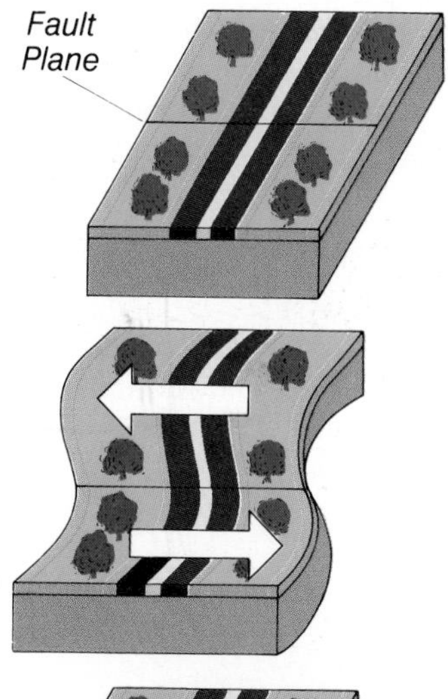

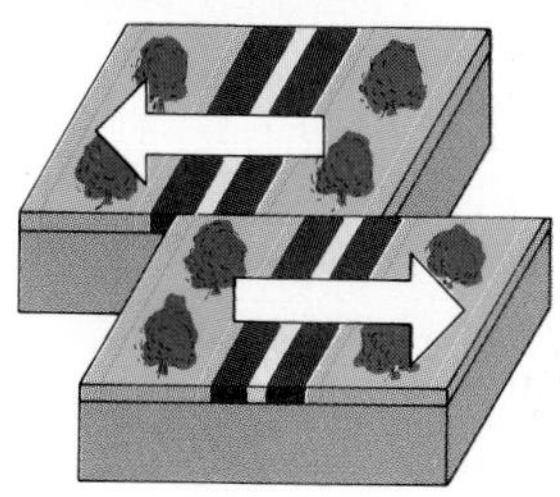

15.1 Earthquakes occur when the stress along a fault plane overcomes the forces of friction. When friction is finally overcome, the plates move suddenly and release earthquake energy. Then the rocks along the plate boundaries snap back to their original shape.

Topic 3 Depth of Earthquakes

The depth inside Earth at which an earthquake occurs depends upon the kind of plate boundary involved. At spreading centers and sliding boundaries, such as the mid-Atlantic Ridge and the San Andreas Fault, most earthquakes are less than 30 kilometers deep. At subduction boundaries, however, where one plate is plunging beneath another plate, earthquakes can be as much as 700 kilometers deep. The plate boundary is also plunging downward, often at about a 45-degree angle. Earthquakes can occur along this boundary until such depths are reached where pressures and temperatures transform rigid rocks into a more flexible material.

The place inside Earth where the earthquake actually occurs is called the **focus** of the earthquake. Shallow-focus earthquakes usually damage only small areas. As the depth of the focus increases, the area damaged by the earthquake increases. The point on Earth's surface directly above the focus of an earthquake is the **epicenter** of the earthquake.

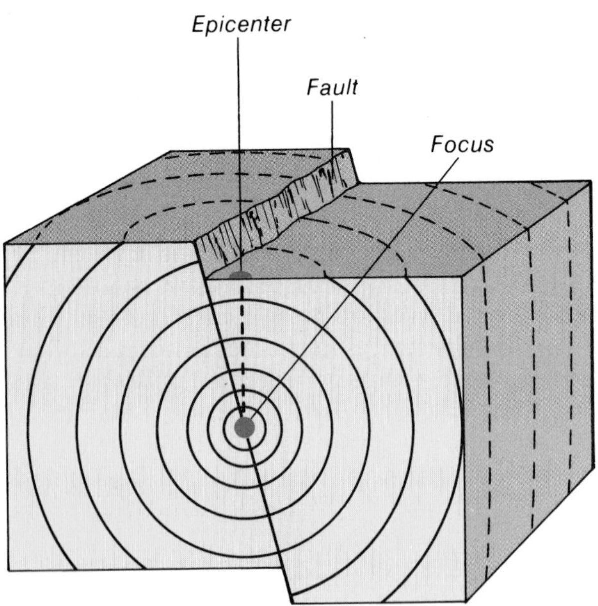

15.2 The focus is the location of the earthquake within Earth. The epicenter is the point on the surface directly above the focus.

Topic 4 Earthquake Waves

Earthquakes produce three basic kinds of wave motions. One motion moves the particles in the rock back and forth, while a second motion moves the particles up and down. The third motion resembles waves in water.

The back-and-forth wave motion alternately squeezes and stretches the rock material through which the wave passes. These waves are called *compressional, primary,* or ***P* waves.** *P* waves can travel through any material—solid rock, magma, ocean water, even air.

The up-and-down wave causes particles to move at right angles to the direction the waves are traveling. These waves are called *shear, secondary,* or **S waves.** *S* waves can travel through solids but not through liquids or gases. Liquids and gases cannot be sheared apart.

The rate at which *P* waves and *S* waves move through the ground depends upon the type and nature of the rock material. The velocity of these waves is greatest if the rock is rigid and dense but slows as the rock becomes less rigid and less dense. No matter what the material, *P* waves always travel about twice as fast as *S* waves.

Both *P* and *S* waves are called body waves because they travel through the body of Earth. When *P* and *S* waves reach the surface, they set up a third type of wave called *surface waves,* or ***L* waves.** These waves, which move like ripples on a pond, travel at about three kilometers per second.

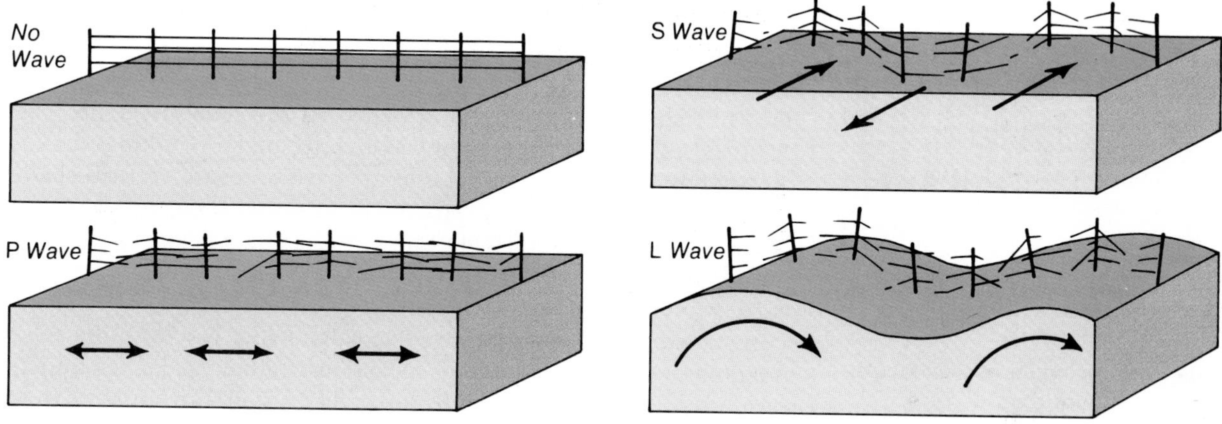

15.3 *P* waves and *S* waves travel through Earth. *L* waves travel along the surface.

TOPIC QUESTIONS

Each topic question refers to the topic of the same number.

1. **(a)** What is an earthquake? **(b)** How many earthquakes occur worldwide each year? **(c)** Name several forms of devastation and hardship that accompany earthquakes.
2. **(a)** List several minor causes of earthquakes. **(b)** What is the major cause of earthquakes? **(c)** Describe how earthquakes occur, according to the elastic-rebound theory.
3. **(a)** What type of plate boundary has the deepest earthquakes? Why? **(b)** What is the focus of an earthquake? How is the focus related to the area damaged by an earthquake? **(c)** Where is the epicenter of an earthquake?
4. **(a)** How do the particles in a *P* wave move? **(b)** What kinds of materials can *P* waves travel through? **(c)** How do the particles move in an *S* wave? **(d)** What materials can *S* waves *not* travel through? **(e)** How do the speeds of the *P* and *S* waves compare? **(f)** What are *L* waves?

OBJECTIVES

A Describe how a seismograph works.

B Discuss the relationship between the arrival time of the *P* and *S* waves at a seismograph station and the distance of the station from the earthquake epicenter.

C Explain how to locate an earthquake epicenter.

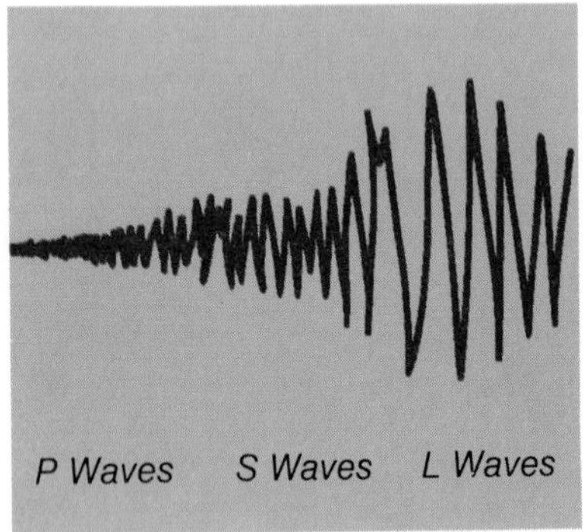

15.4 Seismic waves as they would look on a seismogram

15.5 Different kinds of seismographs record earthquakes by tracing earthquake waves.

II Locating an Earthquake

Topic 5 Seismographs

The instrument that detects and records earthquake waves is called a **seismograph.** Because there are different directions of motion produced by an earthquake—back and forth (horizontal) and up and down (vertical)—there are different kinds of seismographs. Some record horizontal motions and others record vertical motions. The way in which each works is simple.

A heavy weight is attached to a base anchored in bedrock. The weight stays almost perfectly still (due to inertia) even when the bedrock and base are being shaken by an earthquake.

A record sheet, called a **seismogram**, is put on a drum attached to the base. The drum is turned slowly by a clock. A pen attached to the heavy weight rests its point on the drum. As long as the bedrock is quiet, the pen makes a straight line on the turning drum. When the bedrock shakes, the drum shakes slightly. However, the pen does not shake because it is attached to the heavy weight. The result is a zigzag trace that shows an earthquake is taking place.

Different forms of seismographs are used to record vertical shaking and horizontal shaking. Seismograms show three groups of zigzags for a single quake. Each group represents a type of wave. Since the *P* waves travel fastest, they arrive first. *S* waves arrive second, and *L* waves arrive last.

In addition to recording the basic earthquake waves, some seismographs are built to record special earthquakes. For example, some are designed to measure only very small earthquakes that occur near the seismograph station. Others record moderate earthquakes several hundred kilometers away. Still others measure earthquakes anywhere in the world.

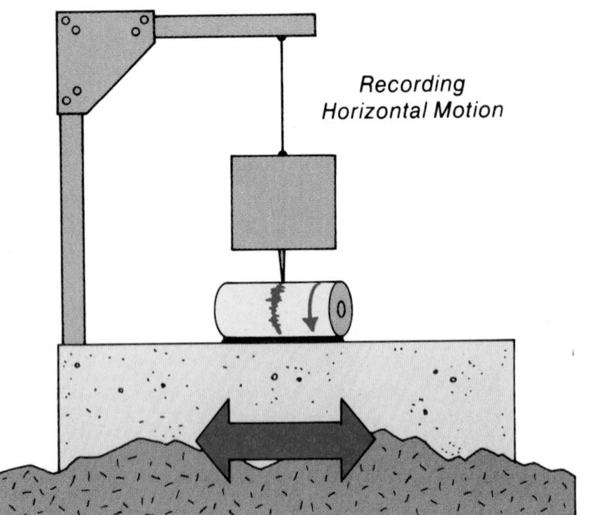

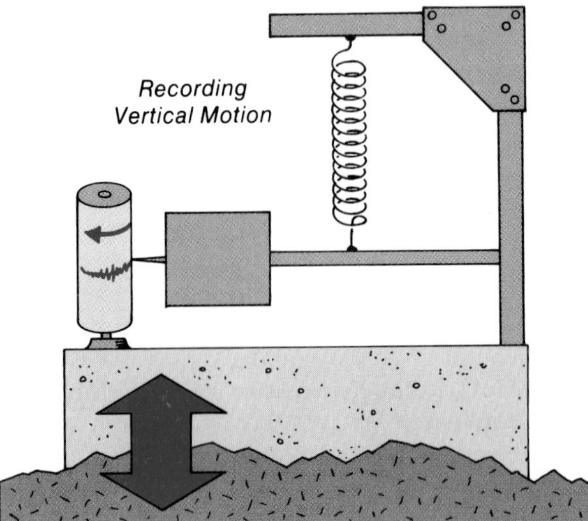

Topic 6 Determining the Distance to the Earthquake Epicenter

The tracing made by a seismograph can be used to tell how far away the earthquake epicenter is from the seismograph station that recorded the tracing. Since *P* waves travel faster than *S* waves (Topic 4), the *P* waves made by the earthquake always arrive at a seismograph station before the *S* waves. The farther the seismograph station is from the earthquake epicenter, the larger the difference is in the arrival times of the two waves. For example, the difference in arrival times for the *P* and *S* waves for an earthquake that occurs 2000 kilometers from a seismograph station is about 3 minutes 10 seconds. The difference for a station 5000 kilometers away is about 6 minutes 40 seconds.

The relationship between *P* and *S* wave travel times and epicenter distance is shown on a **time-travel graph** (Figure 15.6). If the

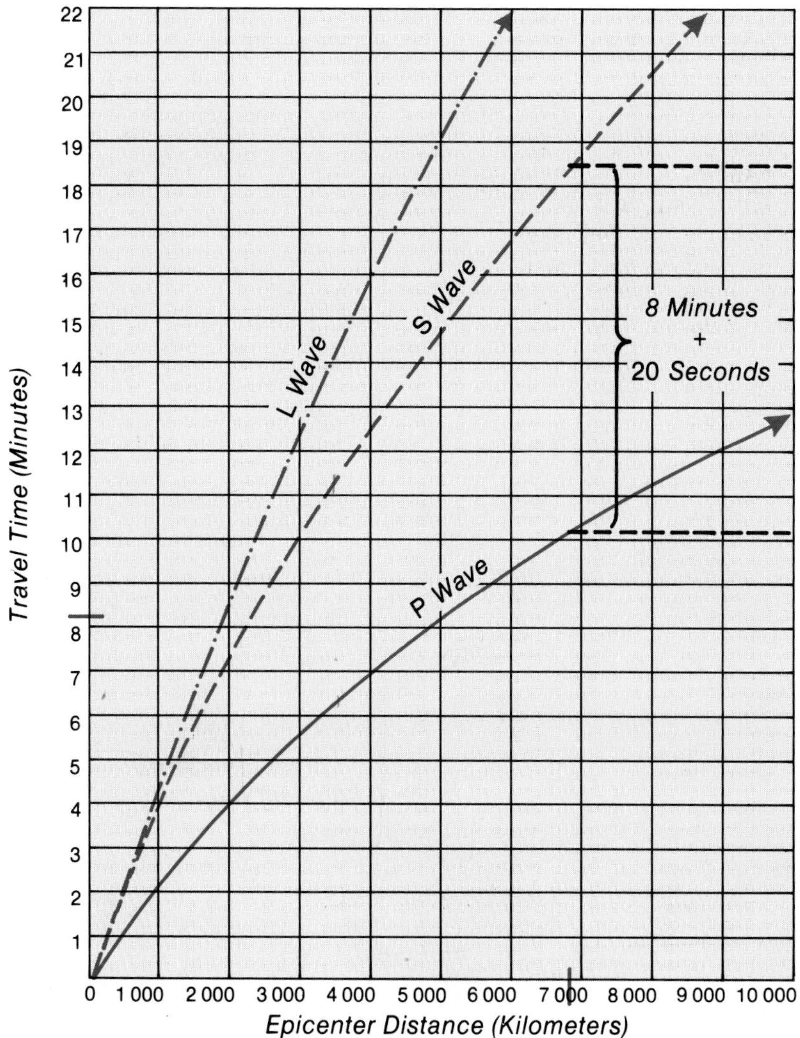

15.6 A time-travel graph can be used to find the distance to an earthquake. For example, if the difference between the arrival times of the *P* and *S* waves is 8 minutes 20 seconds, the earthquake occurred 6800 kilometers from the seismograph station.

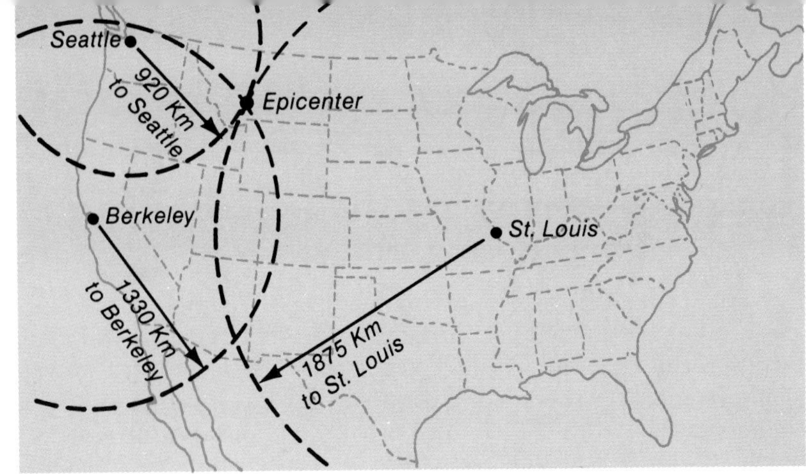

15.7 A single seismograph station can only determine the distance to the epicenter. Three stations are needed to pinpoint the exact location of the epicenter.

difference in the arrival times of the two waves is known, the distance to the epicenter can be read directly from the graph. For example, suppose the time difference between the arrival of the *P* wave and the arrival of the *S* wave is 8 minutes 20 seconds. The distance from the seismograph station to the earthquake epicenter is 6800 kilometers.

Topic 7 **Locating the Epicenter**

Knowing the distance between a single seismograph station and an earthquake epicenter does not locate the epicenter. Instead, distances from three different stations are needed. For example, assume that a seismograph station at St. Louis, Missouri, determines that the epicenter is located 1875 kilometers away. A second station at Berkeley, California, find that the same epicenter is 1330 kilometers away. A third station at Seattle, Washington, finds that the distance to the epicenter is only 920 kilometers.

To locate the epicenter, three circles are drawn on a map. The first circle is drawn around St. Louis at a distance of 1875 kilometers. The epicenter must be located somewhere on this circle. Then a similar 1330-kilometer circle is drawn around Berkeley. The two circles will cross at two points. One of these points must be the epicenter. A similar 920-kilometer circle around Seattle will meet the other two circles at a single point. This point is the location of the earthquake epicenter.

TOPIC QUESTIONS

Each topic question refers to the topic of the same number.

5. **(a)** What does a seismograph detect and record? **(b)** Why is there more than one kind of seismograph? **(c)** How does a seismograph work? **(d)** What is a seismogram?
6. **(a)** What kind of wave arrives at a seismograph station first? **(b)** What is the relationship between the arrival times of *P* and *S* waves and the distance to the earthquake epicenter? **(c)** What is a time-travel graph used to determine?
7. **(a)** How many seismograph stations are needed to locate an epicenter? **(b)** How is the epicenter located?

III Measuring an Earthquake

Topic 8 Earthquake Magnitude

In addition to locating the epicenter, seismograms can be used to determine other facts about an earthquake. For example, seismograms can be used to determine the strength, or magnitude, of the energy produced by the earthquake.

The most widely used scale of earthquake magnitude is the scale developed by Charles F. Richter in the 1940's. The **Richter scale** is designed to be a measure of the amount of energy released by the earthquake itself. Each magnitude number represents an earthquake 32 times stronger than the next lower number. For example, an earthquake with a magnitude of 6 is 32 times stronger than an earthquake with a magnitude of 5 and more than 1000 times stronger than an earthquake with a magnitude of 4.

In recent years, another method of determining earthquake magnitude called **seismic moment** has been developed. The number for the seismic moment is not as easy to measure as Richter magnitude. However, the result is a more accurate indicator of the total energy involved. For example, both the 1906 San Francisco earthquake and the 1964 Alaskan earthquake had Richter magnitudes of 8.3. The Alaskan earthquake, however, released more total energy than the San Francisco earthquake because of larger movements along a much larger fault plane. The seismic moment values reflect these differences. The San Francisco earthquake has a seismic moment of 7.9; the Alaskan earthquake, 9.2. These numbers show that the Alaskan quake was more than 100 times stronger than the San Francisco quake.

The strongest earthquake recorded to date was the Chilean earthquake of 1960. This quake registered 8.3 on the Richter scale and 9.5 on the seismic moment scale.

Topic 9 Earthquake Damage

Even a mild earthquake can cause buildings to collapse. The two major causes of building collapse are ground shaking and foundation failure.

Ground shaking is the result of the waves set in motion by the earthquake. The sudden release of energy in an earthquake causes all of Earth to vibrate in much the same way that a bell vibrates when struck. Some of these vibrations move up and down while others move side to side (Topic 4). Buildings react to these vibrations and begin to shake up and down and sideways too. Most buildings can withstand large up-and-down vibrations. However, the largest motions at Earth's surface are side to side. Few buildings can survive severe side-to-side movements. As a result of these side-to-side movements, they collapse.

OBJECTIVES

A Identify the scales used to describe earthquake magnitude.

B Name the two major causes of building collapse during earthquakes.

C Identify several kinds of data that are being studied for earthquake prediction.

15.8 If the vibration during an earthquake is severe, then building damage will result. The Alaskan earthquake of 1964 had one of the largest magnitudes ever recorded.

Foundation failure is also a result of ground shaking but in a different way. The soils under a building may settle from severe shaking or even become liquified. In either case, the building is no longer safely supported and may collapse.

The importance of the foundation was first noted in the 1906 San Francisco earthquake. Buildings on solid rock experienced little damage. However, buildings located on bog muds or soft fill suffered severe damage. In fact, almost all of the buildings on soft material collapsed completely.

Topic 10 Earthquake Prediction

Many areas of the United States where the risk of an earthquake is great are also areas with large and growing populations. For people in those areas, the need for earthquake prediction is a serious concern.

A successful earthquake prediction must correctly forecast three facts—*where* the earthquake will occur, *when* the earthquake will occur, and what the *magnitude* of the earthquake will be. Seismologists are studying a variety of data to determine how to provide accurate and reliable earthquake warnings.

One kind of data being studied is *P* wave velocities. The discovery was made that *P* waves slow by 10 to 15 percent for a period of time preceding an earthquake. The period might be only a few days, or it could be years. Earthquakes have been found to occur soon after the *P* wave velocity returned to normal. Furthermore, the longer the velocity stays below normal, the stronger the earthquake. This method has correctly predicted a number of earthquakes in Russia, China, and California.

A second kind of earthquake prediction data comes from changes in elevation. In some areas, a slight increase in the elevation of the land has preceded an earthquake. In Japan, an uplift was noted 10 years before a disastrous 7.5-magnitude earthquake. In California, an area called the Palmdale Bulge has been heavily studied for changes that might indicate an earthquake.

A third kind of data comes from measuring the electrical resistance of the ground. This measurement is made by feeding an electrical current through the ground and reading a voltmeter a few kilometers away. A decrease in the readings has been found to precede an earthquake.

Still another kind of earthquake prediction data comes from the amount of radon in well water. *Radon* is a radioactive element. Its concentration in well water has been found to increase significantly before an earthquake. In addition, the water may become cloudy with sediment.

From these and other observable changes, seismologists are hopeful of learning how to predict correctly Earth's movements. Such predictions would both reduce casualties and lower property damage during an earthquake.

TOPIC QUESTIONS

Each topic question refers to the topic of the same number.

8. **(a)** What is meant by the magnitude of an earthquake? **(b)** What is the scale most widely used to find magnitude? **(c)** How is the seismic moment scale different from the scale used to find magnitude?
9. **(a)** What kind of ground shaking is more likely to cause a building to collapse? **(b)** In what two ways can shaking cause foundation failure? **(c)** What effect did type of foundation have on building failure in the 1906 San Francisco earthquake?
10. **(a)** What three facts must an earthquake prediction forecast? **(b)** List four kinds of data that are being used to forecast earthquakes. Identify the change that occurs in each kind of data before an earthquake.

OBJECTIVES

A Explain the changes in *P* and *S* wave velocities inside Earth.

B Locate the Mohorovicic discontinuity and explain how it was discovered.

C Describe the shadow zone and explain its significance.

IV Earthquake Waves inside Earth

Topic 11 *P* and *S* Wave Velocities

Most information about the inside of Earth has come from an analysis of seismogram tracings. These tracings record far more than just the arrival times of the *P*, *S*, and *L* waves. In combination with a time-travel graph (Topic 6), the tracings can be used to determine if a wave has been bent, speeded up, slowed down, or reflected as it traveled through the inside of Earth. From these kinds of data, seismologists have been able to determine the velocities of *P* and *S* waves as they travel through the different layers inside Earth and to define the locations and characteristics of those layers.

A graph of *P* and *S* wave velocities shows the result (Figure 15.9). The most obvious feature of the graph is the sharp change in velocities at a depth of 2900 kilometers. *P* waves are greatly slowed there, and *S* waves are stopped. Since *S* waves do not pass through liquids, the material directly below 2900 kilometers must be liquid. In fact, this is the evidence that was used to show that Earth's outer core is liquid. The partial recovery of the *P* wave velocity at 5200 kilometers suggests that the inner core, like the mantle, is a solid.

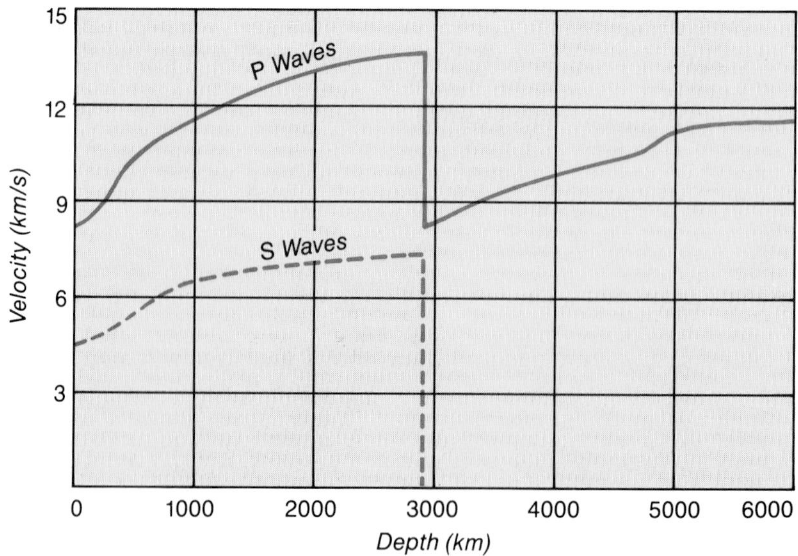

15.9 This graph shows that at a depth of 2900 kilometers the *P* waves slow down and the *S* waves stop. Geologists consider that depth to be the boundary between the mantle and the liquid outer core.

Topic 12 The Moho

Another abrupt change in *P* and *S* wave velocities occurs at the boundary between the crust and the mantle. This change was discovered in 1909 by the Yugoslav seismologist Andrija Mohorovicic from a study of many seismograms of minor earthquakes.

Several of the seismograms showed two distinct groups of *P* and *S* waves. One of the groups had traveled at an average velocity of 7 kilometers per second, but the other had speeded up to 8 kilometers per second. Mohorovicic reasoned that the second group had gone through denser material below the crust. He calculated the depth to the denser material to be about 50 kilometers.

The boundary he discovered is considered to be the boundary between the crust and the mantle. In his honor, the boundary is named the **Mohorovicic discontinuity,** or **Moho** for short.

The Moho, however, is not at a depth of 50 kilometers everywhere. The Moho averages 32 kilometers under the continents but only 8 kilometers under the oceans. Thus the continents stand higher on the crust but also sink deeper into the mantle.

15.10 The Moho is deeper under the continents than under the oceans.

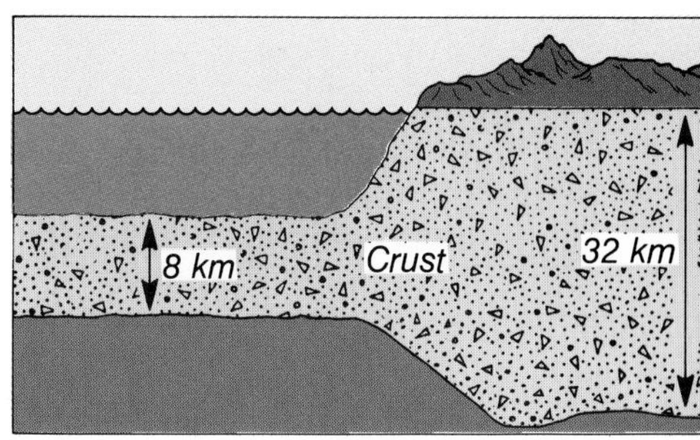

Topic 13 **The Shadow Zone**

Even though an earthquake sends waves throughout all of Earth's interior, not all seismograph stations receive information from all earthquakes. Some receive only *P* waves, while others receive no signal at all.

Seismic stations that receive neither *P* nor *S* waves are said to be in the **shadow zone** of that earthquake (Figure 15.11). The shadow zone is a wide belt around Earth on the side opposite the focus of the earthquake. The cause of the shadow zone is Earth's outer core. *P* waves passing through the mantle are refracted (bent) in a smooth arc back to the surface. However, a *P* wave that travels deep enough to enter the outer core is refracted twice, once when it enters the outer core and again when it leaves. The result is that a broad belt around Earth, the shadow zone, receives no *P* wave information. No

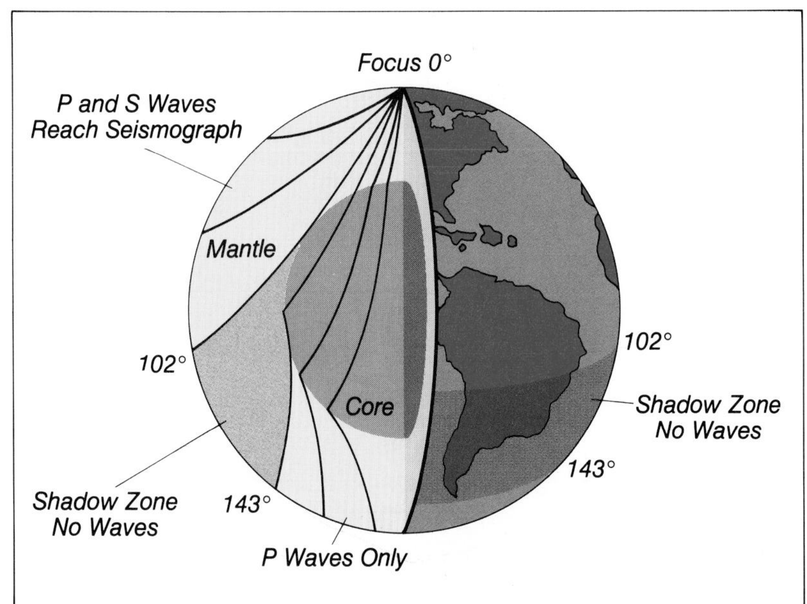

15.11 The shadow zone is caused by Earth's outer core. *S* waves do not reach the shadow zone because they are unable to penetrate the outer core. *P* waves are able to penetrate the outer core, but they are refracted so that none reach the shadow zone.

S wave information arrives in the shadow zone either. *S* waves cannot pass through liquids, and the outer core is a liquid.

Seismograph stations that are between the earthquake epicenter and the shadow zone receive both *P* and *S* waves. Stations within the shadow zone receive neither *P* nor *S* waves. Stations that are beyond the shadow zone on the opposite side of Earth from the earthquake receive only *P* waves. The *S* waves are stopped by the liquid outer core.

TOPIC QUESTIONS

Each topic question refers to the topic of the same number.

11. **(a)** What happens to *P* wave velocities at a depth of 2900 kilometers inside Earth? **(b)** What happens to *S* waves at that depth? Why?

12. **(a)** What is the Moho? **(b)** How did Mohorovicic discover the Moho? **(c)** How does the Moho's depth vary under the continents as compared with its depth under the oceans?

13. **(a)** What is the shadow zone? **(b)** What is the cause of the shadow zone? **(c)** Why do *S* waves *not* come to the surface beyond the shadow zone?

Dr. Waverly Person
Seismologist

The National Earthquake Information Service (NEIS) in Golden, Colorado, is the most important collector of earthquake information in the world. Dr. Waverly Person is a seismologist there. He says that the service regularly computes magnitude and epicenter locations for between 10 000 and 13 000 earthquakes each year.

The data that Dr. Person and other seismologists use in their work arrive in Golden by telegraph, telephone, and even letter from all over the world. However, 90 to 100 seismic stations in the United States, Canada, and other parts of the world are in direct contact with Golden all of the time. Their data are recorded on seismograph drums at NEIS at the same instant they are obtained at the station.

When large or damaging earthquakes occur, the normal routine of epicenter analysis is interrupted in order to determine the location of the earthquake as quickly as possible so that agencies responsible for disaster relief can be alerted. Dr. Person says that for major U.S. earthquakes, the whole staff goes to work, no matter what the hour of the day or night.

NEIS is a part of the U.S. Geological Survey.

V Examples of Earthquakes

Topic 14 Alaska—1964

The Alaskan earthquake of 1964 had one of the largest magnitudes of any earthquake in this century. It began as a gentle rocking motion similar to the kind that Alaskans customarily experience. However, unlike the usual tremors that taper off, this one grew worse until the ground was rolling like huge ocean waves. The rolling continued for five minutes. By the time it ended, Alaska had experienced some frightening changes. Whole blocks of houses were moved, buildings collapsed, and huge fissures opened in the ground. More than 260 000 square kilometers of ground were heaved upward 2 meters and then dropped. Another 65 000 square kilometers were moved sideways.

The Alaskan earthquake was caused by movement along a subduction boundary. All along the Aleutian Islands, the Pacific Plate is pushing under the North American Plate. Some subduction boundaries move by long-term steady creep, so severe earthquakes are rare. The subduction of the Pacific Plate at the Mariana Islands is an example. Other subduction boundaries, however, move by horizontal slippage. This kind of slippage causes earthquakes. Both Alaska and Chile are located on such boundaries.

The main reason the Alaskan earthquake was so severe was that the break on the fault that started the earthquake triggered other breaks. In all, over 800 kilometers of fault plane were affected.

The earthquake was so strong that it caused buildings to shake as far away as Seattle, Washington. Even more surprising, many seismograph stations around the world were unable to record the earthquake because it threw tracking pens off their recording drums. Detectable vibrations were recorded for 18 months after the earthquake. Over 10 000 aftershocks were counted.

The earthquake, however, was just the beginning of the devastation. It generated a series of tsunamis, or seismic sea waves. Coastal villages were flooded again and again at intervals of about 30 minutes. One fishing village simply disappeared after a 21-meter wave swept over it. The waves crossed the Pacific Ocean at more than 600 kilometers per hour and caused severe damage as far away as Hawaii and Japan. Amazingly, only 115 people were killed.

OBJECTIVES

A Identify movement along a subduction boundary as the cause of the 1964 Alaskan earthquake.

B Discuss earthquake activity along the San Andreas fault system.

C Explain the cause and significance of midplate earthquakes such as the 1811–1812 New Madrid earthquakes.

15.12 Buildings in downtown Anchorage were severely damaged during the 1964 Alaskan earthquake.

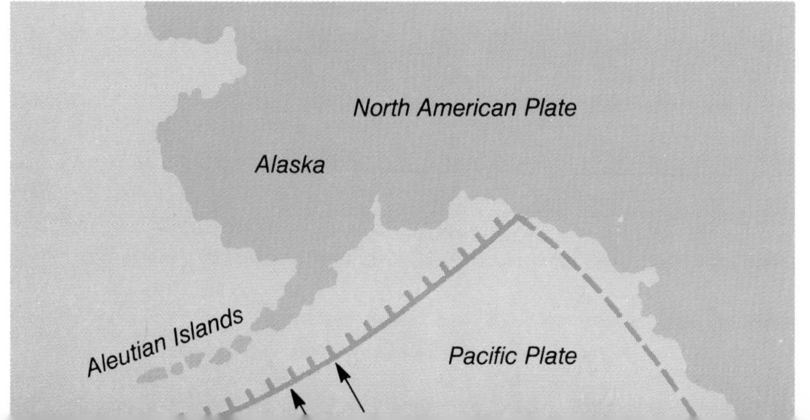

15.13 This map shows the location of the plate boundary that caused the Alaskan earthquake.

15.14 An aerial view of the San Andreas Fault

15.15 Seismologists use the latest technology to detect crustal movements. Here a laser beam is used to keep a precise measurement of the distance between two locations on opposite sides of a fault plane in California. Any change in the measurement would indicate seismic activity.

Topic 15 Earthquakes along the San Andreas Fault

As earthquakes go, neither the 1987 Rosemead earthquake nor the 1971 San Fernando earthquake was a major event. However, they are significant because they both occurred in densely populated southern California. As a result, each of these earthquakes demolished or destroyed thousands of buildings and caused millions of dollars of damage.

The 1971 and 1987 earthquakes were the result of movement on two different faults, both of which are part of the San Andreas Fault system. Prior to 1971, the San Fernando Fault was not considered an active fault. The San Andreas Fault, however, has been active. It has had two major earthquakes in historic times. In 1857, an earthquake centered 120 kilometers from Los Angeles resulted from a 9-meter shift along that portion of the fault. In 1906, the city of San Francisco was destroyed when the fault shifted 6 meters. From a study of fractures in the sediments near the fault, geologists have determined that it has moved nine times between the sixth century and 1857. This means that there has been a major earthquake in California on the average of once every 160 years.

The San Andreas Fault system marks the boundary between the Pacific Plate and the North American Plate (Chapter 13, Topic 9). An 1100-kilometer piece of California is moving north relative to the rest of the United States. If the two plates would slide smoothly past each other as they do in some areas, Californians would not need to be concerned, but in several places the plates are stuck. Tremendous pressures are building up that will cause major earthquakes when they give way. With 18 million people now living along the fault, the risk of a disaster is very high. This region of the United States has a definite need for reliable earthquake forecasting methods.

Topic 16 New Madrid—1811 and 1812

Three of the largest earthquakes in United States history did not occur in either California or Alaska. In fact, they did not even happen at a plate boundary. Instead, they occurred on the Mississippi River near the town of New Madrid, Missouri.

Three earthquakes struck during December, January, and February of 1811 and 1812. Their magnitudes were 8.6, 8.4, and 8.7. Because the crustal rocks in the area conduct seismic waves well, the earthquakes were felt throughout most of the northeastern United States and are reported to have rung church bells in Boston. At New Madrid, two new waterfalls were formed on the Mississippi River, and its surface was littered with the wreckage of boats. The earthquake activity at New Madrid did not end in 1812. Since then, two large but less severe earthquakes have occurred. Even today the area experiences one small earthquake about every other day.

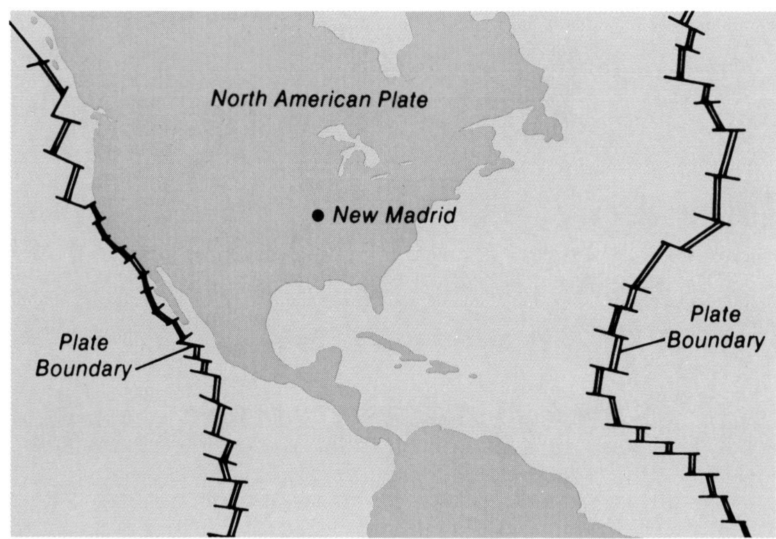

15.16 The faults at New Madrid are buried near the center of the North American Plate. A major earthquake there would affect a huge geographical area.

If New Madrid is not a plate boundary, why is there so much seismic activity there? The cause of the activity is three faults. These faults cannot be seen at Earth's surface. They are deeply buried by Mississippi River sediments and the thick layers of sedimentary rock beneath them. They seem to be related to the craton, the oldest and strongest rocks of the continental crust (Chapter 13, Topic 12). The faults may have been inactive for millions of years before changes in the stresses on the North American Plate caused them to start moving again.

The activity at New Madrid belongs to a class of earthquakes called midplate earthquakes. On a worldwide scale, the class has little significance. To North America, however, the New Madrid earthquakes have great significance because of the size of the area that would be affected by a major earthquake there.

TOPIC QUESTIONS

Each topic question refers to the topic of the same number.

14. **(a)** List some changes that occurred in Alaska because of the 1964 earthquake there. **(b)** What was the cause of the Alaskan earthquake? **(c)** What caused it to be so severe? **(d)** Name some effects of that severity. **(e)** What other devastating force accompanied the earthquake?

15. **(a)** Why was the 1971 San Fernando earthquake important? **(b)** What was its cause? **(c)** Identify some other California earthquakes. **(d)** How often is California thought to have major earthquakes? **(e)** Why is earthquake prediction important in California?

16. **(a)** Why is the location of the New Madrid earthquake unique? **(b)** How large an area felt the three major earthquakes there? **(c)** Why are the New Madrid earthquakes significant?

CHAPTER 15 REVIEW

Summary

An earthquake is a shaking of Earth's crust caused by a release of energy. Severe earthquakes in populated areas can cause serious problems.

Major earthquakes are the result of stresses along the fault plane between two lithospheric plates.

The deepest earthquakes occur at subduction boundaries. The focus is the place inside Earth where the earthquake actually occurs. The epicenter is the point on Earth's surface directly above the focus.

Earthquakes produce *P*, *S*, and *L* waves, each with distinctive properties.

A seismograph is an instrument that detects and records earthquake waves.

The difference in the arrival times of the *P* and *S* waves can be used to determine the distance to the earthquake epicenter. Seismograph tracings from three seismograph stations are needed to locate an epicenter.

Earthquake magnitude is a measure of the strength of an earthquake.

Ground shaking and foundation failure are the two major reasons that buildings collapse during earthquakes.

Several kinds of data are being investigated as earthquake predictors.

P waves travel through all parts of Earth's interior, but *S* waves do not travel through the outer core because the outer core is a liquid.

The Mohorovicic discontinuity, or Moho, is the boundary between the crust and the mantle. The Moho is deeper beneath the continents than beneath the ocean basins.

The shadow zone is a belt around Earth where neither *P* nor *S* waves are received from a particular earthquake.

The Alaskan earthquake of 1964, the California earthquakes of 1971 and 1987, and the earthquakes at New Madrid, Missouri, resulted from different types of crustal plate movements.

Vocabulary

earthquake
elastic-rebound theory
epicenter
focus
L wave
Mohorovicic discontinuity (Moho)
P wave
Richter scale
seismic moment
seismogram
seismograph
shadow zone
S wave
time-travel graph

Review

Choose the word or words that best complete each sentence.

1. The release of energy by an _______ causes Earth's crust to shake.
2. In the elastic-rebound theory, _______ prevents the plates from moving as stresses build up across the fault plane.
3. The deepest earthquakes occur at _______ plate boundaries.
4. The _______ is the place inside Earth where the earthquake occurs. The epicenter is the point directly above it on the surface.
5. _______ waves move particles back and forth, can travel through any material, and arrive at a seismograph station first.
6. *S* waves move particles up and down, travel slower than *P* waves, and cannot travel through _______.
7. *L* waves, or surface waves, travel like ripples on a pond and result when *P* waves and *S* waves reach Earth's _______.
8. Seismographs detect and record _______ waves.
9. The difference in the arrival time of the *P* and *S* waves at a seismograph station increases as the distance from the earthquake epicenter _______.
10. To locate an epicenter, data from _______ seismograph stations are needed.
11. The Richter scale measures the _______ of an earthquake.

12. Severe side-to-side ground shaking is likely to cause buildings to _______ during an earthquake.
13. *P* wave velocities and the electrical resistance of the ground have been found to _______ before earthquakes, while elevation of the ground and the concentration of radon in well water both increase.
14. *P* waves are slowed at the outer core and *S* waves are stopped because the outer core is _______.
15. The Mohorovicic discontinuity, or Moho, is the boundary between the _______ and the mantle.
16. The Moho is deeper beneath the _______ than beneath the ocean basins.
17. Neither *P* nor *S* waves are received in the _______ zone of an earthquake.
18. The Alaskan earthquake of 1964 was the result of the subduction of the _______ Plate beneath the North American Plate.
19. The California earthquakes occur as the _______ Plate slides past the North American Plate.
20. The New Madrid earthquakes may have been the result of _______ in the North American craton.

Interpret and Apply

On your paper, answer each question in complete sentences.

1. The New Madrid earthquake was felt over the northeastern United States. An equally severe earthquake in California, however, would not be felt much beyond California. Why?
2. In what way is the time difference between the arrival of *P* and *S* waves like the time difference between a lightning flash and thunder during a thunderstorm?
3. Using the time-travel graph on page 247, determine the distance to the epicenter if the difference in the arrival times of the *P* and *S* waves is (a) 4 minutes 30 seconds, (b) 6 minutes, and (c) 7 minutes 20 seconds.
4. If scientists wished to drill to the Moho, would it be better to drill on the land or in the ocean? Why?

Critical Thinking

The drawings below are seismogram tracings made at three seismograph stations for the same earthquake. The arrival times of the *P* and *S* waves are indicated on each tracing.

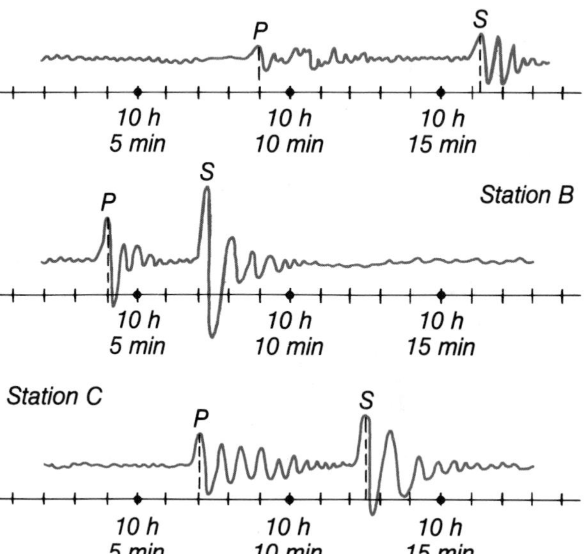

1. Which wave arrived at each seismograph station first? Why?
2. What time did the *P* wave arrive at station *A*?
3. In hours, minutes, and seconds, what time did the *S* wave arrive at station *B*?
4. What is the difference in the arrival times of *P* and *S* waves at station *C*?
5. Station *B* was located nearer to the earthquake epicenter, while station *A* was farthest away. Cite three kinds of evidence from the tracings to support this statement.
6. What time did the earthquake occur? (Use the time-travel graph on page 247.)

CHAPTER

16 Mountains and Plate Tectonics

▲ These Himalayan Mountain peaks formed from the mountain-building collision of lithospheric plates.

How Do You Know That . . .

Rock layers of mountainous areas may be squeezed and crumpled into great wavelike folds? A simple model shows how this movement is possible. Use several different colors of modeling clay to make a plateau of four layers of sedimentary rock. Each layer should be about 1 centimeter thick, 15 centimeters long, and 8 centimeters wide. Gently squeeze the two ends of the plateau toward each other so that the clay forms upfolded layers. Now level out the clay again. This time squeeze the ends of the plateau to form downfolded layers.

I Mountains Result from Collisions

Topic 1 Active and Passive Continental Margins

The margin of a continent is the boundary between oceanic crust and continental crust. There are two basic types of continental margins—active and passive. Both are important to the formation of mountains. The map on pages 588–589 of Appendix B shows the locations of the plate boundaries and major mountain ranges.

Active continental margins are plate boundaries. Earthquakes, volcanoes, and mountain building result as the plates move relative to each other. An excellent example of an active continental margin is the west coast of South America. Here the dense oceanic Nazca Plate is subducting under a less dense continental South American Plate, forming the Andes Mountains. Volcanoes and earthquakes are common features of this area.

Passive continental margins are not plate boundaries. These margins are stable areas of shallow water where the major activity is the buildup of sediments. Some of the sediments come from rivers flowing off the continents. Other sediments come from the skeletons and shells of organisms that live in the water. An example of a passive continental margin is the Atlantic coast of North America. A wedge of sediment 250 kilometers wide and as much as 10 kilometers thick has accumulated there.

How are passive continental margins related to mountain building? The answer is that these margins are the only places where sediments accumulate in a quantity great enough to make a mountain. The mountains of today were passive continental margins in the past. The active continental margin on the west coast of South America was a passive continental margin until about 200 million years ago. The Andes Mountains contain the sediments that were deposited on that passive margin.

Topic 2 Collisions between Oceans and Continents

The Andes Mountains are an example of one type of mountain-building process—the collision of oceanic crustal material with continental crustal material. In this type of collision, oceanic crust plunges, or subducts, under the continent as rock layers on the

OBJECTIVES

A Describe active and passive continental margins and give examples of each.

B Discuss two ways in which mountains are formed during the collision between an ocean and a continent and give examples of each.

C Describe what happens when two continents collide and name places where such collisions are occurring.

continent form mountains. Subduction continues throughout the mountain-building process. Earthquakes are common. Friction from subduction generates a supply of volcanic material to the uplifting mountains.

In some ocean-continent collisions of the past, another process appears to have accompanied subduction. In these cases, pieces of oceanic plate have ridden over the subduction zone rather than plunge into it. These pieces are found attached to the continents. This type of continental collision is thought to have been important to the formation of the west coast of North America. Like the west coast of South America, this area was a passive plate margin until about 200 million years ago. At that time, the Pacific Plate began to subduct under the North American continent. As it subducted, pieces of the Pacific Plate were scraped off and attached to the edge of the continent. Some of the pieces contained oceanic crust, some were islands, and some were fragments of other continents. These pieces became the mountains of the west coast of North America. They are *terranes*, discussed in Chapter 13.

Topic 3 **Collisions between Two Continents**

A second type of mountain building results when two continents come together at a collision boundary (Chapter 13, Topic 10). The collision of India with Eurasia to form the Himalaya Mountains is an example.

Before two continents can collide, the ocean basin between them must close. This change occurs as the oceanic crust subducts beneath one of the continents. Subduction stops, however, once the ocean is gone and the continents are in contact, because continental crust is too light to subduct. Continued movement causes the rocks of the continental margins to be crumpled into mountains.

The formation of the Himalaya Mountains was preceded by the closing of an ocean between India and Tibet, a part of Eurasia. The oceanic crust is thought to have disappeared into a subduction zone that plunged to the north under Tibet. Once the continental crusts

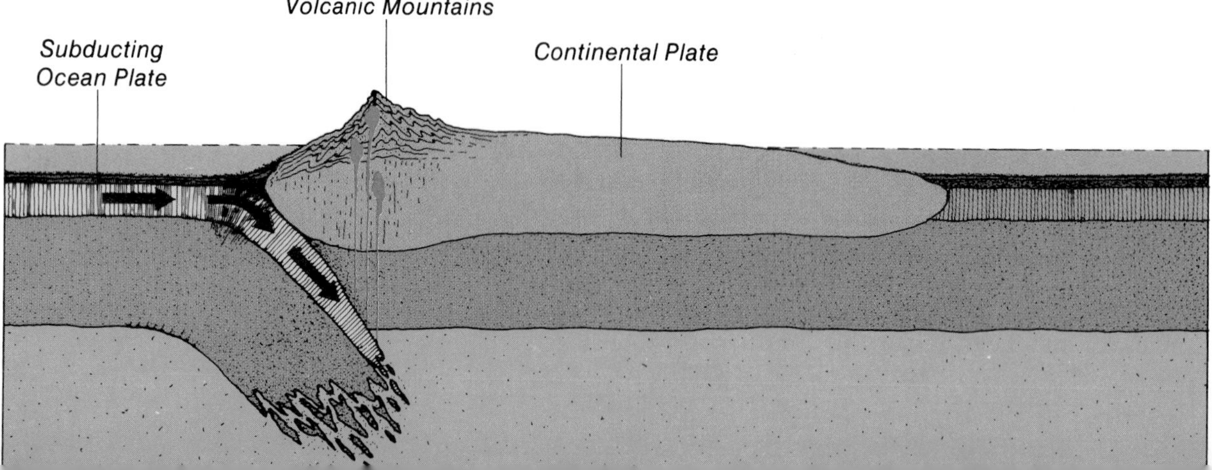

16.1 When an oceanic plate and a continental plate collide, the heavier oceanic plate subducts under the continental plate. The subduction process generates volcanic material near the edge of the continental plate.

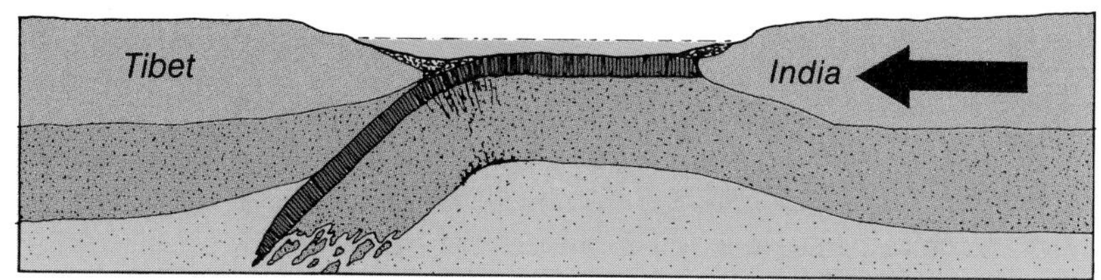

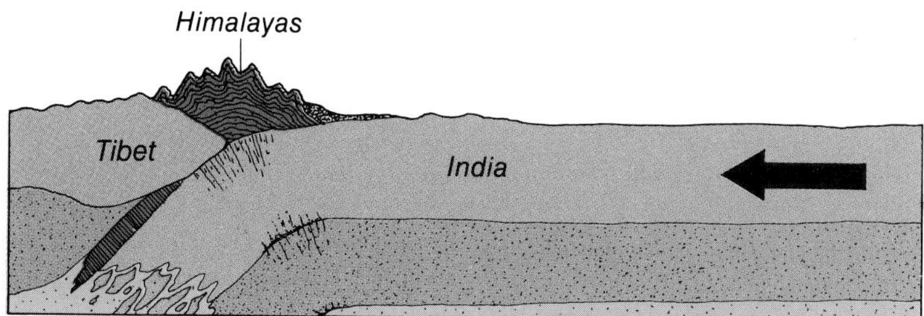

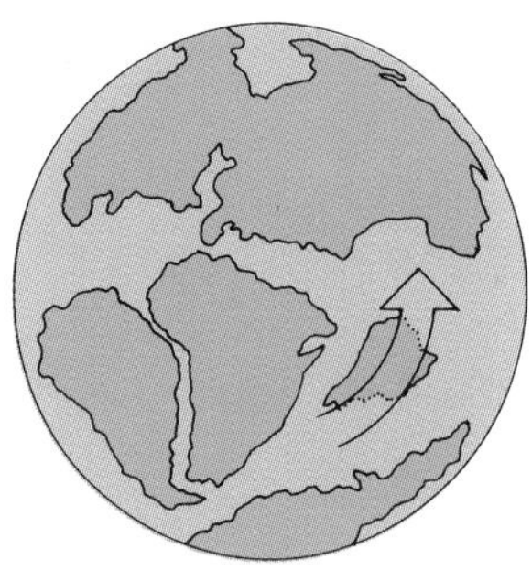

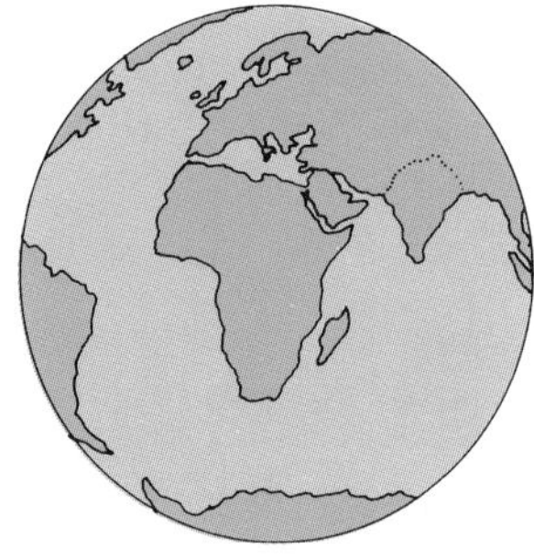

collided, subduction stopped. However, India continued to move north, pushing some rocks aside and crumpling others into mountains. The severe earthquakes that occur in the Himalayas today indicate that the collision is still in progress.

Another example of a mountain range that is forming today by the collision of two continents is the Alps Mountains of Europe. Here the colliding landmass is Italy, which is actually a part of the African Plate. As the Eurasian Plate moves toward the African Plate, closing the Mediterranean Sea, the Eurasian Plate is colliding with Italy.

16.2 When two continental plates collide, a portion of the crust at the collision boundary is crumpled into a mountain formation. The Himalayas formed in this way as the continental crust of the Indian Plate and the Eurasian Plate collided.

TOPIC QUESTIONS

Each topic question refers to the topic of the same number.

1. **(a)** What kinds of earth processes occur at active continental margins? **(b)** Where is there an active continental margin today? **(c)** What is the major activity at passive continental margins? **(d)** Give an example of a passive continental margin. **(e)** How are passive continental margins related to mountain building?

2. **(a)** What happens to oceanic crust in most ocean-continent collisions? **(b)** Where do mountains form in an ocean-continent collision? **(c)** What other processes accompany this kind of collision? **(d)** What has happened to oceanic crust in some ocean-continent collisions of the past? **(e)** Where are mountains thought to have formed by this kind of collision?

3. **(a)** When does subduction occur during the collision of two continents? **(b)** Why does subduction stop? **(c)** Where was the subduction zone thought to be for India's collision with Eurasia? **(d)** What evidence indicates that the Indian-Eurasian collision is still in progress? **(e)** What other mountains, in addition to the Himalayas, are forming from the collision of two continents?

OBJECTIVES

A Name three kinds of faults and give examples of each.

B Identify two kinds of folds, explain how they are described, and name a well-known folded mountain range.

C Discuss the importance of volcanism to the formation of the Himalayas, the Andes, and the Cascades.

II Features of Collision Mountains

Topic 4 Faults

A fault is a break or crack in Earth's crust along which movement has occurred. The surface that separates the two moving pieces is the *fault plane.* Movement along fault planes causes the earthquakes that accompany mountain building (Chapter 15, Topic 2). There are three basic kinds of faults.

A **normal fault** occurs when the rocks on one side of the fault plane drop down with respect to the rocks on the other side. Normal faults occur in areas where tension is pulling the crust apart. An example is the Baikal Rift System, a part of the Himalayan disturbance. Here a piece of crust dropped down between two normal faults. The valley that resulted from the movement now contains Lake Baikal, the deepest lake in the world. Since normal faults are caused by stresses pulling away from each other, they are not common in collision mountains.

A **reverse fault** occurs when one side of the fault plane is driven up over the other side. These faults result from stresses that push toward each other. Reverse faults are important to mountain building because they allow the crust to be shortened as the plates collide. If the fault plane is nearly level, large pieces of crustal material can be moved great distances. This process is the thin-skinned thrusting described in Chapter 13. It is an important feature of most of the world's mountain ranges.

A third kind of fault is a **strike-slip fault.** In this fault, the rocks on opposite sides of the fault plane move horizontally past each other. The San Andreas Fault is a well-known example (Chapter 15, Topic 15).

In the Himalayas, strike-slip faults are more common than reverse faults. These faults result as India pushes rock material aside on its drive into Eurasia. Strike-slip faulting has occurred over a large area. In some cases, the fault planes are over 3000 kilometers away from India. There is even some evidence that earthquakes in China are the result of the Indian-Eurasian collision.

16.3 Three basic types of faults

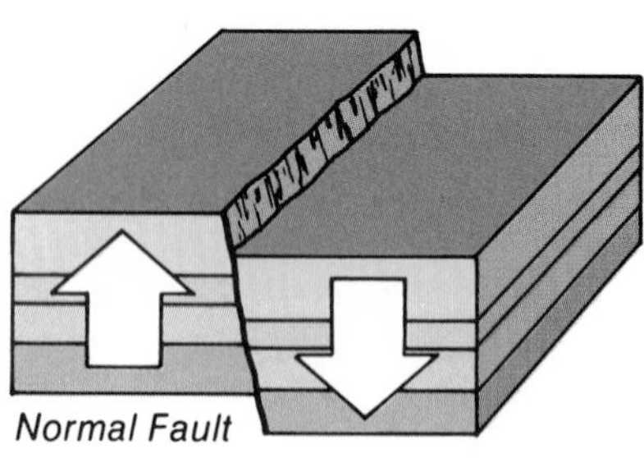

Normal Fault

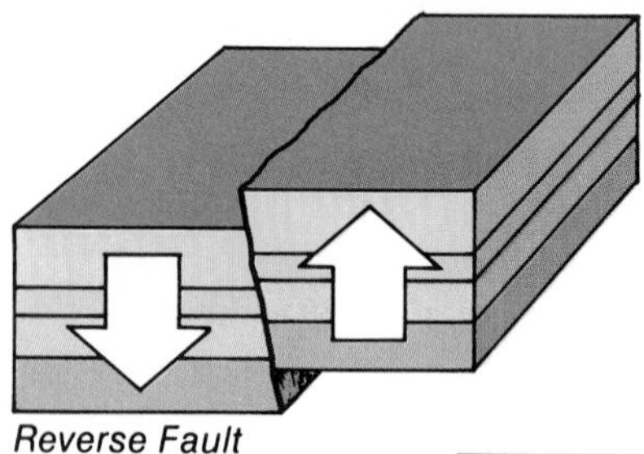

Reverse Fault

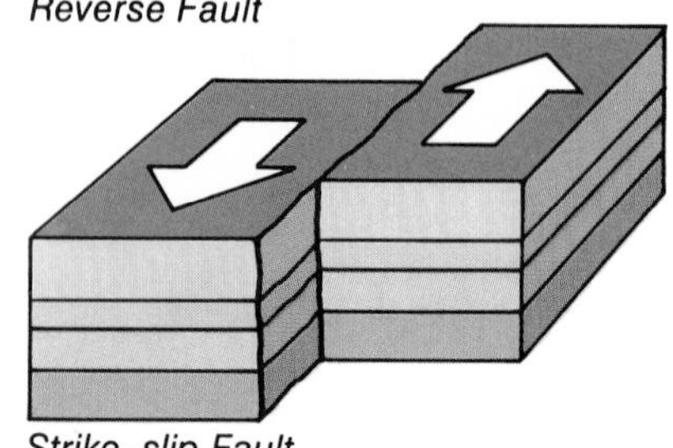

Strike–slip Fault

Topic 5 Folds

During plate collisions, the rock layers along the continental margins are crumpled into folds. A number of terms are used to describe these folds.

An **anticline** is an upfold in the rock layers. A **syncline** is a downfold. The sides of the folds are called *limbs.* The steepness, or *dip,* of the limbs reflects the intensity of folding. Limbs may be gently dipping, steeply dipping, straight up and down, or even overturned.

16.4 **(a)** Normal fault, **(b)** reverse fault

The compass direction of the fold or of the rock layers exposed at the surface along the fold is called the *strike.*

In some folded mountains the folding is severe, and the rock layers are badly deformed. In others, the layers have been pushed into gentle anticlines and synclines.

The most famous example of folded mountains is probably the Valley and Ridge Province of the Appalachian Mountains. The rock layers there have not been badly crumpled. Instead, the stress of collision has formed the layers into long, narrow folds. Interestingly, the valleys between the mountains do not correspond to fold synclines nor the ridges to fold anticlines as one might expect. Instead, the locations of the valleys and ridges are controlled primarily by the weathering rates of the rocks in different areas of the folds.

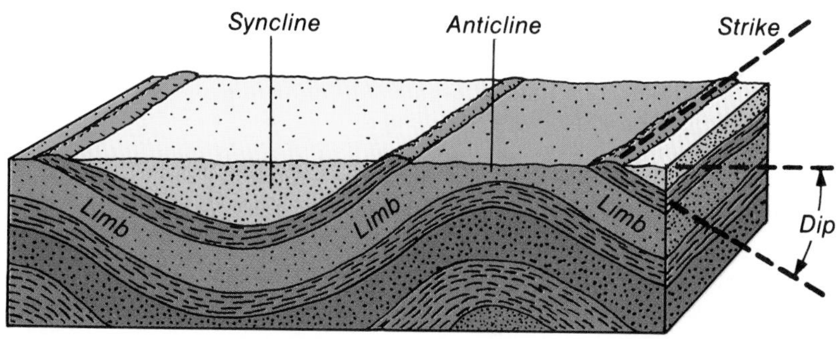

16.5 An anticline is an upfold in rock layers, and a syncline is a downfold. The strike is the direction of the fold, and the dip is the steepness of the fold.

Topic 6 Volcanoes

Volcanic rocks are not common in the Himalayas, but some do occur on the northern edge of the range. These rocks may have formed during the time the Indian Plate was still subducting under the Eurasian Plate but before the two continents collided.

Volcanism has been important throughout the history of the Andes. In fact, the core of the Andes is a granite batholith that apparently supplied magma to many surface volcanoes. Erosion removed the volcanoes long ago, but the batholith and the feeder dikes to the volcanoes are still present. These features are now easily visible at the surface. The batholith is exposed over an area of about 3000 square kilometers and, because granite resists erosion, contains the highest peaks of the Andes. These peaks make up the Cordillera Blanca, or White Range, so named because the mountains are always covered with snow. A similar batholith forms the core of the Sierra Nevada in California. Many geologists believe that the Andes of today resemble the Sierra Nevadas of 100 million years ago and the Northern Appalachians of 450 million years ago.

The eruption of Mount St. Helens in 1980 focused attention on volcanism in North America. The Cascade Range, in which Mount St. Helens is located, is a classic example of an active volcanic mountain range.

TOPIC QUESTIONS

Each topic question refers to the topic of the same number.

4. **(a)** Describe the movement of rocks in a normal fault. **(b)** How did Lake Baikal form? **(c)** How are rocks moved in a reverse fault? Explain why reverse faults are important to mountain building. **(d)** Describe the movement in a strike-slip fault and give an example. **(e)** Which type of fault is most important in the Himalayas?

5. **(a)** How do anticlines and synclines differ? **(b)** Where are the limbs of a fold? **(c)** What is meant by the dip of the limbs of a fold? **(d)** What is strike? **(e)** How are the valleys and ridges of the Appalachians related to the anticlines and synclines that occur there?

6. **(a)** When were the volcanic rocks of the Himalayas thought to have formed? **(b)** What is the Cordillera Blanca and how does it relate to volcanism in the Andes? **(c)** How are the Andes thought to be related to the Sierra Nevadas and to the Northern Appalachians? **(d)** What kind of mountain range is the Cascade Range?

III Other Evidences of Mountain Building

OBJECTIVES

A Name and describe three ways in which uplifting of rock layers can be detected.

B Identify some ways in which rock layers become tilted; describe and give examples of fault-block mountains.

C List and describe several ways to tell if rock layers have been overturned.

Topic 7 Uplifting

Not all sedimentary rock layers of passive continental margins are crumpled into folds. In some areas the layers are raised to higher levels with little deformation. Such uplifting is also a part of mountain building. Several methods can be used to determine whether uplifting has occurred.

Fossils are one indicator of uplift. Some of the sedimentary rocks of passive continental margins contain the skeletons and shells of organisms that lived in the ocean. The presence of these marine skeletons and shells in rocks now located high above sea level is good evidence that uplifting has occurred.

A second evidence of uplift comes from *raised beaches*. In some coastal areas of the world, old shorelines can be seen at elevations above the modern shoreline. One particularly well-developed area of old shorelines is the coast of California near Los Angeles. Here a series of level terraces can be seen, each above and inland from the previous one. The terraces are old beaches that originally formed at sea level. Each must have been raised above sea level as the area was uplifted. Since the highest is about 400 meters above the present sea level, the area must have been uplifted by at least that amount.

A third evidence of uplift can be obtained by making regular *measurements of the elevation* of an area over a period of time. Using bench marks (Chapter 7, Topic 8), a surveying team can determine whether any changes in elevation have occurred since the last survey. Using this technique, a mountain pass 80 kilometers east of Los Angeles has been found to be uplifting at a rate of about 14 centimeters per century. Another area within 3 kilometers of the San Andreas Fault has been rising at a rate of 78 centimeters per century.

16.6 These raised beaches along the California coast are evidence of uplifting.

Topic 8 Tilting

Most sedimentary rocks are formed in level layers. Therefore, the occurrence of tilted layers is an evidence of mountain building.

Layers of rock can become tilted in a number of different ways. The folding of sedimentary rocks into anticlines and synclines is one way. The folded layers of the Valley and Ridge Province of the Appalachian Mountains contain many examples of tilted sedimentary rock layers. Tilting can also result when rocks are pushed upward. The uplift of the Rocky Mountains caused sedimentary layers in Colorado to be steeply inclined.

16.7 (left) The tilted layers of this sandstone formation indicate that a geologic change has occurred. (right) Fault-block mountains are usually quite steep on the faulted side.

In other areas, tilted layers are the result of whole blocks of crust having been faulted and uplifted at the same time. The raised structures are called **fault-block mountains.** Such mountains are usually steep on the faulted side but gently sloping on the opposite side. Examples of fault-block mountains are the Sierra Nevadas of California, the Wasatch Range of Utah, and the Teton Range of Wyoming. In addition, a series of fault-block mountains can be seen in Nevada and western Utah.

Topic 9 Overturning

In some areas of the world, rock layers are so severely tilted that they may be bottom side up. Geologists have several methods of determining whether rock layers have been overturned.

Ripple marks are features that form on the floor of a quiet body of water when waves are moving gently across the surface. These features consist of miniature valleys between sharply pointed tiny hills. The rock containing ripple marks is right side up if the sharp hills point up.

Cross-bedding is a feature of deltas and sand dunes. Although most sediments are deposited in level layers, parts of deltas and sand dunes are not. These parts are deposited at an angle to the other level layers and can be used to tell if the entire layer has been overturned. The layer is right side up if the cross-bedding curves downward and the top of the cross-bedded layer is cut off by the layers above it.

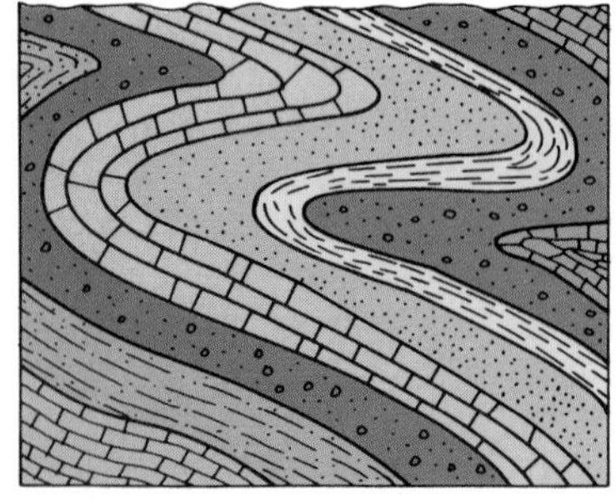

16.8 Some rock layers can become so severely tilted that they are overturned.

Mud cracks develop on the surfaces of such areas as mud flats when the mud and ooze dry. Individual cracks are wider at the top than at the bottom. When these cracks are preserved in rocks, they are still wider at the top if the layer is right side up.

Shells with curved surfaces, such as clam shells, are unstable if their curved side is down. Currents in the water tend to flip over such shells. These shells, however, are very stable if the open side of the shell is down. A layer in which most of the curved shells have their open sides down is right side up.

TOPIC QUESTIONS

Each topic question refers to the topic of the same number.

7. **(a)** How do the fossils of organisms that lived in the ocean show that uplifting has occurred? **(b)** How do old beaches on the California coast show uplifting? **(c)** At what rate have changes in elevation occurred near Los Angeles and near the San Andreas Fault?

8. **(a)** In what position are most sedimentary rocks formed? **(b)** List two ways in which sedimentary rocks can be tilted. **(c)** What are fault-block mountains? **(d)** Give some examples of fault-block mountains including a large area where many occur.

9. **(a)** What is meant by overturning? **(b)** List some sedimentary features that indicate whether overturning has occurred and describe the appearance of each feature if overturning has not occurred.

Dr. Jack Oliver

Geophysicist

How do you find out how a mountain formed? If you are Dr. Jack Oliver, you send a seismic signal into Earth's crust and use a computer to help you interpret the echo.

Dr. Oliver is the director of a group that has been investigating the details of Earth's crust for several years. The group, Consortium for Continental Reflection Profiling (COCORP), has made many exciting discoveries. It found a body of magma under New Mexico, discovered a buried rift valley in Michigan, traced a major fault in Wyoming, discovered younger sediments under the older surface rocks of the Appalachians, and plotted gently sloping fault planes under the fault-block mountains of Nevada and Utah.

Dr. Oliver has been using seismic data to learn about Earth's crust since his college work at Columbia University. While there, he was one of the first to show the relationship between earthquakes and lithospheric plates.

In addition to directing COCORP, Dr. Oliver is former Chairman of the Department of Geological Sciences at Cornell University and is currently director of Cornell's Institute for the Study of the Continents, of which COCORP is a part.

OBJECTIVES

A Distinguish between a fracture and a fault.

B Explain how dome mountains are different from folded mountains and describe two kinds of dome mountains.

IV Other Tectonic Features

Topic 10 Fractures

Like faults, fractures are breaks in the bedrock. Unlike faults, fractures do not involve motion. Thus, a **fracture** is a crack or break in the bedrock along which no movement has occurred. Fractures can be the result of the same stresses that uplift, tilt, and fold rock layers.

The surface of a fracture is usually a plane, although curves sometimes occur. The fracture plane may occur in any position from level to up and down. Like rock layers, a fracture plane can be described by its strike and dip. For example, most of the fractures in the Adirondack Mountains of New York State strike northeast and dip at 90 degrees (straight up and down).

Fractures occur in many sizes. Some fractures are only a few meters long, while others may be traced for hundreds of kilometers. Fractures never occur alone. Instead, they always come in parallel sets that range from a few centimeters apart to hundreds of meters apart. Often, one set of fractures intersects another set of fractures that strike in a different direction. In the Adirondack Mountains, the northeast-striking fractures are intersected by a second set that strikes northwest.

Topic 11 Dome Mountains

A **dome mountain** is a nearly circular folded mountain. However, dome mountains have some fundamental differences from folded mountains like the Andes and the Appalachians. Dome mountains do not form mountain chains. Instead, these mountains are individual, isolated structures. Also, dome mountains are the result of uplifting forces. Folded mountains, on the other hand, are the result of the horizontal forces of plate collisions. The relationship of dome mountains to plate tectonics, if any, is not clear.

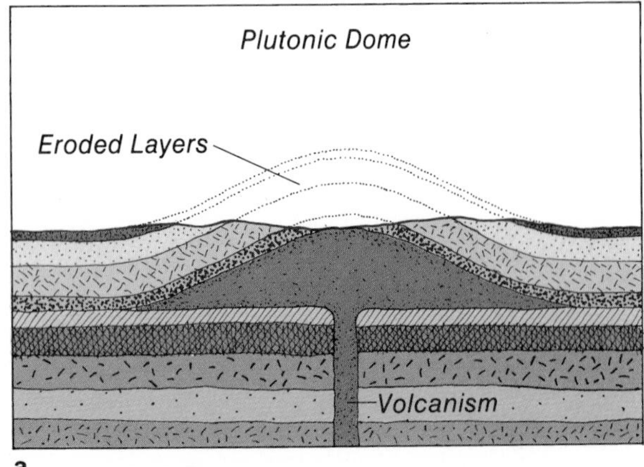

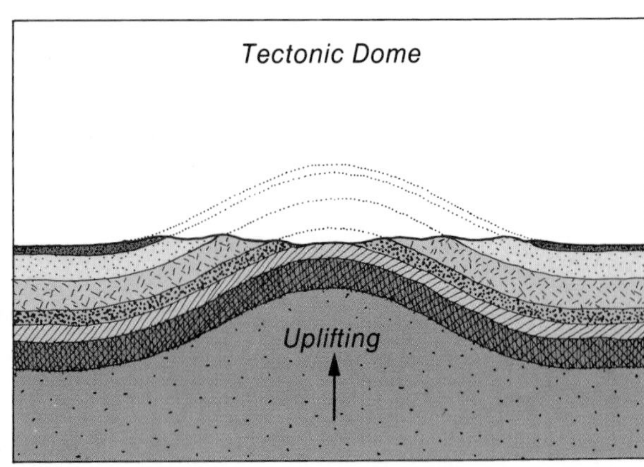

16.9 **(a)** The formation of a plutonic dome, **(b)** the formation of a tectonic dome

Dome mountains may occur in areas of essentially flat-lying sedimentary rocks. However, these layers may be bent sharply upward around the dome as a result of the uplifting forces that formed it. If erosion has removed the rocks over the center of the dome, the layers may stand out as sharp ridges around its edge. Dome mountains may be less than 10 kilometers to more than 180 kilometers across.

There are two basic kinds of dome mountains—plutonic and tectonic. *Plutonic* dome mountains are formed when overlying crustal rocks are pushed upward by the intrusion of an igneous mass, such as a laccolith. Because the intrusion occurred after the rocks were formed, the rocks of the exposed core of the mountain are younger than the sedimentary rocks around the core. An example of a plutonic dome mountain can be found in the Henry Mountains of Utah. Many other examples occur on the border of the Colorado Plateau and the Rocky Mountains.

Tectonic dome mountains are the result of uplifting forces that arched the rock layers upward. All of the rocks in the dome were present before the uplift occurred. The rocks at the core extend under the rocks around the dome and, therefore, must be older. Two excellent examples of tectonic domes are the Adirondack Mountains of New York State and the Black Hills of South Dakota. In both cases, the rocks in the core of the dome are older than the rocks around it.

TOPIC QUESTIONS

Each topic question refers to the topic of the same number.

10. **(a)** What are fractures? **(b)** How is the position of a fracture plane described? **(c)** How large are fractures? **(d)** Describe the pattern in which fractures usually occur.

11. **(a)** What is a dome mountain? **(b)** Name two ways in which dome mountains differ from folded mountains. **(c)** What may happen to the rock layers around a dome? **(d)** How do plutonic domes form? **(e)** What is the age of the rocks at the center of a plutonic dome compared to the rocks around the dome? **(f)** Give an example of a plutonic dome. **(g)** How do tectonic domes form? **(h)** What is the age of the rocks at the center of a tectonic dome compared to the rocks around the dome? **(i)** Give some examples of tectonic domes.

Map Skills

Refer to the map on pages 588–589 to answer these questions.

1. From this map, are the most extensive mountain ranges located on the land or underwater?

2. What type of feature forms the underwater mountain ranges?

CHAPTER 16 REVIEW

Summary

Earthquakes, volcanoes, and mountain building occur at active continental margins. Large quantities of sediments accumulate in the shallow water of passive continental margins.

When an ocean collides with a continent, the ocean plate usually subducts beneath the continent. Pieces of the oceanic plate may be scraped off and become attached to the continent.

When two continents collide, subduction stops. Mountains form as the collision continues.

In a normal fault, one side moves down relative to the other side. In a reverse fault, one side is pushed over the other side. In a strike-slip fault, one side moves horizontally past the other side.

Anticlines are upfolds of rock layers; synclines are downfolds. The dip and strike of the limbs of the fold indicate the shape and orientation of the fold.

Fossils in mountains, raised beaches, and changes in elevation are evidence of uplifting.

Folded and tilted rocks are evidences of mountain building. Fault-block mountains form where pieces of crust have been faulted and uplifted.

Ripple marks, cross-bedding, mud cracks, and fossil shells can provide evidence of overturning.

Fractures are breaks in the crust along which no movement has occurred. They occur in parallel sets and are often intersected by other sets.

Dome mountains are nearly circular folded mountains that result from uplifting. There are two kinds of dome mountains—plutonic and tectonic.

Vocabulary

active continental margin
anticline
dome mountain
fault-block mountain
fracture
normal fault
passive continental margin
reverse fault
strike-slip fault
syncline

Review

Number your paper from *1* to *13*. Write the letter of your answer on your paper.

1. Which is *least* likely to be a feature of an active continental margin? (a) earthquakes (b) volcanism (c) mountain building (d) sediment buildup
2. In time, passive continental margins may become (a) mid-ocean ridges, (b) mountains, (c) deep-ocean floor, (d) volcanoes.
3. Terranes are thought to form when pieces of (a) continental plate plunge into a subduction zone, (b) continental plate ride over a subduction zone, (c) oceanic plate plunge into a subduction zone, (d) oceanic plate ride over a subduction zone.
4. When two continents collide, subduction (a) does not occur, (b) occurs until the continents are in contact, (c) occurs only when the continents are in contact, (d) occurs throughout the collision.
5. A fault in which one side of the fault plane drops down relative to the other side is a (a) normal fault, (b) strike-slip fault, (c) fault-block mountain, (d) dip-slip fault.
6. Anticlines and synclines are kinds of (a) folds, (b) faults, (c) dome mountains, (d) volcanic cones.
7. The dip of a rock layer indicates the (a) age of the rock layer, (b) source of the particles in the rock, (c) kind of fossils in the rock, (d) steepness of slope of the rock layer.
8. Which mountain range contains active volcanoes? (a) Alps (b) Cascades (c) Himalayas (d) Sierra Nevadas
9. Raised beaches and fossils high in mountains are evidence of (a) volcanism, (b) subduction, (c) uplifting, (d) faulting.
10. Mountains that result from the tilting and uplifting of large pieces of crust are called (a) folded mountains, (b) volcanic mountains, (c) tectonic dome mountains, (d) fault-block mountains.

11. If a rock layer is right side up, (a) the sharp hills of ripple marks will point down, (b) cross-bedded layers will curve downward, (c) the narrow part of mud cracks will be up, (d) the open side of curved shells will be up.
12. Cracks or breaks in the bedrock that do not involve motion and that always occur in parallel sets are called (a) bench marks, (b) faults, (c) fractures, (d) strikes.
13. In what way are dome mountains like folded mountains? (a) Both bend rock layers upward. (b) Both form mountain chains. (c) Both involve uplifting forces. (d) Both involve plate collisions.

Interpret and Apply

On your paper, answer each question in complete sentences.

1. Would you expect the west coast of Africa to be an active or a passive continental margin?
2. A geologist standing on a low hill notes that rock layers stand out in sharp ridges all around the edge of the hill and dip gently away in all directions. A study of the rocks shows that the oldest rocks are at the center of the hill, and the rock layers become younger away from the center of the hill. What kind of structure could the geologist be standing on?
3. Both plutonic and tectonic dome mountains can have an igneous rock core. How can thermal, or contact, metamorphism (Chapter 5, Topic 22) be used to distinguish the two kinds of domes?

Critical Thinking

The diagram shows a cross section of the sedimentary rock layers in a folded area. The cross section was drawn from west to east along a line about 50 kilometers long. Points *A* through *F* are locations along the ground surface. The rock layers have not been overturned.

1. On which side of the anticline do the rock layers have the greater dip? Which side of the syncline?
2. How does the resistance to weathering of the rocks at point *B* compare to those at point *C*? Explain.
3. How do the ages of the rocks change from point *B* to point *D*? From point *E* to point *D*?
4. On the basis of your answer to question 3, how does the age of rocks at the center of an anticline compare with the age of rocks at the center of a syncline?
5. If a normal fault occurs at line *XY*, what will be the effect on the distance between *A* and *F*? What will be the effect on the distance if the fault is a reverse fault?

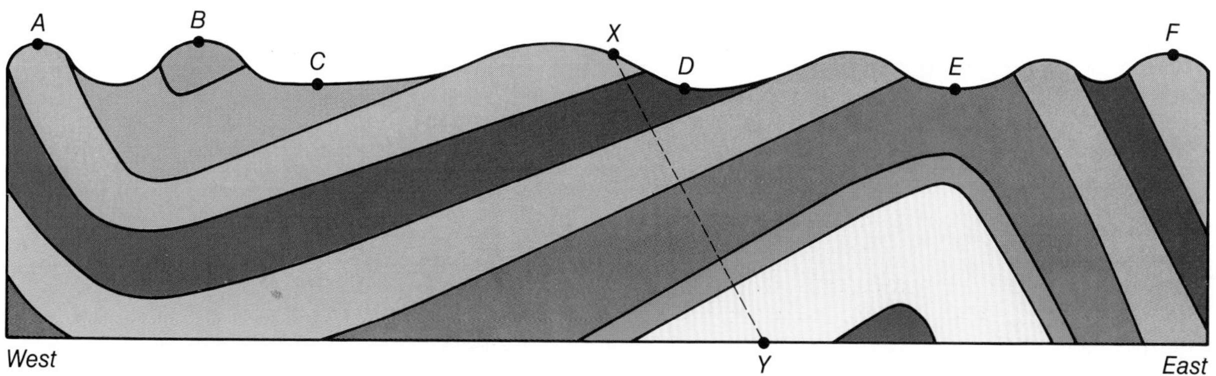

UNIT FOUR
The Ocean

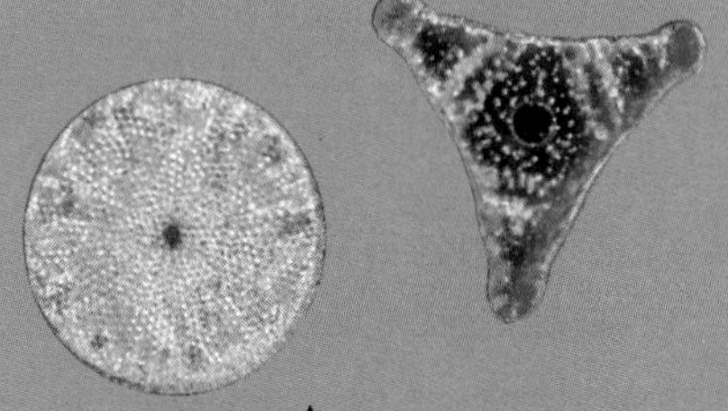

▲ Microscopic fossils of tiny floating organisms lie on the ocean floor worldwide. What do these fossils reveal about the age of the ocean?

◀ People who fish know that parts of the ocean have abundant life, while others have almost none. Why do ocean creatures live where they do?

The remote-controlled robot *Jason Jr.* records images in the ocean depths. What features can be observed by using *J. J.*? ▶

What lies in the ocean?

People have sailed the seas for thousands of years, but little was known about the ocean until fairly recently. Since scientists first began to study the ocean, they have solved many of its mysteries, such as the shape of the ocean floor. Yet the ocean still holds some surprises. What does each picture show about the study of the ocean?

This computer-colored satellite image highlights an ocean current. How are satellites helpful in ocean research? ▼

Scientists on research ships can tell when they have entered the Antarctic Ocean, even though it is surrounded by other oceans. How do differences in water properties define ocean areas? ▼

CHAPTER

17 Properties of Ocean Water

▲
A diver explores a coral reef in the Caribbean Sea.

How Do You Know That . . .

Ocean water is different from fresh water? Swimmers who accidentally get sea water in their mouths know that it has a definite salty taste. Fresh water does not taste salty. Ocean water is also more dense than fresh water. Swimmers can float more easily in sea water than in fresh water. In addition, the oceans are home to many animals and plants that do not live in fresh water. The corals shown with the diver in the photograph are an example.

I Earth—The Water Planet

Topic 1 The World Ocean

Over 70 percent of Earth is covered by oceans. The blue color of the oceans can even be seen from space. For this reason, Earth is sometimes called the water planet. Geographers recognize five different oceans of the world. (The map on pages 588–589 shows the five oceans.) The Pacific Ocean stretches from America's west coast to Asia and Australia. The Atlantic Ocean reaches eastward from the Americas to Europe and Africa. The Indian Ocean lies south of Asia. The Arctic Ocean covers the north polar region. The Antarctic Ocean circles the continent of Antarctica, connecting the Atlantic, Pacific, and Indian oceans in the south polar region.

How does the depth of the ocean compare with the elevation of the continents? The average depth of the ocean is more than four times greater than the average elevation of the continents. Mount Everest, the highest peak on land, would completely disappear in the Marianas Trench, the deepest place in the ocean.

OBJECTIVES

A Explain why Earth is called the "water planet" and name and locate the major oceans.

B Discuss the development of the science of oceanography.

C Name some modern research vessels and describe how each is used to explore the oceans.

17.1 The top of Mount Everest is the highest point on Earth's surface. Marianas Trench is the lowest point.

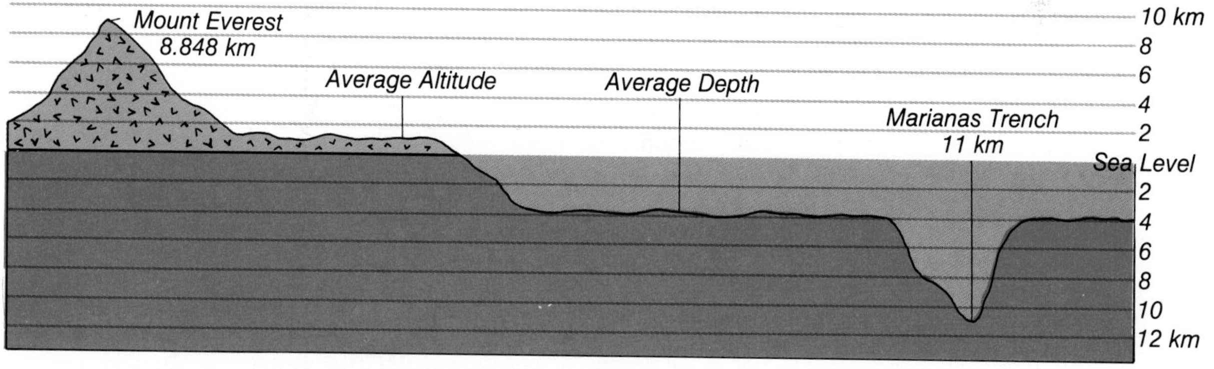

Topic 2 Beginnings of Oceanography

Oceanography is the scientific study of oceans. One of the first modern studies about ocean features was by Matthew Fontaine Maury, a U.S. Navy officer. Because of an injury, Maury was forced to spend most of his career on land. As director of the Navy Department's Depot of Charts and Instruments, he was able to study the logbooks written by the captains of naval vessels. From these records, he compiled worldwide charts of ocean winds and currents.

17.2 H.M.S. *Challenger* was the first ship designed especially for oceanographic research. It sailed the world's ocean from polar waters to the equator.

These charts were published in 1855 in his book *The Physical Geography of the Sea.* This was the first scientific book written in English about the physical features of the ocean.

Seventeen years later, in 1872, the British government sponsored the first great study of the oceans. H.M.S. *Challenger* was outfitted as a laboratory and carried a staff of marine scientists. The scientists measured depths, took water and sediment samples, recorded temperatures, collected plant and animal specimens, and studied ocean currents. The expedition lasted nearly four years and resulted in over 50 volumes of reports, some of which are still in use.

The next great advance in oceanographic research occurred during World War II. The military needs of submarines and surface ships led to better ocean charts, sonar, magnetic recorders, and many other new instruments. These instruments became the basic tools of modern oceanographic research.

Topic 3 Oceanographic Research Today

Many countries, including the United States, are involved in oceanographic research. Although there are many oceanographic ships and submarines studying the sea, three vessels have become particularly well known. They are the drillship JOIDES *Resolution,* the minisubmarine *Alvin,* and the deep-towed vehicle *Argo.*

The JOIDES *Resolution* is a seagoing drilling platform and scientific laboratory. The ship is designed to sample the rocks and sediments of the seafloor, a particularly difficult task where the ocean is several kilometers deep. With the help of computers, the JOIDES *Resolution* can remain on an exact spot while drilling into the ocean floor. An on-board six-story laboratory, which includes a scanning electron microscope and other instruments, is used to analyze the cores of sediment and rock samples obtained.

Alvin is a tiny, battery-powered submarine. *Alvin* is designed to descend to depths of more than 4000 meters with a pilot and two passengers and to return safely to the surface. The small submarine can also collect samples and take photographs and television pictures. Its instruments record such factors as the temperature, electric conductivity, and concentration of dissolved oxygen in the water. One of *Alvin's* first uses was in 1966. It was used to locate a U.S. Air Force hydrogen bomb that had fallen to the seafloor after a mid-air plane collision. Since then, *Alvin* has been used to explore such deep-sea areas as the mid-Atlantic Ridge and the East Pacific Rise. Recently, *Alvin* was used to explore the wreck of the *Titanic,* the "unsinkable" ocean liner that rammed an iceberg and sank on its first voyage in 1912. A small robot submarine carried by *Alvin,* named *Jason, Jr.,* or *J.J.,* was able to go inside the *Titanic* and photograph decks and rooms inside the wreck.

17.3 The minisubmarine *Alvin*

The vehicle *Argo* was also used to explore the *Titanic* wreck. *Argo* is an undersea sled that carries powerful lights, undersea radar, and many cameras. The sled is towed through the water behind a surface vessel. Video pictures and other data travel back to the vessel through a long cable. Although *Argo* was built to explore seafloor features, its first voyage was to photograph the *Titanic* resting on the seafloor.

TOPIC QUESTIONS

Each topic question refers to the topic of the same number.

1. **(a)** What percentage of Earth's surface is covered by oceans? **(b)** Name and describe the locations of the five oceans. **(c)** Compare the average depth of the oceans with the average elevation of the continents.
2. **(a)** What was Maury's contribution to the study of oceanography? **(b)** Name some kinds of information collected by scientists on the *Challenger* expedition. **(c)** How did World War II affect oceanographic research?
3. **(a)** What kinds of samples does the JOIDES *Resolution* obtain? **(b)** Describe *Alvin.* **(c)** What is *Argo?*

Dr. J. R. Heirtzler
Marine Geophysicist

Dr. J. R. Heirtzler has been involved in many exciting discoveries about the oceans. He was at the Lamont-Doherty Geological Observatory of Columbia University when the pattern of magnetic reversals at mid-ocean ridges was first detected. Working with a group of scientists there, he was able to show that this pattern was the result of a moving ocean floor, a revolutionary idea at that time. Dr. Heirtzler labels that "a time as exciting as any in the history of science." He then became chief scientist for Project FAMOUS, the detailed survey of the mid-Atlantic Ridge. Project FAMOUS used *Alvin* and other tools to obtain the first proof that spreading centers were the youngest part of the ocean floor.

Dr. Heirtzler was chairman of the Department of Geology and Geophysics at the Woods Hole Oceanographic Institution for many years. That department, along with other marine geophysicists, is using *Alvin* to study parts of the ridge system in the Atlantic and Pacific. He is continuing his interest in the Antarctic, where a mountain has been named after him. Recently Dr. Heirtzler completed a highly accurate, computer-produced map of the entire surface of Earth. He is currently working on a magnetic anomaly map of North America.

In 1986 Dr. Heirtzler moved to NASA as Head of the Geophysics Branch to study the whole Earth, both land and sea, to compare Earth to the other planets, and to prepare plans for the next geophysical satellites.

II The Salinity of Sea Water

OBJECTIVES

A Define *salinity*, explain how it is determined, and describe some conditions that cause it to vary.

B Explain how electrical conductivity is used to find salinity.

C Name the major ions found in sea water and discuss the relationship between salinity and the relative amounts of these ions.

D Identify some substances that can be removed economically from sea water.

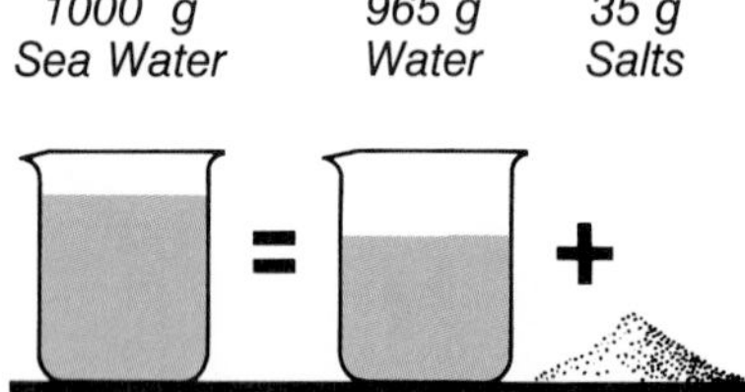

17.4 If you evaporate 1000 grams of sea water, 35 grams of solid minerals (salts) will be left behind.

Topic 4 Salinity

Salinity is a measure of the dissolved solids in sea water. The main solid is common salt, or sodium chloride. Other salts, such as magnesium chloride and calcium sulfate, also occur in sea water. All of these materials contribute to the solids dissolved in sea water.

Salinity can be determined by evaporating a measured quantity of filtered sea water. The white crust that remains in the evaporating dish is made of the salts that were dissolved in the water. The ratio of the mass of this salt crust to the original mass of the water is the salinity. On the average, 1000 grams of sea water contain 35 grams of salts. The salinity of sea water is 35 parts per 1000 parts of sea water. This is written as 35‰.

Ocean water salinity varies. The figure 35‰ is an average. In deeper ocean waters, the salinity is close to the average figure. Near the surface the salinity can vary between 33‰ and 37‰.

Salinity is below average where large amounts of fresh water enter the oceans. Reduced salinity occurs in areas of heavy rainfall, such as at the equator. It also occurs where glaciers enter the oceans and at the mouths of rivers. The Baltic Sea, for example, has a salinity of only 30‰ because many rivers and glaciers drain into it.

Salinity is above average in areas of hot, dry climates. Here the oceans lose water rapidly by evaporation, leaving the salts behind. These areas lie roughly in latitudes 20° to 30° north and south of the equator. The Mediterranean Sea and the Red Sea are in this dry belt. Their salinity can be as high as 40‰ in some areas.

Salinity may also be above average in polar waters near sea ice. When sea water freezes, only freshwater ice forms at first. This leaves the remaining water saltier than before.

Topic 5 Measuring Salinity

Finding salinity by evaporation is a slow, inaccurate process. Oceanographers have a much quicker method. They measure the *electrical conductivity* of the water. The salt dissolved in sea water makes it possible for an electric current to pass through the water. The greater the quantity of dissolved salts, the more easily current flows. Thus, the conductivity increases as the salinity of the water increases. This fact provides oceanographers with a quick, easy, and accurate method of determining salinity.

Why do oceanographers measure the salinity of the oceans when they already know the approximate value they will obtain? Salinity is an important factor in identifying *water masses.* A water mass is a body of water that has certain properties due to conditions at its place of origin. When oceanographers know salinity and other properties of different water masses, they can trace a water mass as it moves through an ocean. Also, when both salinity and water temperature are known, the water's density can be determined. Knowing ocean water density is important to understanding how water masses move through the ocean and mix together.

Topic 6 The Composition of Sea Water

Salt is present in sea water in the form of dissolved ions. Common salt, for example, consists of a positive sodium ion and a negative chloride ion. Dissolved sodium ions make up 30.61 percent of the salinity of sea water while dissolved chloride ions make up 55.04 percent. The table shows the percentage of dissolved ions, including sodium and chloride, found in sea water.

One of the most amazing facts about the composition of sea water is that the percentages shown in the table are the same for all sea water. The relative amounts of the different dissolved ions do not change even though the salinity does change. The percentages shown are the same for ocean water from anywhere in the world.

Composition of Sea Water

Dissolved Ion	Percentage
Chloride (Cl^-)	55.04
Sulfate ($SO_4{}^{2-}$)	7.68
Bicarbonate ($HCO_3{}^-$)	0.41
Bromide (Br^-)	0.19
Sodium (Na^+)	30.61
Magnesium (Mg^{2+})	3.69
Calcium (Ca^{2+})	1.16
Potassium (K^+)	1.10
All others	0.12
	100.00

Topic 7 Mining Sea Water

At least 55 elements are found in sea water, including such metals as gold, copper, and uranium. These metals occur only in tiny amounts. The percentage of gold, for example, is 4 parts per trillion parts of sea water. Mining these metals from the sea is not profitable. An exception is magnesium. This metal is present in sea water in fairly large percentages. Furthermore, magnesium can be taken from sea water more easily and cheaply than it can be taken from magnesium ore on land.

Salt can also be mined cheaply from sea water. The only energy needed to evaporate the sea water is sunlight. One cubic kilometer of sea water contains about 27 million metric tons of salt.

TOPIC QUESTIONS

Each topic question refers to the topic of the same number.

4. **(a)** What is salinity? **(b)** What does 35‰ mean when applied to sea water? **(c)** Identify some factors that cause ocean salinity to fall below 35‰ and to rise above 35‰.

5. **(a)** How is the electrical conductivity of ocean water related to its salinity? **(b)** Why is it important to know the salinity, temperature, and density of a sea water sample?

6. **(a)** What are the two most abundant ions in sea water? **(b)** How are the percentages of each ion in sea water related to the salinity of sea water?

7. **(a)** Why aren't gold and silver mined from sea water? **(b)** Why is magnesium extracted from sea water? **(c)** How is salt extracted from sea water?

OBJECTIVES

A Identify three temperature zones found in the ocean.

B Discuss the formation and movement of polar water.

III The Temperature of Ocean Water

Topic 8 Heating the Oceans

The oceans do not heat up readily. Almost all the energy that heats the oceans comes from the sun. Light and heat do not penetrate very deeply into the oceans. In fact, most solar radiation is absorbed in the top few meters of ocean water.

Because ocean water does not heat readily, ocean temperature decreases rapidly with depth. A typical set of readings for latitude 40° N might be 20°C at the surface, 11°C at 500 meters, 5°C at 1000 meters, and 2°C at 4000 meters. These data show two facts. First, the decrease in temperature with depth is not uniform. Second, with the exception of the water near the surface, all the water in the ocean is very cold.

Based upon temperature changes like these, oceanographers divide the oceans into three temperature zones—a surface zone of warm water with sunlight, a deep zone of very cold water without light, and a middle region between the two in which temperatures change rapidly and there is little light.

Topic 9 The Mixed Layer

The surface layer is called the **mixed layer** because wind and waves mix heat evenly throughout the zone. This warm-water layer makes up only about two percent of the ocean's volume, but it is very important to life in the ocean. The mixed layer is the only place where light is present in enough quantity to grow the marine plants upon which most other ocean life depends.

How thick is the mixed layer? The answer depends in part upon the latitude. At high latitudes and near the equator, the mixed layer may extend to a depth of about 100 meters. In middle latitudes, the mixed layer may be as thick as 300 meters.

The temperature of the mixed layer also depends upon latitude, although seasonal changes can also be a factor. Near the equator, where air temperatures are always high, the mixed layer may be as

17.5 Most marine life depends, either directly or indirectly, on the tiny phytoplankton in the mixed layer.

warm as 30°C all year. Near the poles, where air temperatures are always cold, the temperature of the mixed layer may remain at about −2°C all year. The largest temperature changes in the mixed layer occur in the middle latitudes because these are areas where the air temperature changes with the seasons. At latitude 40° N, for example, a change of 10°C between summer and winter is not unusual.

Topic 10 Temperatures under the Mixed Layer

A thermometer sinking through the mixed layer reads almost the same temperature throughout the layer. However, temperatures drop rapidly below the mixed layer to a depth of about 1000 meters. This water layer in which rapid temperature change occurs is called the **thermocline**.

The water at the bottom of the thermocline is very cold. Even near the equator the temperature may be only about 5°C. The temperature continues to drop, but more slowly, from the bottom of the thermocline to the ocean floor, where temperatures may be only about 2°C.

In polar areas the oceans are cold from top to bottom. Such cold water is denser than other ocean waters and tends to sink beneath them. This cold water moves away from the polar regions along the ocean floor. As a result, polar water is found beneath other ocean water at almost all latitudes. The exceptions are inland seas with high, narrow openings to the ocean. For example, the Straits of Gibraltar prevent polar water from entering the Mediterranean Sea. The temperature at the bottom of the Mediterranean remains warm all year, in some places as high as 12°C.

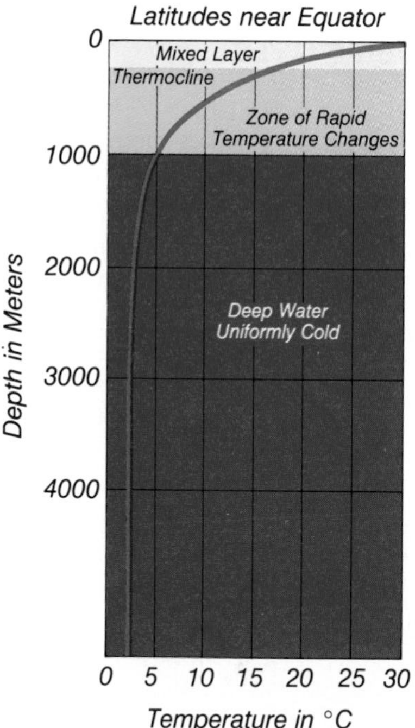

17.6 The graph shows how water temperature changes according to the depth of ocean water near the equator.

TOPIC QUESTIONS

Each topic question refers to the topic of the same number.

8. Locate and describe the three temperature zones in the ocean.

9. **(a)** Where is the mixed layer in the oceans? **(b)** Why is the mixed layer important? **(c)** Describe the thickness or depth of the mixed layer with latitude. **(d)** Identify two factors that determine the temperature of the mixed layer. **(e)** Compare the temperature of the mixed layer at the equator, the poles, and the middle latitudes.

10. **(a)** What is the thermocline and where is it located? **(b)** How cold is the bottom of the thermocline near the equator? **(c)** How does the water temperature change from the bottom of the thermocline to an ocean's floor? **(d)** Where is polar water found?

OBJECTIVES

A Discuss the importance of microscopic plants and animals that live in the mixed layer.

B Describe the distribution of oxygen and carbon dioxide in the ocean.

C Discuss the occurrence of ocean-floor vents and the communities of animals that live around them.

IV Life in the Sea

Topic 11 Sunlight and Marine Life

Sunlight is vital in the oceans. Most sea plants, like land plants, need sunlight to grow. However, sunlight penetration decreases rapidly with depth (Topic 8). Only within the mixed layer at the surface is there enough sunlight for plant growth.

The most important group of plants in the mixed layer is the microscopic **phytoplankton.** These tiny plants are floaters and drifters, moving wherever waves and currents carry them.

One of the most abundant kinds of phytoplankton are the **diatoms.** Diatoms are one-celled organisms that build thick shells made of silica. Many diatoms build two shells that fit together like two halves of a tiny pillbox.

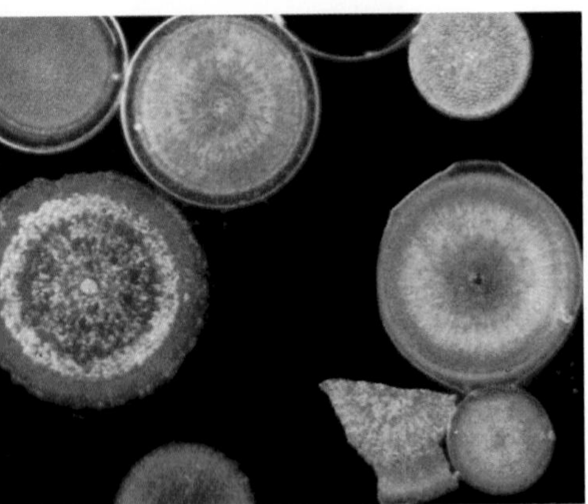

17.7 Diatoms are a common type of phytoplankton. This is a microscopic view.

The phytoplankton, including the diatoms, are important because they are the basic food source for ocean life. Phytoplankton are able to produce their own food from surrounding materials, using sunlight as their energy source. Nearly all other life in the ocean depends on the making of food by the phytoplankton. Billions and billions of phytoplankton grow in the mixed layer. These tiny organisms are then eaten by microscopic floating animals, called **zooplankton.** The zooplankton, in turn, are eaten by everything from tiny fish to giant whales.

Diatoms are important for another reason. When diatoms die, their shells settle to the bottom and become part of the sediment. Marine geologists use shells preserved in this way to trace changes in diatom populations, to determine the age of the sediment, and even to determine the water temperature at the time the diatoms lived.

Topic 12 Oxygen and Marine Life

All living things need oxygen to convert their food into energy. Oxygen in the ocean comes from two sources. Some of the oxygen mixes into the ocean water from the air above the water. Other oxygen is given off by plants that live in the water. The mixed layer contains plenty of oxygen for the abundant marine life that occurs there. However, the oxygen supply decreases with depth.

17.8 Corals can live only in shallow seas where there is sufficient light and oxygen.

Even at the bottom of an ocean's deepest trenches, however, some deep-sea life exists. The oxygen for these depths is provided by the cold, dense water of the polar regions that circulates into all parts of the ocean.

On land, the carbon dioxide produced by animal respiration is consumed by plants in the process of photosynthesis. Although ocean animals also produce carbon dioxide, no plants are found in the deep ocean to consume the carbon dioxide. As a result, deep-ocean waters accumulate carbon dioxide.

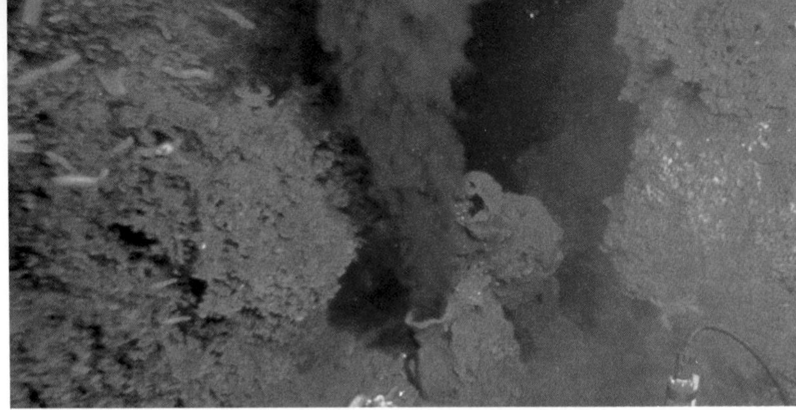

17.9 A black smoker at the East Pacific Rise

Topic 13 Ocean-Floor Vents

Not all living things in the oceans depend upon sunlight. There are some unusual communities of giant clams, white crabs, and giant tube worms that do not require sunlight for energy or phytoplankton for food. These animals live near vents that seep hydrogen sulfide from beneath the ocean floor, often near mid-ocean ridges. The best-known of these vents are hot springs known as **black smokers** that rise from the ocean floor. The first black smokers were discovered by *Alvin* during the exploration of the East Pacific Rise. Since then black smokers have been found on other mid-ocean ridges. Cooler vents have been found in the Gulf of Mexico.

The water that comes from the vent of a black smoker is clear at first. This water quickly mixes with the ocean water around it. A chemical reaction with that water causes fine particles of iron sulfide to form. These particles are black and make the rising plume of hot water appear black. This color change is the origin of the name "black smoker."

Hydrogen sulfide seems to be crucial to life near ocean-floor vents. Certain bacteria live in the digestive systems of the clams, crabs, and tubeworms that live near the vents. The bacteria absorb the hydrogen sulfide from the water and release energy, which is the food supply for the animals in which the bacteria live.

TOPIC QUESTIONS

Each topic question refers to the topic of the same number.

11. **(a)** What are phytoplankton? **(b)** What are diatoms? **(c)** Why are phytoplankton important to life in the oceans? **(d)** What are zooplankton and how do they relate to phytoplankton? **(e)** Why are diatoms important to marine geologists?

12. **(a)** How do all living things use oxygen? **(b)** What are two sources of oxygen for the upper waters of the ocean? **(c)** How does oxygen reach the deep waters of the ocean? **(d)** Why does carbon dioxide accumulate in the deep ocean?

13. **(a)** What are black smokers and where are they found? **(b)** How are the animals that live at ocean-floor vents different from other ocean life? **(c)** What part do bacteria play in life at ocean-floor vents?

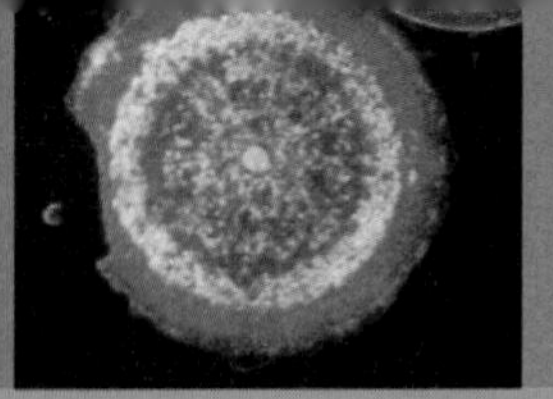

CHAPTER 17 REVIEW

Summary

Seventy percent of Earth's surface is covered by oceans. The average depth of the ocean is more than four times the average elevation of the land.

Oceanography developed through the work of Matthew Fontaine Maury, the voyage of H.M.S. *Challenger*, and the military needs of submarines and surface ships in World War II.

Three vessels now used for oceanography research are the drillship JOIDES *Resolution*, the minisubmarine *Alvin*, and the instrument sled *Argo*.

Salinity is a measure of the dissolved solids in sea water. The average salinity of sea water is 35‰. Oceanographers measure salinity to locate and trace water masses.

The relative proportions of ions in all sea water is the same. Only a few substances can be mined economically from sea water.

The surface mixed layer is the only zone with enough light to grow marine plants. The thickness and temperature of the mixed layer depend upon latitude and season.

The thermocline is a zone of rapid temperature change below the mixed layer. The layer below the thermocline is very cold everywhere. Polar water forms in high latitudes and flows along the ocean floor toward the equator.

Phytoplankton, such as diatoms, are microscopic organisms that grow in the sea. Zooplankton are microscopic organisms that eat the phytoplankton.

Dissolved oxygen is most abundant near the ocean surface and decreases with depth. Deep water flow from high latitudes supplies the ocean floor with oxygen. The concentration of carbon dioxide is high near the ocean floor.

Unique communities of animals live near hydrogen sulfide vents, such as black smokers, near ocean ridges. Hydrogen sulfide, rather than sunlight, is the energy source for these communities.

Vocabulary

black smoker
diatom
mixed layer
oceanography
phytoplankton
salinity
thermocline
zooplankton

Review

Match the terms in List *A* with the phrases in List *B*.

List A

1. *Alvin*
2. Atlantic
3. Arctic
4. bacteria
5. black smokers
6. cause of decreased salinity
7. cause of increased salinity
8. chloride
9. electrical conductivity
10. H.M.S. *Challenger*
11. JOIDES *Resolution*
12. magnesium
13. Mediterranean and Red seas
14. mixed layer
15. phytoplankton
16. high latitude oceans
17. salinity
18. thermocline
19. water mass
20. zooplankton

List B

a. hot springs of mid-ocean ridges
b. only region of ocean with enough heat and light to grow marine plants
c. used to measure salinity; increases as water salinity increases
d. tiny, battery-powered, piloted submarine used to explore mid-ocean ridges
e. a region of the ocean with the same temperature and salinity
f. measure of the dissolved solids in sea water; averages 35‰
g. zone of rapid temperature change
h. heavy rainfall, rivers, and melting glaciers
i. ocean that reaches eastward from the Americas to Europe and Africa
j. microscopic organisms, such as diatoms, that are basic food source of ocean life

k. most abundant ion in sea water
l. first seagoing ocean laboratory
m. microscopic organisms that live off food-producing phytoplankton and are eaten by other organisms
n. converts hydrogen sulfide to energy for giant clams, white crabs, and tube worms of mid-ocean ridges
o. ocean of the north polar region
p. seagoing drilling platform used to obtain sea-floor sediment and rock samples
q. evaporation and freezing
r. origin of cold, dense water that flows toward equator
s. mineral that can be profitably mined from sea
t. areas of high salinity resulting from high evaporation

Interpret and Apply

Answer the following questions on your paper.

1. Why are the bottom waters of the Mediterranean Sea likely to be poor in oxygen?
2. The concentration of silica in rivers flowing into the ocean is more than three times the concentration of silica in the ocean. What could become of the silica that enters the ocean to cause this difference?
3. The percentage of sodium and chloride ions in sea water is much greater than their percentage in Earth's crust. Propose a reason.
4. What relationship would be expected between the amount of dissolved oxygen in a water mass and the "age" of a water mass moving along the bottom of the ocean?

Critical Thinking

The graph shows variations in the density of water masses, in g/cm^3, relative to their temperature and salinity. Salinity, in ‰, increases toward the right on the horizontal scale while temperature, in °C, increases upward on the vertical scale.

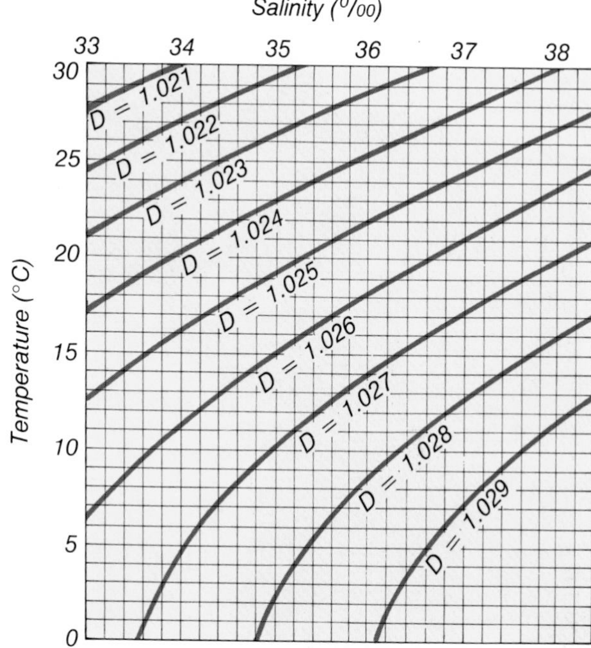

1. The average temperature and salinity of the Atlantic Ocean are 3.7°C and 34.8‰. Water from the Mediterranean Sea that flows into the Atlantic Ocean may have a temperature and salinity of 12°C and 37.2‰. Would this Mediterranean Sea water be expected to rise or to sink when it enters the Atlantic Ocean? Why?
2. The densest water mass in the ocean is the Antarctic Deep Water mass with a temperature of −1.9°C and a salinity of 34.6‰. Extrapolate (extend the information on the graph) to determine the approximate density of this water.
3. When two water masses with the same density but different temperature and salinity mix, the properties of the new water mass are at a point on a straight line joining their original locations on the graph. In general, how does the density of a new water mass compare with the density of the original water masses? (Hint: Lay a straight edge between any two points on the same density line.)

CHAPTER

18

The Ocean Floor and Its Sediments

▲
Scientists use a precision depth recorder to make a profile of the ocean floor.

How Do You Know That . . .

The depth of the seafloor changes from place to place? One evidence of such change can be seen in the photograph. The scientists are looking at a tracing of the seafloor made by a special echo device. The device makes a record of seafloor depth. Over the years, this device has provided an accurate and inexpensive record of the different elevations of the seafloor throughout the world's oceans. Such data has helped scientists better understand the shape and composition of the seafloor and Earth's crust.

I Studying the Ocean Floor

Topic 1 Echo Sounding and Satellites

In the days of the first oceanographic surveys, such as the *Challenger* expedition, the distance to the seafloor was measured with a lead weight on a line. The weight was lowered until it touched bottom, the amount of line let out was determined, and the weight was hauled back to the ship. In deep water a single depth reading might take an entire day. The process was tiresome and produced very limited information.

Today ships use a device called the *precision depth recorder* to find the distance to the ocean floor. The device works by sending a sound signal through the water to the seafloor. The length of time needed for the signal to reach the bottom and echo back to the ship measures the depth of the water. The recorder traces a continuous profile of the area over which the ship is sailing. Such profiles are used to make accurate and detailed maps of the seafloor.

A device similar to the precision depth recorder provides information about the sediment layers on the ocean floor. Lower-pitched sound signals are able to penetrate many layers of seafloor sediment. Scientists produce lower-pitched signals using underwater explosives or compressed air blasts and record the way the signals travel through the sediment layers. Such data reveal the structure of each layer of sediment and of the bedrock beneath. Profiles of all but the thickest sediments have been obtained in this way.

In recent years, satellites have come into use in mapping the ocean floor. Satellites can gather far more data more quickly than a seagoing vessel. Signals sent from satellites cannot reach the ocean floor, but they can bounce off the ocean surface. Using ocean surface data for ocean floor mapping works because the level of the ocean surface varies slightly. Ocean water piles up slightly over undersea mountains and dips slightly over undersea trenches. The ocean surface hills and dips are revealed by precise measurements taken from the satellite. The data are processed by computer to produce an image of the ocean floor.

Topic 2 Sampling the Sediments

Although echo soundings provide data about the ocean floor and its sediments, actual samples of the seafloor yield far more information. Many samples are scooped up by mechanical devices. A *grab sample* is taken by a mechanical device that, as the name suggests,

OBJECTIVES

A Describe past and present methods for determining the depth of the seafloor.

B List direct and indirect methods of studying seafloor sediments and identify some kinds of information obtained from direct samples.

C Name some devices used to make direct observations of the seafloor and discuss their advantages and disadvantages.

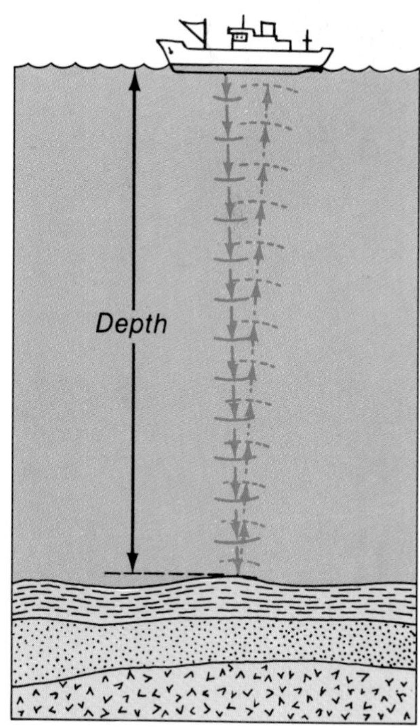

18.1 The sound wave from the ship bounces off the ocean floor and back to the ship. The time it takes to return to the ship indicates the depth of the ocean floor.

a

b

18.2 (a) A specially designed camera sled sinks to the ocean floor. (b) Sedimentologists examine a core of sediment split lengthwise.

grabs a sediment sample off the seafloor. Another device used to obtain samples is a *dredge,* or a large scoop that is dragged along the ocean floor. Dredges are less important for sediment sampling than they once were. However, they are still used to sample rocks lying on seafloor that is bare of sediment. Another sampling device is a *box corer.* Box corers are often used to sample nodules, lumps containing many valuable minerals such as manganese and cobalt, a rare element used in making heat-resistant steel.

Many sediment samples are obtained by drilling a hole in the seafloor. Drilling of the seafloor produces a *core sample,* or *core,* a cylindrical sample of sediment or rock. Most cores are taken by a conventional drill. However, scientists also use a device called a *hydraulic-piston corer.* The JOIDES *Resolution* (Chapter 17, Topic 3) is equipped with such a device. Scientists have taken core samples of sediments that contain the record of millions of years of ocean history. The cores are used to study factors such as ancient water circulation patterns, changes in plankton population over thousands of years, and the rate at which sediment has built up on the seafloor. In addition, the cores can be used to learn about Earth's past climates, especially in relation to the last Ice Age.

Topic 3 **Direct Observations**

The discoveries made by scientists aboard *Alvin* (Chapter 17, Topic 3) point out the benefit of direct observations of the ocean floor. However, despite its many uses, *Alvin* has one major drawback. While exploring the deep ocean, scientists aboard the minisubmarine must spend half of their research time descending to the ocean bottom and returning to the surface. Only a small part of each dive can be spent actually observing the seafloor.

To overcome this problem, more deep-towed vehicles like *Argo* will be used. These vehicles "fly" above the seafloor as they are towed along by a research ship. Supersensitive television cameras send pictures of the seafloor through a cable to televisions on the surface vessel above. A separate robot vehicle is now being planned. The robot vehicle, using *Argo* or another towed vehicle as a base, will be able to take samples. With these devices, scientists will be able to continuously make direct observations of the seafloor. Mechanical devices do not need to return to the surface after only a brief time on the seafloor. They can do in a few days the work that might take a submarine carrying scientists, such as *Alvin,* several weeks. *Alvin* is still needed, however, to transport scientists to the ocean depths so they can observe features discovered by the undersea vehicles.

TOPIC QUESTIONS

Each topic question refers to the topic of the same number.

1. **(a)** How was ocean depth determined in the past? **(b)** How does a precision depth recorder measure depth? **(c)** What is constructed from the data obtained by a precision depth recorder? **(d)** Why are ocean surface data collected by satellites helpful in studying the ocean floor?
2. **(a)** Name three devices used to obtain seafloor samples. **(b)** List some kinds of information that can be obtained from a core of sediment.
3. **(a)** What is the major difficulty in the use of research submarines like *Alvin*? **(b)** How is this problem overcome?

Dr. Maggie Goud
Marine Geologist

The study of the ocean floor yields a great deal of information regarding Earth's past. According to Maggie Goud, a marine geologist at the Woods Hole Oceanographic Institution, studying the ocean floor also yields information regarding Earth's future.

As a marine geologist, Dr. Goud studies the way waves and currents move sand and mud around the ocean floor. This involves placing instruments on the ocean floor to measure currents, waves, and sediment motion. Dr. Goud says that the field work is exhausting but exciting. Placing the instruments requires going to sea for days or weeks at a time and often requires scuba diving. Back on shore, the field data are used to help formulate theoretical models of ocean floor dynamics.

Dr. Goud says that ocean floor research is vital to the understanding of how ancient rock deposits were formed. The research is also useful for understanding why sediments are found where they are on the continental shelf and for predicting where they will move in the future. This has practical as well as scientific value, since development of the continental shelf (for example, in offshore oil drilling) can only be done safely if the processes in the environment are understood. As a result, the work of Maggie Goud and other marine geologists is linked as much to the future as to the past.

OBJECTIVES

A Locate and describe the features of the continental margins.

B Differentiate between passive and active continental margins.

C Discuss the origin and formation of submarine canyons.

II The Continental Margins

Topic 4 Continental Shelves

The ocean floor is usually divided into two major regions: the continental margins and the ocean basins (Topics 8–13). The continental margins, in turn, include the continental shelves, the continental slope (Topic 5), and the continental rise (Topic 7).

The **continental shelves** are a part of the continent that is underwater. Continental shelves are extremely flat. They extend from the shoreline of the continent to the *shelf edge,* the boundary between the continental shelf and the continental slope. The shelf edge marks the place where the water depths begin to increase rapidly. Over most of the world, the depth of the shelf edge is about 130 meters.

The characteristics of a continental shelf depend upon the type of continental margin where it occurs. At active continental margins, the continental shelf is very narrow and bordered by an ocean trench. The shoreline is rugged with coastal mountains. The active continental margin on the Pacific coast of South America is an example of this kind of continental shelf.

At passive continental margins, the continental shelf is broad. Some passive continental shelves are more than 300 kilometers wide. On these shelves, no bordering trench or rugged coastal

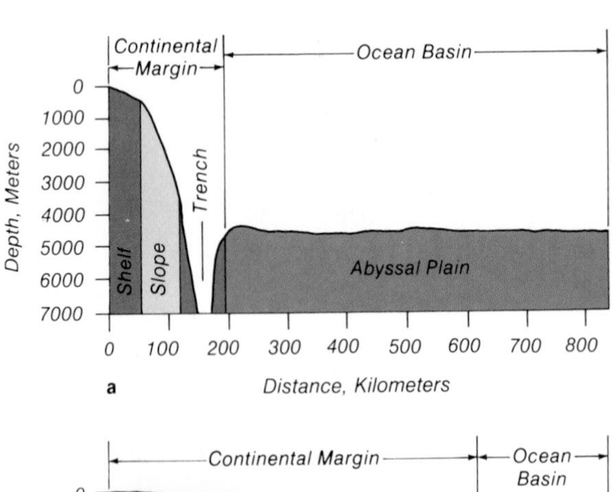

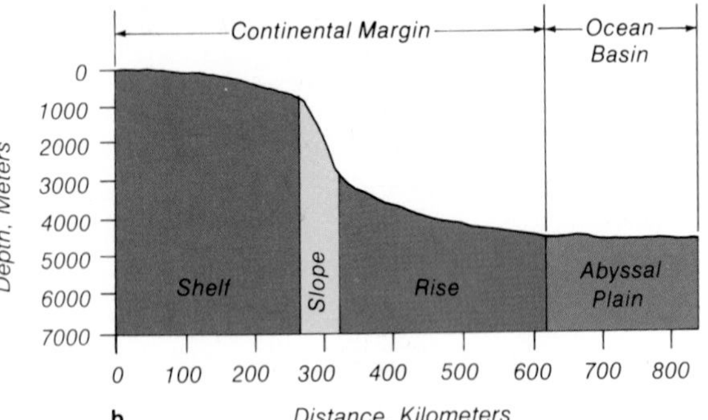

18.3 (a) Ocean floor features at an active continental margin; (b) features at a passive continental margin

mountains are found. Instead, the continental shelf is bordered by a coastal plain. Both the shelf and the coastal plain have generally level surfaces with low hills and shallow depressions. The passive continental margin on the Atlantic coast of North America is a good example of this kind of continental shelf.

Topic 5 Continental Slopes

The **continental slopes** begin at the shelf edge, where water depth starts to increase rapidly. The boundary between the continental shelf and the continental slope is clear and abrupt. Beyond the shelf edge, the seafloor is no longer nearly level but begins to slope toward the deep ocean. The average slope angle is about four degrees, similar to the slope of an aisle in a movie theater. Continental slopes are usually less than 200 kilometers wide and descend to a depth of about 3 kilometers. The change from continental crust to oceanic crust often occurs beneath the continental slope. On an active continental margin, the slope ends in a deep-sea trench. On a passive continental margin, the slope ends in a fan of sediment, the continental rise.

The continental slopes are cut by many gullies and small valleys. These valleys are probably the results of mudslides. The slopes are also cut in places by gigantic gullies called **submarine canyons.** Some of these canyons rival the Grand Canyon of the Colorado River in size. Submarine canyons often begin on the continental shelf and continue to the end of the slope. Some are extensions of river valleys on the coastal plain.

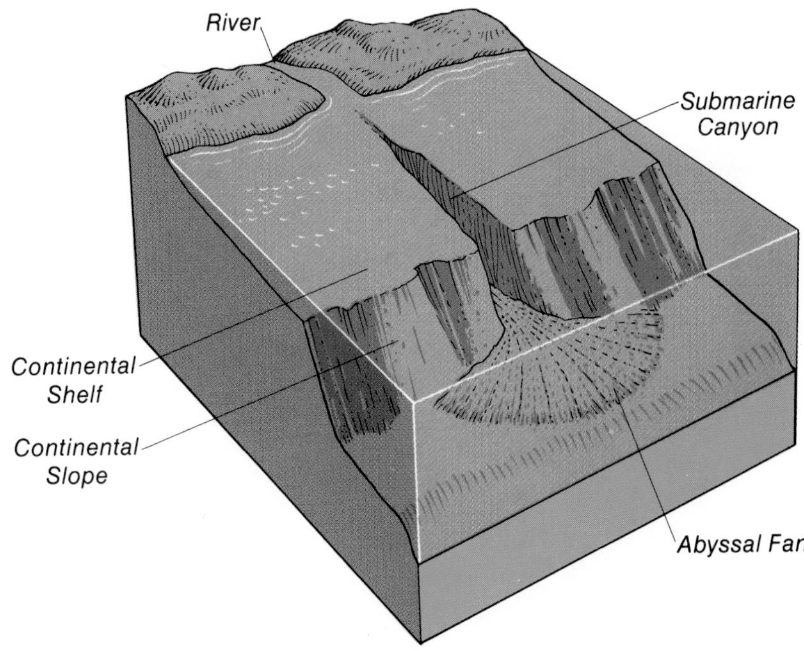

18.4 The upper part of this submarine canyon was formed by a river. The deeper part was formed by undersea currents.

Many submarine canyons occur off the eastern coast of North America. A well-known example is the Hudson River Canyon. This canyon extends about 300 kilometers out to sea from the mouth of the Hudson River. At the end of the continental slope, the canyon is 3 kilometers deep. Another great submarine canyon is the Monterey Canyon off the California coast.

Topic 6 The Origin of Submarine Canyons

How did submarine canyons form? Some, like the Hudson River Canyon, extend out from coastal plain rivers. The upper part of the canyon is on the continental shelf. The lower part cuts deep into the continental slope. Geologists think the upper parts of submarine canyons were formed during the Ice Age. At that time, sea level was perhaps 100 meters lower than now. Broad areas of the present continental shelves were above sea level. Rivers such as the Hudson River cut valleys to the shelf edge. When the glaciers melted, sea level rose and the valleys were drowned. Many Atlantic coast bays were formed in this way.

What about the lower canyons? These canyons extend thousands of meters into the continental slopes, so they cannot be described as drowned valleys. Furthermore, most canyons show no connection with rivers on the continents.

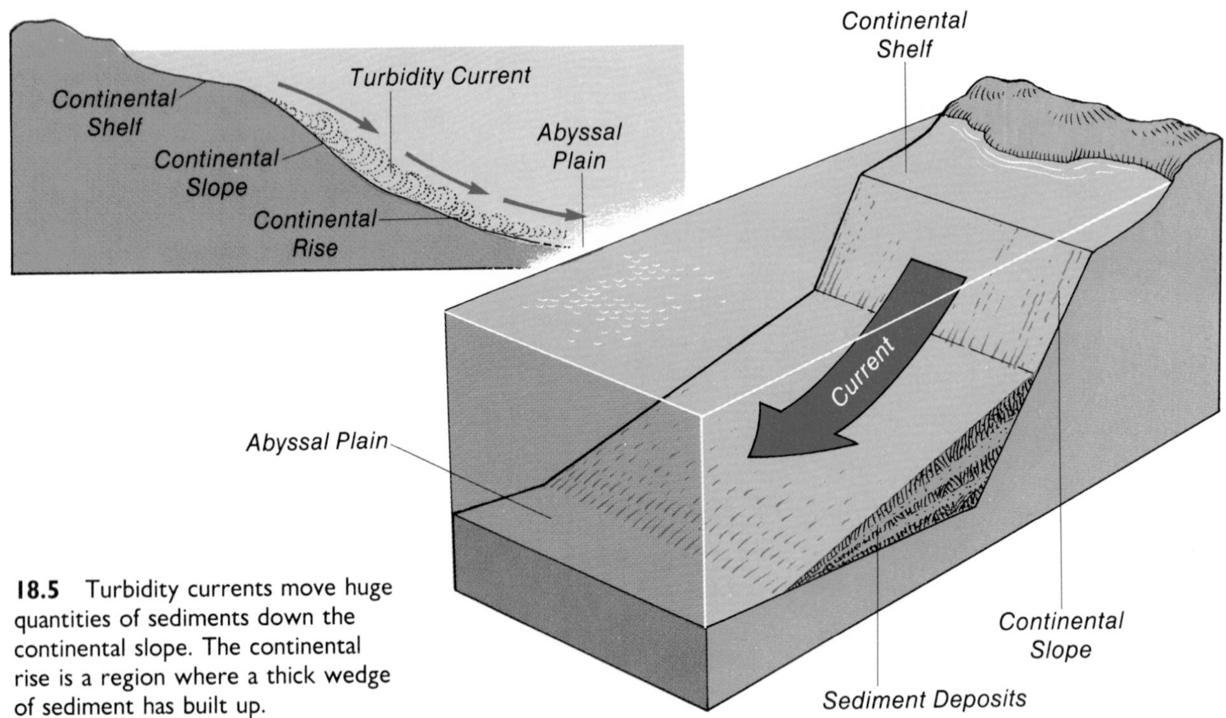

18.5 Turbidity currents move huge quantities of sediments down the continental slope. The continental rise is a region where a thick wedge of sediment has built up.

Geologists think that canyons on the continental slopes have a different origin. They think that these canyons are caused by powerful currents that run like flash floods down the steep continental slopes. Such currents form when great landslides of mud and sand come down the slopes. The landslides may be started by earthquakes or simply by the force of gravity. Such undersea landslides are called **turbidity currents** (*turbid* means "muddy"). The speed of turbidity currents makes these mixtures of water, mud, and sand powerful agents of erosion. Communications cables on the ocean floor between North America and Europe are regularly snapped by turbidity currents, especially near the mouths of large rivers. The turbidity currents also build great fan-shaped deposits at the mouths of many submarine canyons. Some turbidity current deposits can be traced for hundreds of kilometers along the seafloor.

Topic 7 Continental Rises

The **continental rise** is the gently sloping region between the continental slope and the ocean basin. It was formed by the deposition of masses of sediment several kilometers thick. The sediment originally came from the land and was brought to this region by turbidity currents and gravity flows.

Continental rises are not found at active continental margins because the deep-sea trenches that occur there trap the sediments. They are features of passive continental margins such as the Atlantic coast of North America. Here they may be as much as 1000 kilometers wide with a gentle slope.

TOPIC QUESTIONS

Each topic question refers to the topic of the same number.

4. **(a)** What are the continental shelves? **(b)** What is the shelf edge? **(c)** List some features of active continental margins and give an example of such a margin. **(d)** Describe the continental shelf on passive continental margins and give an example.

5. **(a)** Where is the continental slope? **(b)** How is the slope different from the continental shelf? **(c)** Where does the slope end on active continental margins? **(d)** Where does the slope end on passive continental margins? **(e)** What are submarine canyons? Give an example of a submarine canyon.

6. **(a)** What process may have formed the part of a submarine canyon in a continental shelf? **(b)** What process may have formed the part of a submarine canyon in a continental slope?

7. **(a)** What is the continental rise? **(b)** On which type of continental margin are continental rises found? Why are they not found on the other type?

OBJECTIVES

A Locate and describe the various features of the ocean basins.

B Describe and give examples of deep-sea trenches and mid-ocean ridges.

C Discuss the fracture zones of mid-ocean ridges.

III The Ocean Basins

Topic 8 Abyssal Plains

The **abyssal plains** are one feature of the floor of the deep sea. These plains range in depth from 3000 to 6000 meters. Their most remarkable feature is their flatness. In fact, abyssal plains are the flattest areas of Earth's surface.

The abyssal plains are composed of sediments. In some areas, these sediments are more than 1 kilometer thick. Most of this material came from the continents. How could material from the continents reach the deep seafloor? The answer is turbidity currents. Continental rivers deposit material on the edges of continental shelves during times of low sea level, such as Ice Ages. Turbidity currents carry sediment down the continental slopes, and spread it evenly over the continental rise and abyssal plain.

Although abyssal plains are found in all oceans, they are particularly well developed and widespread in the Atlantic Ocean. An example there is the Hatteras Abyssal Plain. This plain is 1000 kilometers long and 150 to 300 kilometers wide. The thick sediment layers that cover it are thought to have come from turbidity currents in the Hatteras and Hudson canyons.

Topic 9 Abyssal Hills

The **abyssal hills** are another part of the floor of the ocean basins. They are small, rolling hills that occur, often in groups, next to continental margins and oceanic ridge systems. In the North Atlantic, abyssal hills form two strips parallel to the mid-Atlantic Ridge for almost its entire length.

Individual hills are generally from 1 to 10 kilometers across and usually extend no higher than a few hundred meters above the abyssal plain. Interestingly, the thick sediments of the abyssal plains have been found to hide a surface of abyssal hills that cover much of the deep ocean floor. For this reason, the abyssal hills are thought to represent the original seafloor surface that forms at the mid-ocean ridges. Sediments from turbidity currents bury this surface as it is carried away from the ridges on the lithospheric plate. Thus, abyssal plain sediments merely cover abyssal hills beneath them.

1000 m

18.6 Seamounts are the peaks of volcanic mountains located on the deep seafloor. Flat-topped peaks are called guyots.

Topic 10 Seamounts, Guyots, and Coral Atolls

Seamounts are cone-shaped mountain peaks that rise high above the deep ocean floor. These peaks may occur alone but more typically are found in clusters or rows, often near plate boundaries. Although they are found on seafloors in all oceans, seamounts are most abundant in the Pacific.

Seamounts are volcanic in origin, and seem to be related to plate boundary activity. However, some seamounts are located away from the edges of lithospheric plates. There is speculation that these isolated groups of seamounts originated over hot spots. In fact, the Hawaiian Islands, a famous chain of hot-spot volcanoes (Chapter 14, Topic 7), are actually a chain of seamounts tall enough to rise above the ocean surface.

Some seamounts look as though they have had their tops sliced off. These flat-topped seamounts are called **guyots** (GHEE ohs). Their tops, thought to have originally been above sea level, were removed by wave action. Later sinking of the oceanic crust lowered the tops of the guyots below the surface. The tops of some guyots are as deep as two kilometers below sea level.

Another result of crustal sinking is the formation of **atolls,** ring-shaped coral islands. An atoll begins to form when a fringing coral reef forms around a volcanic island. Corals are tiny sea animals that live in water less than 80 meters deep (Chapter 12, Topic 15). As the seafloor around the island sinks, the corals sink with it. New corals grow on top of the old, dead corals beneath. As the reef sinks, it "grows" at the top, keeping pace with the lowering of the seafloor. Eventually the mountain is completely below sea level, leaving behind an atoll (circular reef) with a central lagoon.

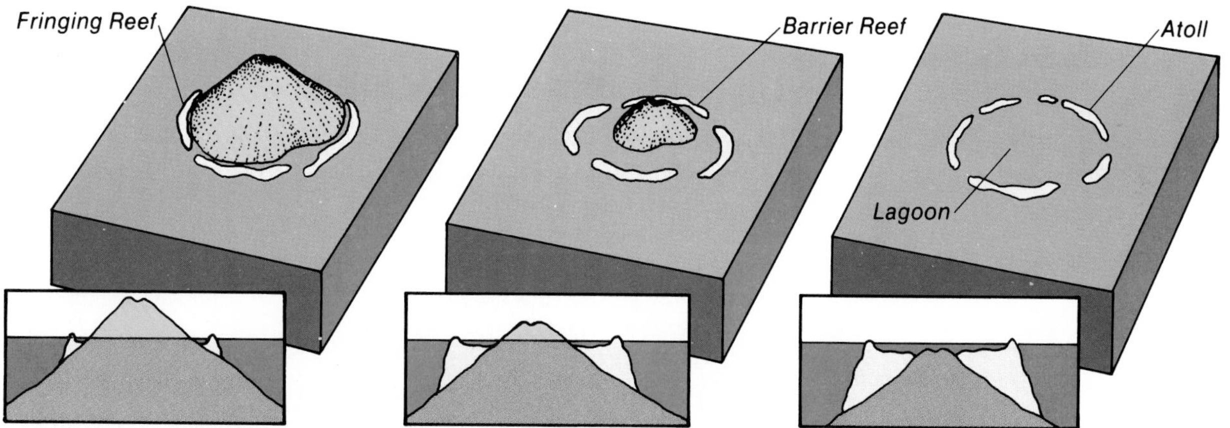

18.7 The three stages in the formation of an atoll

18.8 Kayengel Atoll is located in the South Pacific.

Topic 11 Trenches

Deep-sea *trenches* are long, narrow, steep-sided troughs that parallel either continental margins or chains of volcanic islands. Nearly all trenches occur around the margin of the Pacific Ocean. These trenches mark the places where the crust goes beneath the surface as one lithospheric plate subducts beneath another (Chapter 13, Topic 11). On average, deep-sea trenches are 1500 kilometers long but less than 100 kilometers wide. Their depth may be 2 to 4 kilometers below the neighboring ocean floor. The bottoms of the deep-sea trenches are narrow, flat, and filled with sediment.

The longest trench is the Peru-Chile Trench. This trench parallels the coast of South America for 5900 kilometers. The Peru-Chile Trench is the result of the subduction of the oceanic Nazca Plate eastward beneath the continental South American Plate.

The deepest trench is the Marianas Trench on the west side of the Pacific Ocean. Here the Pacific Plate is subducting westward beneath the Indian Plate (Chapter 13). The deepest place in this trench—the deepest place in any ocean—is 11 kilometers below sea level. Four other Pacific trenches are deeper than 10 kilometers. They are the Kurile-Kamchatka Trench, the Philippine Trench, the Tonga Trench, and the Kermadec Trench. Each marks the subduction of the Pacific Plate beneath another plate.

Topic 12 Mid-Ocean Ridges

The most obvious feature of the ocean basins is the mid-ocean ridges. These are the diverging boundaries introduced in Chapter 13. They are the locations where new oceanic crust forms as two lithospheric plates move apart.

1. *Kurile Trench*
2. *Aleutian Trench*
3. *Philippine Trench*
4. *Marianas Trench*
5. *Tonga Trench*
6. *Peru–Chile Trench*

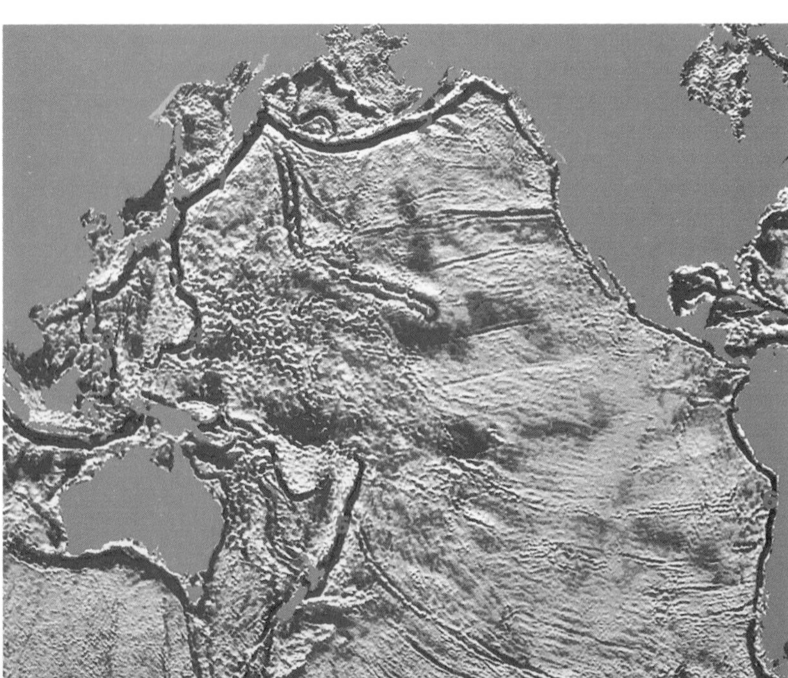

18.9 This portion of a computer-generated satellite image shows some of the major trenches in the Pacific Ocean.

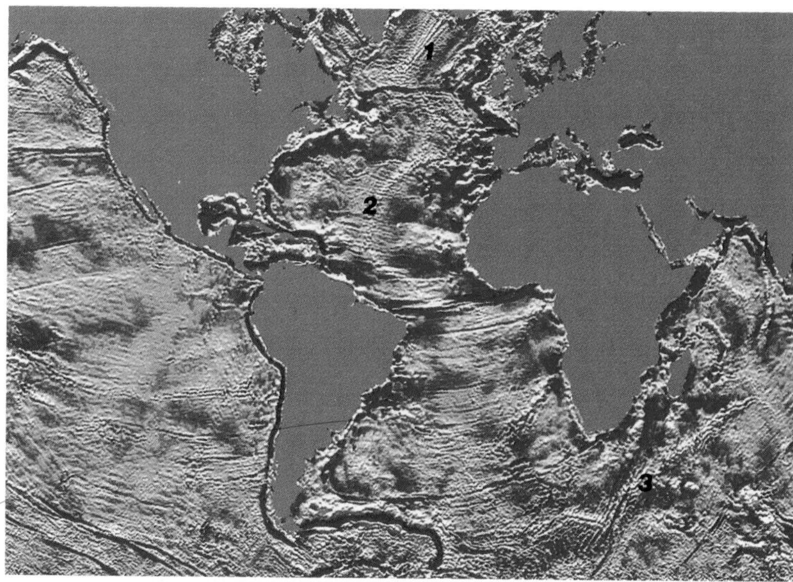

18.10 Another portion of the same satellite image shows the ridge system of the Atlantic Ocean.

1. *Reykjanes Ridge*
2. *Mid–Atlantic Ridge*
3. *Indian Ocean Ridge*

Mid-ocean ridges are great undersea mountain ranges. They form a nearly continuous chain 80 000 kilometers long that crosses every ocean. With the exception of the Pacific, mid-ocean ridges occur in the middle part of each ocean. Their average depth is 2500 meters. In places, however, the highest peaks of mid-ocean ridges reach above sea level as islands. The ridge crest is 1000 to 3000 meters above the neighboring seafloor. Mid-ocean ridges are usually greater than 1000 kilometers wide.

The mid-Atlantic Ridge is the portion of the ridge system in the Atlantic Ocean. This ridge runs roughly parallel to the shoreline of the continents that border the Atlantic. Seamounts rising from the ridge to above sea level include the Azores Islands in the North Atlantic Ocean and Ascension Island in the South Atlantic.

Like some other parts of the ridge system, the mid-Atlantic Ridge has a central rift valley at its crest. This valley is 1 to 2 kilometers deep and tens of kilometers wide. Interestingly, the East Pacific Rise has no rift valley at its crest. The East Pacific Rise is also broader and less rugged than the mid-Atlantic Ridge. The cause of the difference between the two ridge systems is suspected to be their different spreading rates. The mid-Atlantic Ridge is spreading at a rate of about 1 centimeter each year. The rate for the East Pacific Rise is about 6 centimeters each year. In general, ridges with spreading rates of less than 2.5 centimeters per year have rift valleys and rugged profiles. In contrast, ridges with more rapid spreading rates typically lack rift valleys and are less rugged.

Although pieces of ridges may form islands, such as Ascension Island or the Azores, rift valleys rarely appear above sea level. An exception is Iceland. The center of the mid-Atlantic Ridge goes completely across the island of Iceland and is directly responsible for the volcanic activity that occurs there.

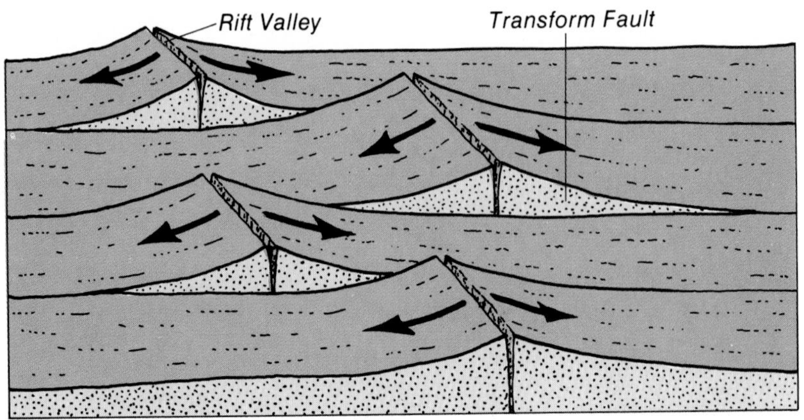

18.11 Fracture zones consist of a series of transform faults. Earthquakes occur where the pieces of lithospheric plate are moving in opposite directions.

Topic 13 **Fracture Zones**

One more important seafloor feature remains—the hundreds of faults that cut across the mid-ocean ridges. They are a kind of strike-slip fault (Chapter 16, Topic 4) called *transform faults.* The transform faults and the rugged seafloor that occur with them make up oceanic *fracture zones.* Although the mid-ocean ridges together make up the longest mountain range on Earth, the ridge is broken by the fracture zones into separate pieces. These pieces, which are 50 to 100 kilometers long, are offset relative to each other. Some of the offset pieces are only a few kilometers apart, but others have moved several hundred kilometers.

Between the pieces of offset ridge, the crustal plates are moving in opposite directions. The grinding and straining that result from these opposing motions cause earthquakes to occur along these sections of the faults. Beyond the offset ridge, the pieces of plate are moving in the same direction. Earthquakes do not occur in those areas.

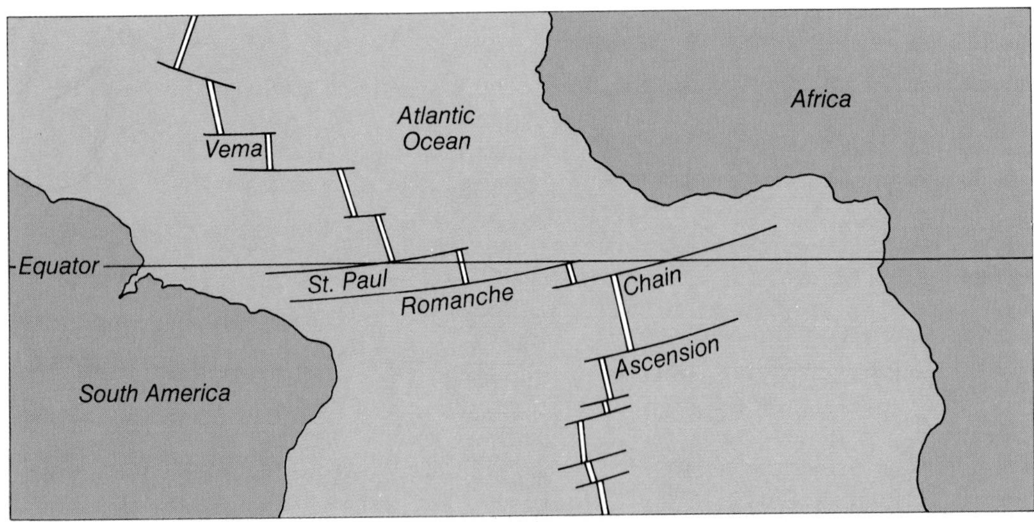

18.12 The mid-Atlantic Ridge is broken by a series of fracture zones.

Fracture zones may be as deep as 1500 meters. Some of the fracture zones form high submarine cliffs, and some extend across an ocean basin. An example is the Romanche Fracture Zone, which crosses the mid-Atlantic Ridge near the equator. Here the ridge is offset by almost 1000 kilometers. The fracture zone forms a trench that, in some areas, is more than 7 kilometers below sea level.

TOPIC QUESTIONS

Each topic question refers to the topic of the same number.

8. **(a)** What are abyssal plains? **(b)** Where does the sediment on the abyssal plains come from? How? **(c)** Name one example of an abyssal plain.

9. **(a)** Where are abyssal hills? **(b)** How are they related to abyssal plains?

10. **(a)** What is a seamount? **(b)** Where are most seamounts located? **(c)** How are seamounts in the middle of plates thought to originate? **(d)** What is a guyot? **(e)** How do atolls form?

11. **(a)** Describe the shape of a deep-sea trench. **(b)** What happens to the lithospheric plates at deep-sea trenches? **(c)** Where are most of the world's deep-sea trenches located? **(d)** Identify the longest trench and the deepest trench.

12. **(a)** What happens to the lithospheric plates at mid-ocean ridges? **(b)** Describe the mid-ocean ridges. **(c)** List some ways in which the structure of the East Pacific Rise is different from that of the mid-Atlantic Ridge. **(d)** What is thought to be the cause of these differences?

13. **(a)** What is a fracture zone? **(b)** What effect do fracture zones have on the mid-ocean ridges? **(c)** Where do earthquakes occur at the transform faults? **(d)** Identify a fracture zone on the mid-Atlantic Ridge.

Map Skills

Questions 1 and 2 refer to the physical world map on pages 588–589.

1. Locate the North Atlantic Ocean. Are the deepest places in the North Atlantic Ocean in the middle of the ocean? Explain.

2. **(a)** What color is used to identify areas of the continental shelf? **(b)** Compare the width of the continental shelf off the coasts of California and Florida. **(c)** Based on the width of the continental shelf, does California lie on an active or passive continental margin? Which kind of margin is Florida on?

IV Ocean Floor Sediments

OBJECTIVES

A Name two types of ooze-making organisms and give examples of both.

B Describe seafloor muds and clays and identify some sources of these sediments.

C Discuss the origin and formation of turbidites.

D Discuss the nature and importance of authigenic sediments.

Topic 14 Oozes

Oozes are one of four main classes of ocean floor sediments. The other classes are muds and clays, turbidites, and authigenic materials. **Oozes** are sediments made from microscopic shells. These shells are the remains of the tiny floating plants and animals that live in the mixed layer at the ocean surface. When the plants and animals die, their shells settle to the bottom.

There are two kinds of oozes—calcareous ooze and siliceous ooze. *Calcareous* oozes contain calcium carbonate. These oozes cover about half of the entire seafloor. The most common ooze comes from the shells of *Globigerina,* a one-celled animal the size of a pinhead. Calcium carbonate dissolves in sea water at certain depths. In the Atlantic, this depth is about 4500 meters. For this reason, calcareous oozes do not occur below those depths.

Siliceous oozes contain silicon dioxide. The two most common siliceous oozes come from the shells of diatoms and radiolaria, microscopic organisms that build elaborate shells. The major area of siliceous ooze deposition is around Antarctica and near the equator. Diatoms are especially abundant in the ocean water in these places and make up most of the ooze that forms.

Topic 15 Muds and Clays

18.13 Icebergs contain rock material that was scoured from the land by the movement of a glacier. When the iceberg melts, this rock material will settle to the ocean floor.

Muds are mixtures of fine particles of various sizes that have settled to the bottom from the ocean surface. They are soft, plastic materials with a greasy feel. **Clays** also settle to the bottom from the ocean surface. The most important are *red clays.* They are common in deep ocean trenches, where calcium carbonate is dissolved and the supply of diatoms and radiolaria is low. Red clays need not be red in color. Red clays can be brown, yellow, gray, green, or even blue. They are, however, made primarily of flakes of clay-sized (0.004 millimeters) material. As a result of their small size, clay particles are slow to settle to the bottom. However, some red clay particles are bound together into tiny pellets by zooplankton. These pellets are much larger and denser than individual flakes, and may sink to the seafloor within a week.

Other muds and clays have a variety of sources outside the ocean. Some extremely fine material from the land takes many years to settle to the ocean floor. A source of coarser material is icebergs. They contain rock material that was ground off the land by a glacier. When an iceberg melts, this material settles to the ocean floor to form *glacial-marine* sediments. A third source is volcanoes. Fine ash and dust from volcanoes may be carried around the world in the atmosphere. After settling to the ocean surface and then to the seafloor, ash and dust can form a measurable sediment layer of fine particles.

Topic 16 Turbidites

Turbidites are deposits made by turbidity currents. These are the currents that sweep material down the submarine canyons and out over the abyssal plains (Topic 6).

The most important feature of turbidites is that they form graded beds. A *graded bed* is a single layer that changes from larger particles at the bottom to smaller particles at the top. For example, a single layer could have pebbles and sand on the bottom and then grade upward into a fine sand at the top. Graded beds form because turbidity currents carry particles of all sizes. Once the current sweeps out over the abyssal plain, the current slows down and these particles settle. The current carries larger particles at a shorter distance above the seafloor. As a result, larger particles reach the bottom first and finer particles are deposited on top of them.

18.14 Manganese nodules

Topic 17 Authigenic Sediments

Authigenic means "formed in place." Authigenic sediments do not settle to the bottom, but form directly on the seafloor.

Probably the best-known example of an authigenic material is **manganese nodules**. These are lumps of material made from minerals rich in manganese and iron oxides, and small amounts of nickel, cobalt, and copper. Originally discovered on the floor of the Pacific Ocean, these nodules have now been found in all of the oceans except the Arctic. Manganese nodules are usually found in areas of red clay deposits where sediments build up slowly. Manganese nodules form, layer by layer, at a rate of 1 millimeter per 1 million years. Most of the material forming the nodule is thought to come from the seafloor sediments around the nodule.

Manganese nodules are important because the materials they contain are needed in industry. In addition, the nodules contain twice the concentration of copper and nickel as do land deposits of these elements.

TOPIC QUESTIONS

Each topic question refers to the topic of the same number.

14. **(a)** What are oozes? **(b)** Identify the material that makes up most calcareous oozes. **(c)** Why do calcareous oozes not occur below a certain depth? **(d)** Describe siliceous oozes.

15. **(a)** What are muds? **(b)** Describe red clays. **(c)** Name three sources of material for muds.

16. **(a)** What are turbidites? **(b)** What is their most important feature? **(c)** Where and how do these features form?

17. **(a)** Where do authigenic sediments form? **(b)** Why are manganese nodules important?

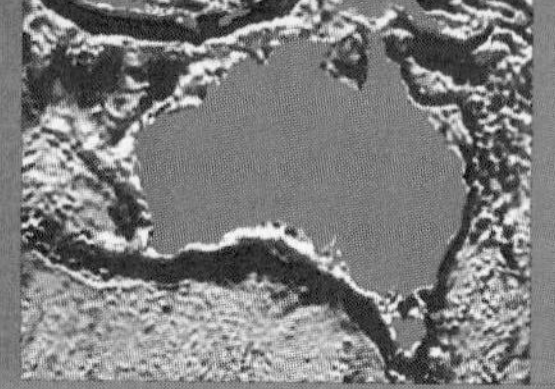

CHAPTER 18 REVIEW

Summary

Early methods of measuring ocean depth were slow and difficult. Today, echo devices trace profiles of the seafloor and satellites gather ocean surface data. This information is then used to draw maps.

Seafloor sediments can be studied by echo sounding, coring, and dredging. Core samples can be used to study an ocean's history.

Piloted and robot submarines make direct observations of the seafloor. Each has advantages and disadvantages.

Continental shelves are the drowned edges of the continents. Continental slopes extend seaward from the shelf edge. Continental rises are found at the base of the slope. Characteristics of each region depend upon the type of continental margin.

Submarine canyons are found on many continental margins. Rivers are thought to have formed the shelf parts of these canyons and turbidity currents the slope parts.

Abyssal plains are the very level plains of the deep sea, found between continental margins and mid-ocean ridges. The thick sediments found there cover a surface of abyssal hills. The abyssal hills may be the original seafloor that forms at mid-ocean ridges.

Seamounts are volcanic peaks that rise from the seafloor. Guyots are flat-topped seamounts. Atolls form when fringing reefs continue to grow upward as an island sinks.

Deep-sea trenches are the deepest places in the ocean floor. Most are found in the Pacific Ocean.

Mid-ocean ridges form an undersea mountain chain. Ridge features are determined by the rate of formation. The ridges are broken into pieces by fracture zones.

The four most important groups of seafloor sediments are oozes, muds and clays, turbidites, and authigenic materials. Each forms in a different way.

Vocabulary

abyssal hill
abyssal plain
atoll
clays
continental rise
continental shelf
continental slope
guyot
manganese nodules
muds
oozes
seamount
submarine canyon
turbidites
turbidity current

Review

On your paper, write the word or words that best complete each statement.

1. In the days of the *Challenger* expedition, the depth of the seafloor was found by lowering a lead ______ on a long line.
2. Core samples of ocean sediment contain a record of the ______ of an ocean over the past several million years.
3. While *Alvin* can spend only a limited time underwater, ______ vehicles, like *Argo*, can observe the seafloor continuously.
4. The continental ______ is a part of the continent that is underwater.
5. Narrow continental shelves, deep-sea trenches, and rugged coastal mountains are features of ______ continental margins.
6. On passive continental margins, the continental shelf and continental slope end in a deposit of sediment called the continental ______.
7. Huge gullies, called submarine ______, cut many continental margins.
8. The lower parts of the giant gullies are thought to have been carved by undersea landslides called turbidity ______.
9. The broad, extremely flat areas of the deep seafloor are called abyssal ______.
10. Abyssal hills are thought to form at mid-ocean ______ and to represent the original seafloor.
11. ______ are cone-shaped volcanic mountain peaks that rise above the deep ocean floor.

12. Guyots are undersea peaks that have had their ______ removed by wave action.
13. Many deep trenches are found on the west side of the ______ Ocean.
14. The mid-ocean ridges are a great undersea ______ range that crosses every ocean.
15. Rapidly forming mid-ocean ridges tend to lack central ______ valleys at their crests.
16. At transform ______, pieces of mid-ocean ridges are offset relative to each other.
17. Oozes are made of microscopic ______ of Globigerina, diatoms, and radiolaria.
18. Examples of source material for muds and clays include ______, ______, and ______.
19. Turbidite deposits are called ______ beds because each sediment layer changes from larger particles at the bottom to finer particles at the top.
20. An example of an authigenic sediment is lumps of material called manganese ______.

Interpret and Apply

On your paper, answer each question in complete sentences.

1. Why are the mouths of rivers likely sources of turbidity currents?
2. Why is the elevation of an abyssal plain likely to be less than that of abyssal hills, even though the abyssal plains are formed from sediments deposited on top of abyssal hills? (Hint: Review Chapter 13, Topic 7.)
3. Unlike the Atlantic Ocean, the Pacific Ocean has few abyssal plains. Propose a reason for this.
4. The rate of turbidite deposition on the abyssal plains of the North Atlantic Ocean dramatically increased during the Ice Age. Propose at least one reason for this increase.
5. **(a)** Sound travels at 1500 m/s in sea water. Find the depth to the ocean floor at a point where it takes a sound pulse 12 seconds to reach bottom and return. **(b)** Over what sea floor features can this point be?

Critical Thinking

The chart below shows some of the sources of sediment for the abyssal plains. Use the chart to answer the questions that follow.

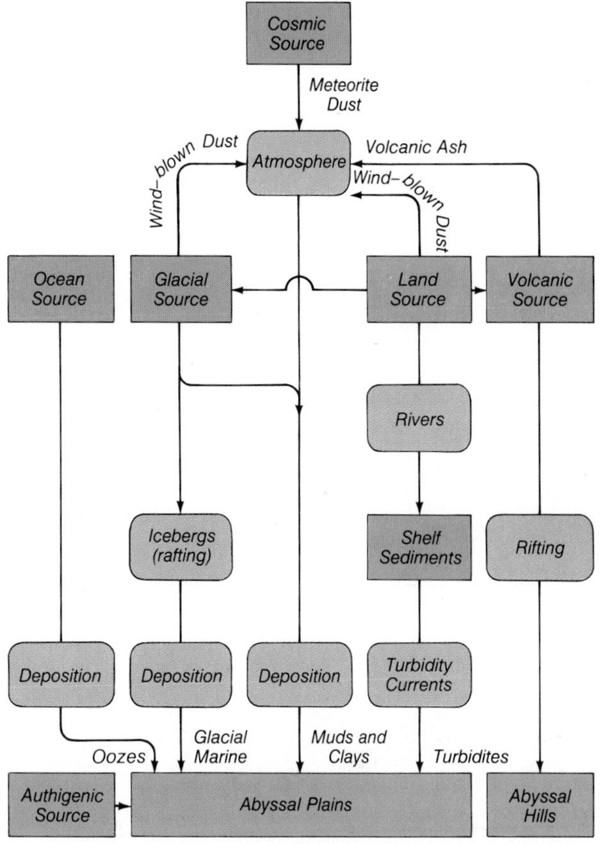

1. What is the process by which oozes, muds, and clays settle from the ocean surface to the seafloor?
2. Which abyssal plain deposit involves ice rafting?
3. List all of the sources shown for the materials that occur in muds and clays.
4. The oozes of the abyssal plain are not likely to be composed of Globigerina. Why not?
5. Why are the authigenic sources shown at the bottom of the chart instead of near the top of the chart with the other sources?

CHAPTER 19

Ocean Currents

▲
Breaking waves are one evidence of a moving ocean.

How Do You Know That . . .

The ocean moves? The waves breaking on this beach are one evidence of a moving ocean. The rise and fall of the tides is another. However, there are other ocean movements that are more difficult to see. These are the great, slow-moving "rivers" of water that circle each of the ocean basins. These currents carry enormous amounts of warm water away from the equator and bring equal amounts of cold water back. Their flow greatly affects the climates of coastal areas. In this chapter, you will learn about currents and their effects.

I Surface Currents

Topic 1 Ocean Currents

An **ocean current** can be defined as any continuous flow of water along a definite path in the ocean. The flow may occur at the surface or far below it. The flow may be up, down, or parallel to the surface.

The general surface currents of the oceans are shown in the map that appears on page 590 in the Appendix. Several observations can be made from the map. First, both the Atlantic Ocean and the Pacific Ocean have two circles of ocean currents, one in the Northern Hemisphere and another in the Southern Hemisphere. The current circles of the North Atlantic and North Pacific turn clockwise. The current circles of the South Atlantic and South Pacific turn counterclockwise. The directions that the current circles turn are caused by Earth's rotation. The way that Earth's rotation affects water and air will be discussed in Chapter 28.

A second observation that can be made from the map is that the temperature of the water within the circles of current follows a pattern. Currents that flow away from the equator carry warmer water. Currents that flow toward the equator carry colder water. This occurs because areas near the equator have warmer temperatures and areas near the poles have colder temperatures.

The result of these patterns of circulation and temperature is that the western sides of ocean basins have warm ocean currents moving away from the equator, while the eastern sides have cool ocean currents moving toward the equator. The western side of the North Atlantic Ocean has the warm, north-flowing Gulf Stream, while the eastern side has the cool, south-flowing Canary Current. The western side of the North Pacific Ocean has the warm, north-flowing Kuroshio Current, while the eastern side has the cool, south-flowing California Current. Other ocean basins show similar patterns.

Topic 2 Currents and Winds

The driving force of the surface ocean currents is wind. Winds tend to blow in fairly constant directions at different latitudes on Earth's surface. Two sets of constant winds are involved in forming most ocean currents – the trade winds and the westerly winds. Both sets occur in belts around the world.

OBJECTIVES

A Define *ocean currents*, describe the general pattern of surface ocean currents within a basin, and describe the effects of some currents.

B Discuss the relationship between winds and ocean currents.

C Locate and describe the Gulf Stream, its features, and its effects on climate.

D Define and give examples of countercurrents.

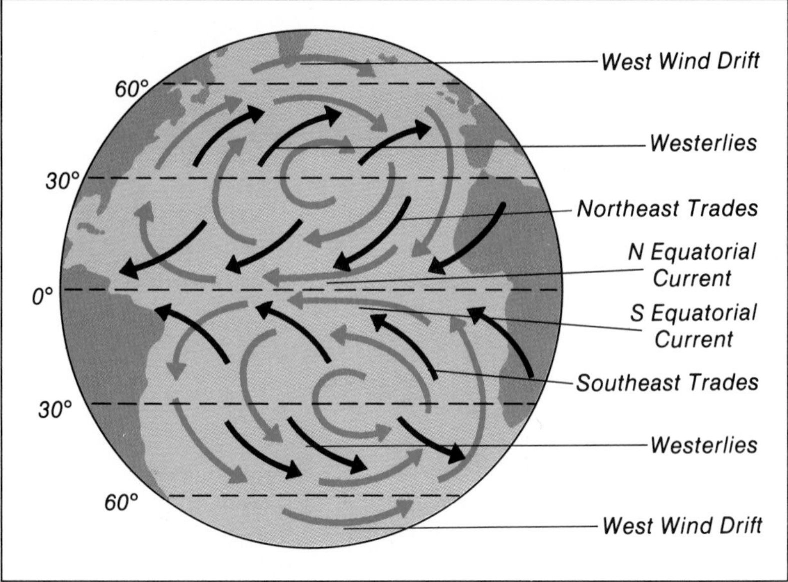

19.1 Winds help drive ocean currents. In the diagram, the black arrows represent winds. The blue arrows represent currents.

The *trade winds* affect the part of each current circle that occurs near the equator. The trade winds are very steady winds. They blow from the northeast in the Northern Hemisphere and from the southeast in the Southern Hemisphere. The trade winds push both the North and South Equatorial Current toward the west.

The *westerly* winds, or westerlies, drive the polar portion of the current circles. The westerlies blow from the southwest in the Northern Hemisphere and from the northwest in the Southern Hemisphere. They drive the currents of the polar regions, the West-Wind Drifts, toward the east.

Although seasonal changes in wind direction do not usually change the direction of ocean currents, one ocean area near India is an exception. India is subject to seasonal winds called monsoons. These winds blow from one direction in summer and from the opposite direction in winter. When the winds reverse direction, the surface ocean currents that they cause also reverse direction.

Topic 3 **Warm Currents**

Warm ocean currents flow away from the equatorial region on the west sides of ocean basins. The Gulf Stream in the North Atlantic, the Kuroshio Current in the North Pacific, the Brazil Current in the South Atlantic, and the East Australia Current in the South Pacific are all warm ocean currents on the west sides of ocean basins. Of the four, the Gulf Stream is best-known.

The Gulf Stream is a narrow, intense flow of water that begins in the Caribbean Sea. The current follows the east coast of the United States northward to the latitude of Cape Hatteras, North Carolina. Then the Gulf Stream swings northeastward across the Atlantic Ocean. Here it is called the North Atlantic Drift. The current carries warm water to Iceland and the British Isles. Because of the

19.2 (left) These currents form a complete circle around the calm waters of the Sargasso Sea. (right) This raft of floating brown seaweed is sargassum.

Gulf Stream, these places have warmer climates than they would otherwise. On average, the Gulf Stream is 240 kilometers wide and 1.6 kilometers deep and can move 100 000 000 cubic meters of water each second. (As a comparison, the Mississippi River is 0.8 kilometers wide, 0.015 kilometers deep, and discharges 20 000 cubic meters per second.)

The Gulf Stream forms the western and northern boundary of the Sargasso Sea. This is an area of warm water, light winds, and relatively calm seas in the middle of the North Atlantic Ocean. Great amounts of floating brown seaweed called *sargassum* are typical of the surface water there. Similar conditions exist in other oceans, but none is as well developed as in the North Atlantic.

Topic 4 **Gulf Stream Rings**

Unlike rivers on continents, the Gulf Stream does not flow in the same channel all the time. Instead, the stream wanders, sends out offshoot streams, speeds up in some areas, and slows down in others. Occasionally the Gulf Stream develops eddies or whirlpools that break away from the edge of the current. These eddies become structures called Gulf Stream rings. Figure 19.3 illustrates how Gulf Stream rings form from a bend in the Gulf Stream. As each ring forms, it takes with it a column of water from the opposite side of the Gulf Stream. This column of water becomes the center, or core, of the ring. A ring that forms on the Sargasso Sea side of the Gulf Stream has a core of cold water from the continent side. These rings are called *cold-core rings*. Conversely, a ring that forms on the continent side of the Gulf Stream has a core of warm water from the Sargasso Sea. These are called *warm-core rings*. Cold-core rings may be 300 kilometers in diameter and extend to a depth of 4000–5000 meters. Warm-core rings are smaller and shallower (150 kilometers in diameter, 1500 meters deep). Usually less than 10 rings form each year. Some rings may last as long as two years.

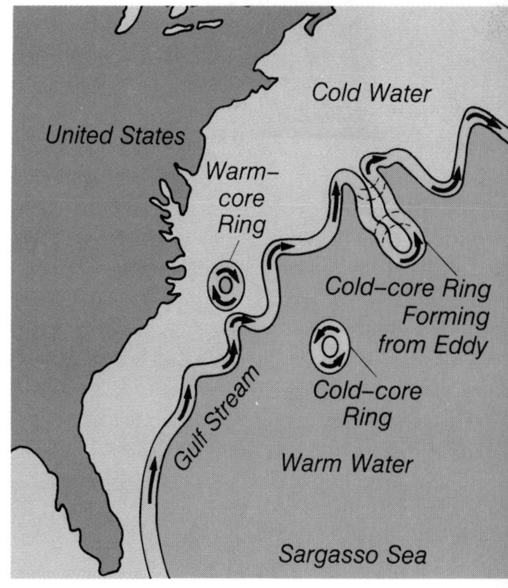

19.3 Rings form when eddies in the Gulf Stream break off. The diagram shows a warm-core ring, a cold-core ring, and an eddy that is becoming a cold-core ring.

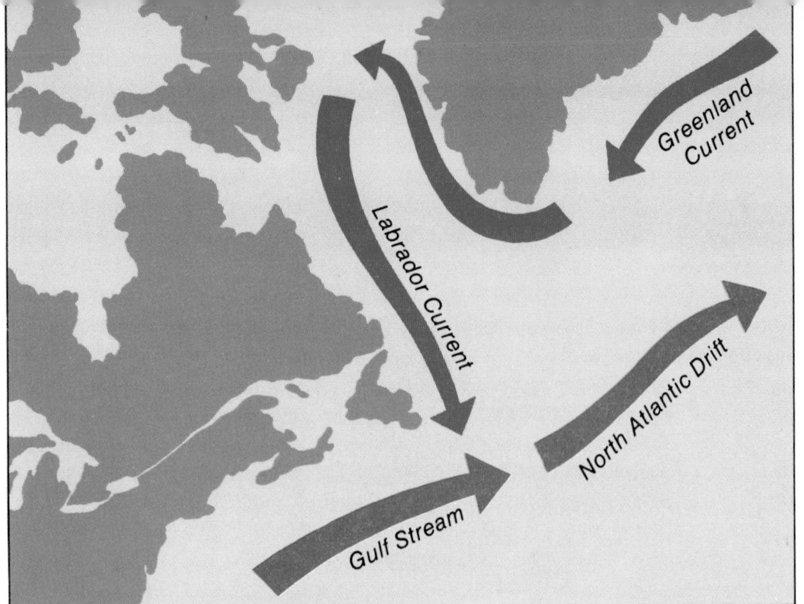

19.4 (left) The presence of icebergs provides an indication of the temperature and direction of an ocean current. (right) The Labrador Current flows out of Baffin Bay between Greenland and Labrador, carrying icebergs and sea ice.

Topic 5 **Cold Currents**

Cold currents flow toward the equator on the east sides of ocean basins. Four examples of cold ocean currents are the Canary Current in the North Atlantic, the California Current in the North Pacific, the Benguela Current in the South Atlantic, and the Peru, or Humboldt, Current in the South Pacific.

Some cold currents also flow out of far northern regions. The Labrador Current flows from Baffin Bay past Labrador, the coastal part of the Canadian province of Newfoundland (Figure 19.4). The current carries icebergs and sea ice from Baffin Bay, creating an iceberg hazard for ships in the North Atlantic. In the sea off the coast of Newfoundland, the Labrador Current meets the Gulf Stream. When warm, moist air from the Gulf Stream blows over the cold Labrador Current, water vapor condenses. The thickest fogs in the world are the result.

Two other important cold currents originate in northern regions. The east Greenland Current flows into the North Atlantic through the Strait of Denmark. The Kamchatka (or Oyashio) Current flows through the Bering Strait between Siberia and Alaska and into the North Pacific.

Topic 6 **Countercurrents**

Countercurrents flow in the opposite direction of the wind-related currents. Some of them flow at the surface, while others flow beneath the surface.

The Equatorial Countercurrents are surface currents. They flow eastward in a narrow belt of calm that occurs between the westward-moving North and South Equatorial currents. The calm belt occurs because the trade winds and the North and South Equatorial currents that flow with them pile water up on the western sides of the ocean basins. The countercurrents return some of that water to the east side of the basin. Equatorial Countercurrents are best developed in the Pacific Ocean but also occur in the Atlantic and Indian Oceans.

The Cromwell Current is a subsurface countercurrent of the Pacific Ocean. This current flows eastward underneath the westward-flowing South Equatorial Current. The Cromwell Current is about 30 meters below the ocean surface. It is about 210 meters thick and 400 kilometers wide. The Cromwell Current has been traced through the Pacific for a distance of nearly 5000 kilometers. Its average rate of flow is about 1.5 meters per second. This is considerably faster than the current that flows westward at the surface above the Cromwell. The size and volume of the Cromwell Current make it a major ocean current. Similar currents also occur in the Atlantic and Indian Oceans. The cause of subsurface countercurrents such as the Cromwell is unclear.

TOPIC QUESTIONS

Each topic question refers to the topic of the same number.

1. **(a)** Define *ocean current.* **(b)** What is the general circulation pattern of ocean currents north and south of the equator? **(c)** Within an ocean basin, where are warm currents generally found? **(d)** Within an ocean basin, where are cool currents generally found?

2. **(a)** What part of the current circles do the trade winds affect? **(b)** What are the currents caused by the trade winds called? **(c)** What part of the current circles do the westerlies affect? **(d)** What are the currents caused by the westerlies called?

3. **(a)** Name and locate several warm currents. **(b)** How does the Gulf Stream affect climates? **(c)** What is the Sargasso Sea?

4. **(a)** Describe how Gulf Stream rings form. **(b)** Locate and describe cold-core rings. **(c)** Locate and describe warm-core rings.

5. **(a)** Within an ocean basin, in what direction do cold currents flow? **(b)** Describe the location and direction of flow of the Labrador Current. **(c)** Name and locate two other cold currents.

6. **(a)** What are countercurrents? **(b)** Describe the location and origin of the Equatorial Countercurrents. **(c)** Locate and describe the Cromwell Current.

Map Skills

Questions 1–3 refer to the map of world ocean currents on page 590 in the Appendix.

1. Where is the Gulf Stream?

2. How does the place where the Gulf Stream begins affect the temperature of the water that the Gulf Stream carries?

3. What current in the South Atlantic Ocean is most like the Gulf Stream? Explain your answer.

II Currents under the Surface

OBJECTIVES

A Discuss ways in which density currents begin and explain why they are important.

B Describe how upwelling occurs and explain why upwelling is important.

Topic 7 Density Currents

In addition to the horizontal currents moving in the world's oceans, vertical currents also occur. Turbidity currents (Chapter 18, Topic 6) are an example. In these currents, sand, silt, clay, and other particles mix with water to form dense water masses that sweep down the continental slopes to the abyssal plains.

Turbidity currents are one form of density current. **Density currents** result when water in an area of the ocean has become more dense than the water around it. The denser water moves beneath the less dense water and forms a density current. Evaporation, cooling, and freezing are other common causes of dense water that can lead to density currents.

Evaporation affects the density of sea water in warm, dry climates. When sea water evaporates, the salt in the water is left behind. The result is an increase in the salinity of the remaining water. As salinity increases, the density of the sea water also increases.

Cooling affects sea water in polar regions. Cooling causes sea water to contract, or to take up less space. When water contracts, its particles are crowded more closely together. Closer particle packing leads to higher water density.

Freezing also occurs in polar regions. When sea water freezes, most of the salt is left behind. As with evaporation, this increases the salinity, and thus the density, of the water that remains.

Density currents that result from these three processes are described in Topics 8–10.

Topic 8 Density Currents by Evaporation

A density current formed by evaporation is found in the Mediterranean Sea. Here the hot, dry climate evaporates far more water than the Mediterranean receives from either rainfall or rivers. This leaves the waters of the Mediterranean Sea with a higher salinity, and thus a higher density, than average ocean water.

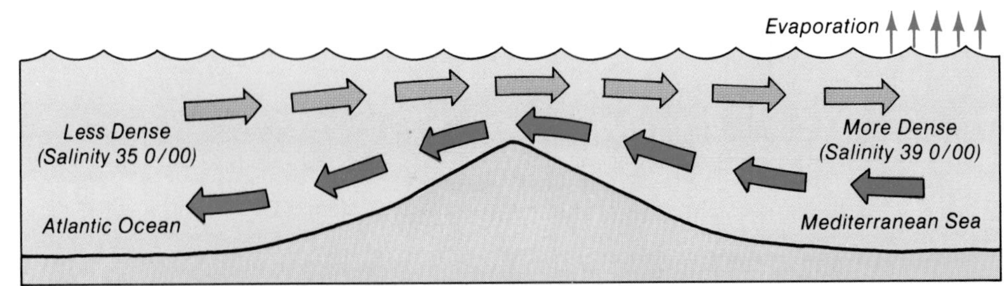

19.5 The denser Mediterranean Sea water flows out of the Mediterranean and down the slope of the Atlantic Ocean. The water is replaced by the less dense Atlantic water.

The Mediterranean Sea and the Atlantic Ocean are connected by the narrow Strait of Gibraltar. On the Atlantic side of the strait, the water salinity is about 35‰. On the Mediterranean side, the salinity is much higher—about 40‰. A two-way flow of water results. The heavy, dense Mediterranean water flows along the bottom of the Mediterranean Sea, over the sill of the Strait of Gibraltar, and into the Atlantic Ocean (Figure 19.5). Less dense Atlantic Ocean water pours into the Mediterranean, over the denser water.

Outside the strait, the dense Mediterranean water sinks in the Atlantic to a depth of 1000 meters. (The floor of the strait is about 275 meters below sea level. The water on both sides of the strait is much deeper.) Dense Mediterranean water forms a stream many times larger than the Mississippi River. Branches of Mediterranean water have been traced to Greenland and Bermuda.

Topic 9 Density Currents from Polar Water

The most dense water in the oceans comes from polar regions because of the intense cooling and freezing that occur there. Three great density currents form in the polar regions. They are Antarctic Bottom Water, North Atlantic Deep Water, and Antarctic Intermediate Water.

Antarctic Bottom Water is the coldest, most dense water in the oceans. This water is produced in large amount in the Weddell and Ross Seas off the coast of Antarctica, especially during winter months. At the time of formation, this water has a temperature of −1.9°C and a salinity of 34.6‰. The water sinks to the ocean floor and spreads northward across the equator to about latitude 40° N. Antarctic Bottom Water is the deepest water in the three major ocean basins.

North Atlantic Deep Water has the second highest density of sea water. This water is believed to form near Greenland by the mixing of higher-salinity Gulf Stream water with cold water from near the Arctic Ocean. The water has a temperature as low as 3°C and a salinity of about 34.5‰. North Atlantic Deep Water is less dense

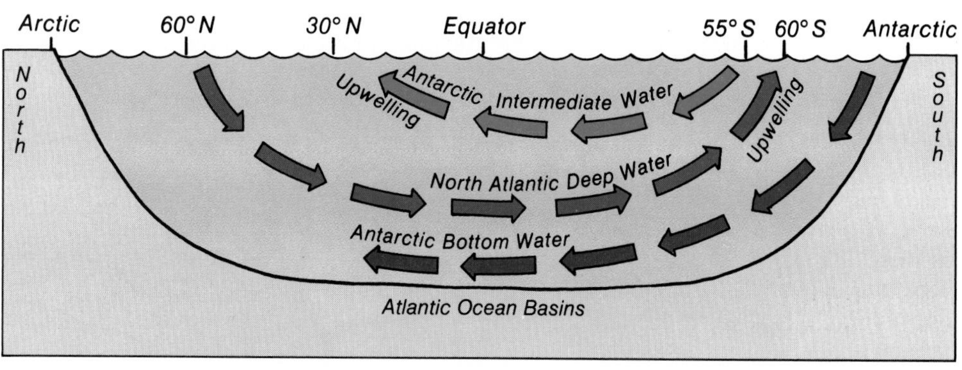

19.6 The arrows show the cold Atlantic subsurface currents that flow from near polar regions.

than Antarctic Bottom Water and thus flows above it. It spreads through the Atlantic to about latitude 60° S, where some returns to the surface. North Atlantic Deep Water also flows west to form deep water in the Indian and Pacific Oceans.

Antarctic Intermediate Water forms at about latitude 55° S. This water has a temperature of 2.2°C and a salinity of 33.8‰. These properties make it the least dense of the three polar currents. Antarctic Intermediate Water spreads northward to about latitude 30° N at a depth of 700 to 800 meters.

Deep currents move very slowly in comparison with surface currents. Despite their slow movements, deep currents are important to animals of the deep ocean. Each current carries oxygen from the surface as well as the temperature, salinity, and density it took on there. Deep currents are the only source of oxygen for life in the deep sea. Without them, there might be no life in the deep sea.

Topic 10 **Upwelling**

Upwelling is another kind of vertical current in the oceans. **Upwelling** occurs when cold deep water comes to the surface. Although upwelling can occur anywhere, it is most common on the western sides of continents. The coast of California is a good example. Upwelling there is caused by wind. The major winds blow toward the south, parallel to the coastline. These winds, together with the effect of Earth's rotation, push the surface water away from the coast. Cold water rises to replace the surface water that has been moved out to sea. Other locations for upwelling of this type are Morocco, southwestern Africa, Peru, and western Australia.

Another kind of upwelling occurs in the Antarctic Ocean at about latitude 60° S. Here the North Atlantic Deep Water returns to the surface. Upwelling in this area has two causes. One cause is winds. Two major wind belts are blowing on either side of this latitude; one wind blows toward the east, the other toward the west. Surface water is pushed away because of the winds, and deeper water upwells. The other cause of upwelling in this area is density currents. Both Antarctic Bottom Water and Antarctic Intermediate Water are sinking nearby. The North Atlantic Deep Water upwells to replace the water that has moved away.

Why is upwelling important? Upwelling water contains large amounts of plant nutrients (phosphates, silicates, nitrates) that

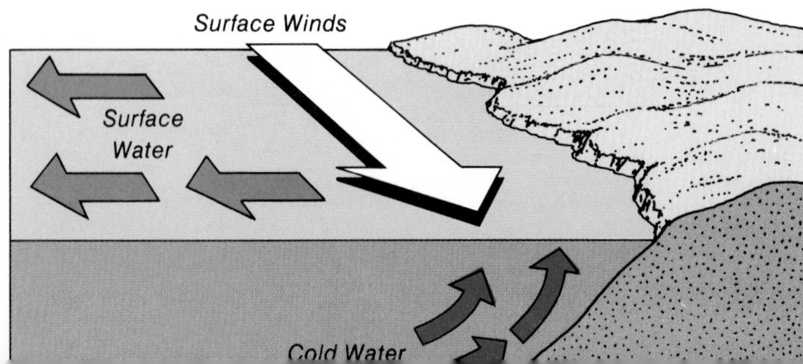

19.7 The remains of fish and plants sink to the bottom of the ocean. Their remains are full of nutrients that plankton need to grow. Upwelling returns these nutrients to the surface. Plankton abound in such areas, and form the base of a large food chain.

phytoplankton need in order to grow. Phytoplankton, the basic food of other living things in the ocean, thrive in areas of upwelling. Animals higher in the food chain live with the phytoplankton in the areas of upwelling. As a result, these areas are usually major commercial fishing areas.

TOPIC QUESTIONS

Each topic question refers to the topic of the same number.

7. **(a)** What is a density current? **(b)** List three ways in which the density of sea water can increase and explain why each occurs.
8. **(a)** Why is water of the Mediterranean Sea more dense than the water of the Atlantic Ocean? **(b)** Describe the two-way water movement through the Strait of Gibraltar.
9. **(a)** What is Antarctic Bottom Water? **(b)** Where and how is North Atlantic Deep Water thought to form? **(c)** Where does Antarctic Intermediate Water form and where does it flow? **(d)** Why are deep ocean currents important to deep-sea life?
10. **(a)** What is upwelling? **(b)** Describe how upwelling occurs near California. **(c)** What two factors contribute to the upwelling of North Atlantic Deep Water at Antarctica? **(d)** Why is upwelling important?

Dr. Taro Takahashi
Chemical Oceanographer

One aspect of oceanography that makes its study so important is the continual exchange of gases between oceans and atmosphere. One of these gases is carbon dioxide. Dr. Taro Takahashi studied that exchange carefully during a cruise that covered the entire Atlantic Ocean between Greenland and Antarctica.

Carbon dioxide dissolves readily in sea water and is easily moved throughout the ocean by currents. For several years the amount of carbon dioxide in the atmosphere has been steadily increasing. Dr. Takahashi points out that the rate of increase has not been as great as would be expected. Based upon his studies, he has proposed that the reason is because the oceans have been absorbing some of the extra carbon dioxide.

Many scientists think that the carbon dioxide concentration of the atmosphere is a major control of Earth's climate. If so, Dr. Takahashi's discovery indicates that the oceans play a different and more important role in world climate than had been realized.

Dr. Takahashi has degrees from the University of Tokyo and Columbia University. He is presently Associate Director of Columbia University's Lamont-Doherty Geological Observatory in Palisades, New York.

CHAPTER 19 REVIEW

Summary

An ocean current is any continuous flow of water along a definite path in an ocean.

Ocean currents move clockwise around Northern Hemisphere ocean basins, and counterclockwise around Southern Hemisphere ocean basins.

The western sides of ocean basins have warm currents moving away from the equator. The eastern sides have cool currents moving toward the equator.

Winds are the driving force for surface ocean currents. The trade winds push the equatorial part of each current circle; the westerly winds push the polar part.

The Gulf Stream is a warm, narrow, intense current in the North Atlantic Ocean. It carries a mild climate with it.

Rings form from eddies in the Gulf Stream. Cold-core rings are found on the ocean side of the Gulf Stream, and warm-core rings are found on the continent side.

The Labrador Current carries icebergs to the North Atlantic Ocean.

Countercurrents flow in the opposite direction of wind-related currents. Countercurrents occur both at the surface and beneath the surface of the ocean.

The density current that flows from the Mediterranean Sea is the result of evaporation.

Density currents that form in polar regions are caused by the cooling and freezing of sea water.

Upwelling occurs where cold currents rise to the surface. Upwelling brings nutrients that support food chains at the surface.

Vocabulary

countercurrent
density current
ocean current
upwelling

Review

Choose the best answer for each question.

1. In which pair of ocean basins do current circles move clockwise? (a) North Atlantic and North Pacific (b) North Pacific and South Pacific (c) South Pacific and South Atlantic (d) South Atlantic and North Atlantic
2. The western sides of ocean basins have (a) cold currents flowing toward the equator, (b) cold currents flowing away from the equator, (c) warm currents flowing away from the equator, (d) warm currents flowing toward the equator.
3. Which current do the trade winds directly affect? (a) Cromwell (b) West-Wind Drift (c) North Equatorial (d) Labrador
4. An example of a warm ocean current is (a) California, (b) East Greenland, (c) Peru, (d) Gulf Stream.
5. In which ocean is the Sargasso Sea located? (a) North Atlantic (b) South Atlantic (c) North Pacific (d) South Pacific
6. Eddies in the Gulf Stream may break off to form (a) rings, (b) countercurrents, (c) upwelling, (d) deep currents.
7. An example of a countercurrent is the (a) South Equatorial, (b) West-Wind Drift, (c) Canary Current, (d) Cromwell Current.
8. Which would NOT cause a density current? (a) trade winds (b) evaporation (c) freezing (d) cooling
9. The density current flowing from the Mediterranean Sea is the result of (a) rainfall, (b) freezing, (c) cooling, (d) evaporation.
10. The salinity of oceans in polar regions is increased by the (a) melting of ice, (b) freezing of water, (c) arrival of warm currents, (d) heavy yearly snowfall.
11. Deep currents are important to life in the deep sea because they (a) carry carbon dioxide to deep water, (b) carry oxygen to deep water, (c) carry carbon dioxide back to the surface, (d) carry oxygen back to the surface.

12. Which is true of upwelling? (a) It occurs only near Antarctica. (b) It is caused by evaporation. (c) It brings nutrients to the surface. (d) It forms cold-core rings.

Interpret and Apply

On your paper, answer each question in complete sentences.

1. If you were standing on the west coast of a continent in the Southern Hemisphere, what kind of ocean current would you expect off-shore? In what direction would the current be flowing?
2. In the Southern Hemisphere, the West-Wind Drift goes completely around the world from west to east. In the Northern Hemisphere it does not. Why is this true?
3. How does the temperature of a south-flowing current in the Northern Hemisphere compare to the temperature of a south-flowing current in the Southern Hemisphere?
4. Laguna Beach, California, and Myrtle Beach, South Carolina, are at nearly the same latitude. How would the water temperature at the two beaches be different? Explain.
5. The Cromwell Current moves 40 million cubic meters of water each second. How does the flow in the Gulf Stream compare to the flow of the Cromwell Current?
6. How are the processes of freezing and evaporation similar in the way they make sea water more dense?
7. Topic 8 states that Mediterranean water entering the Atlantic Ocean sinks to a depth of 1000 meters. At that location, the Atlantic Ocean is 3000 meters deep. Why would Mediterranean water sink only to 1000 meters?

Critical Thinking

The graph shows how the average speed of a deep current in the western Atlantic Ocean changes with height above the seafloor. The horizontal axis of the graph shows the average current speed in centimeters per second. The vertical axis shows height above the seafloor in meters. Refer to the graph to answer questions 1–5.

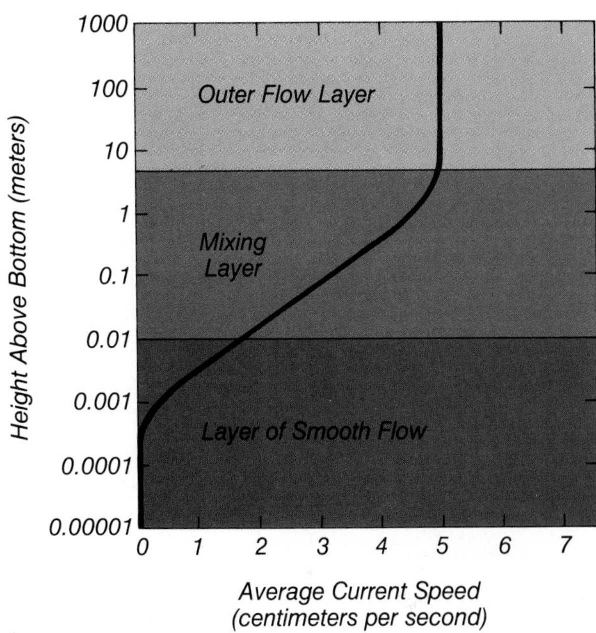

1. (a) Determine the thickness, in meters, of the mixing layer and the layer of smooth flow. (b) How many times thicker is the mixing layer than the layer of smooth flow?
2. (a) What is the average current speed at 1 m above the seafloor? (b) What is the speed at 0.01 m above the seafloor?
3. In which layer is current speed constant with height above the seafloor?
4. Why is current speed nearly zero at the bottom of the graph?
5. The mixing layer is where seawater properties (salinity, temperature, sediment content, etc.) become thoroughly mixed together. If a deep-sea storm causes the speed of the current to increase, what is likely to happen to the thickness of the mixing layer? (Recall the effect of speed on sediment transport from Chapter 10.)

UNIT FIVE
Earth and the Universe

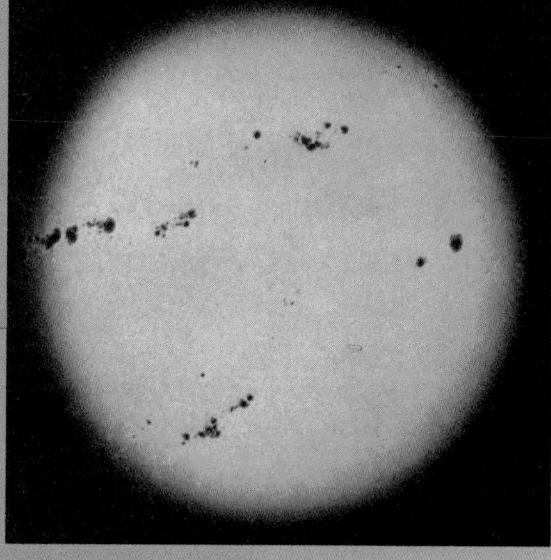

▲ Every eleven years or so, dark spots speckle the sun's surface. During times in between, such spots are few. Why do the spots appear? What are they?

◀ Effort and determination brought humans into space and to the moon. Will people visit a planet next?

Throughout time, people have sought to explain the moon's relationship to Earth. Where did the moon come from? Does it have any effect on Earth? ▶

What's out there?

Few people have been outside Earth's atmosphere. Fewer still have left Earth orbit. Yet astronomers know a great deal about the solar system, the galaxy, and the universe beyond. How can we know so much about places that no one has visited? Look at the photographs. What does each show about the search for knowledge about the universe?

For three hundred years, scientists thought Saturn's rings might be solid disks. How were scientists able to prove otherwise?
▼

▲
The Whirlpool galaxy contains millions of stars. What clues about the origin of the universe do galaxies provide?

▲
Astronomers look at the sky with telescope eyes and listen to it with radio ears. What have they seen and heard in signals from space?

▲
Before computers, devices such as this were used to find the time of sunrise and sunset. Why does the length of a day change throughout a year?

CHAPTER

20 Studying the Universe

▲ This star exploded thousands of years ago.

How Do You Know That . . .

The stars are really as you see them? When you look at the stars, you are really looking at the past. About 170 000 years ago this star exploded, but no one on Earth knew about it until 1987. It took 170 000 years for the light from the explosion to travel to Earth. Energy from distant objects in space provides astronomers with clues about how the universe changes. Telescopes gather these clues and help astronomers learn about the past, present, and possible future of the ever-changing universe.

I Optical Telescopes

Topic 1 The Functions of a Telescope

Stars are seen best on nights with no clouds and no moon and at a place well away from the lights of cities. Under these conditions the sky becomes a breathtaking sight of thousands of stars. What can be seen, however, is only a small number of the stars in the sky. When powerful telescopes are used, billions of stars are visible.

Telescopes help astronomers in three basic ways. First, telescopes collect far more light than the unaided eye can gather. Second, telescopes enable astronomers to visually separate distant objects from one another. Often, for example, astronomers find that what appears to be a single star is really two or more stars. Lastly, telescopes magnify the images they form.

The best locations for optical telescopes are on mountain peaks in dry climates. Thinner air at high elevations and dry, clear skies make observing easier. Because city lights overpower starlight, many observatories are located in remote areas.

OBJECTIVES

A Describe the functions of an optical telescope.

B Describe the relationship between the diameter of a lens or mirror and its ability to gather starlight.

C Name, describe, and locate an example of each kind of optical telescope.

D Discuss the reasons why refractors are less common than reflectors.

E Identify some devices used to improve the image obtained by optical telescopes.

Topic 2 Telescopes and Domes

The earliest telescopes and the ones most used today are optical telescopes. **Optical telescopes** use lenses or mirrors to gather and focus starlight. The light-gathering power of a telescope depends on the area of its lens or mirror. Most lenses or mirrors are circular in shape. The area of a circle varies with the square of its radius. That is, the area of a circle equals πr^2 ($A = \pi r^2$). Doubling the radius of a lens or mirror increases its light-gathering power four times.

Optical telescopes are usually kept in buildings with domed roofs that can be opened for a clear view of the sky. Keeping a telescope in a dome does more than protect it from the weather. Temperature changes, such as those that occur at nightfall, cause the glass of the telescope's lens or mirror to expand or contract. While this is occurring, the image made by the lens or mirror does not focus clearly. Temperature changes around the telescope also lead to air turbulence, another cause of blurred images. Observing time is lost while the telescope adjusts to the new temperature. With a dome the telescope can be kept closer to the nighttime temperature even during the day. It is ready to use as soon as the dome opens.

Telescopes are usually designed such that they can be pointed toward all parts of the sky. This makes it possible to study any

20.1 Telescopes are usually kept in buildings with dome-shaped roofs.

object above the horizon. Few objects, however, remain in the same place in the sky all night. Earth's rotation causes the stars to appear to rise and set, just as the sun appears to rise and set. In order to stay pointed at the same star, a telescope must be able to move at the same rate Earth turns. Its dome must also move. Furthermore, movements must be so smooth that the image is not blurred. The location and design of a telescope and its dome are a major engineering project.

Topic 3 The Refracting Telescope

The simplest **refracting telescope**, or *refractor*, has two lenses. The *objective lens*, located at the front of the tube, is the larger of the two. The objective lens gathers starlight and bends, or refracts, the rays of light to form an image at the rear of the tube. The smaller eyepiece lens magnifies this image for the observer. The objective lens is like a magnifying glass that is used to focus the sun's rays on a piece of paper. The bright spot of sunlight on the paper is an image of the sun.

The world's largest refractor is located at the Yerkes Observatory in Williams Bay, Wisconsin. Its objective lens is 102 centimeters in diameter. A smaller refractor (diameter of 89.5 centimeters) is

20.2 (left) In a refracting telescope, light rays are collected and focused by the large objective lens. The image is viewed through the eyepiece. (right) This refracting telescope has one of the world's largest objective lenses—nearly 1 meter in diameter. The telescope is located at the Lick Observatory in California.

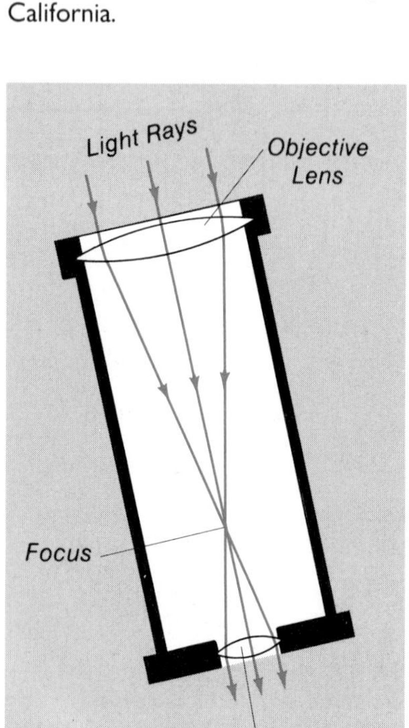

located at the Lick Observatory on Mount Hamilton in southern California.

Almost all major refractors were built before the year 1900. The refractor at the Yerkes Observatory, for example, has been in use since 1897. The refractor at the Lick Observatory has been in use since 1888.

Why aren't large refractors being built today? The primary reason is that telescopes using mirrors are cheaper and easier to build. Why is this the case?

1. Light rays pass through a lens. The glass used to make the lens must be perfect. Mirrors only reflect light, and the glass used does not need to be as pure.
2. Lenses must be ground to a perfectly curved surface on both sides, whereas mirrors need to be ground only on one side.
3. A lens can be supported only at the edges. Over time, a large lens tends to sag under its own weight. This causes the image to blur. A mirror, on the other hand, can be supported over the entire back. It is far less likely to sag and ruin its image.

Topic 4 Single-Mirror Reflectors

The **single-mirror reflecting telescope**, or *single-mirror reflector,* uses one large curved mirror to gather and focus starlight. Like the larger lens of a refracting telescope, this mirror is the objective. The mirror is made of glass or a glasslike substance coated with a thin film of a shiny metal, such as aluminum, to reflect light.

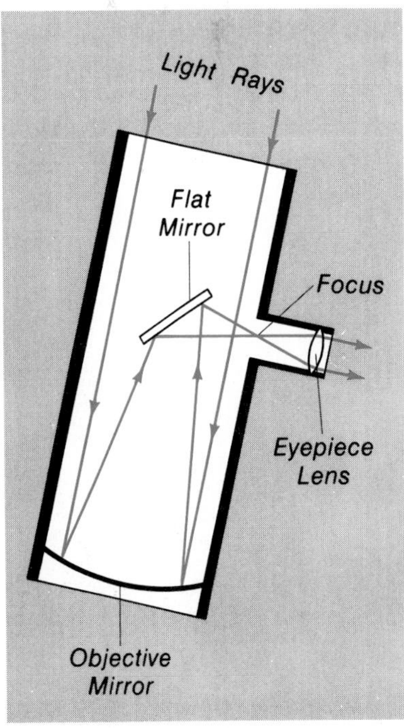

20.3 (left) The Hale reflector at Mount Palomar is one of the largest conventional reflectors in the world. (right) In a reflecting telescope, light passes through the open top of the tube to the bottom, where it is reflected and focused by the large objective mirror. A small flat mirror reflects the light to the eyepiece. Major reflecting telescopes like Hale have openings in the large mirror for use in photography.

The objective mirror is set at the bottom of the telescope tube. When the tube is pointed at a star, a small bright image of the star forms near the top of the tube. This image is reflected to the observer by a smaller mirror. As with the refractor, the observer looks through an eyepiece lens that magnifies the image.

The best-known reflector is the Hale telescope on Palomar Mountain in California. The diameter of its Pyrex mirror is 508 centimeters. It has been in operation since 1948 and, until recently, was the model for all reflecting telescopes built anywhere in the world. Other examples of single-mirror reflectors include a 381-centimeter reflector at Kitt Peak in Arizona and its 400-centimeter twin at Cerro Tololo in Chile. Both were built in the 1970's.

A new method may soon make telescope mirrors much cheaper and easier to form. Until recently telescope mirrors have been made by pouring melted glass into a circular mold. The solid glass disk is then ground down to the proper curve for an objective mirror. The new method is called *spin-casting.* It involves gently rotating the mold as the melted glass is cooling. The rotation pushes some of the molten glass to the outside wall of the mold. When the disk has cooled, its surface is already curved. This method is expected to save months of grinding time. A 350-centimeter spin-cast mirror is planned for a reflector on Apache Point in New Mexico.

Topic 5 Multiple-Mirror Reflectors

The first major change in the design of large telescopes since the building of the Hale reflector came with the development of the **multiple-mirror telescope**, or **MMT**. In this telescope several mirrors take the place of a single large mirror. The image is formed when the light from each of the individual mirrors is combined and focused on a single point. Such telescopes are less expensive to build than a single large-mirror reflector.

20.4 (left) The multiple-mirror telescope at Mount Hopkins, Arizona; (right) In a multiple-mirror telescope, several mirrors reflect light to form one image. Computers assist in keeping each mirror in exactly the right location.

Mirror Segments

Dome

Mirror

Support Structure

The first MMT was built on Mount Hopkins in Arizona in 1979. It consisted of six 180-centimeter mirrors arranged in a ring around a central axis. The six mirrors together had the light-gathering power of a single 450-centimeter mirror. Another MMT, the Keck telescope, is being built on Mauna Kea in Hawaii. Its reflecting surface will be made from 36 6-sided mirrors that fit together closely. A computer will be used to direct each mirror so the light is focused correctly. The total diameter of the multiple mirror is 10 meters, twice the diameter of the single mirror of the Hale telescope.

Several other multiple-mirror telescopes are being planned. The National New Technology Telescope, or NNTT, is to have 4 mirrors, each 7.5 meters in diameter. The 4 mirrors together will have the light-gathering ability of a 15-meter mirror. Each mirror will be able to act alone or combine images with the other three. Another MMT being planned is the Very Large Telescope, or VLT. Its four 8-meter mirrors will be equal to a single 16-meter mirror.

Topic 6 Other Optical Telescopes

Major astronomical observatories have several different kinds of telescopes, each with its own purpose. **Schmidt telescopes** can be found at almost all major observing sites. By using both a reflecting mirror and a refracting lens, these telescopes have an unusually wide field of view. They are used to make wide-angle photographs of the sky. One of the largest Schmidt telescopes in the world is on Palomar Mountain in California.

A telescope can only gather light that reaches it. Earth's atmosphere absorbs and scatters many light waves before they reach any telescope on Earth. In recent years telescopes have been placed in orbit around Earth, above the atmosphere. The *Hubble Space Telescope* is a reflector with a 2.4-meter mirror. When this telescope is placed in orbit (by 1990), it will enable astronomers to see objects 7 times farther away and 50 times fainter than anything visible with telescopes on Earth. The *Hubble Space Telescope* will also detect X rays and gamma rays, which are absorbed by the atmosphere and never reach ground-based observatories.

20.5 The *Hubble Space Telescope* is a reflector designed to orbit high above the interference of Earth's atmosphere. The telescope is about the size of a railroad boxcar. The large fins are solar panels to convert sunlight into electricity for the telescope's electrical system.

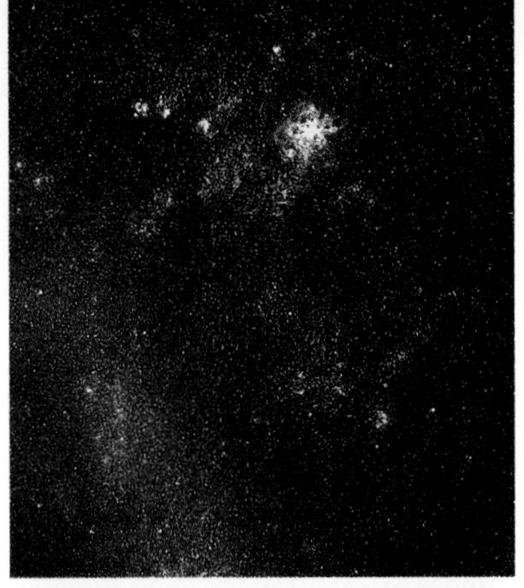

20.6 (top) An image of the Large Magellanic Cloud; (bottom) Much more detail is visible in this image, which was made with the assistance of a charge-coupled device.

Topic 7 **Devices for Improving Images**

A simple telescope enables a viewer to see many more stars than with the eye alone. Photographic plates have been used with telescopes for many years and have proven to be of great value. Photographic film makes it possible to view even more stars. The human eye views incoming light for only a fraction of a second. On film an image can build up over a period of time. Film not only makes it possible to detect stars invisible to the eye but also provides a record that can be studied in the daytime.

Recently an even-better method of collecting data has been developed. The **charge-coupled device**, or **CCD,** is more sensitive to light than photographic film and reacts to a broader range of light rays. A CCD is a group of photocells, which are cells that react to light. Electrons collect where light strikes the cells. The number of electrons that collect on the cells is directly related to the amount of light striking the cell. Periodically the data in each cell are fed to a computer. Astronomers then study the data displayed on computer screens. A CCD can make even a small telescope an important research instrument. A CCD has turned the large Hale telescope into the most powerful optical telescope in the world.

TOPIC QUESTIONS

Each topic question refers to the topic of the same number.

1. **(a)** What are the functions of a telescope? **(b)** Where are optical telescopes best located?
2. **(a)** What is the name for any telescope that uses lenses or mirrors to gather starlight? **(b)** Why does a lens with a 2-cm diameter have 4 times the light-gathering power of a 1-cm lens? **(c)** Why is it important to keep the temperature of a telescope's mirror or lens constant? **(d)** Why must telescopes be able to move at the same rate Earth turns?
3. **(a)** Explain how a refractor works. **(b)** Name two observatories with refractors. **(c)** Explain why refractors are not being built today.
4. **(a)** Explain how a single-mirror reflector works. **(b)** Identify the locations of two major single-mirror reflectors. **(c)** Describe the spin-cast method of making telescope mirrors and the advantages of this method.
5. **(a)** Describe how a multiple-mirror telescope works. **(b)** Identify two multiple-mirror telescopes (present or planned).
6. **(a)** Describe the design and use of a Schmidt telescope. **(b)** What advantages does the *Hubble Space Telescope* have over ground-based telescopes?
7. **(a)** What advantages do observations made with photographic film have over observations made by the human eye? **(b)** What is a charge-coupled device and what does it do?

II Studying Energy Beyond Visible Light

OBJECTIVES

A Identify and compare the wavelengths of the electromagnetic spectrum.

B Discuss the uses and advantages of radio telescopes and radio telescope arrays.

C Identify telescopes used to detect wavelengths other than visible light and radio waves.

Topic 8 The Electromagnetic Spectrum

Optical telescopes are used to study visible light from stars, but not all forms of energy are visible. Stars also emit X rays, radio waves, infrared rays, and other kinds of **electromagnetic energy**. All forms of electromagnetic energy travel through space at a speed of 300 000 kilometers per second, but each has different frequencies and wavelengths. Frequency is the number of waves that pass by a point in a second; wavelength is the distance from the crest of one wave to the crest of the next. Frequency and wavelength are inversely proportional, that is, a low frequency means a long wavelength and a high frequency means a short wavelength. Radio waves have the lowest frequencies and the longest wavelengths, up to several kilometers. Gamma rays have very high frequencies and have wavelengths as short as one millionth of a centimeter. The visible light rays that we see range in wavelength from 0.0004 to 0.0007 millimeters. This range of wavelengths, from radio waves to gamma rays, makes up the **electromagnetic spectrum**.

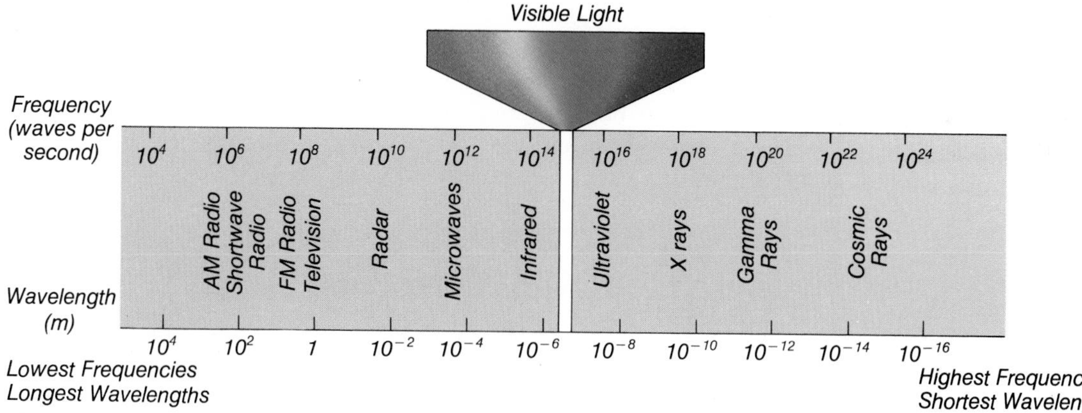

20.7 The electromagnetic spectrum includes heat, light, radio waves, and other forms of energy. Only a small portion of the spectrum is visible light.

Topic 9 Radio Astronomy

Many objects in space send out several kinds of electromagnetic energy. Astronomers study many of these different energies to learn more about the universe. **Radio astronomy** is the study of radio waves from space. Unlike light rays, radio waves can pass through the clouds of fine dust that lie between stars. Radio waves have been detected from the sun and other stars, from some of the planets, from dust clouds within our galaxy, and from other galaxies. More important, radio waves have been received from areas of the sky that appear dark or empty to optical instruments. Some objects can be detected only because of the radio waves they emit.

20.8 The huge radio telescope at Arecibo, Puerto Rico, has a bowl-shaped antenna over 300 meters in diameter. The metal framework above the antenna is the receiver.

In addition to detecting objects that optical telescopes cannot, radio astronomy has other advantages. Radio waves pass unchanged through clouds in the atmosphere. This means radio astronomers can use their instruments when the sky is overcast. Optical astronomers can only observe on clear, cloudless nights. Also, optical astronomers can only work after dark, when stars are visible. Radio wave data can be collected at almost any time, day or night.

Topic 10 The Radio Telescope

Radio telescopes look something like the dishes used to receive television signals from satellites. The curved antenna may be made of solid metal or wire mesh. It collects the radio waves and feeds them to a receiver. The receiver turns the radio waves into electrical signals that produce sound and records the direction, strength, and wavelengths of the signals.

Like an optical telescope, the ability of a radio telescope to gather data depends on its size. Radio waves, however, have much longer wavelengths than visible light rays (Topic 8). As a result, radio antennas must be larger than telescope mirrors. For example, the smallest antenna at the National Radio Astronomy Observatory at Greenbank, West Virginia, is 26 meters in diameter. Remember that the large mirror of the Hale telescope is only 5 meters.

The largest single radio telescope in the world is located in Arecibo, Puerto Rico. Its dish is over 300 meters in diameter and occupies a large natural bowl-shaped area in the ground. The dish cannot be moved or pointed, but the receiver can. This, together with Earth's rotation, makes it possible for the telescope to detect radio signals from a wide area of the sky.

20.9 The Very Large Array radio telescopes near Socorro, New Mexico, work almost as if they were a single telescope with a diameter of 34 kilometers.

Topic 11 Radio Telescope Arrays

The construction of a large radio telescope such as the one at Arecibo is a complicated and expensive task. It is easier to build several small telescopes than a single large one. More important, two small radio telescopes collect data almost as well as if they were a single dish with a diameter equal to the distance between them. For example, two small radio telescopes 100 meters apart act like a single large radio telescope with a 100-meter dish.

Another reason for having more than one radio telescope is the use of **interferometry** to improve the radio image. When two radio telescopes collect data from the same point in space at the same time, the signal that each receives will not be exactly the same. The signals will be slightly "out of phase" and will interfere with each other. This interference between signals can be used to pinpoint locations in the sky with great accuracy—the greater the distance, or **baseline**, between the two radio telescopes the greater the accuracy. Increasing the number of radio telescopes collecting data also improves accuracy.

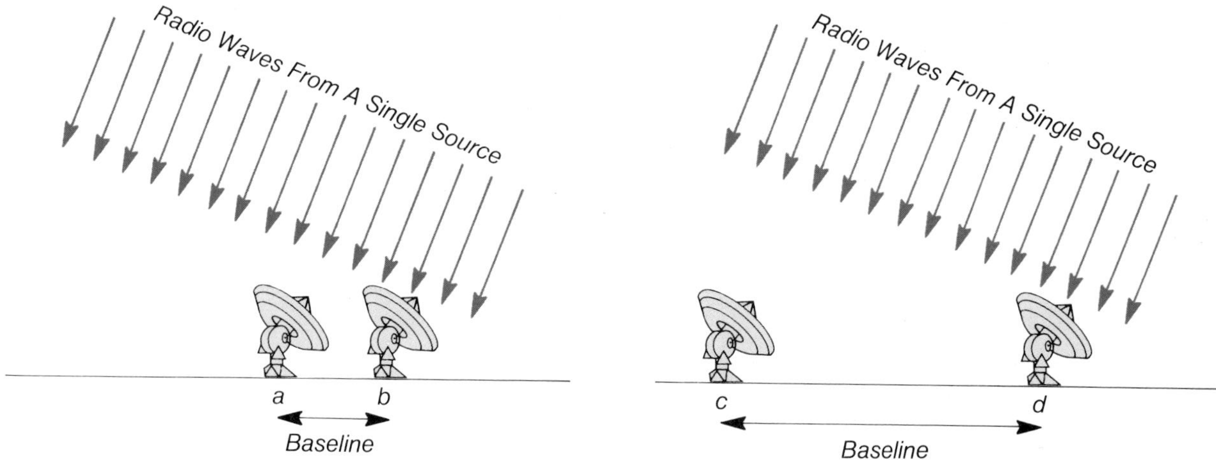

20.10 Two radio telescopes receive signals from the same object, but the signals do not arrive at exactly the same time and thus are out of phase. The greater the distance between telescopes, the more out of phase the signals are, and the more accurately scientists can pinpoint the object giving off signals.

Radio telescopes may be arranged in groups, or **radio telescope arrays**. The Very Large Array, or VLA, in Socorro, New Mexico, consists of 27 antennas each 25 meters in diameter. Together they work like a single antenna with a diameter of 34 kilometers. The Very Long Baseline Array, or VLBA, is even larger. It consists of ten radio telescope antennas located throughout the United States. Its baseline is equal to a single antenna with a diameter of 8000 kilometers. The use of an orbiting radio telescope extends the baseline of VLBA to 1.4 Earth diameters, or about 18 000 kilometers!

Topic 12 Telescopes for Other Wavelengths

Earth's atmosphere makes the study of electromagnetic radiations other than visible light and radio waves very difficult. Most ultraviolet light, X rays, gamma rays, and some infrared wavelengths are absorbed by the atmosphere and do not reach Earth's surface. To collect data on these wavelengths, high-flying aircraft, balloons, rockets, space probes, and even astronauts have been used. The *Infrared Astronomy Satellite,* or *IRAS,* was launched into Earth orbit in 1983. In the ten months it operated, it detected over 250 000 sources of infrared energy including 10 000 previously unknown galaxies. The X-ray satellite, *Exosat,* made over 2000 observations of X-ray sources between 1983 and 1986. Ultraviolet and gamma ray surveys have also been made, and many more surveys are planned.

Some infrared wavelengths can be studied from Earth's surface. Several observatories have infrared telescopes, which are similar to optical telescopes. However, there are two problems to consider when building an infrared telescope. The first is that many infrared wavelengths are absorbed by water vapor in Earth's atmosphere. Because of this, infrared telescopes are placed above the clouds on high mountains. Two infrared telescopes are located on Mauna Kea, Hawaii, an extinct volcano over 4200 meters high. The second

20.11 The *Infrared Astronomy Satellite* was launched early in 1983. It returned data for ten months.

problem is interference from nearby objects. Infrared energy is heat energy. An infrared telescope must be kept very cool. If it is not, it will "see" all of the warm objects around it, including itself and nearby astronomers, and will never be able to detect the weak infrared sources in space. *IRAS* carried liquid helium to cool itself, but only enough to keep it cool for ten months. When the helium ran out, *IRAS* was unable to transmit any more data.

TOPIC QUESTIONS

Each topic question refers to the topic of the same number.

8. **(a)** Identify some forms of electromagnetic energy. **(b)** What property do all forms of electromagnetic radiation have in common? **(c)** How do electromagnetic radiations differ?
9. **(a)** Identify some sources of radio waves from outer space. **(b)** When can radio astronomers collect data? Why?
10. **(a)** How do radio telescopes work? **(b)** Why do radio telescopes have to be much larger than optical telescopes?
11. **(a)** What is the advantage of placing two small radio telescopes 100 meters apart? **(b)** For what purpose is interferometry used? **(c)** Why is the baseline of an array important?
12. **(a)** Why are there no ultraviolet, X-ray, or gamma-ray telescopes on Earth's surface? **(b)** What was *IRAS*? What did astronomers learn from it? **(c)** What was *Exosat*? **(d)** Describe two problems that must be overcome when building an infrared telescope.

Dr. Sidney Wolff
Observatory Director

As director of the Kitt Peak National Observatory in Arizona, Dr. Sidney Wolff rarely gets to use a telescope. Instead, she spends most of her time overseeing a facility that includes seven telescopes, two dormitories, a dining room, an administration building, a machine shop, and a visitor center. All of these things are needed for the seven hundred astronomers who use the Kitt Peak facility annually.

Prior to becoming director of Kitt Peak, Dr. Wolff spent a great deal of time behind the telescope at the University of Hawaii. During her seventeen years there, Dr. Wolff helped to develop the facilities on top of 4300-meter-high Mauna Kea Mountain. It is now the site of the highest astronomical observatory in the world.

How did Dr. Wolff ever become interested in studying the stars? She credits an elementary school spelling lesson on astronomy terms with sparking her interest. Dr. Wolff mastered the spelling and then began to read about the words. She has been reading and studying the heavens ever since.

III A Closer Look at Visible Light

OBJECTIVES

A Describe the visible spectrum and discuss how astronomers use spectroscopes to study stars and planets.

B Name and describe the three types of visible spectra.

C Identify the origin of the red shift in stellar spectra and describe it in terms of the Doppler effect.

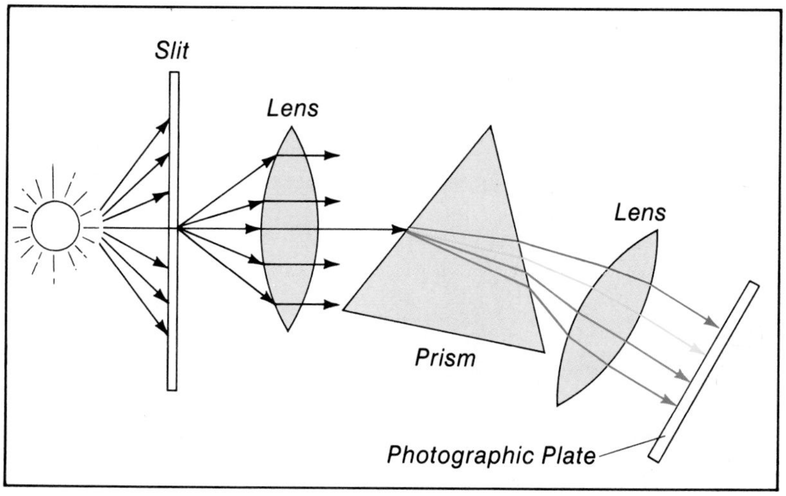

Topic 13 The Spectroscope

Visible light is actually a combination of all colors of light. These are the colors seen in a rainbow or when sunlight passes through a triangular glass prism. Each color has a different wavelength. Red light has the longest wavelength, while violet has the shortest. When light waves pass from air into a glass prism and out again, they are bent, or refracted. Long wavelengths, such as red, are refracted less than short wavelengths, such as violet. The band of colors that forms is called the **visible spectrum**.

Astronomers use the bands of colors from distant stars to learn more about those stars. The tool used to separate starlight into its colors is called a **spectroscope**. It is basically a combination of a prism and a tiny viewing telescope. The prism separates the light it receives into the spectrum of different colors. This spectrum is viewed with the tiny telescope. If the spectrum is to be photographed, the eyepiece of the telescope is replaced with a photographic plate. The instrument is then called a *spectrograph*.

What do astronomers learn from the spectra of stars? For one, the spectra allow astronomers to determine which chemical elements are present in the star's outer layers. Further study of spectra indicates the temperature, pressure, magnetic field, and condition of the gases in the star. Spectra also allow astronomers to learn if the distance between Earth and the star is increasing or decreasing. The study of the spectra of stars and of other objects in the sky is one of the most useful tools that astronomers have for learning about the universe.

Slit

Lens

Lens

Prism

Photographic Plate

20.12 White light can be separated into different colors by a spectroscope. Each color in white light has a different wavelength. As a result each color is refracted a different amount.

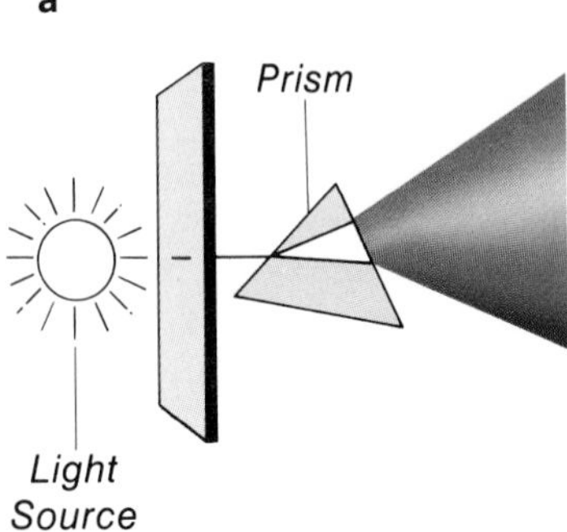

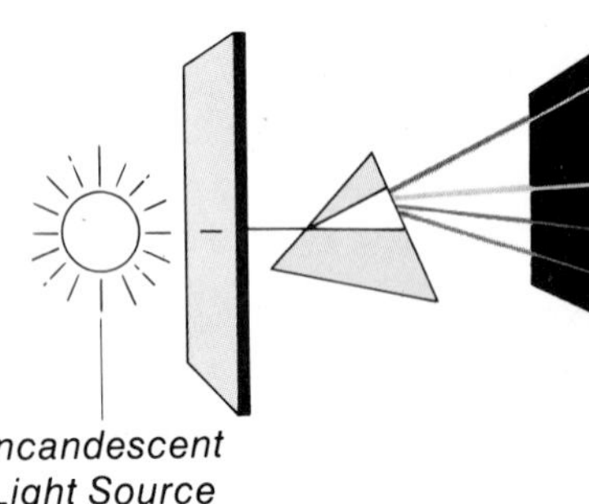

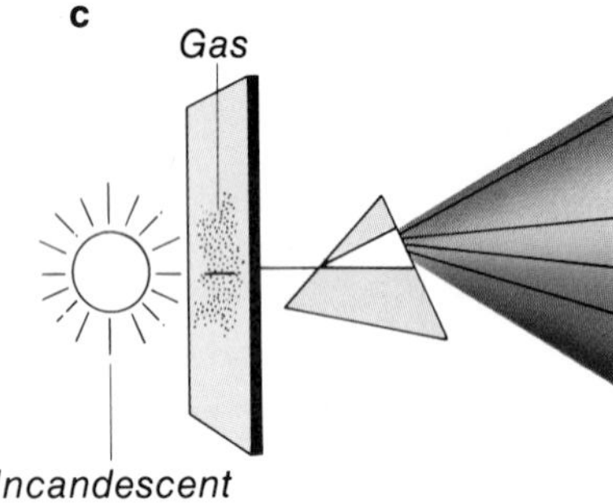

20.13 **(a)** Continuous spectrum, **(b)** bright-line spectrum, **(c)** dark-line spectrum

Topic 14 Kinds of Visible Spectra

Three different types of spectra may be seen in a spectroscope. Each provides information about the source of its light.

A **continuous spectrum** is an unbroken band of colors, which shows that its source is sending out light of all visible wavelengths. Such a spectrum can come from three kinds of materials:

1. a glowing solid, such as the hot filament of an electric light
2. a glowing liquid, such as molten iron
3. the hot, compressed gases deep inside a star

A **bright-line spectrum** is an unevenly spaced series of lines of different colors and brightness. The bright lines show that the source is sending out, or emitting, light in certain wavelengths only. A bright-line spectrum is also called an *emission spectrum.* Bright-line spectra come from chemical elements when they are in the form of a glowing thin gas or vapor. An example is the glowing neon gas in a neon sign. Each element has its own, unique bright-line spectrum. The different wavelengths (seen as colors) appear as bright lines at different places on the spectrum for each element.

A **dark-line spectrum** is a continuous spectrum with dark lines where light is absorbed. The dark lines are in exactly the same place as the bright lines from the same element in a bright-line spectrum. The dark lines form when the light from a continuous spectrum passes through a cooler gas. The gas then absorbs the same wavelengths as it would give off if heated. Since the absorption leaves dark places for these wavelengths in the spectrum, a dark-line spectrum may also be referred to as an *absorption spectrum*. The positions of the dark lines are used to identify the element.

Topic 15 Dark-Line Spectra and the Solar System

A dark-line spectrum from a star or planet shows the composition of the star's outer layer or the planet's atmosphere. The sun's spectrum is a dark-line spectrum. The hot compressed gases of its interior radiate a continuous spectrum. When these radiations pass through the sun's own cooler atmosphere, absorption occurs. As a result the sun's spectrum has thousands of dark lines. When the dark lines are matched with bright-line spectra, the elements in the sun's atmosphere can be identified. More than 80 elements have been identified on the sun. Like the sun, almost all stars form absorption spectra.

20.14 The middle horizontal band is part of the sun's dark-line spectrum. It is being compared with the bright-line spectrum of iron vapor.

Absorption spectra can be used to determine the composition of a planet's atmosphere for the following reason. A planet shines by reflecting sunlight. If the spectrum of a planet shows dark lines that are not found in the sun's spectrum, then they must be caused by substances in the planet's atmosphere.

Topic 16 The Doppler Effect

When the spectrum of a star is compared in a laboratory with the bright-line spectrum of an element, a strange thing is sometimes noted. The black lines of the star's spectrum are shifted to the left or right of the bright lines formed by the element's spectrum as observed in the lab. If the shift is toward the red end of the spectrum, it means that longer wavelengths are coming from the star. If the shift is toward the violet end, it means that shorter wavelengths are coming from the star. Why does the shift occur?

Astronomers explain that these shifts happen because the distance between the star and Earth is increasing or decreasing. If the distance is increasing, the wavelengths the star radiates seem to become longer. This movement causes all of the star's spectral lines to shift toward the red end of the spectrum. The faster the distance between the star and Earth increases, the greater the *red shift* of its spectrum. If a star's spectrum is shifted toward the shorter wavelengths (violet), it means the distance between the star and Earth is decreasing. If a star is moving but the distance is not changing, the spectral lines do not shift.

The principle of the red shift is explained by the **Doppler effect**. It works the same way in sound waves. Think about the sound of a moving train or automobile horn. As it approaches, the wavelengths apparently shorten and the pitch rises. As it recedes, the wavelengths become longer and the pitch becomes lower.

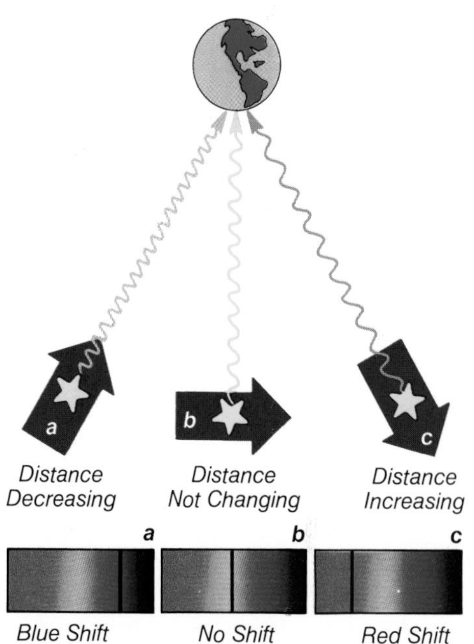

20.15 Stars **a,** **b,** and **c** all emit yellow light. The distance between **a** and Earth is decreasing. The light from **a** appears shifted toward the blue end of the spectrum. Star **b** is moving relative to Earth, but the distance is not changing. The light from **b** has no shift. The distance between **c** and Earth is increasing. The light from **c** is shifted toward red.

TOPIC QUESTIONS

Each topic question refers to the topic of the same number.

13. **(a)** Why does light separate into colors when passing through a glass prism? **(b)** What are the parts of a spectroscope and how are they used? **(c)** What can astronomers learn about stars from their spectra?
14. **(a)** Describe the appearance of each of the three types of spectra. **(b)** How are elements identified from bright-line spectra? **(c)** How are elements identified from dark-line spectra?
15. **(a)** Why does the sun have a dark-line spectrum? **(b)** How does the spectrum of a planet give data about its atmosphere?
16. **(a)** How does a star's spectra appear to be changed if the distance between the star and Earth is decreasing? **(b)** How does a star's spectra appear to be changed if the distance between the star and Earth is increasing? **(c)** Describe how this effect can be heard in sound.

CHAPTER 20 REVIEW

Summary

Telescopes gather more light than the eye, help visually separate objects, and magnify images.

Optical telescopes gather light by means of lenses (refractors) or mirrors (reflectors). Larger lenses or mirrors gather more light.

The image made by an optical telescope is improved by the use of photographic film and the charge-coupled device (CCD).

The electromagnetic spectrum includes radio, infrared, visible, ultraviolet, X-ray, and gamma-ray wavelengths. All electromagnetic energy travels at 300 000 km/s.

Radio telescopes receive and concentrate radio waves from space. Arrays of radio telescopes provide more accurate radio images.

Forms of electromagnetic energy other than light and radio waves are observed with telescopes specially designed to detect them.

Visible light is made of many colors, or wavelengths. Astronomers use spectroscopes to study the colors of visible light from stars.

There are three kinds of spectra: continuous, bright-line, and dark-line. Spectra provide information about the temperature and composition of stars and other objects.

The Doppler effect can be used to determine the movement of a star relative to Earth.

Vocabulary

baseline
bright-line spectrum
charge-coupled device (CCD)
continuous spectrum
dark-line spectrum
Doppler effect
electromagnetic energy
electromagnetic spectrum
interferometry
multiple-mirror telescope (MMT)
optical telescope
radio astronomy
radio telescope array
refracting telescope
Schmidt telescope
single-mirror reflector
spectroscope
visible spectrum

Review

Select the best answer for each item. Write your answer on your paper.

1. Which does a telescope NOT do? (a) speed up the light from distant objects (b) gather more light than the human eye (c) magnify the image (d) show the separation between distant objects
2. Which part of an optical telescope gathers and focuses light? (a) objective lens or mirror (b) eyepiece lens (c) dome (d) telescope tube
3. Compared to a 1-meter lens, what is the light-gathering power of a 2-meter lens? (a) ½ as great (b) 2 times as great (c) ¼ as great (d) 4 times as great
4. Which is true of refracting telescopes? (a) They use mirrors to focus starlight. (b) They are cheaper to build than reflectors. (c) Many are larger than reflectors. (d) Most major ones were built before the year 1900.
5. Which can be made by the process of spin-casting? (a) telescope lenses (b) telescope mirrors (c) radio telescope antenna dish (d) charge-coupled devices
6. Which was the first major change in optical telescope design since the Hale telescope? (a) Schmidt telescope (b) MMT (c) VLA (d) CCD
7. Which is used to make wide-angle sky photographs? (a) Schmidt telescope (b) MMT (c) *Hubble Space Telescope* (d) VLA
8. Which is most sensitive to visible light? (a) human eye (b) photographic plate (c) charge-coupled device (d) Hale's 5-meter telescope mirror
9. Which is NOT true of electromagnetic energy? (a) It includes many wavelengths. (b) Its speed varies with wavelength. (c) Its wavelength varies with its frequency. (d) It includes visible light.
10. Which is observed with optical telescopes? (a) infrared light (b) visible light (c) X rays (d) ultraviolet rays

11. Which is true of radio waves? (a) They can pass through clouds. (b) They can be detected only in daytime. (c) They have very short wavelengths. (d) They cannot be reflected.

12. Why must radio telescopes be larger than optical telescopes? (a) Objects in space emit fewer radio waves than light waves. (b) Radio waves are much longer than optical waves. (c) Static interferes with radio waves. (d) Radio telescopes cannot be moved or pointed.

13. Which is NOT a reason for using radio telescope arrays? (a) Two small radio dishes work almost as well as one large one. (b) It is easier to build several small dishes. (c) Interferometry improves radio images. (d) Radio signals are more in phase when more than one dish is used.

14. Which form of E-M radiation from space can only be detected outside Earth's atmosphere? (a) visible light (b) infrared light (c) ultraviolet waves (d) radio waves

15. Which color of visible light is refracted most by a prism? (a) green (b) red (c) orange (d) violet

16. Which would form a bright-line spectrum? (a) the hot filament of a light bulb (b) a neon sign (c) the sun (d) hot gases deep inside a star

17. What happens to spectral lines from a star when the distance between the star and Earth is increasing? (a) They are unchanged. (b) They shift toward the red end of the visible spectrum. (c) They shift toward the blue end. (d) They become a bright-line spectrum.

Interpret and Apply

On your paper, answer each question in complete sentences.

1. Optical telescopes gather more light than the human eye can. Why is this so?
2. Using math, compare the light-gathering power of a 3-meter reflector with the light-gathering power of the 5-meter Hale telescope and the 4-meter reflector at Cerro Tololo, Chile. Show your calculations.
3. The mirror of the *Hubble Space Telescope* is half the diameter of the mirror of the Hale telescope. How is it that the *Hubble* can gather light from objects 50 times fainter than the faintest object the Hale can detect?
4. How can stars that are invisible to the eye appear on photographs?
5. Why can a radio telescope antenna be made of wire mesh, while an optical telescope needs a smooth, solid lens or mirror?
6. Helium was discovered on the sun 30 years before it was known on Earth. How is this possible?
7. A few stars have bright lines superimposed on their continuous spectra. How can this be explained?
8. Explain why there is no shift in spectral lines of a star moving at right angles to the line of sight.

Critical Thinking

On your paper, answer each item in complete sentences.

1. Assume that you have just been made chairperson of a committee that is to find the best location in the United States for a new astronomical observatory. The observatory will have as many kinds of ground-based telescopes as possible. Make a list of the features that the location should have and explain why each is important.
2. One of the most exciting uses of the Very Large Baseline Array of radio telescopes has been to make very precise measurements of the distances between certain points on Earth's surface. What kinds of information could these measurements reveal about Earth's surface?

CHAPTER

21 Stars and Galaxies

▲ The Big Dipper, part of the constellation Ursa Major

How Do You Know That . . .

Stars change position in the sky? Look at the sky on a clear moonless night. Chart the position of the Big Dipper when darkness falls and again four hours later. Note how its position changes in relation to that of Polaris, the North Star.

Early astronomers noticed how different constellations appeared with the sun at sunrise and sunset through the course of a year. The movement of the sun crossed 12 constellations during this time. Do some library research to find the names of these 12 constellations.

I Stars and Their Characteristics

Topic 1 Constellations

A **constellation** is a group of stars that appears to form a pattern in the sky. A total of 88 different constellations can be seen from the Northern and Southern Hemispheres. The Big Dipper is probably the best-known example. It is actually a part of a much larger constellation known as Ursa Major, or the Big Bear. The dipper can be used to find other constellations. Think of an imaginary line drawn through the two stars on the front of the dipper. This line through the "pointer stars" points to the last star in the handle of the Little Dipper (part of Ursa Minor, the Small Bear). This star is Polaris, or the North Star. At the same distance on the opposite side of the Little Dipper is a large, lopsided M. This is the chair of Queen Cassiopeia (CASS ee o PEE ya).

Ursa Major, Ursa Minor, and Cassiopeia are examples of *circumpolar constellations*. Such constellations never set below the horizon and can be seen all year long. Circumpolar constellations appear to move around Polaris, the star located almost exactly above Earth's North Pole. The number of stars that are seen as circumpolar depends upon the observer's latitude. The farther north the observer lives, the more stars will appear circumpolar.

The apparent movement of the circumpolar constellations is caused by Earth turning on its axis. Earth turns from west to east. As a result the whole sky appears to turn from east to west. That is why the sun, the moon, and the stars are said to rise in the east and set in the west. The part of the sky above Earth's axis, however, does not rise or set. When Earth turns on its axis, Polaris seems stationary in the sky. The stars near Polaris go around in a counterclockwise direction. Their trails can be recorded with ordinary cameras by using time-exposure photography.

Topic 2 Seasonal Changes in Constellations

Although the circumpolar constellations are visible every night, their positions in the sky change with the seasons. The Big Dipper is near the northern horizon in the fall. It is high overhead in the

OBJECTIVES

A Identify and locate some famous constellations and describe their apparent motions in the sky.

B Define and use several units that express distances in space.

C Compare the physical and chemical properties of the sun with those of other stars.

D Discuss the different ways in which star brightness is measured and compare star brightness using these methods.

21.1 The circumpolar stars make circular trails around Polaris on a time-exposure photograph. The brightest trail near the center is Polaris.

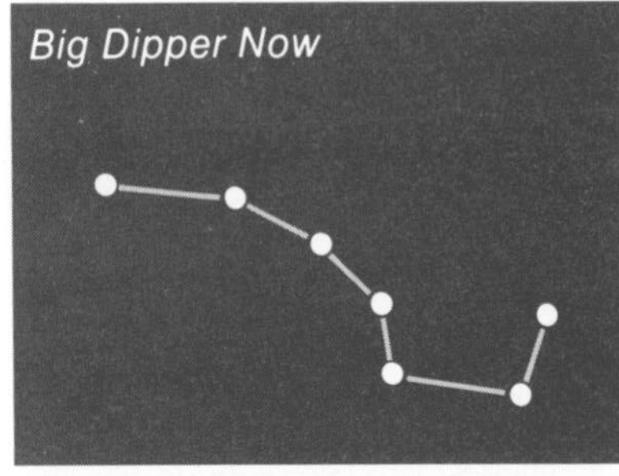

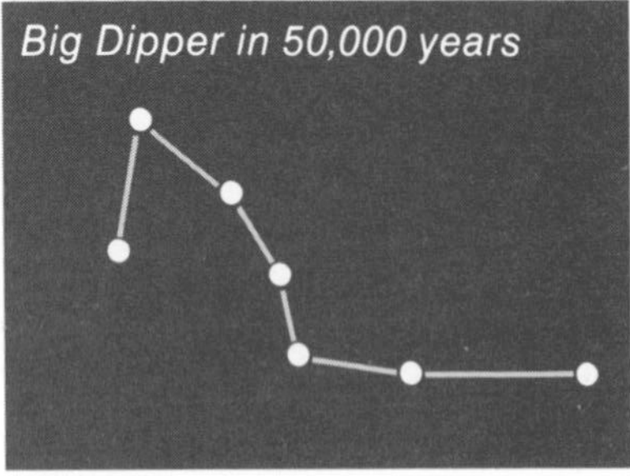

21.2 The Big Dipper will appear quite different 50 000 years from now.

spring. Cassiopeia is nearly straight overhead in the fall but is just above the northern horizon in the spring. These changes are caused by the changing position of Earth in its orbit around the sun.

Of course the stars in most constellations only appear to be together as they are viewed from Earth. Each star is actually moving toward or away from the other stars at high speed. However, because stars are so far away, it takes thousands of years before constellations appear very different. For example, in 50 000 years the Big Dipper will almost reverse its appearance, as shown in Figure 21.2.

Some constellations can be seen only at certain seasons. Constellation maps for all four seasons appear on pages 592–593. In the summer the first three stars that are usually seen in the evening sky form the Summer Triangle. These three stars can be used to locate three different summer constellations. The first star of the triangle to become visible will be Vega (VAY guh) in the small constellation Lyra (LIE ruh), the Lyre or Harp. The second star will be Altair (al TARE) in the constellation Aquila, the Eagle. The third star of the triangle to appear will be Deneb at the top of the Northern Cross. The Northern Cross is part of the constellation Cygnus the Swan.

The most famous winter constellation is Orion the Hunter. Orion contains the red supergiant Betelgeuse (BET el jooz) and the blue supergiant Rigel. The three stars that make up Orion's belt can be used to find two other winter constellations. To the left, the belt points to Sirius, the brightest star in our sky. Sirius is part of the constellation Canis Major, the Large Dog. To the right, Orion's belt points to Taurus the Bull and the famous Pleiades (PLEE uh deez) star cluster.

The change from Orion in winter to Lyra in summer also occurs because of Earth's movement around the sun. Figure 21.3 illustrates the reason. In the wintertime the night side of Earth faces the part of the sky containing Orion and his companions. The winter daytime half of Earth faces Lyra. As a result Orion can be seen at night in the winter, but Lyra is lost in sunlight. Six months later Earth has moved about 180° (halfway around) in its orbit of the sun. In summer the daytime side of Earth faces the part of the sky with Orion. Lyra is easily seen from the summer nighttime side of Earth.

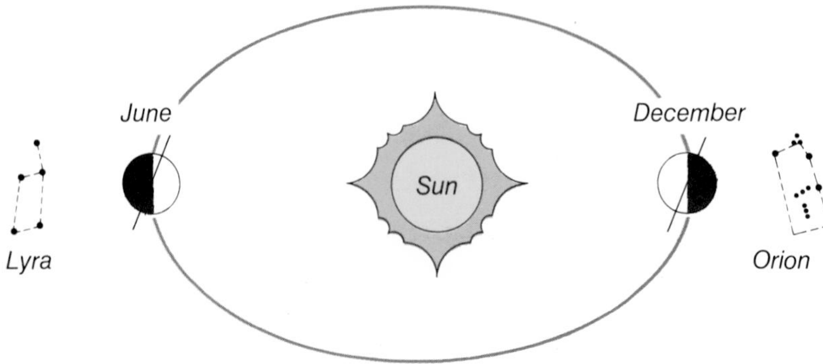

21.3 The constellations visible in different seasons change because of Earth's movement around the sun.

Topic 3 Distances to Stars

The closest star to Earth is, of course, the sun. The average distance between Earth and the sun is about 150 million kilometers. This distance defines one **astronomical unit**, or one **AU**.

How far away is the nearest star? Imagine that Earth is a dot 1 centimeter from the sun. The next nearest star, Alpha Centauri, would be more than 2.5 kilometers away! Alpha Centauri is about 40 trillion (4.0×10^{13}) kilometers away–nearly 300,000 times as far from Earth as is the sun.

Kilometers are not very satisfactory units for expressing the great distances in space. Neither are astonomical units. Instead, astronomers use a unit called a **light-year (LY).** Despite the name, the light-year is a unit of distance and not a unit of time. A light-year is the distance that a ray of light travels in one year. The speed of light is about 300 000 kilometers per second. At this rate light can travel about 9.5 trillion (9.5×10^{12}) kilometers in 1 year. Alpha Centauri is about 4.3 light-years from Earth while Betelgeuse, the red supergiant in Orion, is nearly 490 light-years away.

Topic 4 Physical Properties of Stars

The sun is an average star in many ways. Its diameter is about 1 380 000 kilometers. Its average density is about 1.4 times that of water. Its mass is about 300 000 times that of Earth. How do the other stars in the universe compare with the sun?

Star sizes vary over a great range. The smallest stars may be smaller than Earth. The largest star known is more than 2000 times the diameter of the sun.

Stars differ even more in density. Betelgeuse is one ten-millionth as dense as the sun. Sirius has a neighbor so dense that one teaspoonful of it would weigh more than a ton on Earth!

Stars differ less in mass. Masses larger than 50 times that of the sun are probably very rare. The smallest is about one hundredth the mass of the sun. Most stars are fairly close to the sun in mass.

The color of a star depends on its surface temperature. Betelgeuse is red, the sun is yellow, and Sirius is blue. Hot stars are bluer in color. Cool stars are redder in color. Stars radiate all colors, but hotter stars emit more blue and less red. The same color changes can be seen when an iron bar is heated. As it gets hotter, its color changes from red to orange to yellow to white to blue-white. In stars, red-hot may mean a temperature of only 3000°C at the surface. Stars that are blue-hot may be over 30 000°C. The sun has a surface temperature of about 5500°C.

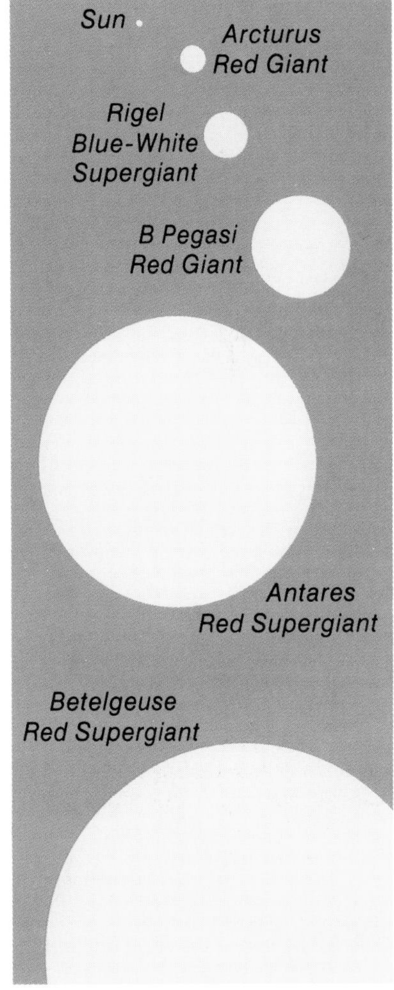

21.4 Notice how tiny the sun is when it is compared to the giants and supergiants.

Topic 5 Elements in Stars

Spectrum analysis helps astronomers determine the composition of stars. Stars are mainly hydrogen and helium. One or two percent of a star's mass may be heavier elements such as iron, titanium,

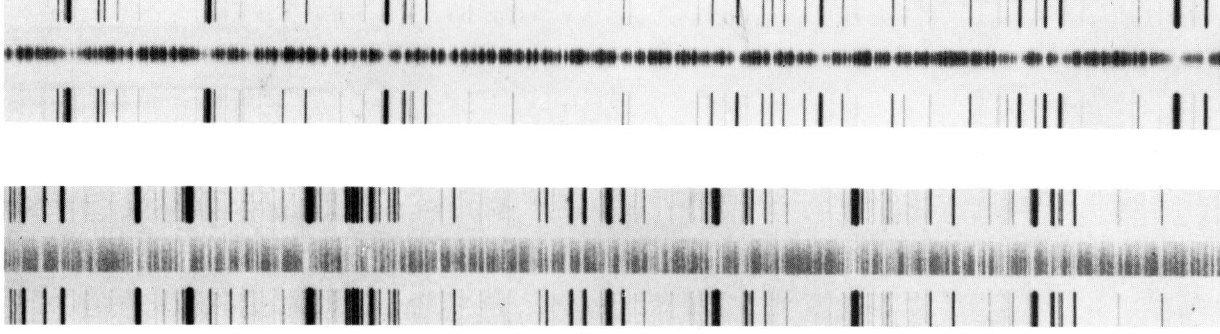

21.5 The spectra of two different stars indicate differences in composition and temperature. Every star has its own unique spectrum.

calcium, sodium, and others. The sun appears to be about 70 percent hydrogen and 28 percent helium. The remaining two percent is heavier elements.

The spectrum radiated by a star depends on both its composition and its temperature. No two stars have exactly the same composition and temperature. Each star has its own individual spectrum.

Topic 6 Star Brightness

Astronomers have several ways of talking about the brightness of a star. One way is the star's **apparent magnitude**. The apparent magnitude is how bright the star appears to an observer on Earth. The brighter stars are first-magnitude stars. The faintest stars that can be seen with the unaided eye are sixth magnitude.

In the star-magnitude system, each magnitude differs from the next by a factor of approximately 2.5. This means that a first-magnitude star is 2.5 times brighter than a second-magnitude star. A second-magnitude star is 2.5 times brighter than a third magnitude star, and so on. A first-magnitude star is 100 times brighter than a sixth-magnitude star (2.5 x 2.5 x 2.5 x 2.5 x 2.5). The apparent magnitudes of stars brighter than first magnitude are expressed as values less than 1.0, such as 0 magnitude. Some stars are even brighter than 0 magnitude and have negative values. For example, Sirius, the brightest star in our sky, has an apparent magnitude of −1.43.

Apparent magnitudes are also used to express the apparent brightness of the planets. At their brightest, Venus, Mars, and Jupiter are brighter than any star. Their brightest apparent magnitudes are −4.4, −2.5, and −2.8, respectively.

Apparent magnitude indicates how bright the star appears to us. It does not tell how bright the star actually is. For example, the apparent magnitude of Sirius is about 10 times brighter than that of Antares. Yet Antares is actually about 250 times brighter than Sirius. Antares is much farther away from Earth than Sirius. The actual or true brightness of a star is its **luminosity**.

The luminosity of a star depends only upon its size and temperature. Apparent magnitude also depends upon a star's distance from Earth. Consider this example. Viewed from the same distance away, a 100-watt light bulb is much brighter than a flashlight bulb. The 100-watt bulb has greater luminosity. However, the flashlight bulb up close would look brighter than the 100-watt bulb a kilometer away. Under those conditions the apparent magnitude of the flashlight is greater than that of the 100-watt bulb.

How do astronomers express the true brightness or luminosity of a star? If all stars could be placed at the same distance from Earth, their true brightness could be compared. Astronomers use the term **absolute magnitude** to express the luminosity of stars as if they were seen from the same distance. Absolute magnitude is the apparent magnitude a star would have if placed at a distance of 32.6 light-years from the sun. The sun is an average star. Its absolute magnitude is 4.8. By contrast, a very bright star such as Rigel in Orion has an absolute magnitude of −6.4.

TOPIC QUESTIONS

Each topic question refers to the topic of the same number.

1. **(a)** What is a constellation? **(b)** What are circumpolar constellations? Give examples. **(c)** Describe and explain the apparent motions of the stars in our sky.
2. **(a)** Name some constellations that can be seen in summer. **(b)** Identify some constellations that can be seen in winter. **(c)** Explain why the constellations that are visible change with the seasons. **(d)** Why will the shapes of constellations be different in the future?
3. **(a)** What is an astronomical unit? How many kilometers equal an astronomical unit? **(b)** Name the star nearest the sun. How far away is this star? **(c)** What is a light-year? How many kilometers equals a light-year?
4. **(a)** What are the sun's diameter, density, and mass? **(b)** Describe how stars vary in size, density, and mass. **(c)** How is the color of a star related to its temperature? Give examples.
5. **(a)** What are the two most abundant elements in stars? **(b)** Identify two factors that determine the spectrum of a star.
6. **(a)** What does apparent magnitude tell about a star? **(b)** How is apparent magnitude written for stars brighter than first magnitude? Give an example. **(c)** What is luminosity? **(d)** What is absolute magnitude? **(e)** Compare the apparent magnitudes, absolute magnitudes, and luminosities of the sun and Rigel.

Map Skills

Use the constellation maps on pages 592–593 to answer these questions. Write your answers on your paper.

1. Locate the Big Dipper in all four seasonal maps. How does the position of the Big Dipper change during the year?
2. Look at the constellations that surround the Big Dipper in each season. Compared to the Big Dipper, do the positions of these constellations change throughout the year?
3. Based on your answers to questions 1 and 2, do stars change position throughout the year when compared to each other?

OBJECTIVES

A Define and describe the properties of giant, supergiant, and dwarf stars and give examples of each.

B Name and describe the kinds of variable stars.

C Discuss the characteristics of pulsars.

II Kinds of Stars

Topic 7 Giants, Supergiants, and Dwarfs

Sirius and Vega are hot blue-white stars. They are highly luminous. However, the cooler red stars Aldebaran and Arcturus are even more luminous because they are so huge. Astronomers call Aldebaran and Arcturus **red giants**.

Some stars are hundreds of times more luminous than the red giants. These stars are **supergiants**. They include blue-white Rigel, white-yellow Canopus, and the red supergiants Antares and Betelgeuse. Again, the red supergiants must be much larger than the blue or white ones to be equally luminous. Red supergiants are the largest of all stars.

Less luminous stars are **dwarf stars**. These stars have an absolute magnitude no brighter than 1. Most dwarfs are red, orange, or yellow. One exception is white dwarfs. *White dwarfs* are very faint, very small, and very dense. The density of white dwarfs is due to tight packing of their atomic nuclei. A typical white dwarf is about as large as Earth, but over 100 000 times more dense.

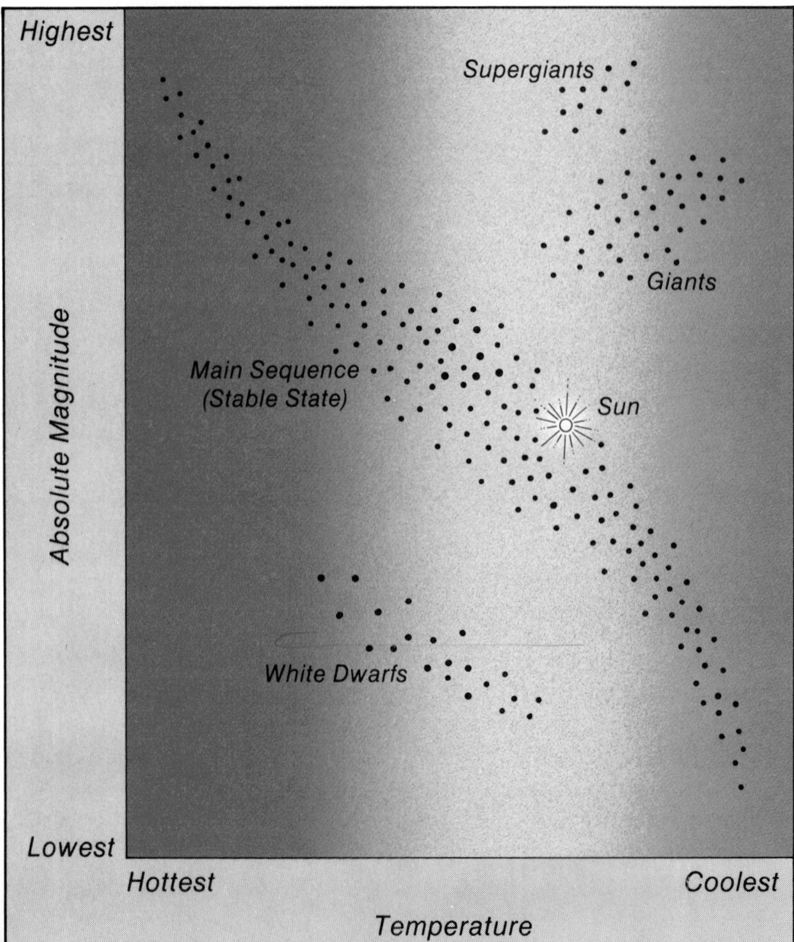

21.6 The diagram shows how the absolute magnitude of a star depends on the star's temperature. If cooler red stars are large enough, they can be as bright as smaller blue stars.

Topic 8 **Variable Stars**

Most stars shine with a steady brightness. Some stars, however, vary in brightness over regular periods or cycles that take from days to years. Such stars are **variable stars**. There are different kinds of variable stars.

Stars that change in brightness as they expand and contract are *pulsating stars.* Contraction causes pulsating stars to become hotter and brighter. Expansion makes them cooler and dimmer. An important example of pulsating stars are the **cepheid** (SEE fee id) **variables**, or *cepheids,* first discovered in the constellation Cepheus. Cepheid variables are yellow supergiants whose bright-dim-bright periods range from about 1 day to 50 days. Most have periods of about five days.

Astronomers have found that the true brightness of a cepheid is related to the time of its bright-dim-bright period. The longer and slower the bright-dim-bright period, the greater the absolute magnitude of the star. Astronomers have worked out the absolute magnitude a cepheid will have for any bright-dim-bright period. Then by comparing a cepheid's apparent and absolute magnitudes, the distance from Earth to the cepheid can be determined. In this way astronomers can calculate the distance to most galaxies in which there is a cepheid.

A nonpulsating star may change in brightness because it is not one star but is two stars of unequal brightness. The two stars revolve around each other. As they do, the dim star eclipses (passes in front of) the bright star. Then the bright star eclipses the dim star. This occurs at regular intervals as seen from Earth. Together, these two stars are called an **eclipsing binary**. The best-known eclipsing binary is the second-magnitude star Algol and its dim companion, in the constellation Perseus. Algol is eclipsed to about one third its normal brightness every 69 hours.

Topic 9 **Pulsars**

In 1967, astronomers discovered strange new objects that gave off powerful bursts of radio waves every second or less. One source of the radio-wave bursts was the Crab Nebula. Astronomers looked closely at the Crab Nebula. They discovered that a very faint star in the nebula was flickering in time with the radio pulses. Apparently both light and radio waves were coming from this star. Astronomers called this star a **pulsar**. They think this star is the remaining core of a neutron star left by the star that became a supernova and produced the Crab Nebula.

Hundreds of pulsars are now known. All pulsars are believed to be neutron stars formed in supernovas. Astronomers think that the radio pulses occur because pulsars are rotating very rapidly. As a pulsar rotates, a beam of radiation is emitted along its magnetic axis and sweeps through space like a searchlight. If Earth is in line with this beam, the pulses can be observed. One pulsar, the fastest yet discovered, pulses 642 times a second!

21.7 The Crab Nebula is a source of radio waves.

TOPIC QUESTIONS

Each topic question refers to the topic of the same number.

7. **(a)** What is a red giant? Give examples. **(b)** How are supergiant stars different from red giant stars? Give examples of supergiants. **(c)** How is a dwarf star defined? **(d)** What is a white dwarf? Why are they so dense?
8. **(a)** What are variable stars? **(b)** What is a pulsating star? **(c)** Why are cepheid variables of great importance to astronomy? **(d)** What is an eclipsing binary? Name an example.
9. **(a)** How was the pulsar in the Crab Nebula discovered? **(b)** How are pulsars related to supernovas? **(c)** What is thought to be the cause of the rapid pulses put out by pulsars?

Alan M. MacRobert

Astronomer

Studying the heavens is a pleasurable hobby for many people. Best of all, getting started does not require expensive equipment. "By far the best way to start out in astronomy is with the naked eye," says astronomer Alan M. MacRobert of Cambridge, Massachusetts. He points out that until the telescope was invented in the 1600's, all astronomy was done by naked eye observations.

Mr. MacRobert suggests that one should start to study the heavens by learning the major constellations, because they are easy to learn and because they serve as guides to the other objects in the sky. The planets can be seen to move in front of the constellations and to have distinctive appearances—Venus is brilliant white, Mars is orange, and so on. Each constellation contains stars—the colors and pulsations of some can be seen with the naked eye. Then other objects can be located with the unaided eye—star clusters (Pleiades, Hyades), nebulae (M42 in Orion), and even galaxies (M31 in Andromeda) are all easy to find. Telescopes are fine, says Mr. MacRobert, but much astronomy can be done and enjoyed with purely naked eye observations.

III Formation of Stars

OBJECTIVES

A Name, describe, and give examples of several kinds of nebulae and explain the relationship between nebula and stars.

B Describe the formation of red giants and dwarfs.

C Describe the formation of novas, supernovas, neutron stars, and black holes.

Topic 10 Origin of a Star

Huge clouds of gas and dust occur in parts of space between stars. The density of these clouds is very low. Nevertheless, because the clouds are so large, they contain at least as much material as stars. These clouds are usually about 99 percent gas, most of which is hydrogen. The remaining 1 percent of the clouds is a strange kind of dust. The grains of this dust are very tiny, with diameters of about one ten-thousandth of a centimeter or less. Astronomers think that the dust grains may consist of hydrogen, carbon, nitrogen, oxygen, and possibly other elements.

Where does this gas and dust come from? One possible source is the explosion of stars that have become novas or supernovas (Topic 13). Such explosions could scatter material over a wide area.

Most of the great **nebulae**, or clouds of gas and dust in space, are invisible. Some are made visible in one of two ways. A nebula near a bright star is made visible by light from the star. Such a nebula is a *diffuse nebula.* The brightest of these is the Great Nebula in the constellation Orion. Close to the middle star in Orion's sword (Figure 21.8(a)), it is visible to the unaided eye under dark skies.

A nebula that is not near a bright star may show up as a dark patch against the more-distant stars. Such a nebula is called a *dark nebula.* The Horsehead Nebula in Orion is a dark nebula.

According to modern theory stars are forming continually wherever clouds of gas and dust exist. An average cloud is about 25 light-years in diameter. Each cloud may contain enough material to form many stars. A force from outside the cloud causes the cloud to begin to condense into stars. The force may be a shockwave from a supernova. The outside force triggers the force of gravity that exists between the gas atoms and dust grains. The attraction of gravity causes the particles in the cloud to move toward each other. Huge areas become denser throughout the cloud. The temperature increases as the areas contract. If the cloud is large enough, parts of it will start to glow. These large glowing cloud sections are called **protostars**. They will eventually become stars.

As contraction continues, the protostars become hotter and brighter. Eventually the center is so hot that a fusion reaction begins. During fusion, light hydrogen atoms unite to form heavier helium atoms. When fusion begins, the protostar has become a star. Huge amounts of energy are radiated during fusion. When the release of energy counterbalances the force of gravity, the star stops contracting and has reached a *stable state.* In the stable state, more-massive stars are so hot that they glow blue or white. Less-massive stars are cooler and glow yellow or orange. Massive blue stars may reach a stable state in a few hundred thousand years. Less-massive yellow and orange stars contract more slowly and may take millions of years to reach this stable state.

a

b

21.8 **(a)** The Great Nebula in Orion is a diffuse nebula. **(b)** Horsehead Nebula is a dark nebula.

21.9 The diagram shows how a stable star first shrinks and then expands to become a red giant. Eventually it collapses and becomes a white dwarf.

Topic 11 Formation of Red Giants

In the stable state a star's diameter and radiation remain the same for millions or even billions of years. Eventually, however, so many of the core's light atoms are used up that the energy of fusion no longer balances the force of gravity. Then the star loses its stability. When this occurs, the center or core of the star contracts again. The core gets so hot that it causes the star's outer layers to expand. This expansion enlarges the star's surface area. The star again radiates more light and appears brighter. In the meantime the fusion reaction starts occurring in the outer layers. The core is now composed mostly of helium formed from the hydrogen fusion reaction. The star expands further and becomes a red giant or supergiant.

If the star's core gets hot enough, helium atoms fuse in a reaction that forms still heavier atoms. If the temperature rise continues after the helium atoms are used up, elements as heavy as iron may be formed.

Topic 12 Formation of White Dwarfs

Finally the stage comes in a star's life when most of the fuel for the fusion reaction is used up. The temperature and pressure of the core can no longer support the weight of its outer layers. The giant collapses. The nuclei of its atoms are squeezed tightly together. The star becomes a white dwarf and is probably no larger than Earth.

With most of its fuel gone, the white dwarf no longer produces energy and cannot maintain its high temperature. It gives off enough leftover heat to glow faintly for perhaps a billion years. The white dwarf will continue to cool until it becomes cold and dark.

Occasionally a white dwarf flares up brilliantly. Astronomers then call it a **nova** (new star). A nova may be the result of bombardment by a companion star. Novas fade to their former luminosity in a few years at most.

The sun is thought to be at least five billion years old. It is still in its stable stage. The sun is expected to remain stable for another five billion years before it swells to a red giant and eventually collapses to a white dwarf.

Topic 13 Supernovas

White dwarfs form from red giants whose masses are about equal to the mass of the sun. However, more-massive red giants have a different life cycle. A massive red giant can become much hotter than a less-massive red giant. It may explode so violently that half its mass is blown away as a great cloud. As this happens, the star flares up into an intensely bright object called a **supernova**. The remaining mass is crushed into an almost incredibly dense core called a **neutron star**.

21.10 The great supernova of 1987 is the best-studied supernova in history. Data from it are still being analyzed. (left) Before the supernova became visible, (right) after the supernova became visible

A supernova may be a billion times more luminous than the sun. Hundreds of supernovas have been seen and photographed through powerful telescopes. Only a few, however, have been near enough to be seen by the unaided eye. The most famous and best-studied supernova occurred in the Large Magellanic Cloud, and was visible during 1987. This supernova was the closest ever observed since modern scientific equipment was developed. Astronomers have been able to test many hypotheses about supernovas by studying data from the 1987 supernova. For example, scientists had predicted that supernovas produce subatomic particles called neutrinos. In fact, instruments did detect a burst of neutrinos just before the supernova became visible. Astronomers were also able to examine old photographs and determine which star had exploded. Data from the 1987 supernova are still being collected and analyzed. The event will be studied in detail for many years to come.

The best record of a supernova before modern times was made by Chinese astronomers in A.D. 1054. The brilliant star faded after a year, but it left behind a great expanding cloud of gas. Today that cloud is known as the Crab Nebula. It is in the constellation of Taurus the Bull.

Topic 14 **Neutron Stars and Black Holes**

What are the materials in the dense core of a supernova? Normally an atomic nucleus contains both protons and neutrons. The space around the nucleus is occupied by a cloud of spinning electrons. Astronomers think that in the core of the supernova, every atom's electrons are crushed into its nucleus. Thus each atom is no larger than its nucleus. This is only about one hundred-thousandth of the diameter of the whole atom! Each electron is thought to have joined a proton, changing the proton to a neutron. The entire core of a neutron star would be made of neutrons. Astronomers calculate that a typical neutron star is only about ten kilometers in diameter, which makes it trillions of times more dense than the sun.

Are neutron stars the densest of all objects in the universe? Scientists do not think so. There is evidence that very massive stars may collapse into cores even denser than neutron stars. These objects have gravitational forces so powerful that even their own light rays cannot escape. Scientists call these invisible objects **black holes**. Many dark areas of the sky may have such bodies.

If black holes do not release light, how can they be located and identified? Astronomers have found what they think may be black holes. The best-known black hole is located in the constellation Cygnus the Swan and is called Cygnus X-1. The *X* means it radiates vast amounts of invisible energy in the form of X rays. These radiations led to the detection of Cygnus X-1 by NASA's *Orbiting Astronomical Observatory-3.* Furthermore, Cygnus X-1 has a visible companion star that revolves with it. Astronomers have detected powerful gravitational effects that Cygnus X-1 causes on its companion. For these reasons astronomers think Cygnus X-1 is a black hole.

21.11 An artist's conception of a black hole

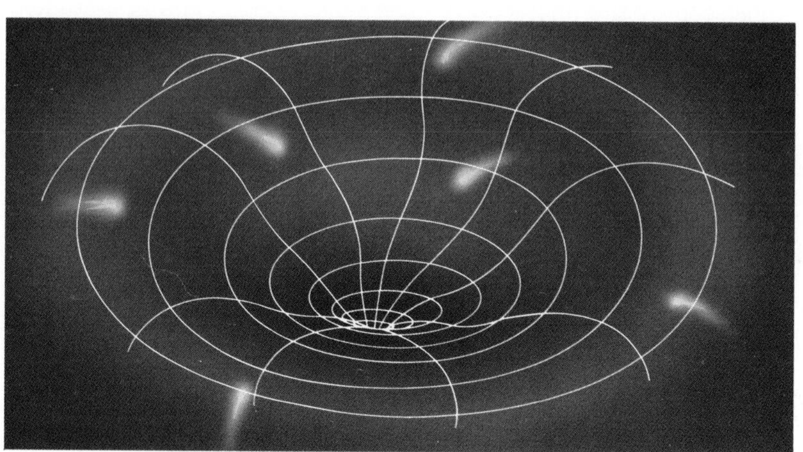

TOPIC QUESTIONS

Each topic question refers to the topic of the same number.

10. **(a)** What is a diffuse nebula? Give an example. **(b)** What is a dark nebula? Give an example. **(c)** Where are stars formed? **(d)** What is a protostar? **(e)** What reaction occurs in a protostar that has become very hot? **(f)** When does a star stop contracting?

11. **(a)** What is the stable state? Why does it end? **(b)** Explain how a star becomes a red giant.

12. **(a)** How does a star become a white dwarf? **(b)** What is a nova? **(c)** Summarize our sun's probable past and future.

13. **(a)** What is the characteristic that determines whether or not a red giant becomes a supernova? **(b)** What is a neutron star? **(c)** Describe a supernova. **(d)** What is the Crab Nebula?

14. **(a)** Explain why a neutron star is very dense. **(b)** How are black holes thought to form? **(c)** Why are black holes thought to be even more dense than neutron stars?

IV Galaxies and the Universe

Topic 15 What Are Galaxies?

Without a telescope you can see several thousand stars. You can also see a few hazy patches of light in the night sky. Small telescopes show thousands more of these patches. Early observers called most of these hazy patches nebulae (clouds).

Today the nebulae described by early observers are studied with powerful telescopes. Modern telescopes show that many of the hazy patches are not nebulae. They are instead systems containing millions or even billions of stars. These systems are **galaxies**. Telescopes show that space contains at least several billion galaxies. Space is so vast that most galaxies are millions of light-years apart.

The galaxy to which the sun belongs is the Milky Way galaxy. In it the sun is one star among 100 billion. Every individual star seen with the unaided eye belongs to the Milky Way.

The Milky Way is shaped like a large, thin magnifying lens with a central bulge. The diameter of the Milky Way is about 120 000 light-years. Its greatest thickness is about 20 000 light-years. The sun is about 30 000 light-years from the galaxy's center.

When looking through the galaxy along its length, so many stars can be seen that the sky looks milky. Observers called this part of the sky the Milky Way long before they actually knew that it was a galaxy.

The Milky Way belongs to a small cluster of 17 galaxies. Astronomers call this cluster the *Local Group*. The nearest neighbors in the Local Group, the two Magellanic Clouds, are in the Southern Hemisphere sky. These galaxies can be seen without a telescope. Another neighbor, the Andromeda Galaxy, is faintly visible to the unaided eye in the Northern Hemisphere sky. The Andromeda Galaxy is larger than the Milky Way and is about two million light-years away.

OBJECTIVES

A Name, describe, and give examples of types of galaxies and quasars that occur in the universe.

B Discuss the big-bang hypothesis and present the evidence for it.

21.12 Notice the approximate location of Earth's solar system in this side view of the Milky Way Galaxy.

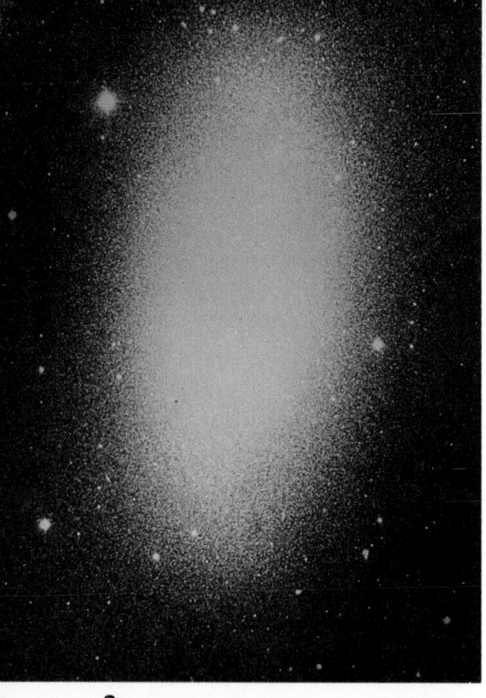

a

b

c

21.13 **(a)** An elliptical galaxy, **(b)** an irregular galaxy, **(c)** a spiral galaxy

Topic 16 **Types of Galaxies**

There are three main types of galaxies. *Spiral galaxies* have a central lens-shaped, bright nucleus made of millions of stars. Around the nucleus may be a fainter, flat disk of stars. Spiral arms, usually two, come out from opposite sides of the nucleus. The arms trail behind the galaxy as it rotates. There are millions of stars in the arms. The arms also contain great clouds of dust and gas. Few stars and almost no dust or gas occur between the arms. About three fourths of all known galaxies are spirals. The Milky Way and the Andromeda galaxies are spirals.

Elliptical galaxies range from nearly spherical to lens-shaped. Their brightness patterns show that most of their stars are close to the center. They have no arms and almost no gas and dust clouds.

Irregular galaxies are smaller, fainter, and less common than the others. Their stars are spread unevenly. The two Magellanic Clouds are irregular galaxies.

Topic 17 **Quasars**

Quasars were discovered in 1961. These objects looked like stars, and they emitted radio waves. Yet these objects were different from stars in several ways. Thus, astronomers named them **quasars** for quasi-stellar radio sources (radio sources like stars).

Quasars appear as very faint objects when viewed through a telescope because they are so far away. However, calculations show them to be the most luminous objects in the universe. Quasars are far larger and more massive than any known star. They radiate light and radio waves at very high rates. Scientists think that quasars may be whole galaxies in an early stage of development.

One quasar is called PKS 2000-330. In a powerful telescope it looks like a very faint star. The red shift of PKS 2000-330, however, shows it to be about 12 billion light-years away. At this distance, no known star can be seen even in the most powerful telescopes. For PKS 2000-330 to be seen from that distance, it must be as bright as 100 trillion suns and be billions of times more massive!

Topic 18 **Origin of the Universe**

How do scientists explain the formation of galaxies? The most widely accepted scientific explanation is the **big-bang hypothesis**. According to the big-bang hypothesis the whole universe was originally packed into one dense sphere of hydrogen. The entire sphere is thought to have been not much larger than the sun is today.

About 15 billion years ago this mass of hydrogen exploded, forming a gigantic expanding cloud. Some parts of the cloud moved faster than others, but all parts moved outward, away from the center. As the cloud parts moved, they condensed into galaxies. Billions of

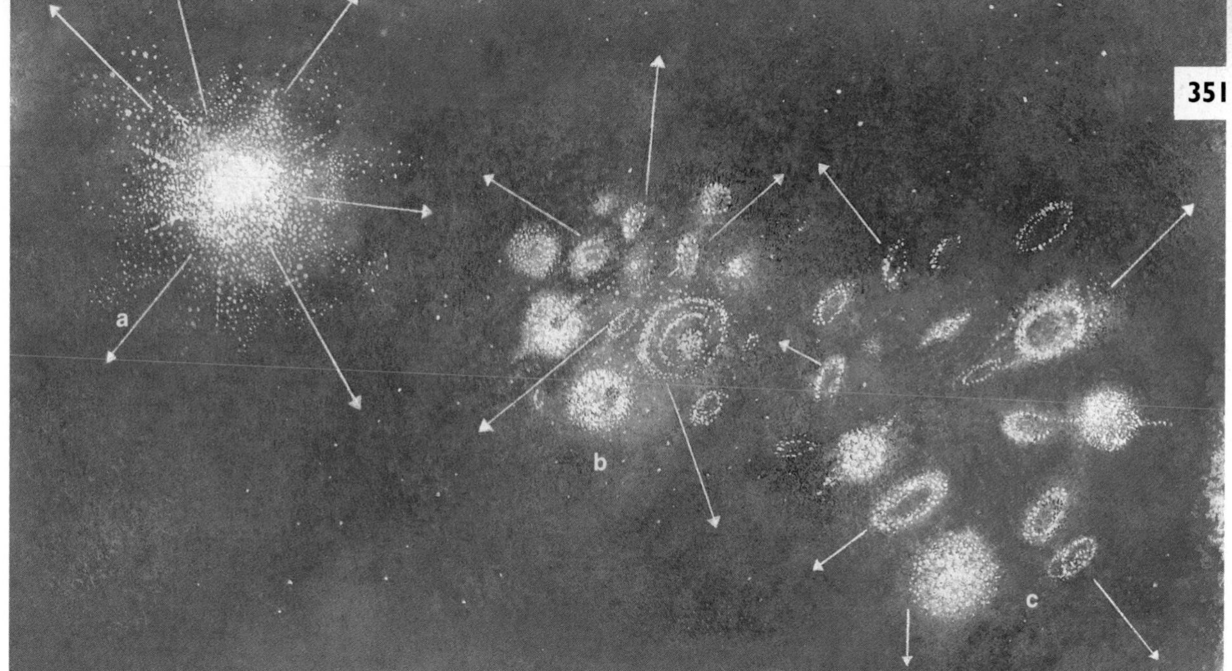

21.14 How did the universe begin? According to the big-bang hypothesis, **(a)** a big ball of hydrogen exploded, **(b)** a huge hydrogen cloud moved outward, with cloud parts condensing to form galaxies, and **(c)** the galaxies continued to move outward.

galaxies were formed. All of the galaxies continued moving outward, away from the center and from each other. Those with the highest speeds are now farthest out in space.

What is the evidence for this hypothesis? Recall from Chapter 20 that when an object is moving away from Earth, its spectrum appears to be shifted toward the red end of the spectrum because of the Doppler effect. In 1929, astronomer Edwin Hubble found red shifts in the spectra of the galaxies he studied. The red shifts showed that most of the galaxies were receding from Earth. Furthermore, Hubble found that the more distant the galaxy, the faster it receded. He concluded that the universe is expanding!

The most distant galaxies seem to be receding at nearly the speed of light. This apparent speed of the galaxies is so great that some astronomers question it. These astronomers think that the observed red shifts may not be due to the Doppler effect. No other explanation has yet been given.

TOPIC QUESTIONS

Each topic question refers to the topic of the same number.

15. (**a**) What are galaxies? (**b**) What is the name of our galaxy? Describe its shape and size. (**c**) What is the Local Group? Identify some members.

16. Name and describe the three main types of galaxies. Give examples where possible.

17. (**a**) In what ways do quasars differ from stars? (**b**) What do astronomers think that quasars may be?

18. (**a**) Summarize the big-bang hypothesis. (**b**) How does the red shift of galaxies provide evidence for the hypothesis?

CHAPTER 21 REVIEW

Summary

The apparent motion of constellations around Polaris is caused by Earth's turning. Earth's movement around the sun causes visible constellations to change through the year.

Distances in space are measured in astronomical units and light-years.

Stars differ in size, density, and color. Hydrogen and helium are the two most abundant elements in stars.

Apparent magnitude, luminosity, and absolute magnitude all describe the brightness of stars.

Giants and supergiants are large stars with low densities. Dwarf stars are small, dense stars.

Variable stars change in brightness. Pulsating variables, such as cepheids, and eclipsing binaries are types of variable stars.

Pulsars are neutron stars that produce bursts of both light and radio waves.

Nebulae are huge clouds of dust and gas in space. Stars are thought to form in nebulae.

A nova is caused by the flare-up of a white dwarf star. Supernovas result from the explosion of a neutron star's outer portions.

Neutron stars are denser than white dwarfs. Black holes are so dense that light cannot escape their gravity. Neutron stars and black holes result from the collapse of large and very large stars.

Galaxies contain millions or billions of stars. Galaxies may be spiral, elliptical, or irregular.

Quasars are distant objects that may be galaxies in the early stages of formation.

The big-bang hypothesis is an explanation for the origin of galaxies and the universe.

Vocabulary

absolute magnitude
apparent magnitude
astronomical unit (AU)
big-bang hypothesis
black holes
cepheid variables
constellation
dwarf stars
eclipsing binary
galaxies
light-year (LY)
luminosity
nebulae
neutron star
nova
protostars
pulsars
quasars
red giants
supergiants
supernova
variable stars

Review

Write the letter of your answer on your paper.

1. An example of a circumpolar constellation is (a) Ursa Major, (b) Orion, (c) Canis Major, (d) Cygnus.
2. Earth turning on its axis causes (a) stars to rise in the west, (b) stars to appear to move around Polaris, (c) Orion to be seen in winter, (d) Cassiopeia to be overhead in autumn.
3. Which is the greatest distance? (a) 1 astronomical unit (b) 1 kilometer (c) 1 light-year (d) 1 millimeter
4. The two most abundant elements in stars are (a) helium and iron, (b) iron and calcium, (c) calcium and hydrogen, (d) hydrogen and helium.
5. How many times brighter is a first-magnitude star than a third-magnitude star? (a) 2 times (b) 2.5 times (c) 2 x 2.5 times (d) 2.5 x 2.5 times
6. Which object has the brightest apparent magnitude? (a) Sirius, −1.43 (b) Venus, −4.4 (c) Procyon, +0.37 (d) Barnard's Star, +9.5
7. Which probably describes a blue-white star? (a) massive, hot (b) massive, cool (c) small, hot (d) small, cool
8. The variable stars used to calculate star distance are (a) pulsating variables, (b) eclipsing binaries, (c) dwarfs, (d) cepheids.
9. A rapidly spinning neutron star is a (a) nova, (b) quasar, (c) pulsar, (d) nebula.
10. What kind of object is the Coal Sack? (a) diffuse nebula (b) dark nebula (c) black hole (d) supernova

11. Which stage follows the stable state for most stars? (a) red giant (b) red dwarf (c) nova (d) white dwarf
12. Stars that have used up their nuclear fuel and shrunk to a tiny size are (a) pulsars, (b) white dwarfs, (c) supernovas, (d) binaries.
13. The object located in the same place as a supernova explosion observed in A.D. 1054 is (a) Horsehead Nebula, (b) Orion Nebula, (c) Crab Nebula, (d) Andromeda Galaxy.
14. Cygnus X-1 is thought to be a (a) black hole, (b) pulsar, (c) variable star, (d) quasar.
15. Which may be distant galaxies in the process of formation? (a) black holes (b) neutron stars (c) pulsars (d) quasars
16. To which system does our sun belong? (a) Andromeda Galaxy (b) Milky Way (c) Big Dipper (d) Lesser Magellanic Cloud
17. What kind of galaxy is the Milky Way? (a) diffuse (b) spiral (c) elliptical (d) irregular
18. How long ago is the big bang thought to have occurred? (a) 5 billion years (b) 15 billion years (c) 25 billion years (d) 100 billion years

Interpret and Apply

Answer each question in complete sentences.

1. Where would an observer have to be in order to photograph star trails that are complete circles? Why?
2. The star Sirius is 4.3 light-years from Earth. Determine the distance to Sirius in kilometers and in astronomical units.
3. The moon's average distance from Earth is about 380 000 kilometers. How long does it take moonlight to reach Earth?
4. Planets shine by reflected sunlight. How can planets be brighter than stars?
5. Approximately how many times brighter than Mars is Earth's full moon? (Moon's apparent magnitude equals −12.6)
6. Could we see the sun if it were 32.6 light-years from Earth?

Critical Thinking

Graph A shows the relationship between the distance to a star in parsecs (1 parsec = 3.26 light-years), and the distance modulus. The distance modulus is the difference between the apparent magnitude (m) of a star and its absolute magnitude (M). Graph B shows the relationship between the period of a cepheid variable and its absolute magnitude.

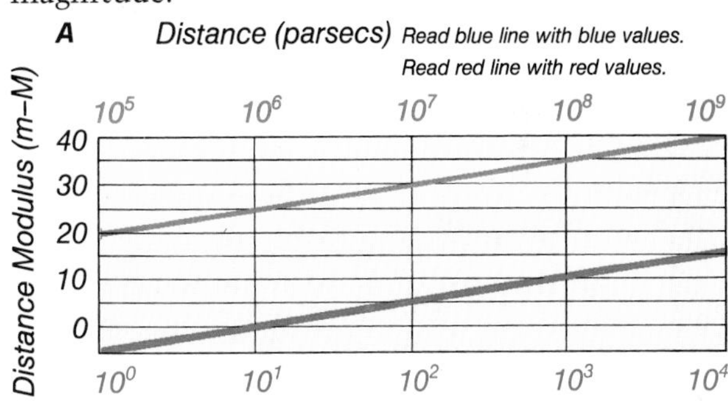

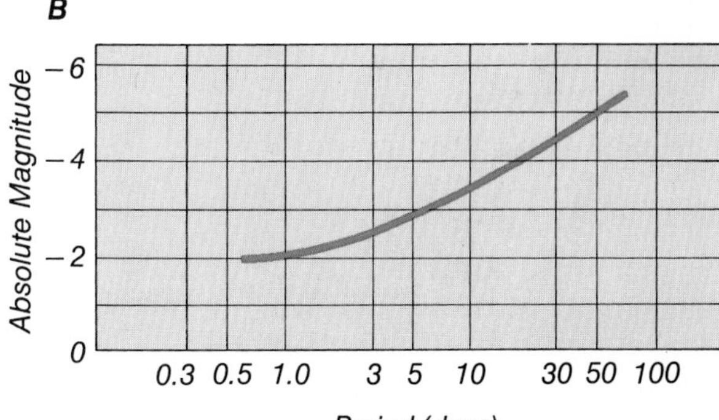

1. The distance modulus for a star is 10. How far is the star?
2. What is the distance modulus for a star that is 10^6 parsecs away?
3. How far away is a star if its apparent magnitude (m) is 10 and its absolute magnitude (M) is −10?
4. What is the absolute magnitude (M) of a cepheid variable star with a period of 5 days?
5. A cepheid variable has a period of 50 days. If its apparent magnitude (m) is +0, how far away is the cepheid?

CHAPTER

22 The Sun and Its Solar System

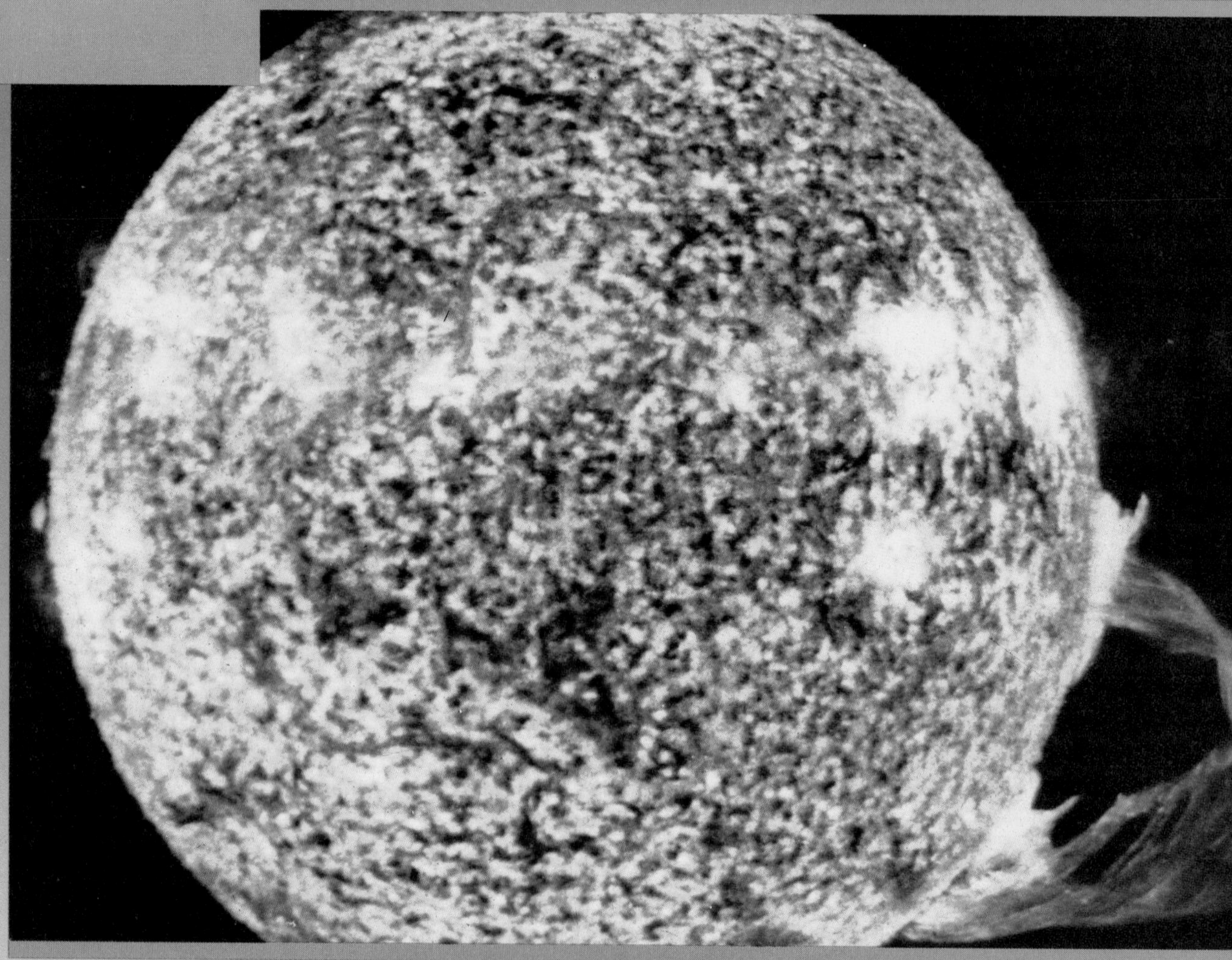

▲ The sun's surface has a mottled, grainy appearance.

How Do You Know That . . .

The sun is constantly changing? To a casual observer, the sun always appears the same. When the sun is observed with special equipment many changes are visible. For example, the surface of the sun appears to be bubbling and boiling. Solar scientists describe the surface of the sun as looking like the surface of a pot of boiling rice in slow motion. When rice boils, individual pieces quickly disappear and others take their place. A similar change appears to occur to the pieces that make up the sun's surface, although the change takes several minutes.

I The Sun

Topic 1 Studying the Sun

Although the sun is the nearest star to Earth, it is both difficult and dangerous to observe. Early astronomers risked blindness by looking directly at the sun. A telescope makes features on the sun's surface appear larger but greatly increases the risk of eye damage. Safe ways of studying the sun had to be developed. For solar astronomers the instrument that provided the first scientific measurements of the sun was the spectroscope (Chapter 20). The spectroscope made it possible nearly 100 years ago for solar scientists to learn about the chemical composition, temperature, and internal pressure of the sun.

Today, in addition to the spectroscope, other instruments are used to study the sun. One is the **solar telescope**. This instrument projects a large image of the sun into a dark underground room. With special glasses similar to those used by welders, solar astronomers can safely watch this image and observe changes that occur on the sun's surface.

Satellites have made it possible to study solar radiation that is absorbed by Earth's atmosphere, such as ultraviolet and X rays. The most organized and intense study of the sun was performed from *Skylab,* an orbiting solar and space observatory designed to carry astronauts. During 1973, three separate crews of astronauts occupied *Skylab* for a total of 172 days. They took photographs and made observations using several solar telescopes on board the spacecraft. Some of the data collected at that time are still being analyzed by solar astronomers.

OBJECTIVES

A Identify and describe some methods of studying the sun and discuss the sun's dimensions.

B Name and describe the layers and features of the sun's atmosphere and describe sunspots and the sunspot cycle.

C Define solar wind, identify sources of solar wind, and describe the effects of solar wind on Earth.

D Explain how the sun produces energy.

22.1 (a) The McMath Telescope is the world's largest solar telescope. It is located at Kitt Peak National Observatory in Arizona. **(b)** A scientist using a solar telescope

a

b

22.2 The most organized and intense study of the sun was performed during the 1970's from *Skylab*, an orbiting solar and space observatory.

Several satellites without astronauts have also been used to study the sun. Eight *Orbiting Solar Observatories* returned data about the sun to Earth from 1962 through 1979. In 1974 and 1976 the solar satellites *Helios A* and *Helios B* were placed in long, oval orbits that carried them inside the orbit of the planet Mercury. The *Solar Maximum Satellite,* or *Solar Max,* was launched in 1980. It is designed to study the output of energy from the sun during periods of high sunspot activity.

Ulysses is a solar satellite planned for the future. This spacecraft will fly over the sun's poles, an area that cannot be seen from Earth or from Earth-orbiting satellites. From these missions, solar scientists hope to learn more about the sun's magnetism.

Topic 2 Properties of the Sun

Even though our sun is just an average-sized star, it is enormous compared to the size of Earth. The sun's diameter, 1 380 000 kilometers, is about 110 times Earth's diameter. The sun's volume could hold more than 1 million Earths. Its mass is 745 times greater than all the planets together.

It is difficult to imagine the huge size of the sun because it is so far away. Even though the sun and the moon appear to be nearly the same size in our sky, the sun is 400 times farther away. The SST (supersonic transport) *Concorde* can fly from Paris to New York in three and one-half hours. If the *Concorde* could fly through space at the same speed, it would take 10 years to reach the sun! Even for a particle traveling at the speed of light (300 000 km/s), it takes 8 minutes and 20 seconds to travel between the sun and Earth.

Temperatures on the sun are extreme. The sun's surface temperature is about 5500°C, about as hot as an electric arc that is used to weld iron. Its interior temperature is even higher, and may be as high as 15 000 000°C.

Topic 3 The Sun's Atmosphere

The only parts of the sun that can be studied directly are the three regions of the sun's atmosphere. These regions are the photosphere, the chromosphere, and the corona.

The **photosphere** is the apparent bright yellow surface of the sun. It is about 400 kilometers thick. The photosphere appears to be made of millions of individual cells, called **granules**. Each granule is about 1500 kilometers across with a bright center and dark edges. Granules are the tops of the columns of gases that form in the region below the photosphere. The gases are rising at the center of the granule and sinking back down at the edges. Because the gases are constantly moving, the surface is constantly changing. Individual granules last about eight minutes before disappearing.

The photosphere is the lower, denser part of the sun's atmosphere. It is not at all like Earth's lower atmosphere. The density

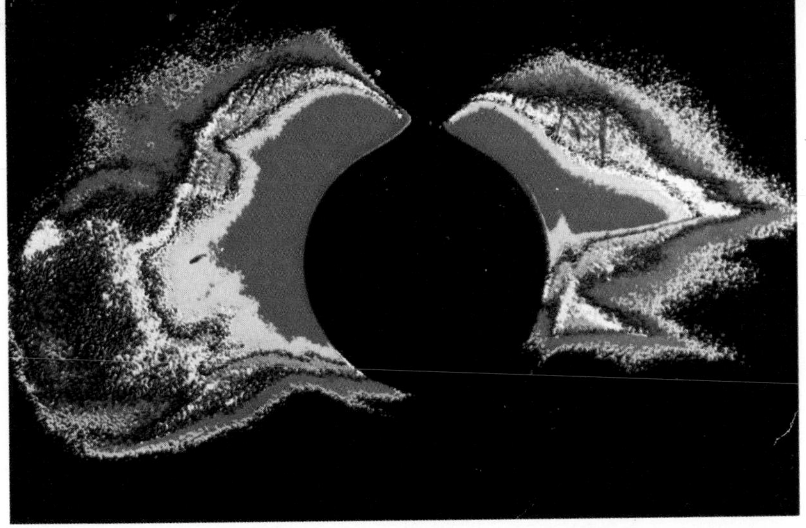

22.3 The sun's corona is visible during a solar eclipse. This image of the corona was taken from *Skylab* by an instrument that masked the sun's disk, creating an artificial eclipse. The image has been colored by a computer to make differences in brightness more visible.

of the photosphere is 28 billionths of a gram per cubic centimeter (2.8×10^{-8} g/cm^3). That is about the same as the density of Earth's outermost atmosphere.

Above the photosphere is the sun's outer, less dense atmosphere. Without special instruments the sun's outer atmosphere can be seen only during a solar eclipse. At the lower part of the outer atmosphere is the **chromosphere**, colored red by glowing hydrogen. The chromosphere extends thousands of kilometers above the photosphere. Above the chromosphere is the **corona**, with so little gas that it would be considered a vacuum on Earth. The corona surrounds the sun to a height of more than 1 million kilometers. It is seen during a total eclipse as a faint, pearly light.

Solar prominences are huge, red, flamelike arches of material that occur in the corona. Although they may look like flames, their light is the result of chemical changes that occur in cooler, denser parts of the corona. Solar prominences may last for many hours. Some extend millions of kilometers above the photosphere.

Topic 4 Sunspots

Sunspots are dark spots on the photosphere. Some sunspots are barely visible in telescopes. Others are larger than Earth's diameter. Some last only a few hours before disappearing, while others may remain visible for a few months. Sunspots typically have a dark center, called an umbra, and a lighter rim, the penumbra.

Sunspots occur in pairs. Like the opposite ends of a bar magnet, one of the pair is a north magnetic pole and the other a south magnetic pole. The concentration of magnetic forces at these locations slows down solar activity and causes the photosphere to cool. The gases in a sunspot may be as much as 1500°C cooler than the surrounding photosphere. That temperature is still hotter than many stars, and sunspots would glow on their own if removed from the sun. Sunspots look dark only because the surrounding photosphere is so much hotter and brighter.

Sunspots appear to move from left to right across the sun's surface. This motion is caused by the sun's rotation. Because the sun is not solid like Earth but is made of gases, its rate of rotation is not

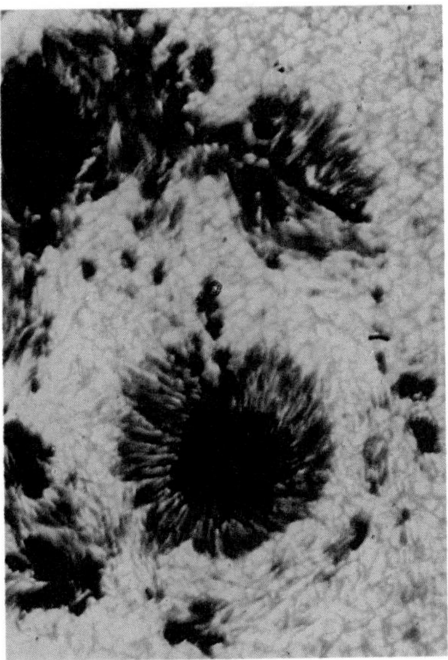

22.4 Sunspots occur on the photosphere. Sunspots appear dark because they are cooler than the surrounding photosphere.

the same everywhere. At the equator the sun takes about 25 days for one rotation. The rate of rotation near the poles is 27 days.

The number of sunspots visible on the photosphere changes from day to day. At times of peak sunspot activity, over 100 may be counted on the sun's surface. During periods of low sunspot activity, several days may pass when no spots are visible. These changes occur in a *sunspot cycle* that averages about 11 years from one period of peak activity to the next.

Topic 5 The Solar Wind and Magnetic Storms

The corona gives off a constant stream of electrically charged particles called **solar wind**. These particles fly into space in all directions, some at an average speed of 400 kilometers per second by the time they reach Earth.

Some solar events produce huge gusts of solar wind. Great tears, called **coronal holes**, sometimes appear in the corona. Some of these holes extend halfway around the sun, and many do not close for several months. Solar wind pours from coronal holes in a great torrent of particles.

Solar flares are another source of solar wind bursts. Solar flares are outbursts of light that rise up suddenly in areas of sunspot activity. Most flare up in a few minutes and then fade rapidly. The number of solar flares increases as the number of sunspots increases.

As the solar wind blows past Earth, some particles interact with Earth's magnetic field and upper atmosphere, causing **auroras**, or northern and southern lights. Auroras are common events in the polar regions near Earth's magnetic poles.

22.5 Solar flares are outbursts of light from regions of sunspot activity. They usually last a few minutes.

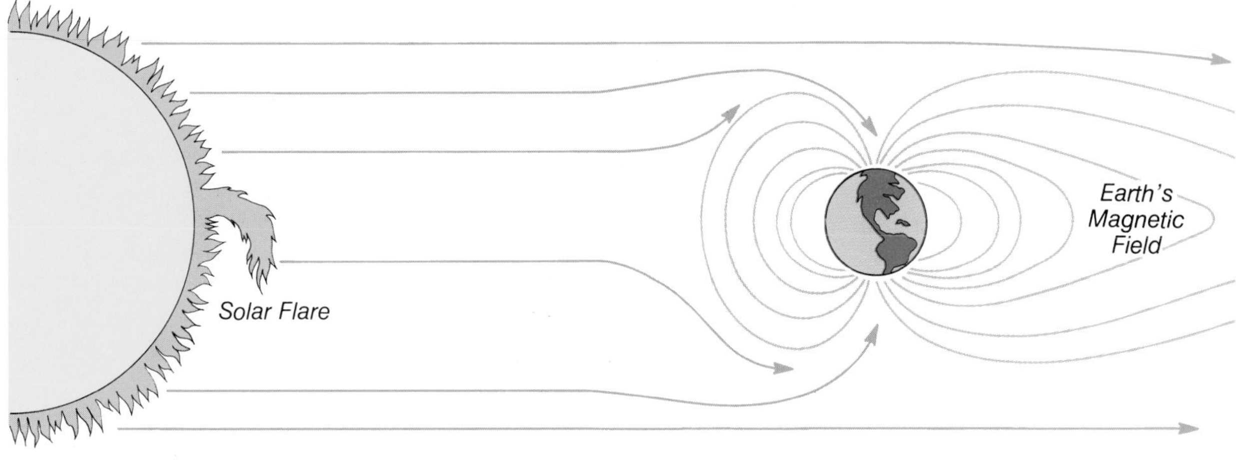

22.6 As solar wind passes Earth, some particles are trapped by Earth's magnetic field and are carried to the magnetic poles. When the particles hit the atmosphere, they cause auroras. During periods of intense solar activity, increased solar wind may lead to auroras at latitudes away from the poles.

Magnetic storms occur on Earth when the particles thrown out by coronal holes and solar flares are added to the constant solar wind produced by the corona. At such times auroras may be seen in middle latitudes as well as in polar areas, and compass needles may give inaccurate readings. Electrical surges following large solar flares may disrupt telephone reception and damage unprotected electrical appliances. Other particles in these outbursts affect the ionosphere, a region in Earth's upper atmosphere that reflects certain radio signals back to Earth. Radio reception of AM, citizen's band (CB), and shortwave frequencies may be affected.

Topic 6 Source of the Sun's Energy

Remember from Chapter 21 that the fusion of light elements into heavier ones is the source of a star's energy. How does this fusion reaction take place? Why does it provide energy?

Albert Einstein gave the key to the answer in 1905 with his famous $E = mc^2$ equation. It stated that *matter can be converted into energy* and vice versa.

The sun is mostly hydrogen. Four hydrogen nuclei have a mass of about 4.030 atomic mass units. In fusion, four hydrogen nuclei join to form a helium nucleus that has a mass of only about 4.003 atomic mass units. Although some mass seems to disappear in the fusion process, it really does not. The mass changes into energy, which is radiated into space.

Calculations show that the total conversion of 1 kilogram of matter would release enough energy to raise a billion metric tons of matter 10 kilometers above Earth's surface. Astronomers calculate that about 4 million tons of matter are being changed to energy every second in the sun. This conversion to energy happens as 564 million tons of hydrogen become 560 million tons of helium. The mass of the sun is so great that this process can continue for another 5 billion years.

TOPIC QUESTIONS

Each topic question refers to the topic of the same number.

1. **(a)** Why is it dangerous to look directly at the sun? **(b)** What instrument provided astronomers with their first scientific observations of the sun? **(c)** How does a solar telescope work? **(d)** What was *Skylab*? **(e)** Identify some satellites that have been used to study the sun. **(f)** What area of the sun do scientists hope to study with *Ulysses*?
2. **(a)** Compare the sun's dimensions with those of Earth. **(b)** How hot is the sun?
3. **(a)** Name and briefly describe the three regions of the sun's atmosphere. **(b)** Describe solar prominences.
4. **(a)** Describe the appearance, size, magnetism, and temperature of sunspots. **(b)** What do sunspots show about the sun's rotation? **(c)** What is the sunspot cycle?
5. **(a)** What is solar wind? **(b)** Name and describe the sources of solar wind bursts. **(c)** What effects does solar wind have on Earth?
6. **(a)** In the fusion reaction in the sun, what happens to the hydrogen that does not convert to helium? **(b)** How much longer is this reaction expected to continue in the sun?

Dr. Barbara Mihalas
Solar Astrophysicist

Knowledge about the sun is increasing rapidly as a result of new methods of observation and calculation. Dr. Barbara Mihalas is a solar astrophysicist at the National Center for Supercomputing Applications (NCSA) in Urbana, Illinois. Together with scientists at the National Center for Atmospheric Research (NCAR) in Boulder, Colorado, she is studying wave and pulsation motions of the sun. Almost all information about the sun comes from its dark-line spectrum. Motions within the sun's atmosphere cause its spectral lines to shift slightly in frequency. These shifts are caused both by waves in the sun's atmosphere and by pulsations of the sun itself. The first step in studying these motions is to observe the sun with a CCD. This is done at sites in New Mexico and Arizona. Then, at NCSA and NCAR, relevant data is extracted from the observations using specially-designed computer programs. With the help of such programs, scientists gather a great deal of information about the sun's wave and pulsation motions.

II Observing the Solar System

OBJECTIVES

A List the members of the solar system and identify those that can be seen with the unaided eye.

B Describe how the motions of the planets across our sky differ from those of stars and explain the cause of this difference.

C Describe the difference between a geocentric and a heliocentric solar system.

Topic 7 The Solar System

The sun's family is known as the **solar system**. It includes objects that range in size from tiny sandlike grains to gigantic spheres many thousands of kilometers in diameter. The solar system includes 9 planets, at least 54 natural satellites (also called moons), thousands of asteroids, millions of meteroids, and many comets. All of these objects travel around the sun at high speeds in paths called **orbits**. Some of the orbits are nearly circular, while others are highly elongated. Some of the orbits are near the sun, while others are billions of kilometers away.

Several members of the solar system can be seen with the unaided eye. Five of the planets can be seen without a telescope—Mercury, Venus, Mars, Jupiter, and Saturn. Meteors can be seen regularly with the unaided eye. A telescope is needed to see all asteroids and most comets.

Topic 8 Planets and Stars

To the unaided eye, planets look very much like stars. However, there is one difference that has been noted since earliest times. Over the lifetime of an observer the positions of stars relative to each other, and thus the shapes of constellations, do not noticeably change. The positions of planets among the constellations, however, change constantly. The reason for the difference is the distances to the two kinds of objects—the planets appear to move

22.7 The solar system includes the sun, planets and their moons, asteroids, meteoroids, and comets.

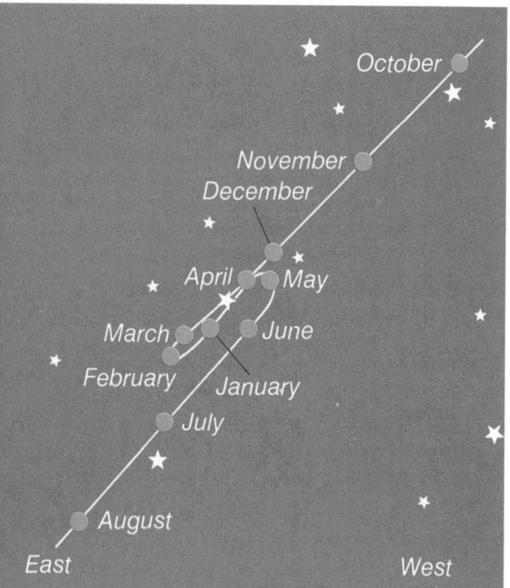

22.8 Planets move eastward against the background of stars but periodically make westward loops called retrograde motion.

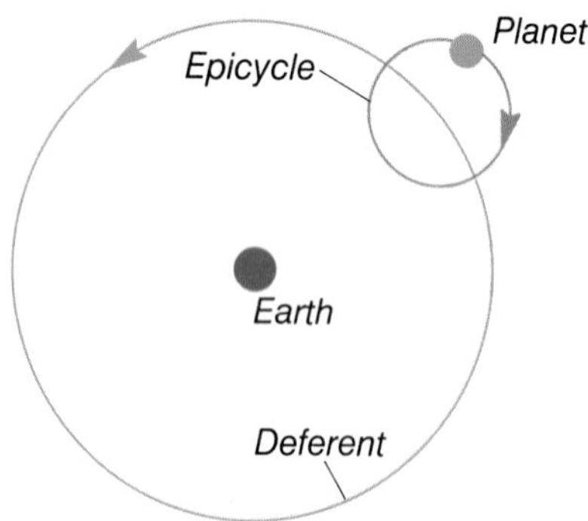

22.9 In Ptolemy's geocentric model of the solar system, the planets traveled on small circles called epicycles, which lay on a larger circle called a deferent.

through the stars because they are so much closer to us than the stars.

Most of the time the planets move eastward in front of the background of constellations, but they periodically make westward loops called **retrograde motion**. These loops occur because each planet travels around the sun at a different speed. Whenever Earth overtakes and passes another planet, that planet appears to move backward, or westward, among the stars. Once the planet has been passed, its eastward motion through the stars continues.

On a single night, a planet will not appear to move in front of the stars. Several days, weeks, or months may be needed to notice a change in the position of a planet. The more distant the planet is from Earth, the more slowly its position changes.

Topic 9 Solar System Models

Ancient people did not recognize the cause of retrograde motion. They thought that Earth was the center of the universe and that the sun, planets, and stars moved around it. Such a system is called a **geocentric**, or earth-centered, system. The Greek astronomer Ptolemy, who lived around A.D. 140, developed an earth-centered model that he used to predict the locations of the planets. He imagined the planets on small orbits, called **epicycles**. The center of each small orbit moved around Earth on a larger orbit called a **deferent**. Retrograde motion occurred when the planet made a trip around the epicycle. Ptolemy's model was accepted until the 1600's.

The Polish astronomer Copernicus is credited with proposing the **heliocentric**, or sun-centered, solar system. Copernicus suggested that Earth and the other planets revolved around the sun. Epicycles were no longer needed to explain planetary motion. Retrograde motion would occur whenever Earth passed another planet. The heliocentric system provided a much simpler explanation of the observed motions in the sky. This system marked the beginning of our modern understanding of the structure of the universe.

TOPIC QUESTIONS

Each topic question refers to the topic of the same number.

7. **(a)** List the kinds of objects that are part of the solar system. **(b)** Which of these objects are visible to the unaided eye?

8. **(a)** How do the movements of planets in our sky differ from the movements of stars? **(b)** What is retrograde motion and why does it occur?

9. **(a)** What is a geocentric solar system? **(b)** Who used the geocentric system to explain planetary motions? How did he explain retrograde motion? **(c)** What is a heliocentric system and who is credited with proposing it? **(d)** What is the advantage of the heliocentric system over the geocentric system?

III Motion in the Solar System

Topic 10 The Contribution of Tycho

Tycho Brahe (TEE koe BRAH hee) was a Danish nobleman who lived on an island. On the island, Tycho built an astronomical observatory. His observatory did not include a telescope because it had not yet been invented. Tycho's observatory contained several kinds of instruments for measuring the positions of objects in the sky. With these instruments Tycho made very careful measurements of the positions of the stars and planets over a period of 20 years. Tycho's observations were the best ever made before the telescope. They were also the first long-term sky observations.

Topic 11 Johannes Kepler and the Laws of Planetary Motion

After Tycho's death, Johannes Kepler inherited all of Tycho's notebooks of data. Kepler spent many years studying those notebooks, and from their data he developed three **laws of planetary motion**.

Kepler's *first law of planetary motion* states that the planets travel in **elliptical orbits** with the sun at one focus. Instead of having a single center, or focus, as a circle does, an ellipse has two foci (foci = plural of focus). An ellipse was an unfamiliar shape at the time, and Copernicus had thought that the orbits were perfect circles. Because the sun is at one focus of the ellipse, a planet's distance from the sun will change throughout its orbit. The point in a planet's orbit where it is farthest from the sun is called its **aphelion**, while the point nearest the sun is its **perihelion**.

Kepler's *second law of planetary motion* is known as the **equal area law**. It states that each planet moves around the sun in such a way that an imaginary line joining the planet to the sun will sweep over equal areas of space in equal periods of time. Because a planet's orbit is an ellipse with the sun at one focus, the equal area law means that the speed at which a planet travels around the sun is not constant. Kepler determined that planets travel more rapidly when they are closer to the sun. He was not able to explain why they did, but later Isaac Newton discovered the reason (Topic 13).

OBJECTIVES

A Describe the work of Tycho Brahe and explain why his work was important.

B Summarize Kepler's laws of planetary motion and demonstrate their use.

C Identify some objects observed by Galileo with his telescopes and explain why his observations were important.

D Define Newton's law of gravitation and identify some factors that can be determined using the law.

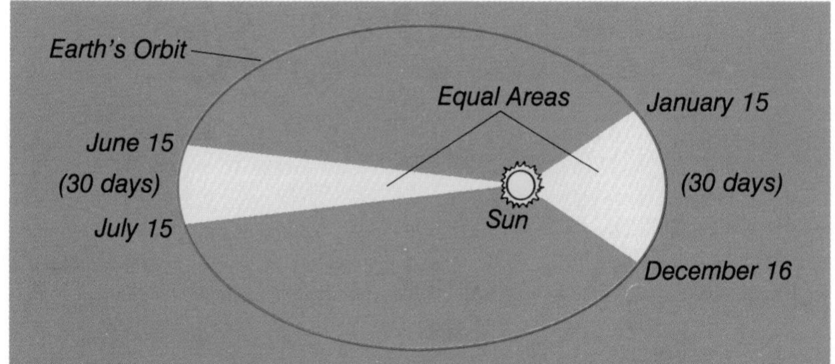

22.10 According to Kepler's law of equal areas, a line connecting Earth to the sun would pass over equal areas of space in equal times. Because Earth's orbit is elliptical, this means that Earth moves faster when it is nearer the sun.

Periods of Revolution

Planet	Distance (AU)	Period
Mercury	0.4	88 days
Venus	0.7	225 days
Earth	1.0	365.25 days
Mars	1.5	687 days
Jupiter	5.2	12 years
Saturn	9.5	29.5 years
Uranus	19.2	84 years
Neptune	30.0	165 years
Pluto	39.4	248 years

Kepler's *third law of planetary motion* is the **harmonic law**. The time it takes a planet to travel one orbit around the sun is its *period*. The third law of planetary motion states that the period (P) of a planet squared is equal to the cube of its distance (D) from the sun, or $\mathbf{P^2 = D^3}$. The formula is used to find the distance between the sun and a planet if the period is known or to find the period if the distance is known. To use the formula, the period must be in Earth years and the distance from the sun must be in astronomical units (AU, the distance between Earth and the sun). What is the period of Jupiter, if its distance from the sun is about 5.2 AU?

By using Kepler's third law:

$$(\text{Jupiter's period})^2 = (\text{Jupiter's Distance})^3$$

Expressing period in years and distance in AUs:

$$\begin{aligned}(\text{Jupiter's Period})^2 &= (5.2\ \text{AU})^3\\ (\text{Jupiter's Period})^2 &= 140.6\ \text{years (approx.)}\\ \text{Jupiter's Period} &= 12\ \text{years (approx.)}\end{aligned}$$

Kepler's third law states that the farther a planet is from the sun, the longer is its period of revolution. One reason is that its orbit is larger. Another is that it moves more slowly than nearer planets. The average speed of Earth in its orbit is about 30 kilometers a second. Mercury, nearest to the sun, moves about 49 kilometers a second. Pluto, usually farthest out, travels 5 kilometers a second.

Topic 12 Galileo and the Telescope

Galileo is believed to be the first astronomer to have a telescope and to turn it toward the sky. He was amazed at what he saw. In parts of the sky where our eyes can see thousands of stars, his telescope allowed him to see millions of stars that had never been suspected to exist. He could clearly see the craters and mountains on the moon. He observed Venus and discovered that it went through phases like our moon. Most important, he discovered four moons in orbit around Jupiter. In an Earth-centered system, all objects should go around Earth, but these moons clearly did not. Galileo's observation gave support to the heliocentric system.

Topic 13 Isaac Newton and the Universal Law of Gravitation

Kepler knew that a force was required to keep the planets in motion around the sun. Isaac Newton identified the force as gravity and determined its mathematical nature. Newton's **universal law of gravitation** shows that the force of gravity between any two objects is directly related to the masses of the two objects but inversely related to the square of the distance between the centers of the two objects. Thus, gravitational force is greater between objects of greater mass, and less between objects of lesser mass. Gravitational attraction also changes in a definite way as the distance between the centers of the two objects changes.

$$\text{change in force} = \frac{1}{\text{distance}^2}$$

The formula indicates that the gravitational attraction between objects changes inversely with the square of the distance between them. For example, if the two objects move to twice their former distance, then the force of attraction between them is one fourth as great. If two objects move to half their original distance, then the force of attraction between them is four times as great.

$$\begin{array}{l}\text{change}\\\text{in force}\end{array} = \frac{1}{2^2} = \frac{1}{4}; \qquad \begin{array}{l}\text{change}\\\text{in force}\end{array} = \frac{1}{(1/2)^2} = 4$$

The law of gravitation explains the changing speed of a planet. The speed of a planet increases when it approaches the sun because the gravitational pull between the sun and the planet is greater at that time. The speed of the planet decreases when it is farther from the sun and the gravitational force is less. The law of gravitation also explains why the planet closest to the sun, Mercury, travels at a higher speed in its orbit than any other planet.

From the law of gravitation Newton calculated the masses of the planets from the dimensions of their orbits. He determined that tides are caused by the force of the moon as it revolves around Earth. Gravitational force explained the long orbits of comets and provided proof that they are part of the solar system.

In this century the law of gravitation is used to determine escape velocity. **Escape velocity** is the minimum velocity needed to escape the gravitational pull of a planet, moon, asteroid, or other object. Escape velocity is directly related to the mass of the object. For example, the velocity needed to escape from Earth is 11.2 kilometers per second. Mars, however, has less mass than Earth and its escape velocity is only 5.0 kilometers per second.

22.11 Even though the sun is many times more massive than Earth, the force of gravity between Earth and the moon is greater than between the moon and the sun because the distance is so much less. This is why the moon revolves around Earth, rather than revolving around the sun on its own.

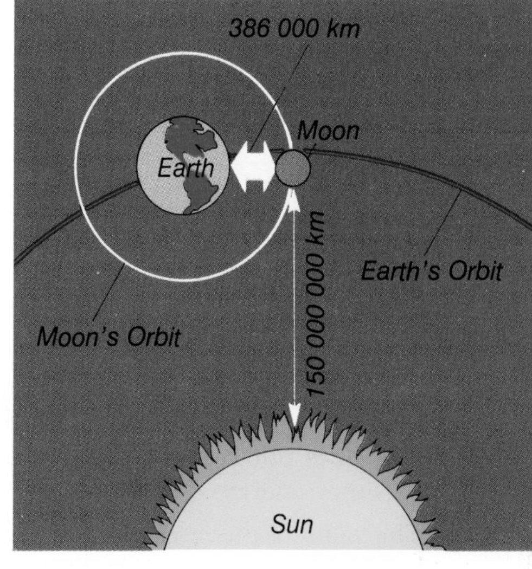

TOPIC QUESTIONS

Each topic question refers to the topic of the same number.

10. What was the contribution of Tycho Brahe to astronomy?

11. **(a)** What conclusions did Kepler draw from Tycho's data? **(b)** Define aphelion and perihelion. **(c)** What does the equal area law tell about the speed of a planet? **(d)** What is Kepler's harmonic law used to determine?

12. **(a)** Identify objects Galileo observed with his telescope. **(b)** Which was his most important observation? Why?

13. **(a)** What happens to the force of gravity between two objects if their masses increase? If the distance between them increases? **(b)** Name some phenomena explained by gravitation. **(c)** What is escape velocity?

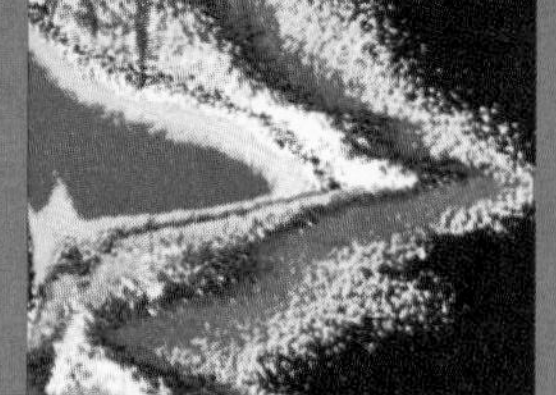

CHAPTER 22 REVIEW

Summary

The spectroscope, the solar telescope, and satellites are used to study the sun.

The sun is enormous compared to Earth. Its surface temperature is about 5500°C; its interior is even hotter.

The photosphere, chromosphere, and corona are layers of the sun's atmosphere. Granules, solar prominences, sunspots, and solar flares appear on the sun's surface.

The solar wind is a stream of charged particles from the sun's corona. Some solar events cause changes in the solar wind that can affect Earth.

The sun's energy is the result of the conversion of hydrogen to helium in nuclear fusion. The mass that does not convert to helium is not lost, but becomes energy.

The planets move eastward in front of the stars but periodically make backward loops called retrograde motion.

Ptolemy proposed a complex geocentric solar system to explain planetary motion. Copernicus proposed a simpler heliocentric system.

Tycho Brahe made careful measurements of the positions of the stars and planets in the sky for a 20-year period.

Kepler used Tycho Brahe's data to develop three laws of planetary motion: the elliptical orbit law, the equal area law, and the harmonic law.

Galileo observed the sky with a telescope. His observations helped to confirm the heliocentric system.

Newton developed the universal law of gravitation, which explained the motions of planets in the solar system.

Vocabulary

aphelion
auroras
chromosphere
corona
laws of planetary motion
orbit
perihelion
photosphere
coronal holes
deferent
elliptical orbit
epicycles
equal area law
escape velocity
geocentric system
granules
harmonic law
heliocentric system
retrograde motion
solar flares
solar prominences
solar system
solar telescope
solar wind
sunspots
universal law of gravitation

Review

On your paper write the word or words that best complete each sentence.

1. The instrument that provided the first scientific measurements of the sun was the ______.
2. A solar ______ projects an image of the sun into a darkened room where it can be safely studied.
3. Granules are found on the ______, the apparent bright-yellow face of the sun.
4. Compared to the photosphere, the temperatures of sunspots are ______.
5. Sunspots show that the sun ______ about once every 25 days.
6. The steady stream of the solar wind from the corona causes frequent ______ at polar latitudes on Earth.
7. Solar ______ are sudden outbursts of light that rise up in areas of sunspot activity.
8. Gusts of solar wind cause ______ storms on Earth.
9. The nuclear reaction in the sun changes ______ to helium.
10. Planets, ______, ______, ______, and ______ are all solar system members.
11. The planets travel eastward against the background of stars but periodically make backward loops called ______ motion.
12. Ptolemy used a ______ solar system to describe the motions of planets in the sky.
13. In a heliocentric solar system, the planets travel around the ______.

14. Kepler used Tycho Brahe's data to show that the orbits of the planets were ________.
15. According to Kepler's equal area law, the speed of a planet ________ when it is nearer to the sun.
16. In Kepler's harmonic law, the period of a planet can be determined if its ________ from the sun is known.
17. Using a ________, Galileo discovered the four largest moons of Jupiter.
18. Increasing the distance between two objects causes the force of gravitation between them to ________.

Interpret and Apply

On your paper answer each question in complete sentences. Show any calculations.

1. Using the data in Topic 2, determine how long it would take the SST *Concorde* to fly from Earth to Jupiter. (Distance from the sun to Earth is about 150 000 000 km; from the sun to Jupiter, about 778 000 000 km.)
2. The average speed of the coronal solar wind is 400 km/s. How long does it take a particle in such a wind to reach Earth? (Assume that the distance from Earth to the sun is 150 000 000 km; there are 86 400 seconds in a day.)
3. *Skylab* entered Earth's atmosphere and burned up in 1979. As *Skylab* spiraled toward Earth, its orbital speed increased. Why?
4. Using Kepler's equal area law, explain why the speed of an object in a perfectly circular orbit is constant.
5. Using Kepler's harmonic law, calculate the period of a planet that is four times farther from the sun than Earth.
6. Using the equation given in Topic 13, demonstrate how the gravitational force between two objects changes when they are moved to **(a)** 3 times their original distance, **(b)** 10 times their original distance, **(c)** ½ their original distance, **(d)** 1/10 their original distance.

Critical Thinking

When Venus is observed from Earth, it is never more than 45° of arc from the sun. Figure A shows the positions of Earth, the sun, and Venus in a geocentric system. Three *phases,* or lighted portions of Venus visible from Earth, are also shown. In the geocentric system Venus and the sun are always on the same side of Earth. Figure B shows the positions of Venus, Earth, and the sun in a heliocentric system, and shows eight phases of Venus. Study Figures A and B and answer questions 1 – 4.

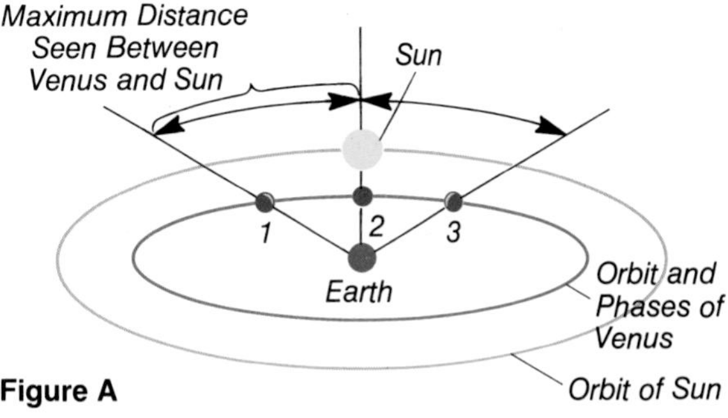

Figure A

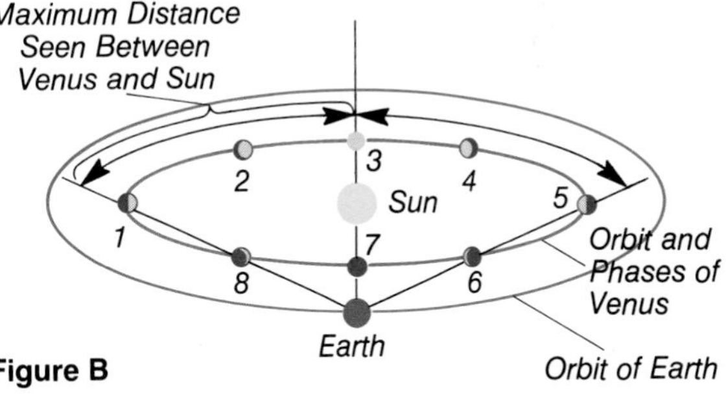

Figure B

1. Which phases in Figure B match phases 1, 2, and 3 shown in Figure A?
2. When Galileo looked at Venus with his telescope, he saw Venus in phases that are impossible in the geocentric system shown in Figure A. What phases did Galileo see?
3. Why did Galileo's observations of Venus help to disprove the geocentric model of the solar system?
4. Are there other planets that would show phases, as Venus does? Explain.

CHAPTER

23 The Planets and the Solar System

▲ The Great Red Spot on Jupiter has long intrigued scientists.

How Do You Know That . . .

Jupiter's atmosphere is stormy and turbulent? A series of close-up photographs taken by the *Voyager* space probes recorded atmospheric movement in swirling bands. A prominent feature of Jupiter's atmosphere is the Great Red Spot, first discovered by telescope over 300 years ago. The large white oval below the Great Red Spot formed only 40 years ago. Over the years, other spots have formed but have later disappeared. Why the Great Red Spot has lasted so long is just one of the many mysteries of the solar system.

I The Inner Planets

Topic 1 Two Groups of Planets

Pioneer, Mariner, Voyager, Venera—these are the names of some of the spacecraft launched from Earth to explore the solar system. Spacecraft bearing these names have flown past Mercury, Venus, Mars, Jupiter, Saturn, and Uranus, and have provided us with a new and exciting view of our neighborhood in space.

Even before the Space Age, scientists knew a great deal about the solar system. The planets are divided into two groups. The four planets nearest the sun—Mercury, Venus, Earth, and Mars—are the **inner planets**, while the other five—Jupiter, Saturn, Uranus, Neptune, and Pluto—are the **outer planets**. The asteroids that orbit between Mars and Jupiter divide the two groups.

The four inner planets are also called the **terrestrial**, or earthlike, **planets**. All have a rocky crust, a denser mantle layer, and a very dense core. All have average densities well above that of water.

Jupiter, Saturn, Uranus, and Neptune are the **Jovian**, or Jupiter-like, **planets**. These planets are huge compared to terrestrial planets. Jovian planets are gaseous and much less dense than the terrestrial planets. Pluto, an outer planet because of its location, is not dense enough to be terrestrial nor large enough to be Jovian.

OBJECTIVES

A Describe methods for grouping planets and give examples of planets in each group.

B Describe the properties and features of Mercury and Venus.

C Explain why some planets are seen only at sunrise or sunset while others can be seen all night.

D Identify the properties and features of Mars and compare Mars with Earth.

Topic 2 Planet Mercury

Mercury is the planet nearest the sun. It orbits the sun in the shortest period of time—88 Earth days. Mercury is the smallest of the four terrestrial planets. Mercury's diameter is one third Earth's, and its gravity is about two fifths of Earth's. Mercury's magnetic field is hundreds of times weaker than Earth's.

Little was known about Mercury until *Mariner 10* photographed it in 1975. These photographs show that craters cover about 75 percent of Mercury's surface. Like the craters on Earth's moon, these **impact craters** probably formed when huge rocks smashed into Mercury. The rest of the surface is smooth plains that may have been formed by lava flowing out of cracks in the surface.

Mercury turns on its axis once every 59 days. This slow rate, combined with Mercury's nearness to the sun, causes a daytime temperature of more than 400°C. In the nighttime, heat radiates away quickly and the temperature may be as low as −200°C.

Mercury has almost no atmosphere. Its weak gravity results in a low escape velocity. High daytime temperatures cause any particles to move at high speeds, allowing gases to escape into space.

23.1 A close-up shows that the surface of Mercury is cratered.

Topic 3 **Planet Venus**

Venus has been called Earth's twin because the two are near each other and are similar in diameter, mass, and gravity. Unlike Earth, however, Venus has a very weak magnetic field. Unlike the other planets, Venus rotates from east to west.

Thick, pale yellow clouds in Venus' atmosphere make its surface impossible to see from Earth. A few photographs have been taken by landers. However, knowledge of most of Venus' surface comes from mapping by radar from Earth and from Soviet *Venera* and U.S. *Pioneer-Venus* spacecraft in orbit around Venus.

Radar images show the surface of Venus to have some remarkable similarities to the surface of Earth. The crumpled and torn structures that are typical of tectonic activity on Earth are also found on Venus. For example, a region of folded and broken crust on Venus looks much like the Appalachian Mountains on Earth. Another area seems to have several large faults resembling the San Andreas Fault in California. Both features would seem to indicate plate motions similar to those on Earth. However, there is no proof of the volcanic activity that goes along with plate motions on Earth. Venus has some features that look like volcanic cones but none appear to have been active within the past 1 billion years.

In 1985, two balloons carrying weather instruments were placed in the atmosphere of Venus to take measurements. The data showed that the dense atmosphere is mostly carbon dioxide with about three percent nitrogen. Venus' yellow clouds are made of droplets of concentrated sulfuric acid. The surface atmospheric pressure is about 90 times greater than that on Earth.

Despite Venus' thick clouds, its surface gets very hot. Carbon dioxide in the atmosphere acts like the glass roof of a greenhouse. About 25 percent of the sunlight striking Venus reaches the surface and heats the rock. Like a blanket, the carbon dioxide atmosphere

23.2 (left) A Russian *Venera* lander provided this photograph of the surface of Venus. (right) This ultraviolet image of Venus from the *Pioneer-Venus Orbiter* shows a turbulent, cloudy atmosphere.

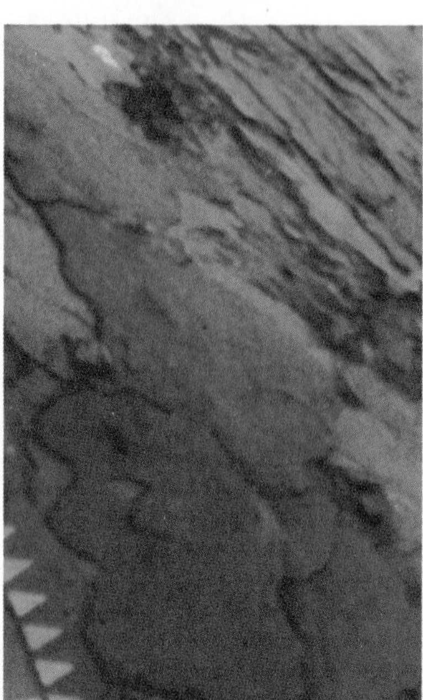

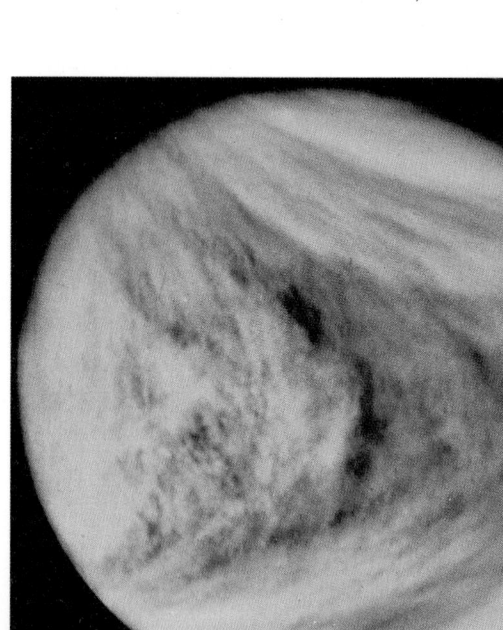

prevents much of this heat from escaping to space. The result of this **greenhouse effect** is a surface temperature of about 460°C. The heating of the atmosphere also leads to strong upper-air winds of over 300 kilometers per hour.

Topic 4 Evening and Morning Stars

Venus is visible to observers on Earth at either evening or morning twilight almost all year. Because Venus is nearer the sun than is Earth, it appears only in parts of the sky near the sun. During most of the daytime, the sun is too bright for Venus to be seen. However, when Venus is east of the sun, the sun sets first and Venus is seen in the evening twilight of the western sky. At such times, Venus is called an **evening star**. It may remain visible as long as three hours after sunset. When Venus is west of the sun, it rises before the sun and is seen in the eastern sky as a **morning star**.

Mercury also can be seen only as a morning or evening star. However, Mercury is much more difficult to see because its orbit is closer to the sun. It is also smaller and less bright than Venus.

When Mars, Jupiter, and Saturn appear close to the sun, they are also seen as morning or evening stars. However, these planets have orbits beyond Earth's and can also appear in the nighttime sky.

23.3 When Venus is east of the sun, the sun sets before it. Then Venus is clearly visible in the evening sky.

Topic 5 Planet Mars

Mars is the fourth planet from the sun and the first planet outside Earth's orbit. Mars takes 687 days to orbit the sun. Its diameter and gravity are about one half those of Earth. Mars has a very weak magnetic field.

Mars' axis is tilted at almost the same angle and in the same direction as Earth's. This tilt gives Mars four seasons similar to Earth's. However, because a Martian year is about twice as long as an Earth year, each Martian season is also twice as long. Because it is farther from the sun, Mars is colder than Earth. By day, Mars may be as warm as 27°C at the surface, but at night the temperature drops as low as −125°C. The thin Martian atmosphere is about 95 percent carbon dioxide and 5 percent nitrogen and argon with traces of other gases. Because the atmosphere is so thin, atmospheric pressure is about 150 times less than on Earth.

Like Earth, Mars has polar ice caps. Unlike Earth, the polar caps are mostly frozen carbon dioxide and some frozen water. The caps increase in size during each Martian winter and shrink during each summer. The temperature difference between the polar caps and soil warmed by the spring sun leads to strong winds and great swirling dust storms that often cover the entire planet.

The surface of Mars has been photographed by half a dozen spacecraft. The *Viking* spacecraft also sent landers to the surface that took close-up photos, recorded quakes and weather, and tested soil samples. Photographs show that Mars' northern hemisphere is

23.4 A photograph of Mars taken from *Viking 1*

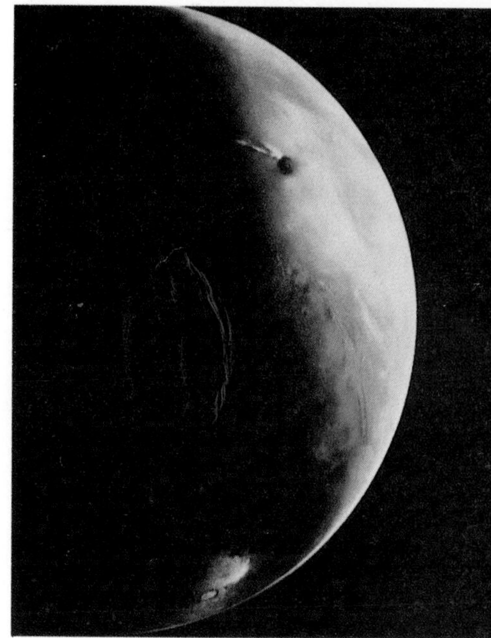

23.5 *Viking* landers photographed the surface of Mars and did tests of its soil and atmosphere. Further exploration of Mars is expected.

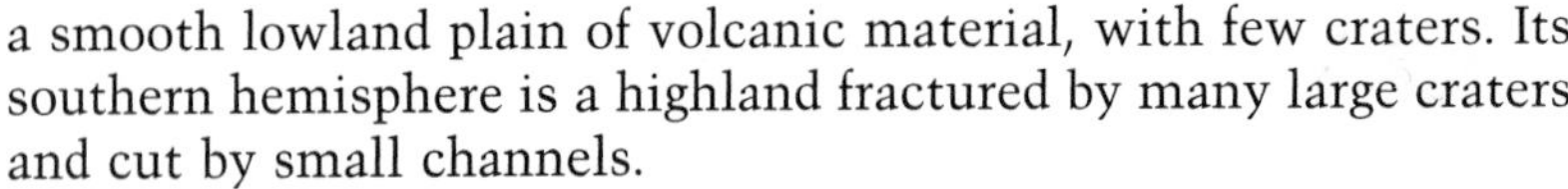

a smooth lowland plain of volcanic material, with few craters. Its southern hemisphere is a highland fractured by many large craters and cut by small channels.

Rising above the northern plains are several extinct volcanoes. The largest, also the largest known volcano in the solar system, is the shield volcano Olympus Mons (Mount Olympus). It is about 600 kilometers across and 25 kilometers high. Earth's highest volcano, Mauna Loa, rises only 8 kilometers above the Pacific Ocean floor. Unlike many of Earth's volcanoes, Martian volcanoes do not seem to be related to plate motions. The crustal rock of Mars appears thick, strong, and unbroken.

Cutting across the craters of the southern hemisphere is the Valles Marineris, a canyon system nearly as long as the United States is wide. While the canyon system appears to have been carved by water, there is no water on the surface of Mars. Some scientists think that water may have been an agent of erosion in the past. Frozen water reservoirs may lie beneath the surface of Mars.

Is there life on Mars? The *Viking* landers made chemical tests on soil samples to find out. The results were not clear, and while some scientists still hope that evidence of life will be found, many now think it very unlikely.

TOPIC QUESTIONS

Each topic question refers to the topic of the same number.

1. **(a)** How are planets classified as inner and outer? **(b)** Name the terrestrial planets and identify ways they are alike. **(c)** Name the Jovian planets and identify ways they are alike.

2. **(a)** Compare Mercury's orbital period, diameter, gravity, and magnetic field with Earth's. **(b)** Identify the two kinds of surface features on Mercury and name the cause of each. **(c)** Why is Mercury so hot by day and so cold at night? **(d)** Why does Mercury have almost no atmosphere?

3. **(a)** How are Venus and Earth alike? Different? **(b)** Why is the surface of Venus difficult to study? What method has been used to learn about it? **(c)** How is the surface of Venus like Earth's? Different from Earth's? **(d)** Describe the composition, temperature, and pressure of Venus' atmosphere.

4. **(a)** Why are Venus and Mercury only seen as evening or morning stars? **(b)** Why can other planets be seen all night?

5. **(a)** Compare Mars' period of revolution, diameter, gravitation, and magnetic field with Earth's. **(b)** How are seasons on Mars like seasons on Earth? How are they different? **(c)** How do polar caps on Mars change with the seasons? **(d)** What causes dust storms on Mars? **(e)** How do the surfaces of the northern and southern hemispheres of Mars differ? **(f)** What is the evidence of water on Mars?

II The Outer Planets

OBJECTIVES

A Contrast the Jovian planets with the terrestrial planets and describe properties common to Jovian planets.

B Discuss the properties and features of Jupiter and Saturn and compare and contrast these two planets.

C Describe the features of Uranus and identify those which are unusual.

D Describe the features of Neptune and Pluto.

Topic 6 The Jovian Planets

The Jovian planets—Jupiter, Saturn, Uranus, and Neptune—are unlike the terrestrial planets in several ways. First, Jovian planets are much larger. The smallest Jovian planet, Uranus, is nearly 15 times more massive than the largest terrestrial planet, Earth. Second, Jovian planets are gas planets and their surface is the top of the gas layer. Third, Jovian planets are composed mainly of the light elements hydrogen and helium, while terrestrial planets are made of iron, silicon, oxygen, and other heavy elements.

All Jovian planets have a three-layered structure. A rocky core may lie at the center of each. The rocky core is surrounded by a liquid mantle. For Jupiter and Saturn, this mantle is thought to be liquid hydrogen. Uranus and Neptune are slightly denser than Jupiter and Saturn, and their mantle layers may contain oxygen, nitrogen, and carbon along with liquid hydrogen. The outer layer of all four planets is mainly gaseous hydrogen and helium.

All the Jovian planets have ring systems, although some rings are very faint and others do not go completely around the planet. The ring systems have three common properties. First, they consist of many particles in independent orbits around the planet. Second, the rings are closer to the planet than its major moons. Third, the rings are centered over the planet's equator. The spectacular rings of Saturn are made of billions of "snowballs" of ice and ice-covered rock. The rings of the other planets are faint and were discovered in the late 1970's by Earth-based telescopes and *Voyagers 1* and *2*. Jupiter's three rings are made of fine bits of dark rock. The 11 rings of Uranus are made of larger rocky chunks. The *ring arcs* of Neptune do not appear to go completely around the planet.

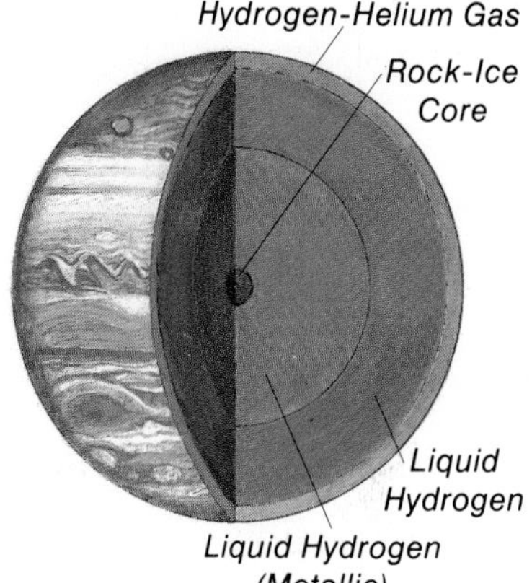

23.6 This diagram shows the possible inner structure of Jupiter. Other Jovian planets have similar inner structures.

Topic 7 Planet Jupiter

Jupiter, the fifth planet from the sun, takes 12 Earth years to complete one orbit. It has the shortest day, equal to only 9.8 Earth hours. It is the largest planet and has twice the total mass of all other planets combined. Jupiter's density is so low that it would float in a tub of water, if a large enough tub existed!

Four spacecraft have flown by Jupiter and returned data and photographs of the planet. These show the structure of Jupiter's gaseous surface. It consists of alternating light- and dark-colored bands that run parallel to its equator. The dark bands are areas of sinking gases while the light bands are areas of rising gases. Between the bands, high velocity winds blow parallel to the equator. The winds at the equator travel eastward at an average speed of 400 kilometers per hour. Directly north and south are narrower bands surrounded by westward winds of about 100 kilometers per hour. Jupiter has five or six such bands in each hemisphere.

23.7 Jupiter's surface consists of a series of light and dark bands. The bands are caused by alternating wind belts.

The Great Red Spot is the most striking feature of Jupiter's surface, and it rises about 8 kilometers above the cloud tops. However, it is just one of several spots. Some spots appear and disappear quickly, while others remain for decades. Photographs indicate that the spots may be relatively calm areas that rotate slowly within the turbulent atmosphere.

Jupiter has the strongest known magnetic field. As on Earth, the interaction between the solar wind and the magnetic field causes brilliant auroras. *Voyager 1* observed these auroras as well as intense lightning storms.

Jupiter radiates between 1.5 and 2.0 times as much heat back to space as it receives from the sun. The extra heat is thought to come from Jupiter's original heat of formation and from contraction due to gravity.

The moons of Jupiter are described in Topic 12.

Topic 8 Planet Saturn

Saturn, the sixth planet from the sun, takes nearly 30 Earth years to complete one orbit. Saturn turns on its axis once every 10.2 hours. Most of what is known about Saturn was learned from the flyby flights of *Pioneer 11* in 1979 and *Voyagers 1* and *2* in 1980 and 1981.

Like Jupiter, the surface of Saturn has colored bands, which are areas of rising and sinking gases, parallel to the equator. Saturn, however, has fewer bands than Jupiter, and the wind speed at its equator is faster—about 1800 kilometers per hour. Saturn's density, like Jupiter's, is low—less than 1 gram per cubic centimeter.

Saturn radiates between 1.5 and 2.5 times as much energy as it receives from the sun. Like Jupiter, it apparently has sources of internal heat. Saturn has a weak magnetic field.

The moons of Saturn are described in Topic 13.

23.8 The surface of Saturn, like that of Jupiter, has alternating wind belts.

Topic 9 **Planet Uranus**

Uranus, the seventh planet from the sun, takes 84 Earth years to complete one orbit. Because Uranus is not easily visible to the unaided eye from Earth, it was not discovered until 1781. Uranus is about 19 times farther from the sun than Earth is. Sunlight there is about 360 times fainter than on Earth, and the average surface temperature is only about −200°C.

Uranus has many unusual features. It turns on its axis once every 17.3 hours, the slowest rate of any Jovian planet. More unusual is its axis of rotation—it is tipped almost completely over, so that Uranus orbits the sun on its side. At the present time, the planet's south pole is pointed almost straight at the sun. Some scientists think that the planet was tipped by a collision with an Earth-sized mass of material early in the history of the solar system.

When *Voyager 2* flew past Uranus in 1986, it discovered something surprising about the planet's magnetic field. Even though the planet is tipped over, the magnetic field is nearly upright. For most planets the axis of rotation and the magnetic field differ by only a few degrees. On Uranus the difference is 60 degrees. This difference causes the planet's magnetic field to trace a spiral pattern in the solar wind as the planet rotates. Scientists used this difference to gain better data about the planet. Usually, rotation rates for Jovian planets are difficult to determine because the movement of the gaseous outer layers may not be the same as the movement of the whole planet. A planet's magnetic field is generated in its core, which does rotate at the same rate as the whole planet. The spiral pattern traced by the magnetic field made it possible to determine Uranus' rate of rotation very accurately.

Voyager scientists were also surprised at the temperatures in the atmosphere of Uranus. The side of the planet facing away from the sun was no cooler than the side facing the sun. In fact, the temperature of the atmosphere is nearly the same over the entire surface of the planet. The reason for this similarity is not yet clear, but some sort of atmospheric currents seem to be at work.

23.9 *Voyager 2* took this photograph of Uranus in 1986.

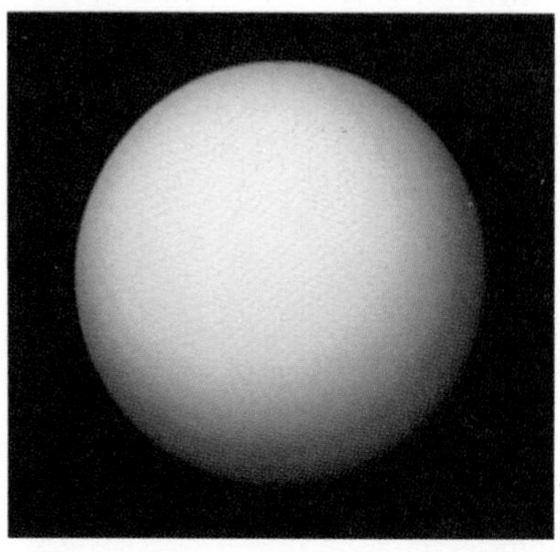

23.10 For most planets, the angle between the axis of rotation and the magnetic field is small. For Uranus, however, the difference is 60°.

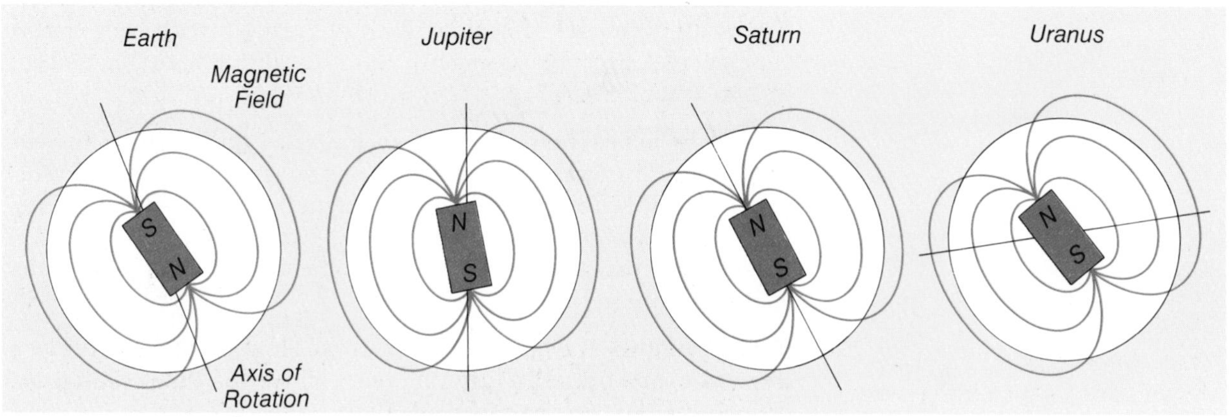

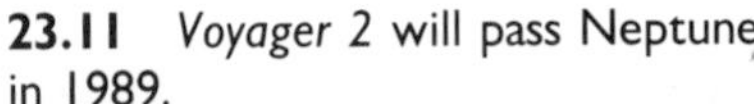

23.11 *Voyager 2* will pass Neptune in 1989.

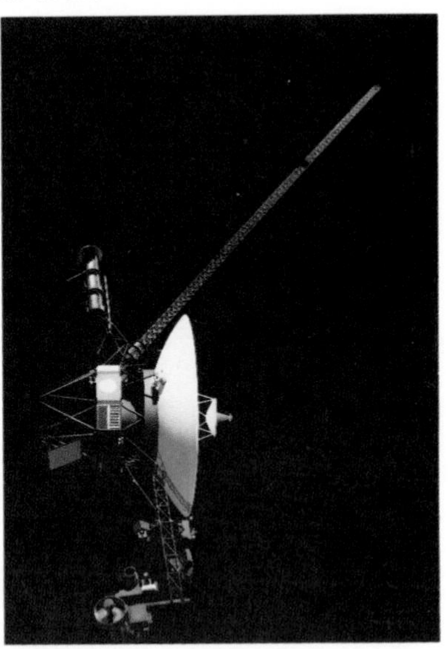

Topic 10 Neptune and Pluto

Neptune is the most distant of the Jovian planets. It was located in 1846 after the behavior of Uranus led some astronomers to think that the force of another planet might be the cause. Neptune turns once on its axis every 18–22 hours. It takes 165 years to orbit the sun. Neptune is thought to be similar in structure and atmosphere to the other Jovian plants. *Voyager 2* will pass Neptune in 1989.

Pluto is the smallest, most distant, and coldest planet. Its surface temperature is probably below −220°C. It appears to be a great snowball of water ice, some rocky material, and frozen gases, one of which is methane. Pluto's thin atmosphere contains methane and helium.

Pluto has the most unusual orbit of any of the planets. Its orbit is a longer ellipse than the orbits of other planets. Also, Pluto's orbit crosses the orbit of Neptune. At present, Pluto is nearer the sun than Neptune is and will be until March of 1999. Pluto's orbital plane is also the most inclined. The plane is tilted 17° when compared to the orbital planes of the majority of the planets.

TOPIC QUESTIONS

Each topic question refers to the topic of the same number.

6. **(a)** List some ways the Jovian planets are different from the terrestrial planets. **(b)** Describe the internal structure of the Jovian planets. **(c)** List three properties common to the Jovian ring systems.
7. **(a)** Identify two ways Jupiter is different from all the other planets. **(b)** Describe Jupiter's winds. **(c)** Describe Jupiter's magnetic field. **(d)** How does the amount of heat that Jupiter radiates to space compare with the amount it receives from the sun?
8. **(a)** How is the surface of Saturn similar to that of Jupiter? How is it different? **(b)** How does the amount of heat Saturn receives from the sun compare to the amount it radiates back to space?
9. **(a)** In what ways is Uranus unusual? **(b)** What is unusual about Uranus' axis of rotation and magnetic field? **(c)** What kind of pattern does Uranus' magnetic field make in space? What were scientists able to determine from the pattern? **(d)** Why are scientists puzzled by the temperatures of Uranus' atmosphere?
10. **(a)** Describe the planet Neptune. **(b)** How are the size, temperature, and orbit of Pluto unique? **(c)** Why is Pluto sometimes nearer the sun than Neptune is?

III Planetary Satellites

Topic 11 Satellites of Earth and Mars

Bodies that revolve around planets are called **satellites**, or **moons**. Except for Mercury and Venus, each planet has at least one natural satellite. The moon is Earth's only natural satellite. At 3476 kilometers across, it is about one fourth Earth's diameter and slightly larger than the planet Mercury. The moon's average distance from Earth is 386 000 kilometers. It circles Earth every 27.3 days. Earth's moon is the subject of Chapter 24.

Mars has two tiny moons, Phobos (FEE bus) and Deimos (DIE mus). Both have irregular shapes and are marked with impact craters. Phobos, the larger of the two, is only 27 kilometers across its widest point. It is closer to Mars and circles the planet three times a day.

OBJECTIVES

A Define *satellite*, identify two planets that have no satellites, and describe the satellites of Mars.

B Name the four Galilean satellites and identify features unique to each.

C Identify and describe the major moons of Saturn, Uranus, Neptune, and Pluto.

Topic 12 Jupiter's Moons

Jupiter has at least 16 moons. Only 13 moons were known until *Voyager* discovered 3 more in 1979. The four largest moons—Io, Europa, Ganymede, and Callisto—are known as the *Galilean satellites* in honor of their discoverer, Galileo. Ganymede is the largest moon in the solar system. Callisto is almost as large. Io and Europa are about the size of Earth's moon. Most of what is known about these moons comes from *Voyager* photographs taken in 1979.

Io, nearest of the Galilean satellites to Jupiter, is one of the most exciting moons. Its color varies from bright yellow-orange to red, and it is geologically active! At least 10 active volcanoes have been filmed in eruptions that reach as high as 320 kilometers. The materials that erupt from the volcanoes—sulfur, sulfur dioxide, and other sulfur compounds—cause Io's yellow-orange color. Unlike most bodies in the solar system, Io shows no signs of impact craters. If craters ever existed on Io, they have been completely covered by material erupted from the volcanoes. Io's density is about 3.5 g/cm^3, which is close to that of Earth's moon. Io is thought to have an atmosphere of sulfur dioxide. Its surface is probably covered by layers of sulfur and frozen sulfur dioxide. Its interior may be molten silicate rock. Io may get its internal heat from friction due to the gravitational pull of Jupiter.

Europa, next out from Jupiter, is also a rock-core moon with a density somewhat less than that of Earth's moon. Europa's strangely smooth and shiny white surface appears to be a crust of ice (mostly frozen water) about 100 kilometers thick. The surface is marked by a crisscross pattern of bright and dark lines that are still a mystery. Scientists think there may be deep oceans of water beneath the ice. If so, it is possible that simple forms of life, like those in the lakes of Antarctica, have developed.

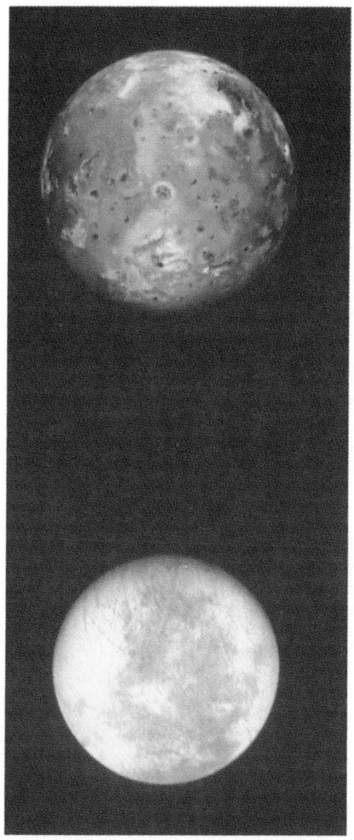

23.12 Two of Jupiter's four Galilean moons: (top) Io, (bottom) Europa

23.13 The Galilean moons (left) Ganymede, (right) Callisto

Ganymede and Callisto, next in order from Jupiter, are very different from Io and Europa. Their densities are less than 2 g/cm^3, which suggests that these moons are mainly ice. Both Ganymede and Callisto appear to be covered by thick layers of ice mixed with rock. Their interiors are probably ice with silicate rock cores. Callisto is the most cratered body in the solar system. Its craters were made some 4 billion years ago. Ganymede's surface has dark areas that are cratered like Callisto, but it also has lighter areas. The lighter areas are marked by many grooves that seem to be long parallel ridges and valleys. The grooves are much younger than the impact craters. Geologists think the grooves may have been formed by movements of crustal plates which—if they do exist—are ice.

Topic 13 **Saturn's Titan**

Until the Space Age, Saturn was known to have nine moons, all discovered before 1900. Recently, new moons have been discovered by both telescopes and spacecraft. The latest count is 17 (with 3 more unconfirmed). The largest and most interesting is Titan.

Titan is the second largest moon in the solar system. Its density is just under 2 g/cm^3, and it seems to be about half rock and half frozen water. Most of the ice is included in a thick shell reaching nearly halfway to the center. The rest of the interior is rock.

Titan is the only moon known to have a substantial atmosphere. Its atmospheric pressure is about 1.5 times Earth's. Like Earth, its principal gas is nitrogen, which is estimated to be from 90 to 99 percent of the total atmosphere. Most of the remaining gas is methane with traces of hydrogen cyanide and acetylene.

Titan's surface temperature is about −180°C. This is cold enough to turn methane and other gases to liquid. The resulting droplets form a dense orange smog that hides Titan's surface.

Topic 14 The Moons of Uranus

Only 5 of Uranus' moons were known until *Voyager 2* discovered 10 additional, small moons in 1986. *Voyager 2* also sent back incredible pictures of the five previously known moons.

The five largest moons of Uranus are Titania, Oberon, Umbriel, Ariel, and Miranda. All are alike in that they are dark, lack atmospheres, and have many impact craters on their surfaces. But differences between the moons are visible in the *Voyager* photographs. Titania has huge, faulted valleys. Oberon's impact craters are partly flooded with dark material. Umbriel has an unusual dark surface, and Ariel's cratered surface is crisscrossed by valleys and faults. Miranda (Figure 23.14) proved to be the most startling of all. It has parallel V-shaped grooves over a third of its surface, with jagged, sometimes parallel ridges over the rest. The causes of these features remains unknown.

23.14 The Uranian moon Miranda, as imaged by *Voyager 2* in 1986

Topic 15 The Moons of Neptune and Pluto

Neptune has two known moons, Triton and Nereid. Until *Voyager 2* reaches Neptune in 1989, very little will be known about these moons or about any other moons Neptune may have. Triton, the larger of Neptune's moons, may be nearly as large as Saturn's Titan. It may also have a very thin methane atmosphere.

Voyager 2 is not expected to pass close enough to Pluto to show much about that planet. Telescopic observations from Earth will remain the best source of information. Such observations have shown that Pluto has at least one moon. This moon, Charon (KARE en), was discovered in 1978. Charon's diameter seems to be about half that of Pluto. Charon orbits Pluto in 6.4 days.

TOPIC QUESTIONS

Each topic question refers to the topic of the same number.

11. **(a)** What is a satellite? **(b)** Which planets have no satellites? **(c)** Describe Mars' satellites.

12. **(a)** Name the Galilean moons of Jupiter. Why are they called Galilean? **(b)** Identify one unique feature for each of the Galilean moons.

13. Describe Saturn's moons.

14. **(a)** List the five largest moons of Uranus. **(b)** Name some ways in which all five moons are alike. **(c)** Identify one unique feature of each.

15. Identify the moons of Neptune and Pluto.

OBJECTIVES

A Describe the appearance of a comet, its orbit, behavior, and composition and identify some comets.

B Describe the sizes, shapes, and orbits of asteroids and discuss their possible origin.

C Define *meteoroid, meteor, meteorite,* and *meteor shower,* and name and describe the three types of meteorites.

D Explain why meteorite craters are rare on Earth.

IV Comets, Asteroids, and Meteoroids

Topic 16 Comets

What are the parts of a **comet**? A photograph of a comet, Figure 23.15, shows a glowing head and a long, bright tail. The head, or *nucleus,* of the comet glows by reflected sunlight. The nucleus is surrounded by a hazy cloud called a *coma.* Some comets are also surrounded by great clouds of hydrogen. Comets have been observed since earliest times, and many new comets are discovered every year. Most comets, however, can be seen only through telescopes.

Most of the time, a comet is barely visible even through a telescope. Comets spend much of the time out beyond the orbit of Pluto, and only shine by reflected sunlight. When a comet comes near the sun, solar wind drives particles and gases away from the coma and forms the tail. Because the tail is formed by solar wind, it always points away from the sun.

Most comets have very large, elongated orbits. Some come near the sun only once in thousands of years. The closest, Encke's comet, returns every 3.3 years. The most famous, Comet Halley (Halley's comet), returns every 76 years. The comet is named for Edmund Halley, an eighteenth-century English astronomer. In studying records of comets, Halley noticed that bright comets had appeared in 1531, 1607, and 1682. He thought that these were all one comet with an orbital period of about 76 years. He correctly predicted its return sometime in 1758 or 1759. It returned again in 1835, 1910, and 1986.

When Comet Halley returned in 1986, it was studied by six different spacecraft in a truly international effort. *VeGa 1* and *VeGa 2,* launched by the Soviet Union, flew past the comet. *Giotto,* launched by the European Space Agency, came within 605 kilometers of the comet's nucleus. Two Japanese spacecraft, *Suisei* and *Sakigake,* and the American *Pioneer-Venus Orbiter* viewed the comet from greater distances. Shortly before the encounters with Halley, the *International Cometary Explorer (ICE)* flew through the tail of another comet, Giacobini-Zinner.

Much was learned from the data and photographs returned by these spacecraft. The nucleus of Halley's comet was found to be about 16 kilometers long and 8 kilometers wide, a bit larger and more irregular than expected. American astronomer Fred Whipple has long described the nucleus of a comet as a dirty snowball, meaning that it is mostly ice with small pieces of other materials, such as rock, in it. The large size of Halley, however, indicates that a comet nucleus is mostly empty space. Whipple now thinks that "dirty snowdrift" is a better model. The nucleus of Comet Halley was found to contain carbon, nitrogen, oxygen, sulfur, and magnesium, elements common throughout the solar system.

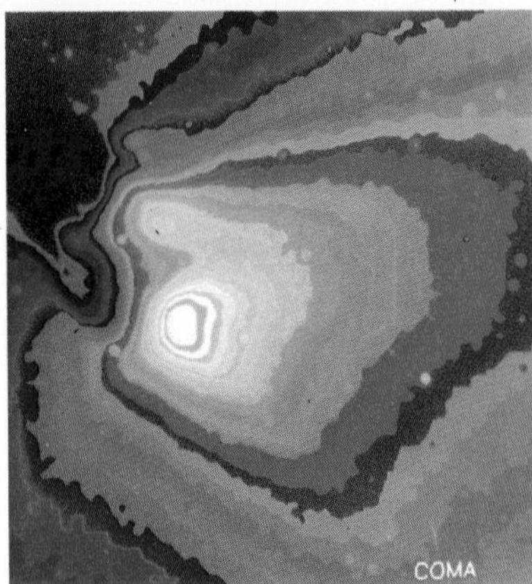

23.15 (top) Comet Halley as photographed through a telescope in 1986 (bottom) A false-color image of Comet Halley made during the *Giotto* mission in 1986.

Topic 17 Asteroids

Early astronomers thought a planet would be found in the great space between Mars and Jupiter. In 1801, the Sicilian clergyman Piazzi discovered the "planet" Ceres. Ceres, however, later proved to be too small to be a planet. It is merely the largest of many small, planetlike bodies called asteroids, of which there are thousands.

Asteroids are solid, rocklike masses. Most seem to have irregular shapes, which explain why their brightness changes as they rotate. Only the two largest, Ceres and Pallas, are spherical. Ceres has a diameter of about 1000 kilometers. Most asteroids are less than 1 kilometer long.

Asteroids revolve around the sun in the same direction as the planets. Most asteroid orbits are nearly circular and lie between Mars and Jupiter. A few, however, have long oval orbits. Some come close to Mercury at perihelion. The most unusual orbit is that of Chiron (KIE ron), discovered in 1977. Its perihelion is inside Saturn's orbit; its aphelion is just inside Uranus' orbit.

How did asteroids originate? Scientists think that some asteroids are left over pieces from the solar system's formation. Others may be extinct or inactive comets.

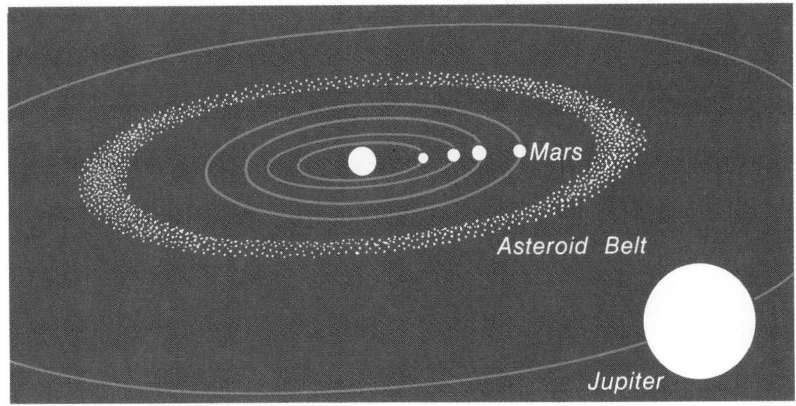

23.16 Most asteroids orbit in a belt located between the orbits of Mars and Jupiter.

Topic 18 Meteors and Meteroids

A **meteoroid** is a rock fragment traveling in space. Meteoroids may be as large as boulders or as small as sand grains. A **meteor** is the light made by a meteoroid as it passes through Earth's atmosphere. The light is caused by friction between the rapidly moving meteoroid and the atmosphere. The friction excites the atoms in the atmosphere and causes them to glow. The meteoroid may burn as it enters the atmosphere. An unusually bright meteor is sometimes called a *fireball.*

On a clear, dark night about 5 to 15 meteors can be seen every hour. However, this is a small portion of all meteors. Scientists estimate that about 100 million meteroids enter the atmosphere daily. Most are tiny and burn or vaporize in the air. The dust and gases from meteoroids add a few metric tons to Earth each day.

Some meteoroids travel through space alone. Others are part of great groups of billions of particles called *meteoroid swarms,* which are associated with the orbits of comets. **Meteor showers** occur when Earth crosses a meteoroid swarm, which happens several times a year. At such times, large numbers of meteors are seen. The meteors of a particular shower appear to come from the same constellation and are named for that constellation. Among the best-known meteor showers are the Perseids about August 12, the Orionids about October 20, the Taurids about November 10, and the Geminids about December 10.

Topic 19 Meteorites

A **meteorite** is part of a large meteoroid that survives its trip through the atmosphere and strikes Earth's surface. There are three basic types of meteorites. Ninety-three percent of all meteorites are *stones.* Stones strongly resemble Earth's dark igneous rocks. They are composed primarily of silicates but include 10 to 15 percent iron. The largest known stone weighs about a metric ton. It landed at Norton County, Kansas, in 1948.

23.17 This large meteorite has a mass of about 34 metric tons. It is on display at the Hayden Planetarium in New York City.

The second group of meteorites are called *irons* because they are 85 to 95 percent iron. The remainder is nickel. Iron meteorites are usually black outside and silvery inside. Since they consist largely of iron and nickel, they are much heavier than stones. One of the largest known irons was found in Greenland. It weighs over 30 metric tons. The third group of meteorites are *stony-irons.* These rare meteorites are a mixture of stone and iron.

The most abundant source of meteorites is the Antarctic ice cap. First discovered in 1969, some meteorites had been buried and preserved in the ice for thousands of years. They are exposed at the surface when wind erosion removes the ice around them. Thousands of meteorites have been recovered from Antarctica, providing an enormous increase in the supply of extraterrestrial material available for study. Some Antarctic meteorites appear to have come from the moon or from Mars. They may have been launched into space as particles by meteoroid impact on those bodies.

Topic 20 Meteorite Craters

Impact craters are common features of some planets and most moons in the solar system. However, impact craters are rare features on Earth. One reason is that Earth's atmosphere burns up most meteroids before they strike the surface. A second reason is that Earth is geologically active and continually erases the marks made by impacts. However, Earth still has some *meteorite craters* that were formed relatively recently.

23.18 Barringer Meteorite Crater in Arizona probably formed when an asteroid crashed into Earth about 25 000 years ago.

The Barringer Meteorite Crater (also called Meteor Crater) in Arizona is thought to have formed 25 000 years ago when an iron meteorite about 20 meters in diameter struck Earth's surface and exploded. The crater is 1300 meters in diameter and nearly 200 meters deep. Fragments of the meteorite were scattered more than a kilometer from the crater. Craters larger than Barringer Meteorite Crater have been found in Australia, Africa, and Canada.

TOPIC QUESTIONS

Each topic question refers to the topic of the same number.

16. **(a)** Describe the parts of a comet. **(b)** What causes a comet to have a tail? Why does the tail always point away from the sun? **(c)** Describe the orbit and period of most comets. **(d)** Describe the comet explorations that took place in 1985–86. **(e)** Describe the composition of comets.

17. **(a)** Describe the general size, shape, and orbit of asteroids. **(b)** How might asteroids have originated?

18. **(a)** Distinguish between a meteoroid and a meteor. **(b)** Why do meteor showers occur? Name and give the dates of several meteor showers.

19. **(a)** What is a meteorite? **(b)** Name and describe three types of meteorites. **(c)** What is unusual about Antarctic meteorites?

20. **(a)** Why are impact craters rare on Earth? **(b)** Describe the shape and possible origin of the Barringer Meteorite Crater.

Guion S. Bluford, Jr.

Aerospace Engineer

At 2:37 A.M. Eastern Standard Time, August 30, 1983, Lieutenant Colonel Guion S. Bluford, Jr., of the U.S. Air Force was launched into space on the successful third flight of the space shuttle *Challenger.* His duties as part of the five-member crew included deployment of the satellite *Insat-1B* for the country of India and assisting the two pilots in the ascent and landing phases of the flight. *Insat-1B* is a combination telecommunication and meteorological satellite. From its position in an orbit nearly 36 000 kilometers above the Indian Ocean, it beams telephone and television communications to all parts of India. Colonel Bluford's other duties included monitoring equipment which is being used in ongoing experiments aboard the space shuttles. Since then, Colonel Bluford has flown other space shuttle missions.

Colonel Bluford is an experienced flyer who flew 144 combat missions in Vietnam. He received a doctorate in aerospace engineering from the Air Force Institute of Technology in 1978.

CHAPTER 23 REVIEW

Summary

The planets are grouped by position as inner or outer and by properties as terrestrial or Jovian.

The terrestrial planets are Mercury, Venus, Earth, and Mars. All are similar in size, all are much more dense than water, and all are thought to have similar inner structures.

Venus and Mercury are seen only at sunrise or sunset; other planets can be seen all night.

The Jovian planets are Jupiter, Saturn, Uranus, and Neptune. All are large, all are less dense than terrestrial planets, and all have similar structures, such as a gaseous outer layer, and features, such as rings.

A planetary satellite or moon is a smaller body that revolves around a planet. Except for Venus and Mercury, each planet has at least one satellite. Many satellites have unusual features.

A comet has a nucleus of ice and debris, a coma of gas surrounding the nucleus, a bright tail caused by solar wind, and a large, elongated orbit.

Asteroids are small, planetlike bodies. Most orbit the sun between Mars and Jupiter. Ceres is the largest asteroid.

A meteoroid is a rock fragment in space. A meteor is a meteoroid glowing as it enters Earth's atmosphere. Meteor showers are regular events that occur when Earth's orbit crosses the orbit of a meteoroid swarm. A meteorite is a meteoroid that has reached Earth's surface.

Vocabulary

asteroid	meteorite
comet	meteoroid
evening star	meteor shower
greenhouse effect	morning star
impact crater	outer planet
inner planet	satellite or moon
Jovian planet	terrestrial planet
meteor	

Review

Choose the best answer. Write the letter of your answer on your paper.

1. Which planet is not considered terrestrial? (a) Mars (b) Mercury (c) Saturn (d) Venus
2. A planet that has no atmosphere because of its high temperature and low gravity is (a) Mars, (b) Pluto, (c) Venus, (d) Mercury.
3. A planet that can be seen ONLY as a morning star or as an evening star is (a) Jupiter, (b) Uranus, (c) Venus, (d) Mars.
4. Which planet has polar caps of frozen carbon dioxide? (a) Pluto (b) Mars (c) Venus (d) Jupiter
5. The Jovian planets do NOT have (a) rocky surfaces, (b) moons, (c) rings, (d) magnetic fields.
6. Two planets that radiate away more energy than they receive from the sun are (a) Mars and Earth, (b) Jupiter and Saturn, (c) Venus and Mercury, (d) Neptune and Uranus.
7. Which planet orbits the sun on its side, although its magnetic field is nearly upright? (a) Jupiter (b) Venus (c) Neptune (d) Uranus
8. Two planets whose orbits cross are (a) Pluto and Neptune, (b) Uranus and Saturn, (c) Jupiter and Mars, (d) Venus and Earth.
9. Two planets with no satellites are (a) Pluto and Mercury, (b) Mercury and Venus, (c) Venus and Mars, (d) Mars and Pluto.
10. Which is a Galilean satellite? (a) Deimos (b) Titan (c) Io (d) Charon
11. What is unusual about the moon Titan? (a) It is Saturn's only moon. (b) It has a substantial atmosphere. (c) It has V-shaped grooves. (d) It is the largest of all moons.
12. Which Uranian moon has V-shaped grooves over one third of its surface? (a) Titan (b) Ariel (c) Miranda (d) Titania
13. Which is Pluto's moon? (a) Charon (b) Chiron (c) Titan (d) Titania
14. What kind of an object is Ceres? (a) moon (b) comet (c) asteroid (d) meteor crater

15. Which is NOT true about comets? (a) Most orbit between Mars and Jupiter. (b) They have glowing heads and bright tails. (c) They are usually seen only with telescopes. (d) Their tails point away from the sun.
16. How is meteor defined? (a) rock fragment in space (b) rock fragment that reached Earth's surface (c) rock fragment with a large orbit that reappears (d) light made by a rock fragment burning in the atmosphere
17. Why are impact craters rare on Earth? (a) Its surface resists impacts. (b) Its orbit seldom crosses objects that make craters. (c) Most objects are attracted to the moon. (d) Most objects burn up in the atmosphere.

Interpret and Apply

On your paper, answer each question.

1. Consider an astronomer with a telescope on Venus and another on Mars. Which would have an easier time learning about Earth and why?
2. Occasionally a planet will pass directly between Earth and the face of the sun. Which planets could do this and why?
3. Photographs taken of Mars by telescopes on Earth show very little or none of the south polar cap. Why is it so difficult to see Mars' south polar cap from Earth?
4. Neptune was discovered in 1846. Since then, a complete orbit of the sun by Neptune has not yet been observed. Why is this the case?
5. Phobos revolves around Mars from west to east faster than Mars rotates on its axis from west to east. In what direction does Phobos rise and set?

Critical Thinking

The straight lines on the graph show the speed (in km/s) needed by several gas molecules to escape a planet relative to the absolute, or kelvin (K), temperature of that planet's atmosphere.* Points representing the planets are also on the graph.

1. If the escape speed of a gas from a planet's atmosphere is directly related to the mass of the planet, then according to the graph which planet has the greatest mass? Is this planet, in fact, the largest planet?
2. According to the graph, which planet has the least mass? Is this planet the smallest?
3. Using the graph, identify two pairs of planets that must have nearly the same masses because gases can escape from their atmospheres at nearly the same speeds.
4. According to the graph, which two planets have no atmosphere? (A gas is not held by a planet if the line for that gas is above the point for the planet.)
5. Which planets have both hydrogen and helium in their atmospheres?
6. According to the graph, how does the atmosphere of Earth differ from that of Mars?
7. The average temperature of the atmosphere of Saturn's moon, Titan, is 100 K. The speed needed for a gas to escape from its atmosphere is 0.5 km/s. Which gases could be held in Titan's atmosphere?

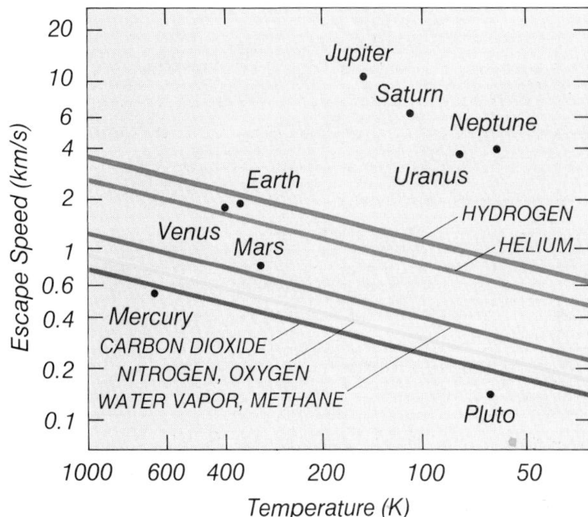

*The speed for a molecule to escape the atmosphere of a planet is not the same as the speed for a spacecraft to escape a planet.

CHAPTER

24 Earth's Moon

▲ The *Apollo* missions were a giant step forward in space exploration.

How Do You Know That . . .

People may someday go back to the moon? Twelve astronauts walked on the moon as part of the *Apollo* program, from 1969–1972. The data and samples that they brought back show that the moon has many potential uses. A lunar mining base could supply materials used up on Earth. A lunar observatory could study the stars without the interference of an atmosphere. A lunar space station could be a stepping stone to other planets. The exploration of the moon has barely begun. Sometime soon, people will return to the moon. Perhaps you will be part of that adventure.

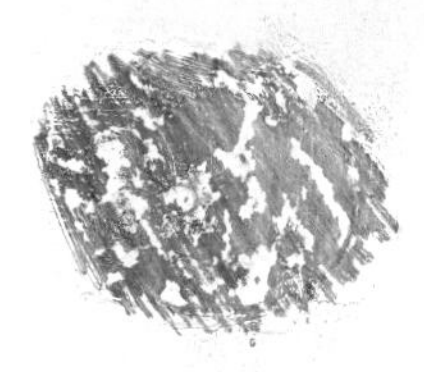

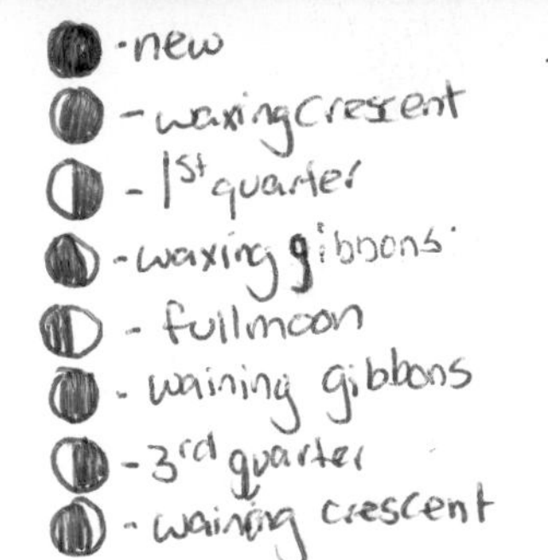

I Lunar Exploration

Topic 1 Getting to the Moon

At 386 000 kilometers away, the moon is Earth's nearest neighbor in space. For more than 350 years, the telescope was the chief instrument for studying the moon. Features on the moon's surface can be observed clearly with a telescope, but such observations are made from a long distance away. The exploration of the moon entered a new phase in 1959 when spacecraft from Earth first flew past the moon and returned data about the lunar surface.

Getting a spacecraft to the moon is a complex task. The rocket used must be large enough to put the spacecraft into Earth orbit before the rocket stops firing (at burnout). Once the spacecraft is in Earth orbit, another rocket fires it out of orbit toward the point where the moon will be when the spacecraft gets there. The aiming and firing of the spacecraft must be precise. If rocket burnout occurs a few seconds too early or too late, or if the spacecraft is not positioned correctly at burnout, the spacecraft will miss the moon and go into orbit around the sun.

OBJECTIVES

A Discuss the steps involved in landing a spacecraft on the moon.

B Identify the kinds of information needed to land an astronaut on the moon and discuss the contributions of the programs leading up to *Apollo*.

C Describe the *Apollo* spacecraft and summarize the accomplishments of the *Apollo* program.

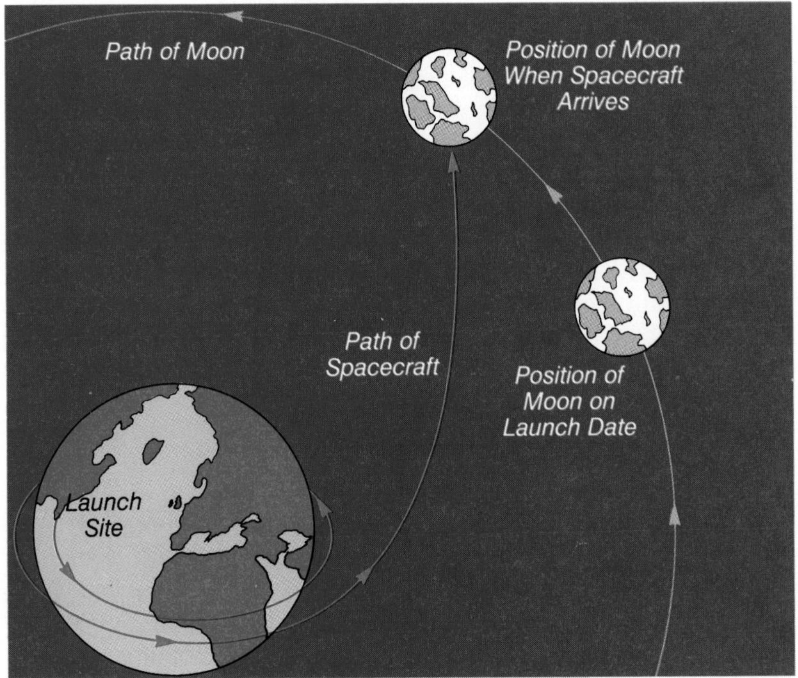

24.1 A lunar spacecraft is aimed at the point where the moon will be when the spacecraft arrives.

Placing a spacecraft in orbit around the moon requires even more precision. Not only must the spacecraft arrive at exactly the right spot at the right time, but at some point above the lunar surface the spacecraft must be slowed to a speed of 1.7 kilometers per second to avoid crashing. This slowing is done with retro engines, that is, rocket engines that fire in the direction opposite from the one in which the spacecraft is moving. If the spacecraft is to land on the lunar surface, the retro engines must be fired longer so that the spacecraft is slowed even more.

Topic 2 First Spacecraft to the Moon

The first spacecraft to leave Earth orbit and reach the moon was part of the ***Luna*** series of space probes launched by the Soviet Union. *Luna 1* performed the first successful flyby of the moon before going into orbit around the sun. Although *Luna 2* crashed into the moon's surface, it was the first artificial object to land on another solar system member. *Luna 3* orbited the moon and returned the first close-up photos of the moon's surface and the first photos ever of the moon's far side.

At the same time the *Luna* series was in progress, the United States launched the ***Pioneer*** space probes. *Pioneers 1, 2,* and *3* were unsuccessful, but *Pioneer 4* reached escape velocity from Earth and returned data as it flew past the moon.

In his State of the Union Address on May 25, 1961, President Kennedy made it a national goal to land an astronaut on the moon and return the astronaut safely to Earth before the end of that decade. At the time, no American had even orbited Earth, although one, Alan Shepard, had been in suborbital flight at an altitude of 186 kilometers before splashing down into the ocean.

The Soviet Union, on the other hand, had already orbited a cosmonaut. Yuri Gagarin became the first human in space by completing one orbit of Earth in a flight that lasted 108 minutes. While American astronauts were still preparing for their first orbital flight, a second Soviet cosmonaut, Gherman Titov, completed a 17-orbit flight that lasted over 25 hours. If there was to be a "race to the moon," the American space effort was far behind at the start.

Two parallel programs were needed to reach the president's goal of landing an astronaut on the moon. First, a safe landing site had to be located. Second, the spacecraft that would carry the astronauts had to be developed.

The task of searching for a safe landing site went to the ***Ranger*** and ***Surveyor*** lunar probes. The *Ranger* probes were designed to send back pictures of the lunar surface, and then crash into it. *Ranger 4* (the first American probe to reach the moon's surface) and *Rangers 7, 8,* and *9* sent back thousands of pictures before completing their missions and crashing. The *Surveyor* missions were able to soft-land on the moon. In addition to taking photographs, *Surveyor* probes had small shovels to scoop up lunar soil and determine the strength of the lunar crust. Together, these two programs returned tens of thousands of pictures and other data about the moon's surface and made the selection of a safe landing place for the astronauts possible.

Topic 3 *Mercury and Gemini*

While *Ranger* and *Surveyor* were providing data on the moon's surface, spacecraft were being developed to carry astronauts to the moon. The first American spacecraft to carry astronauts, called ***Mercury,*** had already flown one successful mission. Alan Shepard's flight in *Mercury 3* was the first of nine *Mercury* flights. John Glenn in *Mercury 6* became the first American to orbit Earth, which he did three times in a flight that lasted nearly five hours. *Mercury 9,* the final flight of the series, completed 22 orbits and lasted over 34 hours. As primitive as these flights were, they turned out to be the first step in getting an astronaut to the moon.

The ***Gemini*** spacecraft were designed for two astronauts. Ten missions were flown between March 1965 and November 1966. The missions had two purposes. The first was to find out if a human could survive and work in the weightlessness of space for the ten days needed to go to the moon and back. The second purpose was to train astronauts to maneuver the spacecraft to rendezvous (meet) and dock with (attach to) another spacecraft, a vital step in all moon missions.

24.2 *Mercury* astronaut Wally Schirra orbited Earth six times in this small capsule. Here, he is being picked up after splashing down in the Pacific Ocean.

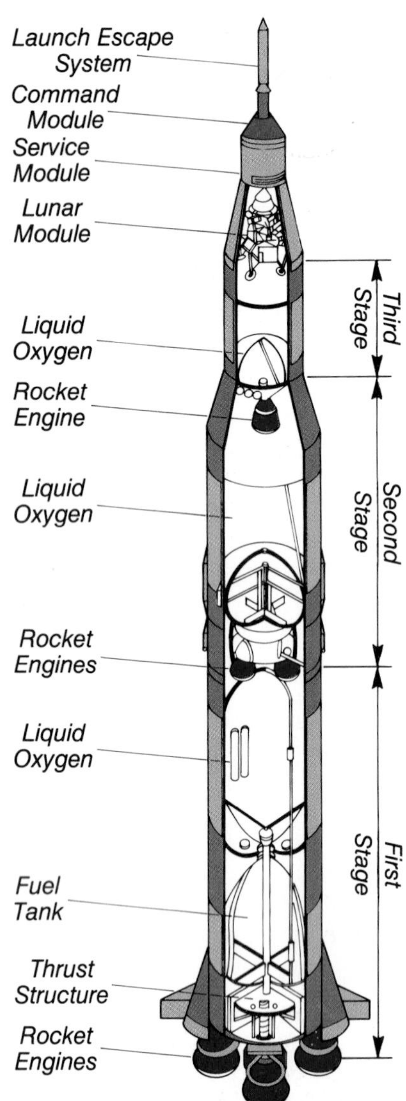

24.3 The *Apollo* command module was only a tiny part of the entire module and rocket assembly.

Topic 4 *Apollo*

The ***Apollo*** missions accomplished President Kennedy's objectives. In 1969, *Apollo 11* astronauts Neil Armstrong and Edwin Aldrin, Jr. became the first people to walk on the moon. In all, six missions traveled to the moon, collected samples, set up instruments, and returned safely to Earth.

The parts of an *Apollo* spacecraft and launch rockets are shown in Figure 24.3. The *Apollo* spacecraft consisted of a *command module* where three astronauts were seated, a *service module* containing the electrical power supply, life-support systems, and small maneuvering rockets, and the *lunar module* for the trip to the moon's surface and back to the orbiting command module. At lift-off the spacecraft and its three stages of launch rockets were over 110 meters tall and had a mass of nearly 3 million kilograms.

Each *Apollo* mission had a crew of three astronauts. One crew member remained in orbit around the moon while the other two went to the surface in the lunar module. The first lunar astronauts spent only 2.5 hours on the moon's surface, but the last two spent over 22 hours there.

At the end of each journey, only the command module with the astronauts inside returned to Earth's surface. All other parts of *Apollo* vehicles were jettisoned (thrown away) once they had been used. Of the total mass that was launched, only about 6000 kilograms, including the mass of the astronauts, returned to Earth.

The *Apollo* astronauts brought back a total of 380 kilograms of rock and soil samples. The instruments they left behind measured such things as moonquakes, the moon's magnetic field, solar wind particles, and the gases present at the moon's surface. Some of these instruments continued to send back data long after the *Apollo* program was over.

TOPIC QUESTIONS

Each topic question refers to the topic of the same number.

1. **(a)** How was the moon studied before 1959? **(b)** List the steps involved in landing a spacecraft on the moon.

2. **(a)** List some accomplishments of the *Luna* space probes. **(b)** What did *Pioneer 4* do? **(c)** What goal did President Kennedy set for the nation in 1961? **(d)** How did *Ranger* and *Surveyor* help to meet this goal?

3. Describe the *Mercury* and *Gemini* missions and identify what each accomplished.

4. **(a)** Summarize the *Apollo* missions. **(b)** Name and identify the purposes of the major parts of an *Apollo* spacecraft. **(c)** What kinds of measurements were made by instruments left on the moon?

II Properties and History of the Moon

OBJECTIVES

A Compare the properties of the moon with those of Earth and describe the internal structure of the moon.

B Explain why the same side of the moon always faces Earth, and compare the front half of the moon with the back half.

C Outline the moon's geologic history.

D Identify some ways moon rocks are different from Earth rocks and relate the ages of moon rocks to the moon's history.

Topic 5 Properties of the Moon

Although Earth's moon is not the largest satellite in the solar system, it is closer in size to its planet than any other satellite (with the possible exception of Pluto's Charon). The moon's diameter is 3476 kilometers, or more than one fourth Earth's diameter. The moon's density, about 3.3 g/cm^3, is less than Earth's, and its mass is only about one eightieth Earth's. The moon's low gravity (about one sixth Earth's) and low escape velocity (one fifth Earth's) means that it is much easier to launch a spacecraft from the moon than from Earth.

Seismometers left on the moon by *Apollo* astronauts continued to operate for nearly eight years. The moonquakes they recorded were very few and feeble compared to earthquakes. Nevertheless, the data were enough for scientists to develop a model of the moon's interior. The moon, like Earth, has a layered structure. The crust is about 60 kilometers thick and is made of rocks similar to gabbros and anorthosites on Earth. The mantle beneath the crust extends to about 800 kilometers. Seismographs were not able to detect the moon's core, but its central part may consist of iron.

Topic 6 The Moon's Front and Back

The moon's period of rotation is the same as its period of revolution—27.3 days. In other words, the moon turns just once on its axis while it goes once around Earth. The effect is that the same side of the moon always faces Earth.

To the unaided eye, the moon is a pattern of light and dark areas. Modern telescopes reveal details of the pattern. The light areas are lunar highlands, rugged mountains pockmarked with craters. The dark areas are great basins and level plains. Galileo had thought the basins were filled with water and had named them **maria** (MAR ee uh), the Latin word for seas (singular *mare,* MAR ay).

The moon's front side is nearly half highlands and half maria. The back of the moon is very different. Photographs taken by lunar probes show the back half to be mostly highlands and craters. There are only a few small maria.

There are other differences between the front and back of the moon. Lasers carried by the orbiting *Apollo* spacecraft were used to measure precisely the elevations of lunar surface features. From these measurements, scientists determined that the moon is not a perfect sphere but is slightly egg-shaped. The small end of the "egg" points toward Earth. Another difference was discovered from the seismic data. The crust is about 60 kilometers thick on the front

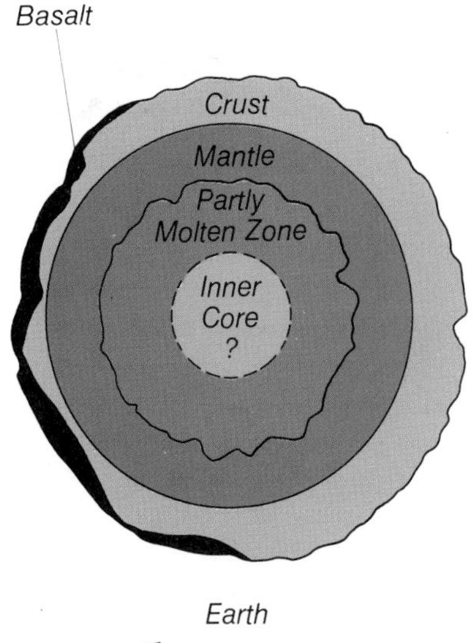

24.4 Data from seismographs left on the moon suggest that it has a layered internal structure.

24.5 This is an *Apollo* photograph of the moon's far side.

side facing Earth. On the side away from Earth the crust is more than 100 kilometers thick. The cause of these differences is unknown but is suspected to be related to Earth's gravitational pull on the moon.

Topic 7 Origin and History of the Moon

The samples of moon rock returned to Earth by *Apollo* astronauts have been thoroughly examined. By studying these rocks, as well as thousands of lunar photographs and other data, scientists have worked out a geologic history of the moon.

One likely theory based on lunar data proposes that the moon formed about 4.6 billion years ago from a collision between Earth and a Mars-sized object. At that time, Earth is thought to have been liquid with a solid crust. In the theory, the collision broke through the solid crust and splashed a huge mass of molten rock into space. This mass cooled and became the moon.

As soon as the lunar crust became solid, a second stage of moon history began. Great showers of rocklike particles bombarded the moon's surface. The largest particles blasted out great basins in many places. Smaller explosions formed smaller craters. Tiny particles ground and pitted the surface. Rock fragments and dust spread over the landscape.

The bombardment lasted for hundreds of millions of years. As it slowed down, a third stage of moon history began. Hot lava poured out of gaps in the great basins. The eruptions continued for nearly a billion years. The basin floors became dark and smooth as the lava hardened. Finally, the moon became geologically inactive.

For 3 billion years the moon's interior has been quiet. No volcanoes have erupted. Few moonquakes have shaken it, and no crustal plates have moved. However, meteoroids have continued to bombard the lunar surface. None of these meteoroids has been large enough to blow out new basins, but smaller ones have dug many new craters in the basins. These basin craters are younger than most of the highland craters. The bombardment going on now is mainly by **micrometeoroids**, tiny objects no larger than sand grains. Micrometeoroids are the major cause of erosion on the moon today.

Topic 8 Lunar Rocks: Evidence of the Moon's History

All lunar rocks differ from Earth rocks in several ways. Lunar rocks contain no water at all. They have greater proportions of elements with high melting points, such as aluminum, titanium, and zirconium. They contain lesser amounts of elements that exist as gases, such as nitrogen and chlorine, and lesser amounts of elements with low melting points, such as sulfur and lead.

24.6 The pitted surfaces of these lunar boulders are a result of constant bombardment by micrometeoroids.

Radioactive dating has been used to find the age of lunar rocks. Most highland rock specimens are between 4.0 and 4.3 billion years old. However, a few specimens collected by the *Apollo 17* mission have been dated at 4.6 billion years, thought to be the age of the moon itself. These ages support the hypothesis that the lunar highlands are the original lunar crust.

The mare basalts are the youngest lunar rocks. They range in age from 3.1 to 3.8 billion years, which supports the idea that the moon has been inactive for the last 3 billion years.

Lunar maria and highland rocks are further described in Topics 9 and 10.

TOPIC QUESTIONS

Each topic question refers to the topic of the same number.

5. **(a)** How does the moon compare in size, mass, surface gravity, and escape velocity to Earth? **(b)** How are moonquakes different from earthquakes? **(c)** Describe the moon's interior.

6. **(a)** Explain why one side of the moon always faces Earth. **(b)** What are the light areas of the moon called? **(c)** What are the dark areas called? Why do they have this name? **(d)** List some ways in which the front of the moon is different from the back of the moon.

7. **(a)** Summarize the four stages of the moon's history. **(b)** What is the major cause of erosion on the moon today?

8. **(a)** Name several ways that moon rocks differ from Earth rocks. **(b)** Where are the oldest moon rocks found? The youngest?

OBJECTIVES

A Discuss the location and probable origin of lunar maria; describe mare rocks, mascons, and rilles.

B Discuss the location and probable origin of lunar highlands; describe the rocks found in lunar highlands.

C Describe lunar craters and give examples; discuss the characteristics and probable origins of rays and of regolith.

III The Moon's Surface Features

Topic 9 The Lunar Maria

Although Galileo thought the dark areas on the moon's surface were seas, the lunar maria contain no water and there is no sign that they ever did. The maria are smooth plains with huge circular basins. Examples are Mare Imbrium (Sea of Rains), Mare Crisium (Sea of Tears), and Mare Serenitatis (Sea of Serenity). The largest mare is the Oceanus Procellarum (Ocean of Storms).

The first three *Apollo* missions to land on the moon explored maria. Rock samples returned by these missions strongly resemble the basalts in lava flows from Hawaiian and Icelandic volcanoes. Like those basalts, the mare basalts are fine-grained crystalline rocks. They are dark gray or black and contain mostly plagioclase feldspar and pyroxene. Some contain olivine and ilmenite (an oxide of iron and titanium).

The first spacecraft to orbit the moon found that the moon's gravity was greater over some of the more circular maria. Gravity readings change if the material beneath the surface has a different density than the surrounding rock. Some lunar geologists suspect that the mass of material that created a mare basin remains buried deep beneath the surface. These areas of higher gravity are called **mascons** for "mass concentrations."

Rilles are long deep clefts or cracks running through maria bedrock. The best known is *Hadley Rille* on the floor of Mare Imbrium, which was explored by *Apollo 15* astronauts. This rille may have formed when the roof of a lava tunnel caved in.

24.7 This lunar rock is a volcanic basalt from one of the maria. What Earth rock does it resemble?

24.8 The brighter areas of the moon are mountainous highlands. The darker areas are the level maria. Rays can be seen around the craters Copernicus and Tycho.

Topic 10 The Lunar Highlands

The final three *Apollo* flights landed in lunar highlands. These areas appear brighter than the maria because their rocks are lighter in color and they reflect more sunlight. Within the lunar highlands are a few mountain ranges and many craters.

Most lunar mountain ranges are at the edges of maria. One great range forms the western border of Mare Imbrium. This range includes the lunar Alps, Apennines, and Caucasus mountains. These mountains are as high as 5 kilometers above the mare floor.

Lunar scientists think that the Apennines were thrown up by the impact that created Mare Imbrium. Perhaps all lunar mountains that border maria were formed in this way. How could such great masses of rock be thrown so far and high? One reason is that the moon has no atmosphere to slow flying particles. A second reason is the moon's weak gravity.

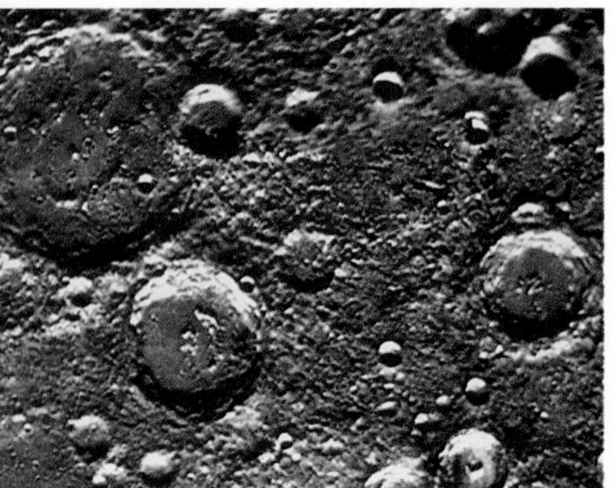

24.9 (top) Lunar craters vary in size. (bottom) A close-up of the crater Copernicus shows the rays that extend from it.

24.10 Lunar regolith is a mixture of small rocks and dust.

Two kinds of rock were returned from the lunar highlands. One is a light-colored, coarsely crystalline igneous rock. The composition of this rock lies somewhere between Earth's gabbro and anorthosite. Scientists think that this anorthositic gabbro makes up all the moon's solid crust except where mare basalts cover it.

The other specimens brought back from the lunar highlands are lunar breccias. Breccias are rocks made of angular fragments cemented together with fine material. On Earth, one source of breccia is volcanic eruptions. On the moon, breccias were probably formed by meteoroid impacts that melted the rocks together. Lunar breccias are mostly gray.

Topic 11 Lunar Craters and Rays

Lunar **craters** are hollows on the moon's surface. The smallest craters are microscopic pits. The largest, Clavius, is about 240 kilometers across. Most craters were formed by the impact of meteoroids.

Craters are roughly circular. Their rims are rugged cliffs. In large craters the rims may be thousands of meters above the plains, while their floors may be a thousand meters lower than the plains. Most crater floors are themselves dotted with many small peaks and craters. Like the highlands, these peaks reflect enough sunlight to look bright. Lunar craters are named after great scholars and scientists, such as Plato, Aristotle, Archimedes, Kepler, and Copernicus.

Bright streaks, called **rays**, radiate from a number of craters. The rays of the crater Tycho and other large craters are thousands of kilometers long, and cross mountains, plains, and other craters. For a long time the rays were a mystery. Scientists now know that they consist of shattered rock and dust splashed out by the meteoroid impacts that formed the craters.

Topic 12 Lunar Soil

Lunar soil is not really soil. Scientists prefer to call it **regolith** which means loose rock materials. Regolith is a grayish-brown mixture of small rock pieces and fine particles that range in size from sand grains to fine dust. Unlike Earth soil, regolith contains no water or organic material. Regolith was made by the smashing impact of meteoroids of all sizes. When large meteoroids explode, they mix rock fragments over broad areas. This stirring of the regolith is called *gardening.*

The regolith ranges in thickness from perhaps 1 to 20 meters. It is likely to consist of chips from many different kinds of rocks and minerals. It also contains tiny beads of glassy material. These formed from rock melted by high-speed meteoroid impacts. Droplets of the melted rock solidified to form glassy beads. Some of the melted rock formed a glaze on other rocks.

TOPIC QUESTIONS

Each topic question refers to the topic of the same number.

9. (**a**) List some examples of maria. (**b**) Describe the mare basalts. (**c**) What are mascons and how were they discovered? (**d**) What is a rille?

10. (**a**) Where are most lunar mountains located? Give some examples. (**b**) Describe the probable origin of the lunar mountains. (**c**) Identify the rocks of the lunar highlands.

11. (**a**) Describe the lunar craters and explain their origin. (**b**) What are lunar rays? How were lunar rays formed?

12. Describe the lunar regolith.

Andrea Mosie
Lunar Geologist

Did you know that geologists and space scientists are still studying the rocks and soil samples collected on the moon by the *Apollo* astronauts? Andrea Mosie is a geologist at the Johnson Space Center in Houston where most of the samples are stored. She is one of several geologists there who continue the detailed analysis of those rocks.

The rocks are kept in special cabinets. The "air" inside the cabinets is nitrogen gas. Nitrogen is used instead of air because the oxygen and water vapor in the air might react with minerals in the rocks and change their composition. In addition, the tweezers and other tools Ms. Mosie uses in studying the rocks must be made of nylon, Teflon, or some other nonreactive substance.

The cabinets are kept in special clean rooms. Before entering, Ms. Mosie must put on white nylon coveralls, booties, gloves, and a cap. She then steps into an air shower to remove all traces of dust and lint, which could contaminate the rooms.

The rock and other samples stored at the Johnson Space Center are considered a national treasure. Even though these samples have already told scientists a great deal about the moon, much remains to be learned.

OBJECTIVES

A Describe all aspects of the moon's orbit; explain why the sun and moon appear to be about the same size in the sky.

B Explain why the moon rises later each day; describe the moon's cycle of phases; locate the positions of the sun, moon, and Earth at each lunar phase.

C Explain why the period of a lunar month is not equal to the moon's period of revolution.

D Identify and describe the different kinds of eclipses and explain why each occurs.

IV The Moon's Motions and Phases

Topic 13 The Moon's Orbit

The moon revolves around Earth from west to east in an elliptical orbit. Its period of revolution is 27 ⅓ days. Its average distance from Earth is about 386 000 kilometers. When the moon is nearest Earth, it is said to be at **perigee** (peri = near, gee = Earth). When farthest from Earth, it is at **apogee**.

The moon's orbit is not in exactly the same plane as Earth's orbit. The angle between the two orbits is about 5 degrees. This difference is very important in determining how often eclipses occur (Topics 17 and 18).

The sun's diameter is nearly 400 times the moon's diameter, yet both appear to be about the same size in the sky. The reason is that the sun is nearly 400 times farther away from Earth than the moon.

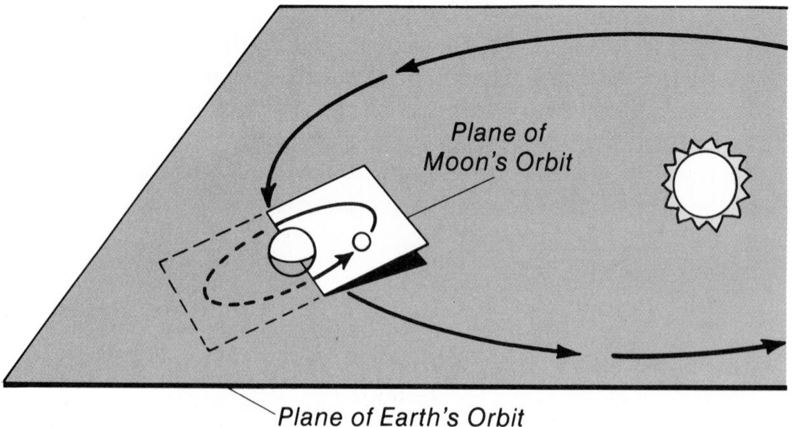

24.11 The moon's orbit is inclined about five degrees to the plane of Earth's orbit.

Topic 14 Moonrise and Moonset

The moon rises in the east and sets in the west. Like the sun's rising and setting, this is an apparent motion caused by Earth's turning on its axis from west to east. Unlike the sun, the moon is in orbit around Earth.

If the moon did not revolve around Earth, it would be seen in about the same place in the sky at the same time each day. However, each day the moon moves about 13° along its orbit. Twenty-four hours later, the moon has not yet returned to the same place in the sky. To catch up, Earth must turn about 13° further on its axis. This takes about 50 minutes. As a result, the moon rises about 50 minutes later each day and sets about 50 minutes later as well.

Since the time of moonrise changes each day, the moon can be seen in the sky during day and night. When the moon is opposite the sun, it is seen mostly in the night sky. When it is between Earth and the sun, it is seen mostly in the daytime sky.

Topic 15 The Moon's Phases

The **phases** of the moon are the daily changes in the moon's appearance. Moon phases occur for two reasons. One is that the moon is seen by reflected sunlight. The other is that the moon is in orbit around Earth.

The sun lights the half of the moon that is facing it. However, except for a short time each month, the half that always faces Earth is not the half lit by the sun. From Earth, the face of the moon changes from all dark to all light, or from new moon to full moon, in about two weeks. During this time, the moon is said to be **waxing**. During the next two weeks, the face of the moon gradually changes from all light back to all dark, or from full moon back to new moon. During this time, the moon is said to be **waning**.

Figure 24.12 shows the moon at eight points in its orbit. Although the half of the moon facing the sun is always fully lighted, a different portion of the lighted half is visible from Earth during each phase. At the new moon phase, the lighted half faces away from Earth and the moon cannot be seen. At the crescent phases, only one edge of the lighted half faces Earth. At the quarter phases, the half of the moon facing Earth is half lighted and half dark. At the gibbous phases, almost all of the bright half faces Earth. When the moon is full, the entire bright half faces Earth.

24.12 The left portion of the diagram shows the appearance of the moon at each of the eight phases. The right portion of the diagram shows the actual illumination of the moon at each phase. No matter what the phase, the same side of the moon is always facing Earth.

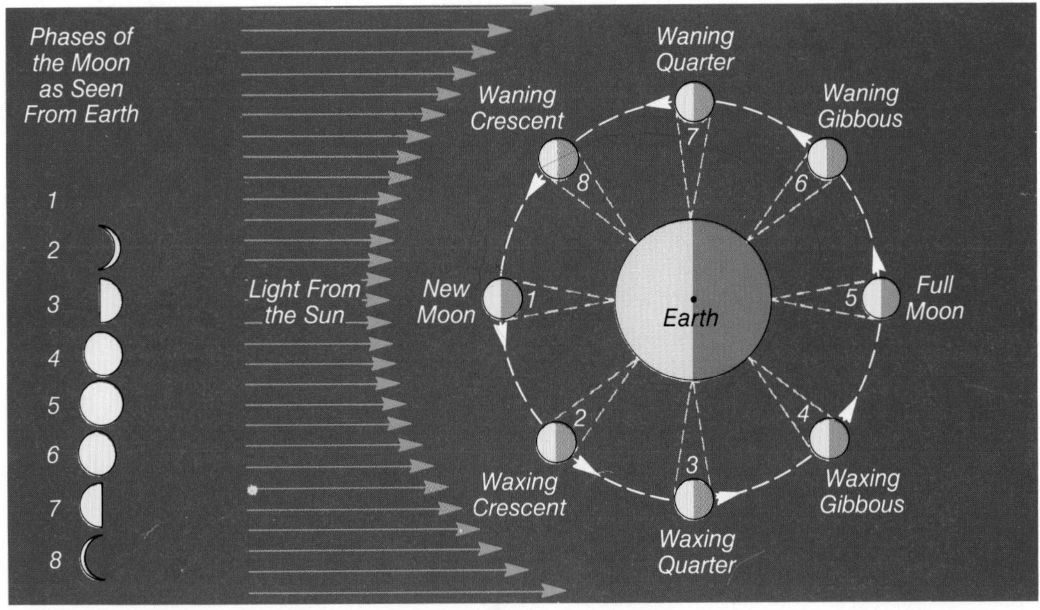

Topic 16 Lunar Months

The time from one new moon to the next new moon is not the same as the time for one revolution of the moon around Earth. The time from one new moon to the next is called the **lunar month** and lasts 29.5 days. One revolution only takes 27.3 days.

The reason for the difference in the two values is Earth's revolution around the sun. While the moon travels in its orbit around Earth, Earth moves about 1° each day in its orbit around the sun. During the 27.3 days that the moon takes to complete one revolution, Earth moves about 27.3° along its orbit. The moon must move another 27.3° along its own orbit to return to the same phase. Since the moon moves about 13° along its orbit each day, it takes slightly more than two extra days to arrive at the same position. Thus, the time from one moon phase to the same phase is about two days longer than the time for the moon to orbit Earth once.

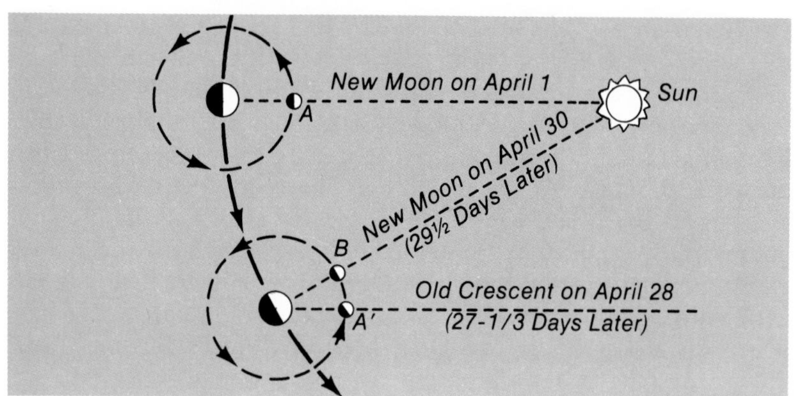

24.13 The lunar month, 29½ days, is the time span from one new moon to the next. The diagram shows why the lunar month is longer than the moon's period of revolution, 27⅓ days.

Topic 17 Lunar Eclipses

The shadow cast by any opaque object has two parts: The **umbra** is the total shadow and the **penumbra** is the partial shadow surrounding the umbra. Both Earth and the moon cast shadows into space. Earth's umbra is a long, narrow cone. The tip of Earth's umbra is nearly 1 400 000 kilometers beyond Earth. The penumbra is also a cone, but it gets wider and lighter in space. Because the moon is smaller than Earth, the moon's shadows are smaller and shorter.

A **lunar eclipse** occurs when the moon passes into Earth's umbra. A total lunar eclipse occurs when the moon is fully within the umbra. When the moon is only partly in the umbra, that is a partial lunar eclipse.

A lunar eclipse can occur only at the full moon phase. Even though a full moon occurs every month, a lunar eclipse does not occur that often. The reason is that the moon's orbit and Earth's orbit are inclined to each other by about 5 degrees. The full moon is usually above or below Earth's umbra, and no eclipse occurs.

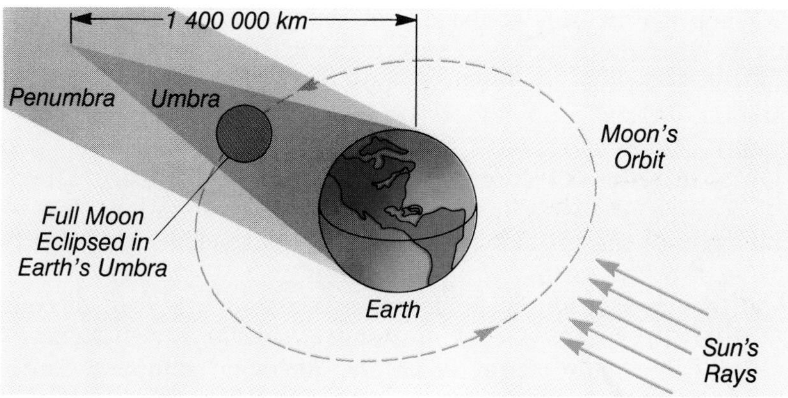

24.14 A lunar eclipse can occur only at the full moon phase. Notice that the umbra is the area of total darkness, while the penumbra is only partially dark. Earth's umbra eclipses the moon.

The moon remains visible during its eclipse, but it has a dusky red or coppery color. This occurs because Earth's atmosphere acts like a lens and bends some sunlight, mostly longer red wavelengths, into the umbra.

On the average, at least one total lunar eclipse occurs every year. With good weather it is visible from the entire nighttime half of Earth. If the moon goes through the center of the umbra, a total lunar eclipse may last for two hours.

Topic 18 **Solar Eclipses**

A **solar eclipse** occurs when the moon's umbra reaches Earth's surface. The moon's umbra is just long enough for its tip to reach Earth at perigee. It is not long enough to reach at apogee. The umbra's greatest width on Earth's surface is about 269 kilometers. The penumbra is much wider and lighter.

Locations on Earth within the umbra experience a total solar eclipse. At that time, the moon blocks the entire photosphere of the sun. The sky is dark. Bright stars and planets can be seen with the unaided eye. The sun's chromosphere and corona glow around the blocked-out disk. A partial solar eclipse is seen at locations within the moon's penumbra shadow. The moon covers only a part of the sun, and often little change in daylight is noticed.

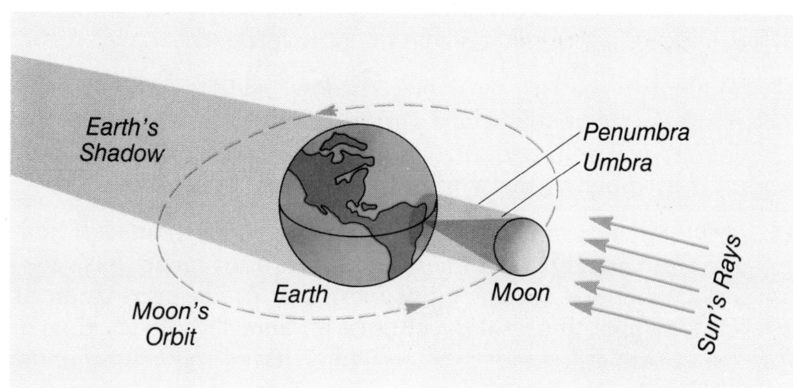

24.15 A solar eclipse occurs only at the new moon phase. It is really an eclipse of part of Earth by the moon's shadow. The eclipse is total in the umbra. It is partial in the penumbra.

24.16 During a total eclipse of the sun, the sun's corona can be seen extending hundreds of thousands of kilometers into space.

When the moon is at apogee, the umbra shadow fails to reach Earth. When this happens, observers in the center of the umbra see the sun as a thin, bright ring around the moon. This is called an **annular**, or ring, eclipse. Observers in the penumbra see a partial eclipse.

A solar eclipse can occur only at the new moon phase. Like a lunar eclipse, a solar eclipse does not occur every month because of the angle of the moon's orbit. The moon's shadow usually falls above or below Earth.

Although at least one solar eclipse occurs every year, a given location can expect to see one only once every 300 years! This rarity is mainly due to the size of the umbra. The moon's umbra on Earth is usually much less than its maximum possible width. Nor does a total solar eclipse last very long. The moon's revolution makes the narrow shadow race across Earth at over 1600 kilometers per hour. The shadow's track on Earth is called the eclipse path. The eclipse path may be thousands of kilometers, but at any one place a total solar eclipse can last only 7.5 minutes. A few minutes is more usual.

TOPIC QUESTIONS

Each topic question refers to the topic of the same number.

13. **(a)** What is the direction of the moon's revolution? **(b)** Define perigee and apogee. **(c)** How is the plane of the moon's orbit related to the plane of Earth's orbit? **(d)** Why do the sun and moon look equally large in the sky?

14. Why does the moon rise about 50 minutes later each day?

15. **(a)** Why is the moon not full all of the time? **(b)** List the eight moon phases in order. **(c)** During which phases is the moon said to be waxing? **(d)** During which phases is the moon said to be waning?

16. **(a)** How long is a lunar month? **(b)** Explain why a lunar month is longer than the moon's period of revolution.

17. **(a)** Identify the two parts of a shadow. **(b)** How does a total eclipse of the moon occur? Partial eclipse? **(c)** At what phase does a lunar eclipse occur? Why doesn't it occur every month? **(d)** How much of the world can see each lunar eclipse?

18. **(a)** Describe the moon's shadow and its relation to total, partial, and annular eclipses of the sun. **(b)** At what lunar phase does a solar eclipse occur? Why doesn't it occur every month? **(c)** Why are total solar eclipses seldom seen even though one occurs almost every year? **(d)** What is the eclipse path? **(e)** How long can a total solar eclipse last?

V Sun, Moon, and Tides

Topic 19 The Moon and Tides

The daily rise and fall of the ocean waters are called **tides**. Like the moon, tides rise 50 minutes later each day (on the average). Tides are unusually large during the new moon and full moon phases. They are unusually small during quarter moon phases. Because of these observations, people have known for many years that the moon and the tides are related.

Sir Isaac Newton first explained how the gravity of the moon causes tides. Recall that gravity is stronger when objects are closer together. Because of this, the water on the side of Earth nearest the moon is pulled by the moon more strongly than Earth itself is pulled by the moon. This difference in force causes a bulge in the ocean on the side of Earth near the moon. This bulge is the *direct high tide.* At the same time, Earth's center is nearer to the moon than the water on the side of Earth opposite the moon. Earth itself, therefore, is pulled more strongly by the moon than is the water on the far side of Earth. Earth is pulled away from the water on the far side, leaving a bulge of water behind, which is the *indirect high tide.* Water has been pulled away from the areas that lie between the two high tides. These areas experience low tides.

OBJECTIVES

A List the evidences that relate tides to the moon and explain how the moon causes high and low tides.

B Describe and explain spring tides and neap tides; define tidal range and identify several factors that influence it.

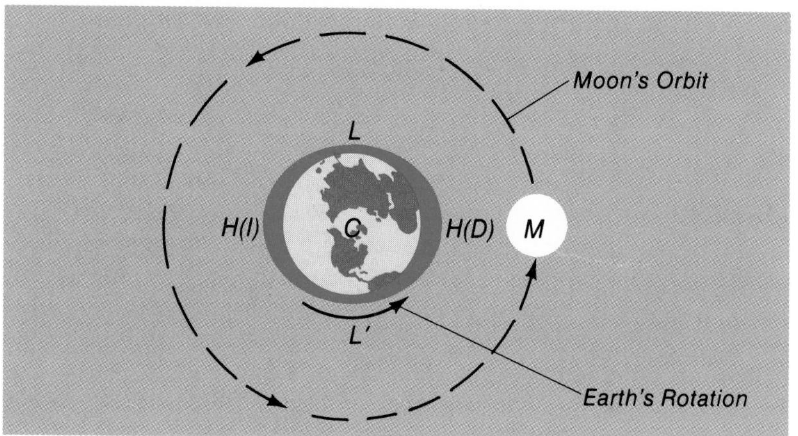

24.17 The moon causes a direct high tide at H(D) and an indirect high tide at H(I). Low tides occur at L and L′.

Topic 20 Rise and Fall of Tides

If Earth and the moon stood still, tides would be in the same places all the time. Earth, however, turns on its axis, and the moon moves around Earth. As Earth rotates, all parts of the oceans pass under the moon in 24 hours and 50 minutes. In one fourth of this time—about 6 hours and 12.5 minutes—the tides change. Each high-tide area gradually rotates to low tide. Each low-tide area gradually rotates to high tide. Six hours and 12.5 minutes later the tides change again.

24.18 (top) At new and full moon phases, sun and moon pull together, causing very high and very low tides called spring tides. (bottom) At quarter moon phases, sun and moon pull against each other, causing a small tidal range, the neap tides.

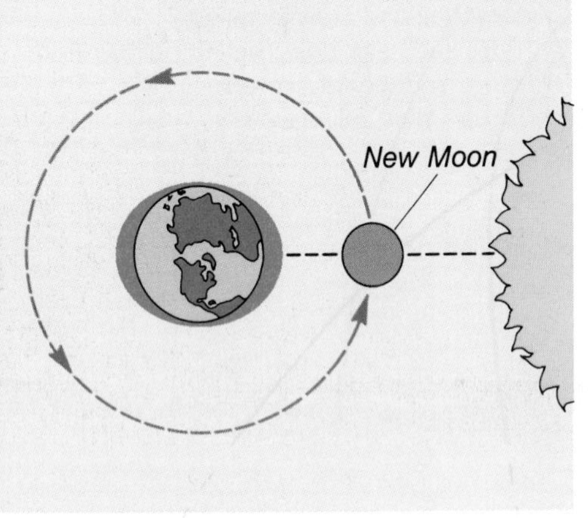

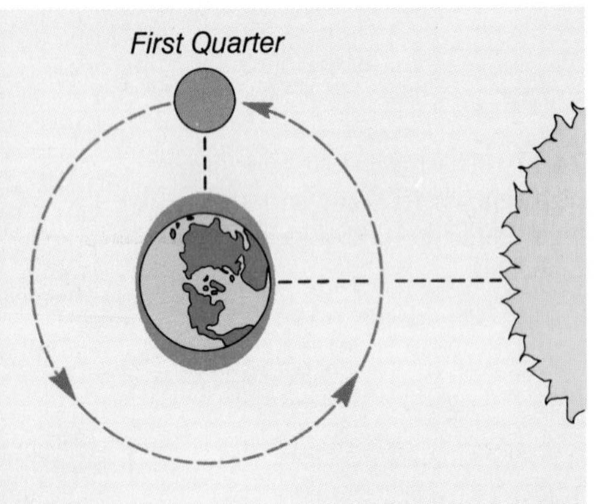

As Earth and the moon move, the tides continue their regular rise and fall. Each day the cycle starts over again, about 50 minutes later than the previous day. The model timetable that follows gives average times for a day of high and low tides. Actual tides are often much more irregular because the shapes of the ocean basins and ocean floors also influence the tides.

Sample Timetable

Tide	Date	Time	Interval Since First High Tide
High	July 4	1:00 A.M.	
Low	July 4	7:13 A.M.	6 h 13 m
High	July 4	1:25 P.M.	12 h 25 m
Low	July 4	7:38 P.M.	18 h 38 m
High	July 5	1:50 A.M.	24 h 50 m

Topic 21 Spring and Neap Tides

The sun has the same kind of effect on Earth's waters as does the moon. However, because it is so much farther away, the sun's tide-making effect is only about half that of the moon. The sun, however, can strengthen or weaken the moon's effects.

Tides are always high in line with the moon and low midway between the high-tide points. When the sun is in line with the moon and Earth, as shown in Figure 24.18 (top), the sun's entire tide-making effect is added to the moon's. When the sun is 90° away from the moon, as in Figure 24.18 (bottom), the entire effect is subtracted from the moon's effect. At new moon and full moon phases, the effects of the sun and moon add together. During these times, high tides are especially high and low tides are especially low. These tides occur twice a month and are called **spring tides**.

At quarter phases the sun is opposing the moon, resulting in high tides that are not very high and low tides that are not very low. These tides also occur twice a month and are called **neap tides**. One other factor that adds to the tidal effect is the moon's nearness to Earth. When the moon is at perigee, the tidal effect is greater, especially if perigee occurs during the new or full moon phases.

Topic 22 Ocean Basins, Shorelines, and Tidal Range

The **tidal range** is the difference in level between high tide and low tide. Tidal ranges vary widely between bodies of water and tend to be more noticeable near the ocean than near lakes. Small lakes show no tides at all. The largest of the Great Lakes, Lake Superior, has a tidal range of only a few centimeters. In the open ocean the tidal range averages less than one meter.

24.19 Because it is long and V-shaped, the Bay of Fundy has a very large tidal range.

Tidal ranges on ocean shores are most noticeable, but they also vary greatly. In the Gulf of Mexico, the tidal range may be only half a meter. In the Bay of Fundy on the coast of Nova Scotia, the range can be as great as 20 meters.

What causes these differences? The Bay of Fundy is a long, V-shaped bay. Water from the ocean tide is funneled into the wide end of the V. When the water reaches the narrow end of the V, it piles up high. In the Gulf of Mexico, the opposite occurs. The Gulf has a shoreline much broader than its mouth. As the ocean tide enters the Gulf, its water spreads out over the long shoreline.

TOPIC QUESTIONS

Each topic question refers to the topic of the same number.

19. (**a**) What obervations indicate a connection between the moon and tides? (**b**) Explain how the moon causes tides. (**c**) What is the bulge of water toward the moon called? The one away from the moon? (**d**) Where do low tides occur?

20. (**a**) Explain why tides rise or fall every 6 hours and 12.5 minutes, on the average. (**b**) Explain why the tides occur 50 minutes later each day.

21. (**a**) How does the sun affect tides? Explain. (**b**) What are spring tides? How and when do they occur? (**c**) What are neap tides? How and when do they occur?

22. (**a**) Define tidal range. (**b**) What is the tidal range of lakes? Of the open ocean? (**c**) Explain the large tidal range of the Bay of Fundy. (**d**) Explain the small tidal range of the Gulf of Mexico.

CHAPTER 24 REVIEW

Summary

Sending spacecraft to the moon requires enough power to escape Earth's gravity, precise aiming and timing, knowledge of a safe landing site, and the ability to prevent the craft from crashing on its arrival.

The *Apollo* program brought back lunar material and photos and left equipment on the moon to gather further data.

The same side of the moon always faces Earth. The front of the moon has smooth plains and a thin crust, while the back has cratered highlands over a thick crust.

One theory of the moon's formation involves a collision between Earth and another object.

Lunar rocks have textures similar to Earth rocks but have differences in composition. Lunar highland rocks are older than mare rocks.

Lunar maria may have formed when large objects hit the lunar surface and broke through the crust, causing lava to flow out.

Lunar highlands surrounding lunar maria may have been thrown up by the impacts that created maria.

Most lunar craters were caused by the impact of meteoroids; rays were splashed out by the impacts. Regolith is the loose rock material covering the moon's surface.

The lunar orbit is tilted 5°. The moon's movement around Earth causes it to rise later each day and to go through phases.

A lunar eclipse occurs when the moon passes through Earth's shadow. A solar eclipse occurs when the moon's shadow falls on Earth. Lunar eclipses are visible more often than solar eclipses.

Tides are caused by the gravitational pull of the moon. The pull of the sun is added to or subtracted from that of the moon.

Tidal range is affected by the pull of the sun, the size of the body of water, and the shape of coastlines.

Vocabulary

annular eclipse	*Mercury*	rilles
apogee	micrometeoroid	solar eclipse
Apollo	neap tide	spring tide
crater	penumbra	*Surveyor*
Gemini	perigee	tidal range
Luna	phases	tides
lunar eclipse	*Pioneer*	umbra
lunar month	*Ranger*	waning
maria	rays	waxing
mascon	regolith	

Review

Match the descriptions in List **A** with the terms in List **B**.

List A

1. Slows down spacecraft during approach to moon
2. First American lunar probes
3. First American craft to carry astronauts
4. Astronaut's home during moon trips
5. Lunar missions that returned rocks
6. Launching from moon is easier because this is less
7. More common on near side of moon
8. Agent of lunar erosion
9. Location of oldest moon rocks
10. Lunar mass concentration
11. Made of cemented angular fragments
12. Lunar soil
13. Bright streaks radiating from craters
14. Point in moon's orbit farthest from Earth
15. Moon rises about this much later each day
16. Full moon to new moon phases
17. Time from one new moon to the next
18. Total shadow of an eclipse
19. Partial eclipse is seen from here
20. Track of moon's umbra on Earth
21. Caused by moon pulling Earth away from water
22. Average time from one high tide to another
23. Tides of new and full moon phases
24. Difference between high and low tide

List B

a. apogee
b. *Apollo*
c. breccia
d. command module
e. eclipse path
f. escape velocity
g. 50 minutes
h. highlands
i. indirect high tide
j. lunar month
k. maria
l. mascon
m. *Mercury*
n. micrometeoroids
o. penumbra
p. perigee
q. *Pioneer*
r. rays
s. regolith
t. retro engine
u. spring tide
v. tidal range
w. 12 hours 25 minutes
x. umbra
y. waning
z. waxing

Interpret and Apply

On your paper, answer each question in complete sentences.

1. Could astronauts on the moon observe a meteor shower? Explain.
2. If both the moon and Earth formed at the same time, why have no 4.6 billion-year-old rocks been found on Earth?
3. If you lived on the moon instead of Earth, how often would the sun rise?
4. For each moon phase, identify the phase that Earth is in as seen from the moon.
5. What effect would there be on the lunar month if the moon revolved east to west rather than west to east?
6. If the moon and Earth kept their present sizes and separation but were at the distance of Jupiter from the sun, how would solar eclipses differ?
7. Direct and indirect high tides measured in the same location are about the same height when the moon is in the plane of Earth's equator. However, these high tides may be very unequal when the moon is above or below the plane of Earth's equator. Using a diagram, explain why this difference occurs.

Critical Thinking

Each moon phase is visible only at a particular time of day or night. For example, a full moon cannot be seen at 12 noon because it is on the side of Earth opposite the sun. The approximate times each phase is visible can be determined. The figure below is similar to Figure 24.12 except that times are shown—12 noon toward the sun, 12 midnight away from the sun, 6 A.M. at sunrise, and so on. Use a piece of paper to cover the daytime side of Earth and the moon phases on that side. The full moon is at its highest point in the sky about midnight. It rises 6 hours earlier, at 6 P.M., and sets 6 hours later, at 6 A.M.

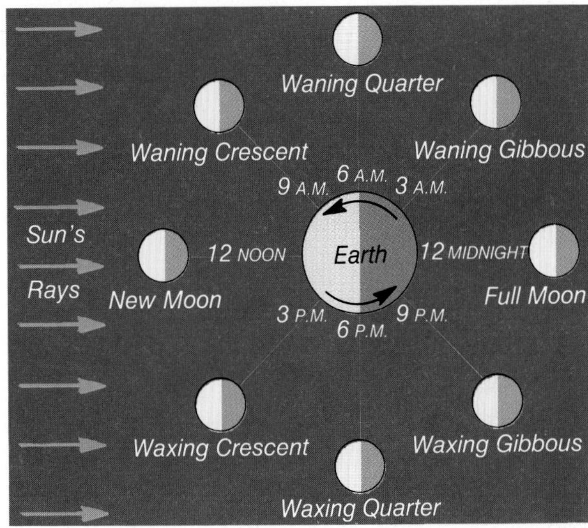

1. Cover the times when the waxing quarter phase CANNOT be seen. At what time is the waxing quarter at its highest point? What time does it rise? What time does it set?
2. Determine the time of moonrise and moonset for the waning gibbous phase.
3. If the waning crescent phase is at its highest point, what time is it?
4. Which phases could never be seen at 3 P.M.?
5. If the waning quarter phase is midway between moonrise and its highest point, what time is it?
6. Which phase rises about 9 A.M.?

CHAPTER

25 Earth's Motions

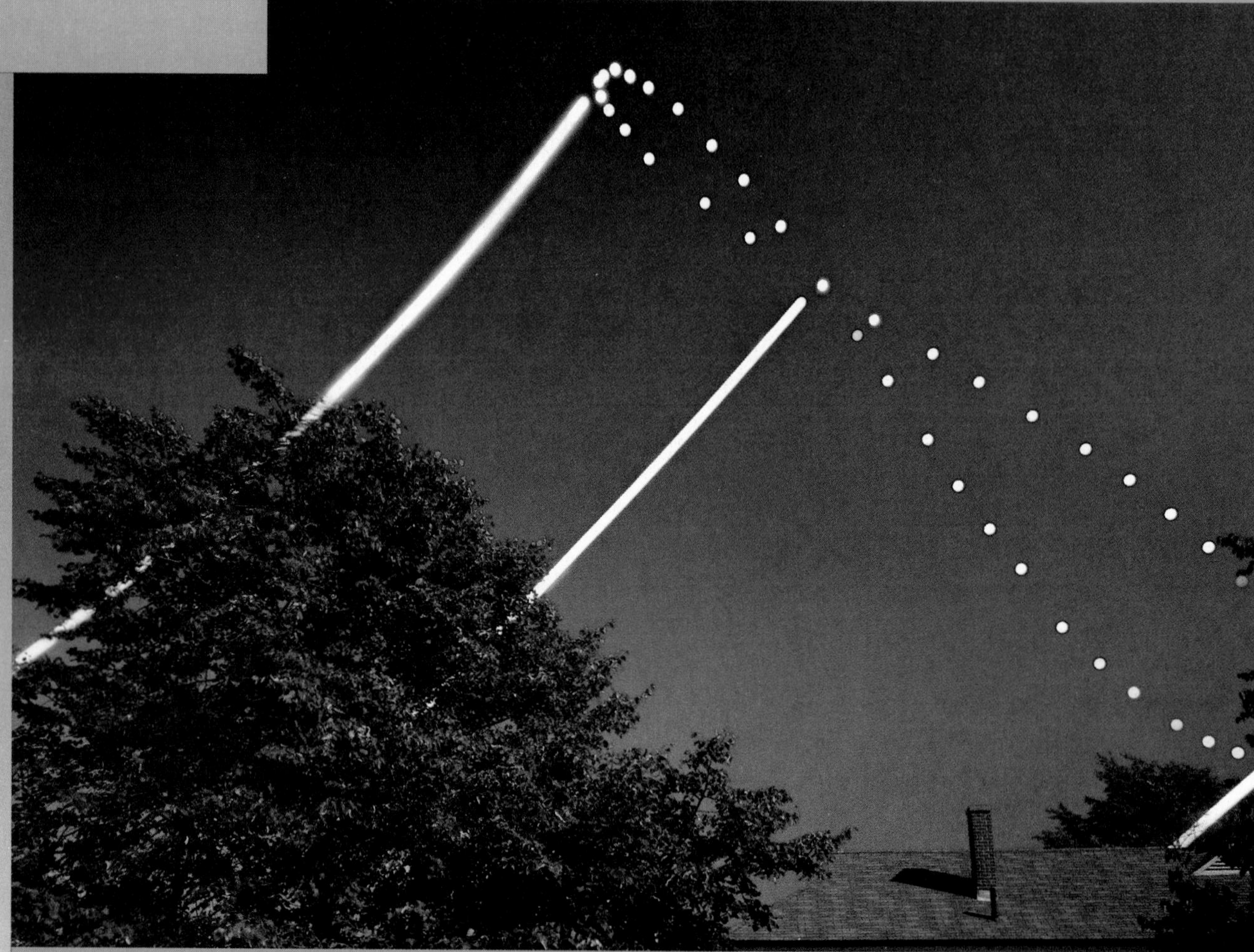

▲ This unusual photo shows the altitude of the sun at the same time of day throughout the year. The photo was taken at 42° N latitude.

How Do You Know That . . .

Earth changes its position in space throughout the year? One clue is the changing position of the sun in the sky. At latitudes away from the equator, the lengths of day and night change as the seasons change. The times and positions of sunrise and sunset also change. The photo above shows the position of the sun at the same time of day over the course of a year. Can you tell which position was photographed around the first day of summer? You will be able to tell by the end of this chapter.

I Earth's Rotation

Topic 1 The Axis of Rotation

Like the other planets in our solar system, Earth turns as it travels around the sun. This turning motion is called **rotation**. The **axis of rotation** is an imaginary straight line through Earth between the North Pole and the South Pole. Earth turns around this axis. Earth's orbit lies within an imaginary flat surface called the *plane of Earth's orbit*. The axis of rotation is not straight up and down when compared to the plane of Earth's orbit, but is slightly tipped. The axis makes an angle of 23.5° from a perpendicular to the plane of Earth's orbit.

The angle that the axis is tilted does not change as Earth moves on its path around the sun. The axis is always aimed toward the same point in the sky near where Polaris, the North Star, is located. Even though Earth's position in its orbit changes each day, the axis always points toward Polaris. To illustrate this change, try this simple experiment. Hold your left fist in front of you to represent the sun. Grasp a pencil in your right hand. Your right hand will represent Earth; the pencil will be its axis. Place "Earth" to the left of the "sun," with its "North Pole" pointing about 23.5° toward the "sun." Keeping the axis parallel to its first position, move "Earth" around the "sun." Notice how the "North Pole" leans away from the "sun" at the opposite (right) end of the orbit. Notice also that neither pole leans toward the "sun" at the two midway points. Every position of Earth's axis is parallel to every other position of the axis. This behavior is called **parallelism of the axis**. Parallelism of the axis is one of the causes of seasons on Earth.

OBJECTIVES

A Define rotation and discuss the evidences for and effects of Earth's rotation.

B Describe Earth's axis of rotation and explain its rate of rotation and speed of rotation.

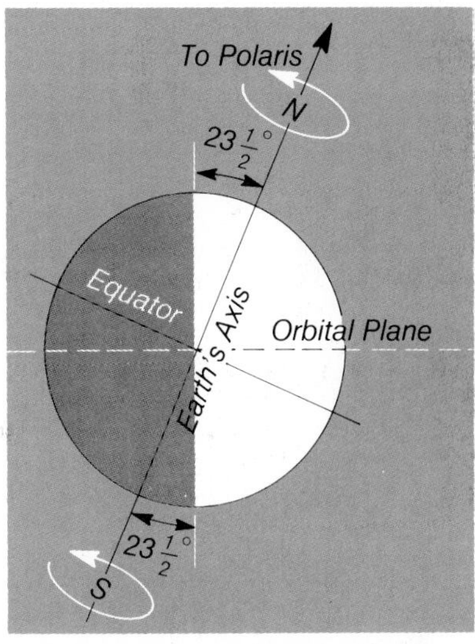

25.1 Earth's axis is inclined by 23½° from a perpendicular to the plane of Earth's orbit.

25.2 Throughout the year, Earth's axis always has the same tilt and points in the same direction. This parallelism of the axis is important in the change of seasons and in the length of daylight and night.

25.3 The Foucault pendulum can be used to demonstrate Earth's rotation.

Topic 2 **Evidences for Earth's Rotation**

How do we know that Earth rotates? Early evidence of rotation was provided by the French physicist Jean Foucault (FOO koe) in 1851. He constructed a pendulum by hanging a large iron sphere on a long wire. Scientists of the time knew that once a pendulum is set in motion, its direction of swing will not change. Foucault, however, observed that the direction of swing of his pendulum did change. Each hour it shifted about 11° in a clockwise direction. After eight hours it was swinging at a right angle to the starting direction. Because the pendulum could not have changed its direction of swing, Foucault concluded that the shift he saw was caused by Earth turning beneath his pendulum. The *Foucault pendulum* is now a famous demonstration of Earth's rotation.

A second evidence of Earth's rotation can be seen by moving air, or wind. Winds blow from areas of high air pressure to areas of low air pressure. If Earth did not rotate, these winds would blow directly from high-pressure areas to low-pressure areas. Because of Earth's rotation, the winds appear to be turned, or deflected. In the Northern Hemisphere, winds are deflected to their right. In the Southern Hemisphere, the direction of deflection is to the winds' left. This apparent deflection is caused by the **Coriolis effect**. Any substance or object that moves freely over Earth's surface, such as ocean currents, winds, and rockets, will be turned when compared to Earth's surface as a result of the Coriolis effect.

What about the rising and setting of the sun? Doesn't that show that Earth rotates? No, it could also result from the sun moving around a stationary Earth. However, the motions of the sun, as well as those of the stars, are much easier to explain with a rotating Earth rather than with a rotating sky.

Topic 3 **Effects of Earth's Rotation**

The Coriolis effect and the behavior of a Foucault pendulum occur because Earth rotates. Another result of rotation is the length of a day. One day is defined as the time needed for Earth to turn once on its axis. One day is divided into 24 parts, or hours.

The daily change from daylight to nighttime also results from Earth's rotation. Only half of Earth can be lighted by the sun at any time. If Earth did not rotate, the half facing the sun would have constant daylight while the other half would have constant nighttime. Earth's rotation causes daylight and nighttime to alternate. Its tilted axis results in unequal sunlight on its Northern and Southern Hemispheres. For all but two days each year either the Northern Hemisphere or the Southern Hemisphere leans more toward the sun. The hemisphere that leans toward the sun has longer daylight periods than nighttime periods, while the one that leans away from the sun has shorter daylight periods.

Yet another result of Earth's rotation is the direction of sunrise and of sunset. Seen from above the North Pole, Earth rotates in a counterclockwise direction, that is, it turns from west to east. This causes the sun to appear to rise in the east and set in the west.

Topic 4 Rate of Earth's Rotation

How fast does Earth turn on its axis? One complete turn occurs every 24 hours. One complete turn is equal to a circle of 360°. Therefore, Earth turns at a rate of 360° in 24 hours, or 15° each hour. The apparent motion of the sun, moon, and stars is caused by Earth's rotation. Thus, these objects move across our sky at the rate at which Earth rotates – 15° each hour.

While every location on Earth's surface moves at a rate of 15° per hour, the speed of rotation in kilometers per hour is not the same everywhere. Speed of rotation depends upon latitude. The greatest speed of rotation occurs at the equator. Here, one rotation is the distance of the equatorial circumference, or 40 074 kilometers. Locations on the equator travel 40 074 kilometers in 24 hours, a speed of nearly 1670 kilometers per hour! The distance required to travel around Earth, and thus the speed of rotation, decreases as the distance from the equator increases. At the latitude of Salt Lake City, Utah, the speed of rotation is only about 1300 kilometers per hour. At the poles, the speed of rotation is almost zero.

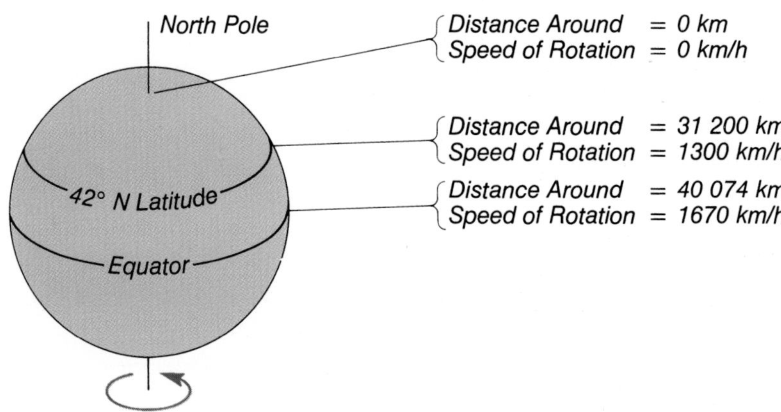

25.4 As distance from the equator increases, the distance around Earth decreases. As a result, Earth's speed of rotation decreases away from the equator.

TOPIC QUESTIONS

Each topic question refers to the topic of the same number.

1. **(a)** What is rotation? **(b)** Describe Earth's axis of rotation. **(c)** What is the angle of tilt of Earth's axis? **(d)** Near what object in space does the axis always point? **(e)** What is parallelism of the axis?
2. **(a)** How does a Foucault pendulum show that Earth rotates? **(b)** In what direction are winds deflected in the Northern Hemisphere? **(c)** What name is given to the cause of this deflection?
3. **(a)** Identify three results of Earth's rotation other than the Coriolis effect and the behavior of a Foucault pendulum. **(b)** In what direction does Earth rotate?
4. **(a)** What is Earth's rate of rotation? **(b)** At what rate do the sun, moon, and stars appear to move across our sky? Why? **(c)** Where on Earth's surface is the speed of rotation greatest? Why? **(d)** Where is the speed of rotation least?

Kathryn Neff
Cartographer

As you have learned, meridians of longitude and parallels of latitude are a system of mapping Earth. Longitude is also used in defining the 24 time zones around the world. According to cartographer Kathryn Neff, the latitude-longitude coordinate system is accepted worldwide as a means of pinpointing a unique spot on the surface of Earth. Ultimately, everything that Kathryn Neff and other cartographers do is based on the latitude-longitude system.

As a cartographer in the Office of Research for the U.S. Geological Survey in Virginia, Kathryn Neff is involved with computerizing maps. She works on converting graphic maps into digital maps that can be used by a computer. The use of computerized maps represents a new and exciting area of cartography called geographic information systems. These systems can provide valuable information to a variety of industries. Recently, a county planning department used geographic information systems to help determine the best location for a new school. A cartographer took the existing graphic map of the county and converted it into a digital map. The digital map was then fed into a computer. Additional types of information pertinent to the placement of the school were also fed into the computer. Such data included population densities, transportation routes, location of waste sites, and industry locations. In a short time, the computer analyzed all the data and predicted the ideal site for the new school. As a result of geographic information systems, a time-consuming task was completed quickly!

II Time Measurement and Earth's Rotation

OBJECTIVES

A Describe the nature of solar time and explain the basis for Earth's standard and daylight time systems.

B Determine the time and day in various locations in the world, given the time and day in one location.

C Locate the international date line and describe the changes that occur there.

Topic 5 Solar Time

The length of a day, 24 hours, is the result of Earth's rotation. How is time determined within that 24-hour period?

For many years, the position of the sun in the sky was the standard for determining the time of day. During a single day, the sun appears on the eastern horizon, seems to move in an arc across the sky, and disappears below the western horizon. **Solar noon** occurs when the sun is at the highest position on this arc. **Solar time** is time by the sun.

Solar noon does not occur at the same time for everyone. Earth's rotation causes solar noon to move westward at a rate of 15° each hour, or 4 minutes of time for each degree of longitude. For example, New York City is located at 74° W longitude, while Philadelphia is at approximately 75° W longitude. Because of this 1° difference, solar noon occurs at New York City about 4 minutes before it occurs in Philadelphia.

25.5 A sundial is a device that indicates local solar time. Because of Earth's tilt and orbit, solar time is the same as clock time only a few days each year.

Topic 6 Standard Time

The problem of different solar times at nearby communities was solved by developing worldwide **standard time zones**. There are 24 time zones, each 15° of longitude wide. The basis for the time zone is the rate at which the sun appears to move across the sky. Each

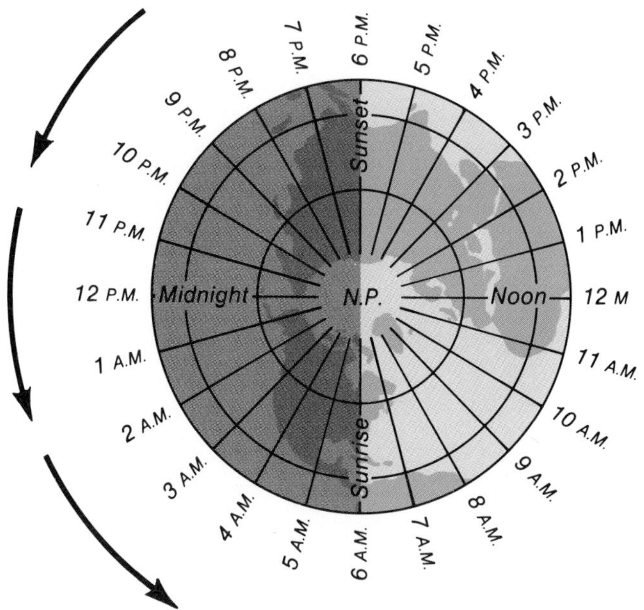

25.6 A map of Earth looking down from above the North Pole, showing Earth's 24 standard time zones; The sun's rays are striking Earth from the right.

standard time zone is roughly centered on a line of longitude exactly divisible by 15°, called a **time meridian**. All areas within a time zone keep the same clock time. Clock time is the average solar time, or *mean time,* at that zone's time meridian.

The starting point for the standard time zones is an arbitrary longitude line called the **prime meridian**. It passes through Greenwich, England, a town outside London and the location of a major observatory. Travelers moving westward from Greenwich move their clocks back to earlier times, while those moving eastward change to later times. For example, when it is 10 A.M. in Greenwich (longitude 0°), it is 11 A.M. in Rome (longitude 15° E), 5 A.M. in Philadelphia (longitude 75° W), and 3 A.M. in Denver (longitude 105° W).

Each standard time zone should be exactly 15° wide. On land, however, such exactness is not always convenient. For example, a time-zone boundary that cuts right through a city would be very awkward for everyone who lived there. Because of this, time-zone boundaries on land are seldom straight lines. Instead, they are shifted east or west to meet the needs of the people living along the true boundary.

25.7 This map illustrates the standard time zones of the United States. The time meridians are 75° W, 90° W, 105° W, 120° W, 150° W and 165° W.

Excluding Alaska and Hawaii, there are four time zones in the United States. The zones and their time meridians are: Eastern (75° W), Central (90° W), Mountain (105° W), and Pacific (120° W). All have highly irregular boundaries. Most of Alaska is in the Alaska time zone (150° W); Hawaii is in the Hawaii-Aleutian time zone (165° W).

Topic 7 Daylight Saving Time

In many places standard time is changed to **daylight saving time** for six months or more of every year. In daylight saving time the standard or clock time is advanced by one hour. This adds an hour of daylight to the part of the day when most people are awake. For example, a sunset that would occur at 8 P.M. standard time would not occur until 9 P.M. daylight saving time. Daylight saving time helps save energy by delaying the need for electric lights until an hour later in the evening.

Where it is used, daylight saving time is usually in effect from April until October. To change from standard time to daylight saving time in April, clocks are set ahead one hour. In October clocks are set back one hour. An easy rule to use in changing from one time to the other is "spring ahead, fall back"; set your clock ahead in the spring, back in the fall.

There have been suggestions that daylight saving time remain in use all year long. The idea has not been popular, however, because it would mean that the winter sun would not rise in some areas until after 8 A.M. The risk to students going to school in the dark is too great. Also, the saving in energy during the winter would be very slight.

Topic 8 The International Date Line

One problem with the standard time system is that travelers going completely around the world gain or lose time at each time zone until they have gained or lost an entire day! How can travelers know where to change from one date to another? This problem was solved by establishing an imaginary line through the Pacific Ocean called the **international date line**. Here travelers change not their watches but their calendars. Travelers moving westward advance their calendars one day, as from Saturday to Sunday. Eastward travelers move their calendars back one day, as from Saturday to Friday.

The international date line lies within a time zone. Places on either side of the date line within the time zone keep the same time, but the western half is one day ahead of the eastern half. Except for the instant when the midnight line crosses the international date line, there are two dates on Earth at any moment. For a good part of each day the continental United States is behind the date in eastern Asia and the Pacific Islands.

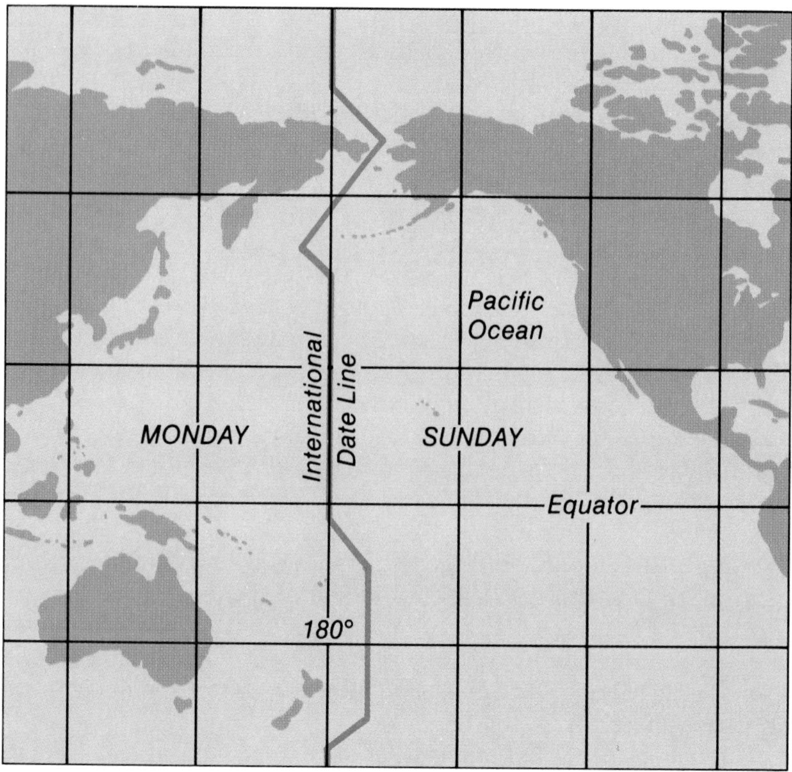

25.8 The international dateline follows the 180th meridian wherever possible, leaving it only where necessary to avoid land.

The international date line roughly follows the 180th meridian on the opposite side of Earth from the prime meridian. The date line zigzags to avoid all land. Because it is located entirely within the ocean, all changes of date are made on a ship or airplane.

TOPIC QUESTIONS

Each topic question refers to the topic of the same number.

5. **(a)** Describe the path of the sun across the sky each day. **(b)** Where is the sun at solar noon each day? **(c)** Why is solar time not the same for everyone?

6. **(a)** Describe the standard time zones. **(b)** Where is the starting point for the standard time zones? **(c)** How does time change westward and eastward of this location? **(d)** Why do standard time zones have irregular boundaries on land?

7. **(a)** What change does daylight saving time make to standard time? **(b)** During what time of the year is daylight saving time usually used?

8. **(a)** Explain the need for an international date line. **(b)** Where is the date line? **(c)** How does a traveler change the date when crossing the date line in each direction?

III Earth's Revolution

OBJECTIVES

A Describe Earth's revolution and discuss the evidences for it and effects from it.

B Discuss the effects of Earth's axial tilt and revolution on the daylight period and temperature at different latitudes.

Topic 9 Evidences for Earth's Revolution

The movement of Earth in its orbit around the sun is called **revolution**. For evidence of Earth's revolution, we look to the stars. As Earth moves around in its orbit, nearby stars appear to shift position when compared to distant stars. This apparent shift in position is called **parallax**. Parallax cannot be seen by eye but it can be measured with precise instruments. You can demonstrate the effect of parallax for yourself. Hold an upright pencil at arm's length and watch what happens when you look at the pencil with first one eye alone and then the other eye alone. The apparent shift of the pencil against the background is the same kind of shift seen in nearby stars when they are compared to distant stars. If Earth did not orbit the sun, no shift would occur. Therefore, the parallax shift of the nearby stars is evidence of Earth's revolution.

Further evidence of Earth's revolution around the sun is the seasonal change in constellations (Chapter 21, Topic 2). If Earth did not move around the sun, we would see the same constellations all year. The regular seasonal change of constellations is evidence of Earth's movement around the sun.

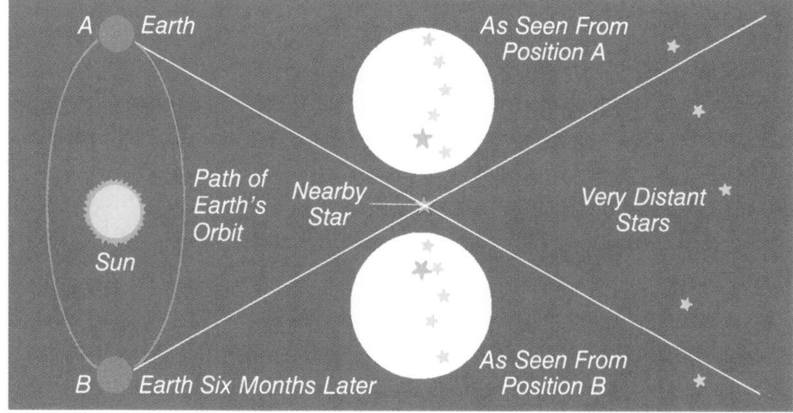

25.9 As Earth revolves around the sun, nearby stars appear to shift position relative to distant stars. This parallax shift is evidence of Earth's revolution.

Topic 10 Path and Rate of Earth's Revolution

The direction of Earth's revolution is the same as the direction of rotation, that is, counterclockwise when viewed from above the North Pole. Like the orbits of the other planets, Earth's orbit is an ellipse with the sun located at one focus. The orbit is in a level plane. Because the orbit is elliptical, the distance between Earth and the sun changes. The average distance is about 150 000 000 kilometers. The sun is about 2 400 000 kilometers from the center

25.10 The level surface in which Earth revolves around the sun is called the plane of Earth's orbit.

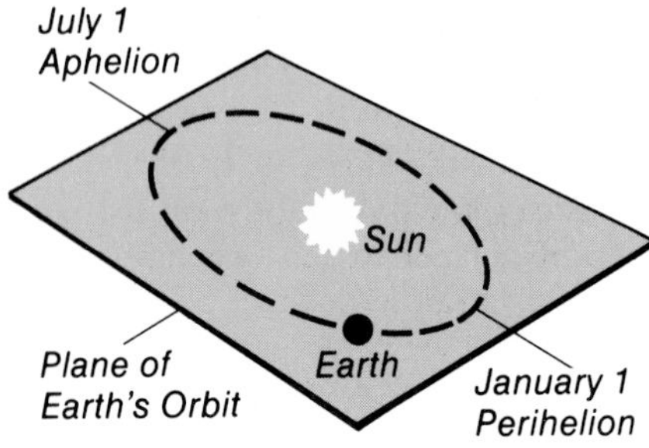

of the orbit, so the distance between Earth and the sun changes by about 2 400 000 kilometers over the period of a year. Earth is closest to the sun about January 1 and farthest away about July 1.

Earth makes one revolution around the sun every 365.24 days. This defines a duration of one year. Since Earth travels 360° (one orbit) in about 365 days, its rate of revolution around the sun is very close to 1° each day.

Topic 11 Effects of Earth's Revolution

Earth's axis is not straight up and down but is inclined at an angle of 23.5° (Topic 1). This tilt, together with Earth's revolution, has a profound effect on Earth. For all but two days a year, either the Northern Hemisphere or Southern Hemisphere leans more toward the sun. The hemisphere that leans toward the sun has a longer period of daylight than the one that leans away from the sun.

The hemisphere that leans toward the sun also has warmer temperatures. The closer to vertical the sun's rays strike a surface, the higher the temperature of the surface becomes. The sun's rays strike Earth closer to vertical in the hemisphere leaning toward the sun. The hemisphere leaning away from the sun has cooler temperatures because the sun's rays are less direct.

The changes in daylight and temperature caused by revolution and tilt lead to the yearly change of seasons at middle latitudes. If the axis were perpendicular to the plane of the orbit, seasons would not occur. Every place on Earth's surface would have 12 hours of daylight and 12 hours of nighttime every day. The average temperature at each location would be the result of its distance from the equator. If Earth's axis were tilted more than 23.5°, each hemisphere would lean more toward the sun in summer and more away from the sun in winter. The result would be warmer summers and colder winters. Thus, increasing the tilt of the axis would make seasons more severe, while decreasing the tilt would make seasons milder. No tilt would result in no seasonal changes.

TOPIC QUESTIONS

Each topic question refers to the topic of the same number.

9. **(a)** What is Earth's revolution? **(b)** Give two evidences for Earth's revolution.

10. **(a)** What are the shape and dimensions of Earth's orbit? **(b)** What is Earth's rate of revolution?

11. **(a)** What effect does the tilt of Earth's axis have on the daylight period and temperature of the hemisphere that leans toward the sun? **(b)** What would seasons on Earth be like if the axis were not tilted at all? **(c)** What would be the effect on seasons if Earth's axis were tilted more?

IV Seasons on Earth

Topic 12 Summer in the Northern Hemisphere

The first day of summer in the Northern Hemisphere occurs on or about June 21 each year. This day has the longest daylight period. The day is called the **summer solstice** (sol = sun; stice = stop) because on that date the sun stops getting higher in the sky at noon. On the summer solstice the Northern Hemisphere is at its maximum tip toward the sun. Because this tip is equal to 23.5°, the sun is straight overhead at 23.5° N latitude. The circle around Earth at 23.5° N latitude is called the *Tropic of Cancer.*

On the same date, every point on Earth within 23.5° of the North Pole is having 24 hours of daylight. This latitude, 66.5° N, is the *Arctic Circle* (the latitude of the North Pole is 90° N; 90° minus 23.5° equals 66.5°). On June 21 in the Southern Hemisphere, every point south of the *Antarctic Circle* (66.5° S latitude) is experiencing 24 hours of darkness. Like the Arctic Circle, the location of the Antarctic Circle is a result of the tilt of Earth's axis.

After June 21 the tilt of the Northern Hemisphere toward the sun decreases as Earth continues on its path around the sun. As the tilt decreases, daylight periods in the Northern Hemisphere decrease while those in the Southern Hemisphere increase.

OBJECTIVES

A Identify the dates, conditions, and positions of the sun at different latitudes on the solstices and equinoxes.

B Describe the daylight and nighttime conditions that occur at each seasonal date worldwide.

C Describe the apparent path of the sun across the sky on the seasonal dates.

D Identify the causes of seasons on Earth.

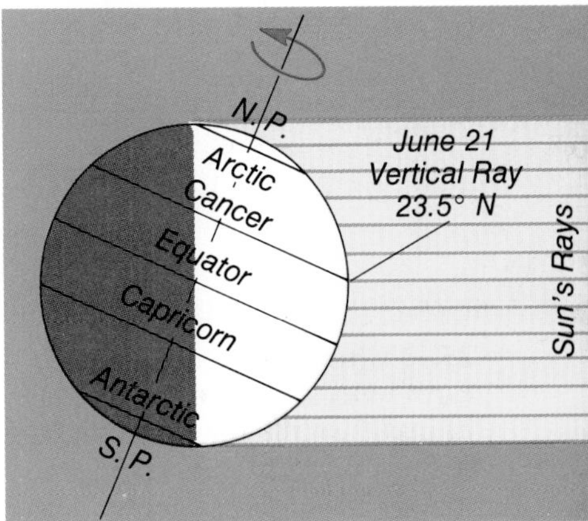

25.11 Because of Earth's axial tilt, latitudes away from the equator experience seasonal temperature differences. On June 21, Earth's Northern Hemisphere is at its greatest tilt toward the sun. June 21 has the longest daylight period in the Northern Hemisphere.

Topic 13 Winter in the Northern Hemisphere

Winter begins in the Northern Hemisphere on or about December 21. This is the **winter solstice**, the shortest day of the year. On that date the Northern Hemisphere is at its maximum tip away from the sun, while the Southern Hemisphere is at its maximum tip toward the sun. The sun is straight overhead at the *Tropic of Capricorn,* which is at 23.5° S latitude. Like the Tropic of Cancer, the location of the Tropic of Capricorn results from the tilt of Earth's axis.

Daylight and nighttime conditions on December 21 are the opposite of those on June 21. On December 21, every point north of the Arctic Circle is experiencing constant darkness while every point

25.12 Bylot Island in Baffin Bay, Canada, is far enough north of the Arctic Circle to have many weeks of continuous daylight in summer. This picture shows the island's midnight sun photographed every fifteen minutes from 11:15 P.M. to 1:00 A.M. on July 25–26.

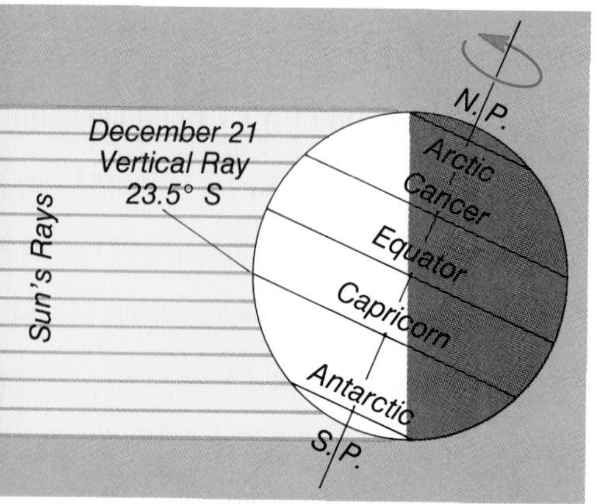

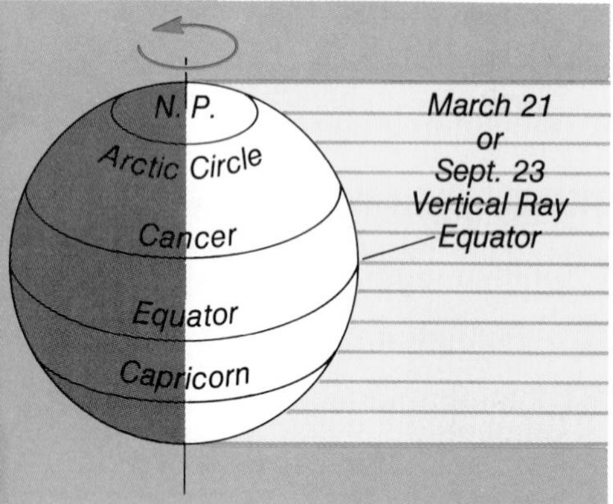

25.13 (top) On December 21, Earth's Northern Hemisphere is at its maximum tilt away from the sun and has its shortest daylight period. (bottom) Daylight and nighttime are equal in length everywhere on Earth only on the two equinoxes.

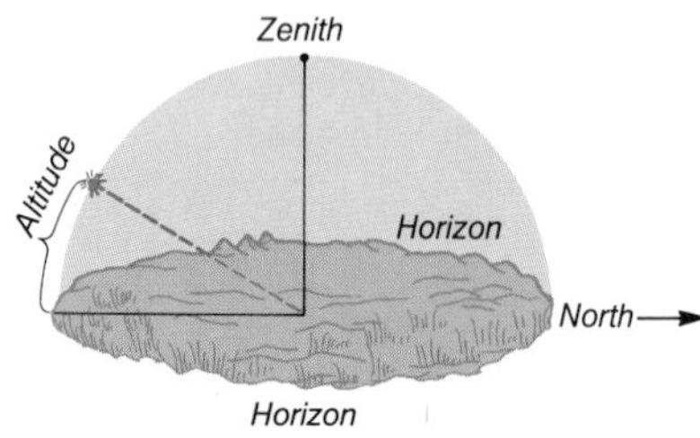

25.14 On the imaginary dome of the sky, the horizon is the rim of the dome and the zenith is the point straight overhead. The altitude of the sun is the vertical angle between the horizon and the sun.

south of the Antarctic Circle is in constant daylight. A traveler moving north on this date will observe that the daylight period becomes shorter, while one moving south will observe increasing daylight periods.

Topic 14 The Equinoxes

There are two days each year when neither hemisphere leans toward the sun. These days occur midway between the solstices. On these dates daylight and nighttime are equal in length all over the world. Each date, therefore, is known as an *equinox* (equi = equal; nox = night). The **spring equinox** occurs on or around March 21. The **autumn equinox** is on or around September 23. The sun is directly overhead at the equator at noon on these dates.

The spring and autumn equinoxes are also the dates when daylight and nighttime reverse at the poles. On March 21, the sun rises above the horizon at the North Pole for the first time in six months. It remains visible at the North Pole for the next six months, while the South Pole begins a six-month period of nighttime. When Earth revolves so the Southern Hemisphere is tipped toward the sun (after September 23) the nighttime period begins at the North Pole and ends at the South Pole.

Topic 15 Sun and the Dome of the Sky

How do the changing positions of the sun appear to an observer on Earth? Think of the sky as a huge bowl over head. The horizon is the circular rim of the bowl. The observer is at the center of the circle. The point straight overhead is the **zenith**. The vertical angle between the horizon and the sun's position is the sun's **altitude**. When the sun is at the zenith, its altitude is 90°. When it is on the horizon, its altitude is 0°. For locations in the United States (except Hawaii) the sun is always below the zenith.

On the first day of summer the sun rises 23.5° north of due east, travels across the dome of the sky to its highest noon position of the year, and sets 23.5° north of due west. This arc is longer and higher than any other path throughout the year. That is why the first day of summer has the longest daylight period of the year. On the first day of winter the sun rises 23.5° south of due east, follows its lowest and shortest path across the dome of the sky, and sets 23.5° south of due west. On equinoxes, the path of the sun is halfway between these two extremes, rising due east and setting due west.

Topic 16 Summary: Causes of Seasons

There are three basic causes of seasons: (1) the revolution of Earth around the sun, (2) the tilt of Earth's axis, and (3) the parallelism of Earth's axis. Because the axis always points in the same direction as

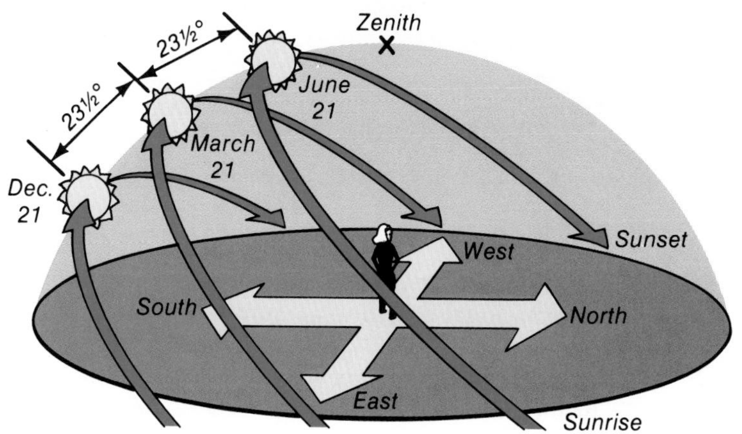

25.15 This diagram shows the path of the sun's apparent motion at latitude 41° N on the solstices and the equinoxes.

Earth travels around the sun, first one hemisphere and then the other hemisphere is tipped toward the sun. The hemisphere tipped toward the sun has longer periods of daylight, more direct sunlight, and thus experiences summer. The hemisphere tipped away from the sun has winter, due to shorter days and less direct sunlight. Areas near the equator do not experience dramatic changes in daylight periods or angle of sunlight, and thus do not have seasons.

Is distance from the sun a cause of seasons? No. We are nearest to the sun on January 1. At that time it is winter in the Northern Hemisphere and summer in the Southern Hemisphere. If distance were a cause of seasons, everyone on Earth would experience the same season at the same time.

TOPIC QUESTIONS

Each topic question refers to the topic of the same number.

12. **(a)** What happens in the Northern Hemisphere on June 21? **(b)** Where is the Tropic of Cancer? Why? **(c)** Where is the Arctic Circle? Why? **(d)** Where is daylight constant on June 21?

13. **(a)** What happens in the Northern Hemisphere on December 21? **(b)** Where is the Tropic of Capricorn? Why? **(c)** Where on Earth is daylight constant on December 21? **(d)** What happens to the daylight period in the Northern Hemisphere after December 21? Why?

14. **(a)** Why are daylight and nighttime of equal length on an equinox? **(b)** Give the names and dates of the equinoxes. **(c)** Where is the sun straight overhead at an equinox? **(d)** Describe what happens at the North Pole and at the South Pole at each equinox.

15. **(a)** What is the zenith? **(b)** What is meant by the altitude of the sun? **(c)** How does the path of the sun across the sky differ on the first day of summer from the first day of winter?

16. **(a)** List the three basic causes of seasons. **(b)** What evidence is there that distance from the sun is not a cause of seasons?

CHAPTER 25 REVIEW

Summary

Rotation is the turning of Earth on its axis. The axis is tilted at an angle of 23.5° from a perpendicular to the plane of Earth's orbit.

The behavior of a Foucault pendulum, the Coriolis effect, the length of a day, the daily change from daylight to nighttime, and the direction of sunrise and sunset are all results of Earth's rotation.

The rate of Earth's rotation is 15° each hour and is the basis for the standard time zones. The speed of Earth's rotation is greatest at the equator and least at the poles.

Solar noon occurs when the sun is at its highest position. Earth's rotation causes solar noon to move 15° W each hour.

There are 24 standard time zones around the world. Each is 15° of longitude wide. The international date line marks where the calendar date changes for world travelers.

Revolution is the movement of Earth in its orbit around the sun. Earth's revolution determines the length of a year.

The tilt of Earth's axis causes the hemispheres to receive different amounts of daylight during the course of a year. The angle at which sunlight strikes Earth affects the temperature.

The Northern Hemisphere is at maximum tip toward the sun on the summer solstice and at maximum tip away from the sun on the winter solstice. Neither hemisphere is tipped toward the sun on the spring and autumn equinoxes.

Seasons are caused by the combined effects of Earth's revolution, the tilt of Earth's axis, and the parallelism of Earth's axis.

Vocabulary

altitude
autumn equinox
axis of rotation
Coriolis effect
rotation
solar noon
solar time
spring equinox
daylight saving time
international date line
parallax
parallelism of the axis
prime meridian
revolution
standard time zones
summer solstice
time meridian
winter solstice
zenith

Review

For each item, select the best answer. Write the letter of your answer on your paper.

1. Toward which star does Earth's axis always point? (a) Sirius (b) Betelgeuse (c) Polaris (d) Vega
2. Which of the following Earth motions is demonstrated by the Foucault pendulum? (a) rotation (b) revolution (c) parallelism (d) perigee
3. Which is NOT caused by Earth's rotation? (a) length of a day (b) direction of sunrise (c) change from day to night (d) location of Arctic Circle
4. What is Earth's rate of rotation? (a) 1° per hour (b) 15° per hour (c) 24° per hour (d) 90° per hour
5. As distance from the equator increases, speed of rotation (a) increases, (b) increases, then decreases, (c) decreases, (d) does not change.
6. Solar noon occurs (a) when the sun is directly overhead, (b) when the sun reaches its highest point for the day, (c) at 12 noon standard time, (d) at 1 P.M. daylight saving time.
7. How many standard time zones are there worldwide? (a) 1 (b) 15 (c) 24 (d) 30
8. What time is it in Chicago if it is 2 P.M. in Los Angeles? (a) 12 noon (b) 1 P.M. (c) 3 P.M. (d) 4 P.M.
9. During daylight saving time, (a) clocks are set 1 hour ahead of standard time, (b) sun does not rise until 8 A.M., (c) clocks are set 1 hour behind standard time, (d) electricity savings are slight.

10. Which is NOT true of the international date line? (a) It is at 0° longitude. (b) It lies within the ocean. (c) People moving west across it lose a day. (d) Areas to its west are one day ahead of areas to its east.
11. Which is NOT true of Earth's revolution? (a) Its path is elliptical. (b) Its rate is 15° per hour. (c) It takes a year to be completed. (d) It occurs in the same direction as revolutions of other planets.
12. Which does NOT occur in the hemisphere that is leaning toward the sun? (a) warmer temperatures (b) longer daylight (c) higher solar altitudes (d) due east point of sunrise
13. Where in the sky is the sun when it is at the zenith? (a) on the horizon, rising (b) directly overhead (c) on the horizon, setting (d) over the prime meridian
14. Which is NOT a cause of seasons? (a) Earth's revolution (b) Earth's distance from sun (c) tilt of axis (d) parallelism of axis

Use the KEY to identify the date when each of the following occurs.

KEY

(a) March 21	**(c)** September 23
(b) June 21	**(d)** December 21

15. Moving northward from the equator causes the daylight period to decrease.
16. The sun is overhead at the equator but will be overhead south of the equator the next day.
17. Shortest day of the year in the Northern Hemisphere
18. Every location north of the Arctic Circle is experiencing a 24-hour daylight period.

Interpret and Apply

On your paper, answer each question in complete sentences.

1. Suppose Earth rotated from east to west and at twice its present rate. How would a day be different?
2. What time is it in each United States standard time zone when the new date is beginning at the international date line?
3. If Earth's axis were tilted at 33.5° instead of 23.5°, where would the Tropics of Cancer and Capricorn and the Arctic and Antarctic Circles be located?
4. How would increasing the tilt of Earth's axis change the length of daylight and nighttime throughout the year?
5. Compare the length of daylight and nighttime on June 21 and December 21 in your city or town with that in Mexico City, Mexico; Montreal, Canada; and Buenos Aires, Argentina.

Critical Thinking

The noon altitude of the sun on the solstices can be calculated for any location if the difference in degrees latitude from that location to the Tropic of Cancer is known. The latitude of Sioux Falls, South Dakota is 43.5° N. Answer questions 1–4. (Refer to information in Lesson IV as needed.)

1. What is the difference in latitude between Sioux Falls and the Tropic of Cancer?

The difference between the zenith and the noon solar altitude on the summer solstice equals the difference in latitude between Sioux Falls and the Tropic of Cancer.

2. Find the altitude of the sun at noon on the summer solstice in Sioux Falls.

The distance of the noon sun from the zenith on the winter solstice is equal to the difference in latitude between Sioux Falls and the Tropic of Capricorn.

3. Find the difference in latitude between Sioux Falls and the Tropic of Capricorn. (Remember that the Tropic of Capricorn is south of the equator.)
4. Find the altitude of the sun at noon in Sioux Falls on the winter solstice.

UNIT SIX
Atmospheric Science

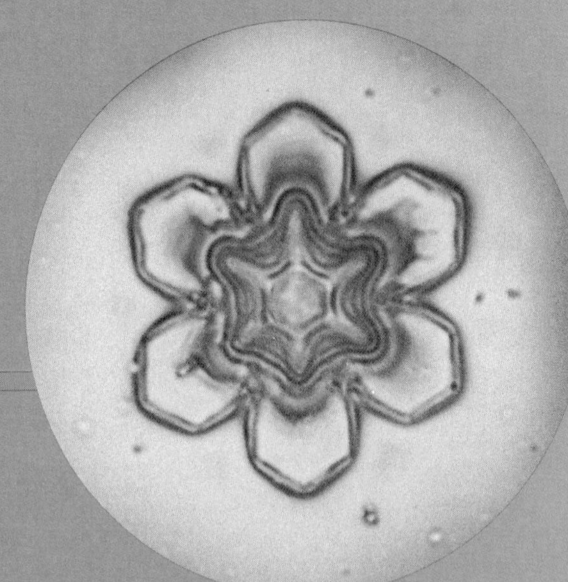

▲
Water may occur as vapor, as liquid droplets, or as solid ice crystals. What determines the form water takes in the atmosphere?

▲
A satellite photo shows atmospheric water in the form of clouds. What do the patterns show about movement in the atmosphere?

Strong winds are evidence of the forces that move water through the atmosphere. How do winds begin?
▼

How does water affect the weather?

Earth's atmosphere holds more water than all the lakes and streams combined. You can see some of this water as clouds, but even on clear days water in the air surrounds you. How does this water affect the weather? What drives the water from place to place? Look at the photographs. What does each show about water in the atmosphere?

Changes in the atmosphere lead to changes in the weather. How do meteorologists predict the weather?

The once-fertile African pastureland that these people depend upon is becoming dry desert. With satellites, computers, and ground surveys, climatologists keep a close watch on these changes. How can modern technology help predict and improve conditions in areas of climate change?

CHAPTER

26 Weather and the Atmosphere

▲ Thunderstorm clouds seen from a jet aircraft flying at a height of 10 kilometers

How Do You Know That . . .

Weather occurs close to Earth's surface? From an airplane, you can look down on the weather. Jet aircraft fly at altitudes greater than 10 kilometers. Passengers looking out the windows can sometimes see the lightning from thunderclouds, whose flat tops are near the level of the aircraft. Smaller, fluffy fair-weather clouds lie around the base of the thunderstorm clouds. Outside the aircraft, the pilot announces, the temperature is about −65°F.

Unlike temperatures near Earth's surface, the temperature 10 kilometers up does not change very much. What causes the temperature changes that are a part of what is called weather?

I Composition and Structure of the Atmosphere

Topic 1 What Is Weather?

Anyone looking outside notices right away whether it is cloudy or clear. From personal experience, people know that cloudy skies bring cooler temperatures. Dark clouds often bring rain. Strong winds and blowing snow mean either heavy coats and boots or a day spent indoors.

Weather is the state of the atmosphere at a given time and place. A complete description of the weather includes the amount and type of clouds. Rain, snow, thunderstorms, lightning, and even dust storms are part of the weather. Measurements of temperature, pressure, wind speed and direction, and the amount of moisture in the air are also included in a description of the weather.

Weather is studied and predicted by scientists called meteorologists. The science of **meteorology** is the study of the entire atmosphere, including its weather. To understand and predict the weather, meteorologists must first understand how the atmosphere heats and cools, how clouds form and produce rain, and what makes the wind blow. Meteorologists also study subjects not obviously related to weather. Such subjects include the composition of the atmosphere, the atmospheres of other planets, and the causes of past and present climates. To study these topics, meteorologists measure the state of the atmosphere using many different kinds of instruments. They also perform laboratory experiments and make mathematical models of the atmosphere using computers.

Topic 2 Observing the Weather

Much can be learned about the weather without numerous instruments. Direct observation tells whether it is cloudy or raining. Wind direction and speed can be estimated with a little practice. It is easy to tell whether the air is warm or cold. Even humidity and pressure have observable effects. Certain clouds come with fair weather and other clouds foretell rain. Farmers, sailors, and others dependent on weather become quite skilled at predicting weather from watching the clouds. For example, in the verse

Mackerel scales and mares' tails
Make lofty ships carry low sails,

a cloud formation predicts a coming storm.

OBJECTIVES

A Identify a number of things meteorologists do in their study of the atmosphere and show how to observe the weather.

B Describe the composition and temperature structure of the atmosphere.

C Discuss the ozone layer, its importance, and its possible reduction by CFCs and nitric oxide.

D Explain the origin and variations of the ionosphere.

26.1 Sailors knew that mares' tails like those pictured here often precede storms.

The wind is also related to weather changes. For example, folk wisdom says that winds blowing out of the east bring rain.

Wind direction is shown by flags or blowing dust. The actual wind speed can be estimated by observing its effects. The **Beaufort scale,** named for Sir Francis Beaufort, relates the wind speed to its effects.

The Beaufort Scale

Beaufort Number	MPH	Knots	Wind Effects Observed on Land	Wind Effects Observed at Sea
0	Less than 1	Less than 1	Calm; smoke rises vertically	Sea like a mirror
1	1–3	1–3	Direction of wind shown by smoke drift but not by vanes	Scalelike ripples; no crests
2	4–7	4–6	Wind felt on face; leaves rustle; vanes moved by wind	Small wavelets; glassy crests, do not break
3	8–12	7–10	Leaves, small twigs in constant motion; wind extends light flag	Large wavelets; crests breaking; foam glassy; scattered whitecaps
4	13–18	11–16	Raises dust, loose paper; small branches moved	Small waves become larger; fairly frequent whitecaps
5	19–24	17–21	Small trees in leaf begin to sway; crested wavelets form on inland waters	Moderate waves form many whitecaps; spray
6	25–31	22–27	Large branches in motion; whistling heard in wires; umbrellas used with difficulty	Large waves form; foam crests more extensive; some spray
7	32–38	28–33	Whole trees in motion; inconvenient walking against wind	Sea heaps up; some foam from waves blows streaks
8	39–46	34–40	Breaks twigs off trees; impedes progress	Moderately high waves; well-marked streaks of foam
9	47–54	41–47	Slight structural damage occurs	High waves; dense foam streaks; spray may affect visibility
10	55–63	48–55	Trees uprooted; considerable damage occurs	Very high waves; long overhanging crests; white foam; has white appearance
11	64–72	56–63	Widespread damage	Exceptionally high waves; sea covered with foam patches; edges of wave crests blow into froth everywhere
12	73–82	64–71	Widespread damage	Air filled with foam and spray; sea completely white with driving spray; visibility very seriously affected

The temperature cannot be guessed accurately, but people feel heat and cold. In the winter, people feel colder when the wind is blowing. The actual temperature can be converted into the temperature the body feels using a chart for the *windchill* factor. This adjusted temperature describes the danger of frostbite. In the winter, weather broadcasts often include temperatures adjusted for windchill.

Increased humidity makes wavy and curly hair curlier. High temperatures seem hotter and low temperatures colder when the air is more humid.

Air pressure cannot be felt, but changes in air pressure can. The most common effect of pressure change is the "popping" of the ears. Ear popping occurs during the takeoff or landing of an airplane, a ride in a rapid elevator, or even a ride in a car over a high mountain pass. In all cases, the ears pop because the air pressure falls with height.

To try to predict weather, you need to observe the clouds, wind, temperature, humidity, air pressure, and precipitation over a period of time. Look for patterns in how these factors change relative to one another. For example, is one sequence of events usually followed by rain? See if you can develop your skills at observing and predicting as you study this Unit.

26.2 Use this table to find the windchill, or cooling effect of the wind. The combined effect of temperature and wind is called the windchill factor.

Wind Velocity (MPH)

Temp. °F	0	5	10	15	20	25	30	35	40	45	50
−10	−10	−15	−31	−45	−52	−58	−63	−67	−69	−70	70
−5	−5	−11	−27	−40	−46	−52	−56	−60	−62	−63	−63
0	0	−6	−22	−33	−40	−45	−49	−52	−54	−54	−56
5	5	1	−15	−25	−32	−37	−41	−43	−45	−46	−47
10	10	7	−9	−18	−24	−29	−33	−35	−36	−38	−38
15	15	12	−2	−11	−17	−22	−26	−27	−29	−31	−31
20	20	16	2	−6	−9	−15	−18	−20	−22	−24	−24
25	25	21	9	1	−4	−7	−11	−13	−15	−17	−17
30	30	27	16	11	3	0	−2	−4	−4	−6	−7
35	35	33	21	16	12	7	5	3	1	1	0
40	40	37	28	22	18	16	13	11	10	9	8

Little danger — *Increasing danger* — *Great danger that exposed flesh will freeze*

Topic 3 Composition of the Atmosphere

Earth's lower atmosphere is a mixture of many gases called *air*. The two main gases in air are nitrogen and oxygen. Together they form about 99 percent of dry air by volume. The remaining 1 percent is mostly argon and carbon dioxide. The atmosphere also contains tiny amounts of helium, hydrogen, neon, ozone, krypton, and other gases. The approximate percentages by volume are nitrogen, 78; oxygen, 21; argon, almost 1; carbon dioxide, 0.03; all others, 0.01.

The air thins out quickly at altitudes high above Earth's surface. Its composition (by percent) remains the same, however, to an altitude of about 80 kilometers. Above this level the air is so thin that it would be considered a vacuum at sea level. Also, above this level the atmosphere changes to layers of different gases. A layer of oxygen reaches to about 1000 kilometers. Above it is a layer of helium to about 2400 kilometers. Above this a layer of hydrogen thins out into space.

Gas molecules at the bottom of the atmosphere are squeezed together by the gases above them. As a result, 99 percent of the atmosphere's weight is found within about 32 kilometers of Earth's surface. Half the atmosphere's weight is within 5.5 kilometers.

Topic 4 Water Vapor, Ozone, and Dust

Air always contains some water vapor. Unlike the other principal gases, however, the amount of water vapor varies. Water vapor enters the air by evaporation from the oceans and from water or plants on land. The amount of water vapor depends mainly on location, season, and time of day. On the average, the percentage of water vapor decreases with height.

Ozone is a form of oxygen gas. A molecule of ozone contains three oxygen atoms; a molecule of oxygen gas contains two oxygen atoms. Ozone forms when ultraviolet rays from the sun act on oxygen in the upper atmosphere.

The amount of ozone in the atmosphere is very small. Nevertheless, ozone is important because it absorbs the sun's ultraviolet rays. If the air had less ozone, the ultraviolet rays would cause bad sunburns and more skin cancer. Ozone is concentrated at heights of about 10 to 50 kilometers. This part of the atmosphere is the ozone layer.

Ozone is destroyed by a number of gases. The most important of these are nitric acid from the exhaust of supersonic aircraft and **chlorofluorocarbons (CFCs)**, gases containing chlorine, fluorine, and carbon atoms. CFCs include the freons used both in aerosol spray cans and as refrigerants. These gases break down the ozone layer and weaken the protection from ultraviolet rays. Measurements of the ozone in the atmosphere reveal a possible decrease of a few percent during the last decade. The reduction is the largest over

Antarctica, where a "hole" in the ozone layer has appeared during September and October of the last few years. The hole became stronger each year until 1986, when it was slightly weaker. This hole may be a natural occurrence in the atmosphere that will go away. On the other hand, it may be related to the increased amount of the gases that reduce ozone.

Dust is also an important part of air. Dust includes tiny grains of rocks and minerals, dirt, pollen grains from plants, crystals of salt from sea spray, chemicals from fires and industrial plants, and bacteria. Microscopic dust grains in the air cause hazy skies. Grains of salt and chemicals help to form fog and rain. Water vapor condenses around them, forming tiny droplets of water.

Topic 5 Structure of the Atmosphere

Scientists divide the atmosphere into four layers that are based on temperature changes. The lowest layer is called the **troposphere**. The troposphere starts at Earth's surface. Its thickness depends on the latitude. At the equator the troposphere is about 18 kilometers thick; at the poles it is only about 8 kilometers thick. The gases of the troposphere are essential to life on Earth. Earth's weather occurs in the troposphere.

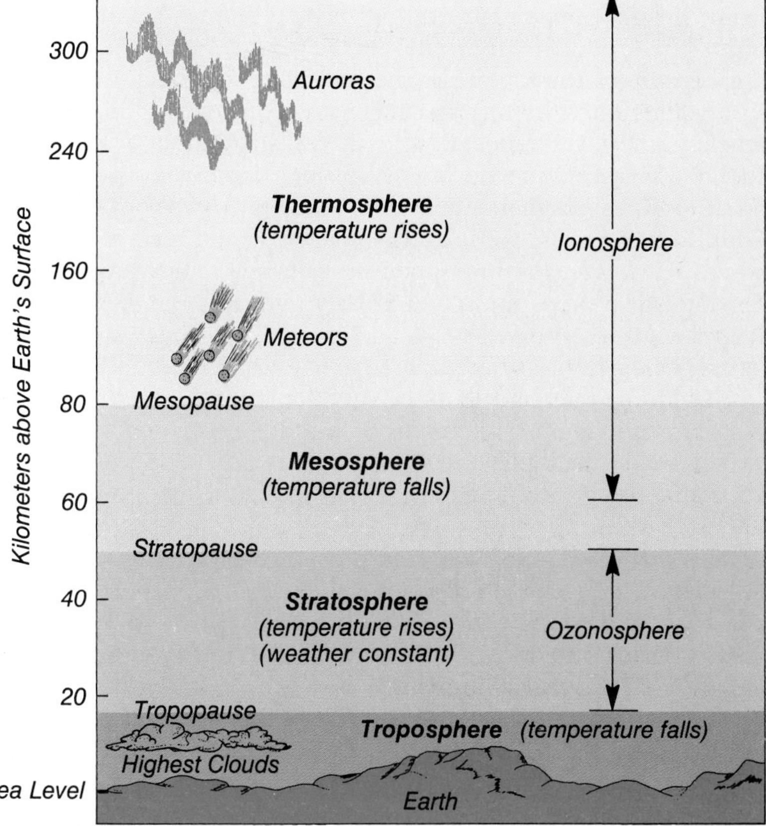

26.3 This diagram shows the temperature layers of the atmosphere. It also shows where auroras form and meteors flare up.

26.4 Reflection of radio waves by the ionosphere extends the range of radio reception.

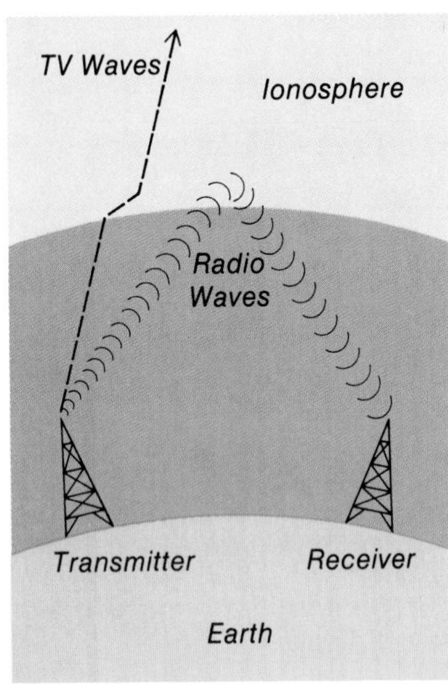

Temperatures gradually decrease with altitude in the troposphere. The top of the troposphere is called the *tropopause*. There the decrease in temperature stops. At the poles the tropopause temperature is about −55°C.

The second layer is the **stratosphere**. It reaches from the tropopause to a height of about 50 kilometers from Earth. The stratosphere is clear and dry. It has strong, steady winds and few weather changes. Because of its steady weather conditions, jet aircraft fly in the stratosphere.

The lower part of the stratosphere is as cold as the tropopause. Then it warms up steadily to its top, or *stratopause*. The absorbing or *absorption* of sunlight by ozone is what makes the stratosphere's temperatures increase with height.

The third and fourth layers are the **mesosphere**, in which temperatures drop again, and the **thermosphere**, in which temperatures rise again. The top of the thermosphere is around 500 kilometers from Earth. The molecules there are so far apart that the word *temperature* no longer has meaning.

Topic 6 The Ionosphere

At heights between about 65 and 500 kilometers above Earth, the air is highly ionized. The ions are formed when ultraviolet rays from the sun knock electrons off oxygen atoms. This part of the atmosphere is called the **ionosphere.** It stretches from the lower mesosphere to the top of the thermosphere.

The ions and electrons are concentrated in layers at four different levels. Each layer reflects radio waves of different wavelengths. Radio waves from broadcasting stations travel in straight lines. Without the ionosphere, the waves would mostly go out into space. Only locations very close to the station would receive any radio waves. However, the ionosphere reflects the radio waves back to Earth. Reflection of the waves greatly increases the area in which they can be received.

The ionosphere is affected by solar events. Huge eruptions on the sun send out large amounts of very short-wave radiation, which disrupts radio communications. Solar eruptions reach a peak each 11 years. Scientists see a relationship between solar eruptions and sunspots, since the number of sunspots also reaches a maximum every 11 years.

The solar eruptions also send out ionized particles. Since they are electrically charged, these particles are deflected by Earth's magnetic field to the North and South Poles. At the poles, the ionized particles interact with air molecules to form *auroras*, colored displays of light in the nighttime sky.

The ionosphere does not reflect the waves used to transmit television. These waves, however, can be picked up and rebroadcast by special satellites orbiting high above Earth. Some radio signals are also relayed by satellite.

26.5 An aurora seen from Alaska

TOPIC QUESTIONS

Each topic question refers to the topic of the same number.

1. **(a)** Define weather. **(b)** What is meteorology?
2. **(a)** Explain how weather can be observed without the use of instruments. **(b)** What two factors make the temperature hard to estimate?
3. **(a)** What is air? **(b)** List the names and the percentages of the main gases for dry air in the lower atmosphere.
4. **(a)** Explain where water vapor comes from. On the average, the most water vapor is at what altitude? **(b)** Why is ozone important? At what height is the most ozone found? What gases destroy ozone? **(c)** List some kinds of particles that are called dust. **(d)** How do salt and chemical grains help to make fog?
5. **(a)** On what basis is the atmosphere divided into four layers? **(b)** Name the four layers.
6. **(a)** On what basis is the ionosphere named? **(b)** How does it help radio communication? **(c)** Explain how radio communication can be disrupted. **(d)** Describe what causes auroras.

Brenda C. Johnson

Research Meteorologist

Did you ever hear of a heat burst? Brenda C. Johnson, formerly of the National Severe Storms Laboratory in Norman, Oklahoma, not only knows what one is but has carefully studied the data from one that moved across central Oklahoma.

A heat burst is a sudden increase in temperature. It usually occurs during nighttime thunderstorms, but it is a rare event. The one in central Oklahoma was unique because it was recorded by a variety of weather instruments over a relatively large land area.

Using the data obtained by the weather instruments, Ms. Johnson was able to trace the heat burst as it moved with a storm northeastward across Oklahoma. She observed that the average temperature increase was 2.6°C, although one weather station recorded an increase of 5°C. At the same time, the amount of moisture in the air decreased by an average of 34 percent, with one station experiencing a decrease of 50 percent. Strong vertical winds, called downdrafts, also developed. Ms. Johnson says that these were a major factor in the occurrence of the heat burst.

II Heating of the Atmosphere

OBJECTIVES

A Differentiate among the three methods of heat transfer.

B Describe the energy balance of Earth and its atmosphere.

C Discuss the greenhouse effect and the potential dangers from increasing amounts of greenhouse gases.

Topic 7 How Heat Moves

Changes in weather involve air movements, formation of clouds, and precipitation. Energy is needed to make all these things happen. That energy comes from the sun. Heat energy enters and moves through the atmosphere in three different ways.

The first way is **radiation**. Hot bodies such as the sun radiate their energy mainly in the form of short waves. These short waves are seen as visible light. Cooler bodies such as Earth radiate their energy as longer waves. These longer waves are called infrared waves, since they are longer than the longest visible light waves, which are red.

The second way is **conduction**. An object receives heat when it comes into contact with a hotter object. A pan on a hot stove is heated mainly by conduction. The air touching a hot radiator is heated mainly by conduction. So is the air that touches warm ground or a warm ocean.

The third way is **convection**. Convection happens only in liquids and gases. Heat is carried by currents in the heated material. A kettle of water on a hot stove is an example. The bottom of the kettle is heated by conduction. The water near the bottom then gets hot, also by conduction. Heat makes the water expand and become less dense. The denser cold water above it sinks, forcing the warm water up. A steady flow called a *convection current* forms. In time, the heat at the bottom reaches all the water. If water is heated from the top, why doesn't convection occur?

Convection is very important in moving heat through the atmosphere. It transfers heat from one place to another. For example, convection removes heat from hot beaches. Winds from the tropics carry heat away and into middle latitudes. The transfer of warm or cold air by horizontal winds is called *advection*.

Topic 8 The Heat Balance of Earth and Atmosphere

Just as much energy enters Earth as leaves it—that is, Earth's heat "budget" is in balance. Otherwise, Earth would gradually heat up or cool down. The only way energy can enter or leave Earth is by radiation. There are not enough molecules in space to carry heat by conduction or convection.

The sun radiates energy into space in all directions. Earth, tiny by comparison and far away from the sun, receives only about one two-billionth of the sun's rays. This *in*coming *sol*ar radi*ation* is called **insolation**.

Suppose 100 units of solar radiation reach the atmosphere. Of these, 30 are reflected back to space, with only about 70 units

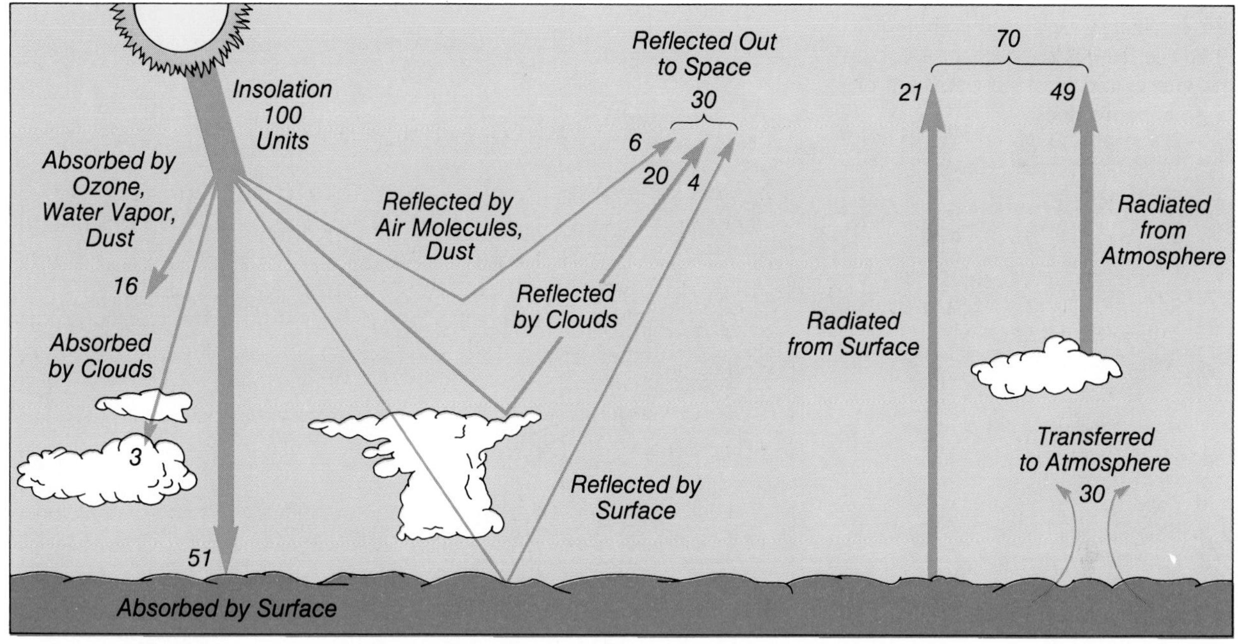

26.6 This diagram shows what happens to 100 units of sunlight entering Earth's atmosphere. Only 51 units are absorbed by the surface.

absorbed. This heat is not absorbed evenly. In the atmosphere, 19 units of sunlight are absorbed by water vapor and clouds, ozone, and dust. Earth's surface absorbs the remaining 51 units of sunlight.

In order to keep Earth's heat budget balanced, 70 units of energy are radiated to space as infrared radiation. The atmosphere and surface also have heat budgets that balance. Of the 51 units of heat absorbed in the form of solar radiation, 21 are radiated back as infrared radiation and 30 are left over. Adding up the complicated radiation budget of the atmosphere, one finds a deficit of 30 units. The 30 units at the surface are transferred from the surface to the atmosphere, so the heat budget balances. How is this done? It is done through the two remaining means of heat transfer, conduction and convection. Conduction from the heated ground heats the very lowest layer of air. Convection currents carry the heat into the atmosphere.

Topic 9 Absorption and the Greenhouse Effect

Earth's surface radiates infrared waves. These infrared waves warm the atmosphere because they are absorbed mainly by the water vapor and carbon dioxide in the air.

In a greenhouse, the glass roof acts like the carbon dioxide and water vapor in the air. It lets in the sun's light to heat the soil. However, it does not allow the longer-wave infrared radiation from the warm soil to escape. Scientists call this trapping of the sun's energy by the atmosphere the **greenhouse effect**. The gases that create this effect are known as greenhouse gases.

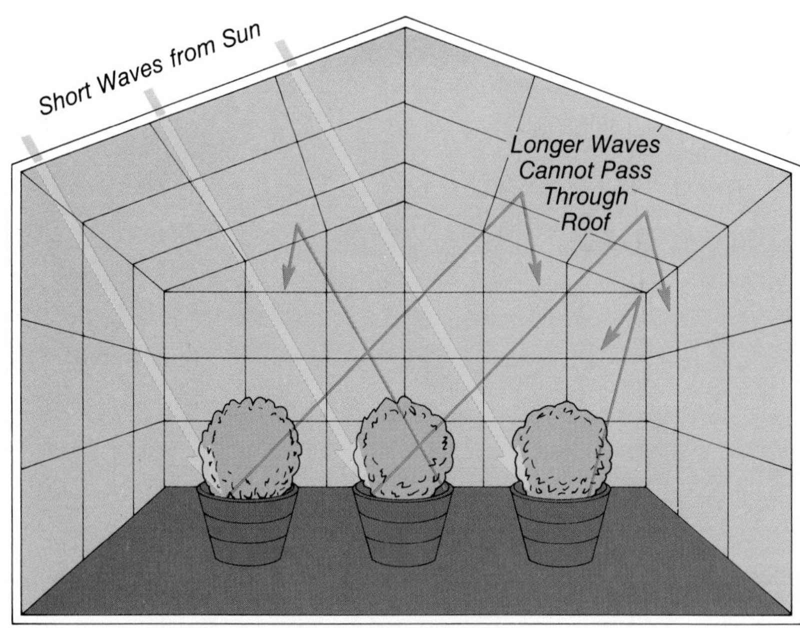

26.7 Water vapor and carbon dioxide in Earth's atmosphere trap solar energy much as the glass roof of a greenhouse does.

The greenhouse effect of Earth's atmosphere is increasing. The burning of fossil fuels—coal, oil, and natural gas—is constantly adding carbon dioxide into the air. There is too much carbon dioxide to be used by green plants or dissolved in the ocean waters. Scientists estimate that if the present rate of burning continues, the percentage of carbon dioxide in the atmosphere will double in about 100 years. Industry is also producing more CFCs, nitrous oxide, and methane, which are also greenhouse gases. The resulting warming of the atmosphere could have serious effects. The glaciers of Greenland and Antarctica could melt enough to raise sea levels all over the world. Such melting would flood low coastal areas such as Miami and New York City. Rainfall patterns could change in ways that would shift desert areas. Obviously, this problem needs serious attention and study.

TOPIC QUESTIONS

Each question refers to the topic of the same number.

7. Name and describe the three ways that heat is transferred through the atmosphere.

8. **(a)** Explain why Earth's heat budget is in balance. **(b)** Describe what happens to sunlight entering Earth's atmosphere. **(c)** What processes balance the heat budget of Earth's surface?

9. **(a)** Describe the greenhouse effect. **(b)** Name the two most important greenhouse gases. **(c)** Why are increased greenhouse gases in the atmosphere a cause for worry?

III How and Why the Temperature Varies

OBJECTIVES

A Explain why the temperature in the troposphere decreases with height.

B Discuss the formation and destruction of temperature inversions near the ground.

C Show how the angle of the sun's rays affects the temperature changes with season, latitude, and hour of day.

D Identify and explain the occurrence of the warmest and coldest hours and the warmest and coldest months.

E Compare the heating and cooling of land and water.

Topic 10 Temperature Drops with Altitude

In summertime some people go to the mountains to escape the heat. The higher they go, the cooler it gets. Scientists have measured the rate of cooling with altitude. It averages about 1°C for every 160 meters. This change is called the **normal lapse rate**.

Why is the troposphere warmest near Earth's surface? Most of the sun's radiation is absorbed at the surface. Heat is transferred from the surface to the air just above by conduction and carried aloft by convection. The rising air in the convection currents cools.

The rising air cools from expansion. Rising air expands because it encounters lower pressure at higher altitudes. Expanding air cools, as anyone knows who has felt the expanding air leaking out of a tire. The air from the tire expands because the pressure outside the tire is lower than the pressure inside the tire. In the atmosphere, rising air outside of clouds cools at a rate of 1°C for every 100 meters. The word *adiabatic* (a-dee-uh-BAT-ic) describes a temperature change caused by expansion, compression, or other changes *within* a substance. The rate of temperature change of rising air outside of clouds is called the *dry-adiabatic lapse rate*. Air sinking toward the surface warms at the same rate.

Why doesn't the troposphere's temperature fall at the dry-adiabatic lapse rate? One important reason is that the convection above about a kilometer is mainly in clouds, which have a lapse rate closer to the normal lapse rate.

Topic 11 Temperature Inversions

Normally the air gets colder with height in the troposphere. Sometimes, however, the air gets warmer with height for a few hundred meters or more. This upside-down temperature condition is called a **temperature inversion**.

26.8 This diagram shows three reasons why the troposphere is warmest near the ground. (At night, the air nearest the ground cools, but it quickly warms during the day.)

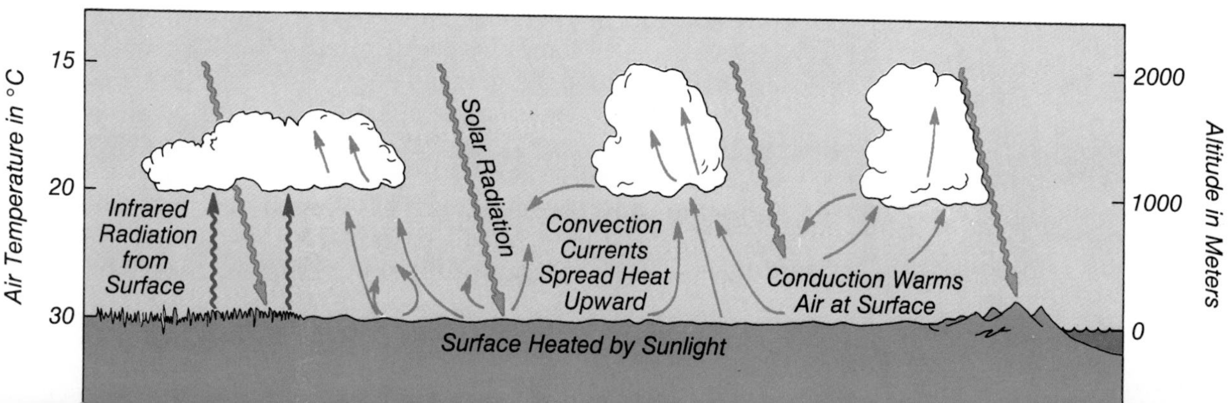

26.9 (a) Normal conditions, and (b) a temperature inversion

Temperature inversions form during clear, dry nights. On these nights, the ground and the air near the ground cool rapidly by radiation from the surface. Since the ground cools faster than the air, the air near the ground cools still more due to contact with the cooler ground. The wind mixes the cold air upward in a layer a few hundred meters deep. This bottom layer is cooler than the air above it. Cold air is heavier than warmer air, so smoke and other pollution are trapped beneath the inversion. Fortunately, if the sky remains clear, the sunlight soon warms the ground and lower atmosphere. The low-level inversion is destroyed by late morning. Mixing of the air by strong winds can also destroy inversions or prevent their formation.

Topic 12 The Sun's Rays and the Seasons

The temperature varies with the seasons because the sun's rays do not heat Earth's surface evenly. Because Earth is round, the sun's rays strike the surface at angles ranging from 0–90°. When the sun is directly overhead, the angle of insolation is 90°. The sun's rays are vertical, and Earth's surface gets all the energy possible. As the angle of insolation decreases, however, the energy of the rays is spread out. As the angle approaches zero, less energy reaches Earth.

Places near the equator get nearly vertical rays all through the year. Thus, these areas have hot climates. Places in middle latitudes (like most of the United States) get near-vertical rays in summer. Their summers are hot. The angle of the rays is less vertical in winter, so winters in middle latitudes are cold. Places in high latitudes (near the poles, for example) never get rays striking the surface at near-vertical angles. These areas may even have no sun at all for part of the year. They are cold all year round.

Topic 13 Warmest and Coldest Hours

Varying insolation also changes the temperature during the day. The highest temperature is not at noon, however, when the sunlight is strongest. Instead, the warmest hour of a sunny day is usually in the afternoon. For several hours after noon, the lower air still receives more heat from the sun and the ground than it loses. Thus, its temperature keeps rising until well into the afternoon. The coldest hour usually comes just before sunrise because the lower air loses heat all through the night.

The difference between the highest and lowest temperatures is the temperature range. For any one day, it is the daily temperature range. For example, a high of 35°C and a low of 10°C give a range of 25°C. The daily temperature range is variable. It is usually large when skies are clear. The clear skies allow strong heating by day. At night they allow rapid loss of heat by radiation.

The daily temperature range is small on cloudy days. The clouds keep out sunshine by day, so the air hardly warms up. At night the clouds keep the air from radiating its heat out into space. This blanket effect keeps the air from cooling much at night.

The average temperature of a day is the sum of the high and low temperatures divided by two. This daily average is then used to compute the average, or mean, temperatures for months, years, or other periods of time.

26.10 The vertical rays of sunlight and the slanted rays are of the same width. They carry equal amounts of energy. However, the vertical rays are concentrated between points A and B, and the slanted rays are spread out between A and C.

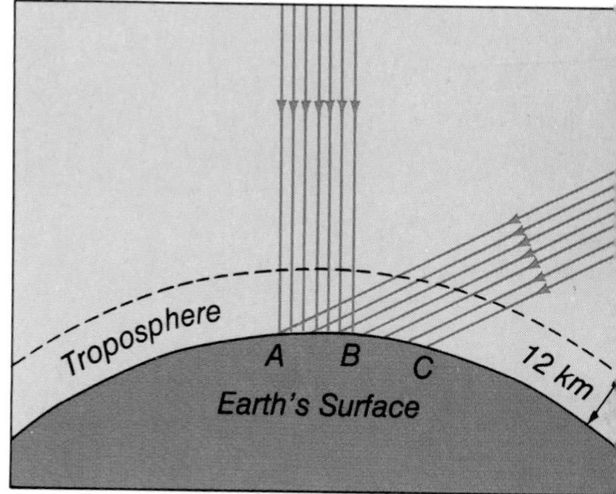

Topic 14 Warmest and Coldest Months

Like the day's highest temperature, the year's highest temperature occurs after the time of strongest sunlight. In middle latitudes of the Northern Hemisphere, June 21 is the time of strongest sunlight. However, July is usually the warmest month. Similarly, December 21 is the time of weakest sunlight, but January is usually the coldest month. In the Southern Hemisphere, the warmest and coldest months are the reverse.

The annual temperature range for an area is the difference between the average temperatures of the warmest and coldest months. Oceans have small annual temperature ranges. They are relatively cool in summer and warm in winter. Continents and large landmasses have large annual temperature ranges. They are relatively hot in summer and cool in winter.

Topic 15 Heating of Land and Water

Why are the daily and annual temperature ranges larger over continents than over oceans? The reason is water and land warm up and cool off at different rates. Water warms much more slowly than land for many reasons.

1. In water, the sun's rays go to a depth of many meters. On land, the sun's rays heat only the top few centimeters of soil.
2. Water can spread heat easily because it is a fluid.
3. Water needs more energy than land to raise its temperature the same amount.
4. Some solar energy is used in the process of evaporation. Thus, less solar energy is available to raise the temperature of the water.

Water cools more slowly than land because it is a slower conductor of heat. It must lose more energy for the same temperature drop. Also, its heat is spread through a greater depth.

Water and land in the same latitude reach very different temperatures. On a sunny day in summer, dry beach sand is much warmer than the nearby water. At night the same sand cools faster than the water and becomes much colder. On a larger scale, continents are warmer than nearby ocean waters in summer. In winter the same continents become much colder than the nearby waters.

26.11 Satellite image of infrared radiation over the southeastern United States. Lighter shades show colder temperatures. Note the warm (darker) water and cooler (lighter) land.

Unlike water, land has many kinds of surface materials. Some of these absorb the sun's rays better than others. Dark soils and rocks absorb more energy than light-colored ones. Rough surfaces absorb more energy than smooth ones. The temperature of dry ground increases faster than wet ground. Meadows warm up more quickly than forests. Pavements get warm long before grassy lawns. Snow and ice reflect sunlight and remain cold.

Surfaces that warm up faster usually also cool off faster. They are warmer in sunshine and cooler at night.

TOPIC QUESTIONS

Each topic question refers to the topic of the same number.

10. **(a)** Explain why the temperature normally drops with altitude in the troposphere. **(b)** Define normal lapse rate. **(c)** Define dry-adiabatic lapse rate.

11. **(a)** What is a temperature inversion? Explain how temperature inversions form at night. **(b)** How are they destroyed in the morning?

12. **(a)** Describe the relationship between the angle of the sun's rays and the heating effect. **(b)** How is this angle related to climates of the low, middle, and high latitudes?

13. **(a)** Explain why the warmest hour of the day is usually in the afternoon. **(b)** Why is the coldest hour just before sunrise? **(c)** Why is the temperature range larger on clear days than on cloudy ones?

14. **(a)** List the warmest and coldest months in the Northern Hemisphere; in the Southern Hemisphere. **(b)** Define annual temperature range.

15. **(a)** List the reasons sunlight warms water more slowly than land. **(b)** Explain why water holds heat longer than land. **(c)** Why does land heat unevenly?

IV Measuring Air Temperature

OBJECTIVES

A Explain how temperature is measured and identify the Celsius temperature scale.

B Describe and explain the pattern of the world's isotherms.

Topic 16 Temperature and Thermometers

Temperature is a measure of the energy of molecules. The more energy the molecules in air have, the hotter it feels. **Thermometers** are the instruments that measure temperature. Common thermometers work on the principle that a rise in temperature causes molecules to move farther apart. Therefore, most materials expand when heated.

Some thermometers contain a liquid such as mercury or alcohol as the expanding material. Mercury is silver in color. Alcohol is clear, so it is usually dyed red or blue to be more visible. The liquid fills the relatively broad bulb end of a long, narrow glass tube. When the temperature rises, the liquid expands into the tube's narrow stem.

Mercury thermometers are more accurate than alcohol thermometers because mercury expands more evenly. However, mercury cannot be used at temperatures below about −40°C, where it freezes. Alcohol freezes at about −129°C.

Metal thermometers have two equally long strips of different metals. Brass and iron are a common pair. The two strips are bonded together, one on top of the other. This forms a device called a *bimetal bar*. Because the metals expand at different rates, a rise in temperature makes the bar curl. A drop in temperature curls it the other way. Usually the bar is shaped into a coil and fastened at one end. As the temperature changes, the coil winds or unwinds.

A *thermograph* is a self-recording thermometer. A *maximum thermometer* shows the highest temperature reached. A *fever thermometer* is a maximum thermometer that has a tiny constriction to keep the mercury from flowing back into the bulb. A *minimum thermometer* indicates the lowest temperature reached.

26.12 The hygrothermograph records temperature and humidity. As the temperature and humidity rise and fall, the pens trace lines on the scale.

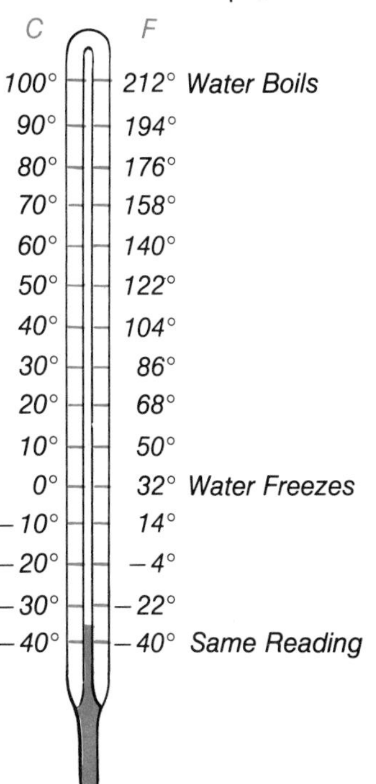

26.13 A comparison of the Celsius and Fahrenheit temperature scales

Topic 17 Temperature Scales

Temperatures are measured in degrees. A **degree** of temperature is a definite fraction of the difference between two fixed temperatures. Usually these points are the temperatures assigned to the melting of ice and the boiling of water at sea level pressure.

On the Celsius scale, the fixed points are labeled as 0 and 100. One degree Celsius is therefore 1/100 of their difference. On the Fahrenheit scale, the fixed points are labeled 32 and 212. One degree Fahrenheit is therefore 1/180 of their difference (212 − 32 = 180).

Note that a Celsius degree is almost twice as large as a Fahrenheit degree. To be exact,

$$1°C = 1.8°F, \text{ or } 1°F = 5/9°C.$$

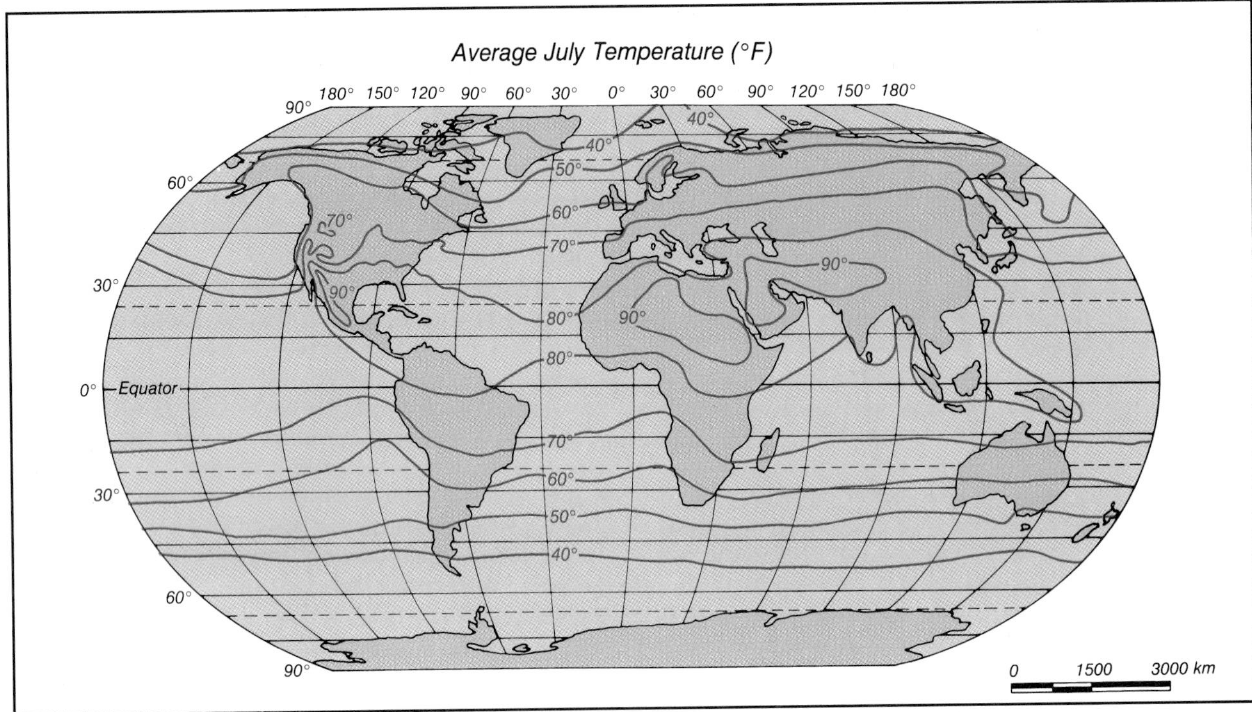

26.14 This map shows isotherms for July.

Topic 18 Isotherms

Isotherms are lines drawn on maps that connect places with the same temperature. Usually isotherms are spaced 5 or 10 degrees apart.

The maps in Figures 26.14 and 26.15 show average world temperatures for January and July. Notice that the warmest temperatures are to the north of the equator in July. The sun's rays are more vertical north of the equator in July. If Earth were all water, the isotherms would be east-west, following the parallels of latitude. However, land heats and cools more easily than water, so the continents are warmer in summer and colder in winter. This makes the isotherms more irregular in the Northern Hemisphere, where there is more land.

Topic 19 Why Isotherms Shift

July is the warmest month in the Northern Hemisphere, and January is the coldest month. Thus, the isotherms shift their positions from January to July.

What else do the temperature maps show?

1. The isotherms shift more over the Northern Hemisphere than over the Southern Hemisphere.
2. The isotherms shift more over continents than over oceans.

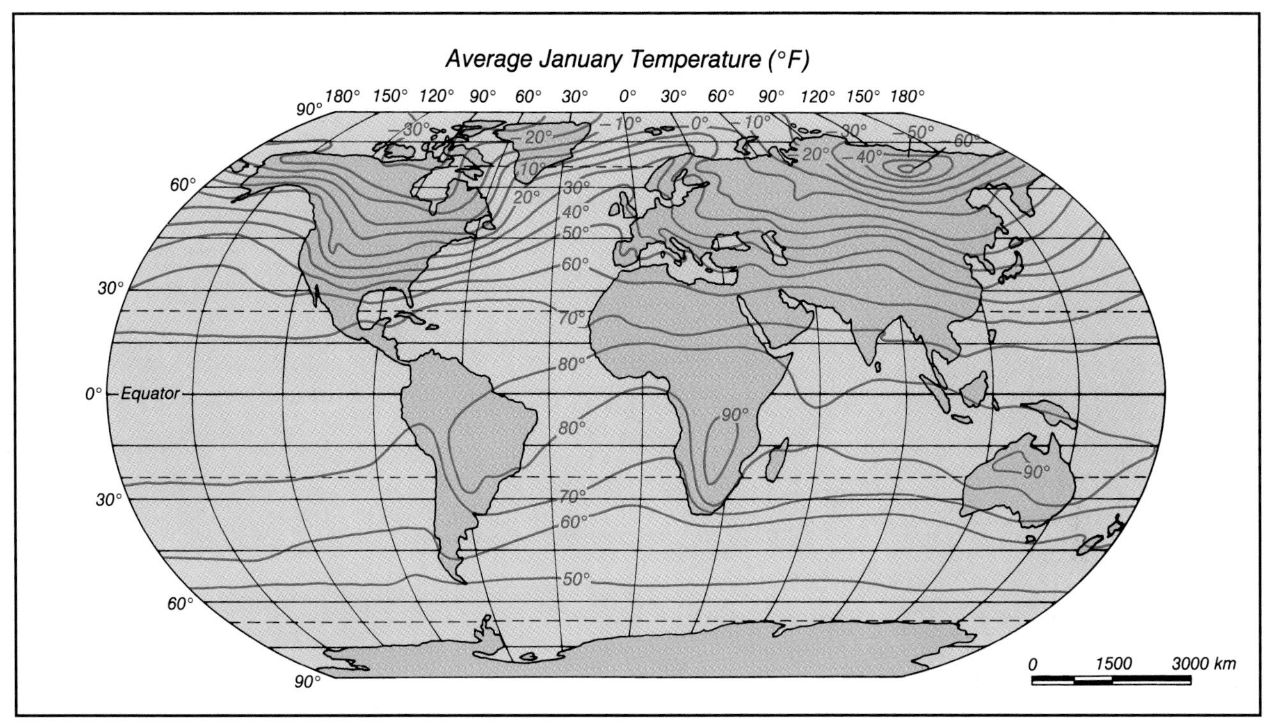

26.15 This map shows isotherms for January.

3. The hottest and coldest places are on land.
4. The coldest spot in the Northern Hemisphere is far south of the North Pole.

What is the explanation of these facts?

TOPIC QUESTIONS

Each topic question refers to the topic of the same number.

16. **(a)** What is the principle used to measure temperature? **(b)** Describe how a liquid thermometer works. **(c)** Describe how a metal thermometer works.

17. **(a)** How are temperature scales determined? **(b)** Express the freezing and boiling temperatures of water in degrees Celsius. **(c)** How do the sizes of a Fahrenheit and Celsius degree compare?

18. **(a)** Explain how isotherms show temperature. **(b)** Why are the hottest temperatures north of the equator in July? **(c)** Why are the isotherms more east-west in the Southern Hemisphere?

19. **(a)** Why do world isotherms shift? **(b)** Compare the shift of isotherms over land and ocean and explain the differences.

CHAPTER 26 REVIEW

Summary

Much can be learned about the weather by direct observation without the use of complicated weather instruments.

Earth's atmosphere is a mixture of gases that thins out with height. It contains mainly nitrogen and oxygen, with small amounts of other gases.

The ozone layer protects life from ultraviolet radiation. CFCs and nitric oxide threaten to reduce the amount of ozone.

The atmosphere is divided into layers based on temperature. The ionosphere contains ionized air.

Heat moves in three ways: by radiation, convection, and conduction.

Earth's heat budget is in balance. Most solar radiation is absorbed at the surface, which warms the air above.

The greenhouse effect traps heat in Earth's atmosphere. An increase in carbon dioxide and other greenhouse gases may cause global warming.

Temperature inversions form on clear nights as the ground and the air just above it cool more rapidly than air higher up.

Climates are warmer at lower latitudes, where the sun is more directly overhead.

The warmest temperatures are generally in the afternoon, and the coldest temperatures just before sunrise.

The warmest month is about a month past the time of maximum sunlight; similarly, the coldest month is about a month past the time of minimum sunlight.

Land heats and cools more readily than water.

Temperature is measured using the principle that materials expand when heated. Celsius and Fahrenheit are two commonly used temperature scales.

Isotherms shift with the seasons, more dramatically over land than over water.

Vocabulary

Beaufort scale
chlorofluorocarbon (CFC)
conduction
convection
degree
greenhouse effect
insolation
ionosphere
isotherm
mesosphere
meteorology
normal lapse rate
radiation
stratosphere
temperature inversion
thermometer
thermosphere
troposphere
weather

Review

Number your paper from 1 to 20. Match the terms in list **A** with the phrases in list **B.**

List A

1. ionosphere
2. greenhouse effect
3. windchill
4. air
5. annual temperature range
6. water
7. isotherm
8. conduction
9. normal lapse rate
10. meteorology
11. thermometer
12. ozone
13. daily temperature range
14. radiation
15. insolation
16. troposphere
17. temperature inversion
18. angle of insolation
19. carbon dioxide
20. convection

List B

a. difference between the average temperatures of the warmest and coldest months
b. heat transfer by currents within the heated material
c. varies due to Earth's roundness
d. temperature the body actually feels when the wind is blowing
e. condition in which the bottom layer of air is colder than the air above it
f. heat transfer in the form of infrared waves
g. based on the principle that a rise in temperature causes most materials to expand

h. the energy Earth receives from the sun
i. reflects radio waves, but not television waves
j. smaller on cloudy days
k. added to the air by the burning of fossil fuels
l. trapping of the sun's energy by the atmosphere
m. a slow conductor of heat
n. line on a map connecting places with the same temperature
o. study of the atmosphere
p. composed mainly of nitrogen and oxygen
q. heat transfer by direct contact
r. layer of the atmosphere where weather occurs
s. absorbs the sun's ultraviolet rays
t. rate at which the troposphere cools with altitude

Interpret and Apply

On your paper, answer each question in complete sentences.

1. Approximately how fast, in miles per hour, is the wind blowing under each of the following conditions? (a) Walking in the wind is difficult and small twigs are breaking off the trees. (b) Pieces of a newspaper are blowing down the street and dust is blown into your eyes. (c) The trees are motionless and smoke is going straight up.
2. The temperature outside is 0°F. How cold does it feel if the wind is blowing (a) 10 mph, (b) 15 mph, (c) 20 mph? (d) Restate these three temperatures in degrees Celsius.
3. How do convection currents help to cool the waters of a lake in autumn?
4. (a) Why are temperature inversions near Earth's surface unlikely on cloudy nights? (b) Under what weather conditions might a temperature inversion NOT disappear in the morning?
5. Why is there very little variation in the time of the warmest and coldest hours of the day at the equator?

Critical Thinking

A student performed an experiment to compare the heating and cooling rates of soil and water. She placed identical containers, one filled with soil and the other filled with water, at equal distances from a light source. A thermometer was placed in each container to record the temperatures. She turned the light on and recorded the temperatures each minute for 10 minutes. Then she turned the light off and again recorded the temperatures each minute for 10 minutes. A graph of her data is shown below. Study the graph and then answer the questions that follow.

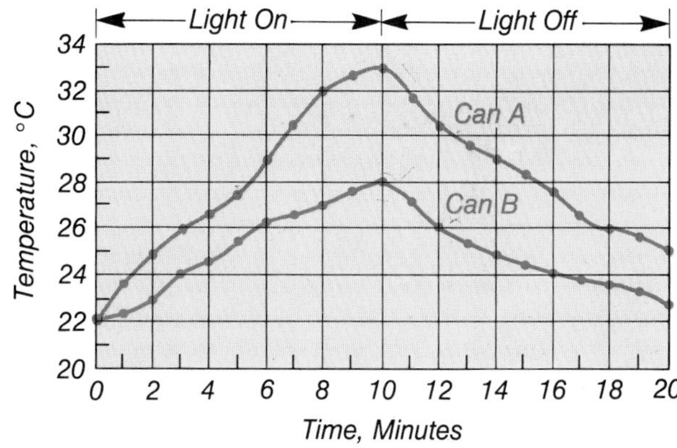

1. In which container did the material heat faster?
2. In which container did the material cool faster?
3. Which container held the water?
4. Did the soil and water both absorb the same amount of energy? Why or why not?
5. The smallest daily temperature ranges at Earth's surface are less than 1°C. Where are they and why? What sort of location would usually have the largest temperature range? Why?

CHAPTER

27 Evaporation, Condensation, and Precipitation

▲
Feathery cirrus clouds and fluffy cumulus clouds look very different, but both are made of forms of water.

How Do You Know That . . .

There is water in the atmosphere? You can observe evidence in the sky. Suppose it is a hot, humid spring day. The morning starts out clear, with some patches of fog that disappear early. By noon, small puffy clouds have formed. By afternoon, the puffy clouds have grown deeper. Their dark, flat bases suggest possible rain showers. The puffy clouds are joined by higher, feathery clouds to make a beautiful sky.

Why do the puffy clouds have such flat bases and tops that look so much like cauliflowers? Why do the high, feathery clouds look so different from the puffy clouds? And what keeps the clouds from falling to the ground?

I Evaporation and Humidity

OBJECTIVES

A Specify the changes in state involved in evaporation and condensation and explain why evaporation is a cooling process.

B Show that warmer air can hold more water vapor.

C Define relative humidity and show how it is measured.

Topic 1 States of Water

Water exists in the atmosphere in all of the three states of matter—solid, as snow, hail, and ice particles; liquid, as rain or cloud droplets; and gas, as invisible water vapor.

Water may change from one state to another. The change from solid ice to liquid water is called melting; the reverse process is freezing. The change from liquid water to water vapor is called **evaporation**. The change from water vapor to liquid water is called **condensation**.

Most water vapor in the atmosphere comes from oceans, lakes, marshes, and glaciers. Some water vapor also comes from moist ground, from the leaves of plants, and from erupting volcanoes.

Water vapor is spread throughout the troposphere by convection currents and winds. Since rising air currents stop at the tropopause, there is little water vapor above the troposphere.

Topic 2 Evaporation

The molecules of liquid water are always in motion. Molecules with sufficient energy to escape the water's surface into the atmosphere are said to evaporate. At ordinary temperatures, evaporation is slow because few molecules have enough energy to escape the liquid's surface. As water molecules absorb heat energy, they speed up. Then more molecules have sufficient energy to escape the water's surface. With increasing temperatures the evaporation rate increases. When water evaporates, it enters the atmosphere in the form of water vapor.

Water and other liquids absorb heat energy from their surroundings when they evaporate. Since the high-energy molecules leave the liquid's surface, the remaining liquid molecules have less average energy. This makes evaporation a cooling process.

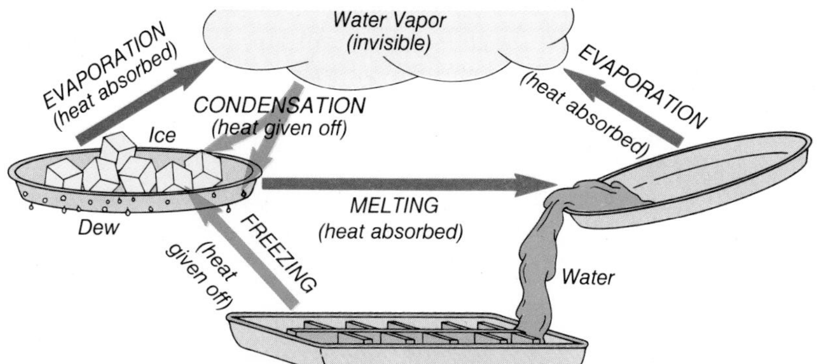

27.1 When water changes from one state to another, it either loses or gains heat.

27.2 This graph shows how air's capacity for water vapor increases with temperature. Note that the capacity roughly doubles for each 11°C.

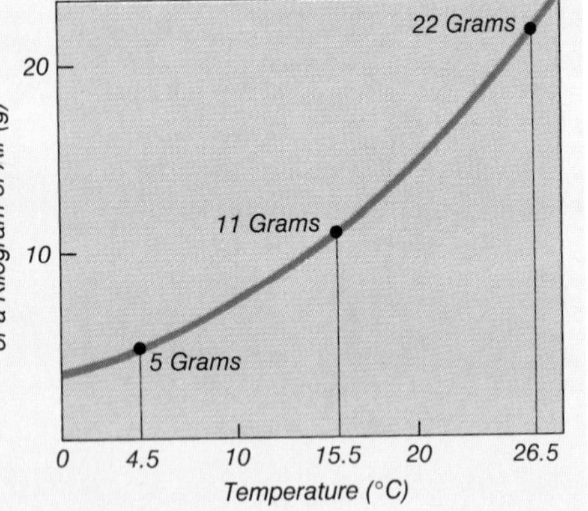

Topic 3 Specific Humidity and Capacity

The capacity of air for holding water vapor depends on the temperature of the air. The warmer the air, the more water vapor it can hold. The amount of water vapor actually present in the air is called **specific humidity**. It is the number of grams of water vapor in one kilogram of air. On a hot, humid summer day, the specific humidity is about 20 grams per kilogram. On a cold winter day, the specific humidity is about 5 grams per kilogram.

When the specific humidity equals the air's capacity for holding water vapor, the air is *saturated*. For example, the air between the water's surface and the glass cover of a fish tank is likely to be saturated. Drops of water hang from the underside of the cover. The drops show that although water continues to evaporate from the warm tank, an equal amount of water condenses from the saturated air.

The air's capacity for holding water vapor roughly doubles for every rise in temperature of about 11°C. For example, a kilogram of air at 15.5°C can hold about 11 grams of water vapor. A kilogram of air at 26.5°C can hold about 22 grams.

27.3 The relationship between specific humidity and relative humidity

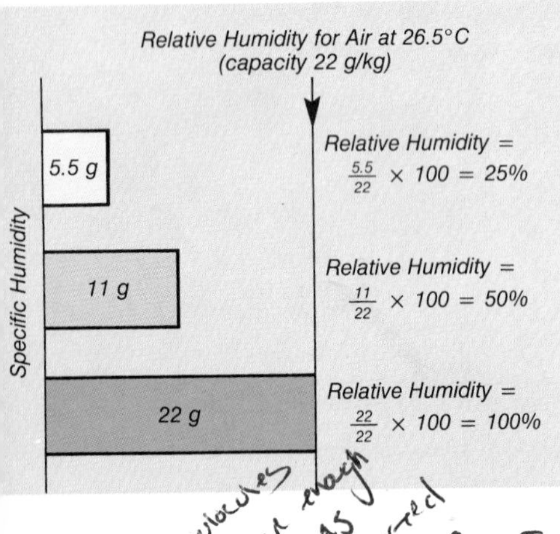

Topic 4 Relative Humidity

Meteorologists need to know how near the air is to its capacity for holding water vapor. This information is known as the relative humidity. **Relative humidity** compares the actual amount of water vapor in the air with the maximum amount of water vapor the air can hold at that temperature.

Relative humidity is usually stated as a percent. It can be calculated by dividing the specific humidity by the capacity. The result is multiplied by 100 to express the answer as a percent.

For example, air at a temperature of 26.5°C has a capacity of 22 grams. If its specific humidity at a particular time is 11 grams, its relative humidity is 50 percent.

$$\frac{11}{22} \times 100 = 50\%$$

Saturated air has a relative humidity of 100 percent.

Topic 5 Finding Relative Humidity

Instruments used to measure relative humidity are called **hygrometers**. One simple type of hygrometer, the hair hygrometer, is based on the principle that human hair stretches when it is humid. One end of a bundle of hairs is fixed. The other end is attached to a pointer. When the air is humid the hair stretches and changes the humidity reading indicated by the pointer. When the air becomes dry again, the hair shrinks back to a shorter length, once again changing the position of the pointer.

Another form of hygrometer is the **psychrometer** (sy-KROM-uh-ter). It works on the principle that evaporation causes cooling. A psychrometer consists of two identical thermometers. One, the wet-bulb thermometer, has a water-soaked wick wrapped around its bulb. The other is the dry-bulb thermometer. The thermometers are whirled or fanned so air circulates past the two bulbs. The dry-bulb thermometer shows the air temperature. The wet-bulb thermometer usually shows a lower temperature. Why are the temperatures different? As the water evaporates from the wick of the wet-bulb thermometer, heat is taken from its bulb. The drier the air, the faster the evaporation, and the lower the reading.

The instrument itself only shows two thermometer readings. These readings give signs of how dry the air is but do not show the relative humidity. With the thermometer readings, however, the relative humidity can be found by using a table. The table has been worked out by actual experiment.

27.4 A psychrometer

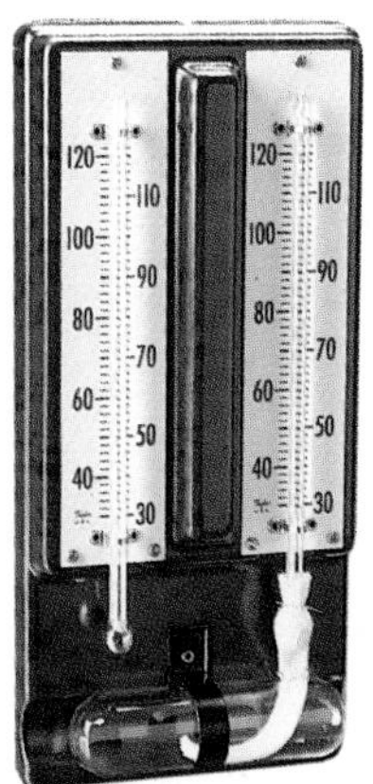

Relative Humidity (%)

Dry-bulb temperature (°C)	Difference between wet-bulb and dry-bulb temperatures (°C)																			
	1	2	3	4	5	6	7	8	9	10	11	12	13	14	15	16	17	18	19	20
0	81	64	46	29	13															
2	84	68	52	37	22	7														
4	85	71	57	43	29	16														
6	86	73	60	48	35	24	11													
8	87	75	63	51	40	29	19	8												
10	88	77	66	55	44	34	24	15	6											
12	89	78	68	58	48	39	29	21	12											
14	90	79	70	60	51	42	34	26	18	10										
16	90	81	71	63	54	46	38	30	23	15	8									
18	91	82	73	65	57	49	41	34	27	20	14	7								
20	91	83	74	66	59	51	44	37	31	24	18	12	6							
22	92	83	76	68	61	54	47	40	34	28	22	17	11	6						
24	92	84	77	69	62	56	49	43	37	31	26	20	15	10	5					
26	92	85	78	71	64	58	51	46	40	34	29	24	19	14	10	5				
28	93	85	78	72	65	59	53	48	42	37	32	27	22	18	13	9	5			
30	93	86	79	73	67	61	55	50	44	39	35	30	25	21	17	13	9	5		
32	93	86	80	74	68	62	57	51	46	41	37	32	28	24	20	16	12	9	5	
34	93	87	81	75	69	63	58	53	48	43	39	35	30	28	23	19	15	12	8	5

A section of a table used with the psychrometer appears above. Assume the dry-bulb reading is 14°C and the wet-bulb reading is 12°C, two degrees lower. First, find 14°C in the column for dry-bulb temperature. Then find 2 (14 − 12 = 2) at the top of the table. At the intersection of 14°C and 2, number 79 indicates the relative humidity, which is stated as a percent.

If both the wet-bulb and dry-bulb thermometers read the same, the air is saturated. The relative humidity at saturation is 100 percent. No evaporation is occurring from the wet bulb.

C° : 5/9 (°F-32) (pg. 441)

F° - 9/5 - C° + 32

Condensation - the molecules of a gas lose energy and return to the liquid state

TOPIC QUESTIONS

Each topic question refers to the topic of the same number.

1. **(a)** In what forms does water exist in the atmosphere? Give examples. **(b)** Define evaporation and condensation. **(c)** What are the sources of water vapor in the atmosphere? **(d)** Why is there so little water vapor above the troposphere?
2. **(a)** Explain why evaporation is a cooling process. **(b)** What causes water to evaporate more rapidly when the temperature is warmer?
3. **(a)** How are the temperature and the water vapor capacity related? **(b)** Define specific humidity. **(c)** When is air saturated?
4. **(a)** What is relative humidity? **(b)** Explain how relative humidity is calculated.
5. **(a)** What is a hygrometer? **(b)** On what principle is a hair hygrometer based? **(c)** What is a psychrometer? What is the principle of its operation? **(d)** How is the psychrometer used to find relative humidity?

Dr. Kristina B. Katsaros
Weather Researcher

Weather satellites have proved to be very valuable tools for day-to-day weather predictions. Dr. Kristina B. Katsaros of the University of Washington has now shown that these satellites can also be used to measure some properties of the air as accurately as conventional weather instruments. She participated in a project called Joint Air Sea Interaction Experiment (JASIN). During the project she studied the water vapor and rate of rain in the JASIN test area of the North Atlantic Ocean.

The conventional method for determining the weather properties of the air above the surface level is to send up several sensors and a radio transmitter on a balloon. The transmitter sends back data as it rises through the atmosphere.

During JASIN three ships stayed on station and released transmitter balloons at regular intervals. Dr. Katsaros compared the results obtained from these instruments with the data obtained by a weather satellite. She found the two readings to show astonishing agreement, making weather satellites even more useful weather predictors and research tools.

II Forms of Condensation

Topic 6 Condensation and Dew Point

How does condensation—the change from vapor to liquid—usually happen in the atmosphere? Consider this example. On a sunny spring afternoon the air temperature is 15.5°C and the specific humidity is 8 grams. The air's capacity at this temperature is 11 grams, so it is not saturated. That night the air cools rapidly. When its temperature reaches 10°C, its capacity is only 8 grams. Since the specific humidity of the air is already 8 grams, the air is saturated.

What happens if the temperature drops below 10°C? All the water vapor above its capacity condenses. If the temperature drops to 4.5°C, the air's capacity is 6 grams. Each kilogram of air releases 2 grams of water vapor, which then condenses. If the water vapor condenses on surfaces such as grass, in the form of a liquid, it is called **dew.** The water vapor could also condense into mist over the ground or droplets in a cloud.

The temperature at which saturation occurs is called the **dew point**. In the example just given, it was 10°C. However, the dew point may be higher or lower depending on the amount of water vapor in the air. The more water vapor air starts with, the higher its dew point. The dew point is an important temperature to meteorologists. When air is cooled below the dew point, condensation of water vapor begins.

Evaporating water molecules absorb heat energy from their surroundings. When water condenses, it returns the same amount of heat energy to its surroundings. Because of this, condensation slows down the cooling of the air in which it is taking place.

In the atmosphere, the temperature rarely falls much below the dew point. Condensation begins as soon as the temperature gets slightly below the dew point. When water condenses in cooling air, the temperature and dew point stay nearly equal.

OBJECTIVES

A Demonstrate how cooling produces condensation and list some of the ways in which air becomes cooler.

B Explain why condensation is a warming process.

C Describe how dew, frost, and fog form.

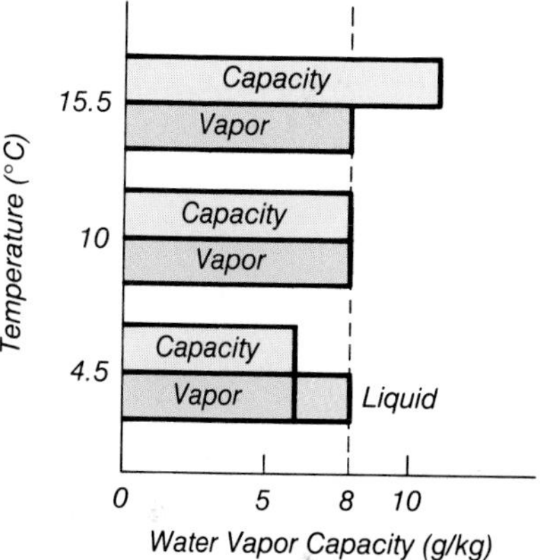

27.5 When a kilogram of unsaturated air (top) is cooled to 10°C, it becomes saturated (middle). Its dew point is therefore 10°C. When further cooling occurs, any excess water condenses as dew, fog, or cloud particles (bottom).

Topic 7 Condensation Requires Cooling and Nuclei

For water vapor to condense, air must be cooled below its dew point. This cooling can happen in four different ways. Air may lose heat by:

1. contacting a colder surface;
2. radiating heat;
3. mixing with colder air; or
4. expanding when it rises.

The last process is most important in producing clouds, rain, or snow. These processes will be discussed further in the next lesson.

Even when air is cooled below its dew point, condensation may not occur. The air is then said to be supersaturated. Water vapor needs to condense on something. The tiny particles on which water vapor condenses are called **condensation nuclei**. If there are no condensation nuclei, condensation cannot occur.

Condensation nuclei are usually substances such as salt, sulfate particles, or nitrate particles. Salt enters the air when fine sea spray evaporates. The sulfates and nitrates come from natural sources and from the burning of fuels. Condensation nuclei are so tiny that a puff of smoke contains millions of them. Similarly, water vapor requires ice nuclei to form ice crystals. Some types of bacteria and clay particles contaminated with organic material are good ice nuclei.

Topic 8 Dew and Frost from Contact

Condensation usually happens when air is cooled below its dew point. If cooling occurs by contact with a colder surface, water vapor condenses directly on that surface. If the temperature is above 0°C, dew forms. The drops of water that form on the outside of a glass of ice water are an often-seen example of dew. Dew may form on the ground, on leaves and grass, and on other surfaces. At night these surfaces become cooler than the air because they lose heat more rapidly. The air reaches its dew point where it touches the cooler objects. Clear nights show greater cooling and heavier dew.

If the temperature at the surface is below 0°C, the water vapor condenses on surfaces as a solid, called **frost.** When the temperatures near the ground drop below −2°C, liquid in the cells of some plants may freeze. This freezing bursts the cell walls and kills the plants. Killing frosts are caused not by atmospheric moisture but by the temperature of the plants themselves.

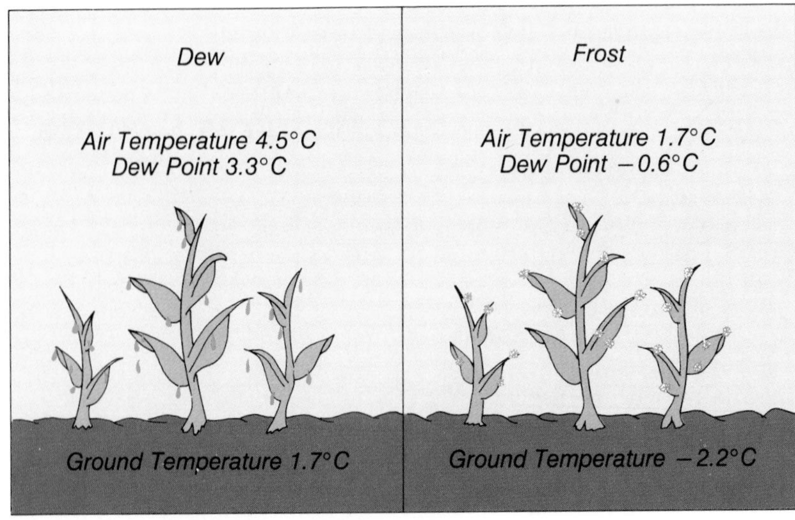

27.6 Dew forms on a cold surface when the surface temperature falls below the dew point of the air touching it but not below 0°C. Frost forms on a surface when the surface temperature at condensation is below 0°C.

Topic 9 Fogs from Radiation and Advection

Often a surface layer of air a few hundred meters thick is cooled below the dew point. As water vapor condenses throughout the entire layer, tiny droplets fill the air and form fog. (If the temperature is well below 0°C the fog droplets will be ice.) Each droplet is centered about a condensation nucleus. The droplets are so tiny that they fall slowly. The lightest air movement keeps them suspended in the air.

Radiation fogs, or *ground fogs,* form under conditions similar to those that form dew. The nighttime sky is clear and the ground loses heat rapidly by radiation. Light winds mix the cold bottom air with the air a short distance from the surface. A whole layer of air is cooled below the dew point, and fog forms.

Radiation fogs are common in humid valleys near rivers or lakes. They are most frequent in the fall of the year. These fogs are thickest in the early morning and are "burned away" by the morning rays of the sun. The surface air in this fog is colder than the air above it. This arrangement of warmer air above cool fog is called a temperature inversion.

Advection fogs result when warm, moist air blows over cool surfaces. In the northern United States or southern Canada, advection fogs form when warm, moist southerly winds blow over snow-covered ground. The famous fogs of Newfoundland form when warm, moist air over the Gulf Stream blows over the cold Labrador Current. Summer fogs in coastal California form when warm ocean air strikes cold coastal waters. Winter fogs form along parts of the Gulf Coast when cold Mississippi River waters chill the warm gulf air at the river's mouth.

TOPIC QUESTIONS

Each topic question refers to the topic of the same number.

6. **(a)** Explain how condensation usually occurs in the atmosphere. **(b)** Define dew point. **(c)** When does condensation occur? **(d)** What does the dew point depend on? **(e)** Why doesn't the temperature ever fall much below the dew point?

7. **(a)** Name four ways the air can lose heat. **(b)** What are condensation nuclei? Give examples. Where do they come from? **(c)** What are ice nuclei? Give examples.

8. Explain how dew and frost form.

9. **(a)** Explain how fog forms and how it stays in the air. **(b)** How do radiation fogs form? **(c)** How do advection fogs form? Name some places advection fogs occur.

OBJECTIVES

A Summarize the main types of clouds.

B Describe the conditions under which clouds with vertical development form.

C Show how to predict the base and highest possible top of cumulus clouds.

D Describe the conditions under which layer clouds form.

III Clouds

Topic 10 The Origin of Clouds

Clouds are simply high fogs, mist, or haze. They form when air above the surface cools below its dew point. The shape of a cloud depends on the air movement that forms it. If air movement is mainly horizontal, clouds form in layers. They are called *stratiform clouds*. If air movement is mainly vertical, clouds grow upward in great piles. These are called *cumuliform clouds*.

At temperatures above freezing, clouds are made entirely of water droplets. Below freezing, clouds are usually mixtures of snow crystals and supercooled water. **Supercooled water** is water that has cooled below 0°C without freezing. When supercooled droplets are disturbed, as by an airplane or a strong wind, they freeze instantly. Below a temperature of about −18°C, clouds are almost entirely snow and ice crystals.

Figure 27.7 and the table below show the four families of clouds. The average height range given in the table is for middle latitudes. The heights are measured above the surface, not above sea level. The heights of cloud tops are greater in equatorial areas and less in polar areas.

Classification of Clouds

Family	Average Height Range	Types	Symbol
High clouds	7000 to 13 000 meters	Cirrus	Ci
		Cirrostratus	Cs
		Cirrocumulus	Cc
Middle clouds	2000 to 7000 meters	Altostratus	As
		Altocumulus	Ac
Low clouds	500 to 2000 meters	Stratocumulus	Sc
		Stratus	St
		Nimbostratus	Ns
Vertical development	500 to 13 000 meters	Cumulus	Cu
		Cumulonimbus	Cb

Topic 11 Cloud Names and Their Meanings

The table includes three simple cloud names—cirrus, stratus, and cumulus. These three names represent the three main cloud types. All the other clouds are combinations or variations of these types.

Cirrus clouds are thin, feathery, or tufted. They are so high that they are always made of ice crystals. All of the high family of clouds

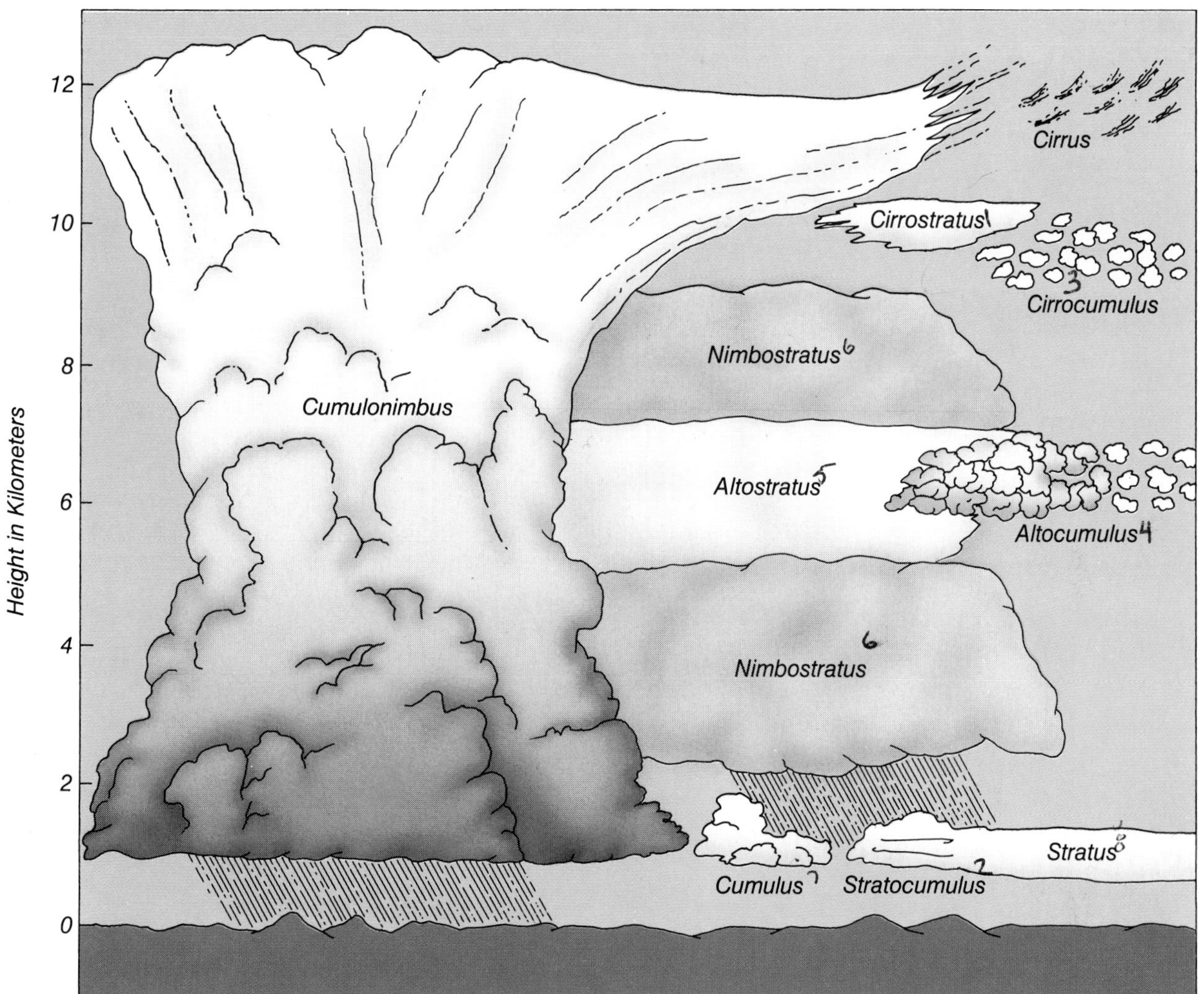

27.7 Cloud types. Cumulus and cumulonimbus belong to the family of clouds of vertical development.

are of the cirrus type. **Stratus** clouds are low sheets or layers of cloud. **Cumulus** clouds are formed by vertically rising air currents. They are piled in thick, puffy masses.

Cirrostratus are high, thin, smooth or fibrous sheets of ice-crystal clouds. They sometimes cause halos, or rings, around the sun or moon. Cirrostratus clouds often mean the approach of rain or snow. *Stratocumulus* clouds are layers made up of round puffs. They often cover the whole sky, especially in the winter. *Cirrocumulus* clouds are small globular patches of cloud made of ice crystals.

The prefix *alto* (high) and the word *nimbus* (rain cloud) are used in cloud names. *Altocumulus* clouds are like stratocumulus clouds. Their puffs look smaller because they are farther away (higher). *Altostratus* clouds are stratus clouds that occur at a higher level. They are gray or bluish and produce no halo around the sun or moon. *Nimbostratus* clouds are dark, gray layers of cloud that produce steady rain.

27.8 Variety of cloud types:
(a) cirrus, (b) cumulus,
(c) altocumulus, (d) cirrostratus,
(e) stratocumulus

Topic 12 Dry- and Moist-Adiabatic Lapse Rates

The shapes of clouds show how the air is moving through them. For example, the air in stratiform clouds flows mostly horizontally, but the air in a growing cumulus cloud is moving upward. The air moves upward because it is buoyant, and it is buoyant because its temperature is warmer than the surrounding air. How long will the cloud be warmer? To answer this question, it is necessary to know how the temperature changes as air rises in a cloud.

Rising dry air cools at a rate of 1°C for every 100 meters (see Chapter 26, Topic 10). This is the dry-adiabatic lapse rate. The cooling is caused only by the air expanding. The air expands as it rises because it is surrounded by lower pressure. Similarly, sinking air is compressed as it encounters higher pressure. This raises the temperature at the same rate, 1°C for every 100 meters. Thus, if an air parcel rises 100 meters and then sinks 100 meters its final temperature will be the same as its starting temperature.

Air rising in a cloud does not cool as fast as rising dry air does. On the average, it cools at 0.6°C for every 100 meters. Why does it cool at a slower rate? The condensing water releases heat to the air, which makes the air cool more slowly. In the same way, sinking air in clouds warms 0.6°C for every 100 meters because the evaporation of cloud droplets slows its warming. Meteorologists call the rate of temperature change of a rising or sinking saturated parcel the **moist-adiabatic lapse rate**.

Topic 13 Clouds with Vertical Development

Cumulus clouds and other clouds with vertical development form when rising air currents are buoyant, or lighter than the surrounding air. How can this happen when air cools as it rises? It can, if the temperature of the surrounding air decreases even faster with height. Suppose a cloud is rising through a layer of air with a lapse rate of 1°C for each hundred meters. Since the air in the cloud is cooling at only 0.6°C for each 100 meters, it will be 0.4°C warmer than the surrounding air after rising 100 meters, 0.8°C warmer after rising 200 meters, and so on. The rising air in the cloud is warmer than the surrounding air even though it gets cooler as it rises. Since the cloud is warmer, it is also lighter or less dense. That is, the air in the cloud is buoyant. The cloud can continue to grow. Meteorologists say that the air surrounding the cloud is *unstable.*

If a shallow layer of air is unstable, cumulus clouds can form. If a deep layer of air is unstable, thunderclouds, or **cumulonimbus** clouds, might form. From these come lightning, thunder, and heavy showers. Violent thunderstorms can have hail, strong winds, and even tornadoes.

27.9 Cumulonimbus cloud

Topic 14 Cumulus and Cumulonimbus Clouds

Rising buoyant air currents form cumulus clouds. These clouds often appear in the late morning or early afternoon on bright sunny days. They have flat bases and billowy tops. Their shape reveals how these clouds form and grow.

How do cumulus and cumulonimbus clouds form? Cumulus clouds form over heated ground. The ground is warm enough so that the air remains buoyant even though it is cooling at the dry-adiabatic lapse rate. The flat cloud base shows where the water vapor began to condense. This height is called the **condensation level**.

Suppose the temperature and dew point of the air at the ground are known. Then the condensation level can be found. For dry air

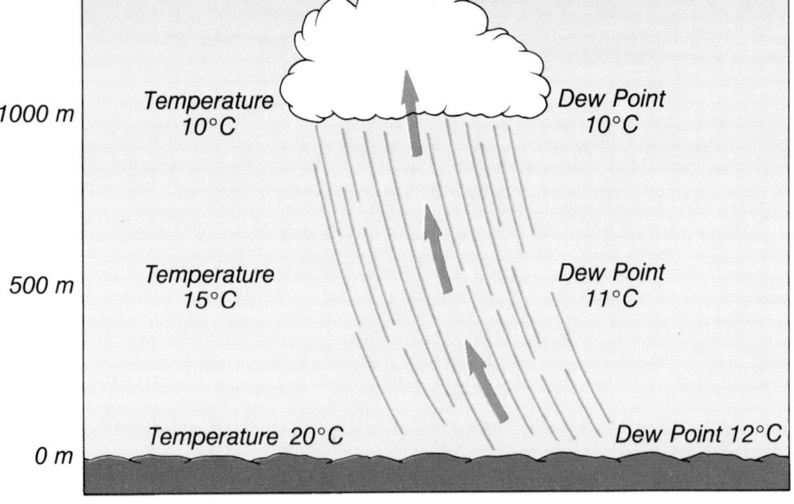

27.10 The condensation level of rising air can be predicted if its temperature and dew point are known. Rising air cools at a rate of 1°C per 100 meters. At the same time, however, its dew point changes, dropping 0.2°C per 100 meters. Where air temperature and dew point meet, condensation begins.

the rate of cooling by expansion is 1°C for every 100 meters. As the air rises, its dew point falls at a rate of 0.2°C for every 100 meters.

Here is an example: At the surface the air temperature is 20°C, the dew point is 12°C, and the difference between these temperatures is 8°C. However, 100 meters higher the air temperature is 19°C and the dew point is 11.8°C. The difference is only 7.2°C. The two temperatures continue to approach each other at a rate of 0.8°C for each 100-meter rise in altitude.

To find where the dew point will reach the air temperature, divide 8°C (the difference between the air temperature at ground level and the dew point) by 0.8°C (the amount per 100 meters at which the dew point approaches the air temperature).

$$\frac{8°\text{C}}{0.8°\text{C}} = 10$$

Thus, 10 multiplied by 100 is the rise necessary in meters (1000 meters) for the beginning of condensation. This level is known as the *lifting condensation level.* It is of great importance in forecasting changes in the weather. A typical value over land in summer is around 1000 meters.

Meteorologists can also estimate the highest possible cloud top. They know that the temperature of the rising air in the cloud starts at the cloud-base temperature and falls with height at the moist-adiabatic lapse rate. They have measurements of the temperature of the surrounding air. The height of the cloud top will be close to the height where the cloud temperature and air temperature are equal. Here, the cloud is no longer buoyant. The rising air spreads out, forming the flat anvil-shaped top characteristic of cumulonimbus clouds.

Topic 15 Layer Clouds

Layer clouds form in stable air, where motions are mainly horizontal. The atmosphere is *stable* when the lapse rate of the air surrounding the clouds is smaller than the moist-adiabatic lapse rate. For example, suppose the temperature of the surrounding air is uniform throughout a thick layer. A cloudy rising current would be

Symbols Showing Percentage of Sky Covered

Tenths of Sky covered	0	1	2–3	4	5	6	7–8	9	10	Sky Obscured
National Weather Service Weather Maps										
Newspaper Maps										

27.11 These symbols are used on weather maps to show how much of the sky is covered by clouds.

cooler than the surrounding air as soon as it started rising and cooling. Being colder and therefore heavier than the surrounding air, the air current would sink back down to where it started. In this case, the air cannot easily move up or down and tends to spread out in layers.

Clouds can form in stable air in two ways. First, the air can be forced slowly upward to its condensation level. Air is forced upward when it moves up rising terrain, such as a mountainside, or over a layer of colder, denser air. And second, layer clouds form if radiation or mixing cools a layer of air to its dew point.

TOPIC QUESTIONS

Each topic question refers to the topic of the same number.

10. **(a)** How are clouds formed? **(b)** What kind of air motions occur in stratiform clouds? Cumuliform clouds? **(c)** At what temperatures do clouds consist of only liquid water? Of only snow and ice? Of both ice and water? **(d)** What is supercooled water? **(e)** List the four families of clouds.

11. Name and describe the three main cloud types.

12. **(a)** Why does rising air cool? Why does sinking air warm? **(b)** Give the numerical value of the dry-adiabatic lapse rate and the moist-adiabatic lapse rate. **(c)** Why is the moist-adiabatic lapse rate smaller?

13. **(a)** Under what conditions do clouds with vertical development form? **(b)** Compare the lapse rate inside and outside the cloud if the air is unstable. **(c)** How does unstable air affect the buoyancy of the rising air in the cloud? **(d)** What kind of cloud forms when the air is unstable through a deep layer?

14. **(a)** How is a cumulus cloud formed? **(b)** How do meteorologists estimate the height of the cloud base? What is this height called? **(c)** Explain how meteorologists estimate the level of the highest possible cloud tops.

15. **(a)** Under what conditions do layer clouds form? **(b)** Compare the lapse rate inside and outside layer clouds.

IV Precipitation

OBJECTIVES

A Describe the process by which precipitation grows in warm and freezing clouds.

B Identify the various types of precipitation, describe how they form, and explain how they are measured.

C Identify areas where precipitation is scarce and areas where precipitation is abundant, and explain why this difference occurs.

D Discuss some ways in which cloud seeding is used to modify precipitation.

E Define acid rain, explain how it forms, and list some of its effects.

Topic 16 How Raindrops Form

Precipitation is the falling of any form of water from the air to Earth's surface. Precipitation occurs when cloud droplets grow into drops heavy enough to fall to Earth.

Raindrops form in two ways: by warm-cloud processes and by ice processes. In the *warm-cloud process,* tiny droplets form by condensation and then grow by bumping into and combining with other droplets. Droplets can collide because they are of different sizes. The bigger drops fall faster than the smaller ones. They catch up with smaller drops, collide with them, and capture them. Some smaller droplets get sucked behind the bigger drop and get captured that way. Still other droplets just bounce off the bigger ones.

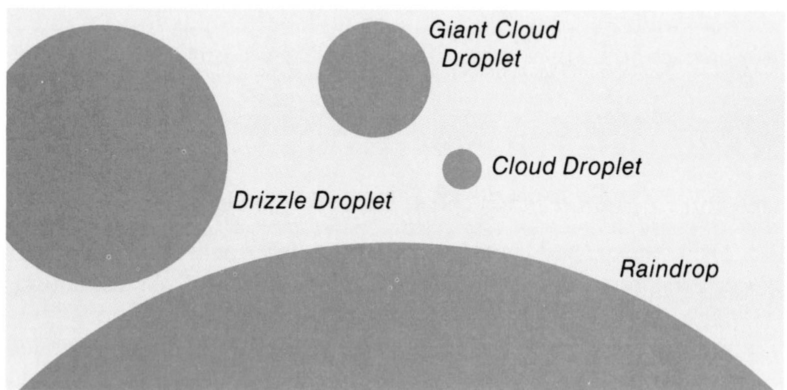

27.12 Compare the relative sizes of cloud droplets, drizzle droplets, and raindrops. A very large raindrop is about 0.25 centimeters in diameter. The diameter of a cloud droplet is only about one hundredth as large.

Why do the droplets have different sizes? Droplets that have been in the cloud longer have had more time to "grow." Some cloud droplets start out larger because they formed around a large salt nucleus. Still other cloud droplets get mixed into air that is less than saturated. The droplets shrink from evaporation. Mixing of air from different parts of the cloud or falling of larger drops from higher up in the cloud brings droplets of different sizes together.

Droplets also grow by *ice processes*. Except for the most shallow clouds in the warm tropics, temperatures in the upper layers of clouds are below freezing. Both ice crystals and supercooled droplets are present. Supercooled water evaporates faster than ice, and this water vapor is deposited on the ice crystals. When the larger ice crystals get heavy enough, they start to fall. The falling crystals can then grow by capturing both the smaller ice crystals and water droplets in their paths. If the temperature in the lower part of the cloud is above freezing, the crystal melts and continues to grow by warm-cloud processes.

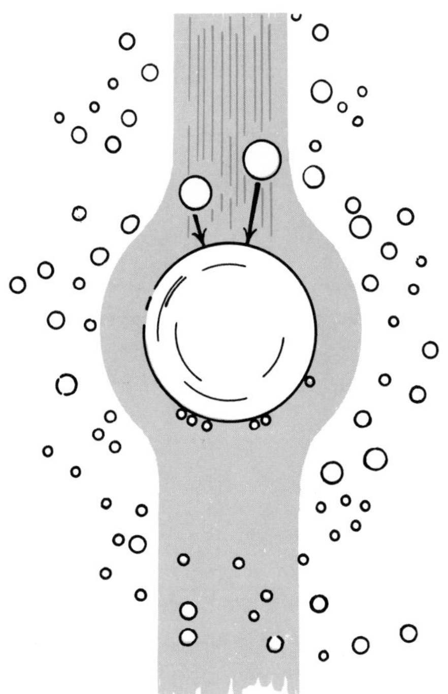

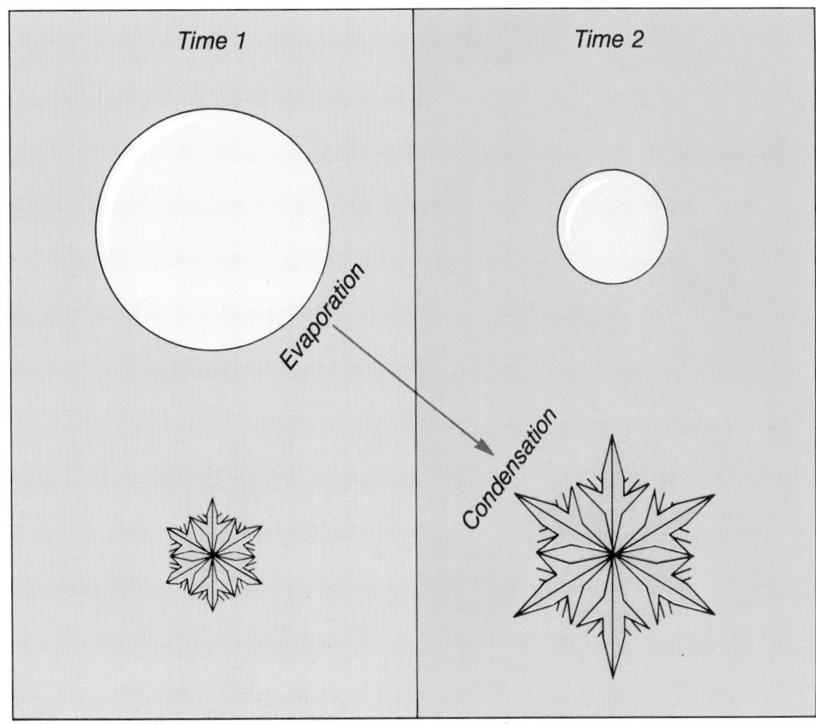

27.13 (a) In the warm-cloud process, large droplets grow by collecting smaller droplets. In this way, they may become heavy enough to fall as rain. (b) In the ice process, supercooled water droplets supply the water vapor that makes ice crystals grow. Thus, from Time 1 to Time 2 the droplet shrinks and the ice crystal grows.

Topic 17 Forms of Precipitation

Precipitation comes in many forms. Drizzle consists of very fine drops that are very close together and fall very slowly. Raindrops are larger, farther apart, and fall much faster. A raindrop may have a maximum diameter of 0.25 centimeter. Larger raindrops may form, but they are torn apart as they fall.

Snow usually falls as clumps of six-sided crystals. The clumps grow by collision. When snowflakes fall into warm air, they partially melt into sticky, wet clusters. If the snowflakes melt completely, they fall as rain.

In some wintertime temperature inversions, warm clouds lie above a layer of air with a temperature below freezing. When raindrops fall through the freezing air, they turn into pellets of ice that fall to the ground as **sleet**. An ice storm, on the other hand, occurs when supercooled rain freezes instantly as it hits surfaces that are below freezing. Sheet ice, or glaze, forms on sidewalks, trees, roofs, and power lines. If the ice becomes heavy enough, trees and power lines may break under the weight of the ice.

Hail forms in cumulonimbus clouds. A hailstone begins as a frozen raindrop or small dense clump of ice crystals. A hailstone grows by collecting smaller ice particles, liquid cloud droplets, and supercooled raindrops that freeze onto it. The growing hailstone is kept aloft by a strong updraft until it becomes too heavy and falls out. In the early stages of its life, the hailstone may fall out of one updraft only to be carried aloft again in another. The size of the hailstone depends on how long it is kept aloft in the cloud and how much moisture it catches. Clearly, the stronger the updraft, the larger the hailstones can be.

Hailstones have a layered structure like an onion. This is because of the different temperatures and different kinds of moisture they meet on their trip through the thundercloud. Hailstones may be as small as buckshot or as large as softballs.

27.14 In this hailstone cross section, each colored area is an individual crystal. Notice the onionlike layers.

Topic 18 Measuring Precipitation

The National Weather Service reports rainfall in hundredths of an inch. The rainfall is measured by an instrument called a **rain gauge**. The measurement represents the depth of water that the rain would leave if it did not soak into the ground.

Snowfall is measured in inches and tenths of an inch. A measuring stick is used. The measurement is usually taken in an open location. The rain equivalent of the snowfall is determined by melting a definite depth of the snow. Dry snows are deeper than equal weights of wet snow. On the average, 10 inches of snow equal 1 inch of rain. This ratio, however, may range from as little as 5 inches of snow to as much as 30 inches. Why is the range so great?

Name	Drizzle	Rain	Shower	Snow	Sleet	Fog	Hail	Thunderstorm
USNWS Symbols	,	●	▽	*	◬	≡	△ ▽	⌈̄ℤ
Newspaper Maps		Ⓡ		Ⓢ		Ⓕ	🌀	Hurricane

27.15 These are the symbols used on weather maps to represent different types of precipitation.

Topic 19 Where Does It Rain?

Precipitation—rain, sleet, hail, or snow—occurs in every part of the world. In some locations it may not rain for years at a time. In other places it may rain almost every day. Parts of Death Valley, California, average only about 1 inch of rain a year. Cherrapunji in India averages 457 inches of rain a year. What accounts for such differences in annual rainfall?

When air rises high enough and in large enough quantities, precipitation often occurs. The warmer the air, the more moisture it may contain. Also, the higher the air rises, the more moisture it can drop.

It follows, therefore, that the rainy areas of Earth will be those where air often rises in large quantities. Such areas are listed below.

1. The windward side of mountain ranges. The normal winds in an area are called prevailing winds. The side of the mountain

range toward which the winds blow is called the windward side. The prevailing winds are forced to climb the windward side of a mountain range to great heights. Because the air cools as it rises, some of its moisture condenses and falls as rain or snow. An example is the rainy western slope of the Cascade Mountains in the northwestern United States.

2. Storm areas of all kinds, including hurricanes, typhoons, low-pressure areas, and fronts. In all of these, air rises and cools to produce precipitation.
3. Areas favored by the global wind belts. As shown in the next chapter, the prevailing winds converge (come together) around the equator. The air can go nowhere but up. The result is almost daily thunderstorms over the land areas. Around the equator lie the dense tropical forests of the Amazon, the Congo, and Indonesia.

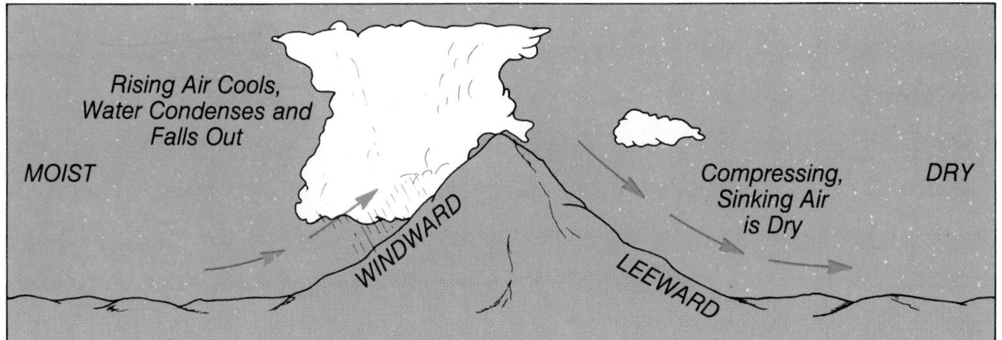

27.16 Rain and snow are usually heavy on the windward side of a tall mountain range and very light on the leeward side.

Topic 20 Where Does It Not Rain?

The answer to this question is almost the exact opposite of "Where does it rain?" In areas of sinking air the air is warmed by compression. Thus no precipitation can occur. If sinking air persists, the dry conditions produce deserts. Sinking air occurs on the downwind or leeward side of mountains and in high-pressure areas. It also occurs where the global wind belts diverge, or blow away from a given area, at the surface. The only way air diverging at the surface can be replaced is by air sinking from above. This happens at the North and South Poles, and at the latitudes of the Sahara Desert.

Topic 21 Weather Modification

Often it does not rain when or where it is needed most. Ever since people have needed rain, they have tried to make it rain. Attempts to change the weather are called weather modification.

There are two methods of rainmaking. In the first method, very cold solid carbon dioxide, or "dry ice," pellets are dropped into a supercooled cloud. These pellets cool the cloud so much that tiny ice crystals form. The crystals grow by the ice process until they are heavy enough to fall. In the second method, artificial ice nuclei (usually crystals of silver iodide or lead iodide) are put into the cloud. Smoke generators are used to make the tiny crystals, which are very much like ice crystals in shape. Once ice crystals form, precipitation again grows by the ice process.

It is hard to prove that rainmaking works, since the precipitation that falls could have fallen naturally. Also, clouds must be present for rain to occur.

Scientists are not only searching for ways to make it rain. They are also trying to prevent hail and to eliminate fog at airports. Supercooled fogs can be cleared by the same techniques used to make rain. In this case, seeding the clouds makes the droplets grow too large and fall out.

27.17 The effects of acid rain on a sandstone statue in Germany. The left-hand picture was taken in 1913; the right-hand picture is from 1984.

Topic 22 Acid Clouds and Acid Rain

Most acid rain contains nitrate or sulfate particles. Sulfates come from sulfur dioxide, which results from the burning of fuels and from natural sources such as volcanoes. Nitrate-forming gases come from those sources and also from automobiles.

Sulfate and nitrate particles make good condensation nuclei. When water condenses on them, they produce nitric or sulfuric acid droplets. As these droplets grow, they remain acid. The drops that fall to the ground are known as **acid rain**. The dry sulfate and nitrate particles that fall to the ground are called dry acid deposition. They combine with groundwater to make acid.

Cloud droplets that form on these nuclei are very acidic. Mountain forests are heavily damaged by acid clouds as well as acid rain because they are often in clouds. Not only does the soil become too acidic, but the leaves may be damaged by acid falling directly on them.

Acid rain is also destroying life in lakes and streams. Fish can no longer live in many lakes in the Adirondack Mountains of New York State because the water is too acidic. In cities, acid rain weathers rock and concrete and damages metals, paints, plastics, and paper.

TOPIC QUESTIONS

Each topic question refers to the topic of the same number.

16. **(a)** What is precipitation? **(b)** Describe how raindrops grow in warm clouds. **(c)** Describe how precipitation grows by ice processes. **(d)** How are mixtures of drop sizes produced?

17. **(a)** Describe drizzle, raindrops, and snow. **(b)** How does sleet form? Sheet ice? **(c)** How does hail form?

18. **(a)** What is a rain gauge? **(b)** How is snow measured?

19. **(a)** Where does precipitation fall? **(b)** Name three kinds of areas in which rising air causes rain.

20. **(a)** Why are areas of sinking air dry? **(b)** Name three kinds of areas in which sinking air usually keeps precipitation from falling.

21. **(a)** Give some examples of weather modification. **(b)** Describe two methods used in rainmaking.

22. **(a)** What is acid rain? **(b)** What condensation nuclei form acid with water? Where do they come from? **(c)** List some ways in which acid rain harms the environment.

CHAPTER 27 REVIEW

Summary

Evaporating water molecules use energy to break away from liquid. This energy is absorbed from the surroundings, which become cooler. When water condenses, this energy is returned to the surroundings.

Warmer air can hold more water vapor. Thus condensation occurs if air is cooled enough.

When the ground temperature drops below the dew point, dew forms if the temperature is above freezing and frost forms if the ground temperature drops below freezing.

Fog and clouds form when water vapor condenses around tiny particles called condensation nuclei.

The three main types of clouds are cumulus, cirrus, and stratus. Cirrus clouds are high, feathery, ice clouds. Cumulus clouds are fluffy clouds with flat bases. Stratus clouds are layered, low clouds.

Rising air cools at the dry-adiabatic lapse rate with no condensation, and at the moist-adiabatic lapse rate with condensation.

Cumuliform clouds form when the rising air in the cloud is buoyant; cumulus clouds form from air currents rising from the heated ground.

Stratiform clouds form when the rising air in the cloud is not buoyant. They form when a layer of air is cooled by lifting or other means.

Precipitation in warm (above-freezing) clouds grows from drop collisions. In cold (below-freezing) clouds, ice crystals grow from collisions and by using water vapor from evaporating supercooled drops.

Precipitation falls in regions where air tends to rise, producing condensation. Air rises going over mountains and when surface air converges.

Cloud seeding starts the ice process to produce precipitation.

Most acid rain comes from sulfate and nitrate particles, which mix with water to form sulfuric or nitric acid.

Vocabulary

acid rain
cirrus
condensation
condensation level
condensation nuclei
cumulonimbus
cumulus
dew
dew point
evaporation
frost
hail
hygrometer
moist-adiabatic lapse rate
precipitation
psychrometer
rain gauge
relative humidity
sleet
specific humidity
stratus
supercooled water

Review

Number your paper from 1 to 18. Select the best answer to complete each statement.

1. Water is found in the atmosphere as (a) water vapor, (b) solid ice particles, (c) liquid cloud droplets, (d) all of the above.
2. The amount of water vapor present in the air is the (a) saturation specific humidity, (b) specific humidity, (c) capacity, (d) relative humidity.
3. A psychrometer works on the principle that (a) evaporation causes cooling, (b) condensation causes cooling, (c) hair stretches when it is humid, (d) relative humidity is stated as a percent.
4. When air cools below the dew point, (a) it is said to be supercooled, (b) condensation occurs, (c) the air can hold more water vapor, (d) water droplets on plants evaporate.
5. The tiny particles on which water condenses are (a) precipitation, (b) hygrometers, (c) condensation nuclei, (d) hailstones.
6. Air loses heat by (a) expanding when it rises, (b) mixing with warmer air, (c) contacting a warm surface, (d) becoming saturated.
7. Dew forms (a) when the air temperature is above the dew point, (b) when water vapor condenses on ice crystals, (c) when the

ground temperature cools below the dew point and the temperature is above 0°C, (d) when the air temperature is below 0°C.

8. When a whole layer of air is cooled below the dew point, the result is (a) rain, (b) snow, (c) fog, (d) supercooled air.
9. Rain falls from (a) cirrostratus clouds, (b) nimbostratus clouds, (c) stratocumulus clouds, (d) cirrocumulus clouds.
10. Buoyant air (a) is cooler than the surrounding air, (b) is cooling at a faster rate than the surrounding air, (c) forms stratus clouds, (d) is warmer than the surrounding air.
11. Cumulus clouds are formed by (a) horizontally moving air, (b) rising buoyant air, (c) sinking saturated air, (d) ice crystals high above the surface.
12. Layer clouds form in (a) stable air, (b) a deep layer of unstable air, (c) a shallow layer of unstable air, (d) sinking air.
13. Which of the following is NOT a way in which raindrops form? (a) Tiny cloud droplets combine. (b) Water vapor is deposited on ice crystals. (c) Cloud droplets shrink from evaporation. (d) Falling ice crystals capture smaller ice crystals and water droplets.
14. Which is NOT a form of precipitation? (a) sleet (b) fog (c) drizzle (d) hail
15. The rainfall equivalent of 20 inches of snow (a) is less than 20 inches, (b) is exactly 20 inches, (c) is more than 20 inches, (d) could be either more or less than 20 inches.
16. Rain occurs (a) in areas where winds diverge at the surface, (b) on the leeward side of mountain ranges, (c) in high-pressure areas where air sinks, (d) in areas where air rises.
17. Attempts to change the weather are known as (a) condensation nuclei, (b) acid rain, (c) ice processes, (d) weather modification.
18. Acid rain forms when (a) silver iodide crystals are put into a cloud, (b) rising air begins to cool, (c) water condenses on nitrate and sulfate particles, (d) warm, moist air blows over cool surfaces.

Interpret and Apply

On your paper, answer each question in complete sentences.

1. Jet traffic at altitudes of 10–13 kilometers has been increasing. (a) What effect would you expect this increase to have on the cloudiness at those altitudes? (b) What kinds of clouds would be produced? (c) What causes them to form?
2. Nighttime and early morning temperatures usually are not very useful for predicting the cloud base. Why not?
3. Why should the average annual precipitation be greater in Mississippi than in Maine?

Critical Thinking

Complete the table by calculating the height at which clouds will form (the lifting condensation level) for the temperatures and dew points shown. Then answer the questions that follow.

Temperature	Dew Point	Condensation Level
16°C	12°C	?
20°C	12°C	1000 m
20°C	16°C	?
28°C	12°C	?
28°C	20°C	?

1. If the dew point stays the same, what effect does a rise in temperature have on the cloud base?
2. If the temperature stays the same, what effect does a rise in the dew point have on the cloud base?
3. Which contains more water vapor, air at 26.5°C with a relative humidity of 50 percent or saturated air at 5°C? Why?
4. From your knowledge of how air's capacity for water vapor increases with temperature, how would you expect the moist-adiabatic lapse rate to change with temperature?

CHAPTER

28 Atmospheric Pressure and Winds

▲ Tropical rain forests like this one in Costa Rica are common near the equator.

How Do You Know That . . .

Weather changes are related to changes in atmospheric pressure? Movies frequently take place in a steamy, tropical rain forest. It is a mysterious place, full of lush plants and unusual animals. Insects and humidity make the tropical rain forest as uncomfortable as it is strange. Rain forests are common in equatorial Africa and Central and South America.

How are these rainy areas related to air pressure? This chapter will explore the global and local wind and pressure patterns and explain how these patterns show where rain should occur. The causes of pressure changes and winds will also be discussed.

I Air Pressure

OBJECTIVES

A Discuss air pressure, describe how it is measured, and compare the different units used to measure air pressure.

B Define *high*, *low*, and *pressure gradient*.

Topic 1 What Is Air Pressure?

Why is the study of air pressure important? Differences in air pressure cause Earth's winds and weather changes.

Pressure is defined as force per unit area. **Air pressure** is simply the weight of the atmosphere per unit area. At the surface, the atmospheric pressure is about 1 kilogram per square centimeter.

A few examples can illustrate the meaning of pressure. Suppose a girl weighing 45 kilograms is standing on one foot. The pressure underneath her foot is the force (her weight) divided by the area of her foot. If her foot is 20 cm long and 8 cm wide, the pressure underneath is 0.28 kilograms per square centimeter. If she stands on two feet, the pressure under each foot is halved. If she balances on one heel of a pair of thin high-heeled shoes (about a square centimeter), the pressure beneath her foot is 45 kilograms per square centimeter!

Air pressure is directed equally in all directions. To envision this, remember that the gases in air are made up of many tiny molecules. The pressure is the sum total effect of the molecules colliding against any surface. The air molecules move in all directions, so the pressure on any surface is the same. This is true whether the surface is horizontal or vertical.

Topic 2 Measuring Air Pressure

The instrument used to measure air pressure is the **barometer**. There are two main types of barometers—mercury and aneroid barometers—which have very different constructions.

Figure 28.1 shows how a mercury barometer works. The air pressure on the surface of the mercury in the dish supports a column of mercury. At sea level, the column is about 76 centimeters (30 inches) high. The space in the column above the mercury is a vacuum. If air pressure increases, the mercury column rises. If air pressure drops, the mercury column falls.

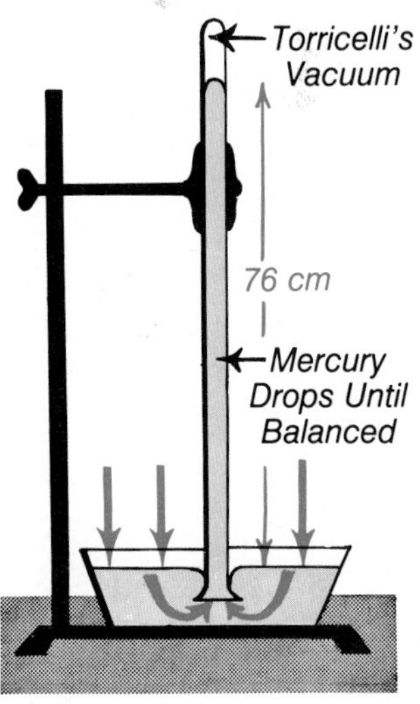

28.1 In the mercury barometer, the atmospheric pressure balances a column of mercury. At sea level, the height of the column is normally 76 centimeters. As air pressure increases and decreases, the column rises and falls.

The aneroid barometer measures pressure with a thin metal can. By pumping most of the air out of the can, the can is made sensitive to air pressure. A spring or similar device keeps the can from collapsing inward. As the shape of the can changes with changes in air pressure, a pointer attached to the can moves over a scale. A *barograph* is a recording aneroid barometer. Its pointer is a pen that writes on a chart.

Since air pressure is the weight of the air overhead, the air pressure drops with height. An *altimeter* (height meter used by aircraft) is an aneroid barometer with a scale that reads height above sea level.

The barometer reading drops about 1 centimeter for every 123 meters (or about 1 inch for every 1000 feet) above sea level. This rate applies only to the first few kilometers of air near Earth's surface. Above this level the air thins out rapidly, and pressure changes more slowly. Half the weight of the atmosphere lies within 5.5 kilometers of Earth's surface.

Topic 3 Air Pressure Units

Air pressure is reported in two different ways. The first way gives the height of the mercury column in the barometer. It may be given in centimeters or in inches.

The second way uses a metric unit of pressure called a **millibar**. A millibar equals about one thousandth of standard sea-level air pressure. The following table shows how inch units and millibars are related. Standard sea-level air pressure is 1013.2 millibars (29.92 inches) of mercury. It is the average air pressure at sea level for the whole world.

Inches of Mercury	Millibars of Pressure
31.00	1050.0
30.00	1015.9
29.92	1013.2
29.53	1000.00
29.00	982.1
1.00*	34.0 (approx.)
0.10	3.4 (approx.)
0.12	4.0** (approx.)
0.03	1.0‡ (approx.)

* Use this value to convert inches of mercury to millibars.
** Pressure interval used on United States weather maps
‡ Use this value to convert millibars to inches of mercury.

The average air pressure at an inland weather station is lower than 1013.2 millibars, because the altitude is higher. At Denver, Colorado (altitude 1600 meters), for example, the normal surface pressure is around 835 millibars. The effect of altitude on pressure is eliminated when surface weather maps are made. The corrected air pressure is called the **sea-level pressure**.

The highest sea-level pressures on a typical weather map are from 1030 to 1050 mb, while the lowest values are from 960 to 1000 mb. The more extreme sea-level pressures occur in the winter. Sea-level pressures as low as 870 millibars have been recorded in strong hurricanes.

The National Weather Service prints a daily weather map. On this map barometer readings are shown in two different ways. The first way shows the actual barometer reading in millibars. This number is placed just to the upper right of the station circle. It shows only the last three numbers (1002.2 millibars would appear as 022). The second way of showing barometer readings uses **isobars.** Isobars are lines that join points having the same air pressure at a given time. Isobars make it easy to see how barometer readings compare over large geographic areas.

28.2 This diagram shows how temperature and air pressure are indicated on a station model. These numbers represent a temperature of 51°F and air pressure of 1013.3 millibars. Notice that only the last three digits of the pressure are given.

Topic 4 Why Air Pressure Changes

A chart from a barograph shows that the air pressure is always changing. The main reason for daily changes in air pressure is changing temperature. Warm air is lighter than cold air because the molecules of warm air are farther apart. So when warm air replaces an equal volume of cold air, the air pressure at the ground falls. In the same way, the arrival of colder air higher up causes the pressure at the ground to rise.

A second reason for changes in air pressure is changing humidity. The more water vapor the air contains, the lighter it is. This statement sounds wrong, but it is easily explained. When water vapor enters the atmosphere, it pushes out an equal volume of dry air. A cubic meter of dry air is about 99 percent nitrogen and oxygen. A cubic meter of humid air with 2 percent water vapor is only 97 percent nitrogen and oxygen. Water vapor is lighter than the nitrogen and oxygen it pushed out. Therefore, humid air weighs less than dry air and exerts less pressure.

In general, meteorologists have found that a falling barometer means warmer weather and more humid air. It may mean rain or snow. A rising barometer usually means cooler, drier weather. This change in barometer readings gives a simple way of forecasting the weather. Meteorologists do not, however, rely on the barometer alone for their forecasts.

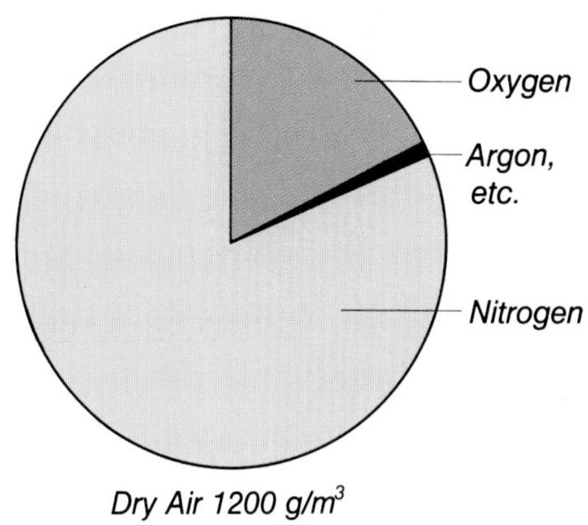

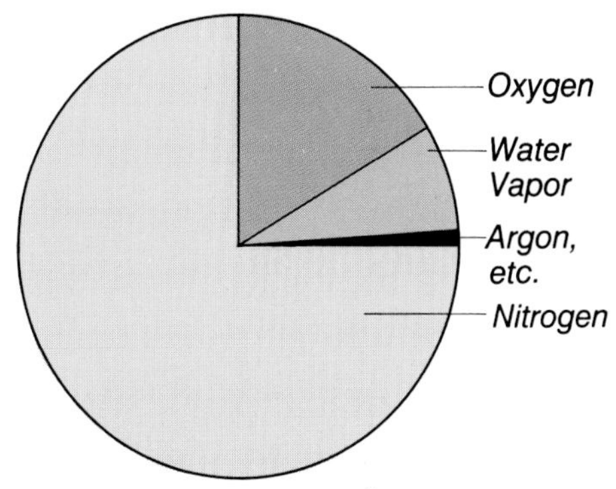

28.3 A cubic meter of air at sea level has a mass of about 1200 grams. When the same volume of air contains water vapor, it has less mass because water vapor is lighter than the nitrogen and oxygen it replaces.

Topic 5 Highs, Lows, and Pressure Gradients

The isobars on a weather map look a lot like the contour lines on the topographic maps discussed in Chapter 7. Both isobars and contour lines form sets of closed curves, one inside the other.

If the values of the isobars steadily increase toward a central area, the area of largest pressure is called the *high-pressure center*. The set of closed isobars surrounding the high-pressure center is called a **high-pressure area (high)**. The pressure in a high is greater than in the surrounding air. (If isobars were contour lines, the high-pressure area would be a hill and the high-pressure center would be the top of the hill.)

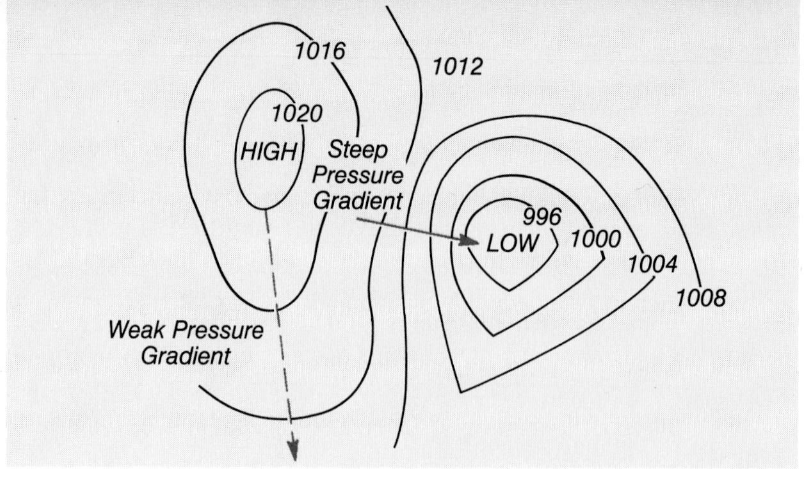

28.4 Isobars on a weather map show areas of high and low pressure, strong pressure gradients, and weak pressure gradients.

Similarly, if the inside isobar has the lowest reading, the set of closed isobars shows a **low-pressure area (low)**. This area has lower pressure than the surrounding air. The low's center is located in the inside isobar, where the pressure is lowest.

High- and low-pressure areas on a weather map are usually more than 1500 kilometers across. Large high-pressure areas can cover most of North America.

When isobars are close together, it means that air pressure changes quickly between two places. When isobars are far apart, air pressure changes slowly. Scientists call this rate of change the **pressure gradient**. Isobars close together are said to have a steep, or strong, pressure gradient. Isobars far apart have a gentle, or weak, pressure gradient. Pressure gradients are measured in millibars per kilometer.

TOPIC QUESTIONS

Each topic question refers to the topic of the same number.

1. **(a)** What is pressure? **(b)** What causes air pressure? **(c)** Explain why air pressure is equal in all directions.
2. **(a)** How do aneroid and mercury barometers work? **(b)** How does air pressure vary with height? How fast does air pressure drop with height near the surface?
3. **(a)** What are the two units of measure commonly used in reporting air pressure? **(b)** How many millibars are in an inch? How many inches are in a millibar? **(c)** What is the sea-level atmospheric pressure in millibars? In inches? List the highest and lowest normal sea-level pressures. **(d)** Why do surface pressures for inland stations need to be corrected before making a weather map?
4. **(a)** How does the temperature of the atmosphere affect the surface air pressure? **(b)** Explain the effect of humidity on air pressure.
5. **(a)** Define high-pressure area, low-pressure area, and pressure gradient. **(b)** How do isobars show a high-pressure center, a low-pressure center, and pressure gradient?

II Winds

Topic 6 What Makes the Wind Blow?

All winds result from uneven heating of the atmosphere. The island in Figure 28.5 is surrounded by cool water. During the day, the island heats faster than the water and so the air above the island becomes warmer. The molecules in the air become farther apart; so the air expands upward and outward. This expansion lowers the air pressure at the island's surface. The cooler ocean air moves in toward the low-pressure area over the island.

There is a pressure gradient between the ocean and the island. The wind moves from high to low pressure. The speed of the wind depends on the pressure gradient. The lower the pressure (the hotter the island), the steeper the pressure gradient and the stronger the wind. The pressure gradient provides the force that makes the wind blow. This force is called the **pressure-gradient force.**

OBJECTIVES

A Show how heating causes low pressure and note that the wind blows from high to low pressure.

B Summarize the causes of land and sea breezes and mountain and valley winds.

C Describe the Coriolis effect.

D Explain why winds are clockwise around highs and counter-clockwise around lows in the Northern Hemisphere and why surface winds blow at an angle to the isobars.

E Describe how winds are named and measured and show how they are depicted on weather maps.

Topic 7 Local Winds

The wind over the island is an example of a *local wind.* A local wind extends over a distance of 100 kilometers or less. A **sea breeze** is a local wind that forms much like the island wind. During the daytime, coastal land is warmer than the nearby water. The air just over the land becomes warmer than the air over the water. The pressure lowers over the land, leading to a pressure gradient between the ocean and the land. The pressure gradient force pushes the cool ocean air inland. This cool wind is the sea breeze.

Over the land, the air rises. It then blows out to sea and sinks to replace the cool air that has flowed inland. As shown in Figure 28.6, the airflow forms a complete circuit—from the sea to the land, up, back to the sea, and down again. Thus the entire wind pattern is sometimes called a *sea-breeze circulation.*

A gentle sea breeze usually begins in the late morning along seacoasts. It increases in speed until midafternoon and dies down toward sunset. The sea breeze is felt inland from 15 to 70 kilometers away from the shoreline. It reaches up to about a kilometer in the atmosphere.

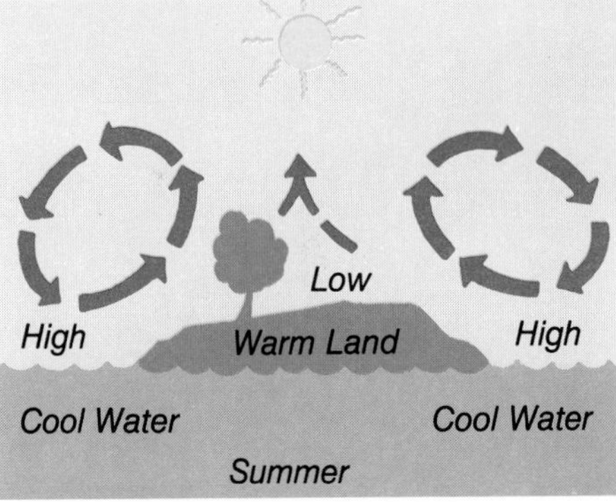

28.5 A heated island surrounded by cooler water becomes a region of low pressure, causing winds to blow toward the land.

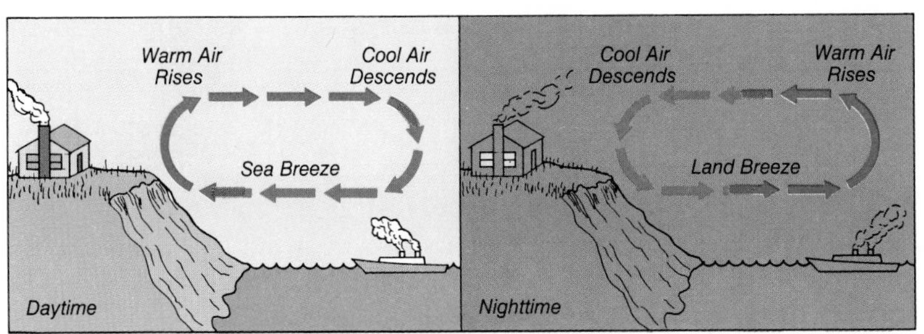

28.6 Sea and land breezes develop through unequal heating of land and nearby water. The land breeze blows from land; the sea breeze blows from the water.

At night, the land cools faster than the water, and the air pressure over the land becomes higher. The resulting pressure gradient causes the cool **land breeze** to blow out to sea. Over the sea the air rises and then flows inland at a higher level. The land breeze starts long before midnight and dies down after sunrise.

Mountain-valley winds are local winds that are driven by buoyancy as well as pressure gradients. At night, cold, heavy air sinks from mountaintops into valleys. The narrower the valley, the stronger the breeze. Coming from the mountains, it is called a mountain breeze.

During the daytime, warm air rises from the sunny mountain slopes. This rising air forms a valley breeze that blows up from the valley. Its speed is generally much less than that of the downhill mountain breeze. People who soar in gliders, hang gliders, and balloons ride the rising warm air in mountain regions.

Topic 8 The Coriolis Effect

In local winds, such as land and sea breezes, the winds flow from high to low pressure. However, a look at a weather map shows that this is not true for the large highs and lows shown. Instead of blowing from high to low pressure, the winds in the Northern Hemisphere flow clockwise around highs and counterclockwise around lows.

Earth's rotation causes the **Coriolis** (kor-ee-OH-lis) **effect**. The effect is felt by all objects, even air, moving toward or away from the equator. Because of the Coriolis effect, winds are turned to the right relative to Earth's surface in the Northern Hemisphere, and to the left relative to Earth's surface in the Southern Hemisphere.

Suppose a rocket fired from the North Pole is aimed straight south toward a point in central Kansas (39° N, 100° W). Also, suppose it takes an hour for the rocket to get that far south. During that hour, Earth has rotated 15 degrees eastward. So the rocket will land 15 degrees to the west. It will end up in eastern Nevada, 1295 kilometers away from the intended target. This deflection is due to the Coriolis effect. It must be taken into account when rocket launches are planned.

The Coriolis effect is larger for higher wind speeds and smaller for lower wind speeds. To understand this, again think of the rocket fired from the North Pole. Suppose its speed is only half of what it was before. In an hour, the rocket will reach only as far as northern Canada. It will still end up 15 degrees to the west of its target, but at these northern latitudes, 15 degrees of longitude is only 718 kilometers. (The distance between longitude lines becomes smaller as they merge at the poles.)

The Coriolis effect is not a force, just as the more familiar centrifugal "force" is not a force. It does, however, act like a force to an observer—or an air parcel—on Earth's surface. The Coriolis effect is important for ocean currents, too.

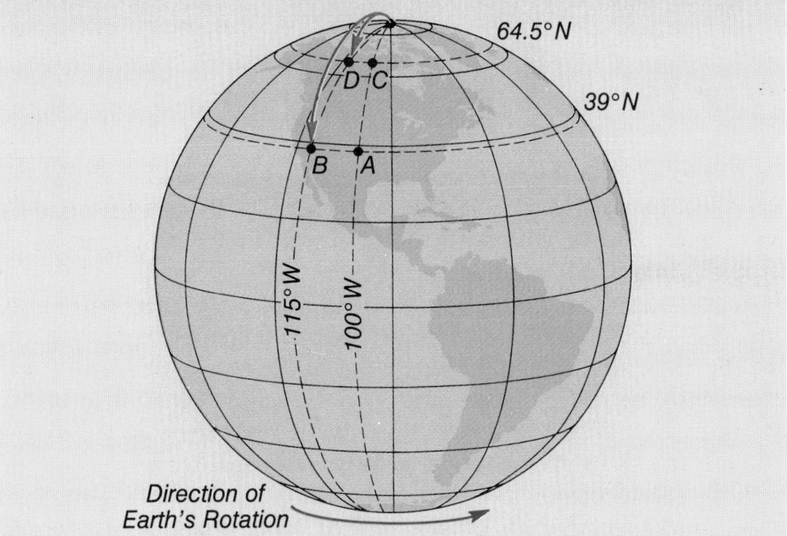

28.7 The Coriolis effect on an object fired from the North Pole. It is aimed toward *A*, but lands at *B* because Earth rotated 15 degrees during the hour the object was airborne. If a second object is fired toward *C* at half the speed of the original object, it lands 15 degrees to the west at *D*. The slower object was only 718 km from its target; the faster object missed by 1295 km.

Topic 9 How the Coriolis Effect Changes the Wind

The Coriolis effect keeps the wind from blowing directly from high to low pressure. Suppose an air parcel begins flowing from high to low pressure. The Coriolis effect turns the wind around to the right. The turning continues until the Coriolis effect exactly balances the pressure gradient force, which occurs when the wind is parallel to the isobars. Thus, in the Northern Hemisphere the air flowing out from a high turns right (clockwise). The air flowing into a low is turned to the right and flows counterclockwise.

At the surface, the wind does not flow exactly parallel to the isobars. This is because friction from the ground slows down the air and lessens the Coriolis effect. Then the air flows at an angle to the isobars, toward lower pressure. If the surface is very smooth, the wind is stronger and more nearly parallel to the isobars. Over the ocean, which is smoother than land, the angle between the surface wind and the isobars is 10 degrees. Over rough land, the surface wind blows at an average angle of about 30 degrees to the isobars. Winds above the surface flow more parallel to the isobars as the effects of surface friction disappear. The wind flows parallel to the isobars above 1 to 2 kilometers above the surface.

Does the Coriolis effect change the local winds? Air parcels have to travel a long time or over a long distance for the effects of Earth's rotation to be felt. Mountain-valley winds cannot be turned to the right because they have to flow up or down valleys. Long-lasting sea breezes, however, do start turning to the right. The Coriolis effect is one of the things that keeps sea breezes from going too far inland.

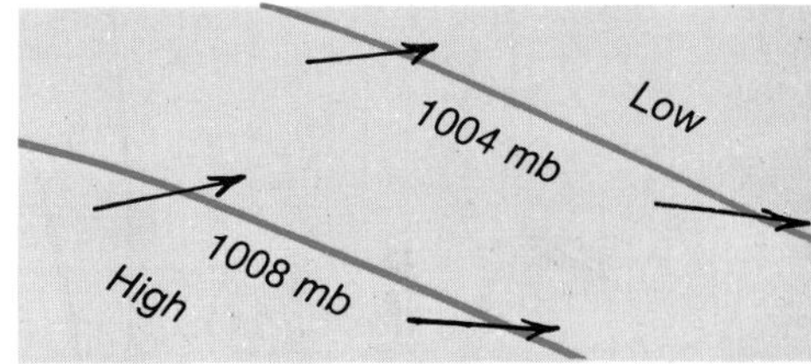

At the Surface

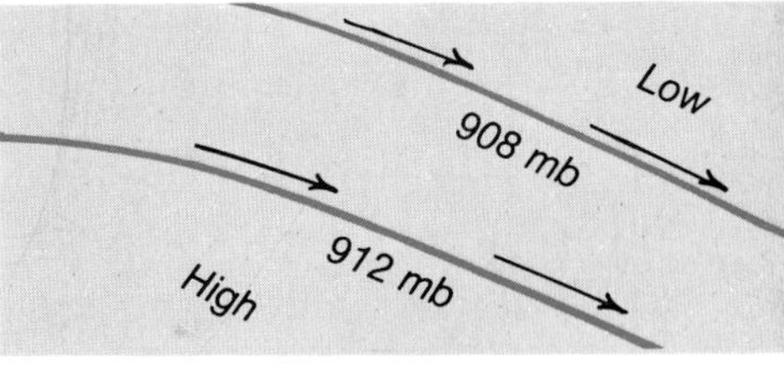

At 1000 m

28.8 Wind changes with altitude. At Earth's surface, winds blow at angles to the isobars. At 1000 meters or higher, they blow along the isobars.

Topic 10 Measuring Wind

The surface wind direction and speed are usually measured at about 10 meters above the ground.

Wind direction is found by use of the **wind vane**. The wind vane has a broad tail that resists the wind more than its slender arrowhead head. If a south wind is blowing, the wind vane will swing the tail to the north. The arrowhead then points south, into the wind. A wind vane always points to the direction from which the wind comes. Thus winds are named for their place of origin.

Wind speed near the surface is measured by an **anemometer**. A cup anemometer consists of hollow cones or hemispheres, all facing the same way, that catch the wind in their open sides from any direction. The speed of the wind is measured by the rate at which the cups turn. The speed and direction of high-altitude winds are found by tracking special upper-atmosphere weather balloons with radar or telescopes.

Wind and weather are closely related. In North America, winds from a northerly direction (north, northeast, or northwest) come from cooler latitudes. Therefore, they are likely to bring cooler weather. Similarly, winds from a southerly direction bring warmer weather. The opposite is true in the Southern Hemisphere.

Wind direction is shown on weather maps by arrows as shown in Figure 28.9. Wind speed is shown by a feather and flags on the arrow's left side. On weather maps the wind speed is given in knots. Each full feather represents a speed of 10 knots. Each half feather represents 5 knots. A flag means a speed of 50 knots. A **knot** is approximately 1.85 kilometers (1.15 miles) per hour. Knots are often used to state the speed of ships and boats.

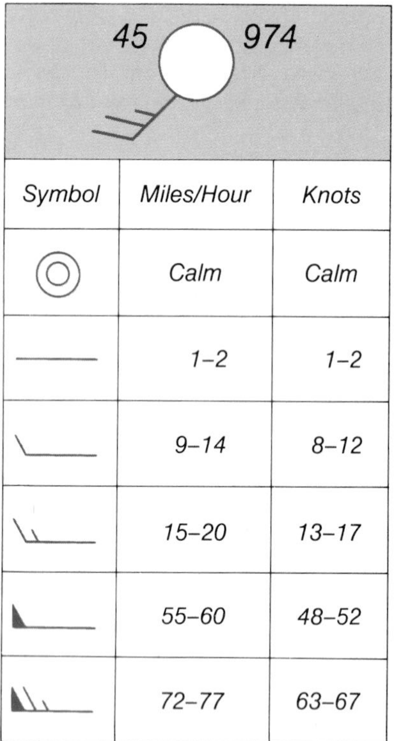

Symbol	Miles/Hour	Knots
	Calm	Calm
	1–2	1–2
	9–14	8–12
	15–20	13–17
	55–60	48–52
	72–77	63–67

28.9 The station model shows a temperature of 45°F, air pressure of 997.4 millibars, and a southwest wind of 25 knots. The symbols show how various wind speeds are represented.

TOPIC QUESTIONS

Each topic question refers to the topic of the same number.

6. **(a)** What is the relationship between air pressure and wind? **(b)** Explain where the pressure-gradient force comes from.

7. **(a)** How do sea and land breezes work? **(b)** Describe mountain and valley winds.

8. **(a)** What is the Coriolis effect? **(b)** What does the Coriolis effect do to a wind in the Northern Hemisphere? How does the Coriolis effect change the path of a southward-moving rocket? **(c)** How does the speed of the wind change the Coriolis effect?

9. **(a)** How does the Coriolis effect change the wind direction relative to the isobars? **(b)** In the Northern Hemisphere, why does the wind flow clockwise around highs and counterclockwise around lows? **(c)** What makes the wind at the surface flow at an angle to the isobars?

10. **(a)** What do an anemometer and wind vane measure? **(b)** How does an anemometer work? **(c)** How does a wind vane work? **(d)** Give some examples of how wind direction is related to weather. **(e)** Explain how wind direction and speed are shown on weather maps.

III Origin of the World Wind Belts

OBJECTIVES

A Characterize the circulation on a nonrotating Earth heated at the equator and describe the three-celled circulation of a rotating Earth.

B Summarize the main pressure belts and their corresponding winds.

C List some effects of the atmospheric circulation on the weather.

Topic 11 Winds on a Nonrotating Earth

Suppose Earth did not rotate and were completely covered with oceans. Then the winds would simply flow from high to low pressure. There would be no Coriolis effect. If Earth were heated around its equator, a low-pressure belt would form beneath the warm air at the surface. The relatively cold poles would have higher pressure. Near the surface, the cool air would flow directly from the poles to the equator. The air from both hemispheres would rise at the equator. At higher levels, the air would then flow toward the poles, where it would sink. The complete circulation would be like that of the sea breeze, only bigger. In the Northern Hemisphere the winds would be from the north at the surface and from the south at higher levels.

Earth's winds do not follow this simple pattern for two reasons. One is that Earth rotates on its axis, causing the Coriolis effect. The other reason is the unequal heating of the land and water.

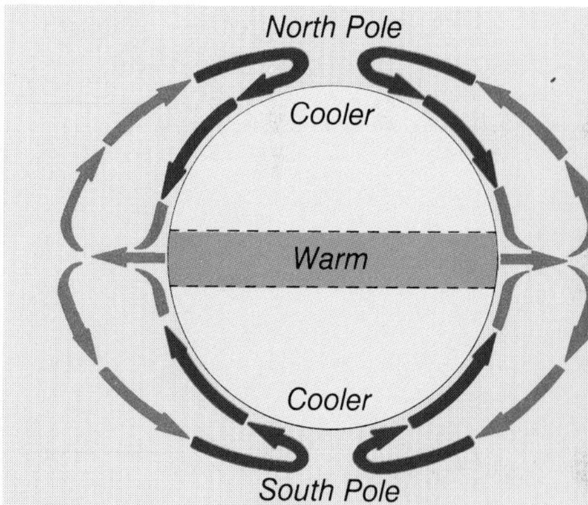

28.10 If Earth's surface were entirely covered by oceans and Earth did not rotate, then heating the equator would produce the simple wind system shown by the arrows.

Topic 12 Latitude Wind Cells

What does Earth's rotation do to the simple circulation pattern described in Topic 11? Imagine the warm air rising at the equator. The rising air splits into two currents. One begins moving northward; the other starts to move southward. However, soon they are turned by the Coriolis effect. The northward-moving air in the Northern Hemisphere is turned to the right, or eastward, and the southward-moving air is turned left (again eastward) in the Southern Hemisphere.

In both cases, the air is flowing almost due east by the time it reaches about 30 degrees latitude. Here, the relatively cool air sinks into a zone of relatively high pressure at the surface. The air at the surface flows from the high pressure at 30 degrees latitude to the low pressure at the equator.

A complete circulation such as this is called a *circulation cell.* The equator-to-30 degree cell just described is also called the **Hadley cell**. It was named for George Hadley, who discovered it in the early 1700's. In each hemisphere, there are two more circulation cells between the Hadley cells and the pole.

Surface high-pressure areas lie at both poles. Cold air flows toward the equator at the surface, turned westward by the Coriolis effect. At higher levels above the poles, the air that comes from lower latitudes sinks to replace the outflowing surface air. Rising air at about 60 degrees latitude completes the circulation. This air is forced to rise because the cold air from the poles collides with warmer air coming from lower latitudes.

28.11 Because Earth rotates on its axis, three pairs of circulation cells develop in the atmosphere. The middle cell is weak and does not show up except in long-term averages, so it is dashed.

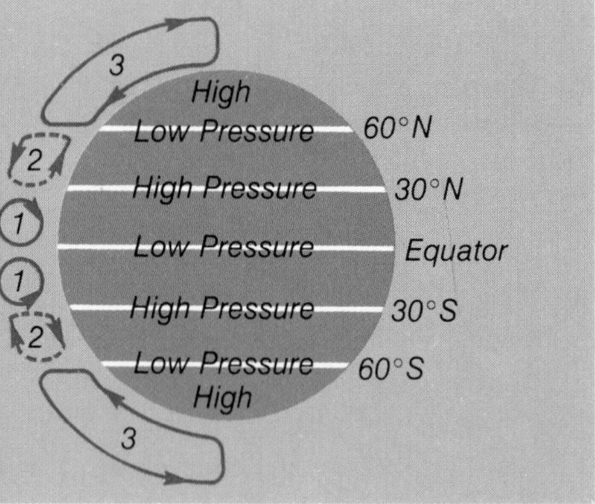

Where the warm and cold air meet, the warm, lighter air flows on top of the cold, heavier air. Meteorologists call the surface between the warm and cold air the **polar front**. Low-pressure areas develop along the polar front. Sixty degrees is only the average latitude of the polar front; it is very irregular.

The circulation cell between 30 and 60 degrees latitude is hard to find. It shows up only in weather data averaged over several years. The air at the bottom of this middle cell flows toward the poles from the high pressure at 30 degrees to the low pressure at 60 degrees. The air at the top of the cell flows toward the equator.

Together, the three circulation cells look like meshing gears. North of 30 degrees, however, the simple pattern is hidden by the passage of highs and lows. Highs and lows will be discussed in the next chapter.

Topic 13 Pressure Belts and Winds

The names of some of the pressure belts survive from the days of the great sailing ships. The low-pressure belt at the equator is called the **doldrums**, and the high-pressure belts at 30 degrees are called the **horse latitudes**.

The scientific names for the pressure belts are less colorful but may be easier to remember. The high-pressure belts at 30 degrees are called the *subtropical highs,* the low-pressure belts at 60 degrees are called the *subpolar lows,* and the high-pressure regions at the poles are simply the *polar highs.* The low-pressure zone at the equator is called the **intertropical convergence zone (ITCZ)** because the winds from the two hemispheres converge (come together) there. Notice that the lows and highs alternate: low at the equator, high at 30 degrees, low at 60 degrees, and high at the poles.

The winds between the pressure zones are named for the directions from which they blow. In the Northern Hemisphere, the winds bend to the right. Thus south winds become southwesterlies, and north winds become northeasterlies. In the Northern Hemisphere the prevailing winds are these:

1. *Polar northeasterlies* blow from the polar high to the subpolar low-pressure belt.
2. *Prevailing southwesterlies* blow from the subtropical highs to the subpolar lows.
3. *Northeast trade winds* blow from the subtropical highs toward the ITCZ.

The Southern Hemisphere has a matching set of winds. However, in the Southern Hemisphere, the Coriolis effect bends winds to the left. South winds become southeasterlies, and north winds become northwesterlies. So the prevailing winds in the Southern Hemisphere are the polar southeasterlies, prevailing northwesterlies, and southeast trade winds. Notice again that the winds blow from highs to lows in both hemispheres.

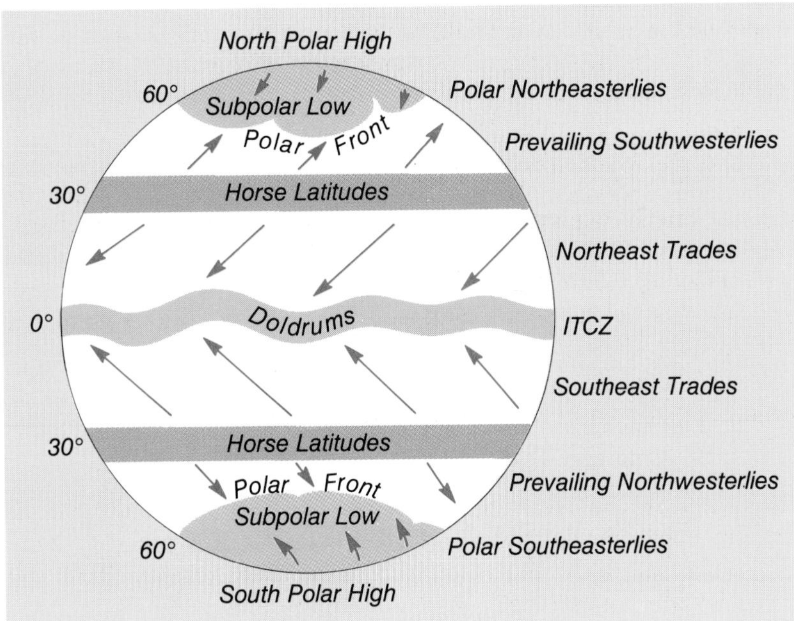

28.12 This diagram gives a general picture of the pressure belts and wind directions at Earth's surface.

Topic 14 Weather in the Wind and Pressure Belts

The air in the doldrums is hot and humid, and slowly rising. There is little or no wind. Sailing vessels have been stuck in the doldrums for days at a time. Rainfall is concentrated in the rising air of the ITCZ.

Dry air sinks from above in the horse latitudes. There is little or no wind. Between the doldrums and the horse latitudes the **trade winds** blow. The trade winds are warm and steady in both direction and speed. In the Northern Hemisphere, they blow from the northeast at 10–20 knots. Because the trade winds are so steady, sailing ships used them whenever possible. In fact, the trade winds got their name because they provided regular trade routes for sailing ships.

The prevailing westerlies are southwesterlies at the surface in the Northern Hemisphere and northwesterlies in the Southern Hemisphere. They change direction and speed frequently. The word "prevailing" means that they blow from the same direction on the average. The speed of the westerlies increases with latitude. The Southern Hemisphere's middle latitudes are almost all ocean. So the westerlies there are very strong, with speeds higher than 40 knots.

The polar easterlies, like the trades, are northeasterly in the Northern Hemisphere and southeasterly in the Southern Hemisphere. Their weather is cold and stormy.

The subpolar low-pressure belts are areas of cold, stormy weather. The polar highs are very cold.

TOPIC QUESTIONS

Each topic question refers to the topic of the same number.

11. What kind of circulation would the atmosphere have on a nonrotating Earth with a heated equator and no continents?

12. **(a)** Briefly explain what happens to the circulation as Earth rotates. **(b)** Describe the Hadley cell. **(c)** Describe the polar cell. **(d)** Compare the 30–60 degree cell with the Hadley cell. **(e)** What is the polar front?

13. **(a)** What are the two causes for the wind directions in the main wind belts? **(b)** Define doldrums, ITCZ, and horse latitudes. **(c)** List the three important wind belts in the Northern Hemisphere and give their locations.

14. What is the weather in **(a)** the doldrums, **(b)** the ITCZ, **(c)** the horse latitudes, **(d)** the subpolar low-pressure belt? **(e)** What are the characteristics of the trade winds? **(f)** Of the prevailing westerlies?

Dr. Robert Harnack
Meteorologist

As a Professor of Meteorology at Rutgers University's Cook College in New Jersey, Dr. Robert Harnack spends a great deal of time with students. His primary responsibility is instructing and guiding individuals who are pursuing a degree in meteorology. With other professors, Dr. Harnack tries to instill in students the knowledge they will need to be professional meteorologists or to go on to graduate study.

Dr. Harnack also spends much of his time on research. Specifically, he has investigated long-range weather prediction for the past 12 years. Currently, meterologists are able to issue reliable short-term weather forecasts. Such forecasts give the expected weather for a maximum of 5 days. Yet, according to Dr. Harnack, there is a need to expand reliable predictions to encompass a longer time period, such as for the next month or season.

Dr. Harnack uses information from a number of sources to formulate long-range winter temperature predictions. He obtains the November surface temperatures of the North Pacific Ocean, the Eastern Tropical Pacific Ocean, and the North Atlantic Ocean. Using relationships calculated based on temperature data from the past 35 years, he is then able to predict the coming winter's temperatures.

IV Winds and Wind Shifts

Topic 15 Effects of Continents

Land heats more in summer and cools more in winter. This heating and cooling has two important effects, which are shown in the maps of Figure 28.13(a) and Figure 28.13(b).

The first effect is that the highest temperatures are not usually at the equator. In the Northern Hemisphere summer, the highest temperatures (and therefore the lowest pressures) are as far north as 30° N in southwest Asia and northern Africa. Air flows into the low-pressure belt from the north and south, so the ITCZ moves north with the high temperatures. In the Southern Hemisphere summer, the ITCZ and the hottest temperatures move southward, reaching their southern point over northern Australia (15–20° S). Away from the continents, the ITCZ does not move as far north or south.

The second effect is that the pressure belts are broken up into highs and lows. In the summer, the pressure is low over the continents and high over the oceans. For example, a low-pressure area forms over the hot southwestern United States. Large high-pressure areas form over both the Atlantic and Pacific Oceans. The Atlantic high brings prevailing south winds to the eastern United States.

In the winter, the patterns reverse. Strong lows form over the northern Atlantic and northern Pacific Oceans. The pressure over North America is high. The low in the northern Pacific is associated with the many storms that reach the western coast of the United States.

OBJECTIVES

A Explain the effects of continents and seasons on Earth's pressure and wind circulation.

B Summarize the characteristics of the jet stream and its relationship to the weather.

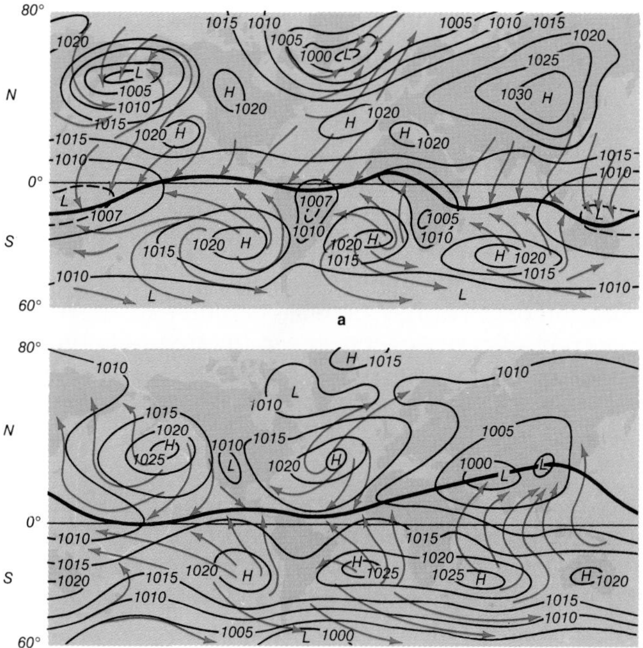

28.13 The effects of the continents and oceans on average sea-level pressure and winds, for (a) January and (b) July. The thin lines are isobars; the thick solid line is the ITCZ.

28.14 (top) India's dry winter monsoon blows from the land to the sea. (bottom) The wet summer monsoon blows from the sea to the land.

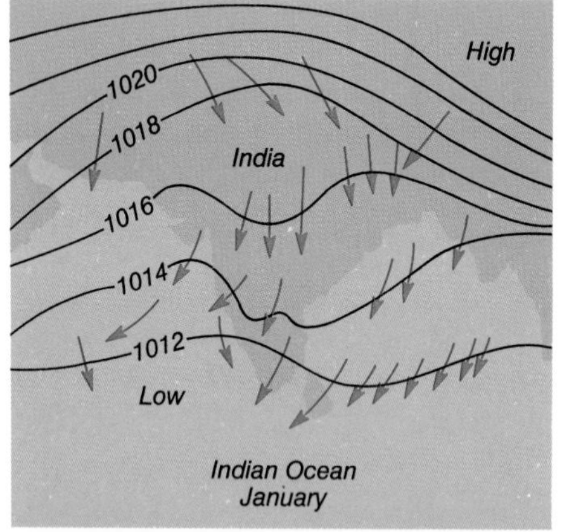

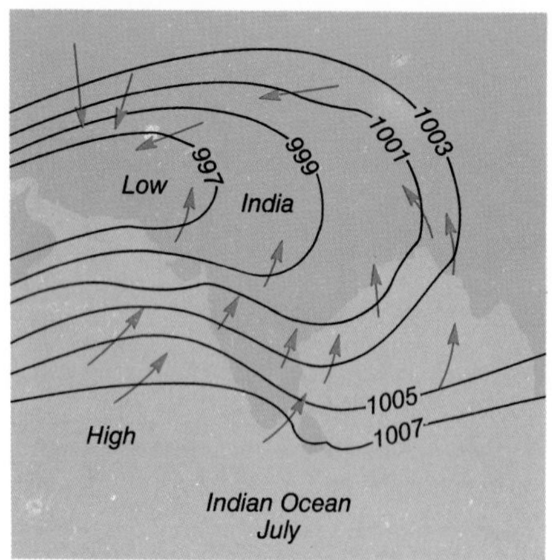

28.15 A typical position of the Northern Hemisphere jet stream over North America

Topic 16 Monsoons

The most dramatic continental effects on wind and pressure occur on the Indian subcontinent. Here the seasonal pressure changes from the heating and cooling of Asia produce a complete wind reversal. During the winter the sinking, cold air over the continent flows toward the lower pressure over the sea. In summer, the low pressure areas over the Indian subcontinent and Southeast Asia become centers of rising warm, moist air from the surrounding waters.

The changing winds are called **monsoons**. The cold, dry winds that flow from the cold interior are the winter monsoon. The warm, moist winds that flow into Asia from the Indian Ocean are called the summer monsoon. When they rise over the highlands of India and Southeast Asia, heavy rains fall.

Other parts of the world, such as northern Australia, west-central Africa, Spain, and the southeastern and southwestern United States, have seasonal wind changes. In most cases, however, the winds do not turn around as strongly as in India.

Topic 17 The Jet Stream

Wind speeds are very high in the upper troposphere. It is here that the spectacular jet stream is found. The **jet stream** is a fairly narrow stream of air in the upper troposphere that moves eastward at a high speed, usually in the middle latitudes. Sometimes it forms a single meandering band around the entire Earth. More often it is made of two or more separate streams.

The height of the jet stream ranges from about 6000 to 12 000 meters. Its strongest winds are about 10 500 meters above Earth. Its separate streams may be from 1600 to 4000 kilometers long, about one tenth as wide, and about 1 kilometer thick. Wind speeds are usually about 150 knots, but they may exceed 300 knots.

Two or more jet streams may be over a continent at once. In the Northern Hemisphere upper-air westerlies, jet streams may reach as far south as 20° N. The jet stream shifts position with the season, moving north in summer and south in winter. Its most common location over North America is around 40° N. A jet stream called the tropical easterly jet forms in the tropics in the Northern Hemisphere summer, but is weaker than the jet stream of the latitudes farther north. Figure 28.15 shows a typical position of the jet stream over North America.

Jet streams help eastward-flying planes to fly faster relative to the ground. Aircraft flying westward are slowed down by the jet streams, so pilots try to avoid them.

Jet streams are closely related to the weather and are strongest during outbreaks of cold polar air. Spring and summer jet streams are related to strong thunderstorms.

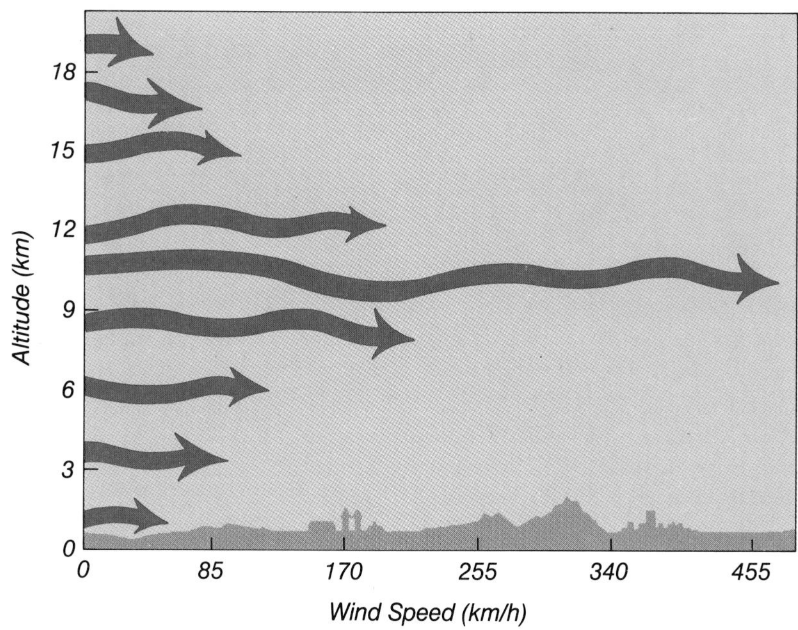

28.16 The arrows show wind speeds above the surface on a winter day in central United States. The very long arrow at about 10.5 kilometers is the jet stream. Its maximum speed is about 400 kilometers per hour.

TOPIC QUESTIONS

Each topic question refers to the topic of the same number.

15. (**a**) How do Earth's continents affect Earth's wind and pressure belts? (**b**) Why does the ITCZ move so far from the equator into the hemisphere where it is summer? (**c**) Describe the pressure pattern around North America for the Northern Hemisphere summer.

16. (**a**) What are monsoons? (**b**) Describe the summer and winter Indian monsoons.

17. (**a**) What is the jet stream? (**b**) List the height, location, and wind speeds of the North-American jet stream. (**c**) How is the jet stream related to the weather at the ground?

Map Skills

The following questions refer to the Prevailing World Winds map on page 591 of Appendix B.

1. (**a**) In the Southern Hemisphere, from what direction do the winds near the equator blow? (**b**) From what direction do the winds south of 40° S blow?

2. How are the winds in the Northern Hemisphere different from those in the Southern Hemisphere?

3. What happens to the southeast trade winds to the south of North Africa and Asia?

CHAPTER 28 REVIEW

Summary

Air pressure is caused by the weight of the atmosphere. It is directed equally in all directions. Air pressure is measured with barometers.

Air pressure changes due to changes in temperature and humidity.

Winds are caused by differences in air pressure. Air flows from high to low pressure.

Uneven heating of land and water results in the sea breeze. At night, the direction of the breeze is reversed.

In the Northern Hemisphere, the Coriolis effect turns winds to the right. It makes winds blow counterclockwise around lows and clockwise around highs.

In the Southern Hemisphere, the Coriolis effect turns winds to the left. It makes winds blow clockwise around lows and counterclockwise around highs.

A wind is defined by its speed and the direction from which it is blowing.

Earth's rotation and the uneven heating between its equator and poles result in the global wind and pressure belts.

Belts of low pressure and rising air lie at the equator and at 60 degrees. Belts of surface high pressure and sinking air lie at 30 degrees and at the poles.

In the Northern Hemisphere, surface northeast winds blow from the North Pole to 60° N, and from 30° N to the equator. Southwesterlies blow from 30 to 60 degrees. The flow north of 30 degrees is very irregular.

In summer, continents have low air pressure and the seas have high air pressure. Winds tend to blow more from the sea to the continents. The pattern reverses in winter. The reversing winds are called monsoons.

Jet streams are localized, very strong winds at heights of 6 to 12 kilometers. They are closely related to the weather.

Vocabulary

air pressure
anemometer
barometer
Coriolis effect
doldrums
Hadley cell
high-pressure area (high)
horse latitudes
intertropical convergence zone (ITCZ)
isobar
jet stream
knot
land breeze
low-pressure area (low)
millibar
monsoon
polar front
pressure gradient
pressure-gradient force
sea breeze
sea-level pressure
trade winds
wind vane

Review

On your paper, write the word or words that best complete each sentence.

1. ______ is the weight of the atmosphere per unit area.
2. Air pressure is measured using an instrument called a ______. An ______ measures height above sea level.
3. The average air pressure at a location with an altitude of 1000 meters would be ______ than average sea-level pressure.
4. Lines on a weather map that connect points with the same air pressure are called ______.
5. Air pressure can be changed by changes in ______ or ______.
6. Dry air weighs ______ than an equal volume of humid air.
7. A set of closed isobars in which the pressures decrease toward the center represents a ______.
8. Isobars that are close together have a ______ pressure gradient, which will result in ______ winds.
9. A ______ is a local wind that blows from the ocean toward the land.
10. Winds in the Northern Hemisphere are turned to the right by the ______.

11. ______ causes surface winds to blow at an angle to the isobars instead of parallel to them.
12. A wind vane points ______ the direction from which the wind blows.
13. Wind speed is measured in units called ______.
14. The Coriolis effect causes the air flow in each hemisphere to form three ______.
15. The equator-to-30 degree cell is called the ______.
16. The ______ is the surface between warm and cold air at about 60 degrees latitude where low-pressure areas develop.
17. The low-pressure zone at the equator is the ______.
18. Winds blow from areas of ______ pressure to areas of ______ pressure.
19. A wind that reverses direction with the seasons is a ______.
20. The North American jet stream flows from ______ to ______.

Interpret and Apply

On your paper, answer each question in complete sentences.

1. The feet of a 4500-kilogram elephant are approximate circles, each about 44 centimeters in diameter. If the elephant is standing on all four feet, what is the pressure under each foot?
2. (a) In what direction do winds circulate around highs in the Southern Hemisphere? (b) In what direction do winds circulate around lows in the Southern Hemisphere?
3. Draw a diagram to show what Earth's major wind belts would look like if Earth rotated from east to west.
4. The Coriolis effect is less at lower latitudes than at high latitudes. How would this reduced Coriolis effect affect a sea breeze at low latitudes?
5. On what time schedule might a fleet of sailboats make the best use of land and sea breezes?
6. Readings of surface air temperature are taken 1–2 meters above ground level, but wind speed and direction are measured about 10 meters above ground level. What is the reason for this difference?
7. Would you or would you not expect the Coriolis effect to affect water going down a drain? Why or why not?
8. How is atmospheric pressure similar to the pressure felt by scuba divers?
9. If you added water vapor to air in a closed container, its pressure would increase. Why then does adding water vapor to air (increasing humidity) lower the air pressure?

Critical Thinking

On your paper, answer each question in complete sentences.

1. Suppose Earth did not rotate, but had one side always toward the sun. Describe the winds and pressure field (a) at the surface and (b) at about 10 kilometers above the surface.
2. Speculate on what the atmospheric circulation would be if Earth's speed of rotation were doubled.
3. Explain what might happen to the air pressure at the surface under each of the following circumstances. (a) A deep cumulonimbus cloud is rapidly growing overhead. (b) A deep, cold downdraft from a squall line cools off the summer afternoon. (c) A dying thunderstorm with heavy rains is overhead. (d) A layer of warm, moist air extending from the surface to 1 kilometer above the surface moves northward, warming the temperature a degree an hour. At the same time, a layer of cool, dry air extending from 5 to 6 kilometers above the ground comes from the north, cooling the temperatures at those heights a degree an hour.

CHAPTER

29

Air Masses and Fronts

▲ A highway near Buffalo, New York, buried by the 1977 blizzard

How Do You Know That . . .

Fronts and air masses affect the local weather? The winter of 1976–1977 was one of the worst winters ever for Buffalo, New York. The worst storm of the winter started in late January 1977, when a strong low-pressure area brought with it cold air, snow, and winds as strong as 70 miles an hour. The storm lasted for 5 days, did 250 million dollars damage, and caused 29 deaths. Nine people froze to death in their cars. The snow in and around Buffalo was 4 feet deep, with drifts 30 feet high in some places. This snowstorm was a spectacular example of what happens when a strong low-pressure area is followed by a very cold air mass.

I Air Masses

Topic 1 Origin of an Air Mass

Air that stays in one area for a long time takes on the weather of that area. If air stays in the Arctic for a few weeks in January, it becomes quite cold. If the air lies over the ocean, it becomes moist.

An **air mass** is a huge section of the lower troposphere that has the same kind of weather throughout. The temperature and humidity are horizontally uniform within an air mass. Air masses may be several thousand kilometers in diameter and several kilometers deep. Two or three air masses can cover all of the continental United States.

How does a huge section of the troposphere become an air mass? It maintains the same position for days or even weeks over a large uniform surface. An air mass over the Gulf of Mexico, for example, would be warm and humid. An air mass over the Great Plains of Canada in winter would be cold and dry.

Air masses originate in parts of the world where winds are light. These are mainly in the polar and subtropical high-pressure belts.

Topic 2 Kinds, Sources, and Paths of Air Masses

The temperature of an air mass depends on whether it comes from the tropics or the polar regions. The humidity of an air mass depends on whether it comes from land or sea.

Air masses are named for their *source regions,* or places of origin. A **maritime tropical** (abbreviated **mT**) air mass comes from tropical seas. It is warm and humid. Maritime tropical air comes into the United States from the Pacific and Atlantic oceans and the Gulf of Mexico. A **continental tropical (cT)** air mass comes from tropical land areas. In North America, these hot, dry air masses originate in the desert area of southwestern United States.

A **maritime polar (mP)** air mass comes from cold ocean waters. It is cold and humid. A **continental polar (cP)** air mass comes from land areas in high latitudes. It is cold and dry. Maritime polar air masses come to the United States from both the Pacific and Atlantic oceans. Continental polar air masses come from Canada and northward.

OBJECTIVES

A Explain how air masses form and list the types of air masses.

B Describe the weather and sky conditions that accompany each type of air mass.

C Describe the techniques used to determine air-mass properties.

29.1 In the summertime, this desert area in southern Utah is part of a source region for hot, dry continental tropical air.

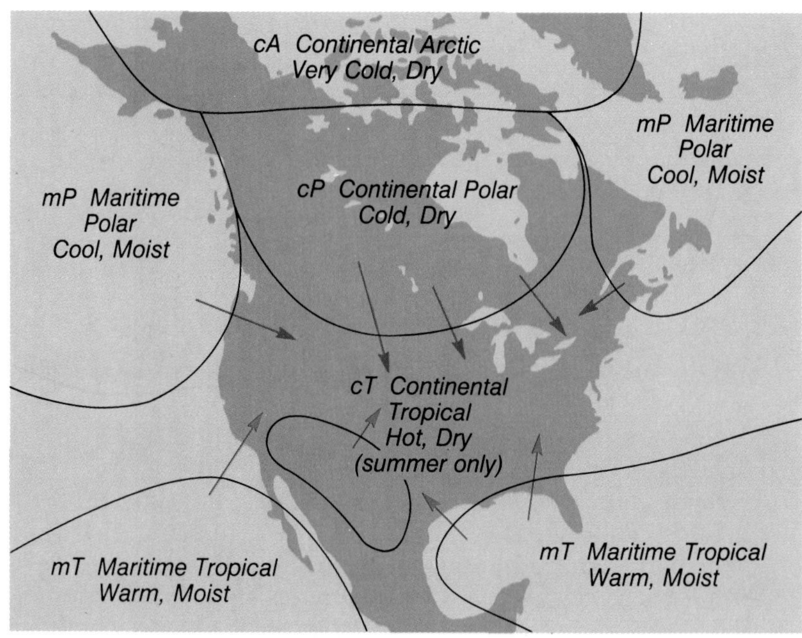

29.2 Air mass source regions and the paths air masses follow across North America

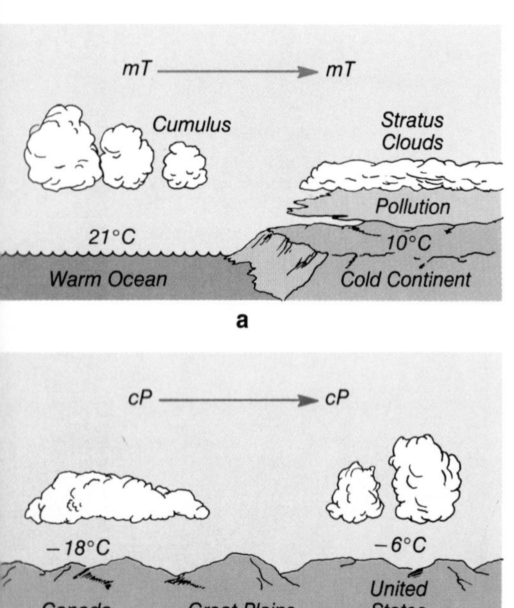

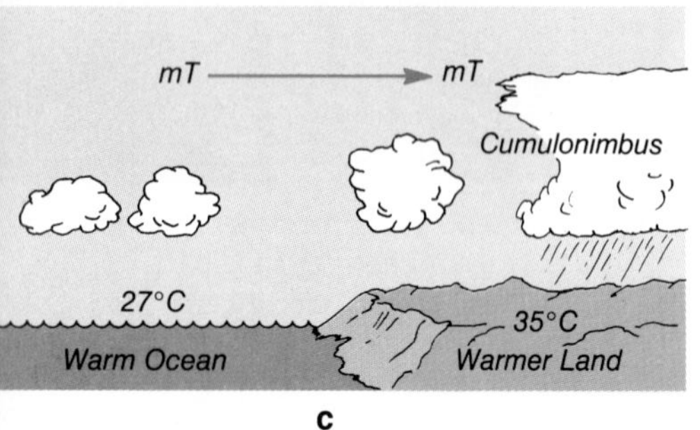

29.3 (a) When a maritime tropical air mass moves from warm sea to cooler land, the air near the surface is stable. Stratus clouds, fog, and drizzle may develop. Pollution may become trapped, forming smog. (b) When a continental polar air mass moves from Canada across the warmer Great Plains in wintertime, fair-weather cumulus clouds form. (c) When a maritime tropical air mass moves from sea to warmer land in summer, cumulonimbus clouds and thunderstorms are likely.

Continental Arctic (cA) air masses are very cold and dry. They come from the ice-covered Arctic regions. There is no maritime Arctic air mass because Arctic air is so dry.

Topic 3 Weather in an Air Mass

Air masses are so large that they may take many days to pass a given place. During this time the weather of the place is like the weather of the region where the air mass originated. In winter, cP air is usually an icy, clear, cold wave. It may reach as far south as Florida. In summer, cP air is felt as a cool spell.

When mP air comes in from the northern oceans, it brings cool, humid weather. The mT air masses bring mild, humid weather in winter. In summer they bring hot, humid spells to central and eastern United States. Maritime tropical air also brings frequent thunderstorms and occasional tornadoes. Continental tropical air masses bring very hot, dry weather.

The weather changes brought by new air masses can be extreme or very slight. Part of the reason for the difference is that air masses change as they move away from their source areas. Polar air masses get warmer as they move southward. Dry air masses become moister over moist ground, and moist air masses become drier over dry ground. Fast-moving air masses spend less time over any one area, so they are usually changed less than slow-moving air masses. Therefore, fast-moving air masses bring more extreme weather changes.

The passage of different air masses is one of the factors that make weather so variable.

Topic 4 Skies in an Air Mass

What kinds of clouds do air masses have? Is the weather fair or rainy, windy or calm?

Meteorologists have found that the conditions in an air mass depend mainly on one thing: Is the surface the air mass lies over warmer or colder than the air mass? If the ground surface is colder, it cools the bottom layer of the air mass, with the following results:

1. The bottom layer of the air is stable. Inversions form. Smoke, dust, and other pollutants do not rise. Visibility is poor. *Smog* may develop.
2. Condensation of water vapor occurs at the surface and in the lower air. This condensation may form dew, fog, stratiform clouds, drizzle, or light rain.

If the ground surface is warmer than the air mass, it warms the bottom layer of the air mass, with these results:

1. The bottom layer is unstable. Convection currents form cumulus clouds. The convection mixes lower-layer air with air at higher levels, so air pollution moves out of the area. Visibility is good.
2. If the air mass is a dry one – such as cP – the weather stays fair. If the air mass is humid or the warm surface is water, showers may form.

Topic 5 Observing an Air Mass

How do meterologists observe the temperature, humidity, and wind at high levels in an air mass? They use a balloon-carried package of instruments called a **rawinsonde**. Rawinsonde measurements are made twice daily, at noon and midnight, Greenwich, England, time (GMT), at weather stations all over the world.

The rawinsonde contains a radio transmitter that sends out signals about the temperature, air pressure, and relative humidity. An automatic radio receiver at the weather station records the signals. The balloon carries the rawinsonde up to a height of more than 30 kilometers, where the balloon bursts. Radar equipment tracks the rawinsonde and determines the speed and direction of the upper-air winds.

Scientists are developing new ways to measure the temperature, humidity, and wind above the surface. The temperature and humidity are estimated by measuring the air's infrared radiation. (Hotter air and more humid air radiate more infrared rays.) These measurements are made both from satellites and from instruments on the ground. The new *radar wind profiler* is a kind of radar that measures the winds through the troposphere. Unlike rawinsondes, the new instruments can take measurements continuously. However, they cannot provide the detail rawinsondes can.

29.4 This rawinsonde, about to be launched, may float upward to an altitude of about 30 kilometers.

TOPIC QUESTIONS

Each topic question refers to the topic of the same number.

1. (a) What is an air mass? (b) Explain how an air mass originates.
2. (a) How are air masses named? Write the full name, characteristics, and source regions of the North American air masses abbreviated by (b) cP, (c) mP, (d) mT, and (e) cT.
3. (a) Briefly describe the weather in each of the following air masses: cP, mP, mT. (b) How does the speed of the air mass affect the expected weather?
4. (a) What is the chief factor that determines the type of skies an air mass will have? (b) Describe the sky conditions in an air mass resting on a cooler surface. (c) Describe the sky conditions in an air mass resting on a warmer surface.
5. (a) How is a rawinsonde used to obtain temperature, humidity, and wind measurements above the surface? (b) How are satellites and ground instruments used to estimate temperatures and humidities aloft? (c) What is the new instrument for measuring wind at upper levels? (d) How do wind measurements made with this instrument differ from wind measurements made with a rawinsonde?

Dr. Robert Sheets
Hurricane Meteorologist

As you will learn in the next chapter, a hurricane is a special kind of air mass. It is a maritime tropical air mass that is capable of great destruction when it strikes land. Dr. Robert Sheets is the acting director of the National Hurricane Center in Miami, a part of the National Weather Service. He and other meteorologists there continually watch for hurricanes, follow their development, and try to predict the paths they will take.

Prior to becoming the acting director of the National Hurricane Center, Dr. Sheets actively studied hurricanes. For 16 years, he worked in the National Hurricane Research Laboratory located with the National Hurricane Center. Gathering research data often involved flying directly into hurricanes. Dr. Sheets estimates that he has flown through the eye of a hurricane over 200 times.

Dr. Sheets' greatest concern is for the nearly 40 million people who now live along the Atlantic Coast and are therefore potential hurricane victims. He wants to make them aware of the great danger from these storms so that they will not wait until it is too late to take action.

II Fronts and the Formation of Lows

OBJECTIVES

A Define *front* and describe the shape of a front.

B Discuss the four kinds of fronts and explain their origin and structure.

C Trace the formation of a typical mid-latitude cyclone.

Topic 6 What Is a Front?

At any given moment several air masses may cover the United States. The boundary between any two air masses is called a **front**. Because the two air masses have different temperatures and humidities, the front is where the temperatures and humidities change. An approaching front means a change in the weather. The greater the differences between the air masses, the greater the change in the weather. On weather maps, fronts are drawn in regions of great change in temperature and wind direction and where isobars tend to bend.

What is the shape of a front? Suppose the front is the boundary between a southward-moving polar air mass and a slower-moving tropical air mass. The polar air is colder and therefore more dense than the tropical air. Therefore, when they meet, the polar air slides under the warmer, lighter tropical air and forces it to rise. The shape that results is a wedge (Figure 29.5). The temperature and humidity changes across the front are not always sudden. Usually, the front is a mixing zone about 30 kilometers thick.

Observations show that fronts have gentle slopes. The slope may range from 1 in 100 to 1 in 400. A slope of 1 in 100 means that the frontal surface rises 1 kilometer for every 100 kilometers of distance on the ground. Frontal surfaces may reach up to higher than 5 kilometers. As a result, fronts affect the weather in an area several hundred kilometers wide. Fronts may be several thousand kilometers in length.

Fronts almost always bring precipitation. At the frontal surface, warm air is rising high into the troposphere. Rising air means cooling, condensation, and then clouds and precipitation.

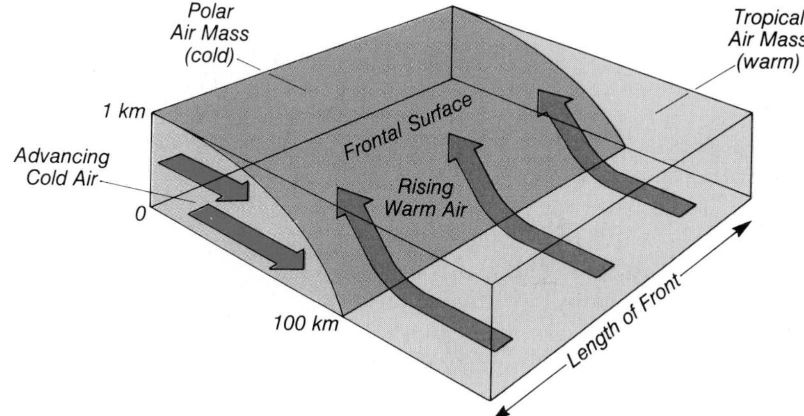

29.5 A front is a boundary between two air masses. At a front, the lighter (less dense) warm air is forced to rise over the heavier cold air. Note that the horizontal and vertical scales are very different. The slope of this front is 1 in 100.

29.6 A cold front passes through Colorado. Dust shows the cold air and the shape of the front. A very steep drop in temperature occurred after this front passed through. The frontal surface in the photo has a very steep slope, about 1 in 2.

Topic 7 Kinds of Fronts

There are three main kinds of fronts. In a **cold front,** the cold air is advancing and displacing warmer air. The front in Figure 29.6 is a cold front. In a **warm front,** warm air is pushing ahead and displacing colder air. If neither air mass is being displaced, the front does not move. It is called a **stationary front.**

Cold fronts have steeper slopes than warm fronts, particularly in the lowest few kilometers. The slope is steepest near the ground. One of the most important reasons for this difference in slope is that the friction at the ground slows down the cold air, as shown in Figure 29.7. Warm fronts have more gentle slopes. Again, friction is important in keeping the slope shallow near the ground. The surface air, slowed down by friction, is left behind by the retreating cold air at higher levels. A warm frontal surface rises about 1 kilometer for every 400 kilometers.

Figure 29.8 shows the symbols used for fronts on weather maps. When a cold front overtakes a warm front, the result is called an **occluded front.** The solid triangles of the cold front and the solid half-circles of the warm front always point in the direction of the front's movement.

Fronts control the weather only at times when one air mass is displacing another. For a much longer time, the weather is air-mass weather. However, most precipitation comes with fronts.

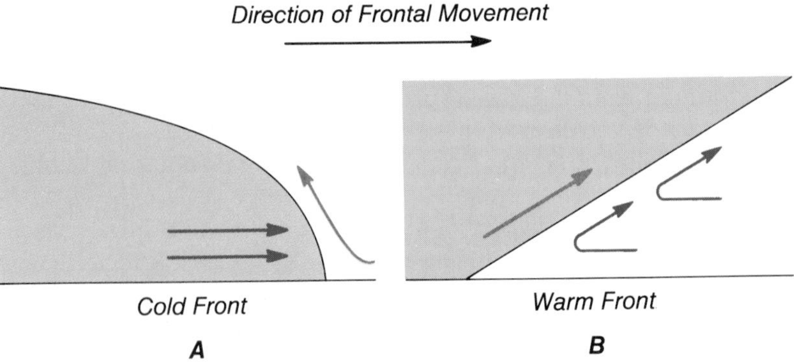

29.7 Slopes of fronts near the ground. The cold front (a) has a much steeper frontal surface than the warm front (b). The blue and red arrows indicate the direction of movement of cold and warm air in each front.

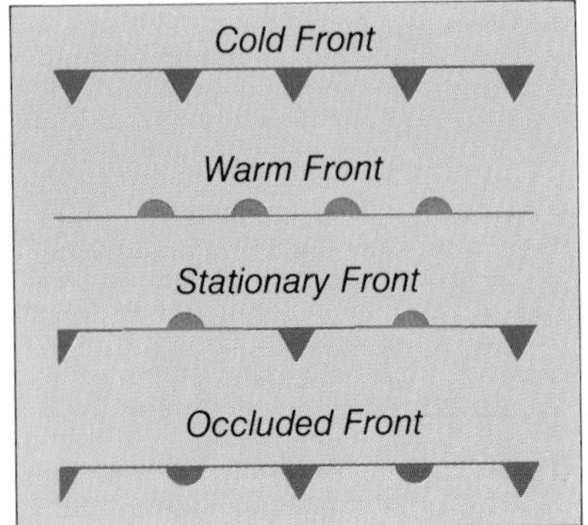

29.8 These are the international standard symbols for fronts.

Topic 8 How Mid-Latitude Lows Form

The polar front, described in Chapter 28, is the boundary between cool air masses in the polar easterlies and warm air masses in the prevailing westerlies. Polar air masses lie to the north of the polar front. Tropical air masses lie to the south of it.

A kink or wave frequently forms somewhere on the polar front. There are many ways such a wave can form. For example, such a wave could be caused by a wave or kink in the jet stream. Also, a kink would develop in the polar front if a cold air mass began moving southward, pushing part of the polar front ahead of it as shown in Figure 29.9(b).

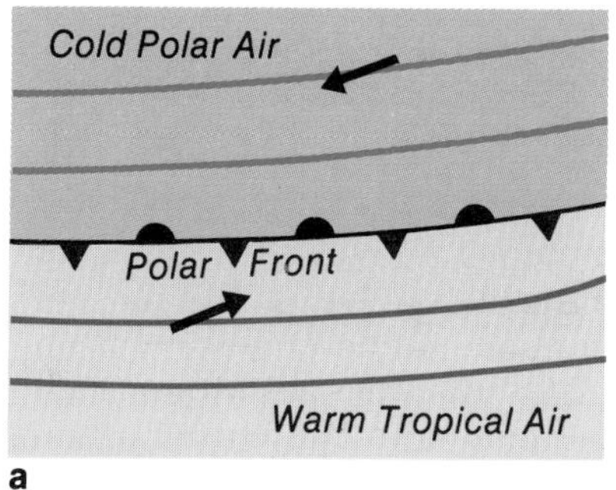

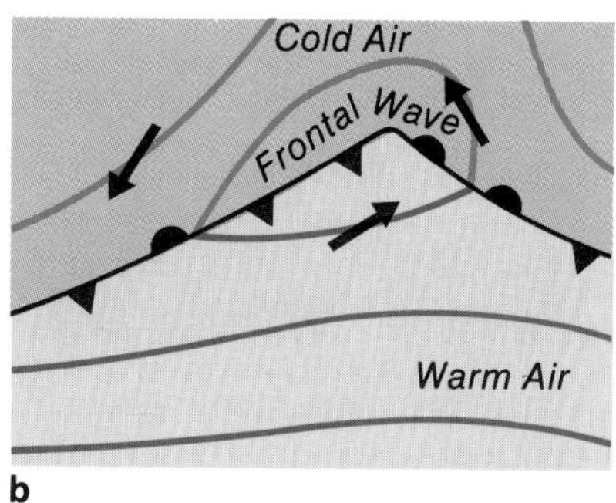

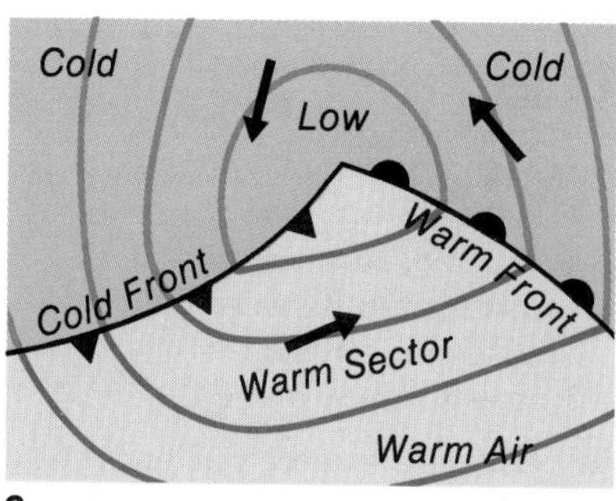

29.9 These four diagrams of the atmosphere at Earth's surface trace the origin and growth of a Northern Hemisphere low. The blue lines are isobars. The arrows are pointed the way the wind is blowing.

The wave moves from west to east, like a wave passing through a stage curtain shaken at one end. The wave ripples the polar front. The front bulges southward on the west side of the wave, where polar air pushes tropical air southward. This southward-moving portion of the polar front is a southward-moving cold front. On the east side of the wave, the polar front bulges northward as a warm front. Here, tropical air pushes the polar air northward.

Between the cold and warm fronts is a large amount of warm tropical air. The warm air bulges into and over the heavier polar air to form a region of low pressure. The lowest air pressure is at the crest of the wave, where the warm and cold fronts meet. A low, or **cyclone,** has formed. The isobars around a low are roughly oval or circular, with a slight bend at the fronts. Winds whirl about the center of the low in a counterclockwise direction in the Northern Hemisphere.

The whole system moves eastward, but the cold front moves more rapidly than the warm front. The front that forms when the cold front overtakes the warm front, shown in Figure 29.9(d), is called an occluded front. The warm air is lifted completely off the surface in an occluded front. *Occlusion* (formation of the occluded front) continues until the low weakens and the two cold air masses mix across the occluded front.

In summary, a low forms from a wave in a nearly stationary front. To form a fully developed low takes only 12 to 24 hours. Complete occlusion usually takes an additional 3 days or more.

TOPIC QUESTIONS

Each topic question refers to the topic of the same number.

6. **(a)** What is a front? **(b)** Describe the relative positions of the air masses at a front and give the slope of a typical front. **(c)** Why do fronts bring precipitation?

7. **(a)** Describe the three main types of fronts. **(b)** Compare the slopes of warm and cold fronts and explain why their slopes are different near the ground.

8. **(a)** Describe how a mid-latitude low forms on the polar front. **(b)** How is the polar front related to warm and cold fronts?

OBJECTIVES

A Describe the winds and weather in a low, including the relationship between condensation and the strengthening of the low.

B List the sequence of clouds and weather associated with both warm and cold fronts.

C Summarize the typical winds and weather in a high.

III Weather Associated with Lows, Fronts, and Highs

Topic 9 Winds and Weather in a Low

In the Northern Hemisphere, the winds near the surface blow counterclockwise and toward the center of a low. The air converging into the low-pressure area rises, resulting in clouds and precipitation. The air also rises at the cold, warm, and occluded fronts, resulting in more clouds and precipitation. Notice the extensive cloudiness in the low shown in Figure 29.10.

The condensation that produces clouds and precipitation also releases heat energy. The air heated by this energy lowers the pressure at the surface, and the low becomes stronger. This increases the pressure gradient, and the winds also become stronger, particularly near the low center. If other factors do not weaken the low, it will continue to strengthen as long as condensation continues.

Figure 29.11 shows a vertical section through a typical low. The following weather changes occur when a low passes to the north of a locality in the Northern Hemisphere:

1. A long period of steady precipitation in advance of the warm front.
2. Warming and slow clearing after the warm front passes. If the air is humid, showery precipitation may occur, particularly nearer the center of the low.
3. Showery precipitation around the time the cold front passes.
4. Cooling and rapid clearing, with a change toward the weather characteristic of the newly arrived cold air mass.

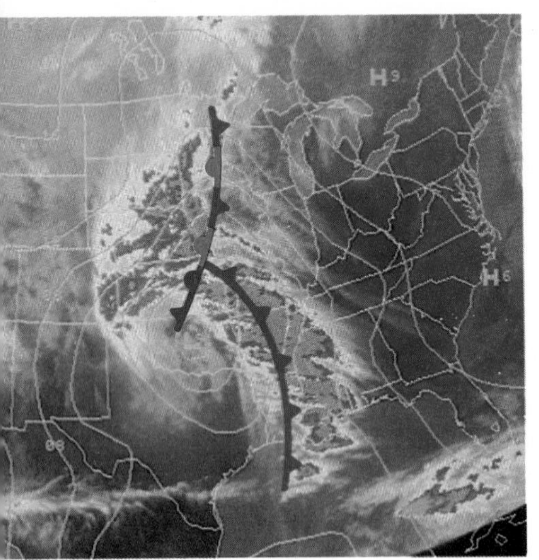

29.10 A strong low-pressure area with cold, stationary, and occluded fronts. Notice that the thick (white) clouds are mostly around the low and fronts. Heavy snows were falling in the Midwest at the time of this picture. The colored areas are probably the tops of precipitating clouds.

Topic 10 Warm-Front Weather

A warm front affects the weather long before the arrival of the rains. As shown in Figure 29.11, high cirrus clouds appear first, followed by cirrostratus and lower and thicker stratiform clouds.

These clouds form in the air sliding up the frontal surface. The warm air may travel 1000 kilometers before rising 2 or 3 kilometers. The air is usually stable, so the rising air forms a vast system of stratiform clouds. The clouds may stretch 1500 kilometers ahead of the place where the warm front touches the ground.

Following the cirrus and cirrostratus are altostratus clouds, which almost screen out the sun and moon. Finally, the heavy nimbostratus clouds arrive, and steady rain or snow begins. This area of rain and snow can stretch hundreds of kilometers ahead of where the front touches the ground. Warming follows the passage of the front at the surface. Thunderstorms may form, but they are not typical of warm fronts. Stationary fronts have the same kind of weather as warm fronts.

Topic 11 Cold-Front Weather

Cold fronts are steeper and move faster than warm fronts. Thus, the air forced upward by the cold front rises quickly. Also, the air ahead of cold fronts is usually unstable. For these reasons, rapidly growing cumuliform clouds grow around the cold front. Precipitation falls from cumulonimbus clouds. Weather is showery, with heavy precipitation starting and ending quickly, and thunderstorms are common. Because of the cold front's steep slope, its precipitation covers at most 300 to 500 kilometers. The precipitation can occur both before and after a cold front passes at the surface.

When a cold front passes, sharp changes of weather occur. Temperatures fall fast as the cold air arrives. The wind rises in speed and may shift suddenly from a southerly direction to a northerly one. The rain usually ends shortly after the front passes.

Sometimes very humid mT air is being pushed forward ahead of a cold front. In such cases, a whole line of thunderstorms may form ahead of the front, creating a squall line that may be hundreds of kilometers long.

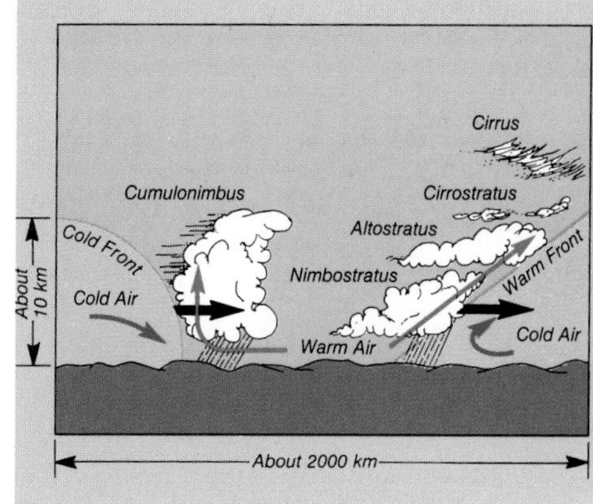

29.11 A cross section through the cold and warm fronts of a fully developed low. The large arrows show the direction of movement of the fronts; the red and blue arrows show the direction of movement of warm and cold air. Notice that the horizontal and vertical scales are very different.

Topic 12 Weather in a High

Between the lows and their fronts lie areas of high pressure, or **anticyclones.** Highs usually appear on weather maps as a series of smooth circular isobars. Unlike a low, a high represents a single air mass. Its diameter may be more than 1500 kilometers. Since the air pressure is highest at its center, the winds in a high blow outward. The air moves in a clockwise direction in the Northern Hemisphere and counterclockwise in the Southern Hemisphere. Isobars are generally farther apart than in lows; therefore, the winds are weaker.

Bright, clear weather is usually present throughout a high because of the sinking dry air at its center. Small cumulus clouds may form over the heated ground during the day. At night, heavy dew, frost, and radiation fogs may form in the quiet lower air. Inversions can also form in the mornings, trapping pollution until the sun warms the ground.

29.12 Squall lines like this one occur ahead of cold fronts in spring and early summer.

TOPIC QUESTIONS

Each topic question refers to the topic of the same number.

9. Give the typical sequence of weather as a low passes to the north.

10. **(a)** List the sequence of clouds and weather that comes before and during the passing of a warm front at the surface. **(b)** Why are the clouds along a warm front stratiform?

11. **(a)** Describe the clouds, precipitation, and weather changes that occur as a cold front passes. **(b)** Why are the clouds along a cold front cumuliform?

12. What is the weather like in a high?

CHAPTER 29 REVIEW

Summary

Air masses are vast areas of air with the same temperature and humidity throughout. They form when air stays for a long time over one place (its source region).

Air masses are named for the climate of their source regions.

The weather in a moving air mass is determined by its humidity and whether its temperature is warmer or colder than the surface beneath.

Rawinsondes are used to measure the temperature, humidity, and wind through the depth of an air mass.

Fronts are boundaries between unlike air masses. There are four kinds of fronts: cold, warm, stationary, and occluded.

A front is shaped like a wedge, with the less dense air on top of the more dense air.

Mid-latitude lows form along waves in the polar front.

Rising air in lows brings condensation and precipitation. The condensation releases heat and lowers the pressure even more.

The sequence of clouds and precipitation when a low passes is determined by the location of the low center and the kinds of fronts that pass.

Clouds on a warm-frontal surface are mostly stratiform; clouds on a cold-frontal surface are cumuliform. Precipitation occurs near the surface fronts.

Sinking air in highs brings fair weather.

Vocabulary

air mass	cyclone
anticyclone	front
cold front	maritime polar (mP)
continental Arctic (cA)	maritime tropical (mT)
continental polar (cP)	occluded front
continental tropical (cT)	rawinsonde
	stationary front
	warm front

Review

Number your paper from 1 to 17. Match the terms in list **A** with the phrases in list **B**.

List A

1. mT
2. front
3. low-pressure area
4. cT
5. air mass
6. polar front
7. anticyclone
8. stable air
9. stationary front
10. cP
11. source region
12. warm front
13. cyclone
14. mP
15. rawinsonde
16. unstable air
17. cold front

List B

a. instrument used to measure weather characteristics high above the surface
b. cold, humid air mass
c. low-pressure area
d. place of origin of an air mass
e. characteristic typical of an air mass resting on a colder ground surface
f. quickly moving front with a steep slope
g. air mass that brings cooler, dry weather
h. characteristic typical of an air mass resting on a warmer ground surface
i. nearly stationary front along which lows form
j. section of the lower troposphere that has the same weather throughout
k. slowly moving front with a gentle slope
l. warm, humid air mass
m. boundary between two air masses
n. high-pressure area

I Thunderstorms and Tornadoes

Topic 1 How Thunderstorms Form

Each day about 44 000 thunderstorms occur across Earth's surface. *Thunderstorms* are small-area storms formed by the strong upward movement of warm, moist air. They are formed from cumulonimbus clouds, are always accompanied by lightning and thunder, and usually produce rain. Strong thunderstorms produce high winds, hail, and even tornadoes. Single thunderstorms are 10–20 kilometers across and 10–20 kilometers deep.

Thunderstorms fall into two groups: local or **air-mass thunderstorms,** and organized or **frontal thunderstorms.**

Air-mass thunderstorms form within a warm, moist air mass. They start when the surface is strongly heated. Often single storms, they occur mostly in spring or summer and usually last less than an hour. Air-mass thunderstorms are widely scattered and form mostly over land. No one can yet predict exactly where an air-mass thunderstorm will form. Some form over mountains, perhaps started by the rising valley breeze, but others form almost anywhere over flat land or water.

Frontal thunderstorms usually form in warm, moist air on or ahead of cold fronts. Some thunderstorms, however, occur around warm fronts. Frontal thunderstorms often occur in lines along the frontal surface. They also occur in lines ahead of the front, called *squall lines.* The lines of thunderstorms can be hundreds of kilometers long. Slowly moving fronts or squall lines can produce heavy rains and flooding. Frontal thunderstorms occur most often in spring and summer. They are often stronger than air-mass thunderstorms and may last for several hours.

OBJECTIVES

A Compare the types of thunderstorms and show how and where they form.

B Describe and explain lightning and thunder, and list places that are safe during lightning storms.

C Describe tornadoes and severe thunderstorms and list the conditions that produce them.

D Differentiate between watches and warnings issued for severe thunderstorms and tornadoes.

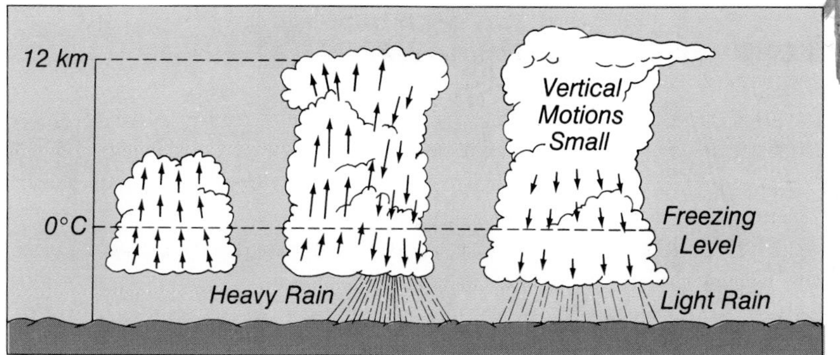

30.1 (left) An air-mass thunderstorm starts when heating of the ground causes vertical motions. (center) The weight of the falling rain and cooling by evaporation cause a downdraft to begin. (right) The downdraft spreads, choking off the vertical motions. The cloud dies.

30.2 Spectacular lightning displays may be seen during a thunderstorm.

Topic 2 Electricity in a Thunderstorm

All thunderstorms produce lightning. Lightning is a discharge of electricity from a thundercloud to the ground or to another cloud.

The temperature inside a channel of a lightning flash is believed to reach about 28 000°C. At this high temperature, the air expands explosively. This sudden expansion makes the tremendous sound wave called thunder. Light travels at 300 000 kilometers a second, so lightning is seen almost instantly. The sound waves from lightning, however, take 3 seconds to travel a kilometer, so you hear the sound of thunder after seeing a lightning flash.

Lightning strokes are often very long, so that some parts are close and some farther away. In this case, the sound is spread out in time, and the thunder rumbles. Rumbling also happens when thunder echoes from mountainsides. The greatest distance at which it is ordinarily possible for thunder to be heard is about 16 kilometers. Heat lightning is the glow of lightning so far away that its thunder cannot be heard.

Lightning Safety Tips

1. *Go indoors, if possible. If you are traveling, stay in your car.*
2. *Stay off bicycles, motorcycles, scooters, golf carts, or farm equipment.*
3. *If you are swimming, get out of the water. Get off small boats.*
4. *Avoid standing near or being the highest object in an area. Outdoors, the best protection is in a cave, ditch, or canyon. If you are out in the open with only isolated trees nearby, crouch in the open as far away from the trees as possible.*
5. *Indoors, stay away from open doors and windows and metal objects such as pipes, sinks, stoves, and radiators. Do not use the telephone or plug–in appliances.*
6. *If you feel lightning is about to strike — your hair stands on end or your skin tingles — drop to your knees and bend forward with your hands on your knees.*

Topic 3 Lightning Danger and Protection

Lightning can be very dangerous. Every year in the United States lightning causes thousands of forest fires and electrocutes about 200 people.

When lightning strikes, it is likely to go from the cloud base to the highest point projecting above the ground. It often strikes tall objects, such as trees, church steeples, and the tops of skyscrapers. Lightning rods are based on this fact. They project above the roofs of houses and are connected to the ground by a good conductor, such as a metal wire. When lightning strikes the rod, the electricity is conducted to the ground. Otherwise it might strike some part of the house and set the house on fire.

Where should one take shelter in a lightning storm? The best shelter is inside a building. Stay away from televisions, telephones, sinks, and bathrooms, since the electrical wiring and metal pipes of your house can conduct electricity. Cars are also very safe. Bathers and boaters should seek shelter as soon as a storm develops. A tree or small group of trees in an open field should be avoided. They attract lightning. If you are out in the open during a lightning storm, crouch on the ground.

30.3 A tornado at the bottom of a thunderstorm cloud

Topic 4 Tornadoes

Tornadoes are much more frequent in the United States than anywhere else in the world. Most tornadoes in the United States occur in the Mississippi River valley and the Great Plains. The conditions that produce strong thunderstorms often also produce tornadoes. Warm, moist air from the Gulf of Mexico moves northward into the Mississippi River valley and the Great Plains. This air extends from the surface up to 3 kilometers deep. Higher up, cool air moves eastward over the Rocky Mountains. So the air is moist at lower levels. It is also very unstable, with the temperature falling rapidly with height through a deep layer. A cold front approaches. This is ideal for producing thunderstorms. Strong wind increasing with height helps to make the thunderstorms stronger.

A **tornado** is a narrow, funnel-shaped column of spiral winds that extends downward from the cloud base and touches the ground. The strengths of tornadoes vary greatly. The strongest winds in a tornado are between 360 and 500 kilometers an hour. The funnel is usually less than 500 meters across at the ground. A tornado travels with its parent thunderstorm, at speeds ranging from 40 to 65 kilometers an hour. Tornado paths are somewhat irregular and usually less than 25 kilometers long. They pass in a few seconds with a thunderous roar. Tornadoes usually last no more than an hour and are accompanied by heavy rain, lightning, and hail.

The tornado funnel is a mixture of cloud and dust. The pressure gets lower closer to the center of the tornado. As air flows toward the funnel, it expands from the lower pressure and cools. When the air cools to its dew point, tiny water drops form. Clouds form in exactly the same way when rising air reaches the condensation level. The low pressure in a tornado causes the condensation level to dip downward, forming the funnel of clouds. Sometimes the dust picked up by the tornado forms a separate funnel surrounding the condensation funnel.

Tornadoes over water are called **waterspouts.** Waterspouts are usually weaker than tornadoes. They occur with weak thunderstorms and even large cumulus clouds.

Tornado Safety Tips

1. *If you live in an area frequented by tornadoes, plan safety rules for your family. Choose the best tornado shelter area in your home and make sure everyone knows where it is. Keep a battery–powered radio that you can use in the event of an emergency. Watch any thunderstorm clouds for signs of a funnel, and know how to reach the local authorities if you spot one. Practice tornado drills.*
2. *In the event of a tornado, stay away from outside walls, windows, and doors. At home, go to the basement or an interior room on the lowest level. If possible, get under a heavy table or mattress.*
3. *In a public place, go to the designated shelter area or sit close to an interior wall on the lowest level.*
4. *Get away from mobile homes or vehicles if possible; find more substantial shelter.*
5. *If you are outdoors in an open area, look for a ravine or ditch. Lie flat and protect your head with your arms.*

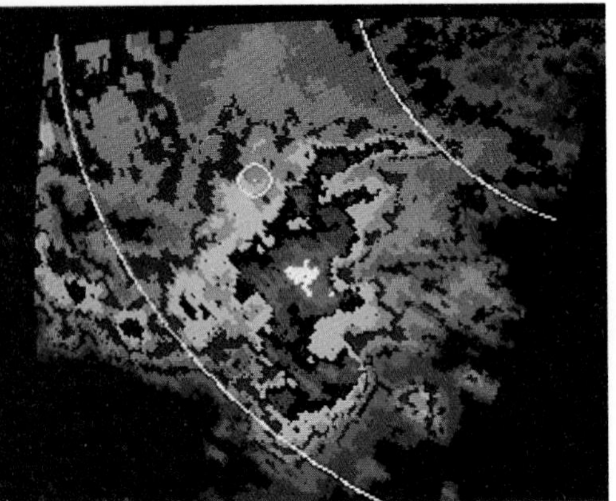

30.4 Radar view of a severe thunderstorm. The inner colors indicate the largest or heaviest precipitation. The heavy precipitation is drawn into two hook shapes; these "hook echoes" indicate possible tornadoes. The existence of a tornado must be confirmed by spotter reports or winds from the Doppler radar. (The curved lines are 40 km apart.)

Topic 5 Severe Weather Watches and Warnings

When conditions favor the formation of severe thunderstorms or tornadoes, the National Severe Storms Forecast Center in Kansas City, Missouri, issues severe thunderstorm or tornado watches. A **severe thunderstorm** has wind gusts at least 80 kilometers per hour and hail about 2 centimeters in diameter or greater.

Local weather stations issue severe thunderstorm or tornado warnings whenever necessary. Watches and warnings are broadcast over radio and television. Watches and warnings are also given for flash floods.

A *watch* covers an area of 100 kilometers by 200 kilometers or larger. It gives the time during which severe thunderstorms and tornadoes are possible.

A *warning* is issued when a tornado or severe thunderstorm has actually been sighted or detected on radar. It gives the location of the storm when detected, the area into which it is likely to move, and the period of time during which the storm could hit.

Tornadoes and severe thunderstorms are most frequent during spring and summer and are most likely to occur in the late afternoon. Tornadoes in the United States kill an average of 104 persons yearly. The worst tornado ever recorded was the Tri-State Tornado, which killed 689 people in Missouri, Illinois, and Indiana in 1925. The number of people killed each year by tornadoes has been dropping in recent years because of improved warnings.

TOPIC QUESTIONS

Each topic question refers to the topic of the same number.

1. **(a)** What is a thunderstorm? **(b)** How are air-mass and frontal thunderstorms different?

2. **(a)** What is lightning? **(b)** What causes the rolling sound of thunder.

3. **(a)** Where does lightning tend to strike? **(b)** Explain how a lightning rod works. **(c)** List the safest places to be during a lightning storm.

4. **(a)** What conditions favor strong thunderstorms and tornadoes? **(b)** Describe a tornado, giving its shape, diameter, path length, speed of travel, and maximum winds. **(c)** What is the funnel made of? **(d)** Where do tornadoes most commonly occur?

5. **(a)** What is a severe thunderstorm? **(b)** What is a severe thunderstorm watch? **(c)** When are warnings given?

II Cyclonic Storms

Topic 6 Hurricanes

People living along the Gulf and Atlantic coasts pay careful attention to weather reports of hurricanes. A **hurricane** is an intense tropical low-pressure area with sustained winds of 120 kilometers per hour or greater. The strong winds and heavy rains produce major damage.

The greatest damage associated with hurricanes, however, is caused by currents called **storm surges.** A storm surge forms when the hurricane piles up water along the shore and then blows it inland. Storm surges are much more damaging during high tide. In November 1970 a tropical cyclone in the Indian Ocean hit Bangladesh at high tide; it caused the death of 300 000 people.

Hurricanes are in some ways like mid-latitude cyclones. They both are low-pressure areas. Winds spiral toward their centers in the same general patterns. As a rule both have areas of heavy precipitation, and both grow larger and more powerful from the vast amounts of energy released in them by condensing water vapor.

In other ways, though, hurricanes are different from mid-latitude lows. A low forms and grows along fronts and gets energy from the air-mass contrast across the fronts. A hurricane has no fronts. Unlike the mid-latitude low, it has a central area of sinking air, known as the **eye** of the storm. The eye is usually 15 to 50 kilometers in diameter. The only clouds in the eye are stratocumulus at low levels and, sometimes, some cirrus at high levels. Because the air in the eye is sinking, there is no rain. There is almost no wind. The eye is surrounded by a bowl of cloudy material called the *eye wall.* Hurricanes have average diameters of 300 to 600 kilometers, smaller than a mid-latitude low. Finally, hurricanes are by definition intense. Their central pressures are lower and their wind speeds are larger than those of typical mid-latitude lows.

The winds increase toward the center of the hurricane and are most violent just outside the eye. Here, wind speeds may be greater than 240 kilometers an hour. The area of destructive winds may be as large as 800 kilometers across and 1600 kilometers long. Tornadoes and severe thunderstorms often occur as hurricanes come ashore.

Like the wind, the rainfall increases toward the center of the storm. It is heaviest just outside the eye.

In recent years, the loss of life due to hurricanes in the United States has been low. Only 30 people were killed during the 1985 hurricane season, even though six hurricanes came inland. Hurricane forecasts and warnings improve every year, but meteorologists think that the low death toll is partially luck. The population has increased so much in many beachfront areas that it is nearly impossible to evacuate everyone in time to avoid a major storm.

OBJECTIVES

- **A** Describe hurricanes and their life cycle.
- **B** Explain how hurricanes produce their damage.
- **C** Show how the Weather Service tracks hurricanes and differentiate between hurricane watches and warnings.
- **D** Specify the conditions necessary to produce a heavy snowfall.

30.5 The 1985 hurricane Elena, photographed from the space shuttle. Notice the cloud spiraling around the eye at the center.

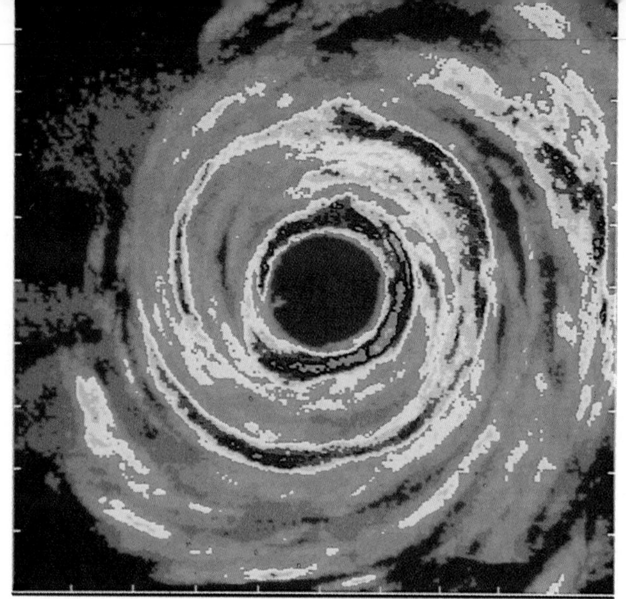

30.6 This image of the 1985 hurricane Elena was made from radar signals collected during several flights through the hurricane. The clear area in the center is the eye. It is surrounded by bands of rain; brighter colors indicate higher rainfall.

Topic 7 Sources and Tracks of Tropical Storms

Tropical storms form from tropical lows along the intertropical convergence zone. They get their energy from the heat and water vapor from the sea surface and from the release of heat by condensing water vapor. The strengthening storms usually move westward at about 10 to 20 kilometers an hour. If they move northward through the horse latitudes into the westerlies, they begin to travel eastward. Here, the hurricanes speed up and usually weaken as they encounter colder water. Cooler water supplies the storm with less heat and moisture. Also, cumulonimbus clouds do not grow as deep over cooler surfaces. Hurricanes also weaken when they move over land.

Many of the Atlantic hurricanes that affect the United States start as lows as far away as West Africa. The lows grow into hurricanes when they reach the warm waters of the western Atlantic, the Caribbean, or the Gulf of Mexico.

Before the days of satellites, North America's Pacific hurricanes were thought to be rare. However, eastern Pacific hurricanes are actually more common than the Atlantic ones. Pacific hurricanes form to the west of Mexico and mostly move westward. Occasionally they move as far north as California or as far west as Hawaii, but usually they weaken in mid-ocean.

Hurricanes are most common in the late summer and early fall because the ITCZ is farther north and the sea surface temperatures are warm. The paths that hurricanes and other tropical cyclones follow are shown in Figure 30.7.

Topic 8 Naming and Forecasting Hurricanes

Before 1953, hurricanes were identified only by their dates. From 1953 to 1979 hurricanes were identified by giving them female

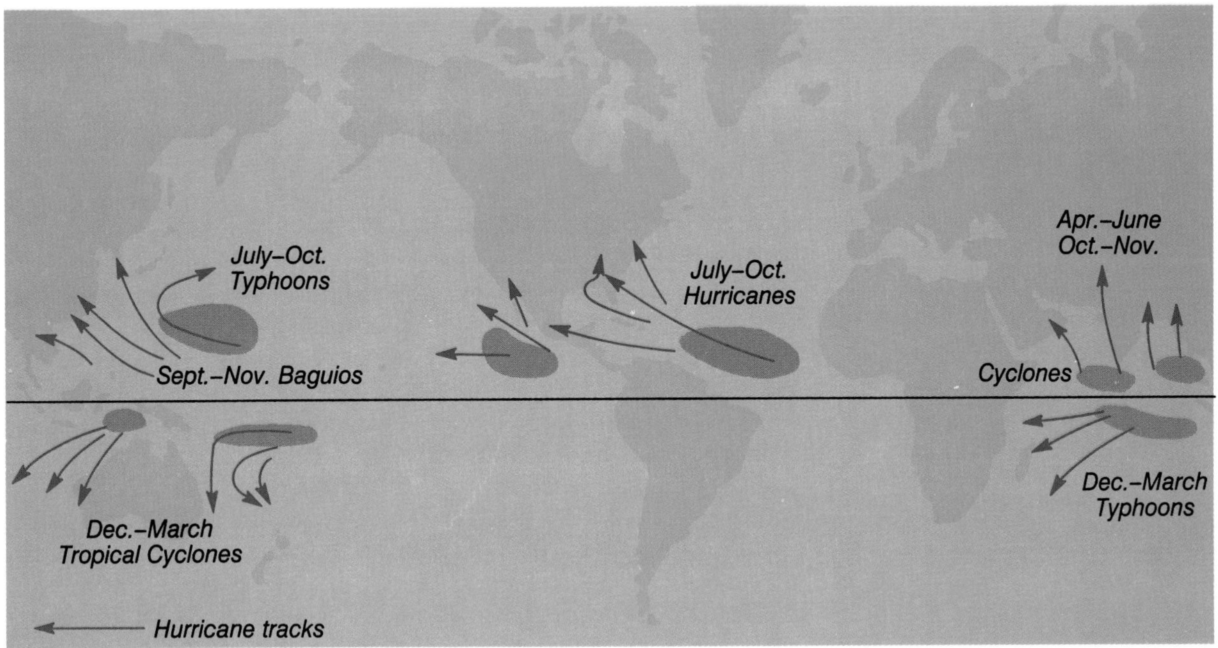

30.7 This map shows the names, tracks, and seasons for tropical storms. Notice the paths of hurricanes around North America.

names. In 1979, however, the National Weather Service began the present practice of using male names too. Two sets of six lists were prepared—one set for Atlantic hurricanes and the other for eastern Pacific hurricanes. Each set was to be used for six years from 1979–1984 and then repeated in each six-year cycle thereafter. If a particular hurricane is an exceptional one, its name will be retired and a new name substituted. Names are arranged alphabetically, with male and female names alternating.

The following is a list of Atlantic hurricane names for 1990 (to be repeated in 1996): Arthur, Bertha, Cesar, Diana, Edouard, Fran, Gustav, Hortense, Isodore, Josephine, Klaus, Lili, Marko, Nana, Omar, Paloma, Rene, Sally, Teddy, Vicky, and Wilfred.

A storm is named once it reaches tropical storm status (sustained winds of 65 kilometers per hour or greater). Once a storm is named, meteorologists watch it closely.

Early hurricane forecasts are important in protecting life and property. Several techniques are used to keep close watch on each hurricane and tropical storm as it grows and moves. Weather satellites are used to track hurricanes and estimate their strength and to spot new storms. Weather reconnaissance aircraft fly through hurricanes for direct measurements of storm strength. Also, when the hurricane is within a few hundred kilometers of a radar, the radar can be used to watch the hurricane.

Hurricane watches and warnings are issued by the National Hurricane Center in Miami, Florida. A watch means that hurricane conditions are expected within 24 hours. A 24-hour warning allows communities in the path of the hurricane to take precautions against potential damage from strong winds and floods.

30.8 A major snowstorm creates work for many people.

Topic 9 Winter Storms

Strong mid-latitude lows bring the winter's major snowstorms. However, two conditions must be met. First, there must be enough moisture. Second, the temperature must be cold enough for snow.

Mid-latitude lows are strongest in winter. Lows form and grow along the polar front. Strong lows form when the polar front is strong. The polar front is the strongest in the winter because the contrast between air masses is strongest. Fronts passing through in the winter give the greatest temperature changes.

Strong mid-latitude lows have minimum pressures around 980 millibars, with some stronger lows having pressures as low as 940 millibars. Since wintertime highs are also stronger, large pressure gradients and strong winds result.

A snowstorm with high winds and low temperatures is called a **blizzard.** The National Weather Service issues winter storm watches and warnings. The definition of winter storm varies with location.

The moisture supply for winter storms differs in different parts of the country. In the midwestern United States, much of the moisture comes from the Gulf of Mexico. To the west, on the Great Plains, water vapor from earlier snowfalls becomes more important. On the East Coast, there is ample moisture over the Atlantic. The West Coast storms are fed by moist air from the Pacific. In the winter, mountains get deep snows as moist air is forced upward on their windward sides.

A temperature difference of a few degrees can be the difference between heavy snow, mixed rain and snow, freezing rain, or rain. For this reason, predicting the amount and type of precipitation expected with a storm is difficult.

TOPIC QUESTIONS

Each topic question refers to the topic of the same number.

6. **(a)** What is a hurricane? How does it cause damage? **(b)** How are hurricanes and mid-latitude lows alike? How are hurricanes and mid-latitude lows different?

7. **(a)** Where and how do tropical storms form? **(b)** Describe the path of a hurricane, from its origin as a low-pressure area to its death. **(c)** When is the best time for Atlantic hurricanes to form? Why?

8. **(a)** How do meteorologists trace the path and strength of a hurricane? **(b)** What is the difference between a hurricane watch and a hurricane warning?

9. List the conditions necessary to produce a heavy snowfall.

III Forecasting and Weather Maps

Topic 10 Weather Forecasts in the United States

Daily weather forecasts are based on the results of computer models of the atmosphere. These computer models use data collected at the surface and data transmitted from the upper atmosphere by rawinsondes. The data are collected around the world at midnight and noon, Greenwich mean time (7:00 P.M. and 7:00 A.M. EST). Other data are provided by satellites and commercial aircraft. The models are run at the National Meteorological Center in Camp Springs, Maryland.

It takes about an hour to put the data in a form usable by the computer and another hour to run the models. Among the results of these models are maps showing highs, lows, and fronts in 12, 24, 36, and 48 hours. Maps are made for the surface and higher levels. Also produced are maps of model-predicted precipitation probabilities and amounts, high and low temperatures, and other aids to the forecaster. Using these data, forecasts are made in 50 Weather Service Forecast Offices around the country. These forecasts are modified to allow for conditions at local Weather Service Offices.

Major forecasts are made as soon as the new model results are ready, around midnight and in the afternoon. Two other forecasts are made in late morning and late evening. These are updates based on more current data. The afternoon and evening forecasts are timed to give television stations the latest information for their evening broadcasts. Forecasts are updated more often during rapid and important weather changes, such as the approach of a snowstorm or other type of severe weather.

Topic 11 Forecasting with Computers

Computer models are very important in making the daily forecasts. Computer models are now better than human forecasters at predicting the movements and strengths of highs and lows. However, human forecasters are still needed to forecast the weather events that come with the highs and lows.

What is a computer model? A **computer model** is a copy of the atmosphere in the computer. It contains data on the wind, temperature, pressure, humidity, clouds, and precipitation. Like most copies, the model lacks the detail of the original. In current models, the data are spaced at height intervals of about a kilometer. Horizontally, data points are 200 kilometers apart. Thus each point stands for a 200 × 200 × 1-kilometer block of atmosphere.

OBJECTIVES

A Explain how computer models, weather maps, satellites, and radars are used in watching and forecasting the weather.

B Describe how weather maps are made.

The model predicts future weather patterns. For example, at each point pressure changes from all possible causes are added up to make a total predicted pressure change. This change is added on to the old pressure to make a new, updated pressure. In the same way, other quantities, such as wind, are updated. This updating is done for each 5–10 minutes of "model time" in forecasting models. Standard forecasting models are used to make predictions from 12 hours to 10 days.

The models are not perfect for many reasons. First, the equations that predict the changes in each quantity are not perfect. Second, there are few measurements over the oceans and other areas where people do not live. Finally, the points in the model are too far apart to catch all the weather changes. For example, a thunderstorm affects the atmosphere in a fairly small area, so it can be missed easily with data spaced at points 200 kilometers apart.

Topic 12 Satellites and Radar in Weather Forecasting

Much of the weather missed by computer models and local weather observations is observed by satellites and radar. Satellites are used more and more to fill in data-poor regions in the models. Scientists are learning to obtain temperature and humidity measurements through much of the atmosphere by measuring the air's infrared radiation from satellite and ground stations.

Satellites provide continuous pictures of the clouds. These pictures make it possible to track lows, hurricanes, and even thunderstorms. Satellites are especially valuable over the ocean, where weather observations are difficult to make by other methods.

If a satellite is placed in an orbit 35 850 kilometers above the equator, its revolution will keep time with Earth's rotation. The satellite will be fixed over the same spot at all times. Such a satellite is said to be *geostationary*, meaning "stationary with respect to Earth." The United States has two such satellites in orbit, called GOES-East and GOES-West. (GOES stands for "Geostationary Operational Environmental Satellite.") They are positioned to get

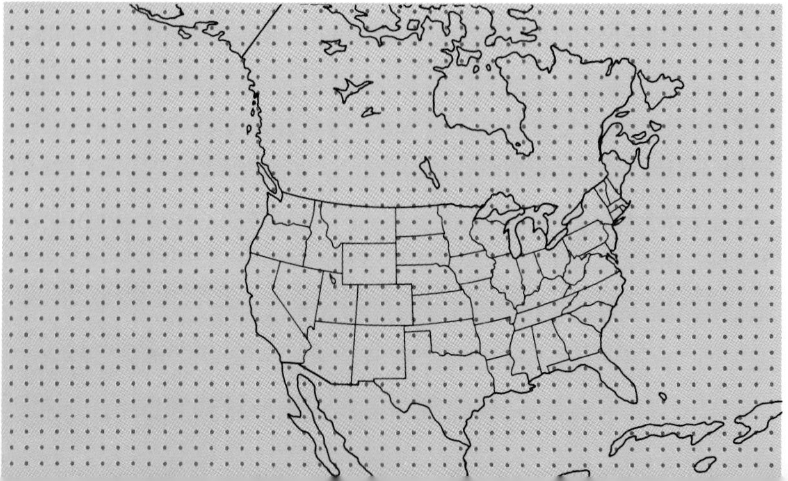

30.9 The widely spaced points or grid used in a forecast model

good pictures of all 50 states. Each satellite can see nearly half of Earth's surface. Every 30 minutes, its television cameras take infrared as well as visible pictures. The use of infrared photography allows good pictures to be taken 24 hours a day. Film loops from these satellites are used on television weather broadcasts.

How is radar used in observing the weather? Radar waves are reflected from precipitation particles. The radar screen shows the location of the precipitation and therefore the shape of precipitation areas. Heavier precipitation or larger particles show up as more intense radar returns, or "echoes." Thus radar can "see" thunderstorms, hurricanes, and other areas of precipitation. It also gives a rough idea of how heavy the precipitation is. Hurricane-penetrating aircraft use radar to locate the eye.

In the 1990's the Weather Service will be installing new Doppler radars around the country. These new radars will show echoes with more detail than before. They will also show the wind toward or away from the radar. How is this possible? Radar waves reflected from particles moving *toward* the radar have shorter wavelengths than radar waves reflected from particles moving *away from* the radar. In the same way, the sound of an approaching train whistle has a higher pitch (shorter-wavelength sound waves) than the sound of a train whistle going away. This effect is called the *Doppler effect,* after its discoverer, Johann Doppler.

The radar echoes and winds will show up on a color screen. Different echo strengths or wind speeds will show up as different colors. The different colors make it easier for the forecaster to spot strong thunderstorms and even tornadoes. Tests of these radars in Oklahoma show that the warning time for tornadoes is increased from around 2 minutes to 20 minutes. They will detect storms as far away as 460 kilometers and winds as far as 230 kilometers.

Topic 13 **Making a Surface Weather Map**

Surface weather maps are essential in following rapidly changing weather or in compensating for poor forecasts from computer models. The data for surface maps are taken hourly at stations all over the world. In the United States alone, surface data are gathered from about 600 National Weather Service Stations.

Official United States weather maps are drawn up every three hours, starting at 1:00 A.M. eastern standard time. After the station reports have been plotted, isobars and fronts are drawn in. Satellite cloud pictures help in finding the fronts and low centers over the ocean. Radar reports are used to add squall lines.

The official maps are made at the National Meteorological Center in Camp Springs, Maryland. They are sent by wire to all forecast centers and by radio or satellite to ships at sea. These maps are available to the public. University weather departments and private forecasters often receive the three-hour maps.

Hourly weather information is also transmitted. With this information, local forecast offices, private forecasters, and others watching the weather can prepare more current maps when needed.

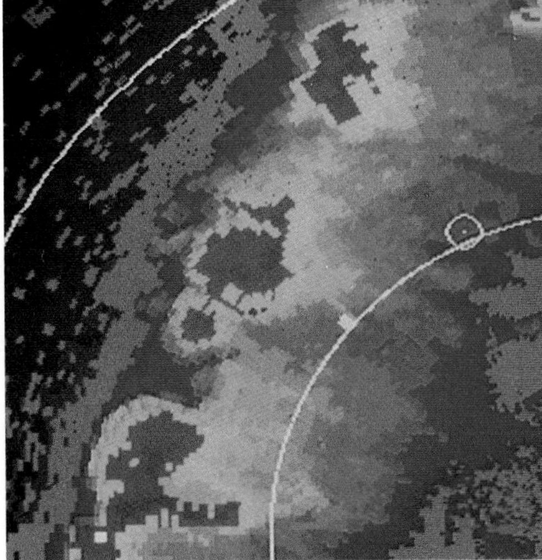

30.10 This is how a line of thunderstorms, or a squall line, appears on radar. From the outside toward the center, the different colors show the strength of the radar echo. Stronger echoes mean higher rainfall or bigger particles, and usually stronger vertical motions.

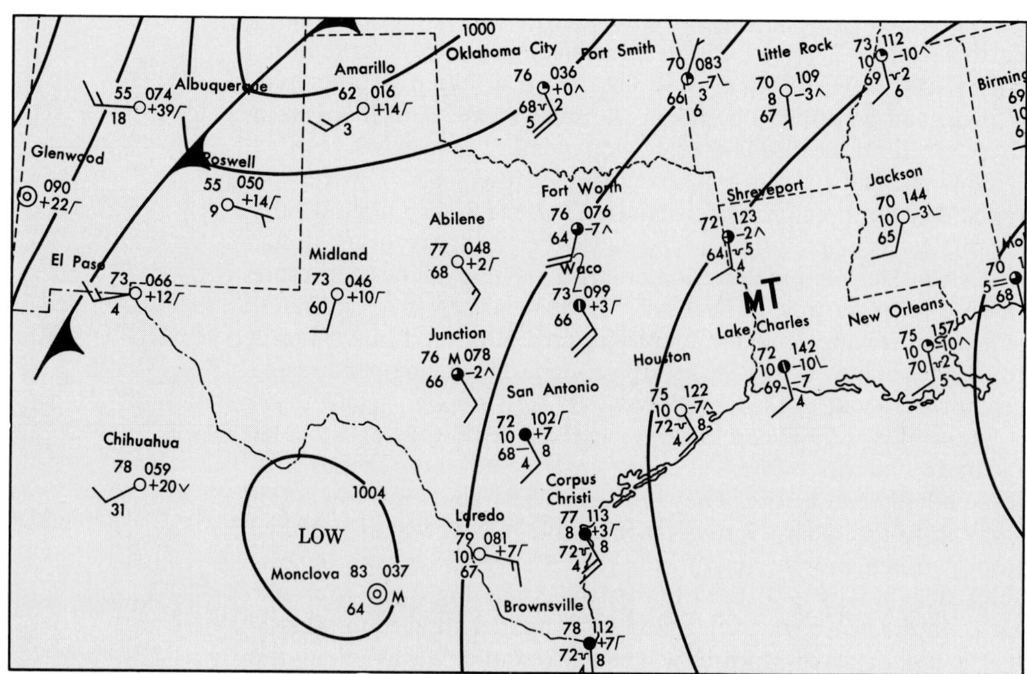

30.11 This is a portion of a printed National Weather Service surface map.

Topic 14 The Station Model

About 20 different weather observations may be plotted next to each station on a weather map. The National Weather Service arranges this information around the station in a form called the **station model.** Where possible, direct readings are given. In all other cases codes are used. Both station model and codes are based on those of the World Meteorological Organization. They can be read by meteorologists of any country. The coded information can be sent by wire or radio.

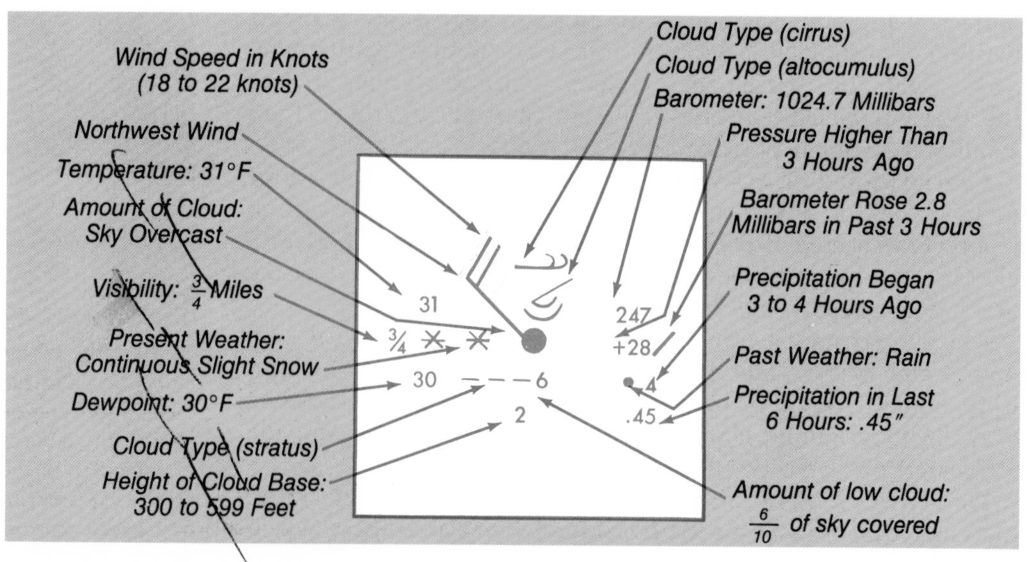

30.12 A station model. Review symbols for cloud cover, wind direction and speed, and precipitation.

TOPIC QUESTIONS

Each topic question refers to the topic of the same number.

10. Describe how daily weather forecasts are made in the United States.

11. **(a)** How does a computer model "copy" the atmosphere? **(b)** List some of the shortcomings of computer models.

12. **(a)** Why are radar and satellites important in observing the weather? **(b)** What do satellites observe? **(c)** What do the new Weather Service Doppler radars observe?

13. Describe how official surface weather maps are prepared in the United States.

14. What is a station model?

Map Skills

The following questions refer to the sequence of weather maps on pages 594–595 of Appendix B.

1. How did the skies over San Antonio change from January 29 to January 30?
2. Where was it snowing on January 31?
3. How many cold fronts are on the map for January 28?

Dr. Charles E. Anderson

Severe Storm Analyst

Can tornadoes be predicted? Dr. Charles E. Anderson of North Carolina State University is trying to learn enough about these severe storms to be able to predict them. He uses information obtained from tornadoes that have occurred in the past. Some of the information comes from photographs taken by satellites above Earth. Other information comes from radar on the ground. All of these data, along with the usual weather information on temperature, pressure, and winds, are placed in a MCIDAS (Man Computer Interactive Data Access System) computer. This special computer allows Dr. Anderson to view images of any level of the storm. In addition, data can be displayed with the image. By studying the air movements within the clouds of past storms, Dr. Anderson hopes to learn how to predict accurately the time and location of future tornadoes and other severe storms.

CHAPTER 30 REVIEW

Summary

Thunderstorms form from warm, moist air rising through unstable air. They can form singly or in groups.

Lightning is an electrical discharge from a thundercloud. Thunder results from the sudden expansion of air in the lightning channel.

Tornadoes are violent, small, funnel-shaped clouds with whirling winds as fast as 500 kilometers/hour. They occur with strong thunderstorms.

Conditions ideal for strong thunderstorms are unstable air that is moist at low levels, strong wind that increases with height, and an approaching cold front. When these conditions occur, the Weather Service issues a severe weather watch. A warning is issued if severe weather is detected.

Hurricanes start as lows along the ITCZ and grow over warm waters. They move with the prevailing winds and die over land or cold water.

Mid-latitude lows and hurricanes have similar pressure and wind patterns, but hurricanes have a central eye, are smaller and more intense, and do not have fronts.

Hurricanes are tracked with satellites, aircraft, and radars. Warnings are given when the hurricane is less than 24 hours offshore.

Heavy snows occur with strong lows when there is enough moisture and the temperature is below freezing.

Daily 12- to 48-hour forecasts are made with the help of computer-predicted weather patterns, updated by current surface maps and other observations.

Satellites provide wind, temperature, and humidity data, as well as cloud pictures.

Radars are used to spot and track severe weather and to locate precipitation areas. Newer radars measure wind toward and away from the radar.

The United States surface weather map has isobars and fronts, based mainly on plotted information from about 600 stations.

Vocabulary

air-mass thunderstorm
blizzard
computer model
eye
frontal thunderstorm
hurricane
severe thunderstorm
station model
storm surge
tornado
waterspout

Review

Number your paper from *1* to *20*. On your paper write the word or words that best complete each sentence.

1. Most frontal thunderstorms are associated with ______ fronts.
2. ______ thunderstorms are usually widely scattered single storms.
3. All thunderstorms produce ______, the discharge of ______ from a thundercloud.
4. Lightning generally strikes the ______ point above the ground.
5. The funnel of a tornado is a mixture of ______ and ______.
6. A ______ is the name given to a tornado that forms over water.
7. When a severe thunderstorm or tornado is possible, a ______ is issued; when a severe thunderstorm or tornado has been seen or detected, a ______ is issued.
8. A ______ is an intense storm, about 300–600 kilometers in diameter, with strong winds, heavy rains, and a central area called the ______.
9. ______ create the greatest damage associated with hurricanes.
10. Hurricanes grow ______ as they move over colder water or land.
11. A tropical storm is named once its winds exceed ______ kilometers per hour.
12. A low produces a major snowfall under two conditions: low ______ and sufficient ______.
13. New model results are used to make ______ major forecasts daily. Updated forecasts are made as many times as needed.

14. A computer ______ contains information about wind, temperature, pressure, humidity, clouds, and precipitation. It is used in making ______.
15. ______ and ______ are used to provide weather data that are missed by computer models and local observations.
16. ______ are especially helpful in collecting data over the oceans.
17. A ______ satellite is always above the same spot on Earth's surface.
18. The new Doppler radar provides information about ______ as well as ______, which is also supplied by earlier weather radars.
19. The data used in drawing surface weather maps are collected from weather stations once each ______.
20. The form in which weather data are arranged around a location on a weather map is called a ______.

Interpret and Apply

On your paper, answer each question in complete sentences.

1. How can the fact that hurricanes have no fronts be explained in terms of air masses?
2. What accounts for the heavy precipitation in tropical cyclones?
3. If thunder is heard 15 seconds after lightning is seen, how far away is the storm?
4. How can the time delay between lightning and thunder be used to prevent injury during a thunderstorm?
5. In what kind of air mass are air-mass thunderstorms most likely to develop?
6. In the Northern Hemisphere, the greatest damage caused by a hurricane occurs along the hurricane's right side. Why is this so?
7. Why do air-mass thunderstorms usually last less than an hour?
8. Heavy winter snowstorms occur on the eastern shores of the Great Lakes. What causes these snowstorms to occur there?

Critical Thinking

On your paper, answer each question in complete sentences.

1. You are a forecaster in Oklahoma. From 24 hours before a major tornado outbreak to the time it occurs, how will you use each of the following to foresee and then watch the tornado? (a) computer-model maps (b) rawinsonde data (c) the surface weather map (d) hourly weather observations (e) satellite data (f) radar
2. A hurricane approaches Florida from the east. Major thunderstorms and tornadoes break out to the north of the hurricane's eye, but things are relatively quiet to the south. What accounts for this difference?
3. The morning satellite pictures show Nebraska half-covered with low clouds and half clear. The 6:00 A.M. rawinsonde data show that both areas have similar temperatures and moisture and that the entire area is unstable aloft. Where are thunderstorms most likely, and why?
4. (a) Why do most thunderstorms occur in the late afternoon? (b) When and why might thunderstorms continue into the night?
5. Below are shown two station models. Interpret the station models and list the following information for each location: temperature, dew point, wind direction and speed, visibility, air pressure, sky conditions, and precipitation.

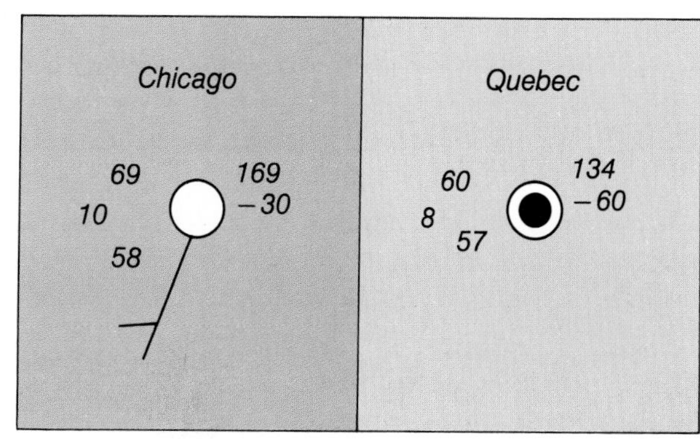

CHAPTER

31

Climate and Climate Change

▲
Home of the Pueblo Indians in a canyon in southwestern Colorado's Mesa Verde plateau

How Do You Know That . . .

The climate has not always been the same as it is today? Around ten centuries ago, the plateaus of Colorado and New Mexico were home to a thriving civilization. Dwellings at Mesa Verde, Chaco Canyon, and faint roads connecting Chaco Canyon to the ruins of outlying villages can still be seen today. The people, however, disappeared around A.D. 1300, victims of a drying climate.

What determines our climate? Will it change in our lifetimes, either naturally or through the effects of people? In order to answer these questions, you need to know about the factors that control the climate of different parts of the world and the factors that cause climate change.

I Climate and Climate Controls

OBJECTIVES

A Define *climate* and explain how to calculate daily and yearly temperature ranges.

B Show how to describe an area's climate.

C Summarize the factors that control climate and climate change.

Topic 1 What Is Climate?

A description of the general weather of an area includes many factors. Among these are how hot the summers are, how cold the winters are, and how much precipitation falls at different times of the year. Such a description also includes how the precipitation occurs—in thunderstorms, as gentle rain, or in the form of snow.

The overall weather of an area is its **climate.** The two main factors that determine climate are temperature and rainfall. However, the number of days and hours of sunlight; the direction, speed, and steadiness of the wind; and even the amount of pollution also help define an area's climate.

Numbers, or statistics, are used to compare climates in different parts of the world. To find out how hot or cold a climate is, an average temperature is useful. *Average temperatures* are found by adding two or more readings and dividing by the number of readings. Average temperatures are calculated daily, monthly, and yearly.

The *daily temperature range* is the difference between the highest and lowest temperatures of the day. The *yearly temperature range* is the difference between the average of the warmest month and the coldest month.

Topic 2 Use of Variation in Describing Climate

Averages and ranges alone do not provide a complete picture of a climate. A description of how the weather varies is also important. For example, Beijing (formerly called Peking), China, and Valdivia, Chile, have almost identical yearly average temperatures of 11.7°C. In Beijing, January averages -4°C and July averages 26°C. Compare these with the mild 8°C and 17°C averages for the coldest and warmest months in Valdivia. In Beijing the annual range in temperature is 30°C; in Valdivia it is only 9°C. Certainly their climates are not the same. Similar contrasts exist in the United States between cities on the East Coast and cities on the West Coast, such as New York City and Portland, Oregon.

Bombay, India, has a yearly rainfall of about 188 centimeters. Mobile, Alabama, has almost as much rain, about 173 centimeters.

31.1 The graph shows that although the average yearly temperatures of Beijing, China, and Valdivia, Chile, are the same, their climates are quite different. The cities are about the same distance from the equator.

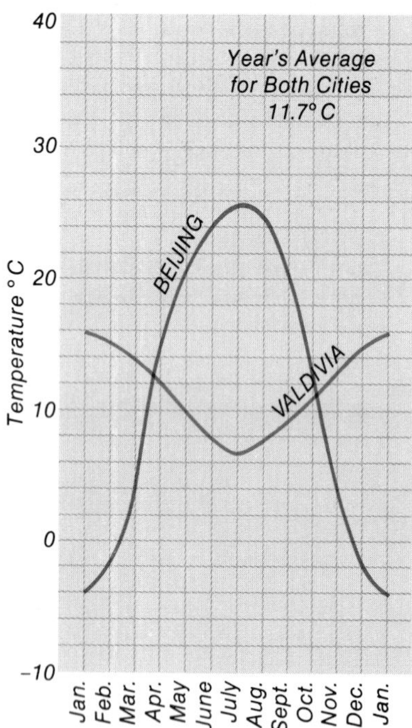

However, almost all of Bombay's rains fall in a monsoon season of four summer months. In Mobile the rains are spread throughout the year. No month averages less than 7.6 centimeters of rain.

It is clear that climate is not necessarily the same as average weather. Climate cannot be described accurately without gathering more information.

Topic 3 Climate Controls

The temperature and rainfall patterns of present-day Earth depend upon a set of conditions called climate controls. The six main climate controls are the following:

1. latitude;
2. altitude;
3. prevailing winds;
4. topography;
5. distance from large bodies of water (oceans, lakes);
6. nearby ocean currents.

For a particular area, some factors are more important than others. For example, nearby ocean currents are not important to the climate high in the Rocky Mountains, but altitude and topography are.

Over long periods of time, the climate changes. The global climate is related to the amount of solar energy Earth absorbs. The local climate is related to the global climate as well as to the six climate controls. All six can change over geologic time. For example, mountain-building and erosion change the topography and altitude of an area. Plate tectonics changes the latitude of land areas and also changes the ocean currents. The positions of continents, ice, and cloud cover are among the factors that determine the amount of sunlight Earth absorbs. All the overlapping causes of climate make sorting the causes of past climates very hard.

TOPIC QUESTIONS

Each topic question refers to the topic of the same number.

1. **(a)** What is climate? **(b)** Define *daily temperature range* and *yearly temperature range.*
2. **(a)** Why don't averages give a complete picture of climate? **(b)** How can two cities have the same average temperature but very different climates? **(c)** How can two cities have nearly the same yearly rainfall but very different climates?
3. **(a)** Name six factors that control climate in a region. **(b)** What controls the global climate?

II Factors That Control Temperature

Topic 4 How Latitude Controls Temperature

Latitude is the distance in degrees (north or south) from the equator. The yearly temperature range and average yearly temperature depend mainly on latitude.

At a location within 5 or 10 degrees of the equator, the sun shines for about 12 hours each day and each night is about 12 hours long. At noon the sun is never very far from being directly overhead. The climate is hot throughout the year, and the average temperature is very high, about 27°C. There are no summers and winters, only rainy seasons and dry seasons. The yearly range of temperature is only 3° or 4°C.

At a location 40 or 45 degrees from the equator, there are 15 or 16 hours of sunshine in July. Nights are only 8 or 9 hours long. Six months later the sun shines only 8 or 9 hours a day and nighttime lasts 15 or 16 hours. On the average the yearly temperature is far lower than it is near the equator. However, the annual range of temperature may be large—as much as 30°C.

In the polar regions most of the sunshine comes in a day that lasts for many months. The winter includes an equally long night. In summer the sun is never high in the sky, so it provides little heating. It goes completely around the sky each day but does not dip below the horizon. Temperatures change very little for days at a time. The summer is comparatively mild. When the long winter night comes, however, the weather becomes very cold. In these latitudes the average annual temperature is very low. The annual temperature range is very large, but the daily temperature range is very small.

Figure 31.2 on page 518 shows the relationship between latitude and yearly temperature range. In general, the higher the latitude, the lower the average yearly temperature and the larger the yearly temperature range.

Topic 5 Altitude and Temperature

Altitude is height above sea level. Its effect on temperature is somewhat like that of latitude. On the average, temperatures drop about 1°C for every 160 meters of altitude. The higher the altitude, the lower the average yearly temperature.

For example, Vera Cruz and Mexico City have the same latitude but very different climates. Vera Cruz, at sea level in the tropics, is hot and humid. Mexico City, 2300 meters above sea level, is pleasantly cool even in summer.

OBJECTIVES

A Show the relationship between latitude and average temperature and between latitude and daily and yearly temperature ranges.

B Differentiate between marine and continental climates.

C Discuss the effects of altitude, prevailing winds, topography, and ocean currents on climate.

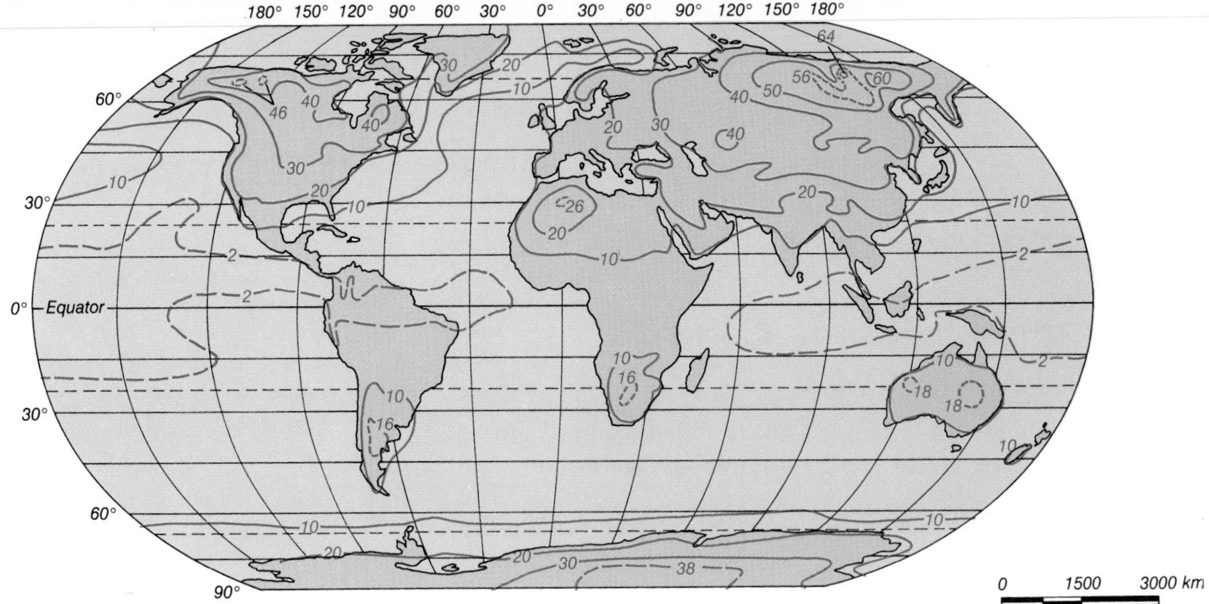

31.2 Average annual range of surface air temperatures (in degrees Celsius)

Topic 6 Land, Sea, and Temperature

Land gains and loses heat much more quickly than water. Land areas in the middle latitudes tend to have hot summers and cold winters. As shown in Figure 31.2, the annual average temperature ranges of land areas are larger than those for the oceans at the same latitudes. These land areas with large yearly temperature ranges have **continental climates**. Areas near the ocean, on the other hand, have small yearly temperature ranges. These areas have **marine climates.**

Reykjavik (RAKE-yuh-vik), Iceland, 64°N, and Verkhoyansk (vyer-koh-YANSK), Siberia, 68°N, are at nearly the same latitude. Reykjavik is on the south coast of Iceland. Its marine climate has an annual temperature range of only 11°C. Verkhoyansk is deep in the interior of the great Asian landmass. It has a continental climate with an annual temperature range of almost 67°C.

In summary, ocean areas have marine climates with small yearly temperature ranges. Continental interiors have continental climates with large yearly temperature ranges.

Topic 7 Prevailing Winds and Temperature

The west coasts of continents in the middle latitudes have marine climates. The prevailing westerlies blow at these latitudes. When they come from the ocean, they carry maritime air masses onto the west coasts of continents and large islands. Air masses from the Pacific Ocean are carried over the west coasts of North America and South America. Air masses from the Atlantic Ocean are carried over the west coasts of the British Isles and Europe. Portland, Oregon, and London, England, have marine climates.

How far inland does a marine climate reach? The distance depends chiefly on the topography. Usually, a marine climate reaches no farther than the first high mountain range. Beyond the mountains, the continental interiors have continental climates.

In middle latitudes, east coasts do not have marine climates. Most of the air masses that come to east coasts are brought by the prevailing westerlies from the interiors of the continents. As a result, east coasts have continental climates. Their temperatures are only slightly moderated by the ocean. Boston and New York, for example, are on the Atlantic Coast. Nevertheless, their summers and winters are nearly as extreme as those of the interior of the continent.

In summary, in the latitudes of the prevailing westerlies, west coasts have marine climates with cool summers and mild winters. East coasts have continental climates with hot summers and cold winters.

Topic 8 Topography and Temperature

Mountain ranges may block wind that could affect temperature. For example, the marine climate of the western United States reaches no farther inland than the Coast Ranges. The Sacramento Valley lies just east of the Coast Ranges, not far from the Pacific Ocean. Nevertheless, it has intensely hot summers and cold winters.

Southern Italy has mild winters, mainly because the Alps keep out cold winds from the north. On the Great Plains of Canada and the United States, just the opposite situation occurs. The plains have no mountain range running across them to block winds from the north. Therefore, winter cold waves, with icy winds from the Arctic, may reach all the way to the Gulf of Mexico.

Topic 9 Ocean Currents and Temperature

Ocean currents may be considerably warmer or colder than the normal surface air temperatures for their latitudes. Warm currents have an effect on the places they pass. Their effect is greatest when the prevailing winds blow from the water to the land. For example, the warm *Gulf Stream* heats the air above it. The prevailing westerlies blow the warmed air to the shores of Iceland, the British Isles, and Scandinavia. As a result, these regions are as warm as places that are closer to the equator. London, England, is about 1100 kilometers nearer the North Pole than Cleveland, Ohio. Nevertheless, its average annual temperature is higher than Cleveland's.

Cold currents also affect temperature. Northern Labrador is chilled by the *Labrador Current*. Its yearly average temperature is more than 11°C lower than that of Stockholm, Sweden, which is at the same latitude.

31.3 Current meters are used to determine the speed, direction, and properties of both surface and subsurface currents.

TOPIC QUESTIONS

Each topic question refers to the topic of the same number.

4. Explain the relationship between latitude and each of the following: **(a)** average yearly temperature, **(b)** average yearly range in temperature, **(c)** average daily range in temperature.
5. **(a)** How does altitude affect temperature? **(b)** Why is Vera Cruz warmer than Mexico City?
6. How do the annual temperature ranges of marine climates and continental climates differ?
7. **(a)** How do prevailing winds determine whether a climate is marine or continental? **(b)** Compare the climates of the eastern and western coasts of the United States.
8. Southern Italy and Nebraska are at the same latitude. How might topography help to explain the difference in their climates?
9. **(a)** How do ocean currents affect temperatures? **(b)** Give examples to show the temperature effects of the Gulf Stream and the Labrador Current.

Marjorie McGuirk
Meteorologist

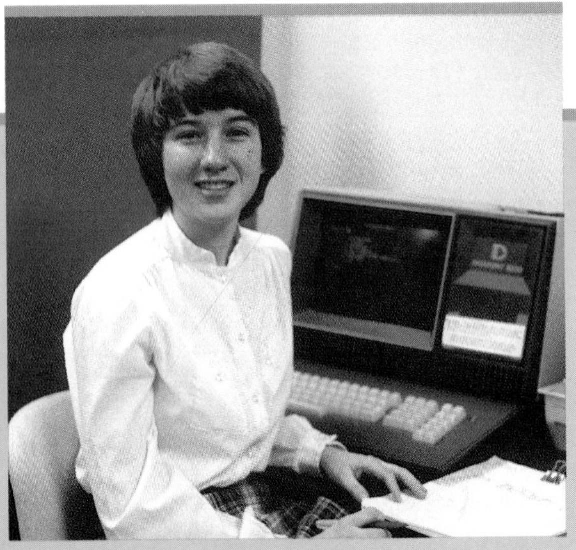

An important part of the study of weather and climate is making and keeping a record of day-to-day conditions. For the United States, that record is collected and kept by the National Climatic Data Center in Asheville, North Carolina. Marjorie McGuirk is a meteorologist there. She says that the center has three primary functions—to collect and record global weather data, to supply these data to anyone who needs them, and to use these data to describe the climate.

Weather data come to the center from a variety of sources. These include the National Weather Service, weather services of the U.S. Air Force and Navy, the Federal Aviation Administration, and the Coast Guard, as well as data from individual observers. With the help of computers, Ms. McGuirk and others at the center study, classify, and organize the data before storing them on magnetic tape or microfiche, or in some other form. At the same time, many of the common weather elements (temperature, precipitation, wind, and so on) are immediately summarized and published. Each year the National Climatic Data Center sends out over one million copies of its many publications to interested subscribers around the world.

III Factors That Control Rainfall

Topic 10 Latitude, Prevailing Winds, and Rainfall

The prevailing wind belts cause precipitation at some latitudes and dryness at other latitudes. Compare the map of the global winds in Figure 28.12 (page 479) to Figures 31.4 and 31.5.

Yearly rainfall is high in the tropics. The precipitation in the tropics follows the pattern of the prevailing winds. The air in the doldrums rises slowly, forced upward by the coming together (convergence) of the northeast and southeast trade winds. This rising air causes almost-daily thunderstorms over the continents. Over the ocean the precipitation is more concentrated in a roughly 300-kilometer-wide band. This band is the most organized part of the intertropical convergence zone (ITCZ), so called because the winds from the two hemispheres mostly converge there (see Chapter 28).

The position of the ITCZ varies with the seasons. The ITCZ reaches its northernmost point around 10° to 20° N in the Northern Hemisphere summer. It moves down to 10°–20° S during the Southern Hemisphere summer. Therefore, in each hemisphere the summer is the rainy season for the area about 10–20 degrees from the equator.

To the north and south of the ITCZ, the rainfall decreases. The air flows outward (diverges) from the horse latitudes. Some of the diverging air flows toward the poles as westerlies; some flows toward the equator as the trade winds. Air sinks to replace the diverging air at the surface. Since clouds and rain cannot form in sinking air, many of the world's great deserts – the desert of Southwest Africa, the desert of the Australian interior, and the Sahara – lie about 20 to 35 degrees from the equator.

OBJECTIVES

A Correlate the world rainfall patterns with the prevailing wind belts.

B Describe the effects of mountains on rainfall and humidity.

C Explain the effects of nearby oceans on precipitation.

D Discuss the relationship between ocean currents and fogs.

31.4 This satellite image of Earth's clouds shows the change of precipitation patterns with latitude. The belt of clouds around the equator is the ITCZ, where much rain falls. At higher latitudes, precipitation falls around traveling low-pressure systems, which look like commas.

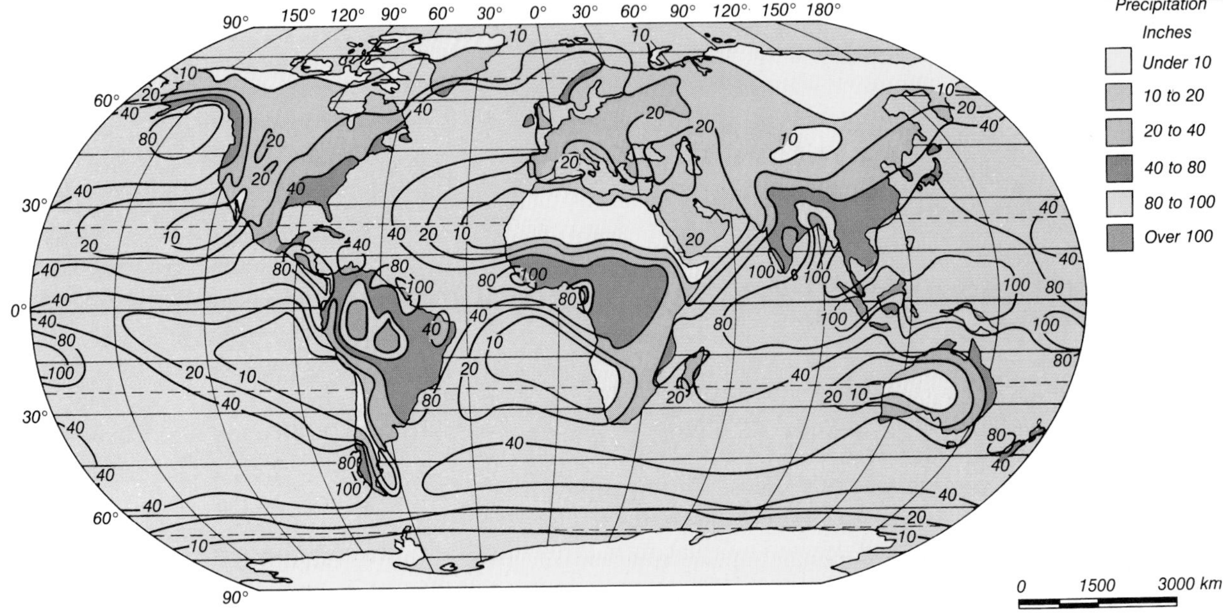

31.5 Earth's pattern of annual precipitation

The pattern of precipitation in the middle latitudes, from about 30 to 65 degrees, is strongly related to the passage of low-pressure areas. A second band of convergence lies between the polar easterlies and the westerlies. The convergence is concentrated in the polar front. Precipitation falls in the rising air along the front, mostly in the traveling low-pressure areas that form along it. The position of the polar front has an enormous range of latitude. In winter it can reach as far south as about 20 degrees from the equator. In summer it is about 65 degrees from the equator. The polar front is also far less regular than the ITCZ.

The polar easterlies flow from the poles to about 65 degrees. This diverging air is replaced by sinking air from above. The very cold air at the poles can hold little water vapor. Therefore, precipitation in the high latitudes (near the poles) is light in all seasons. It comes almost entirely in low-pressure areas.

Topic 11 **Mountains and Rainfall**

The prevailing westerlies and trade winds cause consistent patterns of precipitation along mountain chains. Rising air makes the *windward* side of a mountain – its side toward the wind – rainy. Sinking air makes the side of the mountain away from the wind – its *leeward* side – dry.

The trade winds blow from the northeast in the Northern Hemisphere and from the southeast in the Southern Hemisphere. In the trade-wind belts, the rainy windward sides are:

Northern Hemisphere: northern slopes, eastern slopes
Southern Hemisphere: southern slopes, eastern slopes

For this reason, the east coasts of Africa, South America, and Central America have heavy rains.

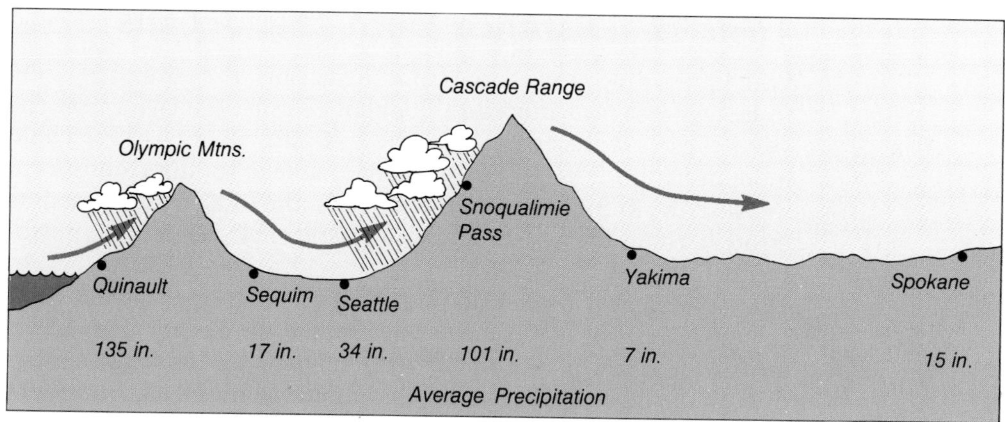

31.6 The distribution of the average annual precipitation in the state of Washington is determined by the mountains and the prevailing west wind.

In the prevailing westerlies, relatively strong highs and lows frequently interrupt the prevailing winds. However, on the average, the rainy windward sides of the mountains are these:

Northern Hemisphere: southern slopes, western slopes
Southern Hemisphere: northern slopes, western slopes

The summer *monsoon* dominates the precipitation pattern in the Himalayan Mountains and India. Southwest monsoon winds bring rain to the western slopes of the Western Ghats range along India's west coast. The monsoon winds become southeasterly in the northern Bay of Bengal to the east of India. These winds bring heavy rain to the southern part of the Himalayan Mountains in summer.

Because the water falls out of the air on the windward side of the mountains, the leeward slopes are very dry. They are also warmer than the windward slopes. The leeward slopes are warmer because the raining air traveling up the mountain cools only 0.6°C for each 100 meters it rises. When the dried-out air sinks on the leeward side of the mountains, it warms at a faster rate – 1°C for each 100 meters. Warm, dry winds formed in this way often blow down the eastern slopes of the Rocky Mountains and the northern part of the Swiss Alps. These winds are called **chinooks** (shin-OOKS) in the Rockies. In Europe, they are called **foehns** (ferns). Similar winds blowing down the Santa Ana Mountains south of Los Angeles are called **Santa Anas.**

When chinooks arrive, they can raise the temperature 20°C in 15 minutes. They melt snow and can cause avalanches. If they blow too long, forests, fields, and buildings dry out. Then a careful watch must be kept against fire. However, chinooks can also make winters milder.

Not all winds blowing down mountains are warm. Some start out so cold that even after heating by compression they remain unpleasantly cold. One such wind is the **mistral** that blows down from the Alps to the Mediterranean Sea. Another is the **bora** that blows down from the mountains of Yugoslavia to the Adriatic Sea. Boras sometimes blow down the eastern slope of the Rockies.

Topic 12 Distance from the Oceans

When prevailing winds blow from the oceans, the rainfall is likely to be heaviest near the shore. Rainfall is usually heavier near the warmer parts of the ocean. Here the air is also warmer and can hold more moisture. The air is also more unstable, so rain clouds form more easily. In the eastern United States, the total yearly rainfall is greatest along the coast. There is less rainfall inland and northward.

Locations near oceans do not always have heavy rainfall. Even though the desert of Peru is located beside the Pacific Ocean, it is one of the driest places in the world. There are three reasons for this. First, the southeast trade winds come from the dry interior of the continent, not from the Pacific Ocean. Second, the desert is on the leeward (western) side of the Andes. Third, the prevailing winds off the coast cause a cold upwelling ocean current. The cold water cools the lowest layer of air. The resulting temperature inversion—warm air from the east over cool air from the nearby ocean—traps the ocean's moisture near the ground and prevents rain clouds from forming.

The eastern interior of North America has more precipitation in the summer than in the winter. The main reason is that in the summer, prevailing winds carry moisture northward from the Gulf of Mexico. A second reason is that thundershowers happen more often in summer because the ground is hotter.

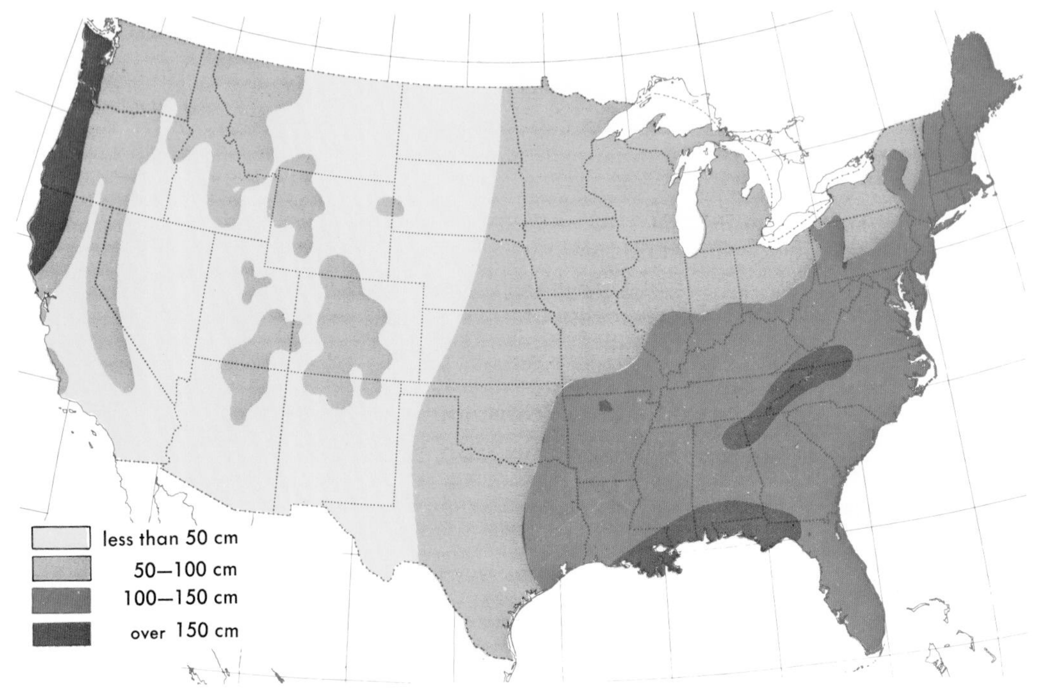

31.7 The map shows average annual rainfall in the continental United States. In the far west, rainfall is controlled mainly by mountain ranges. In the interior and eastern parts of the country, rainfall increases closer to the Atlantic Ocean and the Gulf of Mexico.

Topic 13 Ocean Currents and Fogs

Warm air flowing over cold water makes rainfall unlikely in places like Peru. However, warm moist air over a colder surface often produces fogs. Ocean currents often help set up these conditions. The frequent winter fogs of England and Scotland are an example. These fogs form when warm moist air from the Gulf Stream blows over the cold land.

The summer fogs along the New England coast are another example. They form when warm air moving north is cooled over New England's cold coastal waters. The fogs of Newfoundland form when warm air from the Gulf Stream blows over the icy Labrador Current. The summer fogs of the Pacific coasts of the United States, Peru, and northern Chile are also examples. They form when warm ocean winds blow over cold upwelling coastal waters. In general, fogs form where ocean currents are much warmer or much colder than the adjoining land or water.

TOPIC QUESTIONS

Each topic question refers to the topic of the same number.

10. **(a)** Why do the latitudes near the equator have dry and wet seasons? **(b)** Why are the latitudes from 20–30° N or S dry all year? **(c)** What factors affect rainfall in the middle latitudes? **(d)** What factors affect rainfall in the polar latitudes?

11. **(a)** Which are the dry and rainy sides of mountain chains? **(b)** Which is the rainy side of the Western Ghats Mountains of India? Why is the rainy side different from other mountain chains of the trade-wind zone? **(c)** Explain why a chinook is warm and dry.

12. **(a)** Describe the relationship between wind and rainfall in coastal areas. **(b)** Why does the eastern interior of North America have more precipitation in summer than in winter?

13. **(a)** What conditions produce fogs? **(b)** How are the fogs over England and Scotland formed? **(c)** How are the fogs over New England and Newfoundland formed?

Map Skills

The following questions refer to the map of Earth's Climates on page 596 of Appendix B.

1. At what latitudes are most of the world's major deserts?
2. **(a)** At around 40° N, where are the marine climates? **(b)** Compare the extent of the marine climate in Europe and North America.
3. At what latitudes are the most humid climates?

OBJECTIVES

A Relate changes in climate to Earth's energy budget.

B Identify some causes of short- and long-term climate changes.

C Explain why Earth's climate has been stable for 4 billion years.

IV Climate Change

Topic 14 Sources of Climate Change

The weather varies a lot from day to day and season to season. So it is hard to tell without averaging numbers whether the climate is changing. But what averages are most useful? Is Earth's climate getting warmer? Scientists are using the study of past climate changes to make predictions about future climate changes.

Earth's climate changes with its energy budget. Right now Earth's energy budget is in approximate balance (see Chapter 26, Topic 8). That is, the incoming solar radiation (insolation) is equal to the energy Earth loses to space. To see what can change the balance, one must look at the processes involved. First, solar radiation hits Earth and its atmosphere. Second, Earth loses energy by reflection of sunlight from its surface and from clouds, dust, and air molecules in the atmosphere. Third, Earth's surface, clouds, and atmosphere lose infrared radiation (heat) to space. And fourth, *greenhouse gases,* such as carbon dioxide, let sunlight in but keep infrared radiation from escaping to space. A change in any of these four processes can change the climate.

Scientists know more and more about the climate changes of the past. They have also been able to relate some past climates to specific changes in Earth's heat budget. The next three topics discuss climate changes over three sets of time scales: *short-term* climate changes, which last from 10 to 20 years or less, climate changes that have occurred over *historic time* (within the last 5000 years), and climate changes over geologic time.

Topic 15 Short-Term Climate Changes

Short-term climate changes last from 10 to 20 years or less. They can be seen in official weather records from around the world. A short-term climate change can involve either cooling or warming.

An explosive volcanic eruption can cool the temperatures at Earth's surface a few tenths of a degree Celsius for a period of a few years. Eruptions release dust and sulfur dioxide gas into the stratosphere. The dust and sulfuric acid droplets that form from the sulfur dioxide screen out sunlight but let Earth's heat escape to space. It usually takes several weeks after an eruption for the volcanic material to spread over Earth's stratosphere. The particles remain in the atmosphere for about one to seven years. They stay in the atmosphere so long because the particles cannot be washed out by rain until they fall from the stratosphere into the troposphere. Because of their tiny size and great height, the particles take a long time to settle out of the stratosphere. The greatest cooling occurs during the first year after the eruption. Then temperatures slowly return to normal as the particles settle out.

The Krakatoa eruption in 1883 lowered global temperatures by about 0.5°C, with more cooling at higher latitudes. This is typical of the great eruptions of the last few hundred years, each of which lowered mid-latitude temperatures between 0.1°C and 1°C.

A factor that causes short-term warming is the El Niño. The **El Niño** (ell NEEN-yo) is the warming of the ocean surface off the western coast of South America. Normally, the Pacific high-pressure system causes *upwelling* to occur. Cold, nutrient-rich water rises to the surface and provides a feeding ground for fish. When the Pacific high-pressure system weakens, the upwelling does not occur. The resulting warmer water holds fewer nutrients, and the fish that feed on them disappear. The decrease in the numbers of fish devastates the Peruvian fishing industry.

The warming spreads across the eastern equatorial Pacific Ocean. It covers such a large area that scientists are searching for connections to the weather in the rest of the world. The El Niño may cause abnormal warmth in Alaska and western Canada. It may also cause more Pacific lows to hit the California coast instead of going farther north. El Niños occur between 4 and 12 years apart and last from 1 to 2 years.

31.8 An individual volcanic eruption, such as this eruption of Mt. Veniaminof in Alaska, may cool the atmosphere for two to seven years.

Topic 16 Climate Changes over Historic Time

Historical climate changes are described in the written record. Since the 1600's, thermometers, barometers, and rain gauges have provided climate records. Clues about climate before then come from diaries, records of farming transactions, accounts of battles, and other historical records.

Significant climate changes have taken place in the last thousand years. In Europe and North America there was a very warm period between about A.D. 1000 and 1200. Then some cooling took place from 1200 to 1300. This 100-year period was followed by an even colder period from 1500 to 1900, and then by another warming from 1900 to the present.

During the first warm period, around A.D. 1000, the Scandinavians explored and settled North America and Greenland. Also during this period, American Indians east of the Rockies were able to farm as far north as Wisconsin and Minnesota. In the Colorado Plateau and northern New Mexico, the climate allowed agriculture to flourish. The people who built the pueblos in Chaco Canyon and Mesa Verde reached their greatest numbers.

The cooling from 1200 to 1300 sharply reduced the area of farmland. Glaciers advanced. The cooling of the northern latitudes strengthened the westerlies, causing the dry area on the leeward side of the Rockies to extend as far east as Illinois. The result of the decrease in precipitation was a decrease in population. In the Southwest, the decrease in land for farming caused the people to move to other areas. The human population nearly vanished.

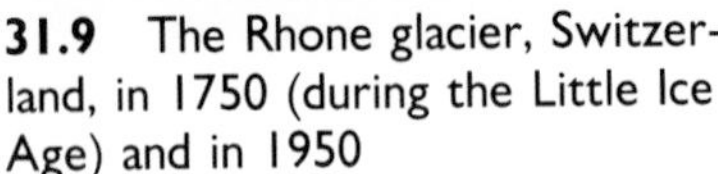

31.9 The Rhone glacier, Switzerland, in 1750 (during the Little Ice Age) and in 1950

Another cool period—the so-called Little Ice Age—occurred between 1500 and 1900. Glaciers in Europe and North America again advanced. Many settlers and American Indians in the northeastern part of the present-day United States died from the extremely cold winters in the 1600's.

The climate became steadily warmer between 1900 and 1950, and then from 1950 to 1970 the average temperature began to lower. Since 1970, however, the trend is not clear. If the increase in carbon dioxide and other greenhouse gases is the most important factor controlling the climate, warming will continue. The concentration of carbon dioxide in the atmosphere increased 13 percent from the 1880's to 1980, and it continues to increase. If this increase continues, scientists predict that the annual average temperature could be 2° to 11°C warmer by the year 2100. This prediction does not account for the other greenhouse gases, such as chlorofluorocarbons, methane, and nitrous oxide, which are also increasing. A warming climate would result in melting of the ice caps and a rise in sea level. Coastal cities would be flooded.

Topic 17 Climate Changes over Geologic Time

Climate changes that occur over periods of 10 thousand years and longer are revealed in the rock record. Fossils of land animals and the glacial deposits are among the clues that reveal air temperature. Sea temperature, also a clue to the past climate, is revealed from fossils of marine animals and plants.

Glacial deposits and fossils for the last billion years show a pattern of alternating periods of mild weather and widespread glaciation. Each period was about 100 million years long. No one knows for certain the causes of climate change at these very long time scales. Of course, there were shorter-term changes during these times as well. However, clues to the shorter-term climate changes become rarer going further back in time.

31.10 Glacial till and striated rock on the Sahara Desert. When the glaciation occurred, about 440 million years ago, part of what is now the Sahara straddled the South Pole.

On these very long time scales, scientists explaining past climates must account for mountain-building, erosion, and especially the positions of the continents. Plate tectonics, for example, makes it much easier to explain why there are glacial features in the Sahara Desert and dinosaur fossils in Antarctica. Volcanic activity also varies over geologic time.

From earlier than 4 billion years ago to the present, Earth's climate has been relatively stable, with alternating warm and cold periods. Two very large and opposite factors – one warming and one cooling – have affected Earth's climate. First, the sun's radiation has increased steadily since about 4.5 billion years ago. At that time, it radiated only about 70 percent of its present-day output. The increased radiation would probably have warmed the atmosphere except for the second factor – the large decrease in carbon dioxide over 2 billion years ago. This decrease was at least partially due to the appearance of early plants. These plants added oxygen to the atmosphere and removed the carbon dioxide.

TOPIC QUESTIONS

Each topic question refers to the topic of the same number.

14. **(a)** What happens when Earth's energy budget changes? **(b)** List four ways in which Earth's energy budget can change.

15. **(a)** Explain how volcanoes cause short-term climate changes. **(b)** How big are the short-term changes? How long do they last? **(c)** What is the El Niño? **(d)** Give some examples of how the weather in North America changes during an El Niño.

16. **(a)** Briefly summarize the climate changes since A.D. 1000. **(b)** List some historical events that might have been related to the warm period from A.D. 1000 to 1200. **(c)** Explain how the cooling from 1200 to 1300 affected the people of North America. **(d)** What is one possible reason that the climate has been warming for most of the twentieth century?

17. **(a)** Explain why Earth's overall climate has not changed significantly for the last 4 billion years. **(b)** Name three geologic processes that affected past climates.

CHAPTER 31 REVIEW

Summary

The climate of a region is the overall description of the weather experienced there.

Many factors act together to determine Earth's climate. They are latitude, altitude, topography, distance from large bodies of water, ocean currents, prevailing winds, and the amount of heat received from the sun.

Temperatures are cooler with larger yearly ranges at high latitudes, but the daily temperature range is lower.

Ocean currents can affect an area's temperature.

The windward sides of mountains are moister than their leeward sides. Mountains can keep cold air from reaching an area, making the winters milder.

Precipitation varies with latitude. The rainfall in the tropics is high because of the rising air in the doldrums. Precipitation in the polar latitudes is low because of sinking air and the low temperatures. Mid-latitude precipitation comes with fronts and low-pressure systems.

Coastal fogs form when warm, moist air from the oceans crosses a colder surface.

Global climate changes are caused by changes in Earth's energy budget. The local climate changes with the global climate and with changes in the factors that determine local climate.

Sulfuric acid and dust from volcanoes cause short-term cooling.

Increases in greenhouse gases warm the climate. These gases come from natural sources and from human activities.

Geologic processes are important in long-term climate changes.

Vocabulary

bora	El Niño
chinook	foehn
climate	marine climate
continental climate	mistral
	Santa Ana

Review

Number your paper from 1 to 17. Select the best answer for each item. Write the letter of your answer on your paper.

1. A good description of climate includes (a) temperature and temperature range, (b) how the temperature varies through the year, (c) how the precipitation varies through the year, (d) all of the above.
2. Climate is controlled by (a) latitude, (b) altitude, (c) ocean currents, (d) all of the above.
3. Areas near the equator have (a) high average temperatures and large yearly temperature ranges, (b) long days and short nights, (c) high average temperatures and small yearly temperature ranges, (d) very long nights during the winter.
4. Denver and Kansas City are at the same latitude, but Denver's altitude is much higher. Denver would be expected to have (a) higher average temperatures, (b) lower average temperatures, (c) more rain, (d) the same average temperatures.
5. Marine climates (a) are warmer than continental climates, (b) are colder than continental climates, (c) have greater yearly temperature ranges than continental climates, (d) have smaller yearly temperature ranges than continental climates.
6. Prevailing winds (a) have no effect on climate, (b) always come from the ocean, (c) may be blocked by mountains, (d) result in lower average temperatures.
7. Ocean currents (a) do not affect temperature, (b) may be colder or warmer than the places they pass, (c) affect areas that have continental climates, (d) always result in milder temperatures.
8. The intertropical convergence zone is (a) a zone of sinking air, (b) a zone of sharp temperature contrast, (c) located in the middle latitudes, (d) a zone of rainfall.
9. Precipitation in the middle latitudes falls (a) during the summer rainy season, (b) in

low-pressure areas, (c) where air diverges, (d) when warm air flows over cold water.

10. The windward sides of mountains are usually (a) rainier and warmer than the leeward sides, (b) cooler and rainier than the leeward sides, (c) cooler and drier than the leeward sides, (d) warmer and drier than the leeward sides.
11. Locations near oceans (a) always have heavy rainfall, (b) have heavy rainfall when the prevailing winds blow from the ocean, (c) are always very dry, (d) have heavy rainfall when the prevailing winds blow from the land.
12. Warm air over cold water results in (a) thunderstorms, (b) unstable weather, (c) warming of the air, (d) fogs.
13. Earth's energy budget (a) is not related to climate, (b) is not in balance right now, (c) has always been the same as it is today, (d) is in overall balance right now.
14. A volcanic eruption may produce (a) cooling for 1–7 years, (b) short-term warming, (c) long-term warming, (d) no effect on climate.
15. The El Niño (a) is associated with cold waters off Peru, (b) is associated with warm waters off Peru, (c) has happened only once in historical times, (d) is caused by greenhouse gases.
16. The warming around A.D. 1000 resulted in (a) farming disasters, (b) population increases in North America, (c) the Norse people sailing farther southward, (d) glaciers advancing.
17. An increase in atmospheric carbon dioxide (a) results in cooling, (b) results in warming, (c) has never occurred, (d) has no effect on climate.

Interpret and Apply

On your paper, answer each question in complete sentences.

1. Volcano A has an explosive eruption that causes large amounts of sulfur dioxide and dust to enter the stratosphere. Volcano B's eruption produces the same amount of material, but it stays mainly in the troposphere. Which volcano will cool the atmosphere for the longer time? Why?
2. Modern civilization is increasing the amounts of carbon dioxide and particulate matter (such as smoke particles) in the atmosphere. Which pollutant might have the greatest effect on the climate? Why?

Critical Thinking

The map shows what North America would look like if it were moved so that the United States lay in the trade-wind zones and Canada was in the horse latitudes.

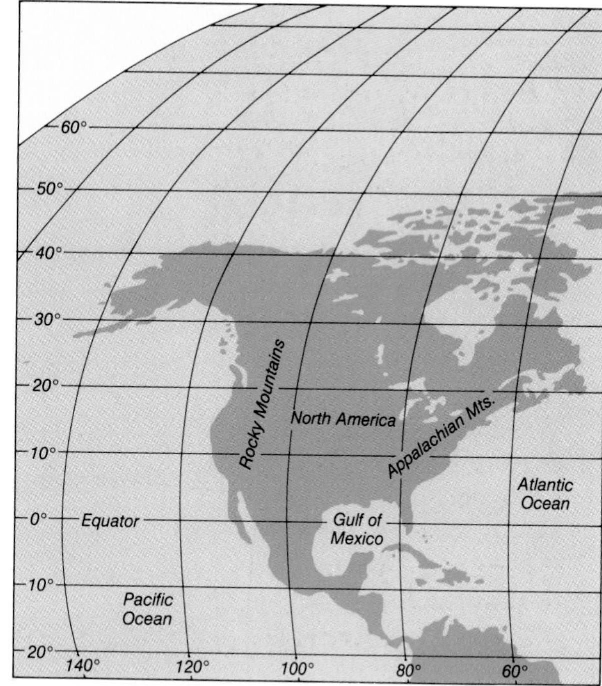

1. Describe the average annual temperature and precipitation (a) on the United States West Coast, (b) just east of the Rocky Mountains in Wyoming, and (c) in Philadelphia, Pennsylvania.
2. What would the climate be like in Canada? Why?

UNIT SEVEN
Earth's History

Geologists have read these rock layers and found that they are ancient sand dunes. Which layers are from older dunes? Which are from younger dunes?

What do these tracks tell about the creature that made them?

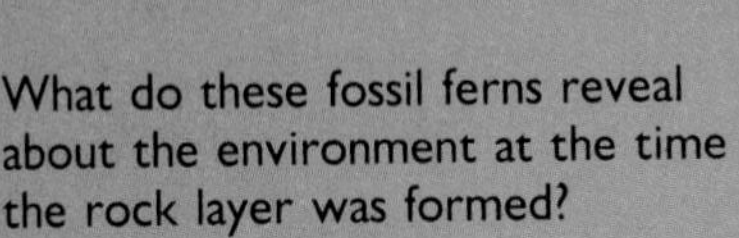

What do these fossil ferns reveal about the environment at the time the rock layer was formed?

Where is Earth's history written?

Rock layers on Earth's surface are like pages in a diary; each layer records an event in Earth's history. But the diary isn't written in English. Geologists have had to learn a different language to read the record. This language includes evidence and events seen on Earth today. Look at the photographs. What does each show about reading the diary of Earth's history?

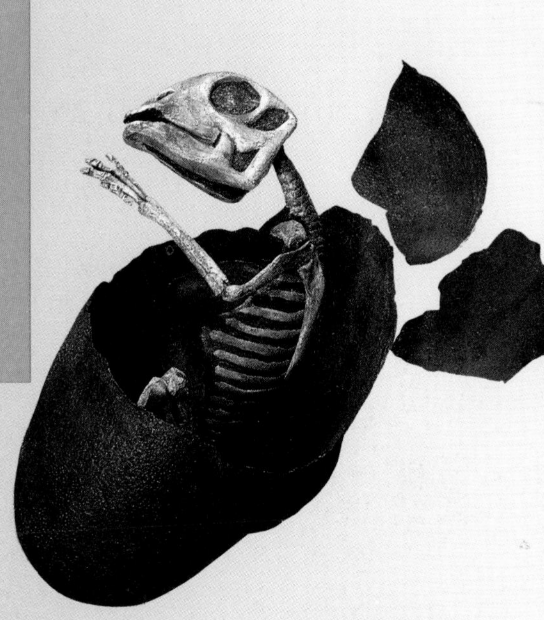

What does this fossil dinosaur show about its life cycle? ▶

How are today's life forms helpful to understanding life forms of the past?
▼

CHAPTER

32 The Rock Record

▲ This fossil plant is more than 200 million years old.

How Do You Know That . . .

Fossil shapes were left in rocks by plants and animals that lived millions of years ago? One way to find out is by learning the age of the sedimentary rock that contains the fossil. The fossil and the rock must have been deposited at the same time in order for the fossil to be a part of the rock layer. Several methods can be used for finding and identifying the age of a rock. First, however, you must learn how to read the rock record and identify the fossils preserved in it.

I Reading the Rock Record

Topic 1 Telling Time

Most of the events earth scientists study took place long before there were people to record them. Without clocks and calendars, it is difficult to determine the order of past events. The ages of past events in Earth's history can be indicated in two different ways. One way records relative time. The other way measures absolute time. Both kinds of time are needed to read the rock record.

Relative time places events in a sequence but does not identify their actual date of occurrence. For example, suppose that several years ago your family took a vacation trip to the Rocky Mountains. Now you cannot remember the exact date of the trip. However, you know that it took place before you entered the fifth grade. In recalling the trip in this way, you are using relative time. Thus relative time does not tell the actual age of an event, but it does indicate the age in comparison with other events.

Absolute time identifies the actual date of an event. The exact date of your visit to the Rocky Mountains would be absolute time. Geologists use absolute time to identify the actual age of rock layers. One rock might be 300 million years old, another rock 200 million years old, and a third rock 50 million years old.

In addition to identifying the actual age of an event, absolute time is important for another reason. If the actual time of two events is known, the length of time between the two events can be calculated. Such values make it possible to determine the rate at which a geologic process such as mountain building occurs.

Absolute time might seem more important than relative time because absolute time gives an actual date. However, absolute dates are difficult and expensive to obtain. Most geologic work is done using relative time.

Topic 2 Finding Relative Time

An important part of reading the rock record is determining the relative ages of events in the record. Several rules for interpreting relative time help to do that.

The *law of superposition* states that in a sequence of undisturbed (that is, not overturned) sedimentary rocks, the oldest rocks will be at the bottom of the sequence and the youngest will be at the top. This is the basis of all relative-time determinations and a fundamental concept in studying Earth's history.

OBJECTIVES

A Explain the difference between relative time and absolute time and list some rules for determining relative time.

B List the eras of the geologic timetable and discuss the basis by which they are defined.

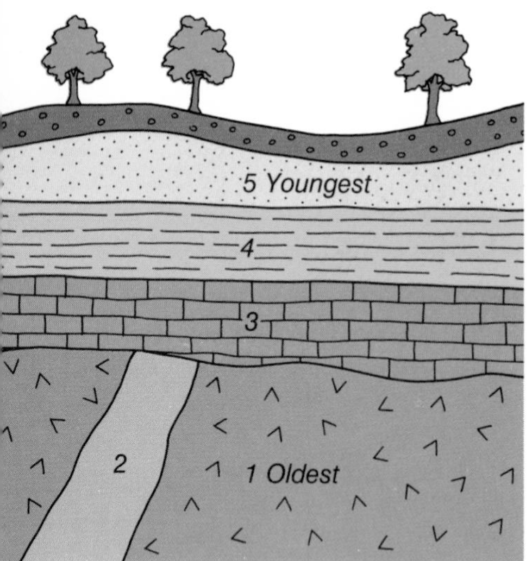

32.1 The relative ages of the rocks are given by numbers. The surface that separates layers 1 and 3 is an unconformity.

The *law of cross-cutting relationships* states that an igneous rock is younger than the rocks it has intruded, or cut across. This law can also be applied to fault surfaces. The event that caused a fault is younger than any rocks the fault has broken, or cut across.

The *law of included fragments* states that pieces of one rock found in another rock must be older than the rock in which they are found. One example would be pebbles in a conglomerate. The pebbles must have existed before the conglomerate formed and, therefore, are older than the conglomerate.

In addition to these rules for reading relative time, unconformities are important. An **unconformity** is a break in the rock record. It represents a surface, like the land surface of today, that was once above sea level. The surface was first eroded and then buried by younger sediments. As a result, the rocks above and below an unconformity are not continuous. There may be a large age difference between the two layers. Their fossils may be quite different. Often the rock layers themselves meet at an angle. An unconformity shows where a part of the rock record is missing.

Topic 3 The Geologic Timetable

A geologist studying the rocks in a particular area can use the rules discussed in Topic 2 to determine the relative ages of the rocks in that area. If these rocks can be matched with the rocks in another area, their relative ages can also be determined. By matching rocks over large areas, geologists have been able to determine the relative ages of most of the rocks on Earth's surface. Over a number of years, geologists have worked out a timetable that subdivides geologic time into units based on the formation of certain rocks.

The **geologic timetable,** shown in Figure 32.3 on pages 538–539, is a summary of the major events of Earth's history preserved in the rock record. Fossils are an important part of that history. In fact, many of the rock layers have been identified and matched based on the fossils in them.

The longest segments of geologic time are called **eras.** The oldest era is the **Archeozoic** era. The Archeozoic Era began when Earth was formed between 4 and 5 billion years ago. The earliest known rocks formed during the Archeozoic Era.

The **Proterozoic** Era began about 2.5 billion years ago. The difference between Archeozoic and Proterozoic rocks is that Proterozoic rocks contain fossils of simple plants and worms that lived in the oceans. No evidence of life on land has been found in Proterozoic rocks.

The **Paleozoic** Era is marked by the start of an abundant fossil record. The rocks formed during the Paleozoic Era contain fossils of both land and ocean plants and animals. The Paleozoic Era began about 570 million years ago.

The **Mesozoic** Era began about 230 million years ago. Dinosaurs thrived during most of Mesozoic time.

32.2 An unconformity in Paleozoic rock layers

The youngest of the eras is the **Cenozoic** Era. This era began about 65 million years ago and is still going on today. Recent events of the era are the Ice Age and the appearance of humans.

Eras are also divided into smaller segments. The divisions of eras are called **periods.** Like eras, periods differ from one another in plant and animal life although less so than between eras. Some of the periods are further divided into **epochs.** These divisions are shorter and less distinct than periods.

TOPIC QUESTIONS

Each topic question refers to the topic of the same number.

1. **(a)** How is the age of an event defined using relative time? **(b)** What is absolute time? **(c)** Why is it important to know the length of time between two geologic events?
2. **(a)** According to the law of superposition, where are the oldest rocks in an undisturbed sequence of sedimentary rocks? **(b)** How does the age of an igneous intrusion compare to the age of the rocks it has intruded? What law describes this age relationship? **(c)** How is the age of the pebbles within a conglomerate related to the age of the conglomerate? What law describes this relationship? **(d)** What is an unconformity? How does it occur? What does it represent?
3. **(a)** List the eras of geologic time, from oldest to most recent. **(b)** What are periods and epochs?

Dr. Thomas R. Waller

Curator

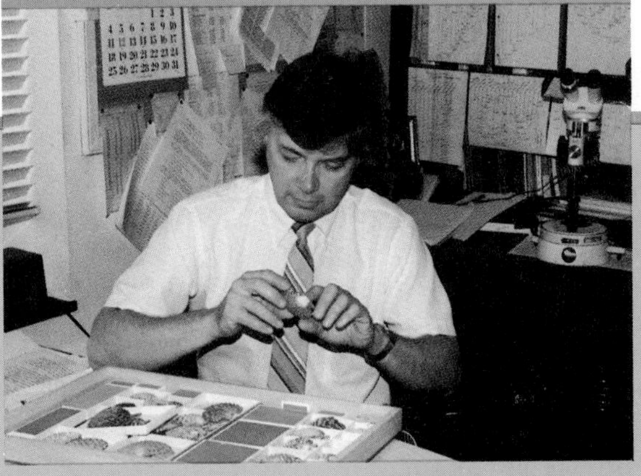

To most people, being a museum curator simply means taking care of specimens. In the case of Dr. Thomas R. Waller, this perception is far from true. As the curator of Cenozoic Mollusca at the Smithsonian Institution's Museum of Natural History in Washington, D.C., Dr. Waller spends most of his time on research. Specifically, he studies the evolutionary patterns of mollusks.

Dr. Waller gathers information on mollusks in three different ways. He learns more about specimens already stored in the museum by examining them under sophisticated microscopes. He also goes on field trips to various parts of the world to search for new fossil specimens. Finally, he examines living counterparts of the ancient fossils at marine laboratories and on scuba-diving expeditions. Sometimes he captures his underwater finds in movies. By studying the current life forms, Dr. Waller is able to relate the past to the present.

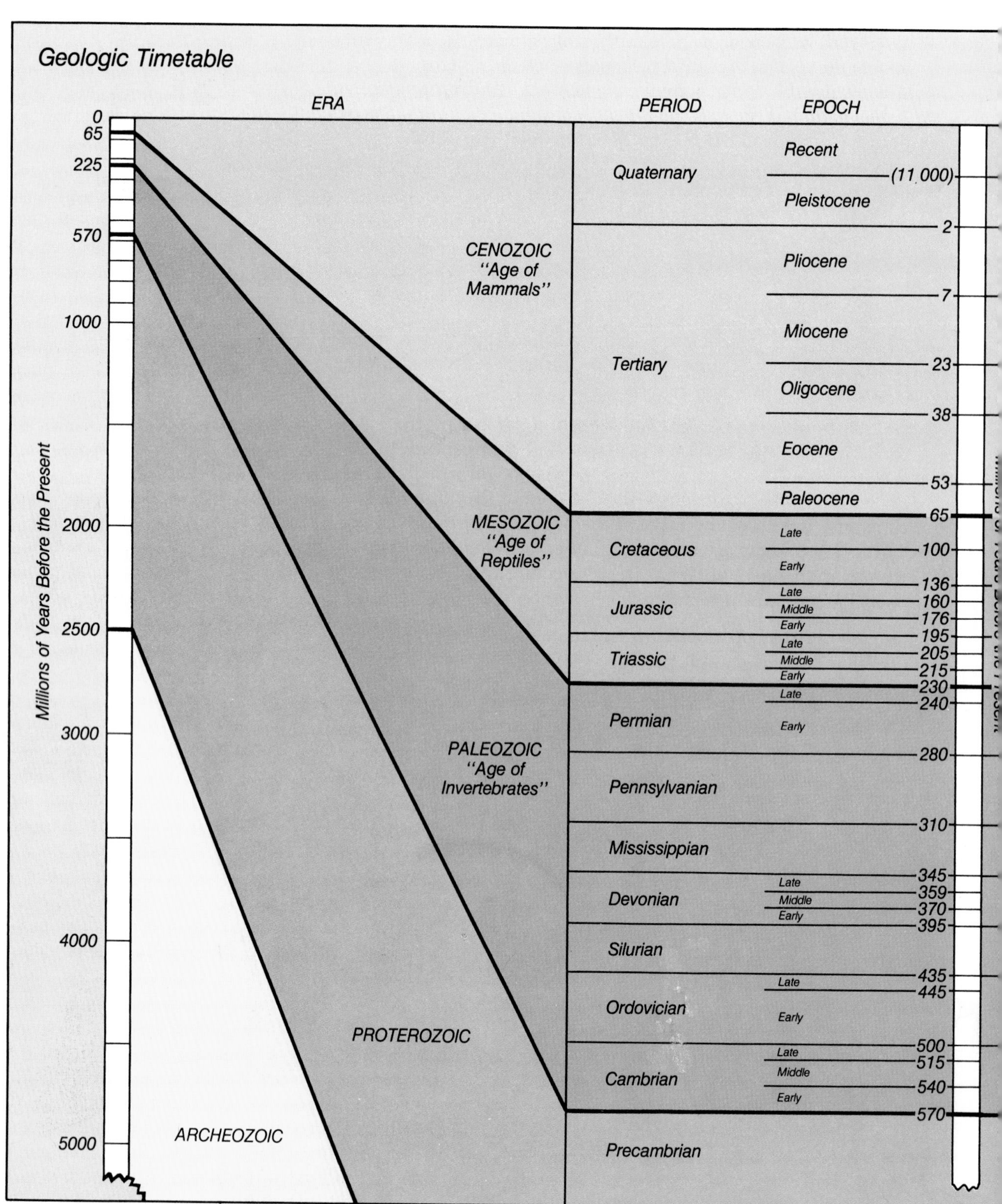

32.3 The geologic timetable summarizes the events of Earth's history.

LIFE	NORTH AMERICAN ROCK RECORD
mans dominant. Domestic animals velop.	West Coast uplift continues in U.S. Great Lakes form.
minids develop. Elephants flourish in America, then die out.	Ice Age. Raising of mountains and plateaus in western U.S.
ominids appear. Modern horse, mel, elephant develop. Sequoias cline; tropical trees driven south.	N. America joined to S. America. Sierras and Appalachians re-elevated.
orse migrates to Asia, elephant to nerica. Grasses, grazing animals thrive.	N. America joined to Asia. Volcanism in northwest United States, Columbia Plateau.
ammals progress. Elephants in Africa. onkeys die out in N. America	Alps and Himalayas forming. Volcanism in western United States.
gmy ancestors of modern horse, other ammals. Diatoms, flowering plants rive.	Coal forming in western U.S.
any new mammals appear.	Uplift in western U.S. continues.
nosaurs, ammonites die out. Mammals, ds advance. Flowering plants, rdwoods rise.	Uplift of Rockies begins. Colorado Plateau raised. Coal swamps in western U.S.
ant dinosaurs. First birds, first mmals. Conifers and cycads abundant.	Rise of Sierra Nevadas, West Coast mountains, Basin and Range mountains.
ptiles thrive. Forests of nifers and cycads.	Volcanism in New England, New Jersey. Palisades of Hudson formed.
lobites, seed ferns, scale trees die out. orals abundant.	"Ancestral Appalachians" formed. Ice Age in South America. Salt-forming deserts in western U.S.
st reptiles. Many giant insects. ore-bearing plants, amphibians urish.	Great coal-forming swamps in North America and Europe.
nphibians and crinoids flourish. Ferns, nifers abundant.	Extensive submergence of continents.
rst amphibians; fishes abound. First land ants, forests.	Mountain building in New England and Canada. White Mountains raised.
rst land animals (spiders, scorpions). sh develop; marine invertebrates thrive.	Salt-and-gypsum-forming deserts in eastern U.S.
st vertebrates (fish). Marine ertebrates thrive: mollusks, trilobites, aptolites.	Taconic and Green Mts. form. Half of N. America submerged.
any marine invertebrates (trilobites, achiopods, snails, sponges). Many aweeds.	Extensive deposition of sediments in inland seas.
life on land. Simple marine plants gae, fungi) and marine worms. romatolites dominant. Others probably isted, but fossil evidence is lacking.	Great volcanic activity, lava flows, metamorphism of rocks. Formation of iron, copper, and nickel ores.

INFERRED POSITION OF EARTH LANDMASSES*

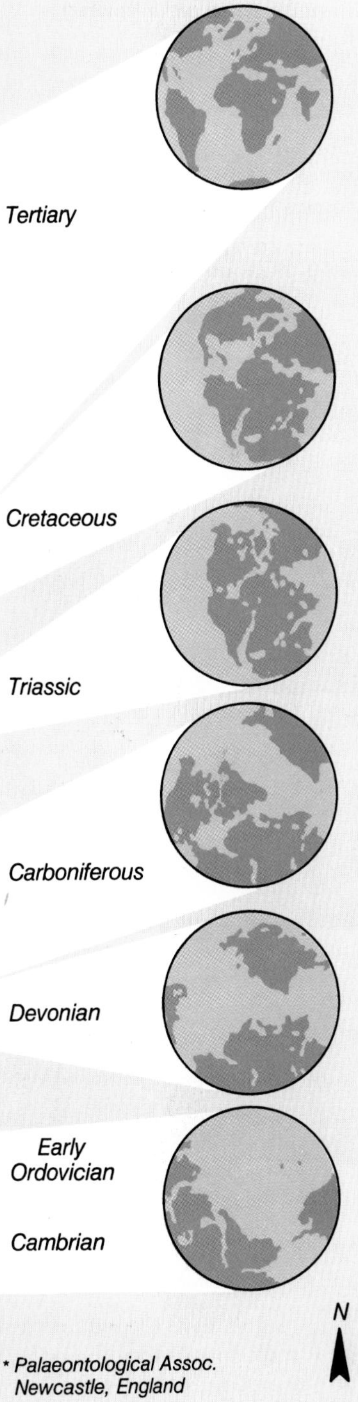

Tertiary

Cretaceous

Triassic

Carboniferous

Devonian

Early Ordovician

Cambrian

N

* Palaeontological Assoc. Newcastle, England

II The Fossil Record

Topic 4 How Fossils Are Formed

OBJECTIVES

A Define *fossil;* identify and describe some ways in which fossils are preserved.

B Summarize Darwin's theory of evolution.

C List some ways in which fossils are used to read the rock record.

D Define *correlation* and identify some methods of correlation.

Fossils are both the basis for the geologic timetable and an important part of the rock record. A **fossil** is any evidence of earlier life preserved in a rock. The evidence can be shells, bones, petrified trees, impressions made by plant leaves, footprints, or even burrows made by worms.

Fossils are preserved in the rock record in several ways. In rare cases, the *original remains*—the actual, unchanged remains—of the plant or animal are preserved. One example includes the large elephantlike creatures, called woolly mammoths, that have been found frozen in permafrost in Siberia and Alaska. These fossils are exceptional because the entire animal has been preserved. More often the soft tissues of an animal decay and disappear, leaving only the original hard parts. The bones and teeth of dinosaurs found in the Rocky Mountains are examples.

The remains of some prehistoric insects have been found in hardened resin. Resin is a sticky sap that oozes from pine trees. A hardened resin is called *amber*. Most amber comes from the shores of the Baltic Sea in Europe. It is used as an ornamental material.

A second way in which fossils can be preserved is as *replaced remains*. In these fossils, the soft parts of the original animal have disappeared and the hard parts have been replaced by mineral material. The replacement is usually the work of underground water. Circulating groundwater removes the original organic material, often an atom at a time, and replaces it with a mineral material. The minerals calcite, silica, and pyrite are common replacement materials. The result is an exact copy of the original plant or animal, which is made from minerals. Petrified wood is a good example of replaced remains.

A third method of fossil preservation is through molds and casts of the original animal or plant. Sometimes a fossil shell or bone is dissolved completely out of the rock in which it has been deposited. This leaves a hollow depression in the rock called a *mold*. The mold shows only the original shape of the fossil. When new mineral material fills the mold, this material forms a *cast* of the original fossil. Molds and casts of shellfish are common fossils. The molds of ferns, leaves, and fish are also found in the rock layers of some areas.

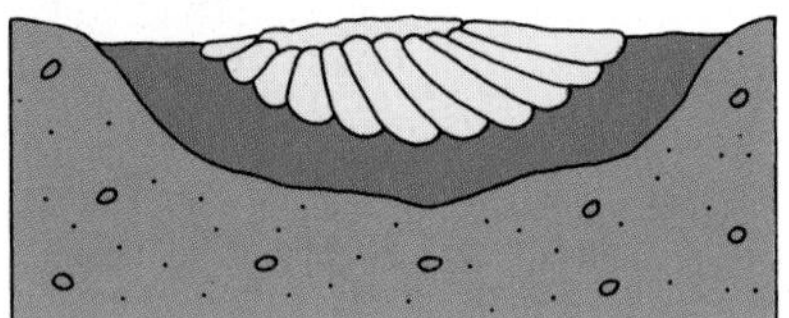

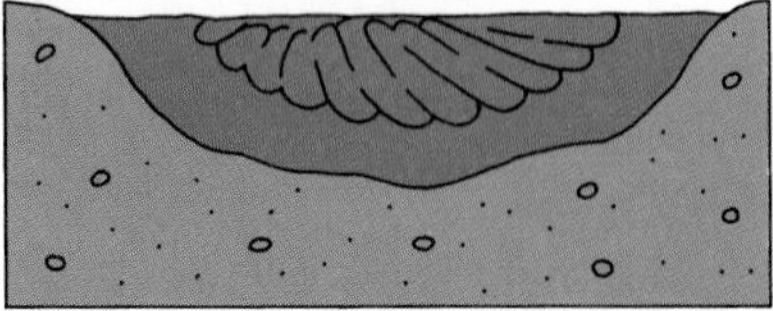

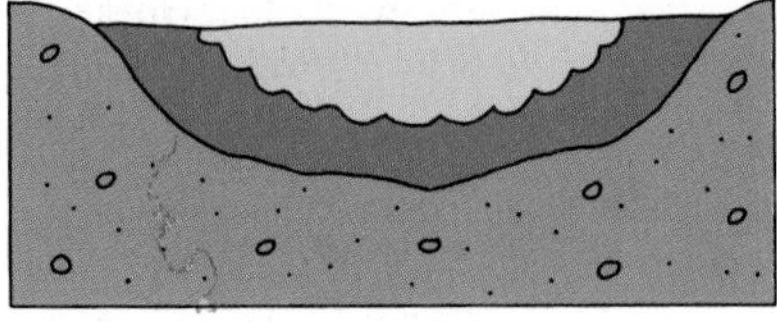

32.4 A mold forms when the original animal or plant dissolves and leaves a hole. New material fills the hole and makes a cast of the original organism.

Trace fossils are evidence of life other than the remains of a plant or animal. Trace fossils include any impression left in the rock by an animal, such as trails, footprints, tracks, burrows, and borings. Many animals are known only by the impressions they have left behind because their remains have not yet been found. For example, some of the earliest fossils in the rock record are trace fossils in the form of borings. The animals that made the borings are unknown, although they are assumed to have been some kind of worm living on the seafloor.

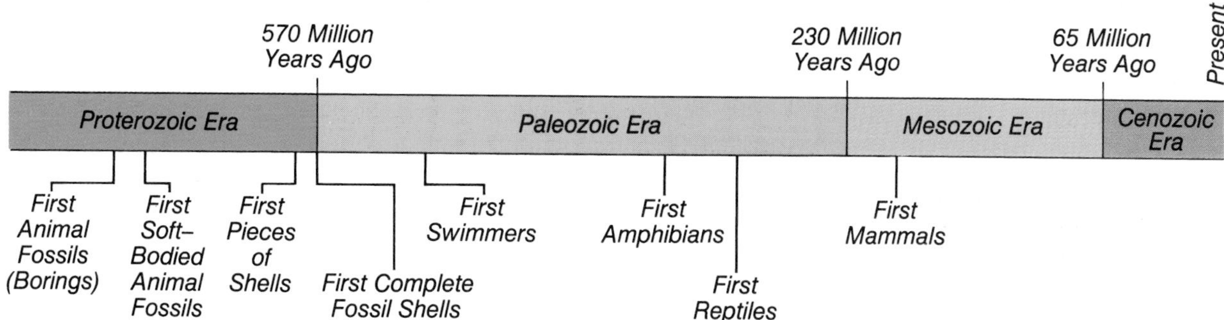

32.5 The fossil record shows that life forms have changed over time.

Topic 5 Fossils as Evidence for Evolution

The fossil record indicates that the first organisms were simple in structure. As time passed, life forms increased in size and complexity. One place that reveals a great deal about the history of living things is the Grand Canyon in Arizona. The youngest rocks, near the top of the canyon, contain imprints of land reptiles, ferns, and insects. A quarter of the way down the canyon is a layer of sedimentary rock containing marine organisms, including fish. Deeper in the canyon layers there are no fish fossils, only a few shells and traces of worms. The oldest rock layers, at the bottom of the canyon, have no fossils at all.

The rock record shows that through time many kinds of organisms disappear and are replaced by new and different organisms. The evidence indicates a changing or evolving pattern of life forms. This process of change that produces new life forms over geologic time is called **evolution.** The *theory of evolution* provides a scientific explanation for the past and present diversity of life on Earth.

32.6 The soft parts of dinosaurs decay, but the hard parts have been preserved unchanged in some areas of the Rocky Mountains.

At one time, most people thought that life forms were fixed and unchanging. However, no existing theory accounted for the fossils of enormous dinosaurs that were no longer living. In the 1800's, several new ideas were proposed to explain the changes in life forms preserved in the fossil record. One theory proposed in 1859 by Charles Darwin, a British naturalist, continues to be the best explanation for most of the existing evidence for evolution. Darwin suggested that *natural selection* accounts for the changes that produced new life forms. By that, Darwin meant that organisms who survive to produce offspring are those who inherited the most beneficial traits for surviving in a particular environment.

Darwin observed a wide diversity of life forms that are adapted to their environment. From his observations, Darwin concluded that life forms evolve gradually over many generations. If this were true, the fossil record should show organisms that are gradually different over geologic time. There should be evidence of small changes in organisms leading to modern-day life. But the fossil record is incomplete. Very few organisms have a complete, unbroken fossil record.

32.7 Petrified wood is an example of replaced remains.

Modern scientists offer another explanation for how quickly evolution occurs. Much of the fossil record shows that several types of organisms lived for very long periods without showing much change. Then "suddenly" a whole new set of different, but clearly related, organisms appeared. These organisms also lasted a long time relatively unchanged. (Remember that "sudden" is relative. A million years is a very short time period in all of geologic time.)

There is considerable debate about whether evolution follows a steady, gradual path or a path interrupted by short periods of dramatic change. The exploration of these theories will continue as more evidence is collected.

32.8 The trilobite *Elrathia* is an index fossil for the middle Cambrian.

Topic 6 Index Fossils and Key Beds

Because animals evolve over time, some fossils are typical of a particular time segment of Earth's history. These fossils are very useful to geologists because they identify the age of the rock in which they occur. Such fossils are called **index fossils,** or **guide fossils.**

An index fossil has three characteristics. First, a good index fossil must be easily recognizable. Such fossils must be unique in some way so that they can easily be told from other similar but nonindex fossils. Second, an index fossil must be widespread in occurrence. That is, an index fossil must be found over a broad geographical area. This makes it possible to use index fossils to match rock layers of a particular age over wide areas. Some index fossils can be used to match rocks between continents. Third, index fossils are limited in time. The organisms only existed for a short period of time, so their fossils occur in only a few rock layers.

A **key bed** is a single rock layer that has the same characteristics as an index fossil. Key beds are easily recognizable and occur over a wide area. A large volcanic eruption is an excellent source of material for key beds. The layer that results from an eruption represents a single instant in time but is unique and widespread.

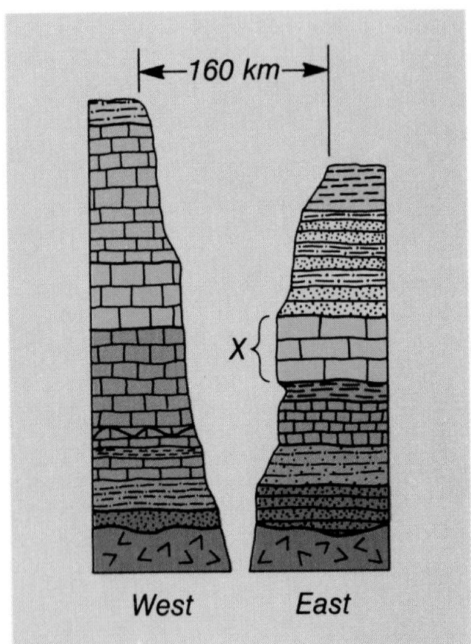

32.9 Which layer on the left correlates with layer X on the right?

Topic 7 Rock Correlation

Correlation is the matching of rock layers from one area to another. For example, a geologist might wish to know if a layer of limestone in New York is the same limestone as one in Michigan.

The simplest and most direct method of correlation is "walking the outcrop." An outcrop is the part of a rock layer that can be seen at Earth's surface. Following along an outcrop is an easy way of finding out if two rock layers are the same. However, walking along the outcrop may be difficult in areas where soils are thick, vegetation is heavy, or extensive erosion has occurred. Also, walking an outcrop is not practical when two outcrops are far apart.

Under these conditions, a second method of correlation, matching similar rock characteristics, might be used. In this method, rocks are matched by such characteristics as appearance, color, composition, or some other unique feature. For example, a rock that weathers with a distinctive rust color might be easy to recognize and, therefore, usable for correlation.

The best method of correlation over long distances is index fossils. Good index fossils are often the remains of creatures that floated in the oceans. Waves and currents can carry such organisms throughout the world to be deposited in any kind of sediment.

Key beds, such as volcanic ash, can also be used to correlate rock formations. Volcanic ash becomes a clay material called *bentonite* in sedimentary rock layers. Beds of bentonite have been used to correlate layers in many areas.

32.10 This layer of volcanic ash is a key bed because it represents an instant in geologic time and is widespread in occurrence.

Topic 8 Other Uses of Fossils

In addition to determining relative time and correlating between rock layers, fossils are important for other reasons as well. One other use of fossils is as indicators of past climate. For example, coral reefs today form only in shallow, warm water between approximately 30° N and 30° S latitudes. When a rock containing fossil coral is found, it can be assumed that the particular area was once an area of shallow warm water.

A second important use of fossils, especially microfossils, occurs in oil exploration. *Microfossils* are fossils so tiny that they have to be studied with a microscope. Foraminifera and diatoms (Chapter 17) are examples of microfossils. In drilling for oil, long cores of sedimentary rock are obtained. The core might contain only bits of large fossils but hundreds of microfossils. The microfossils can then be used to correlate the layers of one core with those of another core taken in a different location.

TOPIC QUESTIONS

Each topic question refers to the topic of the same number.

4. **(a)** What is a fossil? **(b)** Identify two ways in which original remains are preserved. **(c)** Describe how fossils are preserved as replaced remains and give an example of replaced remains. **(d)** How are fossils preserved through molds and casts? **(e)** Give some examples of fossil impressions.

5. **(a)** What is evolution? **(b)** How does the fossil record provide evidence for evolution? **(c)** What did Charles Darwin mean by natural selection? **(d)** Compare the rate at which Darwin thought evolution occurred with the rate at which some scientists of today think it occurred.

6. **(a)** List the three characteristics of an index fossil. **(b)** What is a key bed? Identify a material that forms good key beds.

7. **(a)** Define *correlation.* **(b)** List some methods by which rock layers are correlated.

8. **(a)** How are fossils indicators of past climates? **(b)** How are fossils used in oil exploration?

OBJECTIVES

A Describe how tree rings and varves are used in determining absolute time.

B Explain how radioactive elements can be used to determine absolute time.

C Identify some radiometric dating methods and discuss the advantages of each.

III Measuring Absolute Time

Topic 9 Tree Rings

Methods of measuring absolute time must provide a specific date for the occurrence of an event. One method for determining absolute dates is by counting tree rings. These are the concentric rings seen in a stump or log. Each ring usually represents a single year. Under magnification, each ring can be seen to consist of two kinds of cells—large, thin-walled cells and smaller, thicker-walled cells. The larger cells form in the spring when the tree is starting its yearly growth. The smaller cells form after the tree has leafed out. The width of a ring depends upon the temperature and rainfall that year. Thus tree rings provide not only dates but a record of the weather as well.

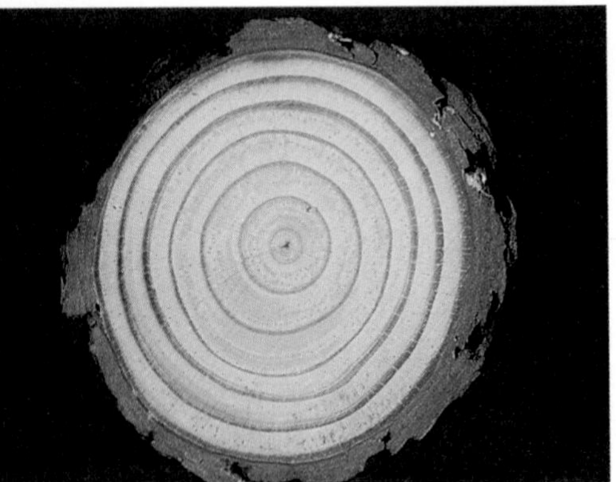

32.11 Tree rings can be counted to determine absolute time.

Because each tree ring is different, the pattern of rings in one tree can be correlated, or matched, with those of another tree. By applying this technique to wood in Indian ruins in the southwestern United States, scientists have determined dates back to almost 2000 B.C.

The bristlecone pine is the oldest living tree to be dated by counting tree rings. Bristlecone pines are slow-growing timberline trees found in the Sierra Nevadas of California. One bristlecone pine was found to be more than 4600 years old.

Topic 10 Varves

A *varve* is any sediment that shows a yearly cycle. Varves can form in any body of water, including the oceans. However, they are clearest in glacial lakes dating from the Ice Age.

Wherever lakes formed at the front of a glacier, streams from the melting ice carried sediments into the lakes. In summer, the ice melted rapidly. Swiftly flowing streams carried a mixture of sands, silts, and clays into the lakes. The sands and silts settled to the bottom of each lake in a thick light-colored layer. Wind blowing across the lakes created currents that kept the fine clays in suspension.

32.12 Varves can be studied to determine how long a glacier was in a particular place before it finally disappeared.

When winter came, the streams slowed or stopped as they froze over. The lakes also froze over. Winds were unable to reach and stir the water. The clays and other fine material that had accumulated in the lake water all summer then settled to the bottom to form a thin layer of fine, dark sediment. Thus each year two distinct layers of sediment were deposited—a thick, light-colored sandy layer in summer and a thin, dark-colored clay layer in winter.

Like tree rings, each annual varve is different. As a result, the varves of one lake can be correlated with the varves of other lakes. By matching deposits, dates back to 15 000 years ago have been determined.

Topic 11 Radioactive Elements and Absolute Time

Tree rings and varves are methods of obtaining absolute dates with good accuracy, but neither method can be used to date very far back in time. For older dates, radioactive isotopes (Chapter 3, Topic 6) are used. These are atoms of elements that give off radiation from their nuclei. Three kinds of radiation are involved—alpha, beta, and gamma. *Alpha* rays have the same structure as the nucleus of a helium atom (two protons and two neutrons). *Beta* rays are high-speed electrons. *Gamma* rays are like X rays.

Each time an alpha ray is released from an atomic nucleus, the atom changes to a new, lighter element. This process is called **radioactive decay.** If the new element is also radioactive, decay takes place again. Radiation continues to be released until an element is formed that is stable, or not radioactive.

Uranium is an element with a radioactive isotope. The most common radioactive isotope of uranium is uranium-238. When U-238 gives off an alpha particle, it becomes an atom of thorium-234, which is also radioactive. The reaction is written as follows:

$$^{238}_{92}\mathrm{U} \rightarrow {}^{4}_{2}\mathrm{He} + {}^{234}_{90}\mathrm{Th}$$

Decay continues with alpha, beta, and gamma rays being given off, until finally an element is formed that is not radioactive. This stable element for U-238 is an isotope of lead, Pb-206.

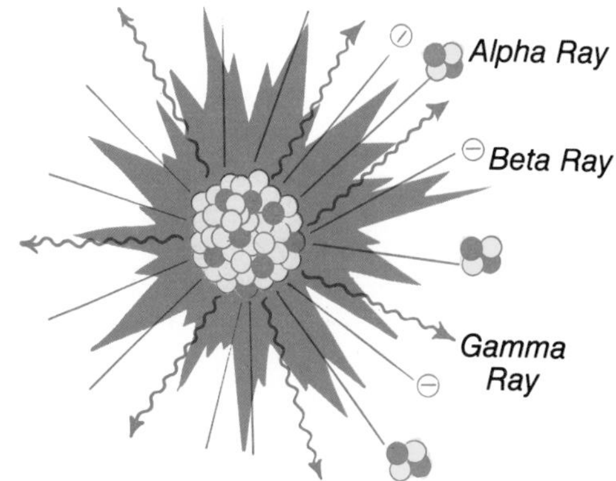

32.13 Radioactive elements produce three different types of radiation. When an alpha ray is emitted, the atom changes to a different element.

Topic 12 Half-Life

Radioactivity can be used to determine absolute time because each radioactive element disintegrates at a constant rate. The rate is not affected by the conditions of temperature or pressure. Scientists assume that the disintegration of a radioactive element begins when a mineral crystallizes. The rate of disintegration is assumed to remain constant throughout Earth's history.

The rate at which a radioactive element disintegrates is called its **half-life.** The half-life is the time that it takes for half of the atoms of an element to decay to a stable end product. Every radioactive isotope has its own rate of decay and half-life. Half-lives range from a fraction of a second to billions of years. For example, the element protactinium has a half-life of about one minute. The half-life of uranium-238 is 4.5 billion years.

An example with thorium-234, shown graphically in Figure 32.15, will show better how half-life can be used to date a material. Thorium-234 has a half-life of about 24 days. In a sample of thorium, half of the atoms will have been converted to a stable product at the end of 24 days and half will remain unchanged. During the next 24 days, half of the remaining unchanged part will decay. During each half-life, half of the radioactive material, no matter how small the amount, will decay to a stable product.

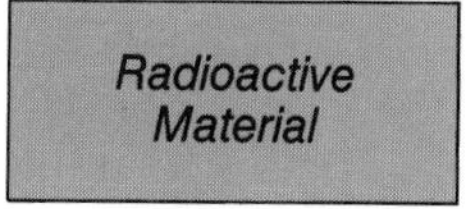

Time 0

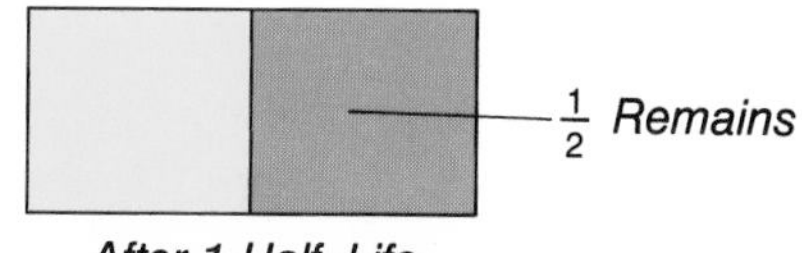

After 1 Half-Life

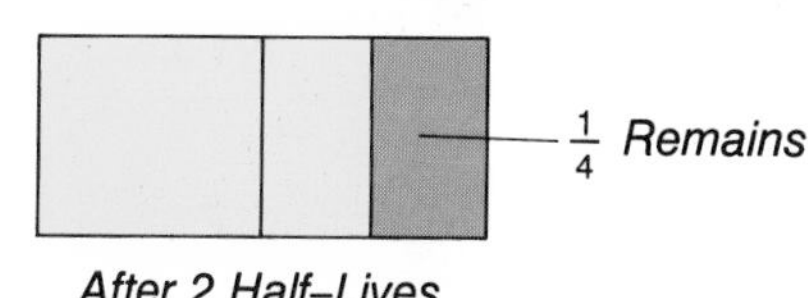

After 2 Half-Lives

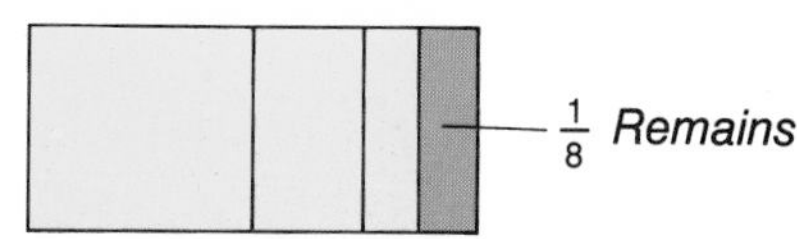

After 3 Half-Lives

32.14 At the end of each half-life, half of the radioactive material remains.

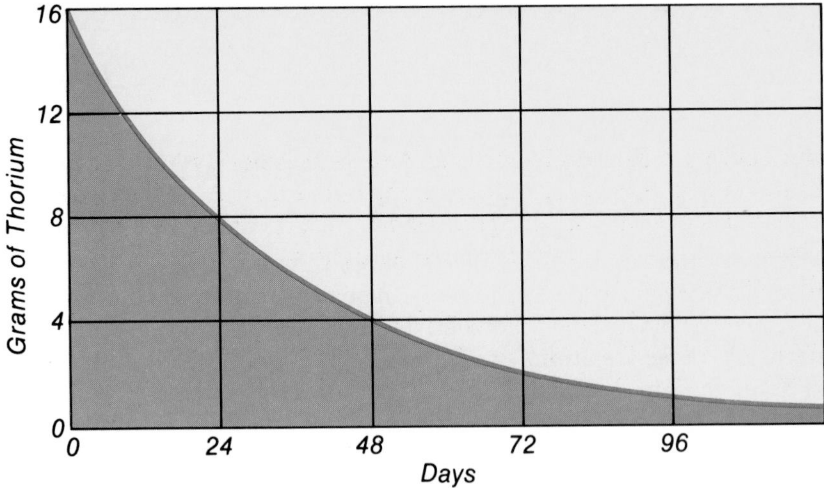

32.15 The radioactive decay of 16 grams of thorium-234. At the end of one half-life (24 days), 8 grams remain. At the end of two half-lives (48 days), 4 grams remain. At the end of three half-lives (72 days), 2 grams remain. At the end of four half-lives (96 days), 1 gram remains.

Topic 13 Radiocarbon Dating

Radiocarbon, an isotope of carbon, is used in radioactive dating. Radiocarbon dating was developed by Dr. Willard F. Libby in 1947. The half-life of the radioactive carbon isotope is about 5700 years. Using radiocarbon, scientists can measure back about 100 000 years.

Radiocarbon dating uses the radioactive isotope carbon-14. All living plant and animal cells contain carbon. Most of that carbon is ordinary carbon-12 but a small percentage is radioactive carbon-14. Libby recognized that the amount of carbon-14 in the cells of a living animal or plant stayed constant as long as the animal or plant was alive. But, as soon as an organism dies, the percentage of carbon-14 decreases at a rate set by its half-life. Thus, the ratio of the amount of ordinary carbon-12 to the amount of radioactive carbon-14 can be used to tell how long ago a plant or animal died and, in turn, when the organism lived.

Radiocarbon dating has two major problems. First, the method cannot be used on rocks but only on things that once were alive, such as logs and bones. Second, because the half-life of carbon-14 is relatively short, the method cannot date very far back in time. Nevertheless, radiocarbon is invaluable for dating such things as the wooden tools and skeletons of prehistoric people. Radiocarbon can also be used to date plant and animal materials buried in Ice Age deposits.

Topic 14 Other Radiometric Methods

The dating of rocks in Earth's crust is done by several radiometric methods. One method is *uranium-lead* in which U-238, the radioactive isotope, decays to lead-206, the stable end product. The half-life of U-238 is 4.5 billion years. This long half-life makes it possible to use this method to date the oldest rocks in the crust. However, the uranium-lead clock cannot be used on every old rock. The reason is that original uranium is rarely found in sedimentary or metamorphic rocks. Neither is it found in all igneous rocks. Thus uranium-lead can be used only on igneous rocks that contain the right kind of uranium isotope. A second difficulty in using uranium-lead is its long half-life. Although the method can be used on very old rocks, it does not give reliable results on rocks less than about 10 million years old because so little of the U-238 will have decayed in that time.

A second method of dating rocks of the crust is the *rubidium-strontium* method. The half-life of rubidium-87 is about 49 billion years, or more than ten times Earth's age! Rubidium-87 decays into the element strontium-87. Rubidium can be used to date almost all igneous rocks because it occurs in common minerals such as the feldspars and micas. If both rubidium-87 and uranium-238 occur in the same rock, one method can be used as a check on the value obtained by the other method.

A third method is the *potassium-argon* method. Potassium-40 decays into the element argon-40. The half-life of potassium-40 is about 1.3 billion years. The potassium-argon method has many advantages. Potassium, unlike uranium and rubidium, is a very common element. It is found in potash feldspar and black mica. Minerals that can be dated by this method are found in metamorphic and sedimentary rocks as well as in igneous rocks. It is possible to date many rocks with potassium-argon that cannot be dated by uranium or rubidium. In some cases, this method can date rocks as young as 50 000 years.

TOPIC QUESTIONS

Each topic question refers to the topic of the same number.

9. **(a)** Describe the two parts of a single tree ring and identify what both parts represent. **(b)** What factors determine the width of a tree ring? **(c)** What are the oldest living trees?

10. **(a)** What are varves? **(b)** Describe the two parts of a varve layer and discuss when each forms. **(c)** How are varves used for dating?

11. **(a)** Name and describe three radiations given off by radioactive elements. **(b)** What is the stable end product from the decay of uranium-238?

12. **(a)** Define *half-life.* **(b)** Describe the radioactive decay of 16 grams of thorium-234.

13. **(a)** What is the half-life of radiocarbon? **(b)** Which carbon isotope is used for radiocarbon dating and how does it work? **(c)** On what kinds of materials can radiocarbon dating be used? **(d)** Identify two problems in using radiocarbon dating.

14. **(a)** What are the disadvantages of the uranium-lead method for measuring geologic time? **(b)** What is the advantage of the rubidium-strontium method? **(c)** What is the advantage of the potassium-argon method?

CHAPTER 32 REVIEW

Summary

Both relative time and absolute time are used to describe geologic time. Several laws are used in the determination of relative time.

The geologic timetable is a summary of the major events of Earth's history.

Unconformities in the rock record represent former erosional surfaces and gaps in the rock record.

Fossils are any evidence of earlier life preserved in the rock record.

The order of appearance of fossils in the rock record supports the evolution of life forms.

Index (guide) fossils are easily recognizable and widespread in occurrence, but limited in time range. Index fossils are the best method of correlating between outcrops.

Key beds are layers with the same properties as index fossils that can be used for correlation. Several other techniques of correlation can also be used.

In addition to evolution and correlation, fossils are also important indicators of past climates. Microfossils are important to oil exploration.

Tree rings and varves can be used to find absolute ages because each shows an annual cycle.

Radioactive isotopes give off alpha, beta, and gamma radiations at a measurable rate. Radiometric dating methods use the rates of natural decay of radioactive isotopes to determine absolute time.

The half-life is the time needed for half of the atoms of a radioactive element to decay to a stable end product. Each radioactive isotope has a different half-life.

Radiocarbon dating is used on material that was once living, such as prehistoric bones.

Uranium-lead, rubidium-strontium, and potassium-argon are radiometric methods that can be used on the oldest rocks in Earth's crust. Each method has its own particular advantages and disadvantages.

Vocabulary

absolute time
Archeozoic
Cenozoic
correlation
era
epoch
evolution
fossil
geologic timetable
half-life
index (guide) fossil
key bed
Mesozoic
Paleozoic
period
Proterozoic
radioactive decay
radiocarbon
relative time
unconformity

Review

Number your paper from *1* to *20*. Match the phrases in list **A** with the terms in list **B.**

List A

1. buried erosional surface
2. used to find age of bristlecone pines
3. method of preservation of woolly mammoths
4. most recent era of geologic time
5. example of a key bed
6. radiometric method with the longest half-life
7. shown by changes in life forms through geologic time
8. divisions within eras
9. best method for correlating over long distances
10. used to date bones and tools of prehistoric people
11. common method of preservation of shells
12. used to search for oil
13. oldest era on the geologic timetable
14. radiometric dating method that works only on igneous rocks containing the right kind of uranium isotope
15. trails, footprints, tracks, and burrows
16. states that the oldest rocks are on the bottom of an undisturbed sequence
17. time for only half of the atoms of a radioactive element to decay

18. deposits in glacial lakes that show seasonal changes
19. the dating of an event by its place in a sequence of events
20. process that releases alpha, beta, and gamma radiations

List B

a.	absolute time	**m.**	periods and epochs
b.	Archeozoic	**n.**	petrified wood
c.	Cenozoic	**o.**	potassium-argon
d.	evolution	**p.**	radioactive decay
e.	freezing	**q.**	radiocarbon
f.	half-life	**r.**	relative time
g.	index fossils	**s.**	rubidium-strontium
h.	law of cross-cutting relationships	**t.**	trace fossil
		u.	tree rings
i.	law of superposition	**v.**	uncomformity
j.	microfossils	**w.**	uranium-lead
k.	molds and casts	**x.**	varves
l.	Paleozoic	**y.**	volcanic ash

Interpret and Apply

On your paper, answer each question in complete sentences.

1. Correlation of rocks is difficult within Archeozoic and Proterozoic rocks. What is a probable reason for this difficulty?
2. Fall-winter varves are usually blackish because they contain more organic matter than do spring-summer varves. Why?
3. Dinosaurs lived during the Mesozoic Era. Could radiocarbon be used to date a dinosaur bone? Explain.
4. Arkose is a sandstone made from feldspar. If the feldspar is dated with potassium-argon, will the date be the time of formation of the arkose? Explain.

Critical Thinking

The diagram is a model for a radioactive decay. The entire circle represents 100 percent of a radioactive material. The relative amount of material that decays during each half-life is indicated. The unshaded portion of the model represents the amount of undecayed material that remains after five half-lives.

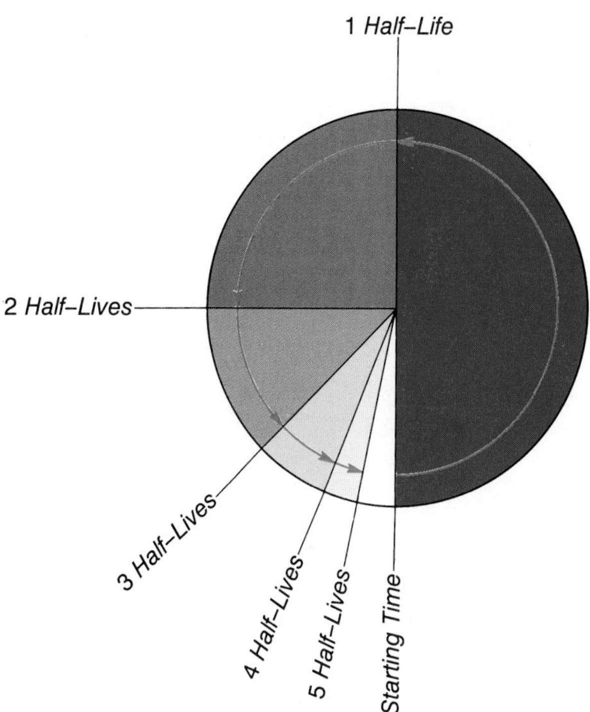

1. What percent of the original material decayed during the first half-life?
2. What percent of the original material remains after the second half-life?
3. If this material has a half-life of 2 billion years, how long will be needed for three half-lives?
4. Will the sixth half-life use all of the unshaded portion that remains? Explain.
5. If the original mass of another radioactive material was 24 grams, how many grams of the radioactive material were left at the end of the third half-life?
6. At the end of the fourth half-life, 10 grams of a third radioactive material remain. What was the total amount of radioactive material at the start?

CHAPTER

33 Precambrian through Paleozoic

▲
Fossil algae near Great Slave Lake, Canada

How Do You Know That . . .

Plants or animals lived on Earth billions of years ago? These rocks near Great Slave Lake in Canada are part of a huge fossil reef made by algae. The algae were living two billion years ago. Similar reefs were being built by other algae in warm, shallow waters around the world at that time. Reefs like this are one kind of evidence of past life.

I Precambrian Time

OBJECTIVES

A Define Precambrian time and identify the two eras that are part of the Precambrian.

B Discuss Precambrian fossils.

C Give some reasons why Precambrian rocks are difficult to interpret and discuss the origin, location, and economic importance of Precambrian rocks.

Topic 1 What Is Precambrian Time?

Precambrian time is all geologic time before the start of the Paleozoic Era. It includes the time span between the origin of Earth and 570 million years ago. The Archeozoic and Proterozoic eras discussed in Chapter 32 are part of Precambrian time. Most of geologic time is Precambrian time.

The single most important characteristic of the rocks formed during Precambrian time is their lack of fossils. This fossil shortage occurs for two major reasons. First, many Precambrian rocks are igneous or metamorphic in origin. The heat and pressure required to form these rocks usually destroy any plant or animal remains that might have been present. Second, the animals of Precambrian time apparently lacked the hard shells and skeletons needed for preservation. In other eras, fossils with hard parts are preserved in sedimentary rocks. Many examples of Precambrian sedimentary rocks do exist. Nevertheless, few Precambrian animals and plants were preserved in these rocks.

Topic 2 Precambrian Life

Despite intensive searching, only about 40 Precambrian fossil locations are known. Even though Precambrian fossils are rare, however, evidence for Precambrian life does exist. The fossil algae reefs of the opening photograph are just one example. These structures are called **stromatolites.** Stromatolites are made of alternating thin layers of silt that settled from the water, and calcium carbonate made by algae. Similar structures are found in Precambrian rocks in many parts of the world. They make up the greatest percentage of Precambrian fossils.

Stromatolites still form today but only in rare locations. Most are found in intertidal or shallow-water areas. Precambrian stromatolites are presumed to have formed in this same kind of environment.

Precambrian fossils are not limited only to stromatolites. A variety of other life forms existed during Precambrian time. Fossil remains of jellyfish, simple fungi, marine worms, and ancestors of modern corals, clams, and starfish have all been found. At one location, 56 different kinds of algae and other soft-bodied organisms were found dating back to late Proterozoic time.

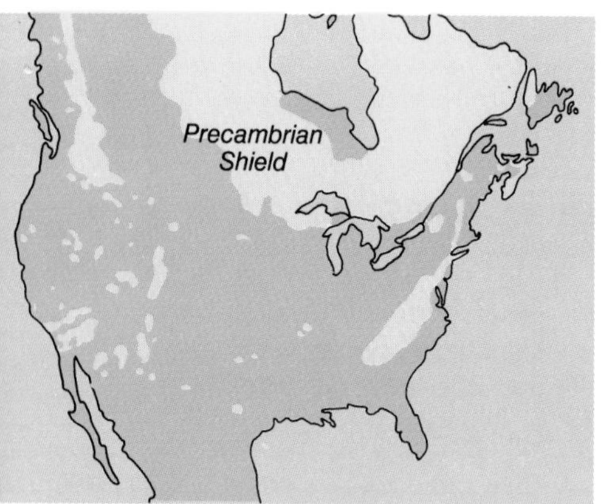

33.1 This map shows the location of Precambrian rocks in the United States.

Topic 3 Precambrian Rock Record

The Precambrian rock record has been very difficult to interpret for three reasons. First, the record covers an incredibly long interval of time. Second, many Precambrian rocks are severely bent and folded. Third and probably most important, the Precambrian is totally lacking in index fossils, which would have made correlations between rock units possible. Despite these problems, geologists have determined that the same processes that occur on Earth today went on during the Precambrian. Volcanism, plate movements, erosion, and deposition went on as they do today.

Most of the rocks that have survived since Precambrian time are found in the craton, the oldest rocks of the continent. These rocks are the remains of Precambrian mountains and highlands. Such Precambrian rocks can be seen on every continent. In fact, about one fifth of the surface rocks of the continents are Precambrian in age. These exposed areas of the craton are called **shields.** The relationship between the Canadian Shield and the North American craton was discussed in Chapter 13.

The details of plate movements during Precambrian time are not known. However, it is known that the continents were moving about. The North America craton experienced at least four *orogenies,* or mountain-building episodes, as a result of plate movements during Precambrian time. The last Precambrian orogeny occurred about a billion years ago when an unknown landmass collided with eastern Canada. This event is called the Grenville Orogeny. The remnants of the mountains that formed from this collision are seen today on the west side of the St. Lawrence River. The rocks of the Adirondack Mountains in New York State were also formed at this time.

Not all Precambrian rocks are part of the craton. Other areas where Precambrian rocks occur are in the Piedmont between the Appalachian Mountains and the Atlantic Ocean, at the bottom of the Grand Canyon in Arizona, in the core of the Rocky Mountains, and in New York City, as well as many other locations.

33.2 Lead and zinc are mined from Precambrian rocks at this mine in the Yukon.

Topic 4 Precambrian Mineral Deposits

The economic importance of Precambrian rocks is considerable. About half of the world's metallic mineral deposits occur in Precambrian rocks. Iron, copper, gold, silver, nickel, chromium, and uranium, as well as many other minerals, are all mined from Precambrian rocks.

Several important deposits are found in the Precambrian rocks of North America. These include the nickel deposits of Sudbury, Ontario, the taconite iron deposits of the Lake Superior region, the uranium ores at Great Bear Lake in northwestern Canada, and the magnetite and ilmenite ores from the Adirondack Mountains in New York State. The world-famous gold ores of South Africa also occur in Precambrian rocks.

TOPIC QUESTIONS

Each topic question refers to the topic of the same number.

1. **(a)** Define Precambrian time and identify the two eras that are part of Precambrian time. **(b)** Give two reasons why Precambrian rocks have few fossils.
2. **(a)** What are stromatolites? **(b)** How does the abundance of stromatolites compare with that of other Precambrian fossils? **(c)** Where are stromatolites found today? **(d)** List some examples of Precambrian life other than stromatolites.
3. **(a)** Give three reasons why the Precambrian rock record is difficult to interpret. **(b)** Where are most Precambrian rocks located on continents? What is the source of these rocks? **(c)** What was the Grenville Orogeny? When and why did it occur? **(d)** Identify some locations in North America where Precambrian rocks can be seen.
4. **(a)** Name some important metals that come from rocks of Precambrian age. **(b)** Locate some Precambrian mining areas.

Eleanor R. Bayley
Fossil Collector

Where could you go to see and study invertebrate fossils? One place is the Paleontological Research Institution in Ithaca, New York. This institution has the third-largest collection of invertebrate fossils in the world. Part of that collection was made by Eleanor R. Bayley. Her particular interest has been the fossils of the Hamilton group. These are well-known rock layers of Middle Devonian age. Her collection contains representative samples of such Hamilton fossil groups as brachiopods, cephalopods, pelecypods, gastropods, and bryozoans.

Ms. Bayley's primary purpose in making the collection was to help others in the identification of their own fossils. To do this, she has put her fossils on display in the institution's museum. She also helps fossil hunters by guiding them to the best collecting locations in the Ithaca area.

In addition to its impressive fossil collection, the institution also regularly publishes books, pamphlets, bulletins, and other materials about fossils. Many of these are used by paleontologists around the world.

OBJECTIVES

A List the periods of the Paleozoic Era, describe the difference between the Precambrian and Paleozoic fossil records, and discuss the location and climate of North America during the Paleozoic Era.

B Identify the major fossils and life changes of each Paleozoic period.

C Discuss the occurrence of mountain-building episodes, the formation of mineral deposits, ice ages, and the formation of Pangaea relative to Paleozoic time.

II The Paleozoic Era

Topic 5 Introduction to the Paleozoic Era

The Paleozoic Era marks the beginning of an abundant fossil record. As a result, geologists know a great deal about this era and have been able to divide the era into smaller segments of time called periods. In order from oldest to youngest, these periods are Cambrian, Ordovician, Silurian, Devonian, Mississippian, Pennsylvanian, and Permian. Most of the names of the Paleozoic periods come from Europe. Cambrian, for example, is named for Cambria, the Roman name for Wales. Wales is the part of Great Britain where rocks of this age were first studied. The Permian is named for an area of Russia called Perm. Mississippian and Pennsylvanian are North American names. In Europe, these two periods combined are called the Carboniferous Period.

The most important difference between the rocks of the Paleozoic Era and rocks of Precambrian time is the record of life preserved in the rocks. Precambrian rocks contain few fossils. The Paleozoic record is markedly different. Starting with the Cambrian, Paleozoic rocks contain an abundance of fossil remains. The Paleozoic animals had hard shells and skeletons that survived burial in the sediment and were preserved in the rocks.

At the beginning of the Paleozoic Era, there were a number of separate continents. They did not look like the continents of today, however. The continent that later became North America was on the equator and was rotated so that what is now the Arctic region faced eastward. As a result, the climate over the entire continent was warm with few seasonal changes. At times, tropical plants and animals lived in what is now Greenland.

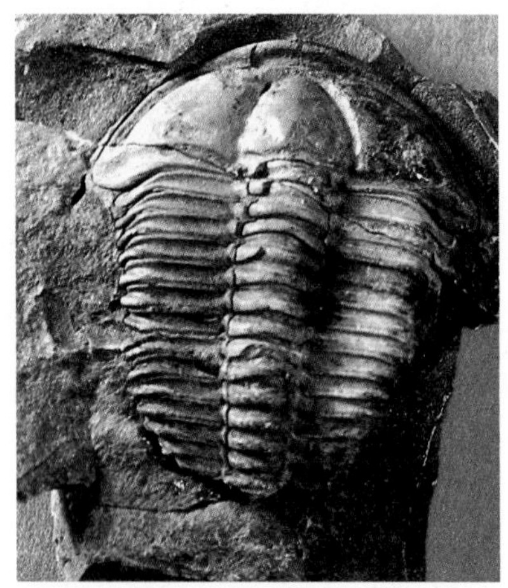

33.3 Trilobites are the most common Cambrian fossil.

Topic 6 The Cambrian Period

The *Cambrian Period* marks the appearance in the fossil record of an abundance of animals with hard preservable parts. The most important of the Cambrian animals is the trilobite. These animals make up more than half of all the Cambrian fossils that have been found. **Trilobites** were crablike animals that are thought to have been bottom scavengers and crawlers rather than swimmers. They became widespread during the Cambrian Period and are therefore good index fossils for that period. Even though trilobites can be found throughout the remainder of the Paleozoic Era, they are relatively unimportant after the Cambrian Period.

The second most common fossil of the Cambrian Period is the **brachiopod.** These are small, shelled animals that are sometimes mistaken for clams. The major brachiopod of the Cambrian Period was the simple smooth-shelled form called *Lingula.* Although other kinds of brachiopods are now extinct, *Lingula* are still found in some oceans today.

There was little mountain building during the Cambrian Period. Much of what is now North America was covered by warm oceans. These conditions enabled marine life to flourish. In fact, all of the fossils of the Cambrian Period are the remains of life forms that lived in the oceans. No land-living plants or animals of Cambrian age have been found.

Although the Cambrian Period marks the appearance in the fossil record of animals with hard preservable parts, soft-bodied animals were apparently still abundant. The evidence for soft-bodied life forms comes from a famous rock formation in the Rocky Mountains of Canada called the *Burgess Shale.* Here, worms and other soft-bodied animals have been preserved in remarkable detail. Over 120 different kind of animals have been found there. The Burgess Shale is middle Cambrian in age.

Topic 7 The Ordovician Period

The major change from life in the Cambrian Period to life in the *Ordovician Period* is a marked increase in the number of kinds of animals. All major groups of animals with hard parts had appeared by the close of the Ordovician Period. Like the organisms of the Cambrian, all Ordovician life forms were also ocean-living.

The important fossil of the Ordovician is the **graptolite.** Graptolites were tiny animals that lived together in floating groups, or colonies. They spread throughout the world's oceans. Although a few have been found in rocks of other periods, their greatest number and distribution occurred during the Ordovician Period. As a result, graptolites are the index fossils for the Ordovician.

During the Ordovician, brachiopods became more numerous than trilobites. A group of colonial animals called *bryozoans* appeared and became as numerous as the brachiopods. Cephalopods (relatives of the modern *Nautilus*), gastropods (snails), and echinoderms (relatives of the modern starfish) were important. One group of cephalopods, which built shells over six meters long, became the first large animals of the sea. Pelecypods (puh-LESS-uh-pods), the group to which clams belong, and corals appeared for the first time.

Earth's first vertebrates appeared in this period. They were primitive fish called *ostracoderms* (OSS-tra-koh-dermz). Fossils of ostracoderms have been found in Colorado and Wyoming.

The end of the Ordovician Period is marked by the Taconian Orogeny. This mountain-building episode occurred as a small plate broke away from northwestern Africa and collided with eastern North America. Part of the ocean subducted under eastern North America, thrusting offshore island arcs and deep-sea trenches onto the continental margins. The Green Mountains of Vermont and the Taconic Mountains of southeastern New York State are remnants of that collision.

a

b

c

33.4 Ordovician life forms. (a) Graptolites were colonial animals. Each sawtooth is the home of one animal. (b) A fossil cephalopod (c) The ostracoderm was the first vertebrate.

33.5 A eurypterid (sea scorpion) from the Silurian Period is shown attacking its prey.

Topic 8 The Silurian Period

The most interesting group of organisms to appear in the oceans during the *Silurian Period* were the **eurypterids,** sometimes called sea scorpions. These animals seem to be distant cousins of the trilobites. Some grew to three meters in length.

In general, Silurian life was similar to that of the Ordovician. Brachiopods and bryozoans were still important. Corals and echinoderms became more numerous. The oldest known coral reefs are Silurian in age.

One of the most significant events of the Silurian was the appearance of plants and animals on land. As far as anyone knows, the land surface was bare until late Silurian time. Rocks of that age are the first to contain any record of land plants. The late Silurian record is well preserved and unmistakable. Although vertebrate animals, such as amphibians, do not appear in the land fossil record until the Devonian Period, animals such as spiders, millipedes, and scorpions were living on the land in late Silurian time.

Also during the late Silurian, the climate of what is now the northern United States became very dry. Shallow seas in eastern North America evaporated continuously. Thick beds of rock salt and gypsum were left from central New York State to Lake Michigan. The salt deposits near Detroit, Michigan, and Syracuse, New York, are in this belt. The famous Lockport dolomite, the cap rock of Niagara Falls, also formed during this time.

Topic 9 The Devonian Period

Coral reefs reached their greatest development in the *Devonian Period* as North America remained equatorial. At the same time, calcite-forming sponges that lived in warm oceans built reefs.

The major event of the Devonian Period was the appearance of several kinds of fish. Although they were not abundant in this period, fish are still important. The earliest fish were jawless and covered with heavy plates. They are presumed to have been poor swimmers. Some armored fish were giants of the Devonian seas, reaching lengths of nine meters. Because fish first appeared during the Devonian, it is called the *Age of Fishes.*

The first fossils of lungfish are found in Devonian rocks. When they are out of the water, lungfish can breathe air. Lungfish still exist today. Before the Devonian Period ended, a group of fish similar to lungfish developed very strong fins. With these fins, they crawled out of the water and lived briefly on land. These lobe-finned fish gave rise to the first amphibians.

Land plants multiplied in both number and variety during the Devonian Period. True (spore-bearing) ferns, seed-bearing ferns, and giant rushes (horsetails) developed. Trees appeared with scaly bark resembling snakeskin. Primitive conifers, ancestors of today's cone-bearing pines and fir trees, have also been found. The first forests date from the Devonian Period.

Devonian rocks indicate that the Devonian Period was relatively quiet. Thick limestone formations were deposited in widespread shallow seas. The close of the Devonian, however, is marked by the collision of North America with the northwest coast of Africa. These landmasses had been moving slowly toward each other during the previous periods. The collision raised mountains from Newfoundland to the Appalachian region. Igneous activity that accompanied the collision helped to build the White Mountains of New Hampshire. This episode is known as the Acadian Orogeny.

Topic 10 The Mississippian Period

Although advances in the evolution of life were not so striking in the *Mississippian Period* as in earlier periods, two groups did become important at that time. They are the crinoids and the foraminifera.

Crinoids (CRY-noydz) are the most abundant Mississippian fossils. Although crinoids look like plants and are called sea lilies, they are actually invertebrate animals. Crinoids are related to starfish. Unlike starfish, however, crinoids spend most of their lives attached to the seafloor. Crinoids are found today in all of the world's oceans but not nearly in the numbers that lived during the Mississippian.

Foraminifera are one-celled animals related to the amoeba. Foraminifera build tiny calcite shells that are usually less than one millimeter in diameter. Foraminifera first appear in the fossil record during the Cambrian Period, but they became common during the Mississippian Period. They are still found in the oceans.

Like the Devonian Period, much of the Mississippian Period was a rather quiet time. It was not until late in the period that the Allegheny Orogeny began. During this mountain building episode, uplift occurred in the middle and southern Appalachians and the ancestral Rockies appeared.

a

b

33.6 Mississippian life forms. (a) Although they look like plants, crinoids are actually animals. They are relatives of modern starfish. (b) The eye of the needle shows how tiny the foraminifera are.

Topic 11 The Pennsylvanian Period

During the *Pennsylvanian Period,* the interior basins of what is now the eastern United States were almost always underwater. When they were below sea level, the basins held inland seas. When they were above sea level, they became freshwater swamps.

Because North America still straddled the equator at this time, the climate was warm and rainy. Trees, ferns, and rushes filled swamps and forests. In the swamps, the dead trees and ferns slowly changed to peat, which in time changed to coal. Today these deposits form the rich coal fields of Pennsylvania, Ohio, West Virginia, Indiana, and Illinois.

When inland seas covered the interior basins, no coal was formed. Instead of trees, there were deposits of sand, mud, and lime. In time, these deposits became the layers of sandstone, shale, and limestone that now separate the coal beds.

33.7 The swampy forests of the Pennsylvanian Period became a major source of coal in the United States.

In the animal world, the first reptiles appeared. These reptiles resembled today's lizards. The reptiles were the first true land vertebrates. They spread into areas where amphibians could not live.

Insects had appeared in the Silurian Period. In the Pennsylvanian Period, however, insects thrived. The largest insects were giant dragonflies with a wingspan of almost a meter. Cockroaches abounded and reached lengths of ten centimeters. Their number and variety is the reason that the Pennsylvanian Period has become known as the *Age of Cockroaches.*

The Allegheny Orogeny reached its peak during the Pennsylvanian Period. As the continents collided, causing this mountain building episode, one great supercontinent was taking shape.

Topic 12 The Permian Period

The *Permian Period* is noted for its dry climate. Sea water that had filled shallow inland seas steadily evaporated. Great deposits of salt and gypsum formed in many parts of the world. In the United States, Permian beds of rock salt and gypsum are widespread. These deposits run through Nebraska, Kansas, Oklahoma, and Texas.

Corals thrived in the warm waters of the oceans and in the deeper inland seas. Large coral reefs of Permian age are found in the Guadalupe Mountains of West Texas.

During the Permian Period, a great ice age took place, mostly in the Southern Hemisphere. The ice covered parts of South America, Australia, South Africa, and India.

Topic 13 The Close of the Paleozoic Era

The close of the Permian is marked by a time of unusually widespread mountain building as the result of continental collisions. The Appalachians were probably fully elevated and appeared all along the eastern border of North America. Siberia and Europe collided to form the Ural Mountains. Other collisions involved southeast Asia, South America, Australia, and Antarctica. Before the end of the Permian, most of the continental crust in the world had welded together into one supercontinent. Alfred Wegener, in his theory of continental drift, named this continent Pangaea.

However, the most significant feature of the end of the Paleozoic is the great number of life forms that died out at that time. By the close of the Paleozoic Era, nearly half of all known animal groups became extinct. The worst losses were among the marine invertebrates. Trilobites and eurypterids, two groups that had been important in earlier periods of the Paleozoic Era, were extinct by the end of the Paleozoic. Other groups, including corals, brachiopods, and crinoids, were greatly reduced in number and variety.

Among the land plants, the seed ferns, scale trees, and primitive conifers that had been so important to the formation of the coal beds of Mississippian and Pennsylvanian times were almost all extinct by the end of the Permian.

Among the survivors of the Paleozoic extinctions were two groups that became important in the Mesozoic Era. These groups are the cephalopods in the oceans and the reptiles on the land.

TOPIC QUESTIONS

Each topic question refers to the topic of the same number.

5. **(a)** What is the most important difference between Precambrian rocks and Paleozoic rocks? **(b)** Describe the climate of North America during the Paleozoic Era.

6. **(a)** Why are trilobites important to Cambrian time? **(b)** What is the evidence that Cambrian life forms all lived in the oceans?

7. **(a)** What is the basic difference between Cambrian and Ordovician life? **(b)** Why are graptolites important to Ordovician time? **(c)** What caused the Taconian Orogeny and what mountains were formed by it?

8. **(a)** Compare Silurian life to that of the Ordovician. **(b)** Describe the cause and location of the late Silurian salt and gypsum deposits.

9. **(a)** Why is the Devonian called the Age of Fishes? **(b)** Why were the lobe-finned fish important? **(c)** What caused the Acadian Orogeny and what mountains resulted?

10. Identify and describe the two groups of organisms that were important during Mississippian time.

11. What conditions of sea level and climate resulted in the formation of the Pennsylvanian coal fields?

12. **(a)** In which states did rock salt and gypsum deposits form in Permian time? **(b)** Which modern land areas were affected by the Permian ice age?

13. **(a)** What was Pangaea and when did it form? **(b)** List some groups that died out at the close of the Paleozoic. **(c)** List some life forms that were reduced in number.

CHAPTER 33 REVIEW

Summary

All geologic time before the Paleozoic Era is called Precambrian. Fossils are rare in Precambrian rocks. Stromatolites are the most important Precambrian fossils.

The Precambrian rock record is difficult to interpret for several reasons.

Shield areas contain exposures of Precambrian rocks from a continent's craton.

Precambrian rocks are the source of about half of the world's metallic mineral deposits.

The Paleozoic Era is divided into seven periods.

During the Paleozoic Era, North America was located over the equator.

The Cambrian Period marks the start of an abundant fossil record. Trilobites and brachiopods were most important. The Burgess Shale is Cambrian in age.

Animal life increased in variety during Ordovician time. Graptolites are the index fossil for the period. Other groups, including primitive fish, also appeared for the first time. The Taconian Orogeny closed the period.

Eurypterids were important during the Silurian, along with the first land plants and animals. The dry climate allowed salt and gypsum to form in the northeastern United States.

Corals reached their peak in Devonian time. Several kinds of fish developed, one of which gave rise to the first amphibians. Land plants thrived. The Acadian Orogeny closed the period.

Crinoids and foraminifera were important during the Mississippian Period. The Allegheny Orogeny began late in the period.

Swamps of the Pennsylvanian Period became the rich coal fields of today. The first reptiles also appeared during the Pennsylvanian. Insects thrived.

Rock salt and gypsum formed in some western states during the Permian, and an ice age occurred in the Southern Hemisphere.

Many animals and plant groups became extinct or nearly extinct at the close of the Paleozoic Era. Cephalopods and reptiles survived.

Pangaea formed before the close of Paleozoic time.

Vocabulary

brachiopod	foraminifera	shield
crinoid	graptolite	stromatolites
eurypterid	Precambrian	trilobite

Review

On your paper, write the word or words that best complete each sentence.

1. The single most important characteristic of Precambrian rocks is that they contain few _____ remains.
2. Stromatolites, the most common fossil of the Precambrian, form today in areas where the water depth is _____.
3. The major reason that the Precambrian rock record is difficult to interpret is that these rocks lack _____ fossils.
4. The Canadian _____ is the exposed part of the North American craton.
5. The nickel deposits at Sudbury, Ontario, and the gold ores of South Africa both formed during _____ time.
6. The Carboniferous Period of Europe is the Mississippian and Pennsylvanian periods of North _____.
7. The two most important fossils of the Cambrian Period were crablike animals called _____ and shelled animals called brachiopods.
8. No land-living animals are known for either the _____ or Ordovician periods.
9. Tiny floating animals called graptolites are the index _____ for the Ordovician Period.
10. The first vertebrate, a primitive _____ called ostracoderm, is found in Ordovician rocks of Colorado and Wyoming.

11. The first fossil record of land plants and animals comes from the ____ Period.
12. The Devonian Period is known as the Age of Fishes because of the appearance of ____ ____ fish in the fossil record.
13. The collision of North America with Africa at the close of the Devonian raised mountains all along the ____ coast of North America.
14. Crinoids, the most abundant fossil of the Mississippian Period, are also called ____ lilies.
15. Foraminifera, one-celled animals of the Mississippian Period, build tiny ____ made of calcite.
16. The great swamps of the Pennsylvanian Period became the rich ____ beds of today.
17. Insects thrived in the Pennsylvanian, including a giant ____ with a wingspan of almost one meter.
18. The ____ climate of the Permian resulted in deposits of rock salt and gypsum in Nebraska, Kansas, Oklahoma, and Texas.
19. The Southern Hemisphere had an ____ age in the Permian Period.
20. Trilobites and eurypterids had become ____ by the end of the Permian Period.

Interpret and Apply

On your paper, answer each question in complete sentences.

1. Why are there no Precambrian coal beds?
2. The oldest known rock is a sedimentary rock. How do you know that even older rocks must have existed at one time?
3. Why are graptolites likely to be better index fossils than crinoids?
4. Imagine yourself standing in the Pennsylvanian swampy forest shown in Figure 33.7. If you had stood in that exact same spot during the Cambrian Period, how would the view have been different?
5. What effect would a supercontinent like Pangaea be expected to have on the distribution of land plants and animals?

Critical Thinking

The chart shows the occurrence in the rock record of 10 different Paleozoic fossils. The periods of the Paleozoic are indicated across the top of the chart—*C* stands for Cambrian, *O* for Ordovician, *S* for Silurian, *D* for Devonian, *M* for Mississippian, *P* for Pennsylvanian, and *PR* for Permian. The fossils are indicated along the left side of the chart. The specific name of each fossil is shown in parenthesis after the name of the group to which it belongs.

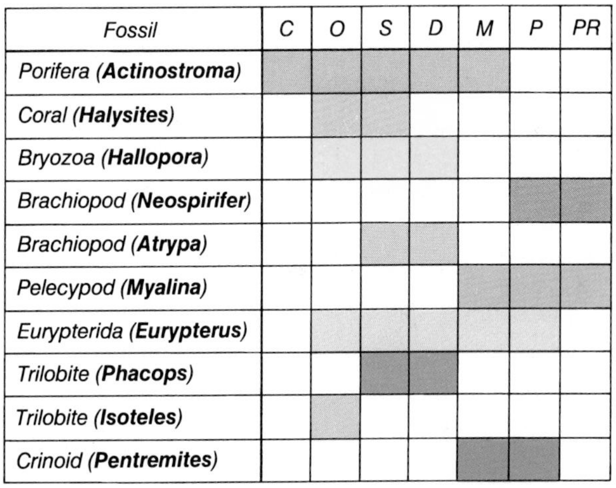

Fossil	*C*	*O*	*S*	*D*	*M*	*P*	*PR*
Porifera (***Actinostroma***)	■	■	■	■	■		
Coral (***Halysites***)		■	■				
Bryozoa (***Hallopora***)		■	■	■			
Brachiopod (***Neospirifer***)						■	■
Brachiopod (***Atrypa***)			■	■			
Pelecypod (***Myalina***)					■	■	■
Eurypterida (***Eurypterus***)		■	■	■	■	■	
Trilobite (***Phacops***)			■	■			
Trilobite (***Isoteles***)		■					
Crinoid (***Pentremites***)					■	■	

1. During which geologic period(s) did the trilobite *Isoteles* live?
2. What is the range of geologic periods for the porifera *Actinostroma*?
3. Two brachiopods appear in the list. Neither brachiopod can be used to identify a Mississippian age rock. Why?
4. What is the probable age of a rock layer that contains the porifera *Actinostroma* and the crinoid *Pentremites*?
5. What is the possible age of a rock layer that contains *Halysites* and *Atrypa*?
6. List the fossils that might be expected to occur in a rock of Devonian age.
7. Two trilobites are shown on the list. How do you know that at least one other kind of trilobite must exist?

CHAPTER

34

The Mesozoic and Cenozoic Eras

▲ Based on fossil evidence, scientists have been able to construct full-scale models of dinosaurs like this Triceratops.

How Do You Know That . . .

Dinosaurs were not warm-blooded? One way to find out the temperature of an animal that has been extinct for 65 million years is by the structure of its bones. The bones of active, warm-blooded animals are full of tiny channels where blood vessels were located. Less active cold-blooded animals have few blood vessel channels in their bones. Surprisingly, the bones of many dinosaurs are full of the tiny channels common to warm-blooded animals. Although some scientists vigorously disagree, others now think that at least some dinosaurs were warm-blooded like modern mammals and birds rather than cold-blooded like modern reptiles.

I The Mesozoic Era

Topic 1 Highlights of the Mesozoic Era

Dinosaur bones are probably the most famous fossil remains. However, the rise and fall of the dinosaurs was just one event of the Mesozoic Era. Other groups of animals as well as plants also appeared for the first time in the Mesozoic. Some, like dinosaurs, were extinct by the close of the era. Others went on to become important in the Cenozoic Era.

The Mesozoic Era began 230 million years ago and ended 65 million years ago. This span of 165 million years is the second shortest of the five geologic eras. Mesozoic time is divided into three periods – Triassic, Jurassic, and Cretaceous.

Throughout most of Mesozoic time, the Appalachian Mountains and eastern North America were being worn down. However, new mountains were raised in western North America. Pangaea, the supercontinent that had formed at the end of the Paleozoic Era, broke into the familiar continents of today.

The Mesozoic climate was mild. Coral grew in what is now Europe. The poles were free of glacial ice. Some evidence indicates that ocean surface temperatures, even in the Arctic, were 10°C to 20°C warmer than today.

Several areas of geologic interest were formed in the western and southwestern United States during the Mesozoic Era. The Navajo Sandstone, a widespread deposit of fossil sand dunes, was formed during the Triassic Period. The Morrison formation, a rock unit famous for dinosaur bones, was formed during the Jurassic Period. The famous aquifer of the Great Plains, the Dakota Sandstone, is Cretaceous in age.

OBJECTIVES

A Name the periods of the Mesozoic Era and a famous rock unit that formed during each, discuss the changes in Pangaea during the Mesozoic, and summarize the Mesozoic climate.

B Explain why dinosaurs are important to the Mesozoic Era, name the different kinds of dinosaurs and give examples of each, and identify some locations where dinosaur bones are found.

C Discuss other Mesozoic animal and plant life; explain the importance of ammonites.

D Identify some animal groups that died out at the close of the Mesozoic Era and list some possible causes of their extinction.

34.1 The Dakota Sandstone is a closely studied Mesozoic formation.

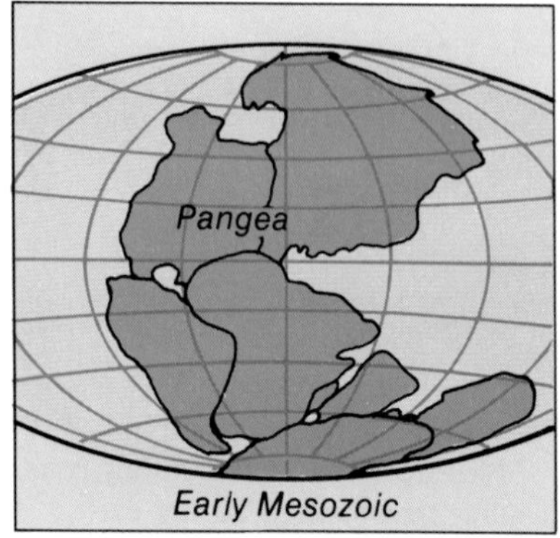

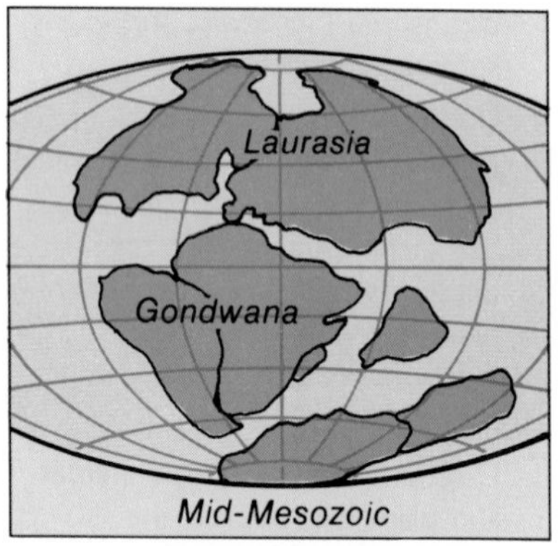

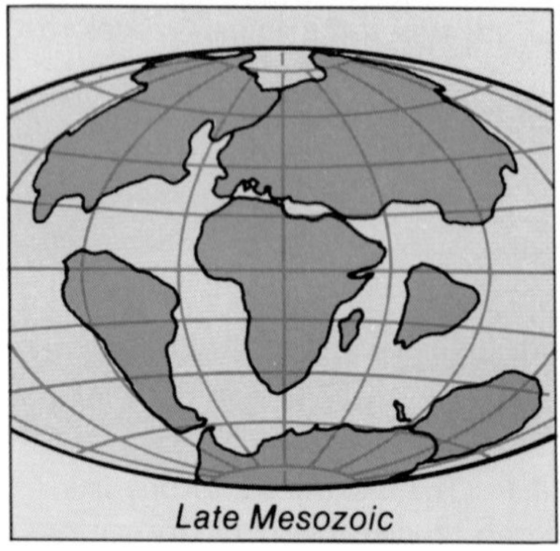

34.2 During the Mesozoic Era, Pangaea split apart forming smaller continents that resembled the continents of today.

Topic 2 Continent Formation

At the close of the Paleozoic Era and continuing into the Mesozoic Era, almost all of Earth's land areas were joined together into a single large continent, Pangaea. The total land area of that continent was about the same as the total land area of all of the continents today. A large bay called the *Tethys Sea* separated what are now the continents of Africa and Eurasia.

Starting about 180 million years ago, in late Triassic, faulting and igneous activity in Europe, North America, South America, and Africa split Pangaea into two parts. The northern part, containing the future continents of North America and Eurasia, is called *Laurasia*. The southern part, with the remainder of the continents, is called *Gondwana*. The basaltic lavas of the Palisades Sill in New Jersey as well as the igneous rocks of several other east coast locations formed at this time.

By the close of Jurassic time 135 million years ago, the North Atlantic and Indian oceans had both formed. The South Atlantic Ocean between South America and Africa was just starting to open. India had begun to move toward Asia. The uplift that formed the Sierra Nevadas occurred at the end of the Jurassic Period.

During most of the Cretaceous Period, much of central and southeastern North America was underwater. The close of the period, however, saw the birth of the Rocky Mountain chain and the re-elevation of the Appalachians.

When the Mesozoic Era ended 65 million years ago, the South Atlantic had become a major ocean, and all of the continents had taken on their present appearance. However, North America and Eurasia were still joined together. Australia and Antarctica also remained connected.

Topic 3 The Rise of the Dinosaurs

The most common land vertebrates of the Mesozoic Era were the **dinosaurs,** a group of large terrestrial reptiles. Dinosaurs lived on all of the continents. The western United States seems to have been a particularly good environment for dinosaurs and, as a result, most dinosaur fossils come from there. Montana, Utah, Wyoming, Colorado, Kansas, Texas, Oklahoma, and New Mexico all have yielded important dinosaur fossils. The richest dinosaur graveyard known is at Como Bluff, Wyoming. The major digging there occurred between 1877 and 1889. Universities and museums throughout North America are still sorting and studying bones removed from the Como Bluff quarry at that time.

The oldest known dinosaur fossil is 225 million years old. The youngest dinosaur fossil is 65 million years old. Thus dinosaurs dominated Earth for 160 million years. By comparison, humans developed only during the last 2 to 3 million years.

The first dinosaurs were small, some no larger than rabbits. Although some dinosaurs were 1.5 to 2 meters long by the end of

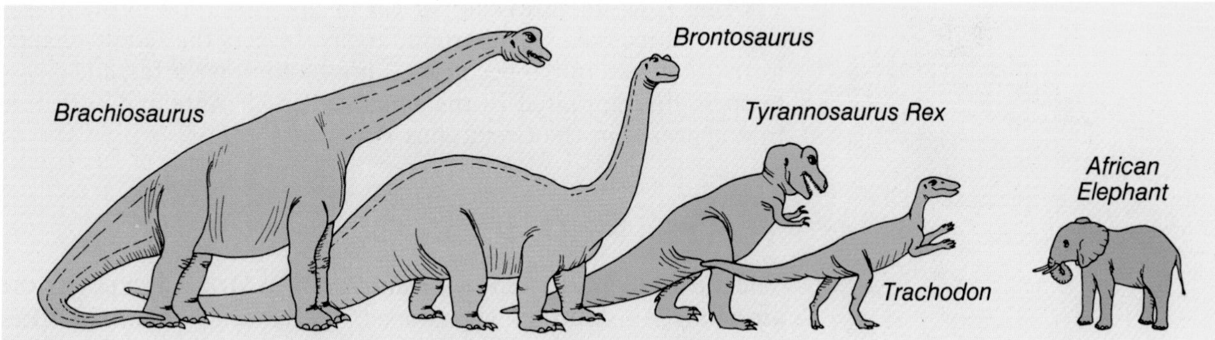

34.3 Compared to elephants, some dinosaurs were enormous in size.

the Triassic, the largest dinosaurs lived during the Cretaceous. These dinosaurs averaged 25 to 30 meters in length. The largest dinosaur known came from the Dry Mesa quarry near Delta, Colorado. This dinosaur could have seen *over* a five-story building.

Dinosaurs were either meat eaters (carnivores) or plant eaters (herbivores). The largest of the meat eaters was *Tyrannosaurus rex.* This dinosaur walked on its rear feet, stood about 6 meters high, and had a huge head with razor-sharp, banana-size teeth. Although carnivorous dinosaurs lived throughout the Mesozoic Era, *Tyrannosaurus rex* did not appear until the Cretaceous Period. *Allosaurus,* another carnivore, lived in the Jurassic Period.

The plant-eating dinosaurs are often divided into four groups: armored dinosaurs, horned dinosaurs, duck-billed dinosaurs, and sauropods. *Stegosaurus,* with a long row of bony plates down its back, was an armored dinosaur. Three-horned *Triceratops* was a horned dinosaur, and the strange-looking *Trachodon* was a duck-billed dinosaur. The sauropods were the largest of the dinosaurs and the largest land animals that ever lived. *Brontosaurus* (whose correct name is actually *Apatosaurus*) is the most familiar example. Other sauropods included *Diplodocus* and *Brachiosaurus.* The five-story monster from Dry Mesa quarry was a kind of *Brachiosaurus.*

34.4 *Stegosaurus* was an armored dinosaur.

Topic 4 Other Land Animals

Although the dinosaurs were the most important Mesozoic land animals, there were other land animals. Mammals first appeared in the Jurassic Period. The first of these were tiny, primitive, rodent-like creatures. Mammals developed throughout the Mesozoic and became the dominant land animal of the Cenozoic.

The Jurassic Period also marks the appearance of the first birds. For many years, the oldest known bird was *Archeopteryx.* The fossil record clearly shows that the immediate ancestor of this bird was a dinosaur. Although *Archeopteryx* had wings and feathers, it probably could not fly. It also had teeth and is assumed to have laid eggs. In 1984, fossils of an even older bird, called *Protoavis,* were found in Texas. The pelvis, tail, hindlegs, and claws of *Protoavis* resemble those of dinosaurs, but other features are more birdlike than similar features on *Archeopteryx.* Two *Protoavis* skeletons were found, both about the size of a modern crow.

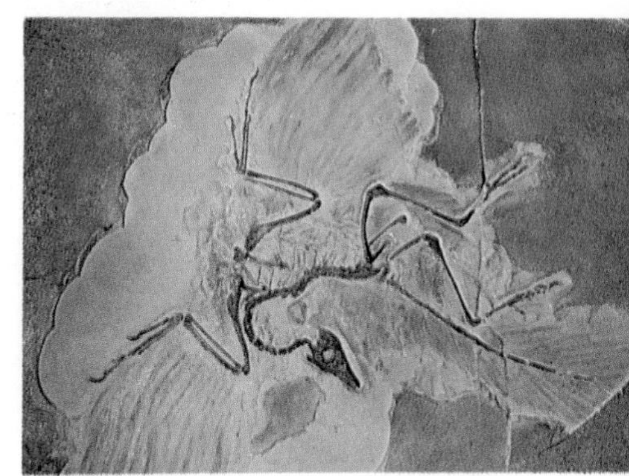

34.5 *Archeopteryx* had wings and feathers but probably could not fly.

Other land creatures that appear for the first time in the Mesozoic fossil record are still around today. Insects that could change form (like a caterpillar becoming a moth), flies, termites, and grasshoppers first appeared in the Jurassic Period. Ants and anteaters first appeared in the Cretaceous Period.

Topic 5 Marine Life

The most important marine organism of the Mesozoic Era was the **ammonite,** a kind of cephalopod. Many kinds of ammonites occurred worldwide during the Triassic Period, but almost all became extinct at the close of that period. A single group that survived gave rise to even more new varieties in the Jurassic and Cretaceous periods. Ammonites are excellent index fossils for the Mesozoic Era.

Some of the Mesozoic reptiles invaded the seas. *Ichthyosaurs* were reptiles that looked like swordfish. Some grew to lengths of 8 meters. Snakelike *plesiosaurs* were even longer, up to 15 meters.

Some Paleozoic invertebrates become more numerous during the Mesozoic Era. Corals almost became extinct at the end of the Paleozoic Era. The survivors gave rise to a new group of corals in the Triassic Period that developed a modern appearance by the Cretaceous Period. Bryozoans, along with certain varieties of clams, became important again during the Cretaceous.

34.6 The giant redwoods are a remnant of the warmer climates of the early Cenozoic Era.

Topic 6 Land Plants

Early Mesozoic plant life was based upon the survivors of the Paleozoic Era. These plants included tree ferns, spore-bearing ferns, rushes, and conifers. New plants of the early Mesozoic Era were pines, yews, and cypresses.

Plant life made its greatest change during the Cretaceous Period, when flowering plants appeared. Chief among these were the deciduous trees. These trees developed rapidly until they crowded the forests. First came magnolia, sassafras, fig, willow, laurel, and the tulip tree. Later came oak, maple, beech, birch, walnut, chestnut, and other modern trees. Evergreen conifers continued. The sequoia, ancestor of California's giant redwoods, first appeared.

Topic 7 The Mesozoic Era Closes

One of the great puzzles of the rock record is the cause of the disappearance of many kinds of plants and animals at the close of the Mesozoic Era. All of the dinosaurs vanished along with the flying and swimming reptiles, most marine turtles, crocodiles, lizards, and many others. Scientists believe that over 50 percent of the plant and animal groups on Earth were wiped out at that time.

Many reasons have been suggested for this mass extinction. These reasons include a change in climate, the rise of mammals, the uplift of mountains from plate motions, and worldwide disease. In recent years, a new theory has been proposed that is still being debated. This new theory came with the accidental discovery that the rocks at the boundary between Mesozoic time and Cenozoic time contained enormous amounts of the element iridium. This element does not occur in any great amount in Earth's crust. It does, however, occur abundantly in rocks of extraterrestrial origin such as meteorites. The suggestion was made that the iridium at the boundary came from the impact of a very large asteroid with Earth. The dust from the impact filled the atmosphere, blocking sunlight for several years. Land plants and marine plankton died because they needed sunlight to live and grow. Animals that use the plants for food then died of starvation.

TOPIC QUESTIONS

Each topic question refers to the topic of the same number.

1. **(a)** How long was the Mesozoic Era? **(b)** List the three periods of the Mesozoic. **(c)** Describe what was happening to the land in North America during Mesozoic time. **(d)** List some evidence for a mild Mesozoic climate.

2. **(a)** How did the total land area of Pangaea compare to the total land area on Earth today? **(b)** Which continents made up Laurasia? Which made up Gondwana? **(c)** What was the Tethys Seaway? **(d)** Which two oceans had formed by the close of Jurassic time? **(e)** Identify two pairs of modern continents that were still joined at the end of the Mesozoic Era.

3. **(a)** Compare the duration of dinosaur history with human history. **(b)** How did the size of typical dinosaurs change during the Mesozoic? **(c)** What name is applied to meat-eating dinosaurs? List two examples. **(d)** What are plant-eating dinosaurs called? **(e)** Name the four groups of plant-eating dinosaurs and give an example of each.

4. **(a)** When did the first mammals appear? What were they like? **(b)** Name the two earliest birds. Which was found first? Which lived earliest? **(c)** When did the first anteater appear?

5. **(a)** What is the most important marine organism of the Mesozoic Era? **(b)** List two Mesozoic marine reptiles. **(c)** Name two Paleozoic invertebrates that did well in the Mesozoic Era.

6. Describe the changes that took place in plant life during the Mesozoic Era.

7. **(a)** Name some animal groups that became extinct at the close of the Mesozoic Era. **(b)** What reasons have been suggested for these extinctions? **(c)** What element has been discovered in the rocks at the boundary between Mesozoic and Cenozoic time? **(d)** What is thought to be the source of that element and how is it related to the Mesozoic extinctions?

OBJECTIVES

A List the periods and epochs of the Cenozoic Era, summarize the crustal activity of the era, and describe the changes in climate that occurred over the era.

B Explain why mammals were important to Cenozoic time; give some examples of mammals that evolved but died out and of mammals that evolved and continue today.

C Summarize other Cenozoic plant and animal life.

D Define and give the characteristics of hominids, trace the development of hominids, and describe the effect of humans on animal life since the end of the Ice Age.

II The Cenozoic Era

Topic 8 Highlights of the Cenozoic Era

The Cenozoic Era is called the Age of Mammals. The tiny mammals that survived extinction at the close of the Mesozoic evolved into the familiar animals of today. Modern plants also evolved. At the same time, the plate movements that began with the breakup of Pangaea in the Mesozoic continued into the Cenozoic, leaving the continents in their present locations. And finally, ice moved from the polar regions to cover large parts of several continents, including North America.

The Cenozoic Era began 65 million years ago. Early geologists divided the era into two periods. The first, covering the time before the Ice Age, was called the *Tertiary*. The second, from the Ice Age to the present, was named the *Quaternary* (qua-TUR-na-ry). Because the Cenozoic is the most recent of the eras, more is known about events of that era than about events of any other. As a result, Cenozoic time is divided into smaller segments. Geologists divide the Tertiary Period into five epochs—*Paleocene*, *Eocene*, *Oligocene*, *Miocene*, and *Pliocene*. The Quaternary contains two epochs, the *Pleistocene*, or Ice Age, and the *Recent*.

Like the climate throughout the Mesozoic, early Cenozoic climates were also warm and humid. Then mountain building activity raised large portions of the continents. With much of the land at higher elevations, temperatures began to fall. By the Pleistocene Epoch, the climate had become very cold. Great sheets of ice covered the northern parts of North America, Europe, Asia, and all of Greenland and Antarctica. Altogether, about one fourth of all the land was covered by ice at that time. (One tenth of the land is covered by ice now.)

Topic 9 Crustal Activity in the Cenozoic Era

When the Cenozoic Era began, North America looked much as it does today. Only the Atlantic and Gulf coastal plains and parts of California were submerged. These areas were covered and uncovered by seawater several times during the Cenozoic Era.

Both the Appalachian and Rocky mountains were worn down and raised again in this era. The Colorado Plateau was raised a number of times. During its last uplift, the Colorado River carved out the Grand Canyon. Faulting created the fault-block mountains of the Basin and Range of Nevada and the Sierra Nevadas of California and Nevada.

Volcanism was also active during the Cenozoic. Lava flows built up the Columbia Plateau in what is now Washington, Oregon, Idaho, and California. Erupting volcanoes were common features of the landscape from the Cascade Mountains to the Southwest. In the Yellowstone National Park area, lava and ash buried whole forests of trees several times. Later these trees were petrified by minerals in groundwater.

Mountain building also took place on other continents besides North America. The highest mountains of today, the Himalayas, were uplifted as India crashed into Asia. The Alps were formed as Africa pushed into Europe. The Andes Mountains in South America already existed but were raised higher in late Cenozoic time, as the Nazca Plate subducted under the South American Plate.

34.7 Liberty Bell Mountain and the rest of the Cascades were formed during the Cenozoic Era.

Topic 10 Rise of the Mammals

Mammals have left the most extensive fossil record of any plant or animal group. Although the first mammal fossils were found in rocks of early Jurassic age, these animals were often very difficult to tell from reptiles. They were also very tiny—the largest were only the size of mice or squirrels. With the extinction of the dinosaurs at the end of the Mesozoic, mammals began to increase in number, variety, and size.

Among the first mammals of the Cenozoic were the *creodonts.* These primitive carnivores flourished in the early Tertiary. Some resembled modern cats or dogs, but all died out during the Oligocene, the fourth epoch of the Tertiary. Other mammals that appeared in the Cretaceous and are now extinct are the *oreodon,* an early grazing animal that resembled modern deer; the mastodon, a kind of elephant; *brontotherium,* a giant animal with a head like a rhinoceros and a body like an elephant; *baluchitherium,* a giant rhinoceros and the largest land mammal of all time; the giant armadillo; and the giant ground sloth.

34.8 This oreodon fossil was found in Wyoming, near the White River.

Some animals that first appeared in the Cenozoic continue today. In almost every case, the first animal of each group to appear was very much smaller than the modern animal. Horses, for example, first appeared in the Eocene and were about the size of a large cat. Other examples of animals that appeared and remain today are camels, rhinoceroses, pigs, dogs, beavers, and rabbits.

34.9 *Brontotherium* stood nearly 3 meters high at the shoulder.

34.10 Invertebrates like these starfish were common during the Cenozoic Era.

Topic 11 Other Cenozoic Animals

Throughout the Cenozoic Era, the oceans were home to nearly the same invertebrate animals as today. Foraminifera were very abundant in the early half of the era. Sponges, corals, starfish, sea urchins, and sand dollars were fairly common then. Brachiopods and cephalopods were rare. Mollusks—clams, oysters, mussels, and snails—thrived throughout the era. Crabs and barnacles were common as well.

On land, the spiders, centipedes, scorpions, and insects continued to thrive. Insects included butterflies, moths, bees, wasps, ants, beetles, and many others.

Most Cenozoic fish were like those of Late Mesozoic time. Sharks and rays were abundant and gigantic. Some sharks were 20 meters long with jaws nearly 2 meters wide.

Amphibians, such as frogs, toads, and salamanders, were about as common as they are now. The reptiles—turtles, lizards, snakes, and crocodiles—resembled those of today.

Birds developed that were similar to those of today. Early in the era, however, there were many ostrichlike types. Some were three meters tall. None of them could fly.

Topic 12 Plant Life

Many modern trees had developed in the Cretaceous Period. Most of them still exist today. At the beginning of the Cenozoic Era, the warm and humid climate favored the growth of tropical plants even in the northern United States. These included palm, fern, fig, and camphor trees. Cypress, laurel, and sequoia grew as far north as Greenland.

As the temperatures cooled late in the era, tropical plants died off except in equatorial areas. By the end of the era, these plants had disappeared from western North America. Sequoia trees remained although they were reduced to only two kinds. The big trees of the California Sierras and the redwoods of coastal California and Oregon are examples.

Replacing the forests in colder, drier areas were grasses. Grasses began to appear in about the middle of the Cenozoic Era. Animals that grazed on the grasses thrived. These grasses are thought to be the cause of the almost explosive evolution of grazing animals such as horses. Some of the grasses developed into the familiar grains of today, such as wheat, corn, barley, rye, oats, and rice.

Topic 13 The Rise of Hominids

The fossil record contains extensive traces of early human life. Over 3000 fossils, consisting of jaws, teeth, skulls, and other bones, have been found. Many of these fossils are dated to be between 2.5 and 7 million years old.

34.11 These footprints in volcanic ash were made by a hominid 3.5 million years ago.

Two chief characteristics distinguish humanlike fossils from apelike fossils. One is brain size. Modern humans have brains that occupy a volume of about 1300 cubic centimeters, larger than the brains of apes. The other distinguishing characteristic is that humans are bipedal. That is, they walk on two legs rather than four. The term **hominids** is used to refer to humanlike, bipedal primates.

The oldest generally accepted hominids are known as *Australopithecus. Australopithecus* skeletons show that they had apelike brains, humanlike jaws, and were bipedal. *Australopithecus* is thought to have lived from 3.8 to 2.8 million years ago. The skeleton of a 20-year-old female *Australopithecus* found in Africa in the early 1970's has become famous as *Lucy.*

In the 1960's and 1970's, hominid fossils were found with a brain size of about 700 cubic centimeters—much larger than that of *Australopithecus.* This fossil was given the name *Homo habilis. Homo habilis* was able to make and use simple tools. They lived from about 2 to 1.5 million years ago.

Homo erectus is another species of hominid. This hominid had a brain volume of about 1000 cubic centimeters. *Homo erectus* lived from 1.5 million years to 400 000 years ago and is thought to be the first hominid to control fire. *Homo erectus* is thought to have first appeared in Africa and then migrated to Asia and Europe.

Hominid fossils from the last 125 000 years have been placed in the species *Homo sapiens.* Modern humans are *Homo sapiens.* But early *Homo sapiens* were somewhat different from those of today. One group of Homo sapiens is referred to as *Neanderthal.* Neanderthals were somewhat shorter and more robust than modern

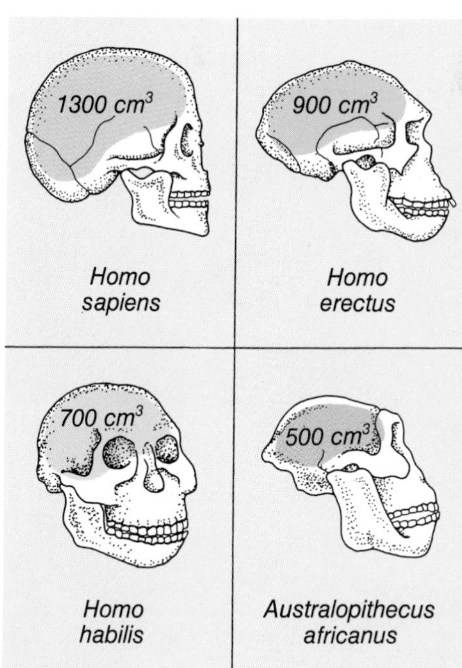

34.12 The brain size of hominids has increased over time.

humans. The other group of early *Homo sapiens,* known as *Cro-Magnons,* had skeletons almost identical to modern humans.

Tracing human evolution from the fossil record is difficult. In one hypothesis, *Australopithecus* is considered to be an ancestor of modern humans. In another hypothesis, *Australopithecus* is considered to be an offshoot, not in the direct line that led to humans. Scientists are in agreement on the broad outlines of human evolution. However, more research is necessary before they agree on all the details.

34.13 The dodo became extinct during the 1600's.

Topic 14 The Past 11 000 Years

The Pleistocene Epoch came to an end when the last ice sheets disappeared from North America, Europe, and Siberia about 11 000 years ago. That time marks the beginning of the Recent Epoch.

In the Recent Epoch, humans have been the main cause for the extinction of animal species. Within the past 400 years, the Great Auk, passenger pigeon, Dodo, and Moa have become extinct. The America bison was nearly wiped out. The great whales and many more species such as the golden eagle, whooping crane, American alligator, and rhinoceros have become endangered species.

Hunting is not the only reason that some animal groups have become extinct or nearly extinct. Civilization itself is also a cause. As swamps are filled and forests are cut down, the breeding grounds of many animals are destroyed.

How can endangered species be saved? Conservation groups all over the world have been formed to protect these species. Many governments have adopted protective programs for both animals and plants. Wildlife sanctuaries have been created. Attempts are being made to establish international agreements to regulate commercial hunting, fishing, and whaling.

TOPIC QUESTIONS

Each topic question refers to the topic of the same number.

8. **(a)** Why is the Cenozoic called the Age of Mammals? **(b)** How is the Cenozoic Era divided? **(c)** What changes in climate occurred during the Cenozoic?

9. **(a)** At the start of the Cenozoic, how did North America look different from the way it looks today? **(b)** What happened to the Appalachian and Rocky mountains during the Cenozoic? **(c)** How was the Colorado Plateau formed? The Columbia Plateau? **(d)** List some mountain ranges that were formed or raised higher during the Cenozoic Era.

10. **(a)** List and describe some examples of mammals that appeared in the Cenozoic but are now extinct. **(b)** List some animals that appeared in the Cenozoic and continue today. **(c)** How did the size of Cenozoic mammals change with time?

11. **(a)** What invertebrates of the Cenozoic Era lived in the seas? On land? **(b)** List examples of Cenozoic fish, amphibians, and reptiles. **(c)** How did Cenozoic birds differ from modern birds?
12. **(a)** Describe the change in plant life at northern latitudes during the Cenozoic. **(b)** What effect did this change have on animal life?
13. **(a)** What does *hominid* mean? **(b)** What two characteristics distinguish hominids?
14. **(a)** Name some animals that people have caused to become extinct or endangered. **(b)** In what ways do people cause animals to become extinct? **(c)** List some ways in which endangered species can be saved.

Dr. Meyer Rubin
Radiocarbon Expert

Radiocarbon dating has recently undergone a revolution that has greatly increased the number and kinds of carbon specimens whose age can be determined by this method. The major change has been in the size of the specimen needed for analysis. The older method, in which a sample was burned and its gas analyzed with a kind of Geiger counter, required amounts up to ten or more grams of material. The new method utilizes a particle accelerator and requires samples of only a few milligrams in size. Two other advantages of the accelerator method over the counter method are that results are obtained much more quickly and that older samples can be dated.

Dr. Meyer Rubin of the U.S. Geological Survey uses both methods, but he is most enthusiastic about the accelerator method because a greater number of events can be dated with it. For example, he says that a tiny scoop of charcoal from under a lava flow will make it possible to date the eruption that caused the flow. He adds that dating such events as lava flows or faults may make it possible to establish a timetable for them and thus to predict their occurrence in the future.

CHAPTER 34 REVIEW

Summary

The Mesozoic Era consists of three periods. During the Mesozoic, Pangaea broke up into Laurasia in the north and Gondwana in the south with the Tethys Sea between them. Several factors indicate that the climate was mild throughout the Mesozoic.

Dinosaurs were the most common land vertebrate of the Mesozoic. The first dinosaurs were small but they evolved to large sizes before the close of the era. There were several kinds of dinosaurs.

The first birds appeared during the Mesozoic. Other land animals were also important.

Ammonites are the index fossil for the Mesozoic Era. Other groups also thrived in the oceans.

The evolution of flowering plants in the Cretaceous led to the development of deciduous trees.

Dinosaurs as well as many other groups died out at the end of the Mesozoic Era. Several causes for their extinction have been proposed.

The Cenozoic Era is divided into two periods and seven epochs.

During the Cenozoic, the continents moved to their present locations, several new mountain ranges formed or were raised higher, and other land areas were formed.

The climate of the Cenozoic was mild at first but gradually cooled to an Ice Age.

Mammals thrived during the Cenozoic Era and left an extensive fossil record. Some groups evolved and died out while others continue today. Other plant and animal groups took on modern characteristics during the Cenozoic.

The development of grasses during the Cenozoic Era led to the rapid evolution of many different kinds of grazing animals.

Hominids began to develop in late Cenozoic time.

Humans have caused the extinction or near extinction of many animal groups. Efforts are now being made to save endangered groups.

Vocabulary

ammonite dinosaur hominid

Review

Number your paper from 1 to 16. Select the best answer to complete each statement.

1. Which is evidence for a mild Mesozoic climate? (a) glaciers in Africa (b) iridium in sediments (c) palm trees in Florida (d) corals in Europe
2. Laurasia consisted of (a) North America and Eurasia, (b) Eurasia and Africa, (c) Africa and South America, (d) South America and North America.
3. Como Bluff and Dry Mesa are famous quarries for (a) flightless birds, (b) flowering plants, (c) iron ore, (d) dinosaur bones.
4. The largest dinosaurs were the (a) sauropod dinosaurs, (b) armored dinosaurs, (c) duck-billed dinosaurs, (d) carnivorous dinosaurs.
5. *Archeopteryx* and *Protoavis* are early (a) mammals, (b) dinosaurs, (c) birds, (d) trees.
6. Ammonites are (a) flying reptiles of the Cenozoic, (b) grazing mammals of the Cenozoic, (c) carnivorous dinosaurs of the Mesozoic, (d) index fossils of the Mesozoic.
7. Flowering plants appeared during the (a) Paleocene Epoch, (b) Cretaceous Period, (c) Triassic Period, (d) Quaternary Period.
8. Iridium in sedimentary rocks at the Mesozoic-Cenozoic boundary is thought to be evidence of (a) asteroid impact, (b) cooler climates, (c) volcanic activity, (d) flowering plants.
9. The Cenozoic is the Age of (a) Reptiles, (b) Ammonites, (c) Mammals, (d) Cockroaches.
10. The two periods of the Cenozoic are (a) Tertiary and Quaternary, (b) Archeozoic and Proterozoic, (c) Mississippian and Pennsylvanian, (d) Triassic and Jurassic.
11. Two mountain ranges that formed during the Cenozoic are (a) Adirondacks and Appalachians, (b) Appalachians and Urals, (c) Urals and Alps, (d) Alps and Himalayas.

12. Creodonts and oreodons are examples of (a) Precambrian stromatolites, (b) Cambrian trilobites, (c) Mesozoic dinosaurs, (d) Cenozoic mammals.
13. Cenozoic invertebrates that lived in the ocean (a) were nearly the same as marine invertebrates of today, (b) were much smaller than marine invertebrates of today, (c) were rare, (d) were nearly the same as Triassic marine invertebrates.
14. Which animal groups benefited most during the change from trees to grasses in the Cenozoic? (a) grazing mammals (b) herbivorous dinosaurs (c) egg-laying amphibians (d) nest-building birds
15. The two main factors that distinguish hominids from other primates are (a) tooth size and erect posture, (b) robust skeletons and use of fire, (c) prominent eyebrows and large arm muscles, (d) bipedal movement and a large brain.
16. What do the Great Auk, passenger pigeon, and Dodo have in common? (a) All thrived during the late Mesozoic. (b) All are marine invertebrates. (c) All died out within the past 400 years. (d) All were saved from extinction by conservation groups.

Interpret and Apply

On your paper, answer each question in complete sentences.

1. What might the plant and animal life of the world be like today if Pangaea had not rifted apart?
2. Aside from radioactivity, in what ways might a nuclear war today be similar to the asteroid impact that is theorized to have occurred at the close of the Mesozoic Era?
3. During the Miocene Epoch, horses migrated from Alaska to Siberia while mastodons moved from Asia to North America. Today the Bering Strait separates Alaska and Siberia. How did the animals get from one continent to the other?

Critical Thinking

The chart shows the geologic time ranges for ten groups of Mesozoic and Cenozoic plants and animals. The width of each column on the chart represents the relative abundance of each group.

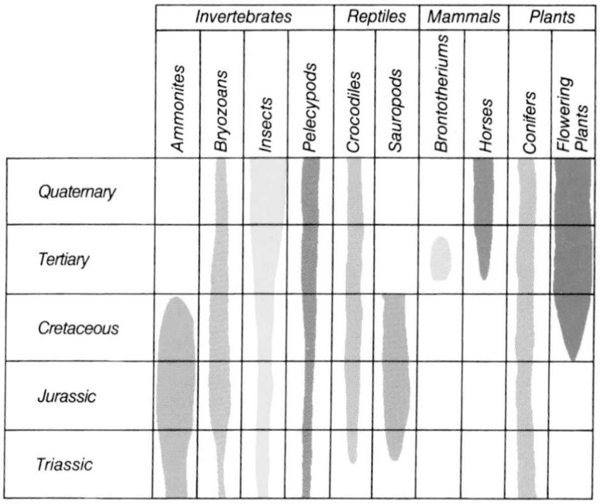

1. Which groups have steadily increased in abundance since the early Triassic Period?
2. According to the chart, which group(s) died out at the end of the Mesozoic?
3. Which group expanded rapidly in the Cretaceous and remained abundant during the Tertiary and Quaternary periods?
4. Which group existed only during the Mesozoic Era?
5. Which group still found today was more abundant in the Jurassic?
6. What is the most likely age of a rock layer that contains the fossil remains of sauropods, conifers, and flowering plants?
7. According to the chart, which group would be the best index fossil?
8. Compared to the abundance of insects today, how abundant were insects during the Jurassic Period?
9. Could a rock that contains sauropods also contain impressions of flowering plants? Why or why not?

Appendix A Properties of Some Common Minerals

The minerals are arranged alphabetically, and the most useful properties in identification are printed in italic type. Most minerals can be identified by means of two or three of the properties listed below. In some minerals, color is important; in others, cleavage is characteristic; and in others, the crystal shape identifies the mineral.

Name and Chemical Composition	Hard-ness	Color	Streak	Type of Cleavage	Remarks
Amphibole (complex ferromagnesian silicate)	5–6	*Dark green to black*	Greenish black	Two directions at angles of 56° and 124°	Vitreous luster. Hornblende is the common variety. Long, slender, six-sided crystals. *Black with shiny cleavage surfaces at 56° and 124°.*
Apatite (calcium fluorophosphate)	5	Green, brown, red, variegated	White	Indistinct	Crystals are common as are granular masses; vitreous luster.
Beryl (beryllium silicate)	8	*Greenish*	Colorless	None	*Hardness, greenish color, six-sided crystals.* Aquamarine and emerald are gem varieties. Nonmetallic luster.
Biotite mica (complex silicate)	2.5–3	Black, brown, dark green	Colorless	*Excellent in one direction*	*Thin elastic films peel off easily.* Nonmetallic luster.
Calcite ($CaCO_3$)	3	Varies	Colorless	*Excellent, three directions, not at 90° angles*	*Fizzes in dilute hydrochloric acid. Hardness.* Nonmetallic luster.
Chalcopyrite ($CuFeS_2$)	3.5–4	*Golden yellow*	Greenish black	None	*Hardness and color distinguish from pyrite.* Metallic luster.
Copper (Cu)	2.5–3	*Copper red*	Red	None	*Metallic luster on fresh surface. Ductile and malleable. Sp. gr. 8.5 to 9.*
Corundum (Al_2O_3)	9	Dark grays or browns common	Colorless	Parting resembles cleavage	*Barrel-shaped, six-sided crystals with flat ends.*
Diamond (C)	10	Colorless to black	Colorless	Excellent, four directions	Hardest of all minerals.
Chlorite (complex silicate)	1–2.5	*Greenish*	Colorless	Excellent, one direction	*Nonelastic flakes, scaly, micaceous.*
Dolomite ($CaMg(CO_3)_2$)	3.5–4	Varies	Colorless	*Good, three directions, not at 90°*	*Scratched surface fizzes in dilute hydrochloric acid. Cleavage surfaces curved.*
Feldspar (Potassium variety)(silicate)	6	*Salmon pink, and red are diagnostic;* may be white and light gray	Colorless	*Good, two directions, 90° intersection*	*Hardness, color, and cleavage taken together are diagnostic.*
Feldspar (sodium plagioclase variety) (silicate)	6	*White to light gray*	Colorless	*Good, two directions, about 90°*	*If striations are visible, they are diagnostic.* Nonmetallic luster.
Feldspar (calcium plagioclase variety) (silicate)	6	*Gray to dark gray*	Colorless	*Good, two directions, about 90°*	*Striations commonly visible;* may show iridescence. Associated with augite, whereas other feldspars are associated with hornblende. Nonmetallic luster.
Fluorite (CaF_2)	4	Varies	Colorless	*Excellent, four directions*	Nonmetallic luster. In cubes or octahedrons as crystals and in cleavable masses.
Galena (PbS)	2+	*Bluish lead gray*	Lead gray	*Excellent, three directions, intersect 90°*	*Metallic luster.* Occurs as crystals and cleavable masses. *Very dense.*
Gold (Au)	2.5–	*Gold*	Gold	None	Malleable, ductile, *dense.* Metallic luster.
Graphite (C)	1–2	*Silver gray to black*	Grayish black	Good, one direction	Metallic or earthy luster. *Foliated, scaly masses common. Greasy feel, marks paper.* This is the "lead" in a pencil (mixed with clay).

Properties of Some Common Minerals *(cont.)*

Name and Chemical Composition	Hardness	Color	Streak	Type of Cleavage	Remarks
Gypsum (hydrous calcium sulfate)	2	White, yellowish, reddish	Colorless	*Very good in one direction*	Vitreous luster. *Can be scratched easily by fingernail.*
Halite (NaCl)	2–2.5	Colorless and various colors	Colorless	*Excellent, three directions, intersect at 90°*	*Taste, cleavage, hardness.*
Hematite (Fe_2O_3)	5–6 (may appear softer)	*Reddish or silvery*	*Reddish*	None	Sp. gr. 5.3. Metallic *or earthy luster.*
Kaolinite (hydrous aluminum silicate)	2–2.5	White	Colorless	None (without a microscope)	Dull, earthy luster. Claylike masses.
Limonite (group of hydrous iron oxides)	1–5.5	*Yellowish brown*	*Yellowish brown*	None	Earthy, granular. Rust stains.
Magnetite (Fe_3O_4)	5.5–6.5	*Black*	Black	None	Metallic luster. Occurs in eight-sided crystals and granular masses. *Magnetic. Sp. gr. 5.2.*
Muscovite mica (complex silicate)	2–2.5	Colorless in thin films; yellow, red, green, and brown in thicker pieces	Colorless	*Excellent, one direction*	*Thin elastic films peel off readily.* Nonmetallic luster.
Olivine (iron magnesium silicate)	6.5–7	*Yellowish and greenish*	*White to light green*	None	*Green, glassy, granular.*
Opal (hydrous silica)	5–6.5	Varies	Colorless	None	*Glassy and pearly lusters, conchoidal fracture.*
Pyrite (FeS_2)	6–6.5	*Brass yellow*	Greenish black	None	*Cubic crystals* and granular masses. Metallic *luster.* Crystals may be striated. *Hardness important.*
Pyroxene (complex silicate)	5–6	Greenish black	Greenish gray	*Two, nearly at 90°*	*Stubby eight-sided crystals and cleavable masses. Augite* is a common variety. Nonmetallic.
Quartz (SiO_2)	7	Varies from white to black and colors	Colorless	None	Vitreous luster. *Conchoidal fracture. Six-sided crystals common.* Many varieties. Very common mineral. *Hardness.*
Serpentine (hydrous magnesium silicate)	2.5–4	*Greenish (variegated)*	Colorless	Indistinct	*Luster resinous to greasy. Conchoidal fracture.* The most common kind of asbestos is a variety of serpentine.
Sphalerite (ZnS)	3.5–4	Yellowish brown to black	White to yellow	*Good, six directions*	*Color, hardness, cleavage, and resinous luster.*
Sulfur (S)	1.5–2.5	*Yellow*	White to yellow	Indistinct	Granular, earthy.
Talc (hydrous magnesium silicate)	1+	White, green, gray	Colorless	Good, one direction	Nonelastic flakes, *greasy feel. Soft.* Nonmetallic luster.
Topaz (complex silicate)	8	Varies	Colorless	*One distinct (basal)*	Vitreous. *Crystals commonly striated lengthwise.*
Tourmaline (complex silicate)	7–7.5	Varies; *black* is common	Colorless	Indistinct	*Elongated, striated crystals with triangular-shaped cross sections are common.*

PERIODIC TABLE OF THE ELEMENTS

(based on $^{12}_{6}C$ = 12.0000)

Solid | Liquid | Gas

14	Atomic number
Si	Symbol
Silicon	Name
28.0855	Atomic mass

1*	2
1 H Hydrogen 1.007	
3 Li Lithium 6.941	4 Be Beryllium 9.012
11 Na Sodium 22.98977	12 Mg Magnesium 24.305

TRANSITION METALS

1*	2	3	4	5	6	7	8	9
19 K Potassium 39.098	20 Ca Calcium 40.08	21 Sc Scandium 44.955	22 Ti Titanium 47.88	23 V Vanadium 50.9415	24 Cr Chromium 51.996	25 Mn Manganese 54.938	26 Fe Iron 55.847	27 Co Cobalt 58.933
37 Rb Rubidium 85.467	38 Sr Strontium 87.62	39 Y Yttrium 88.905	40 Zr Zirconium 91.224	41 Nb Niobium 92.906	42 Mo Molybdenum 95.94	43 Tc Technetium (98)	44 Ru Ruthenium 101.07	45 Rh Rhodium 102.906
55 Cs Cesium 132.905	56 Ba Barium 137.3	57 La Lanthanum 138.906	72 Hf Hafnium 178.49	73 Ta Tantalum 180.948	74 W Tungsten 183.85	75 Re Rhenium 186.207	76 Os Osmium 190.2	77 Ir Iridium 192.22
87 Fr Francium (223)†	88 Ra Radium (226.0)	89 Ac Actinium 227.028	104 (261)	105 (262)	106 (263)	107 (262)	108	109 (266)

INNER TRANSITION METALS

Lanthanide series

58 Ce Cerium 140.12	59 Pr Praseodymium 140.908	60 Nd Neodymium 144.24	61 Pm Promethium (145)	62 Sm Samarium 150.36
90 Th Thorium 232.038	91 Pa Protactinium 231.036	92 U Uranium 238.029	93 Np Neptunium (244)	94 Pu Plutonium (244)

Actinide series

*The numbers heading each column represent group numbers recommended by the American Chemical Society Committee on nomenclature.
†Masses in parentheses are the mass numbers of the most stable isotope.

10	11	12	13	14	15	16	17	18
								2 **He** Helium 4.0026
			5 **B** Boron 10.81	6 **C** Carbon 12.0111	7 **N** Nitrogen 14.0067	8 **O** Oxygen 15.9994	9 **F** Fluorine 18.998	10 **Ne** Neon 20.179
			13 **Al** Aluminum 26.9815	14 **Si** Silicon 28.0855	15 **P** Phosphorus 30.973	16 **S** Sulfur 32.06	17 **Cl** Chlorine 35.453	18 **Ar** Argon 39.948
28 **Ni** Nickel 58.69	29 **Cu** Copper 63.546	30 **Zn** Zinc 65.39	31 **Ga** Gallium 69.72	32 **Ge** Germanium 72.59	33 **As** Arsenic 74.92	34 **Se** Selenium 78.96	35 **Br** Bromine 79.904	36 **Kr** Krypton 83.80
46 **Pd** Palladium 106.42	47 **Ag** Silver 107.868	48 **Cd** Cadmium 112.41	49 **In** Indium 114.82	50 **Sn** Tin 118.71	51 **Sb** Antimony 121.75	52 **Te** Tellurium 127.60	53 **I** Iodine 126.905	54 **Xe** Xenon 131.29
78 **Pt** Platinum 195.08	79 **Au** Gold 196.967	80 **Hg** Mercury 200.59	81 **Tl** Thallium 204.383	82 **Pb** Lead 207.2	83 **Bi** Bismuth 208.980	84 **Po** Polonium (209)	85 **At** Astatine (210)	86 **Rn** Radon (222)

63 **Eu** Europium 151.96	64 **Gd** Gadolinium 157.25	65 **Tb** Terbium 158.925	66 **Dy** Dysprosium 162.50	67 **Ho** Holmium 164.930	68 **Er** Erbium 167.26	69 **Tm** Thulium 168.934	70 **Yb** Ytterbium 173.04	71 **Lu** Lutetium 174.96
95 **Am** Americium (243)	96 **Cm** Curium (247)	97 **Bk** Berkelium (247)	98 **Cf** Californium (251)	99 **Es** Einsteinium (252)	100 **Fm** Fermium (257)	101 **Md** Mendelevium (258)	102 **No** Nobelium (259)	103 **Lr** Lawrencium (260)

The Metric System and SI Units

Some Base Units of Measurement in the SI (International System of Units)

Quantity	Name	Symbol
length	meter	m
mass	kilogram	kg
time	second	s
temperature	kelvin	K*

Metric System Prefixes

Prefix	Symbol	Multiples
kilo	k	1000
hecto	h	100
deka	da	10
		Divisions
deci	d	0.1 (1/10)
centi	c	0.01 (1/100)
milli	m	0.001 (1/1000)

Examples Using the Meter

Name	Symbol	Equivalent
kilometer	km	1000 m
meter	m	1 m
centimeter	cm	0.01 m
millimeter	mm	0.001 m

Metric and American Equivalents in the SI (International System)

Length

1 meter = 39.37 in
= 3.280 ft
= 1.093 yd
= 0.00062 mi

1 cm = 0.393 in
1 km = 0.62 mi

1 inch = 0.0254 m or 2.54 cm
1 foot = 0.3048 m or 30.48 cm
1 yard = 0.9144 m or 91.44 cm
1 mile = 1609 mi or 1.609 km

Area

1 square meter = 1550.0 in^2
= 10.76 ft^2
= 1.19 yd^2

1 sq in = 0.000645 m^2 or 6.45 cm^2
1 sq ft = 0.09290 m^2
1 sq yd = 0.8361 m^2
1 sq mi = 2589900 m^2 or 2.589 km^2

Volume

1 liter = 1.06 qt
= 33.9 oz

1 quart = 0.95 L

1 cu in = 0.000016 m^3
or 16.38 cm^3

Mass

1 kilogram = 2.204 lb
= 35.374 oz

1 pound = 0.4536 kg
= 453.6 g

Temperature*

*Even though kelvin is the SI base unit for temperature, the unit "degree Celsius" is most often used in your study of earth science. The relationship between the two scales is 0° C = 273 K.

°C or Celsius = 5/9 × (°F or Fahrenheit − 32)

0° C or 32° F = freezing point of water
100° C or 212° F = boiling point of water
37° C or 98.6° F = normal human body temperature
20° C or 68° F = room temperature

Appendix B Map Atlas

Reading and interpreting maps are important skills to develop during your study of earth science. A map represents all or part of Earth's surface, another planet, or even the sky. A map may show relatively permanent features, such as continents, oceans, and land features. Or it may show features that change more quickly, such as daily weather conditions. Once you know how to read maps, you can use them for many purposes. For example, by interpreting the information in a weather map, you could predict what kind of clothing you'll need for tomorrow's football game, camping trip, or other outdoor event. Topographic maps are useful in planning vacations, new houses, and swimming pools. Maps can even be used to help plan improvements in radio and television reception. The skills learned in studying the maps in this book will be useful in many ways.

This Map Atlas contains maps from every branch of earth science: geology, oceanography, astronomy, and meteorology.

Topographic Map Symbols

Symbol		Symbol	
Buildings		*Woodland*	
School		*Orchard*	
Church		*Marsh*	
Cemetery		*Wooded Marsh*	
Many Buildings		*Submerged Marsh*	
Road		*Stream*	
Railroad		*Quarry or Mine*	
Trail		*Gravel Pit*	
Bridge		*Bench Mark*	BM × 176
Tunnel		*Spot Elevation*	× 475
Town Border		*Distance Check Point*	△

Topographic Map: Monadnock, NH

(Partial)

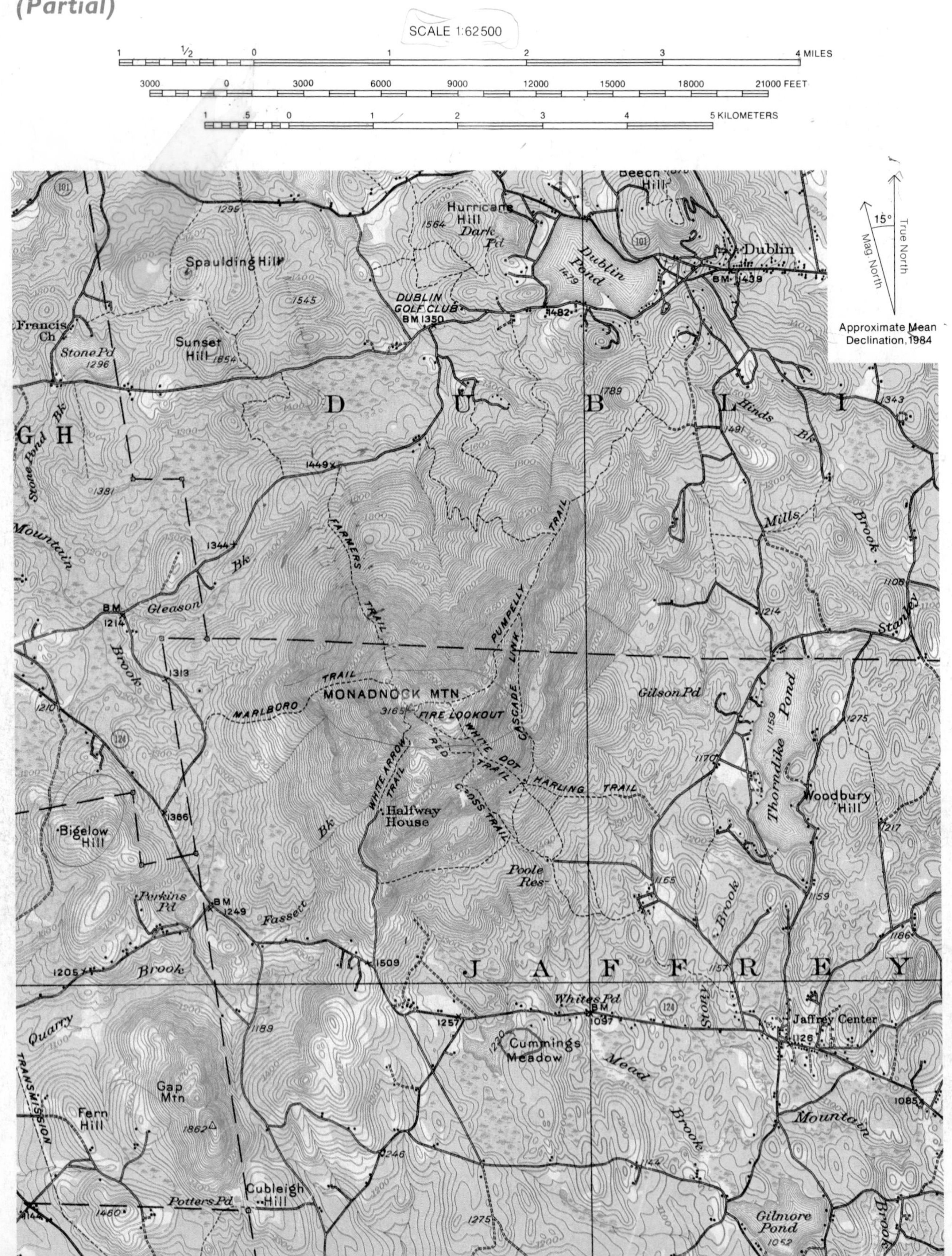

Stereophotos: Monadnock, NH

Two aerial photographs of the same location, each taken from a slightly different angle, can be viewed as a stereoimage. The photos shown were taken, one right after the other, from an airplane as it flew over Monadnock Mountain. To view the stereoimage, you will need a stereoscope like the one shown in the sketch at right. Turn the book sideways. Place the stereoscope over the two images of the mountain. The center of the stereoscope should be over the white space between the photos. Look through the stereoscope and adjust the distance between the two lenses until the mountain appears in 3-D.

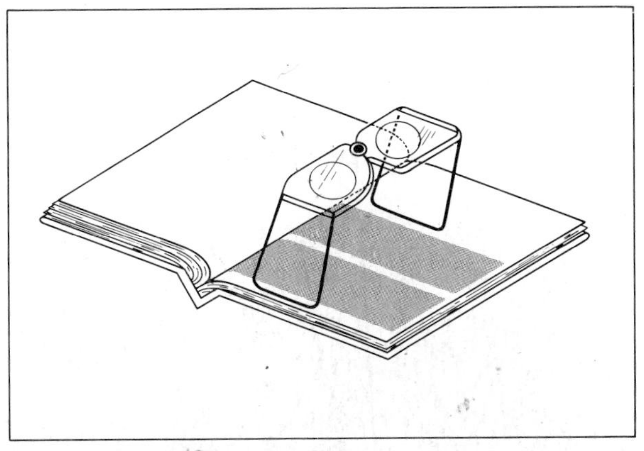

Topographic Map: Harrisburg, PA

(15-minute series, partial)

Refer to map scales on page 582 when using this map.

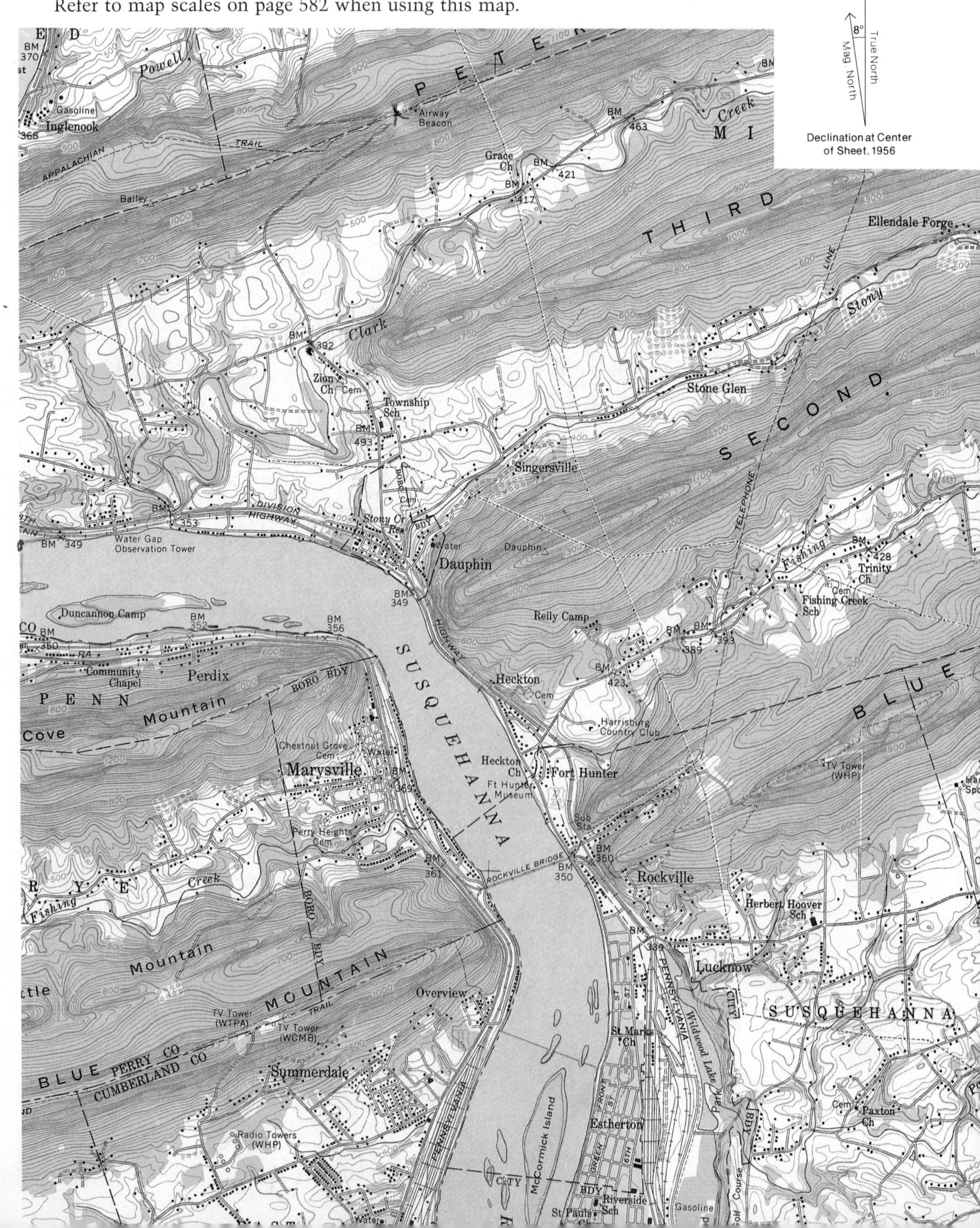

Geologic Map: Flaming Gorge, UT

(Simplified, partial)

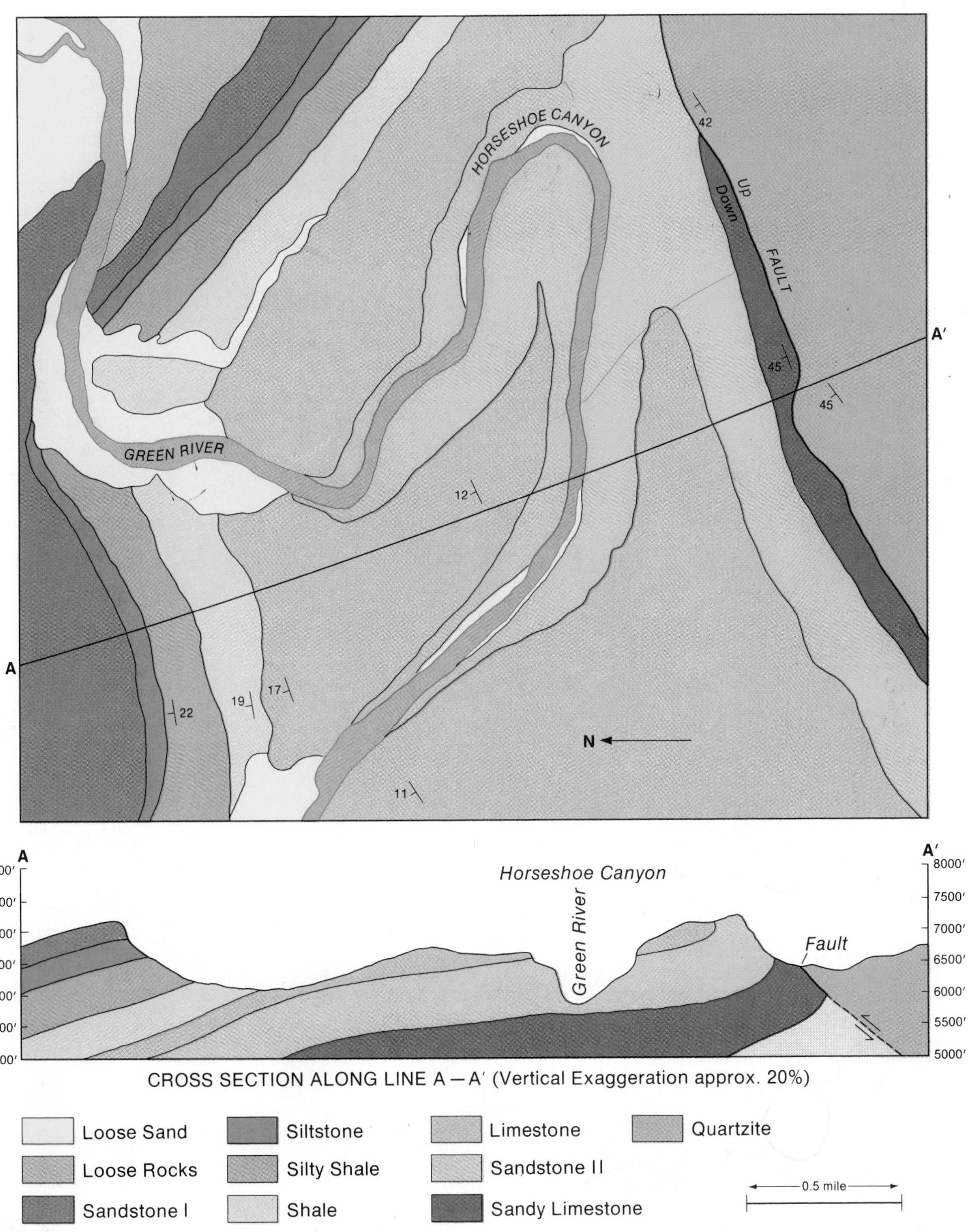

CROSS SECTION ALONG LINE A — A′ (Vertical Exaggeration approx. 20%)

Physical United States

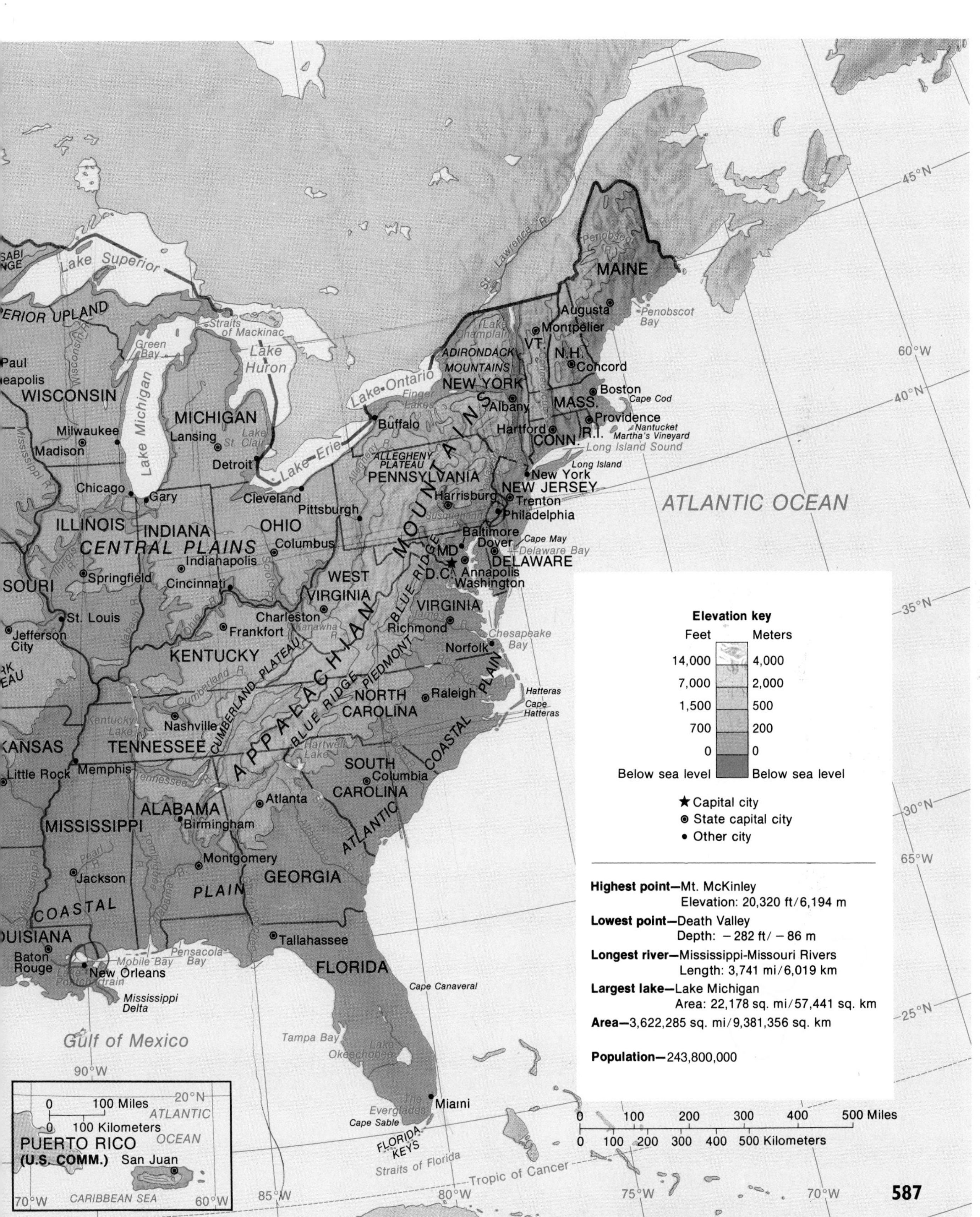

Lake Superior
SUPERIOR UPLAND
Straits of Mackinac
Green Bay
Lake Huron
Lake Michigan
Lake Ontario
Lake Erie
Lake St. Clair
Lake Champlain
Finger Lakes
St. Lawrence R.
Penobscot R.
Penobscot Bay
MAINE
Augusta
Montpelier
VT.
N.H.
Concord
Boston
Cape Cod
MASS.
Providence
R.I.
Nantucket
Martha's Vineyard
Hartford
CONN.
Long Island Sound
Long Island
Albany
ADIRONDACK MOUNTAINS
NEW YORK
Buffalo
New York
NEW JERSEY
Trenton
Philadelphia
ALLEGHENY PLATEAU
PENNSYLVANIA
Harrisburg
Pittsburgh
Cleveland
Detroit
Lansing
MICHIGAN
WISCONSIN
Milwaukee
Madison
Chicago
Gary
ILLINOIS
INDIANA
OHIO
Columbus
CENTRAL PLAINS
Indianapolis
Springfield
Cincinnati
St. Louis
Jefferson City
Baltimore
Cape May
Dover
Delaware Bay
DELAWARE
MD
D.C.
Annapolis
Washington
WEST VIRGINIA
Charleston
Frankfort
KENTUCKY
VIRGINIA
Richmond
Norfolk
Chesapeake Bay
APPALACHIAN MOUNTAINS
BLUE RIDGE
PIEDMONT
CUMBERLAND PLATEAU
Hatteras
Cape Hatteras
NORTH CAROLINA
Raleigh
Nashville
TENNESSEE
Memphis
Little Rock
SOUTH CAROLINA
Columbia
Atlanta
ALABAMA
Birmingham
MISSISSIPPI
Montgomery
Jackson
GEORGIA
COASTAL PLAIN
ATLANTIC COASTAL PLAIN
Tallahassee
FLORIDA
Baton Rouge
New Orleans
Pensacola Bay
Mobile Bay
Lake Pontchartrain
Mississippi Delta
Gulf of Mexico
Cape Canaveral
Tampa Bay
Lake Okeechobee
The Everglades
Miami
Cape Sable
FLORIDA KEYS
Straits of Florida
Tropic of Cancer
ATLANTIC OCEAN
45°N
40°N
35°N
30°N
25°N
60°W
65°W
70°W
75°W
80°W
85°W
90°W
0 100 200 300 400 500 Miles
0 100 200 300 400 500 Kilometers
PUERTO RICO (U.S. COMM.)
San Juan
ATLANTIC OCEAN
CARIBBEAN SEA
0 100 Miles
0 100 Kilometers
20°N
70°W
60°W
Elevation key
Feet Meters
14,000 4,000
7,000 2,000
1,500 500
700 200
0 0
Below sea level Below sea level
★ Capital city
◉ State capital city
• Other city
Highest point—Mt. McKinley
Elevation: 20,320 ft/6,194 m
Lowest point—Death Valley
Depth: −282 ft/−86 m
Longest river—Mississippi-Missouri Rivers
Length: 3,741 mi/6,019 km
Largest lake—Lake Michigan
Area: 22,178 sq. mi/57,441 sq. km
Area—3,622,285 sq. mi/9,381,356 sq. km
Population—243,800,000

Physical World: Continents and Ocean Floor

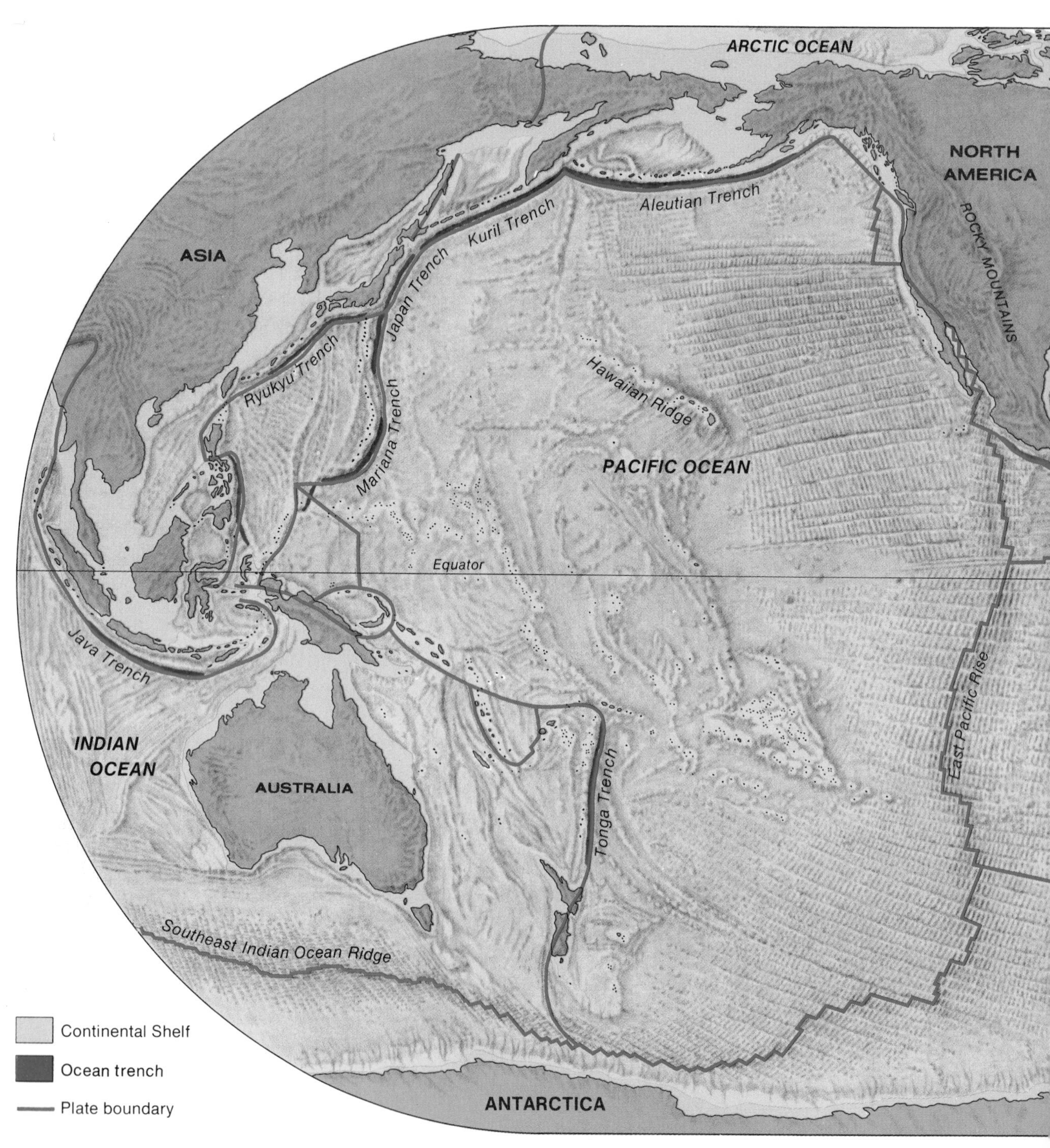

Continental Shelf

Ocean trench

Plate boundary

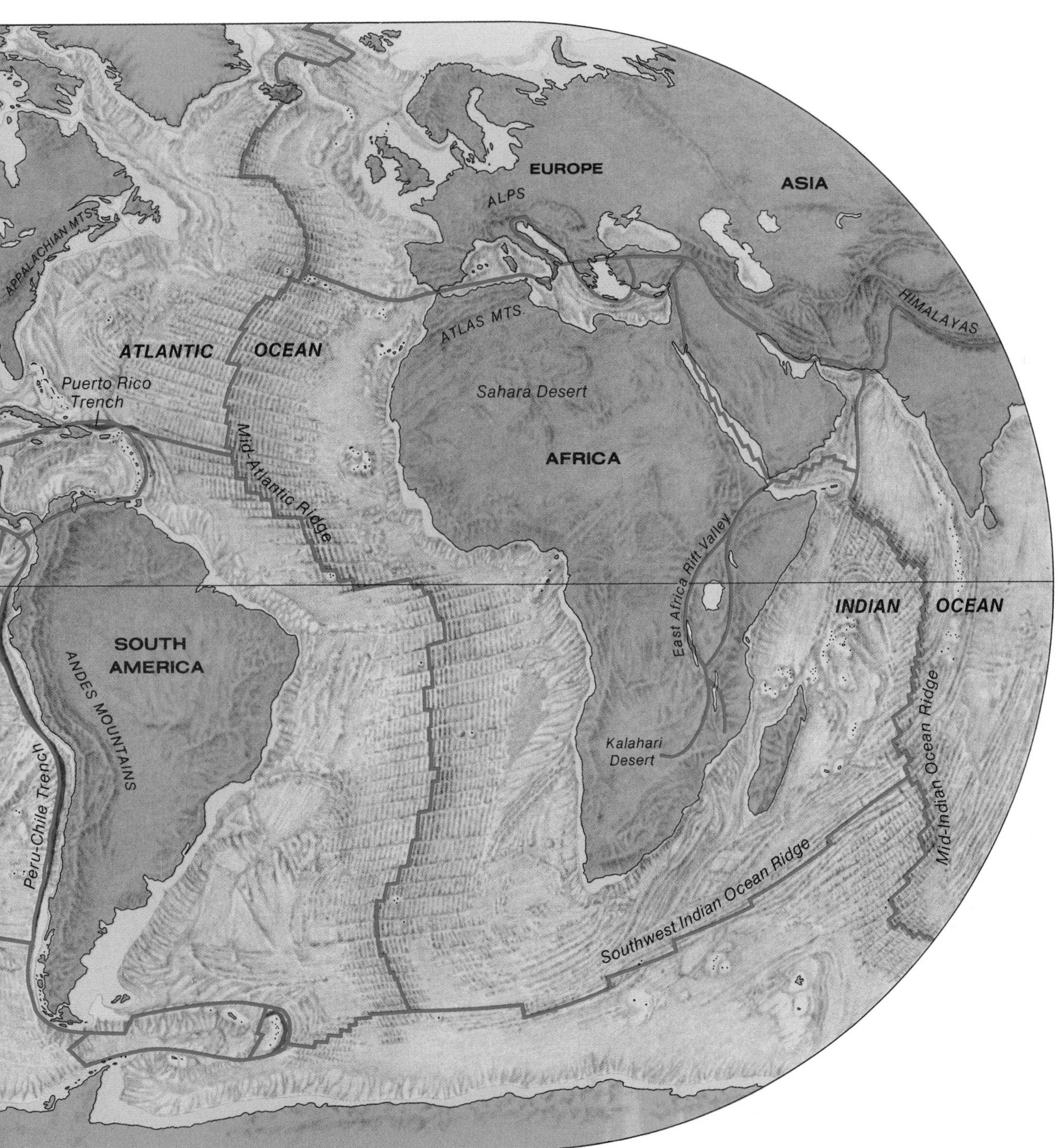

EUROPE
ASIA
ALPS
APPALACHIAN MTS.
HIMALAYAS
ATLAS MTS.
ATLANTIC OCEAN
Puerto Rico Trench
Sahara Desert
AFRICA
Mid-Atlantic Ridge
East Africa Rift Valley
INDIAN OCEAN
SOUTH AMERICA
ANDES MOUNTAINS
Mid-Indian Ocean Ridge
Kalahari Desert
Peru-Chile Trench
Southwest Indian Ocean Ridge

Surface Ocean Currents

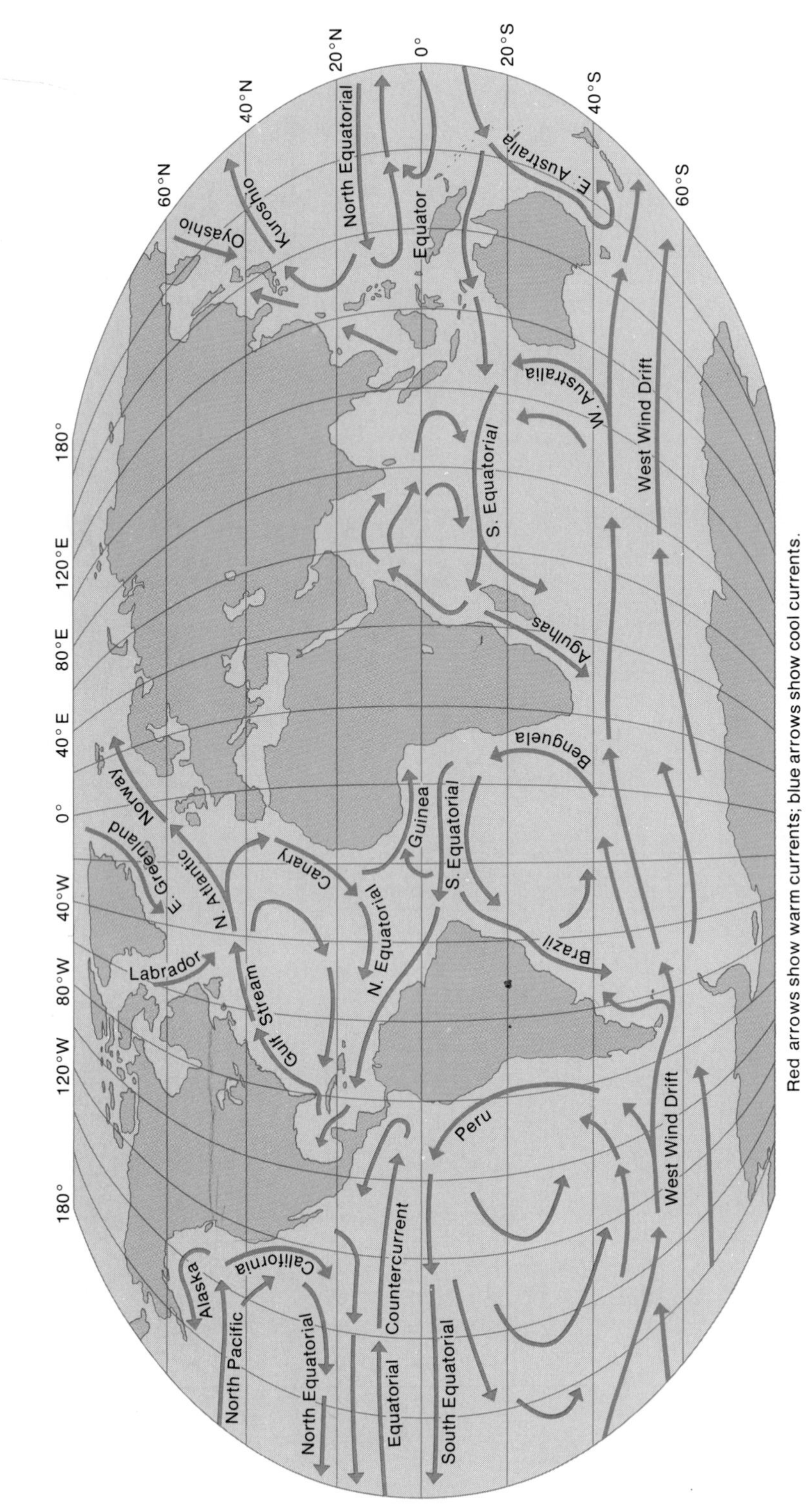

Red arrows show warm currents; blue arrows show cool currents.

Prevailing World Winds
(July average)

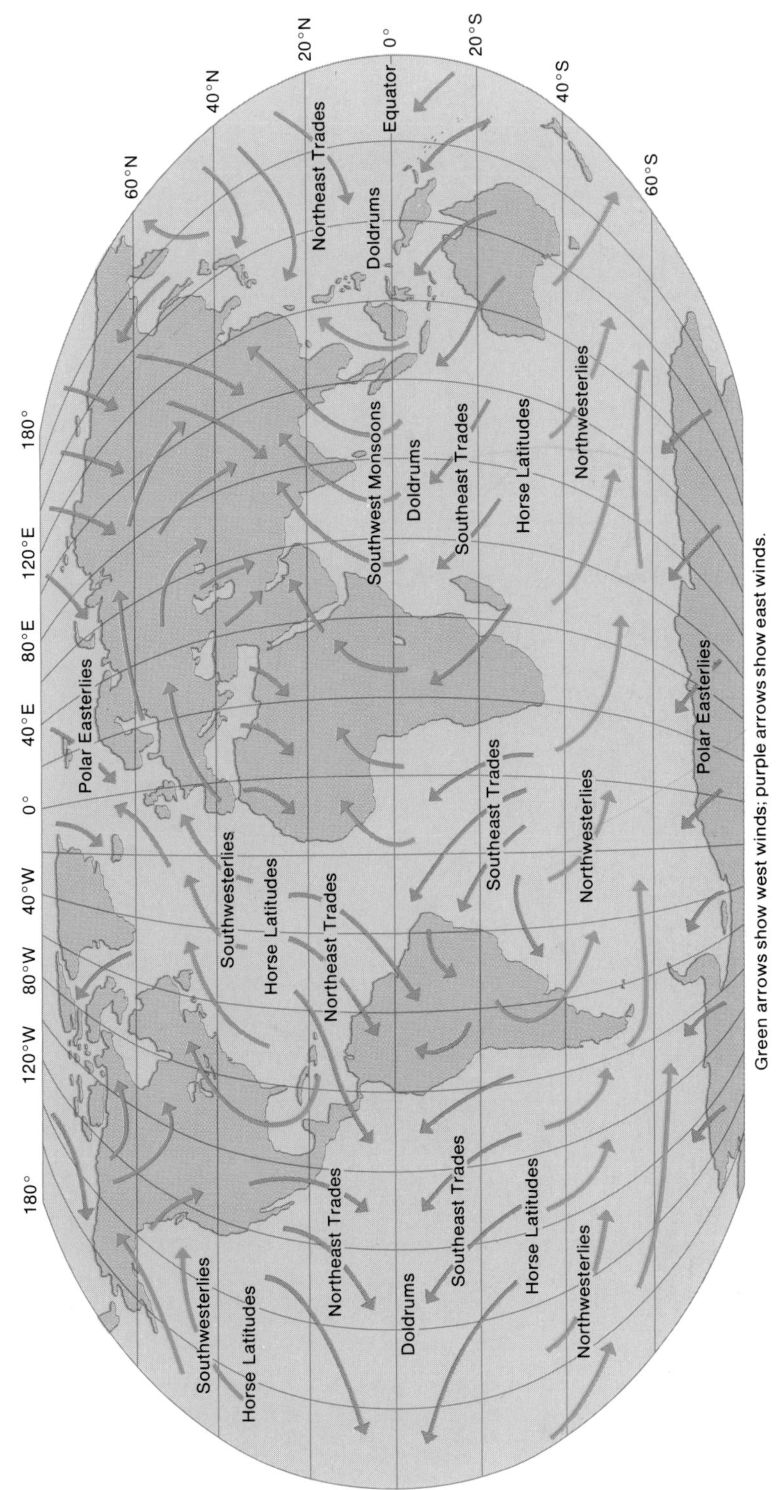

Green arrows show west winds; purple arrows show east winds.

Seasonal Star Maps

Viewed in evening skies from mid-latitude North America

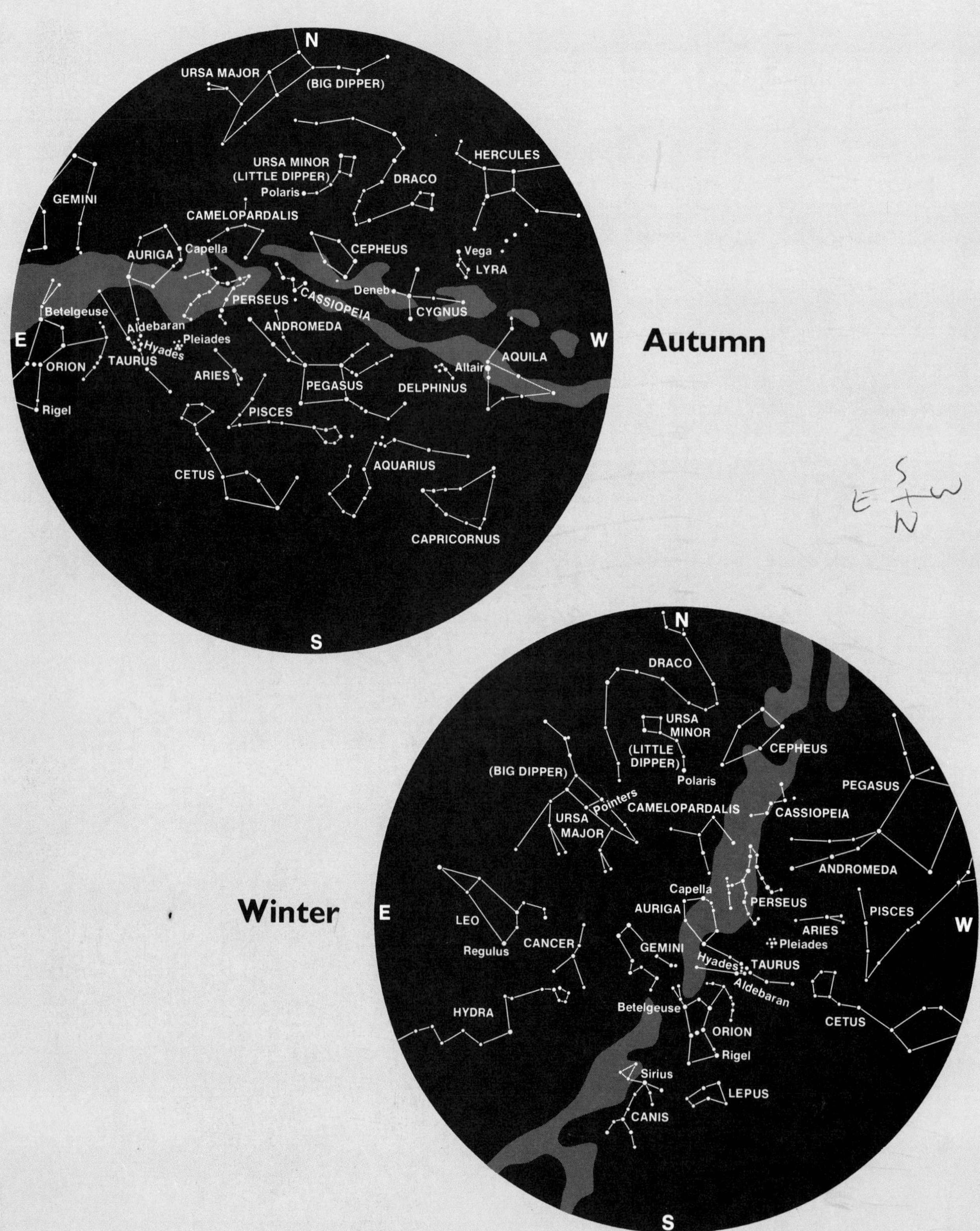

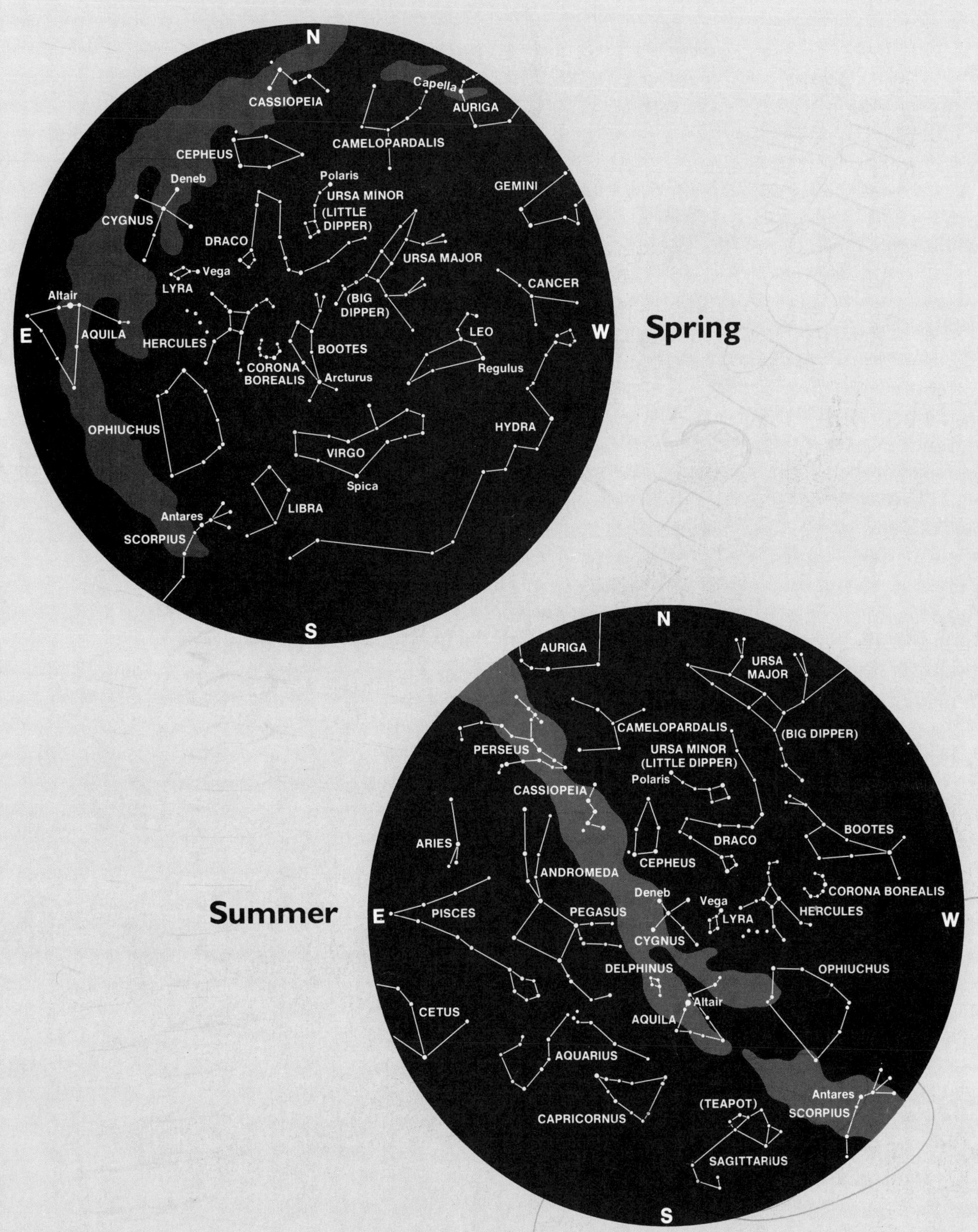
N
CASSIOPEIA
Capella
AURIGA
CAMELOPARDALIS
CEPHEUS
Deneb
Polaris
URSA MINOR
(LITTLE
DIPPER)
GEMINI
CYGNUS
DRACO
URSA MAJOR
Vega
LYRA
CANCER
Altair
(BIG
DIPPER)
E
AQUILA
HERCULES
LEO
W
Spring
BOOTES
CORONA
BOREALIS
Arcturus
Regulus
OPHIUCHUS
HYDRA
VIRGO
Spica
Antares
LIBRA
SCORPIUS
S
N
AURIGA
URSA
MAJOR
PERSEUS
CAMELOPARDALIS
(BIG DIPPER)
URSA MINOR
(LITTLE DIPPER)
Polaris
CASSIOPEIA
ARIES
DRACO
BOOTES
ANDROMEDA
CEPHEUS
Deneb
CORONA BOREALIS
Summer
E
PISCES
PEGASUS
Vega
LYRA
HERCULES
W
CYGNUS
DELPHINUS
OPHIUCHUS
Altair
CETUS
AQUILA
AQUARIUS
Antares
(TEAPOT)
SCORPIUS
CAPRICORNUS
SAGITTARIUS
S

Weather Maps: Four-Day Series

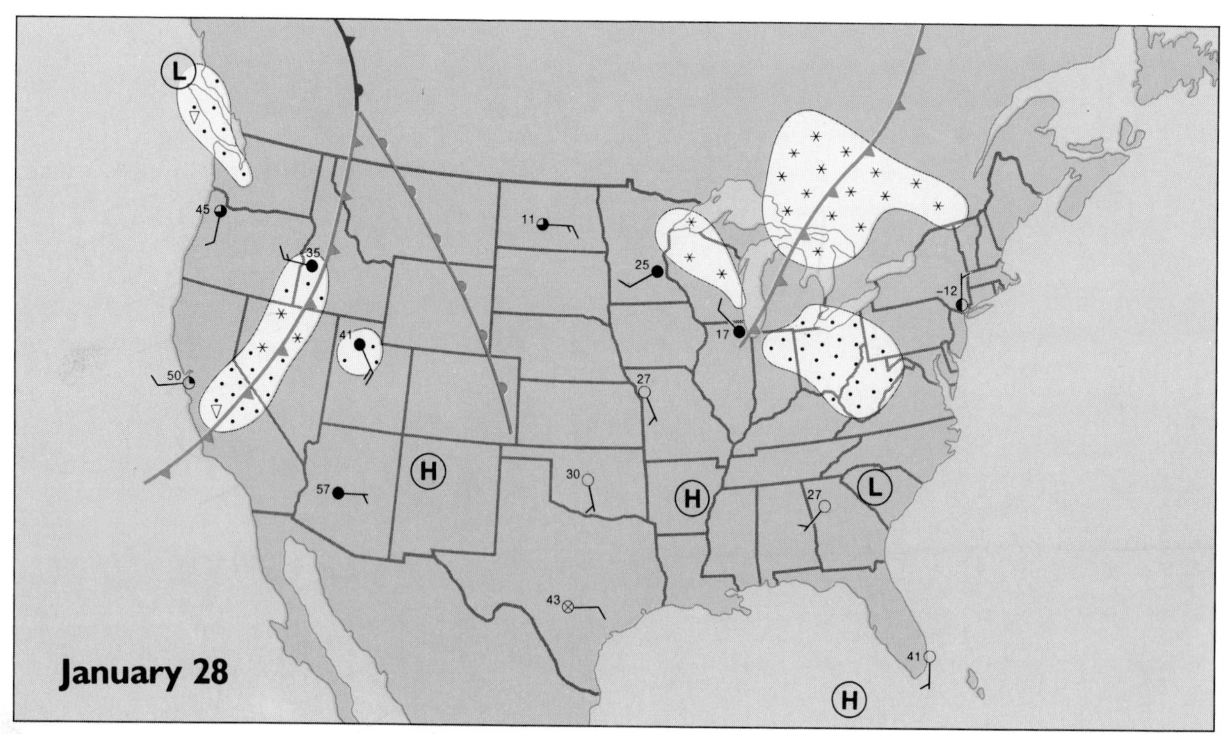

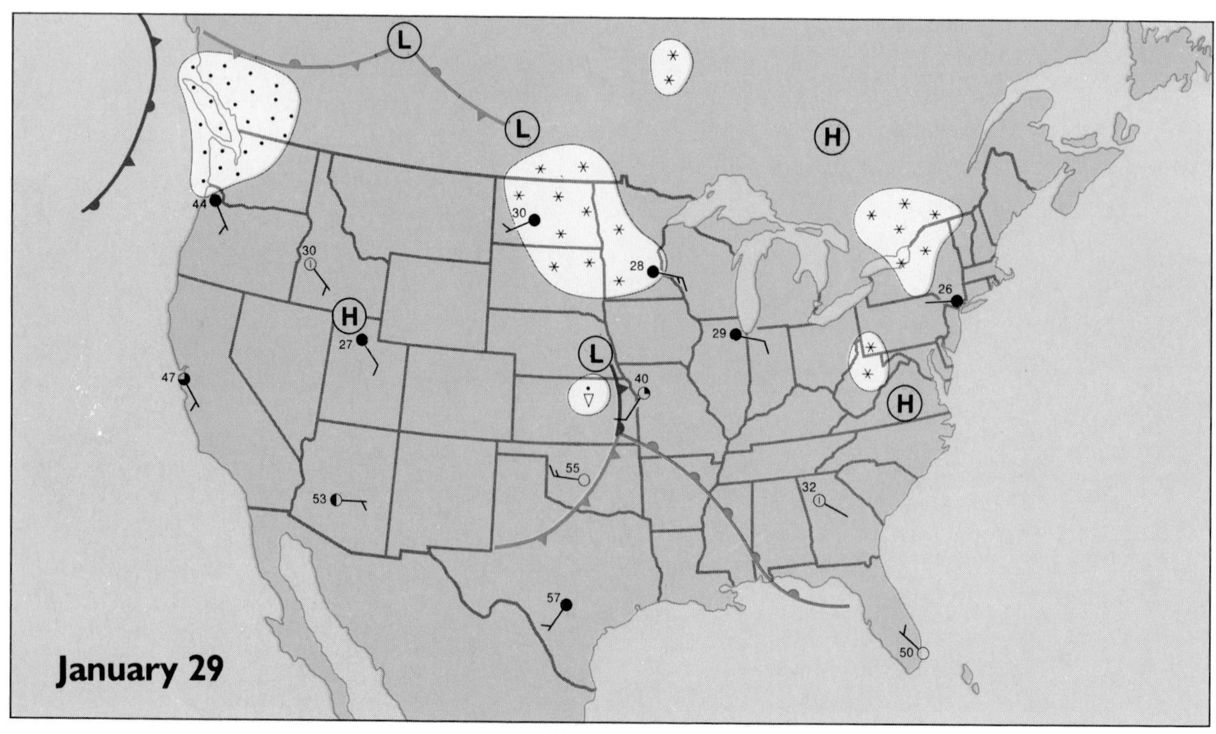

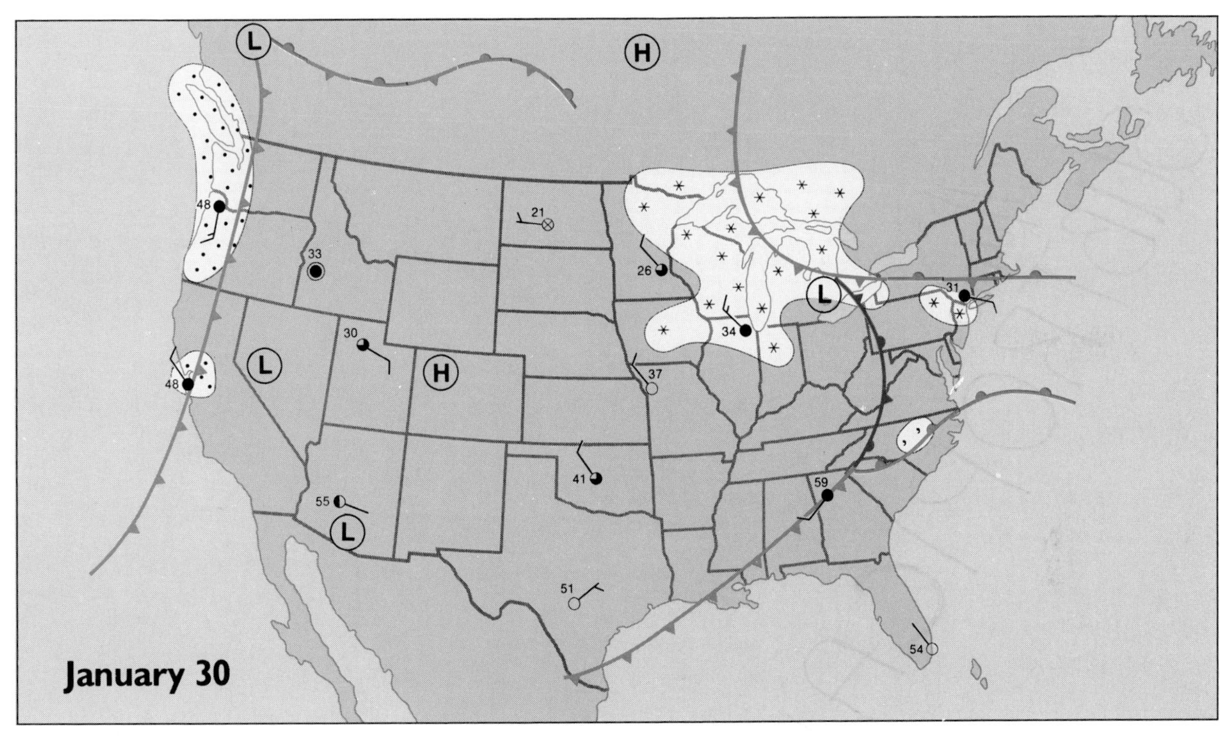
January 30

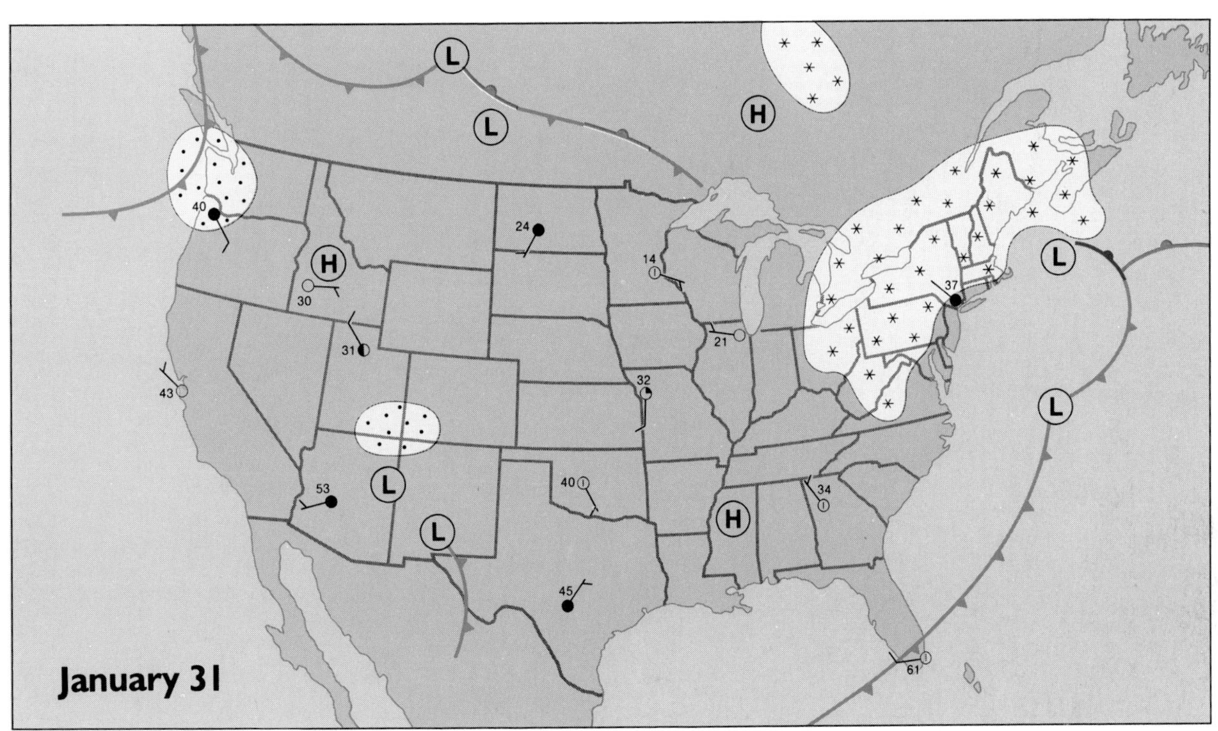
January 31

Earth's Climates

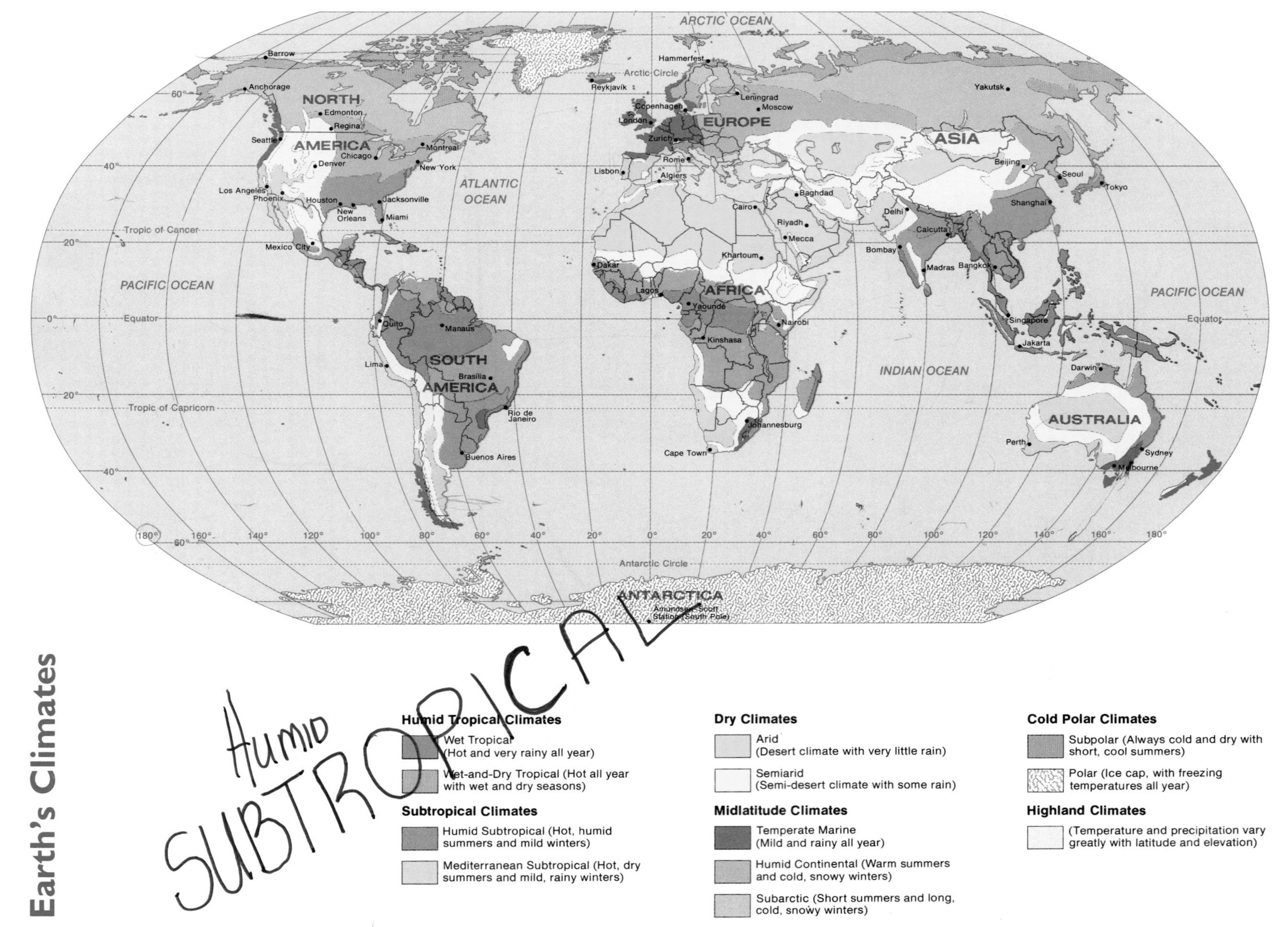

Glossary

A

abrasion: wearing away of rock by grinding action (p. 151)

absolute magnitude: the apparent magnitude of a star if placed 32.6 light-years from the sun (p. 341)

absolute time: the method of recording events that identifies the actual date of an event (p. 535)

acid rain: rain that contains dissolved sulfur or nitrogen gases; a dangerous pollutant (p. 91)

active continental margin: a boundary between oceanic crust and continental crust, also a plate boundary (p. 261)

air mass: a large section of the lower troposphere that has the same weather throughout (p. 487)

air-mass thunderstorms: widely scattered thunderstorms that form within a warm, moist air mass, usually lasting less than an hour (p. 499)

air pressure: weight of the atmosphere per unit area (p. 469)

alluvial fans: sloping deposits of sediment located where a mountain stream reaches level land (p. 163)

amphiboles: a family of complex silicate minerals that tend to form long, needlelike crystals (p. 48)

anemometer: an instrument that measures wind speed (p. 476)

annular eclipse: an eclipse that occurs when the moon's shadow fails to reach Earth, causing the sun to be seen as a thin, bright ring around the moon; also called a ring eclipse (p. 402)

anticline: an upfold in rock layers (p. 264)

anticyclone: an area of high pressure (p. 495)

aphelion: the point in orbit farthest from the sun (p. 363)

apogee: the point farthest from Earth in the orbit of an Earth satellite (p. 398)

apparent magnitude: how bright a star appears to an observer on Earth (p. 340)

artesian formation: the arrangement of a permeable layer of rock (aquifer) sandwiched between two layers of impermeable rock (p. 140)

asteroids: many small planetlike bodies revolving around the sun between the orbits of Mars and Jupiter (p. 381)

asthenosphere: the partially melted layer of the mantle that underlies the lithosphere (p. 210)

astronomical unit (AU): the average distance between Earth and the sun, about 150 million kilometers (p. 339)

astronomy: the study of the universe (p. 3)

atoll: a ring-shaped island or chain of islands, usually of coral limestone, nearly encircling a lagoon (p. 203)

atom: the smallest part of an element that has all of the properties of that element (p. 25)

atomic number: number of protons in the nucleus of an atom (p. 27)

aurora: a glow in the nighttime sky produced in the upper atmosphere by solar radiations (p. 358)

autumn equinox: the first day of fall in the Northern Hemisphere, about September 23; daylight and nighttime are equal in length (p. 420)

average slope: the slope, or gradient, between any two points on a hill; easily determined from a contour map (p. 107)

axis of rotation: an imaginary straight line through Earth between the North Pole and the South Pole on which Earth rotates; it is tilted 23½° from the plane of Earth's orbit (p. 409)

B

backwash: a gentle current of water that runs down a beach under an oncoming wave (p. 196)

barometer: an instrument that measures atmospheric pressure (p. 469)

base level: the level of the body of water into which a stream flows (p. 154)

baseline: the distance between two radio telescopes that are used for interferometry (p. 328)

batholith: name for the largest of all igneous intrusions; batholiths form the cores of many mountain ranges (p. 239)

Beaufort scale: a scale that relates the wind speed to its effects both on land and at sea (p. 428)

bed load: sand, pebbles, and boulders that are moved along the bed of a stream and are too heavy to be carried in suspension (p. 152)

bench mark: a marker in the ground indicating the exact elevation above sea level (p. 104)

big-bang hypothesis: states that the universe was originally a dense sphere of hydrogen that exploded into a gigantic expanding cloud that condensed into galaxies (p. 350)

black holes: objects in space with gravitational forces so powerful that not even their light rays can escape (p. 347)

black smokers: hot springs on the floor of the Pacific Ocean (p. 285)

blizzard: a snowstorm with high winds and low temperatures (p. 506)

C

carbonate: an ion group made of one carbon atom combined with three oxygen atoms and having a negative charge of two (p. 49)

carbonic acid: a weak acid formed when carbon dioxide dissolves in water (p. 120)

carrying power: the total amount of sediment in a stream together with the size of the particles being moved by the stream (p. 153)

cepheid variable: a pulsating star whose distance can be determined from its period of pulsation (p. 343)

charge-coupled device (CCD): photocells more sensitive to light than a photographic plate used with an optical telescope, and thereby improving the image (p. 326)

chemical rocks: sedimentary rocks formed from mineral grains that fall out of a solution (precipitate) by evaporation or by chemical action (p. 61)

chemical weathering: decomposition that takes place when a rock's minerals are changed into different substances (p. 117)

chlorofluorocarbons (CFCs): gases containing chlorine, fluorine, and carbon atoms that break down the ozone layer and weaken protection from ultraviolet waves (p. 430)

chromosphere: the layer of the sun's atmosphere just above the photosphere (p. 357)

cirrus clouds: thin, feathery, or tufted clouds of ice crystals at high altitudes (p. 454)

clastic rocks: sedimentary rocks formed from fragments of other rocks (p. 61)

clays: a seafloor sediment consisting of flakes of clay-sized material that settle to the bottom of the ocean (p. 302)

cleavage: the tendency of a mineral to split easily along planes parallel to the crystal faces, leaving smooth, flat surfaces in one or more directions (p. 43)

climate: the overall weather of a region (p. 515)

collision boundary: a converging boundary that is formed when two continents collide and are welded together into a single, larger continent (p. 218)

cold front: leading edge of a mass of relatively cold air (p. 492)

comet: a mass of rock, ice, dust, and gas revolving around the sun, usually in a highly eccentric orbit (p. 380)

compound: a substance consisting of two or more elements chemically combined (p. 28)

condensation: change from water vapor to liquid water (p. 447)

condensation level: altitude at which water vapor begins to condense; where dew point reaches air temperature (p. 457)
condensation nuclei: microscopic particles on which water vapor condenses, forming cloud droplets (p. 452)
conduction: the movement of heat to an object by its contact with a hotter object (p. 434)
constellation: a group of stars that appears to form a pattern in the sky (p. 337)
continental climate: a climate with great extremes of temperature; it has hot summers and cold winters (p. 518)
continental glaciers: the large ice sheets of Greenland and Antarctica (p. 175)
contour interval: the difference in elevation between two consecutive contour lines (p. 103)
contour line: a line drawn through points that are all the same height above sea level (p. 103)
convection: the movement of heat by currents within a heated material (p. 434)
converging boundary: a boundary that forms when two lithospheric plates come together, or converge (p. 218)
core (inner): spherical center of Earth, about 2800 kilometers in diameter and made of solid iron and nickel (p. 10)
core (outer): the zone of Earth's interior, extending about 2100 kilometers between Earth's inner core and mantle and made of liquid iron and nickel (p. 10)
Coriolis effect: the effect of Earth's rotation that causes the deflection of moving objects toward or away from the equator (p. 410)
corona: sun's outer atmosphere above the chromosphere (p. 357)
correlation: the matching of rock layers from one area to another (p. 542)
countercurrent: a current flowing in a direction opposite to that of the wind-related current (p. 310)
covalent bond: the bond formed from the sharing of electrons by atoms (p. 32)
craters: depressions on the surface of a moon or planet, usually caused by the impact of huge rocks (p. 396)
craton: the ancient core of a continent, usually the oldest and most altered rocks of the continent (p. 221)
creep: slow, invisible, downhill movement of soil (p. 127)
crust: layer of lighter rock that covers Earth's mantle (p. 11)
crystal shape: the pattern a mineral's ions or atoms form if there is enough time and room to grow (p. 42)
cumulonimbus: a cloud formed from a deep layer of unstable air that brings lightning, thunder, and heavy showers; also called thundercloud (p. 457)
cumulus clouds: thick, puffy masses of clouds formed by vertically rising air currents (p. 455)
cyclone: any counterclockwise movement of air (p. 493)

D

daylight saving time: standard time advanced one hour for six or more months each year, adding an hour of daylight to the part of the day when people are awake (p. 415)
deferent: orbit on which the center of an epicycle moved around Earth in Ptolemy's model of the solar system (p. 362)
deficit: a condition in which soil water storage is gone and the need for moisture is greater than the rainfall (p. 135)
deflation: removal of loose rock particles by the wind (p. 190)
degree: unit used in measuring temperature; a definite fraction of the difference between two fixed temperatures (p. 441)
delta: a level, fan-shaped deposit formed at the mouth of a river (p. 163)
density current: a subsurface current that is heavier, or more dense, than the surrounding water (p. 312)
depression contour: a contour line joining points of equal elevation within a depression (p. 104)
desertification: the removal of soil by wind or rain in areas left exposed by the removal of plant covers (p. 77)
dew: water vapor that has condensed on a surface as a liquid (p. 451)
dew point: the temperature at which air becomes saturated with water vapor (p. 451)
dike: an igneous intrusion that cuts across rock layers, formed when magma intrudes into vertical or nearly vertical fissures in bedrock (p. 238)
discharge: the volume of water flowing past a given point in a stream at a given time (p. 153)
diverging boundary: the spreading center where two lithospheric plates are moving apart (p. 216)
divide: the higher land separating two adjacent drainage basins (p. 156)
doldrums: a rainy equatorial belt of low air pressure and slowly rising air (p. 478)
dome mountain: a nearly circular folded mountain (p. 270)
Doppler effect: an apparent change in the wavelength of radiation, where there is relative motion between the source of radiation and the receiver (p. 333)
drainage basin: the land drained by a river system (p. 156)
dust storm: a storm with strong, steady winds that lift great amounts of silt and clay from topsoil (p. 189)
dynamic metamorphism: process of rock-forming that results from large areas of rocks being under the intense heat and pressure of mountain-building movements (p. 68)
dwarf stars: stars of an absolute magnitude of +1 or less (p. 342)

E

earthquake: the shaking of Earth's crust caused by a release of energy (p. 243)
eclipsing binary: two stars of unequal brightness that revolve around and pass in front of each other at regular intervals (p. 343)
elastic-rebound theory: the theory that earthquakes occur when the stress that builds up between two lithospheric plates overcomes the force of friction, causing the plates to suddenly move and then snap back to their former shapes (p. 243)
electron: a negatively charged particle that spins around the nucleus of an atom (p. 26)
electromagnetic energy: forms of energy that travel at a speed of 300 000 kilometers per second, each form having a different frequency and wavelength (p. 327)
element: a substance that cannot be broken down into simpler substances by ordinary chemical or physical means (p. 25)
elliptical orbits: ellipse-shaped orbits with two foci (p. 363)
El Niño: the warming of the ocean surface off the western coast of South America, which contributes to a short-term warming trend (p. 527)
environment: all of the resources, influences, and conditions that surround you (p. 75)
epicenter: the point on Earth's surface directly above the focus of an earthquake (p. 244)
epicycle: a small orbit on which a planet traveled in Ptolemy's model of the solar system (p. 362)
epoch: a subdivision of a geological period of Earth's history (p. 537)
equal area law: law that states that as a planet moves around the sun, an imaginary line joining the two will sweep over equal areas of space in equal periods of time (p. 363)
era: a major division of geologic time (p. 536)
erosion: the process of breakup and transport of earth materials by moving natural agents (p. 117)
escape velocity: the minimum velocity needed for an object to escape from another object to which it is held by the force of gravitation (p. 365)
eutrophication: the destruction of a lake as it is gradually filled in by sediments and plants (p. 78)

evaporation: change of liquid water to water vapor (p. 447)
evapotranspiration: the loss of moisture as water vapor from the ground or from plant leaves (p. 133)
evolution: the process of change that produces new life forms over geologic time (p. 541)
exfoliation: peeling of surface layers of exposed bedrock (p. 119)
eye (of a storm): calm, clear center of a tropical low (p. 503)

F

false-color image: a computer image that assigns different colors for each wavelength of light, each of which depicts a certain surface feature (p. 110)
fault: a break or crack in Earth's crust along which movement has occurred (p. 217)
fault-block mountains: blocks of crust that have been faulted and tilted at the same time (p. 268)
feldspar: a family of the most common and abundant of all minerals; formed by silica tetrahedrons joined together by ions of aluminum and other metals (p. 47)
felsic rocks: light-colored, high-silica rocks (p. 57)
ferromagnesian silicate: a silicate mineral containing atoms of iron and magnesium and dark in color (p. 48)
fertility: the ability of the soil to support plant life (p. 76)
fetch: the length of open water over which the wind blows steadily (p. 193)
flash flood: a sudden rush of water, usually caused by a single cloudburst, over the narrow valley of a young mountain stream (p. 166)
flood plain: any plain that borders a stream and is covered by its water in time of flood (p. 161)
focus: (1) a point within Earth at which an earthquake originates (p. 244); (2) one of two points in an elliptical orbit; the position of the sun inside Earth's elliptical orbit is at one focus (p. 363)
fossil: the remains, impressions, or any evidence of the former existence of life preserved in rock (p. 65)
fossil fuels: nonrenewable fuels formed from the remains of plants and animals that lived long ago (p. 83)
fracture: (1) appearance of a mineral surface where it breaks along other than cleavage planes (p. 43); (2) a crack in bedrock along which no movement has occurred (p. 270)
front: the boundary between two unlike air masses (p. 491)
frontal thunderstorms: thunderstorms that usually form in warm, moist air on or ahead of a cold front and last for several hours (p. 499)
frost: water vapor that has condensed on a surface as a solid when the temperature is at or below 0°C (p. 452)

G

galaxy: a system containing millions, or even billions, of stars (p. 349)
geologic timetable: a summary of the major events of Earth's history preserved in the rock record (p. 536)
geology: the study of Earth's surface and interior (p. 3)
geyser: a boiling hot spring that erupts periodically (p. 143)
granules: individual cells about 1500 kilometers across that are the tops of gas columns that form below the sun's photosphere (p. 356)
great circle: a circle whose plane passes through the center of a sphere (p. 100)
greenhouse effect: the ability of the air to absorb long heat waves from Earth after allowing the sun's short waves to pass through it (p. 371)
gully: a miniature valley formed by heavy rains (p. 155)

H

Hadley cell: the circulation cell in which air flows between the equator and 30 degrees latitude (p. 477)
hail: precipitation in the form of irregular balls or lumps made of concentric layers of ice (p. 461)
half-life: the time required for half of the atoms of a radioactive substance to decay to a stable end product (p. 545)
hardness: the resistance of a mineral to scratching (p. 43)
harmonic law: law that states that the period of a planet squared is equal to the cube of its distance from the sun (p. 364)
headward erosion: the wearing away of land at the head of a gully or stream valley (p. 155)
high-pressure area (high): an area where the pressure is greater than the surrounding air (p. 471)
horse latitudes: belts of high air pressure and very dry descending air, located at about 30 degrees latitude north and south of the equator (p. 478)
hot spots: areas of volcanic activity near the center of lithospheric plates (p. 231)
hurricane: a tropical cyclone with sustained winds of 120 kilometers per hour or greater (p. 503)
hydrolysis: any chemical reaction of water with other substances (p. 120)
hydrosphere: the water of Earth, including surface and subsurface water (p. 133)
hygrometer: an instrument that measures relative humidity (p. 448)
hypothesis: an informed guess that tries to explain known facts (p. 7)

I

ice front: the location where a glacier melts as fast as it moves forward (p. 176)
ice wedging: the process of mechanical weathering in which water held in cracks of rocks wedges the rocks apart when it freezes (p. 118)
igneous rocks: rocks formed by the solidification of hot molten rock material called magma (p. 55)
imaging radar: the radar system in which a signal is sent out and then "heard" echoing off Earth's surface, a method of remote sensing (p. 109)
impermeable: describes a rock material through which water does not pass easily (p. 137)
index (guide) fossils: fossils that identify the age of the rock in which they occur (p. 542)
inner planets: the four planets nearest the sun, separated from the outer planets by the asteroid belt (p. 369)
insolation: the solar energy that reaches Earth (p. 434)
interferometry: the use of two radio telescopes to detect a radio signal from the same point in space and to determine the signal's location (p. 328)
international date line: an imaginary line through the Pacific Ocean, roughly following the 180th meridian; travelers moving westward advance the date, while travelers moving eastward set the date back (p. 415)
intertropical convergence zone (ITCZ): the low-pressure zone at the equator, where the winds from the two hemispheres converge (p. 478)
ion: an atom or group of atoms that is electrically charged (p. 31)
ionic bond: the force of attraction between oppositely charged ions that holds them together (p. 31)
ionosphere: the part of Earth's atmosphere from about 65 kilometers to 500 kilometers above the surface, in which layers rich in electrified particles exist (p. 432)
isobar: a line on a map connecting places of the same atmospheric pressure at a given time (p. 471)
isotherm: a line drawn on a map through places having the same atmospheric temperature at a given time (p. 442)
isotopes: atoms of the same chemical element with different atomic masses (p. 28)

J

jet stream: a narrow band of very strong westerly winds at high levels in the middle latitudes, usually at heights of 6000 to 12 000 meters (p. 482)

Jovian planets: gaseous planets that are much larger and less dense than terrestrial planets; all outer planets except Pluto are terrestrial planets (p. 369)

K

key bed: a single rock layer that has the same characteristics as an index fossil (p. 542)

knot: a speed of approximately 1.85 kilometers (1.15 miles) per hour (p. 476)

L

laccolith: a dome-shaped intruded mass of igneous rock (p. 239)

land breeze: a cool, local wind blowing out to sea that occurs when the air pressure over land becomes higher than the air pressure over the water (p. 474)

landslide: sudden movement of a mass of bedrock or loose rock down the slope of a hill, mountain, or cliff (p. 127)

latitude: distance in degrees north or south of equator (p. 99)

lava: molten rock that reaches Earth's surface (p. 228)

levee: a bank confining a stream or river channel, either natural or artificial (p. 165)

light-year (LY): the distance a ray of light travels in one year (p. 339)

lithosphere: the outer solid shell of Earth that extends to a depth of about 100 kilometers (p. 210)

longitude: the distance in degrees east and west of the prime meridian (p. 99)

longshore current: a current that flows parallel to the shoreline (p. 196)

low-pressure area (low): an area that has lower pressure than the surrounding air (p. 472)

luminosity: the actual, or true, brightness of a star (p. 341)

lunar eclipse: an eclipse that occurs when the moon passes into Earth's total shadow, or umbra (p. 400)

lunar month: the time from one new moon to the next new moon, about 29.5 days (p. 400)

luster: the shine of a mineral surface (p. 41)

***L* wave:** an earthquake wave that travels along Earth's surface (p. 245)

M

mafic rocks: dark-colored, low-silica rocks (p. 57)

magma: the hot liquid rock beneath Earth's surface (p. 55)

magnetic variation or declination: the angle by which the compass needle varies from true north (p. 106)

mantle: the layer of rock in Earth extending from the crust downward 2850 kilometers (p. 10)

manganese nodules: potato-shaped masses 1 to 10 centimeters in diameter; the best-known example of authigenic material (p. 303)

map projections: ways of showing the curved Earth on a flat surface (p. 97)

map scale: the ratio of distance on the map to distance on Earth (p. 100)

maria: the Latin word for *seas;* extensive dark areas that represent great basins on the moon (p. 391)

marine climate: the climate of areas near oceans, with a small yearly temperature range (p. 518)

mascon: an area of higher gravity, existing over the moon's more circular maria (p. 394)

mass movement: the downslope movement of large masses of earth materials (p. 127)

mass number: the number of protons and neutrons in an atom (p. 27)

matter: anything that has mass and volume (p. 25)

meander: one of a series of broad, looping bends in a stream (p. 161)

mechanical weathering: disintegration that takes place when rock is split or broken into smaller pieces of the same material without changing its composition (p. 117)

meridian: an imaginary half circle that runs in a north-south direction from the North Pole to the South Pole (p. 99)

mesosphere: the layer of Earth's atmosphere between the stratosphere and the thermosphere (p. 432)

metamorphic rocks: rocks formed by the effect of heat, pressure, and chemical action on other rocks (p. 56)

meteor: a light produced when a meteorite streaks through Earth's atmosphere (p. 381)

meteorite: the part of a meteoroid that reaches Earth's surface (p. 382)

meteoroid: a rock fragment traveling in space (p. 381)

meteorology: the study of Earth's atmosphere (p. 3)

meteor shower: a time when many meteoroids enter Earth's atmosphere (p. 382)

mica: soft silicate minerals with flat, shiny flakes that are found in many rocks such as granite and gneiss (p. 48)

minerals: elements or compounds that occur naturally in Earth's crust in solid, inorganic, crystalline states (p. 30)

mineralogy: study of minerals and their properties (p. 41)

millibar: a unit used by meteorologists to measure air pressure; 34 millibars equal 1 inch of mercury (p. 470)

mixed layer: the surface layer of ocean water (p. 282)

Mohorovicic discontinuity (Moho): the boundary between Earth's crust and mantle (p. 253)

moist-adiabatic lapse rate: the rate at which the temperature of saturated air changes when it rises or sinks (usually 0.6°C per 100 meters) (p. 457)

molecule: the smallest part of a compound that has all the properties of the compound (p. 28)

moraines: accumulations of glacial till (p. 177)

muds: fine particles that settle to the bottom of oceans to form sediments (p. 302)

mudflow: the rapid movement of a water-saturated mass of clay and silt (p. 128)

multiple-mirror telescope (MMT): a reflector that forms an image by combining the light from each of several mirrors and focusing it on a single point (p. 324)

N

native minerals: minerals composed of single elements; also called native elements (p. 31)

neap tide: a tide of small range occurring at the quarter phase of the moon (p. 404)

nebula: a great cloud of gas and dust in space (p. 345)

neutron: one of three basic atomic particles; has a mass slightly greater than a proton, but no electric charge (p. 26)

neutron star: the dense core remaining after a large star explodes (p. 346)

nonrenewable resource: a resource that is used up faster than it can be replaced in nature (p. 75)

normal lapse rate: the rate at which atmospheric temperature changes with altitude; about 1°C for every 160 meters (p. 437)

normal fault: a fault in which the rocks on one side of the fault plane move down with respect to the rocks on the other side; caused by stresses pulling away from each other (p. 264)

nova: a star that has flared into intense brightness (p. 346)

O

oblate spheroid: a sphere that flattens at its poles and bulges at its equator (p. 16)

ocean current: any continuous flow of water along a definite path in the oceans (p. 307)
oceanography: the study of the world's oceans (p. 3)
occluded front: a front formed when a cold front overtakes a warm front (p. 492)
oozes: fine lime or silica muds found on the deep ocean floor (p. 302)
optical telescope: a tool that uses a large lens or mirror to gather rays of light and focus them on one spot, and smaller lenses to magnify the image (p. 321)
orbit: the path of a revolving body, like that of Earth around the sun (p. 361)
organic rocks: sedimentary rocks formed from the remains of plants and animals (p. 61)
outer planets: the five planets farthest from the sun, separated from the inner planets of the solar system by the asteroid belt (p. 369)
outwash plain: a broad, stratified, gently sloping deposit formed beyond the terminal moraine by streams from a melting glacier (p. 181)
oxbow lake: the crescent-shaped lake remaining after a meandering river has formed a cutoff and the ends of the original bend have been silted up (p. 162)
oxidation: the chemical reaction of oxygen with other substances (p. 120)

P

parallax: the apparent shift in positions of nearby stars when compared to distant stars as Earth moves in its orbit (p. 417)
parallelism of the axis: the behavior of Earth's axis during its revolution (p. 409)
parallels: east-west circles around Earth, parallel to the equator (p. 99)
parent material: material from which a soil is formed (p. 124)
passive continental margins: boundaries between oceanic crust and continental crust whose major activity is the buildup of sediments (p. 261)
penumbra: the part of a shadow that is only partly illuminated; partial shadow (p. 400)
perigee: the point nearest Earth in the orbit of an Earth satellite (p. 398)
perihelion: the point in orbit nearest the sun (p. 363)
period: a subdivision of a geologic era (p. 537)
period (of a wave): the time needed for one full wavelength to pass a given point (p. 194)
permeability: the ability of rock to transmit water or other liquids (p. 137)
phases: daily changes in the moon's appearance (p. 399)
photosphere: the bright yellow surface of the sun (p. 356)
photosynthesis: the process by which green plants manufacture sugars and starches from carbon dioxide and water in the presence of sunlight (p. 10)
plate tectonics: study of the formation and movement of the rigid pieces, or plates, that cover Earth's surface (p. 209)
plutons: igneous intrusions, or rock masses, that form when magma cools beneath other rocks (p. 56)
polar front: a permanent front between the prevailing westerlies and polar easterlies (p. 478)
pollution: a condition in which some part of the environment is changed so that it is unfit for human, plant, or animal use (p. 76)
porosity: percentage of a material that is pore space (p. 137)
precipitation: the falling of any form of water from the air to Earth's surface, occurring when cloud droplets become heavy enough to fall to Earth (p. 460)
pressure-gradient force: the force that causes the wind to blow, which is produced by a pressure gradient (p. 473)
prime meridian: zero meridian; the meridian that passes through Greenwich, England, and from which longitude is measured (p. 414)
profile: a line that shows the changes in elevation across a section of a topographic map (p. 108)
proton: a positively charged particle in the nucleus of an atom (p. 26)
protoplanets: hypothetical whirling gaseous masses within a giant cloud of gas and dust rotating around a sun; protoplanets are thought to have given rise to planets and moons (p. 8)
protostar: a large glowing cloud that eventually becomes a star (p. 345)
psychrometer: an instrument that measures relative humidity by using wet-bulb and dry-bulb thermometers (p. 449)
pulsar: a distant heavenly object that emits rapid pulses of light and radio waves (p. 343)
***P* waves:** primary earthquake waves, which can travel through any material (p. 244)
pyroxenes: silicate minerals that have cleavage surfaces that meet nearly at right angles (p. 48)

Q

quasars: very distant radio sources that resemble stars but are far larger, more luminous, and more massive; also called quasi-stellar radio sources (p. 350)

R

radiation: transfer of heat in the form of short waves (p. 434)
radioactive decay: the process in which alpha rays are released from an atomic nucleus, thus changing an atom to a new, lighter element (p. 545)
radiocarbon: the radioactive isotope of carbon with atomic mass 14, which is used in radioactive dating of plant and animal materials (p. 546)
radio telescope array: a group of radio telescopes, instruments that pick up radio waves emitted by bodies in space (p. 329)
rain gauge: an instrument for measuring the amount of precipitation (p. 462)
rawinsonde: a small balloon-carried observatory, which carries a radio transmitter that sends out signals about temperature, air pressure, and relative humidity (p. 489)
rays: bright streaks of shattered rock and dust that radiate from a number of the moon's craters (p. 396)
recharge: the refilling of soil water supply at times when plants need little moisture (p. 135)
red giants: large, cooler red stars that are more luminous than hotter blue-white stars and have low densities (p. 342)
refracting telescope: a telescope that uses a convex lens as its objective; also called a refractor (p. 322)
refraction: the bending of waves when they pass from one kind of substance to another of different density, or when they reach shallow water (ocean waves) (p. 194)
regolith: lunar "soil," a grayish-brown mixture of small pieces and fine particles (p. 396)
relative time: the method of recording events that places events in a sequence but does not identify their actual date of occurrence (p. 535)
relative humidity: the extent to which air is saturated with water vapor; it is expressed in percent (p. 448)
remote sensing: mapmaking done by gathering data about the land from above Earth's surface (p. 109)
renewable resource: a resource that can be replaced in nature at a rate close to its rate of use (p. 75)
reserves: the amount of known deposits of a mineral in ores that are worth mining at the present time (p. 80)
residual soil: soil that has bedrock as its parent material (p. 124)
respiration: the process by which food is changed to energy (p. 75)

retrograde motion: a periodic backward, or westward, loop made by a planet in front of the background of constellations (p. 362)
reverse fault: a fault in which one side of the fault plane has been driven up over the other side; caused by stresses pushing toward each other (p. 264)
revolution: the movement of Earth in its orbit around the sun (p. 417)
Richter scale: a method of determining earthquake magnitude by measuring the amount of energy an earthquake releases (p. 249)
rift eruptions: volcanic eruptions that occur at long, narrow fractures in Earth's crust (p. 230)
rilles: long deep clefts, or cracks, running through the moon's maria bedrock (p. 394)
rip current: a strong surface current that flows away from the beach in a channel through oncoming breakers (p. 196)
rock: a group of minerals bound together (p. 55)
rock-forming minerals: minerals that make up most of the rocks in Earth's crust (p. 41)
rotation: the turning of an object on its axis (p. 409)

S

salinity: a measure of the dissolved solids in sea water (p. 280)
salinization: a soil condition caused by the evaporation of irrigation water, which leaves too much mineral matter on the soil's surface for crops to grow (p. 77)
sandbar: a bar of sand carried by ocean currents and deposited near shore (p. 199)
satellite: a smaller body revolving around a larger body; a natural satellite is also called a moon (p. 377)
Schmidt telescope: an optical telescope that uses both a reflecting mirror and a refracting lens for an unusually wide field of view (p. 325)
sea breeze: a local wind carrying cool ocean air inland, occurs when the air pressure over land decreases (p. 473)
sea-level pressure: corrected air pressure calculated by the removal of the effect that altitude has on pressure (p. 470)
seamount: a submerged, steep-sloped peak rising from the ocean floor; flat-topped peaks are called guyots (p. 296)
sedimentary rocks: rocks formed from sediments bound together in some way (p. 56)
seismic moment: a more accurate indicator of determining earthquake magnitude than the Richter scale (p. 249)
seismogram: the record sheet of a seismograph; it records when an earthquake is taking place and the type of earthquake wave (p. 246)
seismograph: an instrument that detects and records earthquake waves (p. 246)
severe thunderstorm: a storm that has wind gusts of at least 80 kilometers per hour and hail 2 or more centimeters in diameter (p. 502)
shadow zone: a wide area around Earth on the side opposite the focus of an earthquake where neither *P* nor *S* waves are received (p. 253)
shield: the exposed area of the oldest rocks, or craton, of a continent (p. 552)
silicates: compounds of the elements silica and oxygen; they include more than 90 percent of the minerals in Earth's crust (p. 35)
silica tetrahedron: a grouping of one silicon ion and four oxygen ions that forms the building blocks of silicate minerals (p. 35)
sill: a sheet of intrusive igneous rock forced between rock layers parallel to the rock layers it intrudes (p. 238)
single-mirror reflecting telescope: a telescope that uses one concave mirror as its objective; also called a single-mirror reflector (p. 323)
sleet: frozen raindrops (p. 461)
snow line: the lowest level that permanent snow reaches in summer (p. 173)
soil: loose, weathered rock and organic material in which plants with roots can grow (p. 124)
soil depletion: a condition in which soil no longer can grow usable crops, brought on by the removal of nutrients during harvesting (p. 77)
soil profile: cross section of earth above the parent material, usually consisting of the A-, B-, and C-horizons (p. 124)
solar eclipse: an eclipse that occurs when the moon's total shadow, or umbra, falls on Earth (p. 401)
solar flare: an outburst of light that rises up suddenly in areas of sunspot activity (p. 358)
solar prominences: huge, red, flamelike arches of material that occur in the corona of the sun (p. 357)
solar telescope: an instrument used to observe changes on the sun's surface; it projects a large image of the sun into a dark underground room (p. 355)
solar time: time that is kept by the sun's location in the sky (p. 413)
solar wind: a stream of electrically charged particles that are blown out from the sun in all directions (p. 358)
solution: the state in which mineral matter dissolved from bedrock is carried in a river (p. 152)
specific gravity: the ratio of the weight of a substance to the weight of an equal volume of water (p. 44)
specific humidity: the number of grams of water vapor in one kilogram of air (p. 448)
spectroscope: an instrument that can disperse a beam of light into a spectrum of its component wavelengths (p. 331)
spreading center: the area where lithospheric plates are moving apart (p. 214)
spring equinox: the first day of spring in the Northern Hemisphere, about March 21, when daylight and nighttime are equal in length (p. 420)
spring tide: a tide of large range occurring at new-moon and full-moon phases (p. 404)
standard time zone: an area in which time is based on average solar time at one particular meridian but used over a belt of about 15 degrees of longitude (p. 413)
stationary front: the boundary between two air masses that are not moving (p. 492)
station model: a listing of about 20 different weather observations around the location of a National Weather Service station on a weather map (p. 510)
stock: a large igneous intrusion, similar to a batholith, but with an exposed surface area of less than 100 square kilometers (p. 239)
storm surges: currents formed when a hurricane piles up water along the shore and blows it inland (p. 503)
stratification: the arrangement of rock beds in visible layers (p. 64)
stratus clouds: clouds that are arranged in unbroken, low, horizontal layers, or sheets (p. 455)
stratosphere: the layer of Earth's atmosphere that extends from the troposphere to the mesosphere (p. 432)
streak: the color of a mineral when powdered or rubbed on a streak plate (p. 42)
stream piracy: the diversion of the upper part of one stream by the headward growth of another stream (p. 157)
striations: scratches on rocks and bedrock due to glacier movement (p. 178)
strike-slip fault: a fault in which the rocks on opposite sides of the fault plane move horizontally with respect to each other (p. 264)
subduction boundary: a converging boundary where one plate is plunging down beneath another, overriding plate (p. 219)
submarine canyons: gigantic gullies that cut into continental slopes (p. 293)

subsoil: the B-horizon of soil whose color is usually red or brown, including clay and iron oxides that washed from the topsoil (p. 124)

summer solstice: the first day of summer in the Northern Hemisphere, about June 21; it has the longest period of daylight (p. 419)

sunspot: a dark area on the sun's photosphere (p. 357)

supercooled water: water that has cooled below 0°C without freezing (p. 454)

supergiants: large, low-density stars that are hundreds of times more luminous than the red giants (p. 342)

supernova: an intensely bright object that results from the explosion of a massive red giant star (p. 346)

surplus: the condition of having rainfall greater than the need for moisture when the soil is already saturated (p. 135)

suspension: the state in which rock materials carried by a river are stirred up and kept from sinking by the turbulence of stream flow (p. 152)

swash: the motion of water pushed up a beach by breaking waves (p. 196)

***S* waves:** secondary, or shear, earthquake waves, which can travel through solids, but not liquids or gases (p. 245)

syncline: a downfold of rock layers (p. 264)

T

temperature inversion: the increase in temperature with an increase in altitude; occurs when a layer of cold air is trapped beneath a layer of warm air (p. 437)

terrane: a large block of lithosphere that has been moved, often thousands of kilometers, and attached to the edge of a continent (p. 222)

terrestrial planets: another name for inner planets; they have a rocky crust, a dense mantle layer, and a very dense core (p. 369)

texture: the characteristic structure of a rock given by its size, shape, and the arrangement of its mineral crystals (p. 57)

thermal metamorphism: the process of rock-forming that results when hot magma forces its way into overlying rock and changes the rock (p. 70)

thermocline: the transitional layer between warm surface waters and cold bottom waters in oceans or lakes (p. 283)

thermosphere: the layer of Earth's atmosphere above the mesosphere (p. 432)

thin-skinned thrusting: the pushing of thin, horizontal sheets of rock from continental margins over great distances along nearly level fault surfaces (p. 222)

tidal range: the distance in level between low and high tide in a given area (p. 404)

tides: the daily rise and fall of ocean waters (p. 403)

till: unsorted and unstratified rock materials carried in the bottom of a glacier (p. 180)

time-travel graph: a graph that shows the relationship between *P* and *S* wave travel times and epicenter distance (p. 247)

topsoil: the A-horizon of soil; contains organic material, or humus, that forms from decayed plant and animal materials (p. 124)

tornado: a narrow, violent, funnel-shaped column of spiral winds that entends downward from the cloud base to Earth (p. 501)

toxic waste: a poisonous chemical waste that must be disposed of extremely carefully (p. 92)

trade winds: winds that originate in the horse latitudes and blow toward the doldrums (p. 479)

transported soil: soil deposits that formed from materials left by winds, rivers, or glaciers (p. 124)

troposphere: the convective region of the atmosphere that extends from Earth's surface to the stratosphere; its height ranges from 8 kilometers at the poles to 18 kilometers at the equator (p. 431)

tsunami: a gigantic wave that results from an earthquake or landslide on the ocean floor (p. 194)

turbidity currents: undersea landslides of mud and sand that form currents that carve canyons into continental slopes (p. 295)

U

umbra: the darkest part of the shadow of the moon or Earth (p. 400)

unconformity: a surface between two rock layers that represents a gap in the rock record (p. 536)

uniformitarianism: the concept that the present is the key to the past (p. 55)

universal law of gravitation: Newton's law that states that gravitational force is greater between objects of greater mass and less between objects of lesser mass (p. 364)

upwelling: the vertical movement of cold ocean water toward the surface (p. 314)

usage: the condition where plants draw water from the soil at times when the need for moisture is greater than the rainfall (p. 135)

V

valley glacier: a long, slow-moving, wedge-shaped stream of ice (p. 172)

variable stars: stars that change in brightness at regular periods, or cycles (p. 343)

visible spectrum: band of visible colors; they are the colors of the rainbow and have different wavelengths (p. 331)

volcanic (extrusive) rock: igneous rock that forms from cooled lava, or from volcanic dust and ash (p. 56)

volcanic neck: the solidified lava filling the central vent of an extinct volcano (p. 239)

volcano: an opening in Earth's crust through which an eruption takes place (p. 240)

W

waning: the decreasing of the moon's visible illuminated surface, from full moon to new moon (p. 399)

water budget: describes the income and the outgo of water in a region (p. 134)

water cycle: the hydrologic cycle; a never-ending movement of water from one part of the hydrosphere to another (p. 133)

warm front: the leading edge of a mass of relatively warm air (p. 492)

water gap: a pass in a mountain ridge through which a stream flows (p. 158)

watershed: the entire area drained by a stream and its tributaries (p. 156)

water table: the surface below which the ground is saturated with water (p. 138)

wave height: vertical distance from crest to trough (p. 193)

wavelength: the distance between two successive wave crests (p. 193)

waxing: the increasing of the moon's visible illuminated surface, from new moon to full moon (p. 399)

weather: the state of the atmosphere at a given time and place (p. 427)

weathering: the process in which rocks are broken up by the action of water, the atmosphere, and organisms (p. 117)

winter solstice: the first day of winter in the Northern Hemisphere, about December 21; it has the shortest daylight period (p. 419)

Z

zenith: point in the sky directly above observer (p. 420)

Index

Acknowledgments

DESIGN CREDITS:

Cover: Hannus Design Associates
Cartography in Appendices: 581, 585, 588–595: Sanderson Associates
Photo Research: Martha Friedman

ABBREVIATION KEY

MWLCO – Mt. Wilson and Las Campanas Observatories, Carnegie Institute of Washington
NASA–National Aeronautics and Space Administration
NCAR–National Center for Atmospheric Research
NOAA/AOML–National Oceanic and Atmospheric Administration/Atlantic Oceanographic and Meteorological Laboratory
NOAA/NESDIS/SDSD–National Oceanic and Atmospheric Administration/National Environmental Satellite Data, and Information Service/Satellite Data Services Division
NOAA/PROFS–National Oceanic and Atmospheric Administration/Program for Regional Forecasting and Observing Services
NOAO–National Optical Astronomy Observatories
USGS–United States Geological Services
WHOI–Woods Hole Oceanographic Institution

PHOTO CREDITS:

Cover Photo: Galen Rowell(Peter Arnold, Inc.)**UNIT ONE:** x: *l* Burr(Gamma-Liaison); *tr, br* Breck Kent. 1: *l* Jack Fields(Photo Researchers, Inc.); *r* ©Elliot Varner Smith. 2: Wide World Photo. 3: Chuck Place(The Image Bank). 4: *t* Kraft-Explorer(Photo Researchers, Inc.); *b* NASA. 5: *t* Howard Bluestein; *b* Bob Evans(Peter Arnold, Inc.). 6: Courtesy of Peggy LeMone. 12: Howard Bluestein. 14: Gray Baskerville(*Hot Rod* Magazine). 16: NASA. 19: Ken O'Donoghue/©D.C. Heath. 20: H. Gritscher(Peter Arnold, Inc.). 21: Courtesy of Dr. James W. Head. 22: NASA. 24: H. Stein(Photo Researchers, Inc.). 26: Russ Kinne(Photo Researchers, Inc.). 28: *t* E.R. Degginger; *b* Ken O'Donoghue/© D.C. Heath. 29: Breck Kent. 31: Tom McHugh(Photo Researchers, Inc.). 33: Courtesy of Dr. Kenneth Cox. 38: Breck Kent. 40: Mary Root(Root Resources). 41: *t,b* Jerome Wyckoff. 42: *t* Breck Kent; *b Encyclopedia of Minerals* by Roberts. 43: *l, br* Breck Kent; *tr* Hubbard Scientific Co. 45: Photo courtesy of Ward's Natural Science. 46: Courtesy of Lawrence Gittleman. 47: *tr* Jerome Wyckoff; *bl, br* Breck Kent. 48: *t* Hubbard Scientific Co.; *m Encyclopedia of Minerals* by Roberts; *bl* Lee Boltin Picture Library; *br* Jerome Wyckoff. 49: *tl* Hubbard Scientific Co.; *tr, m* Jerome Wyckoff; *br* Breck Kent. 50: Hubbard Scientific Co. 51–54: Breck Kent. 55: The Granger Collection, NY. 56: Krafft-Explorer(Photo Researchers, Inc.). 57: *t,b* Breck Kent. 58: *t,m,b* Jerome Wyckoff. 59: *t, tm* Breck Kent; *bm, b* Jerome Wyckoff. 61: David Davidson(Tom Stack & Associates). 62: Hubbard Scientific Co. 63: *all* Jerome Wyckoff. 64: *t* Breck Kent; *m* Randall Chew(Photo Researchers, Inc.); *b* Samuel Namowitz. 65: *t* Jerome Wyckoff. *m,br* Breck Kent; *bl* Michael Collier. 67: Courtesy of Suzanne Webel. 68: *tl* Michael Collier; *bl, br* Hubbard Scientific Co. 69: tr Hubbard Scientific Co.; *rm, bl, bm, br* Jerome Wyckoff. 72: Krafft-Explorer(Photo Researchers, Inc.). 74: Larry Lefever(Grant Heilman Photography). 76: William E. Ferguson. 77–78: Harold Hungerford. 79: Gerhardt Scheiola(Peter Arnold, Inc.). 80: Breck Kent. 81: Don Green(Copper Development Association). 82: M.P. Kahl(Photo Researchers, Inc.). 83: Breck Kent. 88: Rochester Gas and Electric Company. 89: Jerome Wyckoff. 90: Tom McHugh(Photo Researchers, Inc.). 91: Bill Weedmark(Panographics). 92: Joe Bator(The Stock Market). 93: Courtesy of Dr. Betty Miller. 94: M.P. Kahl(Photo Researchers, Inc.). 96: Jonathan Goldberg(Hurricane Island Outward Bound School). 102: Courtesy of Peg Rawson. 104: Jerome Wyckoff. 110: *t* NASA; *b* from SCIENCE: 20 July 1987, Vol.232, #4757, Submitted with "Overview of Shuttle Imaging Radar-B Preliminary Scientific Results" Elachi, C. et al., pp. 1511–1516. (Courtesy of M. Kobrick). Copyright 1986 by the AAAS. 111: Photri. 112: Jerome Wyckoff.

UNIT TWO: 114: *tl* Wide World Photo; *tr* Breck Kent; *br* Mark S. Wexler(Woodfin Camp & Associates). 115: *t* Stephen J. Krasemann(DRK PHOTO); *b* B. Bartholomew(Black Star). 116: R.B. Sanchez(The Stock Market); *inset* The Bettmann Archive. 118: Todd Gerstein(Photo Researchers, Inc.). 119: *t, br* Samuel Namowitz; *bl* Jerome Wyckoff. 120: Courtesy of Luray Caverns. 122: Jerome Wyckoff. 123: Courtesy of Dr. Juergen Reinhardt. 125: Kevin Schafer(Tom Stack & Associates). 127: Samuel Namowitz. 128: Jerome Wyckoff. 129: George Gerster(Photo Researchers, Inc.). 130: Courtesy of Luray Caverns. 132: Breck Kent. 142: Courtesy of Dr. Ruth Patrick. 143: Breck Kent. 146: Jerome Wyckoff. 147: Ray Seyd. 148: Breck Kent. 150: Harold Hungerford. 155: *l* Maurice Rosalsky; *r* Samuel Namowitz. 156–158: Breck Kent. 159: Jerome Wyckoff. 160: Niagara Falls Chamber of Commerce. 161: Jerome Wyckoff. 162: USGS/EROS Data Center. 163: Jerome Wyckoff. 164: Courtesy of Sandra Duncan. 165: U.S. Air Force. 166: Joe Rychetnik(Photo Researchers, Inc.). 167: Don Getsus(Photo Researchers, Inc.). 168: Samuel Namowitz. 170: Tom Bean. 172: Gary Milburn(Tom Stack & Associates). 173: E.R. Degginger. 174: Samuel Namowitz. 175: Jerome Wyckoff. 176: Tom Bean. 177: *t* Maurice Rosalsky; *b* Stephen J. Krasemann(Peter Arnold, Inc.). 178: B.F. Molnia(Terraphotographics/BPS). 179: Tom Stack(Tom Stack & Associates). 180–182: E.R. Degginger. 185: Tom McHugh(Photo Researchers, Inc.). 185: Courtesy of Luanne Whitbeck. 186: Gary Milburn(Tom Stack & Associates). 188: Tom Bean 189: M. Brandenburg(Bruce Coleman Inc.). 190: Jerome Wyckoff. 191: E. R. Degginger. 193: Randy Hufford(Tom Stack and Associates). 194: *t, b* NOAA. 196: Alex McLean(Landslides). 197: Courtesy of Dr. Orrin Pilkey, Jr. 198: Breck Kent. 199: John S. Shelton. 202: Stephen J. Krasemann(Peter Arnold, Inc.). 203: *l* Al Grotell; *r* G.R. Roberts. 204: Randy Hufford(Tom Stack & Associates).

UNIT THREE: 206: *l* David Weintraub(Photo Researchers, Inc.); *tr* Tom Bean (DRK PHOTO); *br* Breck Kent. 207: *t* Stephen J. Krasemann(DRK PHOTO); *b* Owen Franken(The Picture Group, Inc.). 208: Museum of Comparative Zoology, Harvard University, Photograph by Ron Eng. © Presidents and Fellows of Harvard University. 211: Courtesy of Dr. Anita G. Harris. 215: NASA. 217: *tl* Randall Hyman; *tr* Fred Grassle(WHOI); *br* WHOI. 218: John S. Shelton. 219: USGS/EROS Data Center. 222: Randall Hyman. 223: D.L. Jones(USGS). 224: USGS/EROS Data Center. 226: S. Jonasson & Frank Lane(Bruce Coleman Inc.). 228: Keith Gunnar(Bruce Coleman Inc.). 229: Harold Hungerford. 230: E.R. Degginger. 232: Courtesy of Robert Decker. 233: Westmanner-Inseln(Peter Arnold, Inc.). 234: William E. Ferguson. 235: Don King(The Image Bank). 236: F. Gohier(Photo Researchers, Inc.). 237: NASA. 238: G.R. Roberts. 239: *l* Tom Bean; *r* Breck Kent. 240: E.R. Degginger. 242: Jeff Slocum(The Picture Group, Inc.). 250: Steve McCutcheon(Alaska Pictorial Service). 254: Courtesy of Dr. Waverly Person. 255: Wide World Photo. 256: *t* Peter Menzel(Stock, Boston); *b* Chuck O'Rear(West Light). 258: Chuck O'Rear(West Light). 260: Keith Gunnar(Bruce Coleman Inc.). 265: *l* Jerome Wyckoff; *r* Peter Dunwiddle(Visuals Unlimited). 267: John S. Shelton. 268: *l* Steinberg(Photo Researchers, Inc.); *r* Jerome Wyckoff. 269: Courtesy of Dr. Jack Oliver. 272: Steinberg(Photo Researchers, Inc.).

UNIT FOUR: 274: *l* Terry Domico(Earth Images); *tr* Alfred Pasieka(Taurus Photos); *br* WHOI. 275: *t* NOAA/NESDIS/SDSD; *b* M.P. Kahl(DRK PHOTO). 276: © Jeffrey L. Rottman. 278: *t* The Granger Collection, NY; *b* Rod Catanach(WHOI). 279: Courtesy of J.R. Heirtzer. 282: Lewis Trusty(Animals Animals). 284: *t* Richard Hoover; *b* Editorial Photo Color Archives(Art Resource). 285: Dudley Foster(WHOI). 286: Richard Hoover. 288: WHOI. 290: Peter Wiebe(WHOI). 291: Courtesy of Dr. Maggie Goud. 297: Douglas Faulkner(Photo Researchers, Inc.). 298–299: William Haxby(Lamont-Doherty Geological Observatory). 302: Tom Bean(Tom Stack and Associates). 303: Robert Hessler(WHOI). 304: William Haxby(Lamont-Doherty Geological Observatory). 306: Frederik D. Bodin(Stock, Boston). 309: Dr. James Butler. 310: R.J. Bowen(WHOI). 315: Courtesy of Dr. Taro Takahashi. 316: R.J. Bowen(WHOI).

UNIT FIVE: 318: *l* NASA; *tr* © Hale Observatories; *br* Kaz Mori(Taurus Photos). 319: *t* © 1984 Regents, University of Hawaii; *bl* © Roger Ressmeyer(Starlight); *tr* NASA; *br* Smithsonian Institution Photo no. 50.471. 320: AAT No. 48A Photographed with the 3.9m Anglo-Australian Telescope by D.F. Malin/Anglo-Australian Telescope Board. 321: Jay Pasachoff (© Pasachoff Educational Trust). 322: Lick Observatory Photograph. 323: California Institute of Technology & Carnegie Institute of Washington. 324: © Roger Ressmeyer(Starlight). 325: NASA. 326: NOAO. 328: *t* Commonwealth of Puerto Rico; *b* National Radio Astronomy Observatory. 329: NASA. 330: Courtesy of Dr. Sidney Wolff. 332: MWLCO. 334: NOAO. 336: Dennis di Cicco. 337: Hansen Planetarium. 340:MWLCO. 344: *t* California Institute of Technology & Carnegie Institute of Washington: *b* Courtesy of Alan M. MacRobert. 345: *t* Lick Observatory Photograph, *b* Hansen Planetarium. 347: AAT No. 48 Photographed with 3.9m Anglo-Australian Telescope by D.F. Malin & R. Sharpies/Anglo-Australian Telescope Board. 350: *t* Jet Propulsion Lab(California Institute of Technology); *m* Lick Observatory Photograph; *b* © 1984 Regents, University of Hawaii. 352: Hansen Planetarium. 354: NASA. 355: NOAO. 356: NASA. 357: *t* NASA; *b* ISIS(Visuals Unlimited). 358: NASA. 360: Courtesy of Dr. Barbara Mihalas. 366–368: NASA. 369: Lunar & Planetary Institute. 370: *l* Sovfoto; *r* Lunar & Planetary Institute. 371: *t* Dennis di Cicco; *b* NASA. 372–374: NASA. 375: Jet Propulsion Lab/NASA. 376–378: NASA. 379: Jet Propulsion Lab/NASA. 380: *t* The Planetarium, Armagh-Northern Ireland; *b* NASA. 382: *t* Neg. #1449, Dept. of Library Services, American Museum of Natural History; *b* Grant Heilman Photography. 383: Courtesy of Guion S. Bluford, Jr. 384: The Planetarium, Armargh-Northern Ireland. 386: NASA. 389: World Wide Photo. 391–394: NASA. 395: MWLCO. 396: *t, b* Lunar & Planetary Institute; *m* Palomar Observatory Photograph. 397: Courtesy of Andrea Mosie. 402: Tom Pantages. 405: Clyde Smith(Peter Arnold, Inc.). 406: Lunar and Planetary Institute. 408: Dennis di Cicco. 410: Courtesy of Smith College. 412: Courtesy of Kathryn Neff. 413: Dennis di Cicco. 419 & 422: SSC-Photo Centre-ASC/Photo by Chris Brunn

UNIT SIX: 424: *l* NASA; *tr* Roger J. Cheng, Atmospheric Sciences Research Center, at SUNY Albany; *br* Siskind(Gamma-Liason). 425: *tl* NASA-Goddard Institute for Space Studies, NY; *tr* Michael Giannechini(Photo Researchers, Inc.); *b* © Steve McCurry(Magnum Photos). 426: © George Hall(Imagery Unlimited). 427: Breck Kent. 432: F.J. Baker(Dembinsky Photo Associates). 433: Courtesy of Brenda Johnson. 440: NOAA/NESDIS/SDSD. 441: Roger J. Cheng, Atmospheric Sciences Research Center, at SUNY Albany. 444: F.J. Baker(Dembinsky Photo Associates). 446: Tom Bean(DRK PHOTO). 449: Taylor/Thermometer Corporation of America. 450: Courtesy of Kristina Katzaros. 456: *tl* Tom Bean (DRK PHOTO); *bl* Breck Kent; *tm, tr, br* E.R. Degginger. 457: Jim Brandenburg(DRK PHOTO). 462: NCAR. 464: Deutsches Nationalkomitee für Denkmalschutz(Geschäftstelle beim Bundesminister des Innern, Bonn). 466: E.R. Degginger. 468: Gregroy G. Dimijian(Photo Researchers, Inc.). 480: Courtesy of Dr. Robert Harnack. 484: Gregory G. Dimijian(Photo Researchers, Inc.). 486: Ira Block. 487: B. Wilcox, Stanford Univ./BPS. 489: NOAA. 490: Courtesy of Dr. Robert Sheets. 492: Edward J. Szoke. 494: NOAA/PROFS. 495: John D. Cunningham(Visuals Unlimited). 496: NOAA/PROFS. 498: Edi Ann Otto. 500: Ralph Wetmore(Photo Researchers, Inc.). 501: Allan Moller(National Weather Service). 502: NCAR. 503: NASA. 504: NOAA/AOML. 506: Ira Block. 509: NCAR. 511: Courtesy of Dr. Charles E. Anderson. 512: NCAR. 514: David Hiser(Photographters Aspen). 519: WHOI. 520: Courtesy of Majorie McGuirk. 521: NOAA/NESDIS/SDSD. 527: Norris J. Klesman(The Picture Group, Inc.). 528: *l* The Bridgeman Art Library, Victoria and Albert Museum, *r* Paolo Koch(VISION INTERNATIONAL). 529: Rhodes Fairbridge. 530: Norris J. Klesman(The Picture Group, Inc.).

UNIT SEVEN: 532: *l* Tom Bean; *tr* Henry D. Meyer(Berg & Associates); *bl* T.A. Wiewandt(DRK PHOTO). 533: *t* E.R. Degginger; *bl* Carl Roessler(Bruce Coleman Inc.); *br* Breck Kent. 534: William E. Ferguson. 536: Jerome Wyckoff. 541: *t* Breck Kent; *b* National Park Service Photo. 542: A.J. Copley(Visuals Unlimited). 543: G.R. Roberts. 544: *t* H.A. Miller(Visuals Unlimited); *b* Samuel Namowitz. 547: Courtesy of Thomas R. Walker. 548: G.R. Roberts. 550: Paul Hoffman(Geological Survey of Canada). 552: John Fowler(VALAN PHOTOS). 553: Courtesy of Eleanor R. Bayley. 554: Photo courtesy of Ward's Scientific. 555: *t* Jane Burton(Bruce Coleman Inc.); *m* Photo courtesy of Ward's Scientific; *b* D. Schwimmer(Bruce Coleman Inc.) 556: Neg. #K10250 Dept. of Library Services, American Museum of Natural History. 557: *t* Breck Kent; *b* Bruce Iverson. 558: Neg. #K10234, Dept. of Library Services, American Museum of Natural History. 560: Neg. # K10250, Dept. of Library Services, American Museum of Natural History. 562: E.R. Degginger. 563: Jerome Wyckoff. 565: *t* Model by Stephan Czerkas; *b* William E. Ferguson. 566: Jerome Wyckoff. 569: *t* E.R. Degginger; *m* T.A. Wiedwandt(DRK PHOTO); *b* Field Museum of Natural History. 570: William E. Ferguson. 571: Photograph by John Reader, courtesy of Mary Leakey. 572: The Bettmann Archive. 573: Courtesy of Dr. Meyer Rubin. 574: T.A. Weinandt(DRK PHOTO).